The Colour of Democracy

The Colour of Democracy

Racism in Canadian Society

Second Edition

Frances Henry Carol Tator

Winston Mattis Tim Rees

HARCOURT
BRACE
CANADA

Harcourt Brace & Company, Canada

Toronto Montreal Fort Worth New York Orlando
Philadelphia San Diego London Sydney Tokyo

Canadian Cataloguing in Publication Data

Main entry under title:

The colour of democracy : racism in Canadian society

2nd ed.
Includes index.
ISBN 0-7747-3648-8

1. Racism — Canada. 2. Canada — Race relations. 3. Canada — Social conditions. I. Henry, Frances, 1931– . II. Title.

FC104.C63 1999   305.8'00971   C99-930238-8
F1035.A1C63 1999

New Editions Editor: Megan Mueller
Senior Developmental Editor: Martina van de Velde
Production Editor: Semareh Al-Hillal
Production Co-ordinator: Cheryl Tiongson

Copy Editor: John Eerkes
Cover and Interior Design: The Brookview Group
Typesetting and Assembly: Carolyn Hutchings
Printing and Binding: Transcontinental Printing Inc.

Cover Art: Cylla von Tiedemann, *Untitled* (1994). Image provided by the artist. Reproduced with the permission of the artist.

Harcourt Canada Ltd.
55 Horner Avenue, Toronto, ON, Canada M8Z 4X6
Customer Service
Toll-Free Tel.: 1-800-387-7278
Toll-Free Fax: 1-800-665-7307

This book was printed in Canada.

1 2 3 4 5   03 02 01 00 99

This book is dedicated to the memory of Dr. Wilson Head,
whose life was committed to the pursuit of a more just
and equitable society and to the elimination of racism in Canada.
His vision and tireless efforts have inspired and guided all of us
engaged in anti-racism.

About the Authors

▼▼▼▼▼▼▼▼▼▼▼▼▼▼▼▼▼▼▼▼▼▼▼▼▼▼▼▼▼

Frances Henry, a professor emerita of social anthropology and scholar in the field of race and ethnic relations, is one of the first researchers in Canada to carry out studies on the dynamics of racism. One of her earliest studies on racist attitudes found that 51 percent of Canadians had somewhat or very racist beliefs (Henry, 1978). Her ground-breaking field study of racial discrimination in employment provided dramatic evidence of the extensive barriers that affect Black jobseekers (Henry and Ginzberg, 1984). She is also the author of a major ethnographic study (1994) of the Caribbean Canadian community in Toronto. As a professor at York University, she has taught courses on racism for more than two decades and published widely on the subject.

Carol Tator worked on the frontlines of the anti-racism movement in one of the first voluntary race relations organizations in Canada. She has participated in many coalitions formed by people of colour and other equality seekers and has been involved in many organizations working to dismantle racist structures and systems. Ms. Tator has contributed to a number of government inquiries and task forces on racism and has worked in the areas of anti-racist policy development, program implementation and evaluation, strategic planning, training, and research. She is a co-author, with Frances Henry and Winston Mattis, of a new text on racism and the arts (1998). Carol Tator is currently a course director in the Department of Anthropology at York University.

Winston Mattis has experience in community development, employment equity, organizational change, and public administration. He has a particular understanding of racism as it affects the Black community in Canada and has worked on the frontlines of both the voluntary and the private sector. His particular interest is in policing, justice, and the law. Winston Mattis is lawyer specializing in employment law.

Tim Rees has worked in the race-relations field in a variety of capacities in the public, private, and voluntary sectors for the past two decades. As a policy and program manager with the Ontario government, he assisted in the development of Ontario's first policies on multiculturalism and race relations. He currently works with the City of Toronto as a senior policy consultant on anti-racism. Mr. Rees is also the editor of the first and only anti-racism journal in Canada, *Currents: Readings in Race Relations*, published by the Urban Alliance on Race Relations.

As private consultants, all four authors have worked extensively with public-sector institutions to address racism in the institutions' policies, programs, and practices. Their work with large and complex organizations has focussed on assisting these agencies to analyze barriers to access, participation, and equity in the major arenas of Canadian society. They have provided consultation to municipal, provincial, and federal government agencies, boards of education, colleges and universities, human-service delivery organizations, media corporations, and law enforcement and justice agencies. As anti-racism consultants, they have conducted numerous research studies and surveys, directed community consultations, reviewed organizational systems, and provided training to staff and management of major mainstream organizations.

REFERENCES

Henry, F. (1978). *Dynamics of Racism in Toronto*. North York: York University.

———. (1994). *The Caribbean Diaspora in Toronto: Learning to Live with Racism*. Toronto: University of Toronto Press.

———, and E. Ginzberg. (1984). *Who Gets the Work? A Test of Racial Discrimination in Employment*. Toronto: Urban Alliance on Race Relations.

Tator, C., F. Henry, and W. Mattis. (1998). *Challenging Racism in the Arts: Case Studies of Controversy and Conflict*. Toronto: University of Toronto Press.

Preface

▼▼▼▼▼▼▼▼▼▼

This book's approach to the subject of racism in Canada attempts to link theory to practice, thought to experience, the personal to the political, the community to the state, and advocacy to social change. Its authors reflect both academic and practical perspectives.

The text provides a multidimensional analysis of racism by discussing, first, how dominant or majority group values, norms, and conflicting ideologies affect the development and maintenance of inequitable social, economic, and cultural systems and structures in Canada. Second, racism is analyzed by looking at how it is manifested in government, education, media, human services, employment, justice, and law enforcement. Third, the concept of democratic racism is applied to explain why racism continues to flourish in the policies and practices of media and cultural organizations, schools and universities, social and health care agencies, police forces, and justice agencies. Fourth, the text examines the ways in which Canadian society has responded to racism. It documents the struggle for racial justice and equity and the obstacles that prevent them from becoming a reality.

Finally, a word about the authors' purpose in writing this book. The objective of writing a book on racism in Canada was to link the growing theoretical knowledge of the academic community with the first-hand experience of those involved in the struggle against racism. The challenge of writing this text was to make it accessible to students of various disciplines who wish to deepen their understanding of racism as both ideology and practice. It was also written to enhance the knowledge and skills of those who work in fields related to the practice of anti-racism. The authors hope that *The Colour of Democracy: Racism in Canadian Society* will challenge racist beliefs and ideologies, behaviours, and practices and lead to the development, implementation, and institutionalization of new strategies, models, and mechanisms for the development of a more just and equitable society.

ACKNOWLEDGEMENTS

This book documents the nature and dynamics of racism as it affects the everyday life of people of colour in Canada and as it is manifested in Canadian culture and institutions. Across Canada, there are individuals who have been steadfast in their efforts to challenge racial prejudice and discrimination in all its insidious forms. They come from various walks of life and include community activists, writers and artists, educators, bureaucrats, advocates and consultants, academics and practitioners. They are people of colour, Aboriginal people, and "mainstream" Canadians. They are Muslims, Jews, Christians, Hindus, and members of other faiths.

We are deeply indebted to the contribution of our many friends and colleagues who share our vision of making Canada a more just and equitable society for all Canadians. We owe our sincere thanks to all those who shared suggestions for the development of this book.

The authors would also like to thank Li Zong, professor of sociology at the University of Saskatchewan, and Audrey Kobayashi, director of the Institute of Women's Studies at Queen's University. Their helpful comments and suggestions assisted in the fine-tuning of this book.

Statistics Canada information is used with the permission of the Minister of Industry, as minister responsible for Statistics Canada. Information on the availability of the wide range of data from Statistics Canada can be obtained from Statistics Canada's regional offices, its Web site at <http://www.statscan.ca>, and its toll-free access number, 1-800-263-1136.

A NOTE FROM THE PUBLISHER

Thank you for selecting *The Colour of Democracy: Racism in Canadian Society*, Second Edition, by Frances Henry, Carol Tator, Winston Mattis, and Tim Rees. The authors and publisher have devoted considerable time to the careful development of this book. We appreciate your recognition of this effort and accomplishment.

We want to hear what you think about *The Colour of Democracy*. Please take a few minutes to fill out the stamped reader reply card at the back of the book. Your comments and suggestions will be valuable to us as we prepare new editions and other books.

Brief Contents

▼▼▼▼▼▼▼▼▼▼▼▼▼▼▼▼▼▼▼▼▼

Contents

▼ ▼ ▼ ▼ ▼ ▼ ▼ ▼ ▼

PART TWO
Racism in Canadian Public-Sector Organizations

CHAPTER 13
THE PARADOX OF DEMOCRATIC RACISM

Introduction

▼ ▼ ▼ ▼ ▼ ▼ ▼ ▼ ▼ ▼ ▼ ▼ ▼

"I am not a racist."

"She/he is not a racist."

"This is not a racist institution."

"Canada is not a racist society."

In spite of the historical and contemporary evidence of racism as a pervasive and intractable reality in Canada, the above statements have become mantras, which, when repeated, cast an illusory spell that has allowed Canadians to ignore the harsh reality of a society divided by colour and ethnicity. Canada suffers from historical amnesia. Its citizens and institutions function in a state of collective denial. Canadians have obliterated from their collective memory the racist laws, policies, and practices that have shaped their major social, cultural, political, and economic institutions for three hundred years.

Racist beliefs and practices, although widespread and persistent, are frequently invisible to everyone but those who suffer from them. White Canadians tend to dismiss evidence of their racial prejudice and their differential treatment of minorities. Victims' testimonies are unheard and their experiences unacknowledged. Public-sector agencies conduct extensive consultations and then fail to translate their knowledge into substantive initiatives. Government bodies establish task forces and commissions of inquiry on racism to demonstrate their grave concern; their findings and recommendations are ignored. Academics produce empirical studies documenting the ways in which **people of colour** are denied power, equity, and rights, and the studies are then buried. Politicians and the power elite rationalize the racial barriers that prevent people of colour from fully participating in the political process, education, employment, media, justice, human services, and the arts.

In recent years, racism has received increased attention. Racial unrest in Vancouver, Toronto, Montreal, and Halifax, and the demands of **racial-minority** communities for greater participation in Canadian society, have become difficult to ignore. As a result, various levels of government and public-sector organizations such as boards of education, police forces, and human-services and cultural organizations have developed policies and programs and modified some of their traditional practices to respond to demands for equity. Money has been allocated, racial-minority communities have been consulted, and people of colour have been hired and appointed to serve in previously all-White organizations and institutions.

However, fundamental racial inequality continues to affect the lives of people of colour in Canada. Racial prejudice and discrimination exist in the workplace and the classroom. The racist assumptions and practices of the print and electronic media marginalize racial minorities by portraying them as invisible and by depicting them as outsiders. Arts and cultural organizations ignore and exclude the creative images, words, and voices of people of colour. Patterns of policing and the attitudes and behaviour of police officers are marked by overt prejudice and the differential treatment of people of colour, particularly Blacks. The school and university are sites of struggle and inequity for ethno-racial minority students and staff. The justice system fails to give fair and equal treatment to Aboriginal peoples and people of colour. Eurocentric barriers impair the delivery of appropriate services by social and health-care agencies. The state, through its legislation and public policies, further reinforces racist ideology and practices.

In each of these sectors, resistance to **equity** policies and programs and the backlash against **anti-racism** initiatives is found among individuals, organizations, and systems. Widespread opposition to any change in the status quo dramatically reduces the effectiveness of any efforts to promote equity.

At the federal level of government, there is no policy to deal with racism. Some argue that **multiculturalism**, as a public policy enshrined in legislation, provides a framework for legitimizing cultural and racial diversity and for ensuring the rights of all Canadians. Yet, despite the Multiculturalism Act's affirmation of the pluralistic nature of Canadian society, Canadians appear deeply ambivalent about the public recognition of other cultures, the freedom of non-White racial and non-European cultural groups to maintain their unique identities, and the right of minorities to function in a society free of racism.

Canada's racist heritage has bequeathed to both earlier and present generations of Canadians a powerful set of perceptions and behavioural patterns regarding people of colour. A deeply entrenched system of White dominance perpetuates inequity and oppression against the socially and economically disadvantaged.

However, racism as a commanding force in this country is constantly challenged and denied by applying the arguments of democratic liberalism. In a society that espouses equality, tolerance, social harmony, and respect for individual rights, the existence of racial prejudice, discrimination, and disadvantage is difficult to acknowledge and therefore remedy. Canadians have a deep attachment to the assumptions that in a democratic society individuals are rewarded solely on the basis of their individual merit and that no one group is singled out for discrimination. Consistent with these liberal, democratic values is the assumption that physical differences such as **skin colour** are irrelevant in determining one's status.

Therefore, those who experience racial bias or differential treatment are considered somehow responsible for their state, resulting in a "blame it on the victim" syndrome.

This conflict between democratic liberalism and the collective racism of the dominant culture creates a dissonance in Canadian society. There is a constant and fundamental moral tension between the everyday experiences of people of colour and the perceptions of those who have the power to redefine that reality — politicians, bureaucrats, educators, judges, journalists, and the corporate elite. While lip service is paid to the need to ensure equality in a pluralistic society, most Canadian individuals, organizations, and institutions are far more committed to maintaining or increasing their own power.

The multiplicity of ways in which these values conflict is the subject of this book. It examines this phenomenon and analyzes the impact of "democratic racism" on Canadian society and its institutions.

The second edition of this book continues to explore the changing face of racism and the dynamics of democratic racism. The major change in the text is a new focus on the construct of **racist discourse**, that is, an exploration of the link between the collective values, beliefs, and practices of culture and the discourse of racism buried in our language, national narratives and myths, public accounts, and everyday commonsense interpretations, explanations, and rationalizations. Smitherman-Donaldson and van Dijk (1988) contend that discourse is not just a symptom of the problem of racism. It essentially reinforces and reproduces the racist beliefs and actions of the dominant culture. This edition of the text analyzes more fully the relationship between two conflicting ideologies — racism and liberalism — and examines how these tensions are expressed in racialized discourse.

In the chapters dealing with institutions such as policing, justice, human services, education, arts and culture, and the state, the authors explore how liberal principles such as individualism, universalism, equal opportunity, and tolerance become the language and conceptual framework through which intolerance and exclusion are defined and defended (Mackey, 1996; Goldberg, 1993).

In this edition, the authors have added a new chapter, "Racism and Aboriginal Peoples." The evidence of racism in Canada is most graphically manifested in the four-hundred-year relationship between White society and indigenous peoples. Woven into this book are numerous references to the impact of racism on indigenous peoples, but the focus in most chapters is on people of colour or racial minorities who are relatively recent arrivals in Canada. In this edition, the authors felt it was important to apply their conceptual framework of democratic racism to the experiences of Aboriginal peoples in this country. It is important to underscore the fact that no one chapter in any text can deal with the complexity of histories and issues that are part of the Aboriginal experience in Canada. The authors encourage readers to explore further the well-documented studies of racism against Aboriginal peoples.

TERMINOLOGY

One of the first challenges that confronts anyone analyzing racism is iden-tifying an appropriate terminology. One must search for words that them-selves are not viewed as racist and, at the same time, clearly and accurately communicate what racism means. As the phenomenon of racism continues to show diverse manifestations, so too does the language evolve. Not only do new words emerge, but the historical context of "old" words affects the ways in which they are used.

The sometimes radical changes that language undergoes suggest there is no fixed or correct meaning for any term (Williams, 1983). Apple ex-presses the challenge of language in this way: "Concepts do not remain still very long. They have wings so to speak, and can be induced to fly from place to place" (1993:25). One therefore needs to look for the meanings of particular terms in their specific contextual use. Concepts such as culture, race, history, truth, freedom of expression, and universalism, for example, are not neutral; rather, they exist as part of many different social and inter-pretative frameworks. There are powerful currents that alter interpreta-tions, depending on the situation, location, and social context (Lentricchia and McLaughlin, 1990; Fiske, 1994).

Although colour remains the nucleus of the race classification system, paradoxically, it bears little relation to the actual skin tones of human be-ings. No White person is truly white, nor is any Black individual truly black. Whites do not consider themselves part of the colour spectrum but rather identify their group as constituting the universal norm. Howev-er, the gradations of colour from white to black associated with various racial groups have economic, social, and cultural consequences. The ideol-ogy that defines Whites as superior renders people of different colours in-ferior.

As we demonstrate in every chapter of this book, skin colour has an im-portant relationship to status and position in Canadian society. Razack ar-gues that the language of colour delineates the politics of domination and subordination, observing that "White ... is the colour of domina-tion" (1998:11). Making this point in terms of her personal experience as a person of colour, St. Lewis observes: "In conversations about race, all of my being is telescoped to my skin. The colour of my skin drives the engine of my public life. It defines relationships and sets out possibilities. Attitudes and beliefs make it real" (1996:28).

It is for these reasons that references to colour in this text are used in their political sense, and the terms "Black" and "White" are capitalized to reflect this context. The reader will note that references citing British liter-ature or experiences use the term Black inclusively, to refer to people of colour. However, in all other discussions, Black refers specifically to people of African descent.

The terms "**mainstream**," "Anglo," and "the **dominant group**" are used interchangeably throughout this book to refer to the group in Canadian so-ciety that maintains the power to define itself and its culture as the norm.

Although the phrases "racial minorities" and "people of colour" appear frequently in this book, they are used cautiously. Referring to groups of people who represent four fifths of the world's population as minorities is, at the very least, inaccurate. Furthermore, huge distinctions exist among racial minorities or people of colour. There are, for example, in each of the groups examined in this book, significant differences that relate to class and gender. The experiences of recent affluent immigrants from Hong Kong, who come to Canada with significant resources and business skills, bear little similarity to those of the unskilled worker who is a third-generation Canadian or the Chinese refugee fleeing from political persecution.

In using the phrases "racial minorities" and "people of colour," we are referring to groups of people who because of their physical characteristics are subjected to differential and unequal treatment in Canada. Their minority status is the result of a lack of access to power, privilege, and prestige in relation to the White majority group. Although there are significant differences among "racial minorities" or "people of colour," as there are within any ethno-racial group, members of these diverse communities share a history of exposure to racial bias and discriminatory barriers based on the colour of their skin. So, for the purposes of this book, they are grouped together. The term "Aboriginal peoples" is used most commonly in this text, although there are also references to "First Nations" and "indigenous peoples." Again, these terms refer to an extremely heterogeneous population.

Finally, what do we mean by "race" and "racism"? Our theoretical perspective is that race is a socially constructed phenomenon (see Chapters 1 and 2 for more detailed definitions) based on the erroneous assumption that physical differences such as skin colour, hair colour and texture, and facial features are related to intellectual, moral, or cultural superiority. The concept of race has no basis in biological reality and, as such, has no meaning independent of its social definitions. But, as a social construction, race significantly affects the lives of people of colour.

Racism (more correctly, "social racism") refers to the assumptions, attitudes, beliefs, and behaviours of individuals as well as to the institutional policies, processes, and practices that flow from those understandings. Racism as racialized language or discourse is manifested in the articulation of ideologies and policies through euphemisms, metaphors, omissions, and passive language. It is reflected in the collective belief systems of the dominant culture, and it is woven into the laws, language, rules, and norms of Canadian society.

Another term frequently used in this book, "racialization," often appears in studies on racism produced in the United Kingdom, particularly those that use a political economy perspective. The terms "racialized" and "racist" are sometimes used interchangeably in this book in reference to discourse (as both language and social practice). "Racialized," less familiar to North American readers, has been defined as "processes by which meanings are attributed to particular objects, features and processes, in such a way that the latter are given special significance and carry or are embodied with a set of additional meanings" (Miles, 1989:70).

Skin colour as a feature of race therefore carries with it more than the signification of "colour"; it also includes a set of meanings attached to the cultural traits of those who are a certain colour, and these meanings are incorporated into everyday language and the discursive practices of politicians, bureaucrats, institutional authorities, the media, and other opinion shapers (Stam, 1993). The assertion that "Blacks are prone to commit crimes" therefore signifies that members of a racial group, identified by their skin colour, have a propensity for certain behaviour. Ideological racialization refers to the ways in which discourse concerning a set of principles becomes imbued with racial dimensions.

For example, in Canada, the debate about immigration has become racialized because substantial numbers of immigrants are now people of colour. Restricting immigration therefore becomes a means of excluding these groups. The racialization of crime results in the stigmatization of certain groups. For example, racialization in the media results in news stories and editorials in which Blacks figure prominently in crimes that are also committed by members of other groups.

PERSPECTIVE

Before embarking on an analysis of racism in Canadian society, some of the text's limitations should be noted. The authors have tried to provide a national perspective on racism in Canada and, wherever possible, to draw on the experiences and expertise of theoreticians and practitioners across the country. However, for the past two decades, Ontario has been one of the primary sites of the anti-racism struggle in Canada. It has the greatest number of people of colour in its population, and its minority communities, especially in Toronto, have perhaps been more politicized and more insistent on ensuring that racism become part of the public agenda.

The authors' work as anti-racism and equity educators, consultants, and practitioners has provided them with direct knowledge of the organizational and institutional processes occurring in each of the arenas described in Part Two. Although they document the events, issues, and activities in other Canadian jurisdictions as well as in the United States and the United Kingdom, they believe that the text's focus on Ontario will be of interest and educational value to readers everywhere.

Throughout this text, there are frequent references to the British experience with racism and anti-racism. Although important differences exist between Canada and the United Kingdom, many similarities exist with respect to the patterns of bias and discrimination against people of colour. Moreover, an extensive body of literature documents racism in British society, its effects on the victims, and various strategies for dismantling racist ideologies, structures, and practices (Rex, 1988; Benyon and Solomos, 1987; Hall, 1991; Gilroy, 1987). The British evidence, therefore, is both timely and relevant to the discussion of racism and anti-racism in Canadian society.

The United Kingdom is, in many ways, a paradigm for Canadian society. It has had a similar pattern of immigration from the Commonwealth of Nations. Immigrants of colour from the Caribbean and Asia began arriving in large numbers in Britain more than twenty years before they did so in Canada. Thinking that they would be well received as members of the Commonwealth, immigrants of colour in Britain were shocked at the racism they faced in employment, housing, social services, policing, and the justice system (Gilroy, 1982; Hall et al., 1978).

FRAMEWORK

Part One establishes a framework for understanding the nature of democratic racism. Chapter 1 introduces the reader to the concept of democratic racism by examining a central ideological struggle in Canadian society: the conflict between the image of a country with a strong and cherished tradition of democratic liberalism and the reality of persistent and pervasive inequality based on colour. While individuals, organizations, institutions, and the state vigorously deny the presence of racism, it flourishes in this liberal democratic country, deeply affecting the daily lives of people of colour. This chapter looks at how democratic racism functions in terms of individual and collective belief systems and behaviour. It challenges the many myths that prevent Canadians from confronting and responding to racism.

Chapter 2 provides a brief overview of theories of racism developed in the United States, the United Kingdom, and Canada. It also provides definitions of terms used in the study of racism. It then turns to the problems of assessing and measuring racism.

Chapter 3 reviews some of the evidence of racism in Canada by looking at the experiences of specific groups in the history of this country. It also draws on the findings of task forces, government inquiries, research, and polls and surveys conducted over the past two decades. One of the main thrusts of this chapter, however, is to demonstrate the extent of individual and everyday racism in Canada. The documented experiences of people of colour provide commanding evidence of racism in Canada. Hate-group activity and the proliferation of White-supremacist groups further demonstrate individual prejudice and discrimination in Canadian society. The final section of this chapter draws on the evidence of employment and housing discrimination to demonstrate how deeply embedded racism is in the fabric of Canadian society.

Chapter 4 examines democratic racism and its impact on Aboriginal communities of Canada. It is important to point out that the relationship between Aboriginal peoples and the state is significantly different from the relationship between racial minorities and the state. The position of Aboriginal peoples is governed by treaties and legislation. Their role and status is determined by formal mechanisms, and the solutions to their systemic racial oppression lie in a unique set of strategies (for example, self-government) that are unavailable to other people of colour. Nevertheless, there are some common elements in the politics of race, racism, and cultural hegemony in the context of both the democratic liberalism and the hierarchical social relations that characterize Canadian society.

Part Two examines a number of key institutions in Canadian society — particularly service providers in the public sector — within which racism continues to be a significant source of tension, conflict, and oppression. The chapters in this part — on policing, the justice system, and the human services — demonstrate how the policies, programs, procedures, and delivery systems of the major institutions in Canada discriminate against people of colour. The analysis of these key institutions illuminates the nature of racism in Canada as it is articulated in both overt and covert organizational and discursive practices.

Chapter 5 examines the justice system from the perspective of the differential treatment of racial minorities in the granting of bail, sentencing, and minority representation in the system. Case studies highlight the attitudes of justice system officials.

Chapter 6 analyzes racism in Canadian law-enforcement agencies. It explores the culture of policing, the racialization of crime, and the over-policing and underpolicing of minority communities. The chapter then critically examines the responses of police forces across Canada in areas such as training, policy development, employment equity, community relations, and the use of force.

Chapter 7 examines the models and delivery of human services. It shows how racism is reflected in the professional values, assumptions, and practices of social workers and other human-services practitioners. It emphasizes the role, position, and status of "minority" workers as an example of how mainstream organizations operate in a racist manner.

In continuing to examine the institutional arenas in Canadian social structure, Part Three analyzes racism in education (schools, colleges, and universities), the media, and the arts. These areas develop, protect, and support a society's values, beliefs, and systems. The chapters in this part focus on the ways in which the ideology of racism is supported and sustained in these institutional defenders of Canada's collective belief system. They also show how the myths and assumptions of democratic racism are employed as discursive strategies to avoid the necessity of acknowledging that the ideology of racism is central to the definition of Canada.

Chapter 8 looks at one of the most powerful socializing agents in society, the educational system, and at the ways in which racism pervades the teaching process and the learning environment and forms an intrinsic part of the organizational structure of schools and classrooms. It explores the ways in which Eurocentric and assimilationist values and ideologies influence curriculum and teaching practices. Examples are presented of the ways in which racial bias and differential treatment affect the educational opportunities of students of colour, particularly Black students. The analysis related to postsecondary institutions challenges the widespread notion that colleges and universities are free of racism by discussing the lack of minority representation in hiring, promotion, and tenure decisions; the prevalence of Eurocentric curriculum and pedagogy; racial tensions and harassment in the schools; and the "chilly climate" among students and between students and faculty in colleges and universities. This examination of racism in education draws upon the theory of discourse analysis to demonstrate that schools and universities are discursive sites, where educators employ a variety of discursive strategies to avoid dealing with the reality of racism within the system.

Chapter 9 analyzes cultural racism by looking at the Eurocentric values and assumptions of arts and cultural organizations in Canada. The power of White culture to define the standards of excellence and professionalism in the arts and to determine what images and voices are outside the boundaries of mainstream culture is an important dimension of cultural racism. This chapter analyzes the **appropriation** of minority cultural experiences and symbols by people outside those cultures as another manifestation of racism. It examines the barriers to participation in the arts in the context of the underrepresentation of racial-minority artists and writers in art galleries, museums, publishing houses, art councils, unions, and associations. The chapter's three case studies illustrate the how people of colour do not have control over cultural systems constructed by the dominant culture, which promotes, supports, and affirms forms of marginalization and exclusion. The chapter also analyzes the response of the dominant group to those who challenge racist representations in cultural production.

Chapter 10 focuses on the mass media and explores how the print and electronic media use their enormous influence to marginalize racial minorities in Canada. It shows how the media, contrary to public myth, are linked to political, social, and corporate elites and legitimate White power structures. It provides an analysis and examples of influential power-brokers shaping the agendas, information, and images circulated by media organizations in the public domain. The chapter concludes with an examination of the discursive strategies used by the media to silence criticism, resistance, and dissent by minorities. In this process, people of colour are labelled as "other" and excluded from definitions of Canadian identity and the national culture.

Part Four provides an analysis of the impact of democratic racism on the state and society by focussing on the ways in which organizational authorities, politicians, bureaucrats, the legal system, and public policies maintain, reinforce, and reproduce racist ideologies and discursive practices. By examining the change process used by many of these agencies, it is possible to identify some of the powerful and widespread forms of resistance to organizational and institutional change, despite these agencies' stated commitment to the liberal principles of fairness, tolerance, and equality.

Chapter 11 examines the rhetorical strategies underlying the development of central state policies, doctrines, and legislative frameworks. Through this analysis, it is possible to identify the powerful but invisible ambivalence that characterizes democratic racism at the level of the state. This chapter poses the question, What role does the state play in perpetuating and reproducing racism? It looks at the laws, policies, and processes of various levels of government that affect the lives of people of colour in Canadian society. Multiculturalism in its many forms is examined as ideology, legislative act, and discursive practice. The Canadian Charter of Rights and Freedoms and provincial human rights codes and commissions are briefly analyzed. The examination of state responses includes an analysis of employment equity legislation and of the resistance to it as a prime example of the politics of resistance engaged in by the dominant culture. The discursive analysis of this resistance incorporates a discussion of the impact of the rise of neoconservative ideology, particularly in Ontario and elsewhere in Canada. (It is also a growing phenomenon in most other Western industrialized nations.) This ideology reinforces hegemonic ideologies and relations, but is articulated in a refashioned liberal discourse.

Chapter 12 analyzes the weaknesses of the approaches and strategies identified in the preceding chapters in dealing with racism in Canadian society and institutions. In exploring resistance to change, it shows again how democratic racism works in terms of discursive practices and organizational structures, policies, values, and norms: individuals and organizations continue to assert their commitment to fairness and equality for all, while at the same time opposing measures that would ensure racial equity.

Chapter 13 concludes the book by discussing how democratic racism has often led to the failure of new policies, programs, and practices to alleviate the oppression of people of colour in the social, cultural, economic, and political arenas. Analyzing the weaknesses of many of the current approaches also allows for some reflection on strategies for change. A number of measures are examined as possible future directions: the development of critical self-awareness, reflective skills and practices on the part of educators, media practitioners, human-service workers, cultural workers, police, judges, employers, decision-makers in public and private institutions, and others; community empowerment; mechanisms for monitoring and evaluating new policies, programs, and practices and for responding to institutional resistance; and the development of organizational and administrative measures and accountability systems based on a recognition of the pervasiveness of racism in the central institutions of Canadian society.

Readers may notice an occasional dearth of research documentation on Canada in some of the chapters. One of the main reasons for this omission is that there is relatively little published research on racism in Canadian institutions. The authors therefore cite many American and British sources and rely extensively on their professional expertise in this field and their own field research. For example, extensive interviews were conducted for the analysis of racism in the arts and culture chapter.

REFERENCES

Apple, M. (1993). "Constructing the 'Other': Rightist Reconstructions of Common Sense." In C. McCarthy and W. Crichlow (eds.), *Race, Identity and Representation in Education.* New York and London: Routledge. 24–39.

Benyon J., and J. Solomos (eds.). (1987). *The Roots of Urban Unrest*. Oxford: Pergamon Press.

Fiske, J. (1994). *Media Matters: Everyday Culture and Political Change*. Minneapolis: University of Minnesota Press.

Gilroy, P. (1982). In Centre for Contemporary Cultural Studies, *The Empire Strikes Back: Race and Racism in 70's Britain*. London: Hutchinson.

——. (1987). *There Ain't No Black in the Union Jack: The Cultural Politics of Race and Nation*. London: Hutchinson.

Goldberg, D.S. (1993). *Racist Culture: Philosophy and Politics of Meaning*. Oxford, UK, and Cambridge, MA: Blackwell.

Hall, S. (1991). "Old and New Identities: Old and New Ethnicities." In A. King (ed.), *Culture, Globalization, and the World System*. Binghampton: Department of Art History, State University of New York.

——, et al. (1978). *Policing the Crisis*. London: Macmillan.

Lentricchia, F., and T. McLaughlin (eds.). (1990). *Critical Terms for Literary Study*. 2nd ed. Chicago: University of Chicago Press.

Mackey, E. (1996). "Managing and Imagining Diversity: Multiculturalism and the Construction of National Identity in Canada." Ph.D. thesis, University of Sussex.

Miles, R. (1989). *Racism*. London: Routledge.

Razack, S. (1998). *Looking White People in the Eye: Gender, Race and Culture in Courtrooms and Classrooms*. Toronto: University of Toronto Press.

Rex, J. (1988). *The Ghetto and the Underclass*. Aldershot, UK, and Brookfield, VT: Avebury.

St. Lewis, J. (1996). "Identity and Black Consciousness in North America." In J. Littleton (ed.), *Clash of Identities: Essays on Media, Manipulation and Politics of Self*. Englewood Cliffs, NJ: Prentice Hall. 21-30.

Smitherman-Donaldson, G., and T. van Dijk. (1988). *Discourse and Discrimination*. Detroit: Wayne State University.

Stam, R. (1993). "From Stereotype to Discourse." *Cine-Action* (23)(Fall): 12–29.

Williams, R. (1983). *Keywords: A Vocabulary of Culture and Society*. 2nd ed. London: Fontana.

PART
ONE

▼▼▼

Perspectives
on Racism

▼▼▼▼▼▼▼▼▼▼▼▼▼▼▼▼▼▼▼▼▼▼▼▼▼

*This part introduces the concept of democratic racism and
provides a general perspective on racism. A discussion of the theoretical
explanations of racism, as documented by social science literature,
is presented in Chapter 2. Chapter 3 reviews the evidence of racism
in Canadian society, drawing on historical examples
as well as current studies, polls, and surveys.
Chapter 4 reviews the history of racism in relation to
Canada's Aboriginal peoples.*

▼▼▼

Chapter 1

▼▼▼▼▼▼▼▼▼▼▼▼

The Ideology of Racism

We are at one of those critical junctures where two ideals are in conflict. There's the principle of the legal equality of all. There's the fact that there are serious inequalities in our society, many of which can only be remedied by treating people unequally. Which puts liberals like myself at war with ourselves. (Gwyn, 1993)

This chapter examines the **ideology** of **racism** in Canada today. It begins with a brief examination of the function of ideology as the basis of social behaviour and then explores the nature of **racist ideology**. This ideology provides the foundation for understanding the racist **attitudes** and behaviours of individuals, the maintenance of racist policies and practices in Canadian **institutions**, and the promulgation of racist doctrines and laws by the state. The chapter analyzes the role and functions of racist ideology and introduces the concept of **democratic racism**. The last section of this chapter examines the discourse of democratic racism and some of the myths that support and reinforce racism as ideology and praxis.

Democratic racism is an ideology that permits and sustains people's ability to maintain two apparently conflicting sets of values. One set consists of a commitment to a liberal, democratic society motivated by the egalitarian values of fairness, justice, and equality. Conflicting with these values are attitudes and behaviours that include negative feelings about people of colour and that result in differential treatment of them, or **discrimination** against them. Democratic racism, in its simplest form, is an ideology that reduces the conflict between maintaining a commitment to both egalitarian and non-egalitarian values.

INTRODUCTION

WHAT IS IDEOLOGY?

Ideology is a set of beliefs, perceptions, assumptions, and values that provide members of a group with an understanding and an explanation of their world. At another level, ideology provides a framework for "organizing, maintaining and transforming relations of power and dominance in society" (Fleras and Elliott, 1992:54).

Ideology influences the ways in which people interpret social, cultural, political, and economic systems and structures, and it is linked to their perceived needs, hopes, and fears. Ideological formations are not static but organic and constantly evolving, often as a result of contradictory experiences (Hall, 1983).

People are often unaware of their ideologies:

> It is indeed a peculiarity of ideology that it imposes (without appearing to do so) obviousness as obviousness which we cannot fail to recognize and before which we have the inevitable and natural reaction of crying out (aloud or in the still small voice of conscience): "That's obvious! That's right! That's true!" (Althusser, 1971:127)

Within these everyday ideological constructs, ideas about **race**, gender, and class are produced, preserved, and promoted. These ideas form the basis for social behaviour. Therefore, understanding ideology is crucial to an understanding of the marginalization, **exclusion**, and domination of people of colour in Canadian society.

THE DEFINITION AND FUNCTION OF RACIST IDEOLOGY

Racist ideology provides the conceptual framework for the political, social, and cultural structures of inequality and systems of dominance based on race, as well as the processes of exclusion and marginalization of people of colour that characterize Canadian society.

The cognitive dimensions of racism are located in collective patterns of thought, knowledge, and beliefs as well as individual attitudes, perceptions, and behaviours. "Racism as ideology includes the whole range of concepts, ideas, images and institutions that provide the framework of interpretation and meaning for racial thought in society" (Essed, 1990:44). Racist ideology therefore organizes, preserves, and perpetuates the power structures in a society. It creates and preserves a system of dominance based on race and is communicated and reproduced through agencies of socialization and cultural transmission, such as the mass media, schools and universities, religious doctrines, symbols and images, art, music, and literature. It is reflected and regenerated in the very language we read, write, and speak.

THE ELUSIVE NATURE OF RACISM

One of the most complex aspects of racism is its elusive and changing nature. The most commonly accepted concept of racism in Canada is one that refers to the individual expression of overt feelings or actions. Racism is generally understood to refer to physical assaults that have been perpetrated by bigoted individuals, racial slurs and **harassment** in

Figure 1.1
IDEOLOGY AND ITS EFFECTS

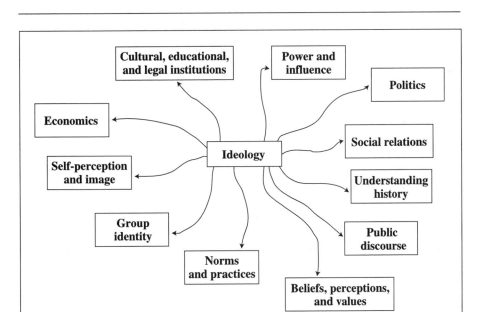

schools or in the workplace, defacing property with racial graffiti, and similar overt acts. There seems to be an extremely limited understanding of racism in public discourse. Racism manifests itself not only within individuals, but also in groups, organizations, institutions, at the state level, and in the value system of society. In each arena, racism assumes a different form. This will be discussed in more detail in Chapter 2. It has "a geographic, social and historical specificity. In any country, at any point of time, the realization of racist practice will be of a specific nature" (Brandt, 1986:67–68).

Racism is not a natural element in society, just waiting for a series of events to trigger its manifestations:

> It has no natural and universal law of development. It does not always assume the same shape. There have been many significantly different *racisms* — each historically specific and articulated in a different way. Racism is always historically specific in this way, whatever common features it may appear to share with other similar social phenomena. It always assumes specific forms which arise out of the *present* — not the past — conditions and organization of society. (Hall, 1978:26)

Thus the ways in which racism manifests itself at any particular time are fluid, dynamic, and ever-changing. They are affected by the social contexts in which racism develops.

In a similar vein, the study of racism provides "a picture ... of historically variant racism both continuously and discontinuously transformed from one period to another. Subject, objects, and modes alter. Developments and changes in racist discourse are demonstrated to be functions of dominant interests, aims, and purposes" (Goldberg, 1990:xiii).

Another important dimension of racism is its ability to be so subtly expressed or indirectly implied that its targets are not even aware of it. Conversely, racism is sometimes visible only to its victims. It remains indiscernible to others, who therefore deny its existence.

The subtle and ever-changing nature of racism helps to explain both its persistence over time and the difficulties of defining and measuring it. However, although many are confused by the term, racism rests on this mystification of social relations — the necessary illusions that secure the order of public authority (Gilroy, 1987).

Racist ideology forms part of "common sense." Racist thinking, according to this view, is natural and forms part of the ways in which ordinary people view the world — they do not need to have specialized knowledge about **minority groups** to be racist. "Commonsense" racism is not based on theory, nor does it have a unified body of knowledge to support it; it contains a "storehouse of knowledge" that guides the thinking of "the practical struggle of everyday life of the popular masses" (Lawrence, 1982:49).

The construction of and belief in a racist ideology helps people to understand the increasingly complex societies in which they live. Thus, recently unemployed people can easily blame the new immigrants who have taken their jobs away. People who are fearful in their homes and on the streets can now blame all those Black or Asian people who commit crimes. Teachers whose Black students are underachieving can believe that it has nothing to do with their racial attitudes or classroom practices. The corporate manager is able to justify a refusal to hire those who are racially "different" on the basis of not wanting to disrupt the harmony of the work force.

Racist assumptions and beliefs provide a ready explanation for the stress experienced by people who live in a country undergoing rapid social and cultural change:

> Racism is not a set of a false pleas which swim around in the head. They're not a set of mistaken perceptions. They have their basis in real material conditions of existence. They arise because of concrete problems of different classes and groups in society. Racism represents the attempt ideologically to construct those conditions, contradictions, and problems in such a way that they can be dealt with and deflected in the same moment. (Hall, 1978:35)

Ideology may go far beyond individual beliefs and attitudes; it carries with it a predisposition to behave in negative, derogatory, or discriminatory ways toward members of the targeted group. An ideology of racism therefore is more powerful than mere attitudes or beliefs (Hall et al., 1978). Ideology denotes a set of ideas and values that legitimate particular economic and social conditions. It penetrates and saturates everyday discourses in the form of common sense and provides codes of meaning (Hebridge, 1993:363).

THE CONCEPT OF DEMOCRATIC RACISM

The primary characteristic of democratic racism — the most appropriate model for understanding how and why racism continues in Canada — is the justification of the inherent conflict between the egalitarian values of justice and fairness and the racist ideologies reflected in the collective mass-belief system as well as the racist attitudes, perceptions, and assumptions of individuals.

Racist beliefs and practices continue to pervade Canadian society. Attitude surveys have found that many Canadians hold racist views. In the first such survey carried out in Canada, about 16 percent of Canadian adults were found to be confirmed bigots, while a further 35 percent held somewhat intolerant views. Another 30 percent leaned toward tolerance, and the remaining 20 percent were extremely tolerant (Henry, 1978). Later surveys and polls support these findings (see Chapter 3). Most Canadians therefore hold some degree of racist attitudes. But, living in a society that believes in democracy, most Canadians also recognize that these attitudes are socially unacceptable. In order to maintain their racist beliefs while championing democratic values, Canadians have developed the ideology of democratic racism — a set of justificatory arguments and mechanisms that permit these contradictory ideologies to coexist.

Democratic racism, therefore, results from the retention of racist beliefs and behaviours in a "democratic" society. The obfuscation and justificatory arguments of democratic racism are deployed to demonstrate continuing faith in the principles of an egalitarian society while at the same time undermining and sabotaging those ideals.

Before discussing this ideology as it pertains to Canada, it is useful to analyze it in the context of the United Kingdom and the United States. In the former the concept of "new racism" has been elaborated, while in the latter "aversive racism" has appeared in the literature. These aspects of racism, identified by critical theorists in the United Kingdom, are also relevant to Canada and are included in democratic racism.

NEW RACISM IN THE UNITED KINGDOM

Distancing themselves from the crude ideas of biological inferiority and superiority, "new racists" have defined a national British **culture** that is homogeneously White. It is concerned with

mechanisms of inclusion and exclusion. It specifies who may legitimately belong to the national community and simultaneously advances reasons for the segregation or banishment of those whose "origin"... assigns
them elsewhere. [West Indians, and Asians, for different reasons] are
judged to be incompatible with authentic forms of Englishness. Alien
cultures come to embody a threat which, in turn, invites the conclusion
that national decline and weakness have been precipitated by the arrival
of Blacks. (Gilroy, 1987:45–46)

Scholars in the United Kingdom have analyzed the trend toward the increasing racialization of state policies "in all areas of social life" (CCCS,
1982:19). For at least the past two decades, observers have noted the central government's lack of sympathy and support for racial-equality initiatives (Ball and Solomos, 1990). The policy interventions of the central government have tended to affirm a deep-seated commitment to the rights of
the White majority rather than those of minority communities. Herman
Ouseley notes that the failure "to implement radical race equality policies
was the result of inadequate attempts by national and local politicians"
(Ball and Solomos, 1990). Such state policies reinforce the racist thinking
of much of the population.

Lawrence (1982) identified a number of racial ideologies characteristic
of the Conservative-run state in Great Britain. At their heart is a definition
of "British" that clearly excludes people of colour who come from former
(and present) Commonwealth countries. This definition affirms the "natu-
ralness" of British values, British culture, and especially British family life.
Within the politics of nationalism, sovereignty, and cultural **identity**, it defines the nation as a unified *cultural* community (Gilroy, 1987). Thus,
White anti-racists are regarded as having been influenced by "alien" ideas.

Although new racism no longer espouses doctrines of racial superiority (there are exceptions, particularly in academia and the extreme right), it
nevertheless denigrates people of colour. The myths that fuel new racism
often derive from a negative evaluation of other cultures rather than from a
focus on race. This ideology, for example, expresses itself in a negative evaluation of Black culture, particularly the "deviant" Black family and the
"aberrant" behaviour of Black youth. Thus, although police officials do not
consider themselves racist, they believe that Blacks are culturally disposed
to criminal behaviour. Further, the media, while not admitting racism, publish report after report in which derogatory cultural characteristics are highlighted.

New racism cites pathological cultural patterns as major reasons for
criminal behaviour, poverty, poor achievement in school, and an assortment
of other social problems. Blacks show their inferiority by having a propensity for loud music and raucous conversation. New racists therefore cloak
their negative attitudes toward other groups by claiming that while they do
not believe in racial superiority, not all cultures are equally valid. The cultural behaviour of the "others," such as Blacks, demonstrates that they are
not the same as Whites and cannot be part of the national culture.

When race is identified with identity and culture, careful language enables people to "speak about race without mentioning the word" (Gilroy, 1987:53). The crude and overtly racist labels of the far right are avoided, but the new racism can be articulated by the choice of carefully coded language: "'They,' despite the good qualities of some of 'them,' are held to be different from 'us' and would, on the whole, be better off back in 'their' countries" (Billig et al., 1988:107).

Another form of discourse in which overt racism is avoided occurs in the "two-handedness of the 'on the one hand, on the other hand' formulation. Having stated an opposition to racism or to **prejudice**, the way is then opened for an expression of racist or prejudiced views" (Billig et al., 1988:109). These formulations appear in an ideology in which traditional racism is eschewed but a newer, masked, and more subtle form is allowed expression. Modern racism is expressed in a rhetorical context, demonstrated in comments such as "I'm not a racist, but...," which are followed by an overtly racist statement.

AVERSIVE RACISM IN THE UNITED STATES

In the United States, a new form of democratic racism has been explored by social psychologists, who analyze the individual's attitudes. Gaertner and Dovidio (1986) present the results of studies of racism among the "well intentioned":

> Our work has focused on those White Americans, who, in terms of racism and public policy, seem "well intentioned." That is, they genuinely profess egalitarianism, as well as the desire to ameliorate the consequences of racism and poverty. However, we believe that the racial attitudes of many of these well-intentioned people may be characterized by a special type of ambivalence: aversiveness. (Gaertner and Dovidio, 1981:208)

Their analysis builds on what was earlier identified as "aversive racism" (Kovel, 1970). In this pioneering work, Kovel distinguished "dominative" racists — strong hard-core bigots who are prepared to act on their attitudes — from "aversive" racists. The latter also believe in White supremacy, but do nothing about it. Aversive racists are prejudiced but do not act in discriminatory ways. Some avoid contact with Blacks and other minorities, but when contact is unavoidable, they are polite.

Other aversive racists, however, "are impelled by a strong social conscience, consider themselves liberals and, despite their sense of aversion (which may not be admitted inwardly) do their best within the given structure of society to ameliorate the conditions of the Negro" (Kovel, 1970:55). They believe in fairness and equality for all and pride themselves on their strong social conscience. They may not be aware of their aversion to Blacks (or other minorities) and appear to have a positive racial attitude. Gaertner and Dovidio note that this attitude is superficial, ambiguous, and complex.

Their studies have identified a number of characteristics of aversive racists, including the following:

- Aversive racists consider themselves prejudice-free but attempt to avoid contact with the minority group to which they are averse.
- Aversive racists think of themselves as politically liberal and non-discriminatory. In a situation in which clearly prescribed norms call for tolerant behaviour, they will behave appropriately. However, in situations in which there are no clear prescriptive norms, they may indulge in discriminatory behaviour because it would not be obvious.
- Aversive racists' positive actions toward minority groups relate less to a genuine effort to help minorities or to implement egalitarian values than to reaffirm their own lack of prejudice. This attitude may result in tokenism: aversive racists affirm that they are prejudice-free by making trivial gestures that preclude the necessity for extensive, costly action. (Gaertner, 1976:208)

Aversive racism therefore "represents a particular type of ambivalence in which the conflict is between feelings and beliefs associated with a sincerely egalitarian value system and unacknowledged negative feelings and beliefs about Blacks" (Gaertner and Dovidio, 1986:62). Moreover, this type of racism does not necessarily include feelings of hate or hostility, nor will it usually express itself in hostile or discriminatory behaviour. Aversive racism involves "discomfort, uneasiness, disgust, and sometimes fear, which tend to motivate avoidance rather than intentionally destructive behaviours" (Gaertner and Dovidio, 1986:63).

Aversive racism stems from socialization and is reinforced by social and cultural factors. In the United States, for example, the denigration of Black culture, Black **stereotypes**, and the constant association of Black people with poverty, crime, and delinquency reinforces negative racial attitudes. Moreover, the differential distribution of social, economic, and political power between Blacks and Whites further reinforces these attitudes.

SYMBOLIC RACISM

Closely aligned to the aversive form, symbolic racism is an attitude in which "abstract moral assertions are made about Blacks' behaviour as a group, concerning what Blacks deserve, how they ought to act, whether or not they are treated equitably, and so on" (Sears and McConahay, 1973:138). Symbolic racism manifests itself in "acts that are rationalized on a non-racial basis but that actually maintain the racial status quo by continuing discrimination against Blacks" (Sears and McConahay, 1973:24). In the United States, these acts include voting for White rather than Black candidates, opposing affirmative-action programs, and opposing desegregation in housing and education. In Canada, opposing **affirmative action** and **employment equity** is an act of symbolic racism.

Other aspects of symbolic racism have relevance for Canada. For example, unlike the older "redneck" bigotry, which denied equal rights and opportunities for people of colour, symbolic racism allows a person to uphold these values but still believe that Blacks are "too pushy" because they are making too many demands for equality too quickly. Moreover, Whites who hold these views may not feel personally threatened by Black claims to equality but feel that their values are endangered: Black assertiveness may be regarded as a threat to the very fabric of society. Another important component of symbolic racism is that, as its name implies, it operates through symbols rather than overt discrimination. Thus, there is opposition to welfare, Black politicians, and fair housing laws because they symbolize the unreasonable demands being made by Blacks. In sum, then, symbolic racism is the expression in terms of abstract ideological symbols and symbolic behaviours of the feeling that Blacks are violating cherished values and making illegitimate demands for changes in the racial status quo (McConahay and Hough, 1976:38).

DEMOCRATIC RACISM

Although democratic racism pertains largely to ideology and stresses the role of value differences as these are reflected in systems and institutions, individuals are largely responsible for the development of policies and the implementation of procedures that regulate systems and institutions. Thus democratic racism is related to new racism, aversive racism, and symbolic racism. It differs from them by positing a value conflict.

Democratic racism is an ideology in which two conflicting sets of values are made congruent to each other. Commitments to democratic principles such as justice, equality, and fairness conflict but coexist with attitudes and behaviours that include negative feelings about minority groups, differential treatment, and discrimination against them.

One of the consequences of the conflict is a lack of support for policies and practices that might ameliorate the low status of people of colour. These policies and practices tend to require changes in the existing social, economic, and political order, usually by state intervention. The intervention, however, is perceived to be in conflict with and a threat to liberal democracy. Thus democratic racism holds that the spread of racism should only be dealt with — if at all — by leaving basic economic structures and societal relations essentially unchanged (Gilroy, 1987). Efforts to combat racism that require intervention to change the cultural, social, economic, and political order will lack political support. More importantly, they will lack legitimacy, according to the egalitarian principles of liberal democracy.

THE DISCOURSE OF DEMOCRATIC RACISM

How is democratic racism manifested in the daily lives, opinions, and feelings of people? What are the values, assumptions, and arguments of democratic racism? As Wellman (1977) noted, the maintenance of a wide array of myths and misconceptions about racism has permitted a pattern of denial that has led to a wholly inadequate response to racism.

Democratic racism in its ideological and discursive form is deeply embedded in popular culture and popular discourse. It is located within what has been called society's frames of reference (Hebridge, 1993). These frames of reference are a largely unacknowledged set of beliefs, assumptions, feelings, stories, and quasi-memories that underlie, sustain, and inform perceptions, thoughts, and actions. Democratic racism as racist discourse begins in the families that nurture us, the communities that socialize us, the schools and universities that educate us, the media that communicate ideas and images to us, and the popular culture that entertains us.

Goldberg (1993) contends that racist discourse covers a wide spectrum of expressions and representations, including a nation's recorded history; scientific forms of racist explanations (such as Rushton's theory of racial differences); economic, legal, and bureaucratic forms of doctrine; cultural representations in the form of national narratives, images, and symbols, and so on. Social power is reflected in racist discourse.

The conflict between the ideology of democratic liberalism and the racist ideology present in the collective belief system of the dominant culture is reflected in the racist discourse that operates in the schools, the media, the courts, law enforcement agencies, arts organizations and cultural institutions, human services, government bureaucracies, and political authorities. The school, the university, the newspaper and the television station, the courtroom, police headquarters, the hospital, and the government office are discursive spaces. Within these spaces, controlled mainly by a dominant White culture, there exists a constant moral tension: the everyday experiences of people of colour, juxtaposed with the perceptions and responses of those who have the power to redefine that reality.

Many people resist anti-racism and equity initiatives because they are unwilling to question *their* own belief and value systems and discursive practices, *their* organizational and professional norms, *their* positions of power and privilege within the workplace and society. Thus, they are unable to examine the relation between cultural and racial differences and the power dynamics constructed around ideas about those differences. Acknowledging that ethno-racial differences make a difference in the lives of people is to concede that Euro-Canadian hegemony continues to function and organize the structures within which the delivery of mainstream programs and services operates (Dei, 1996). In each of these discursive spaces we see tension and resistance in relation to how multicultural and anti-racism ideologies and policies are "imagined, internalized and acted upon" (Yon, 1995:315).

Resistance may manifest itself as active opposition, expressed openly, but it is more commonly articulated in more subtle forms of discourse. Discourses on race and racism converge with concerns about Canadian identity, national unity, ethnicity, multiculturalism, and so on. Discourse provides the conceptual models for mapping the world around us and incorporates both social relationships and power relations (Goldberg, 1993), but as Yon (1995) demonstrates in his ethnographic study of students and teachers in a Toronto high school, discourse about identity and nation that never mentions the word "race" can also be considered racist discourse.

Increasingly, the discourse of liberalism is juxtaposed with popular conservative ideology, and individuals slide ambivalently between the two. As Yon (1995) points out: "Resistance and accommodation can be present in the same moment. Discourse often reveals ambivalence, contradiction and subtleties in relation to the issues of difference. For example, discussions about culture are often framed in the context of being 'tolerant,' 'sensitive' and sufficiently enlightened to appreciate and respect the diverse cultures of the 'others'." Cultural discourse tends to cover up the "unpleasantness" of domination and inequity (Wetherell and Potter, 1992).

The following section outlines a framework for examining the discourse of dominance, which includes myths, explanations, codes of meaning, and rationalizations that have the effect of establishing, sustaining, and reinforcing democratic racism. In this analysis and throughout the text, note how this discourse is contextualized within liberal democratic, humanistic values. As the following chapters show, the central values of liberal ideologies carry different meanings and connotations, depending on the context. Goldberg (1993) contends that tolerance, equality, and liberty, central concepts in liberal discourse, have immensely flexible meanings.

The paradox of a postmodern liberal society is that as modernity commits itself to these liberal ideals and to the moral irrelevance of race, there is a proliferation of racial identities and an assortment of exclusions they support and sustain. Making a similar point, Mackey contends that "liberal principles are the very language and conceptual framework through which intolerance and exclusion are enabled, reinforced, defined and defended" (Mackey, 1996:305).

The elusive nature of the dominant discourse allows it to mask its racialized ideas (Fiske, 1994). Within it are unchallenged assumptions, or myths. These myths attempt to explain, rationalize, and resolve unsupportable contradictions and problems in society. Myths arise at particular historical moments in response to a perceived need within society. They function as a guideline for new ideas and behaviours. The final section of this chapter explores some of the prevailing myths that underpin democratic racism.

THE DISCOURSE OF POLITICAL CORRECTNESS

"Politically correct" is defined by *Merriam-Webster's Collegiate Dictionary* as "conforming to a belief that language and practices which could offend political sensibilities (as in matters of sex or race) should be eliminated." Political correctness is, however, an elusive concept and, as Fleras and Elliott (1996) point out, difficult to define because of its lack of tangible reference points. It is neither an ideology nor a coherent social movement.

Political correctness is a phrase that in recent years has become a central part of the public discourse of neoconservatives as an expression of their resistance to forms of social change. The demands of marginalized minorities for inclusive language and pro-active policies (such as employment equity) and practices are discredited as an "overdose of political correctness." Those opposed to pro-active measures that would ensure the inclusion of non-dominant voices, stories, and perspectives dismiss these concerns as the wailing and whining of radicals whose polemics (and actions) threaten the cornerstones of democratic liberalism. Political correctness is a term commonly used by culturally conservative academics, journalists, politicians, writers, and cultural critics. The phrase is commonly employed to deride the aspirations of minorities and the pedagogical goals of liberal or radical teachers or professors.

The discourse of political correctness is part of a larger and ongoing debate about very different visions of society and diverse paradigms of social change. It is a rhetoric that has intensified and polarized positions with respect to issues of **inclusion**, **representation** (language and images), multiculturalism, equity, racism, and sexism in universities, schools, and human-service and government agencies (Srivastava, 1996).

Toni Morrison suggests that political correctness is a "weighty phrase with a pseudo-intellectual cast" designed to make people desist from having certain kinds of discussion. It serves to stifle dissent. "The political correctness debate is really about ... the power to be able to redefine. The definers want the power to name. And the defined are now taking the power away from them" (Miller, Swift, and Maggio, 1997:54).

THE DISCOURSE OF DENIAL

Within this discourse the principle assumption is that racism simply does not exist in a democratic society. There is a refusal to accept the reality of racism, despite the evidence of racial prejudice and discrimination in, and the effects of racism on, the lives of people of colour. The assumption here is that because Canada is a society that upholds the ideals of a liberal democracy, it could not possibly be racist. When racism is shown to exist, it tends to be identified as an isolated phenomenon relating to a limited number of social deviants, economic instability, or the consequence of "undemocratic" traditions that are disappearing from the Canadian scene. This discourse resists the notion that racism is systemic and inherently embedded in Canada's cultural values and democratic institutions.

THE DISCOURSE OF COLOUR BLINDNESS

Colour blindness is a powerful and appealing liberal discourse in which White people insist that they do not notice the skin colour of a racial-minority person. But, as Gotanda (1991) suggests, this technique of observing but not considering "race" is a "technical fiction. It is impossible not to think about a subject without having first thought about it a little" (101). The refusal to recognize that race is part of the "baggage" that people of colour carry with them, and the refusal to recognize racism as part of everyday values, policies, programs, and practices, is part of the psychological and cultural power of racial constructions (James, 1994). Colour-blindness or colour evasion leads to power evasion (Frankenberg, 1993).

THE DISCOURSE OF EQUAL OPPORTUNITY

This discourse suggests that all we need to do is treat everyone the same, and fairness will be ensured. This notion is based on an ahistorical premise, that is, we all begin from the same starting point; everyone competes on a level playing field. Society merely provides the conditions within which individuals differentially endowed can make their mark. All have an equal opportunity to succeed and the same rights. Thus, individual merit determines who will succeed in the workplace, school, politics, the arts.

This view ignores the social construction of race, in which power and privilege belongs to those who are White (among other social markers of privilege, including gender, class, sexual orientation, and able-bodiedness). Equal opportunity represents a passive approach and does not require the dismantling of White institutional power or the redistribution of White social capital (Crenshaw, 1997). This paradigm demands no form of pro-active institutional or state intervention such as employment equity or anti-racism policies.

THE DISCOURSE OF BLAMING THE VICTIM

If equal opportunity and racial equality are assumed to exist, then a minority population's lack of success must be attributed to some other set of conditions. One explanation used by the dominant culture is the notion that certain minority communities themselves are culturally deficient — they may be lacking intellectual prowess or be more prone to aggressive behaviour or other forms of "deviant behaviour." In this form of dominant discourse, it is assumed that certain communities (such as African Canadians) lack the motivation, education, or skills to participate fully in the workplace, educational system, and other arenas of Canadian society.

Alternatively, it is argued that the failure of certain groups to succeed and integrate into the mainstream dominant culture is largely due to recalcitrant members of these groups refusing to adapt their "traditional," "different" cultural values and norms to fit into Canadian society and making unreasonable demands on the "host" society.

THE DISCOURSE OF WHITE VICTIMIZATION

In this discourse it is argued that White European immigrants also experience prejudice and discrimination in Canada. According to this view, the social system is open but all immigrant groups must expect to start at the bottom of the social and economic ladder. It is only through their own initiative that they can achieve upward mobility and thereby receive full and equal treatment. Therefore there is no need for preferential policies or programs.

This assumption is based on the traditional view that race, ethnicity, and the immigrant experience are one and the same phenomenon. It does not recognize that genetic racial features such as skin colour do not simply disappear over time. It ignores the fact that second- and third-generation Canadian people of colour continue to experience the same prejudiced attitudes and discriminatory behaviour as their parents and grandparents. They continue to be severely impeded in their opportunities for upward mobility. Equating racial **disadvantage** and discrimination with the experiences of White European immigrants ignores the importance of the history of colonization, subjugation, and **oppression** of people of colour by Canadians of European origin.

THE DISCOURSE OF REVERSE RACISM

In a semantic reversal, those associated with the dominant culture contend that they are *now* the victims of a new form of oppression and exclusion. Anti-racism and equity policies are discredited by suggesting in strong, emotive language that they are nothing more than "apartheid in reverse," a "new inquisition," or "McCarthyite witch-hunts."

Positive and pro-active policies and programs are thus aligned with creeping totalitarianism and accused of incorporating the anti-democratic, authoritarian methods of the extreme right. "These are fertile times for hate-mongers and reactionaries. The defenders of the status quo have discovered a wonderful refuge in their opposition to the excesses of political correctness" (DiManno, 1993).

Those concerned with addressing racial inequalities have frequently been accused of belonging to radical, extremist groups. The implication of these reproaches is that the issue of race is being used as a cover for promoting conflict in pursuit of other questionable political ends. Those concerned with racial injustice have been labelled as radicals who are using an anti-racism platform to subvert Canada's fundamental institutions, values, and beliefs.

THE DISCOURSE OF BINARY POLARIZATION

The fragmentation into "we" and "they" groups is usually framed in the context of an examination of the relative values and norms of the majority versus minority populations. "We" are the White dominant culture or the culture of the organization (police, school, workplace); "they" are the communities who are the "other," possessing "different" (undesirable) values, beliefs, and norms. "We" are law-abiding, hardworking, decent, and homogeneous. We are the "Canadian-Canadians" (Mackey, 1996), the "birthright Canadians" (Dabydeen, 1994). The "theys" are very different and therefore undeserving (Apple, 1993). Those marked as "other" are positioned outside of the "imagined" community (Anderson, 1983) of Canada and national identity of Canadians.

The discourse of "otherness" is supported by stereotypical images embedded in the fabric of the dominant culture. Although these stereotypes have little basis in reality, they nevertheless have a significant social impact. When minorities have no power to produce or disseminate other real and more positive images in the public domain, these stereotypes increase their vulnerability in terms of cultural, social, economic, and political participation in the mainstream of Canadian society (Pieterse, 1992).

THE DISCOURSE OF MORAL PANIC

The economic and political destabilization and social dislocations experienced by societies such as Canada, the United States, the United Kingdom, and Germany have created a climate of uncertainty, fear, and threat. Some scholars have identified this phenomenon as "moral panic" (Husband, 1994; Hall, 1978), in which those identified with the mainstream population or the dominant culture experience a loss of control, authority, and equilibrium. The country is described as being in crisis or under siege: "We are not who we used to be" (McFarlane, 1995:20).

This siege mentality is most evident in the public sphere, among groups such as the police, government, academia, and the media. The anti-racism initiatives of the late 1980s and early 1990s have been either significantly weakened or eliminated. Equality is being redefined — and is less and less considered the responsibility of the state. It is no longer linked to group oppression and systemic disadvantage and discrimination (Apple, 1993).

These new "moral panics" are based mainly on fears about cultural and racial differences that imperil the national culture and identity. They take the form of "propaganda" campaigns in which a group is perceived, represented, and constructed as an imminent threat to "normal, civilized" society. The subtext in the discourse of "moral panic" is almost invariably ethnic or racial exclusionism.

THE DISCOURSE OF MULTICULTURALISM: TOLERANCE, ACCOMMODATION, HARMONY, AND DIVERSITY

The concepts of tolerance, accommodation, sensitivity, harmony, and diversity lie at the core of multicultural ideology and are firmly embedded in multicultural policy and discourse (see Chapter 11 on the state). The emphasis on tolerance and sensitivity suggests that while one must accept the idiosyncrasies of the "others," the underlying premise is that the dominant way is superior.

Within this minimal form of recognition of difference, the dominant culture creates a ceiling on tolerance, that is, it stipulates what differences are tolerable. This ceiling is reflected in responses in public opinion polls and in surveys dealing with multiculturalism (Mirchandani and Tastsoglou, 1998), in which a significant number of respondents take a position that "we" cannot tolerate too much difference because it generates dissent, disruption, and conflict. According to this view, paying unnecessary attention to "differences" leads to division, disharmony, and disorder in society. Where possible, the dominant culture attempts to accommodate *their* idiosyncratic cultural differences.

Declarations of the need for tolerance and harmony tend to conceal the messy business of structural and systemic inequality and the unequal relations of power that continue to exist in a democratic liberal society. Mohanty contends that "differences defined as asymmetrical and incommensurate cultural spheres situated within hierarchies of domination and resistance cannot be accommodated with a discourse of 'harmony in diversity'" (1993:72).

THE DISCOURSE OF LIBERAL VALUES: INDIVIDUALISM, TRUTH, TRADITION, UNIVERSALISM, AND FREEDOM OF EXPRESSION

Democratic liberalism is distinguished by set of beliefs that include: the primacy of individual rights over collective or group rights; the power of (one) truth, tradition, and history; an appeal to universalism; the sacredness of the principle of freedom of expression; and a commitment to human rights and equality, among many other ideals. But as many scholars observe, liberalism is full of paradoxes and contradictions and assumes different meanings, depending on one's social location and angle of vision (Hall, 1986; Goldberg, 1993; Apple, 1993; Winant, 1997). As Parekh argues, "Liberalism is both egalitarian and inegalitarian." It simultaneously supports the unity of humankind and the hierarchy of cultures. It is both tolerant and intolerant (1986:82). Ignatieff claims, "We live by liberal fictions"; despite the fact that human beings are "incorrigibly different ... equality is a moral story which governs our hypotheses" (1998:19).

From the perspective of the marginalized and excluded, traditional liberal values have been found wanting. In the interests of expanding liberal democratic principles and extending the promises of liberalism to those who have not enjoyed its benefits, minority communities are demanding an "affirmative" correction of historical injustices (Stam, 1993).

However, those individuals and groups who invoke the validity of alternative voices, experiences, traditions, perspectives, and histories are seen to be violating a sacred body of principles, values, and beliefs. There is only one truth, a single "authentic" history, a noble Euro-American tradition, a universal form of human understanding and expression that includes and transcends all cultural and racial boundaries.

THE DISCOURSE OF NATIONAL IDENTITY

The discourse of national identity is marked by erasures, omissions, and silences. Ethno-racial minorities have been placed outside the "national project" of Canada and excluded from the "imagined community" (Anderson, 1983) of Canadian society. From Canada's earliest history, the idea of "hyphenated" Canadians has been a fundamental part of the national discourse, but it has been limited to two identities: English Canada and French Canada. The Fathers of Confederation ignored the cultural plurality that existed even at that time. Aboriginal and other cultures were omitted from the national discourse and thereby rendered invisible. Later, a category of "others" was added — but only two of these had constitutional rights.

National discourse constructs meanings and influences "our actions and our conceptions of ourselves" (Hall, 1992:292). National culture defines identity by "producing meanings about the nation with which we can identify; these are contained in the stories which are told about it, memories which connect it with its past, and the images which are constructed of it" (Hall, 1992:282).

The debate over national identity is fundamental to Canadian discourse. Canada's search for national unity is really a search for cultural stability. The question of cultural identity is influenced by the politics of difference, a politics shaped by the interplay of history, culture, race, and power. In the struggle over national identity, the dominant culture is reluctant to include identities of "others" that it has constructed, perpetuated, and used to its advantage. To discard "otherness" would in a sense be to abandon the vehicles through which inequalities and imbalances are legitimized.

Many Canadians see themselves as egalitarian and have little difficulty in rejecting the more overt expressions of racism. They may make symbolic gestures of inclusivity. However, beyond these token efforts, the struggles of people of colour are met with the arbitrary use of political, economic, and cultural institutional power in the interests of "maintaining democracy."

This book explores this fundamental tension in Canadian discourse, policies, and practices as an expression of democratic racism. Anti-racism, ethno-racial access, and equity are a necessary part of the legitimization of a new ideology requiring a commitment to a different set of values, discourses, and practices.

REFERENCES

Althusser, L. (1971). "Ideology and Ideological State. *Philos* Apparatuses." In *Lenin and Philosophy and Other Essays*. London: Monthly Review.

Anderson, B. (1983). *Imagined Communities*. London: Verso.

Apple, M. (1993). "Constructing the 'Other': Rightist Reconstructions of Common Sense." In C. McCarthy and W. Crichlow (eds.), *Race, Identity and Representation in Education*. New York and London: Routledge.

Ball, W., and J. Solomos. (1990). *Race and Local Politics*. London: Macmillan.

Billig, M., et al. (1988). *Ideological Dilemmas: A Social Psychology of Everyday Thinking*. London: Sage.

Brandt, G. (1986). *The Realization of Anti-Racist Education*. London: Falmer Press.

CCCS (Centre for Contemporary Cultural Studies). (1982). "The Organic Crisis of British Capitalism and Race." In CCCS, *The Empire Strikes Back: Race and Racism in 70's Britain*. London: Hutchinson.

Crenshaw, K. (1997). "Color-blind Dreams and Racial Nitemares: Reconfiguring Racism in the Post-Civil Rights Era." In T. Morrison and C. Brodsky Lacour (eds.), *Birth of a Nation'hood: Gaze, Script, and Spectacle in the O.J. Simpson Case*. New York: Pantheon Books. 97–168.

Dabydeen, Cyril. 1994. "Citizenship Is More Than a Birthright." *Toronto Star* (September 20):A23.

Dei, G. (1996). *Anti-Racism Education: Theory and Practice*. Halifax: Fernwood.

DiManno, R. (1993). *Toronto Star* (September 6).

Essed, P. (1990). *Everyday Racism: Reports from Women of Two Cultures*. Alameda, CA: Hunter House.

Fiske, J. (1994). *Media Matters: Everyday Culture and Political Change*. Minneapolis: University of Minnesota Press.

Fleras, A., and J. Elliott. (1992). *Multiculturalism in Canada.* Scarborough, ON: Nelson.

———. (1996). *Unequal Relations: An Introduction to Race, Ethnic and Aboriginal Dynamics in Canada*. 2nd ed. Scarborough, ON: Prentice Hall.

Frankenberg, R. (1993). *White Women Race Matters: The Social Construction of Whiteness*. Minneapolis: University of Minnesota Press.

Gaertner, S.L. (1976). "Nonreactive Measures in Racial Attitude Research: A Focus on Liberals." In P. Katz (ed.), *Towards the Elimination of Racism*. New York: Pergamon Press.

Gaertner, S.L., and J.F. Dovidio. (1981). "Racism among the Well Intentioned." In E.G. Clausen and J. Bermingham (eds.), *Pluralism, Racism and Public Policy*. Boston: G.K. Hall.

———. (1986). "The Aversive Forms of Racism." In S.L. Gaertner and J.F. Dovidio (eds.), *Prejudice, Discrimination and Racism*. New York: Academic Press.

Gilroy, P. (1987). *There Ain't No Black in the Union Jack*. Chicago: University of Chicago Press.

Goldberg, D.S. (ed.). (1990). *The Anatomy of Racism*. Minneapolis: University of Minnesota Press.

———. (1993). *Racist Culture: Philosophy and the Politics of Meaning*. Oxford: Blackwell.

Gotanda, N. (1991). "A Critique of 'Our Constitution Is Color-Blind'." *Stanford Law Review* 44(1):1–73.

Gwyn, Richard. (1993). *Toronto Star* (July 18).

Hall, S. (1978). "Racism and Reaction." In *Five Views of Multi-Racial Britain*. London: Commission for Racial Equality.

———, et al. (1978). *Policing the Crisis*. London: Macmillan.

———. (1983). "The Great Moving Show." In S. Hall and M. Jacques (eds.), *The Politics of Thatcherism*. London: Lawrence and Wishart.

————. (1986). "Variants of Liberalism." In J. Donald and S. Hall (eds.), *Politics and Ideology*. Milton Keynes: Open University Press.

————. (1992). "The Question of Cultural Identity." In S. Hall, D. Held, and T. McGrew (eds.), *Modernity and Its Future*. Cambridge, UK: Polity Press in association with Open University. 273–326.

Hebridge, D. (1993). "From Culture to Hegemony." In S. During (ed.), *The Cultural Studies Reader*. London: Routledge.

Henry, F. (1978). *Dynamics of Racism in Toronto*. North York, ON: York University.

Husband, C. (1994). "Crisis of National Identity as the 'New Moral Panics': Political Agenda-Setting about Definitions of Nationhood." *New Community* (Warwick) 20(2)(January):191–206.

Ignatieff, M. (1998). "Identity Parades." *Prospect* (April):19–23.

James, C. (1994). "The Paradox of Power and Privilege: Race, Gender and Occupational Position." *Canadian Woman Studies: Race and Gender* 14(2):47–51.

Kovel, J. (1970). *White Racism: A Psychohistory*. New York: Pantheon.

Lawrence, E. (1982). "Just Plain Common Sense: The 'Roots' of Racism." In CCCS, *The Empire Strikes Back: Race and Racism in 70's Britain*. London: Hutchinson.

London, J. (1993). "Word for Word." Toronto: CBC Radio (broadcast July 18).

Mackey, E. (1996). "Managing and Imagining Diversity: Multiculturalism and the Construction of National Identity in Canada." Ph.D. thesis, Department of Social Anthropology, University of Sussex.

McConahay, J.B., and J.C. Hough, Jr. (1976). "Symbolic Racism." *Journal of Social Issues* 32(2):23–45.

McFarlane, S. (1995). "The Haunt of Race: Canada's Multiculturalism Act, the Politics of Incorporation and Writing Thru Race." *Fuse* 18(3)(Spring):18–31.

Miller, C., K. Swift, and R. Maggio. (1997). "Liberating Language." *MS.* (September–October):51–54.

Mirchandani, K., and E. Tastsoglou. (1998). "Toward a Diversity beyond Tolerance." Manuscript submitted to the *Journal of Status in Political Economy*.

Mohanty, T.C. (1993). *Beyond a Dream: Deferred Multicultural Education and the Politics of Excellence*. Minneapolis: University of Minnesota Press.

Parekh, B. (1986). "The 'New Right' and the Politics of Nationhood." In *The New Right: Image and Reality*. London: Runnymede Trust.

Pieterse, N.J. (1992). *White on Black: Images of Africa and Blacks in Western Popular Culture*. New Haven and London: Yale University Press.

Sears, D., and J. McConahay, Jr. (1973). *The Politics of Violence: The New Urban Blacks and the Watts Riot*. Boston: Houghton Mifflin.

Srivastava, S. (1996). "Song and Dance? The Performance of Antiracist Workshops." *CRSA/RCSA* 33(3):291–315.

Stam, R. (1993). "From Stereotype to Discourse." *Cine-Action* 23(Fall):12–29.

Wellman, D. (1977). *Portraits of White Racism*. Cambridge: Cambridge University Press.

Wetherell, M., and J. Potter (1992). *Mapping the Language of Racism*. New York: Columbia University Press.

Winant, H. (1997). "Behind Blue Eyes: Whiteness and Contemporary U.S. Racial Politics." In M. Fine, et al. (eds.), *Off White: Readings on Race, Power and Society*. New York and London: Routledge. 40–56.

Yon, D. (1995). "Unstable Terrain: Explorations in Identity, Race and Culture in a Toronto High School." Ph.D. thesis, Department of Anthropology, York University.

Chapter 2

▼▼▼▼▼▼▼▼▼▼▼▼

Theoretical Perspectives

Theory is always a (necessary) detour on the way to something more important. (Hall, 1991)

Today, the theory of race has been utterly transformed. The socially constructed status of the concept of race ... is widely recognized, so much so that it is now often conservatives who argue that race is an illusion.... Our central work is to focus attention on the *continuing significance and changing meaning of race.* (Omi and Winant, 1993)

This chapter reviews the substantial theoretical literature on the subject of race and racism. It begins with theories of biological and cultural superiority and ends with sophisticated societal paradigms. A brief review of some of the critical developments in the history of racial theory is presented in the first section of this chapter. To expedite the review, the theories are presented chronologically and identify the major trends in the United Kingdom, the United States, and Canada. In addition to conventional theories, the newer approaches of cultural studies and discourse analysis are briefly presented. The various forms of racism — individual, systemic, and ideological — are defined. The chapter concludes by examining some of the methodological and measurement problems in the study of racism.

INTRODUCTION

As they have done in other areas of human behaviour, social scientists have attempted to explain racist behaviour by constructing theories. It is by constructing general as well as specific theories that we can understand human behaviour. Sociological and psychological theories, especially those focusing on White superiority, were heavily influenced by the emergence of racial classifications.

FROM THE NINETEENTH CENTURY TO THE MID-TWENTIETH CENTURY: RACE AND RACIAL CLASSIFICATION

Race as a biological classification has a long history, but in the nineteenth century the biological classification of human beings into "races" became prominent. When social theorists such as Herbert Spencer began to apply the concept of race to social categories, a new school, Social Darwinism, was created. Although Social Darwinists did not intend their work to be racist, others such as Joseph Arthur de Gobineau and Houston Stewart Chamberlain applied the theory to construct a school of social racism in which the supremacy of the White race and European civilization was dramatically featured (Banton, 1983).

Throughout the nineteenth century and most of the twentieth century, the term "race" was used not only to distinguish between groups but also to establish a hierarchical division of races. Physical appearances were thought to correlate with social, psychological, intellectual, moral, and cultural differences. Characteristics such as skin colour were used to establish a racial classification system. This racial order and discourse was then used to rationalize and legitimize the exploitation and oppression of racial minorities.

Not until the mid-twentieth century was the concept of the inferiority of people of colour fundamentally altered. In the 1950s and 1960s, many biologists and social scientists met to produce new theoretical models to explain "race." In addition, a number of conferences were organized by the United Nations Educational, Scientific and Cultural Organization to address the issue (UNESCO, 1972). Clear messages and definitive statements emerged from these forums to challenge popular myths about race. There was a consensus among scientists that all humans belonged to a single species, that is, one race.

The concepts of race and racial classification can be rejected as unnecessary and unscientific because they add nothing to the understanding of the human species. Humanity cannot be divided into discrete portions distinguished by biological properties (Rex, 1983). All races are mixtures of populations, and "the term 'pure' race is an absurdity" (Mayr, 1963). In fact, some social scientists have suggested that "race" should be removed from the vocabulary of the field (Banton, 1977). It has been called "man's most dangerous myth" (Montagu, 1964).

However, the consequences of the discourse on race and the social relations within which it has been embedded for the past two centuries cannot be ignored. Human societies continue to function as if races do exist. Racial differentiation continues to affect all areas of social interaction. For all practical purposes, then, race is not so much a biological phenomenon as a social myth that has had devastating consequences (Bolaria and Li, 1988).

Thus, while the concept of race as such may be irrelevant, racism is one of the most important causes of human inequality.

THE 1950S AND 1960S: ASSIMILATION AND INTEGRATION

"**Race relations**" have a long history in the United States. Park (1950) and his associates at the University of Chicago developed the concept of "a race relations cycle" in which **assimilation** into mainstream society was the final stage for ethnic and racial groups. The theory was largely based on the study of the adaptation of **ethnic groups** of European origin. It was also applied to racial groups, primarily "American negroes."

The assimilationist perspective, which conceptualized the **integration** of all groups into mainstream society, was popular for many years. An earlier important work in the assimilationist tradition was *An American Dilemma,* by the Swedish scholar Gunnar Myrdal (1944), which propounded the view that prejudice and racial conflict were a "White problem" that could only be resolved by changing the attitudes and behaviours of Whites toward Blacks. The "dilemma" had occurred, according to this pioneering work, because America had allowed a series of racial discriminatory practices and policies to develop that were in direct conflict with the "American Creed," which emphasized freedom, equality, and justice. Myrdal was the first to call attention to this fundamental value conflict.

In another important theoretical development stemming from the discipline of social psychology, the distinction between prejudice — the attitudes held by individuals — and discrimination — the behaviour prompted by these prejudices — was examined by Gordon Allport's seminal work, *The Nature of Prejudice* (1954).

The psychological nature of prejudice as defined by Allport was reviewed by Black scholars such as Jones, who in *Prejudice and Racism* (1972) took the view that attitudes are less important than unequal power relations and institutional practices. However, other social psychologists, such as Gaertner and Dovidio, Katz, and McConahay and Hough, moved beyond the study of prejudice and began to develop theories of racism (see Chapter 1).

Another earlier development of some theoretical importance was the work of Frantz Fanon, who, influenced by Marxian, Freudian, and existential philosophy, in 1952 published *Black Skin, White Masks* (Fanon, 1967). In this work, he called attention to the symbolic analysis of racism and dealt with the duality between Blacks and Whites as expressed in real and symbolic terms. As well, Fanon called attention to the oppressive role of colonization in structuring relations between racial groups.

THE LATE 1960S AND 1970S: FROM RACE RELATIONS TO RACISM

In the 1960s, Black scholars in the United States were instrumental in changing the focus from "race relations," with its assimilationist, value-conflict approach in which attitudinal prejudice was stressed, to "racism."

This shift in perspective resulted in a focus on power relations, in which social, economic, and political inequalities between groups become the centre of attention. It examined in greater depth the role of institutions in both the public and private sectors.

A landmark in the understanding of structural racism was the publication of *Black Power*, by Stokely Carmichael and Charles Hamilton, in 1967. The authors defined racism as "the predication of decisions and policies on considerations of race for purposes of subordinating a racial group"(Drake, 1991:33). They also drew an important distinction between individual and institutional racism. Whereas the former related to individual attitudes and behaviours, the latter drew attention to the importance of institutions in creating and maintaining policies and practices that, even inadvertently, may exclude a group and result in unequal distributions of economic, social, and political power. Later, the term "systemic" racism came to mean any form of discriminatory policy or practice in a system, whether advertent or inadvertent.

The impetus for the development of institutional or systematic racism came from the mercantilist expansion of European countries into Asia, Africa, and the Americas.

> The empirical evidence ... supports the view that prejudice and discrimination based upon skin colour existed [before European expansion] but were not accompanied by any systematic doctrines of racial inferiority or superiority, that is, "racism." ... Nor were colour prejudice and discrimination institutionalized as structural principles defining systems of slavery, caste, or class. Slavery is a phenomenon that has existed in many times and places without any connection with either skin colour prejudice or racism. (Drake, 1991:7)

MARXIST ORIENTATIONS: CLASS PRIMACY THEORIES

During the 1950s, writings on racism, especially in the United Kingdom, tended to focus on race relations. Assimilationists were, however, increasingly challenged by a number of theorists who applied Marxian perspectives to their analysis of race relations. Since neither Karl Marx nor Friedrich Engels wrote about race (or gender, for that matter), most neo-Marxists subsumed issues of race and racism into the more traditional class analysis. A prominent Marxist writing in the 1950s argued that modern racism was a product of capitalism and provided European countries with a rationale for exploiting "native people" and their resources (Cox, 1976).

More recently, however, several important theoretical developments in the United Kingdom have inspired considerable controversy. Partially in reaction to the traditional functionalist,[1] assimilationist "race relations" approach, there is a strong neo-Marxist thrust apparent in the writings of Miles and Phizacklea (1984) and others. Neo-Marxists in the United Kingdom, the United States, and Canada have explored the links between immigrant workers and racism by highlighting the exploitation of wage labour, capital accumulation, and resultant class division. Rex (1983), one of the pioneers in the field in Britain, has attempted to bridge functionalism with a neo-Marxist approach, and Marxist-inspired writers such as Hall et al. (1978) have gained prominence. There is a continuing controversy in the U.K. literature with respect to the primacy of class versus the autonomy of race in the analysis of racism.

Another important perspective, largely stimulated by the work of Solomos (1987, 1993) and Black scholars associated with the Centre for Contemporary Cultural Studies (CCCS, 1982) in Birmingham, emphasizes the role of the state in developing a "politics of racism." This analysis of the state's role in producing and reproducing racism has been stimulated by the increasing association of the British state with the doctrines of Thatcherism.[2]

Whereas traditional Marxists give primacy to class and the means of production, neo-Marxists focus on the process of racialization that occurs in capitalist systems. Thus Canadian scholars such as Bolaria and Li (1988:7) note that "race problems begin as labour problems." Racism as an ideology therefore emerged particularly in earlier periods of history in colonial societies. This analysis of racism argues that because capitalist employers needed large pools of labour to maximize their profits, racism served as a rationale for labour exploitation.

Satzewich (1989), writing about racism in Canadian immigration practices, argues that racism is "an ideology imposed from above by those who own the means of production on those who do not: racism acts to mystify social reality, justifies the exploitation of certain groups of peoples' labour power, and contributes to the maintenance of the status quo." He stresses the relationship between racism and immigrant labour in industrial societies, including Canada. According to this view, racist ideology is preserved in order to maintain a cheap labour supply. Racism is something imposed from above, from the privileged members of society, and is received by the lower orders.

There are a number of weaknesses in this approach; the main weakness is that it does not apply to all situations. For example, racism can work to the disadvantage of employers, particularly with respect to work-force disruptions and work-force harassment based on race. It says little, if anything, about racism and other divisions in the working class.

Neo-Marxist approaches are also popular in the United States. The debate about race and class, in particular, is still an important issue. For example, Franklin (1991:xiii) poses the question: Is the subordinate position of the Black population ultimately derived from the stigma of colour, or is it due to the Black population's inferior class or economic position?

Franklin argues that the choice of emphasis influences Blacks' status as well as the nature of discrimination in the United States. Moreover, choosing one or the other of the race–class dichotomy influences the policies and strategies for overcoming racial inequity. Franklin believes that only by creating equality in income and job allocations will the "dominant–subordinate" patterns that maintain racism be eliminated. He looks to the revitalization of American cities, where most African Americans live, to bring this about.

In the United Kingdom, Miles and Phizacklea (1984) attempted to refine some of these earlier notions while maintaining that race and race relations emerge from class — as an epiphenomenon of class and its relation to the means of production. They note that a high demand for labour characterized the British economy during the 1970s and 1980s. People of colour from the Commonwealth provided the necessary labour, but they were relegated to lower-level semiskilled and unskilled jobs. Thus, part of the working class became racialized. Race, in this model, is an ideological construction rather than an analytical category. The primary focus should be on the capitalist relations of production, which become more important than race (Ben-Tovin and Gabriel, 1986).

A more recent Marxist-influenced approach considers racism and other forms of oppression as part of the hegemonic order. This approach has been particularly well received in the United Kingdom, most notably by Stuart Hall (1991). Although Hall considers race a construct, he argues that racism cannot be reduced to classicism or any other phenomenon but must be understood as part of the broad socioeconomic and political context within which it flourishes: race and class have an interactive relationship.

In attempting to bridge several neo-Marxian approaches, Rex focused on "race relations situations," which he defined as

> situations in which two or more groups with distinct identities and recognisable characteristics are forced by economic and political circumstances to live together in society.... There is a high degree of conflict between the groups and ascriptive criteria are used to mark out the members of each group in order that one group may pursue one of a number of hostile policies against the other.... [T]he ascriptive allocation of roles and rights referred to are justified in terms of some kind of deterministic theory ... scientific, religious, historical, ideological or sociological. (1983:159–60)

Rex and his colleagues attempted to analyze racism by specifying the situations in which it occurs, including those in which race is not a factor. For example, the conflict in Ireland, which is largely based on ethnicity rather than race, would nevertheless qualify as a "race-relations situation" according to this view. Rex's primary aim was to call attention to the unequal access of Black migrants in the United Kingdom to goods and services as well as to examine the consequences of inequality among both the White and Black working classes (Rex and Moore, 1967; Rex and Tomlinson, 1979).

In summary, a basic change in perspective occurred in the late 1960s and 1970s — from the assimilationist race-relations approach in both the United States and the United Kingdom to an emphasis on racism.[3] Analysts concluded that "it was not black people who should be examined but white society; it was not a question of educating blacks and whites for integration, but of fighting institutional racism; it was not race relations that was the field of study, but racism" (Bourne and Sivanandan, 1974:339).

THE 1980S: FROM RACISM TO ANTI-RACISM

Another important shift in the study of race relations occurred in the 1980s. Although many still use the term "racism" to describe the social construction of the biological concept of race, the designation "anti-racism" has taken on some currency.

The word "race" — however positively used (for example, in "multi-racial education") — validates the basic ideas upon which racism is built (Brandt, 1986). Its use negatively influences the development of both policy and practices. Therefore, a more appropriate vocabulary would include "anti-racism," which counters the notion of "races."

The development of a theoretical framework underlying anti-racism focusses on an integrative and critical approach to the examination of the discourses of race and racism and an analysis of the systems of differential and unequal treatment (Calliste, 1996). It is also "an educational political action-oriented strategy for institutional and systemic change to address racism and the interlocking systems of social oppression" (Dei, 1996:25).

"Anti-racism" suggests, in the first instance, that racist institutional policies and practices are the locus of the problem of racism in contemporary society. Thus, in a general sense, anti-racism refers to measures and mechanisms designed — by the state, institutions, organizations, groups, and individuals — to counteract racism. Some social scientists point out that the aims of anti-racism are, by definition, oppositional: its intention is to oppose any organizational or institutional policy or practice that oppresses, represses, or disenfranchises members of a racial group (Brandt, 1986). An anti-racism praxis is oppositional to White hegemony and the attending social, economic, and political interests of the dominant culture (Dei, 1996). At the same time, anti-racism examines the meaning of **Whiteness** and the power and privilege of White skin, which is largely invisible to those who possess it (McIntosh, 1990; Dines, 1994; Fine et al., 1997).

A further important dimension of anti-racism theory and practice is a critique of liberalism. Relying on traditional liberal principles, concepts, and approaches (such as "individualism," "equal opportunity," "colour-blindness," or "education") is flawed because it focusses on incremental change rather than on the more radical notion of transforming social action (Crenshaw, 1997).

Anti-racism is a strong trend in both the United Kingdom and the United States, and more recently in Canada. Anti-racism education in these jurisdictions is aimed primarily at dismantling structures and systems that have generated and perpetuated racial barriers and inequities in the policies, programs, and practices of the educational system. Anti-racism also targets administrative procedures that exclude racial-minority educators from full and equal participation in educational institutions. It assumes that a system of inequality exists and that legislation, policy-making, program implementation, and monitoring are required to dismantle it.

Anti-racism theory provides a vehicle for critically examining the role of both the state and societal institutions (such as legislative and bureaucratic agencies, the workplace, schools, justice, and the media) in reproducing racial, gender, and class-based inequalities. It recognizes the need to address the social construction of difference and the interlocking systems of oppression that result from these beliefs. Anti-racism situates power relations at the centre of the analysis of race and social difference. It focusses on the urgent need for a social system that is more representative, equitable, inclusive, and capable of responding to the concerns and aspirations of marginalized communities (Dei, 1996).

SOCIAL RESEARCH IN CANADA: ETHNICITY, MULTICULTURALISM, AND RACISM

The field of race relations and its recent emphasis on racism and anti-racist approaches are often combined with studies of ethnicity and multiculturalism (Frideres, 1989). In North American universities, for example, "Race and Ethnic Relations" has been a popular course in sociology. This approach assumes that race and ethnicity are closely related and that a racial group is simply another kind of ethnic group.

Thus a textbook in this field may include the study of Greeks, Italians, Scots, Germans, Blacks, and Chinese. Its assimilationist perspective suggests that the experiences of all groups are similar. In Canada, the experiences of European immigrants who arrived here after 1945 and who suffered discrimination are often cited. It is implied that they overcame discrimination because they were industrious and worked hard, and that this eased their eventual adaptation to Canadian society. This view suggests that, in the long run, race and colour will become unimportant in much the same way that ethnic origins become less important as time goes on and generations change.

The study of race and ethnic relations gradually began to give way to the study of ethnicity. American scholars in particular noticed that people whose ancestors had migrated to the United States in the last part of the nineteenth century and in the early twentieth century were reclaiming their origins. Ethnicity, it was discovered, is not totally lost as generations change. Third- and fourth-generation immigrants who had successfully integrated experienced a renewed interest in their origins (Reitz, 1980). Moreover, some ethnic cultural patterns, particularly food habits, had carried over to successive generations. Meanwhile, the United States was receiving migrants from countries such as Mexico, Puerto Rico, and other Hispanic countries. These groups continued to value their ethnic origins and culture in the face of racism directed against them and their relative exclusion from American institutions.

An important work establishing the credibility of the study of ethnicity was Glazer and Moynihan's *Ethnicity: Theory and Experience* (1975), which defined the field of study as "all the groups of a society characterized by a distinctive sense of difference owing to culture and descent." Ethnicity was a central concept in understanding the many subgroups in society and was as important as social class as a segmenting variable. In this formulation, race and colour were not considered important factors in maintaining ethnicity. It essentially ignored the differential treatment that racial minorities would continue to experience. In response, Black scholars took the view that emphasizing ethnicity was simply another way of not dealing with the central issue of racism.

Race and ethnicity are often considered to be closely related because both variables differentiate groups in plural or heterogeneous societies. However, considering the two concepts as equal partners, or tagging race onto ethnicity, subsumes race under ethnicity. Ethnicity involves a notion of blood, kinship, a common sense of belonging, and often a common geographic or national origin. It refers to the social origins of groups, whereas race refers to the biological status of groups and the social construction of racism, which often follows.

Race and ethnicity do overlap at times, particularly in areas in which Blacks and Whites are members of the same ethnic group. The most obvious example occurs in the United States, where both racial groups are ethnically American yet do not share equally in the distribution of wealth, power, and privilege. It is not surprising, therefore, that those who have a strong commitment to the elimination of racism perceive ethnicity studies as drawing attention away from racism. This belief has affected Black studies programs at American universities:

> There was pressure on some campuses to transform [Black Studies programs] into Ethnic Studies programs. In some instances, Black Studies publications were reconceived as Ethnic Studies publications.... One response to the Black Consciousness and Black Power movements in the United States was to try to deracialize them, to argue that the Black Experience was similar to that of European ethnic groups and that the passage of time would make race and colour increasingly irrelevant. (Drake, 1991:59)

In the United Kingdom, a similar movement toward multiculturalism has taken place, particularly in the schools, where multicultural education consists of learning about the heritage and cultures of people rather than dealing with structural racism. One of the most powerful critics of that movement notes that

> anti-racism in the seventies was only fought and resisted in the community, in the localities, behind the slogan of a Black politics and the Black experience. In that moment, the enemy was ethnicity. The enemy had to be what we called "multiculturalism." Because multiculturalism was precisely what I called the exotic. The exotica of difference. Nobody would talk about racism but they were prepared to have "international evenings" when we would all come and cook our native dishes, sing our own native songs and appear in our own native costumes. (Hall, 1991:56)

In describing the situation in the United Kingdom, Hall equates the concepts of ethnicity and multiculturalism. In Canadian studies, however, multiculturalism has a more applied meaning because its main impetus comes from the state, in the form of federal legislation. There has been some work on ethnicity in Canada (e.g., Breton, 1989; Isajiw, 1997; Bibby, 1990; Anderson and Frideres, 1981), but more attention has been paid to multiculturalism (e.g., Fleras and Elliott, 1992, 1996; Kymlicka, 1998).

THE 1990S: CULTURAL STUDIES AND DISCOURSE ANALYSIS

One of the most intriguing theoretical developments in the social sciences in recent years has been the growth of a field of inquiry called **cultural studies**. Strongly influenced by postmodern perspectives, it is an approach to the study of culture that began in the United Kingdom more than twenty years ago because it was recognized that the traditional disciplines that study culture — anthropology, sociology, history, literature, and so on — had become so fragmented and formalized into separate disciplines that culture came to be studied in disparate pieces (During, 1994). Moreover, traditional academic disciplines and their practitioners were isolated from the public sphere, where popular culture, one of the distinguishing characteristics of postmodern society, has its nexus.

The field of cultural studies encourages a critical examination of dominant culture and an effective resistance to its hegemonic control. It is inherently oppositional in its approach to dominance. Although it has been difficult to define the boundaries of this field because of its overwhelming subject matter, a useful approach emphasizes the function of cultural studies

> largely as a term of convenience for a fairly dispersed array of theoretical and political positions which, however widely divergent they might be in other respects, share a commitment to examining cultural practices from the point of view of their intrication with, and within, relations of power. (Bennett, 1992:23)

Of major concern to the field of cultural studies are questions relating to race, national identity, and ethnicity as these operate in a transnational, new world order. The increasing movement of people and ideas among nations has created conditions of multiculturalism and diversity in countries that had earlier enjoyed a monocultural existence, but it has also created concerns about race, ethnicity, and the politics of diversity. This new field breaks with the conventions of traditional social science in many ways.

In its emphasis on subjectivity, it studies culture in relation to the way it affects the daily experiences of people rather than as an abstraction divorced from the reality of everyday experience. Culture is not a social construct, nor is it meant to be defined by high culture and its forms. Cultural studies analyzes the impact of societal inequality on the lives of those most affected, such as women and racial minorities. It is very much concerned with diversity's effects on mainstream traditional institutions and organizations and with how ethno-racial and women's groups are maintaining and elaborating their autonomous values, identities, and cultural products. Thus, cultural studies affirms otherness and difference in what has been called the "politics of survival" (During, 1994) and the "politics of difference" (West, 1990). This approach is part of a theory of society in which difference and otherness are central and in which the dynamic of pluralism and heterogeneity are emphasized. Theoretical explanation in the field of cultural studies does not necessarily depend upon the forces of capitalism or a free-market economy as central causes of structural inequality but works toward creating conditions of autonomy for all "othered" groups. In this view, society does not need a total revolution in its mode of production, but it does need to create conditions of equality and equity. Cultural studies focusses on a critical view of multiculturalism in denying the singular or privileged position of the traditional Eurocentric state and its culture, and it values alternative forms of culture and their expression.

Another significant feature of the cultural studies approach is its opposition to the values of the "new right" and its moral agenda, which emphasizes the preservation of traditional values and the maintenance of existing power relations. A cultural studies approach criticizes the homogeneous image of the national culture and its images of a monocultural society. It supports a competing set of insurgent values with an emphasis on collective rights and freedoms. Cultural studies also underscores the important role of popular culture in the transmission and reproduction of values. The traditional difference between "high" and popular culture, so characteristic of Eurocentred discourses of the past, is de-emphasized. There is also a strong emphasis on identifying those ideologies operating in a specific **cultural artifact** or project that make inequalities appear natural and just; thus marking the ways in which power and domination are encoded in cultural **texts**, images, and narratives (Kellner, 1995).

Cultural studies provides a framework for critically examining the artifacts of contemporary culture, including cultural institutional policies, practices, norms, and values that affect cultural production. Systems of representation such as film, theatre, publishing, the visual arts, music, media, and academia are the subject of public scrutiny and cultural criticism by those who have been marginalized, excluded, and silenced by Eurocentric cultural traditions and practices (Hutcheon, 1988, 1991). Indeed, a critique of the discursive practices buried within these cultural institutions provides an illuminating and powerful form of analysis. The new dimension of the second edition of this text is to include an analysis of how forms of discourse create, reinforce, and reproduce systems of inequality.

DISCOURSE AND DISCOURSE ANALYSIS

Central to a cultural studies perspective is the notion of "**discourse**," which stems from Foucault's seminal work (1980). "Discourse" is, however, elusive and difficult to define. There are at least two basic meanings of the term. It is most closely associated with language and the written or oral text, and it emphasizes the relationship between the speaker and those being addressed, or between the writer and the reader. Sometimes, discourse refers more narrowly to the differences between spoken dialogue and written text. Or, it may refer to the style of language used in a particular situation ("e.g., newspaper discourse, classroom discourse," Fairclough, 1992:3). Fiske (1994) defines the notion of discourse as language in social use and observes that it is a language marked by its history of domination, subordination, and resistance and shaped by the social conditions of those who use it.

Discourse analysis goes beyond the social origins of linguistic forms, however, since it also includes those sets of social relations ordered by a particular discourse. Thus, in addition to texts, there are values, norms, attitudes, and behavioral practices associated with a specific discourse.

In its second basic meaning, "discourse" is used in social theory and analysis following the pioneering theorizing of Foucault to refer to "different ways of structuring knowledge and social practice" (Fiske, 1994). Thus, for example, the dominant discourse of immigration in Canadian society today differs markedly from earlier discourses. Moreover, there are also alternative discourses on this topic espoused by immigrants, people of colour, and other non-dominant groups in Canadian society.

Discourses do more than represent social beings and social relations, since they actually construct or define systems of beliefs and ideologies and position the players within it (as, for example, the difference in positioning between the immigration officer and the would-be immigrant). Thus, discourse contains within it power, which is used to expand or defend the interests of its discursive community.

Discourse analysis is often used as a tool to identify and define social, economic, and historical power relations between dominant and subordinate groups. The field of discourse involves, as D. Goldberg (1993:295) notes, "discursive formation," which is the totality of ordered relations and correlations of subject to each other and to objects; of economic production and reproduction; of cultural symbols and signification; of laws and moral rules; and of social, political, economic, or legal inclusion or exclusion.

Discourses in a modern transglobal and multicultural world are always dynamic, shifting and ever changing. The main function of discourse is to make sense of the reality of experience.

RACIST DISCOURSE

Racist discourse, or the discourse of racism, advances the interests of Whites. It has an identifiable repertoire of words, images, and practices through which racial power is directed against minorities. D. Goldberg (1993:47) contends that racialized discourse includes far more than a set of overt descriptive representations about minority people (e.g., describ-

ing African Canadians as "criminals," refugees as "gate-crashers and welfare abusers," and Chinese Canadians as the builders of "monster houses"). These representations are merely the tip of the iceberg of a series of
racist assumptions and ideas that form the foundation of a racialized discourse.

Racist discourse includes the idea that human beings can be hierarchically classified according to their intellectual and physical abilities;
that people can exclude, disrespect, and dominate those whom they consider inferior to themselves; and that institutional regulations and practices can restrict equal access to education, employment, and other benefits of society. Racialized discourse is expressed in many ways, but all
serve to support patterns of domination, exclusion, and marginalization.

Smitherman-Donaldson and van Dijk (1988) argue that the links between language and discourse and between discrimination and racism are
complex and varied, forming part of an intricate network of social relationships in which power plays a pivotal role. Discourse is vital in the reproduction of the racial oppression and control of people of colour and
other minorities. Racist discourse as part of culture may be understood as
the fundamental form of racism because it includes ideas that are deeply
embedded in the value system of society. It is part of the invisible network
of beliefs, attitudes, and assumptions that define the cultural value system
of society (Wetherell and Potter, 1992; Kellner, 1995; Tator et al., 1998).

Central to racialized discourse is **Eurocentrism**, or the belief in the
dominance of everything European in origin. It is a form of racism in
which certain cultures are perceived to be superior while others are and
will always be inferior (Shohat and Stam, 1994). This is an important element in the racist discourse that characterizes Western societies. Because
this discourse is so central to thought and behaviour, its effects are deep-
rooted and pervasive. The belief in European superiority pervades Western society and exerts a strong influence on the behaviour of the people
who work in institutions and organizations and, as well, on the everyday
behaviour of the citizenry. As will be demonstrated throughout this text,
discourses on minorities, race, and racism converge with questions about
national and cultural identity and raise provocative questions about the
meaning of such cherished liberal democratic values as individualism,
freedom of expression, and tolerance.

THE DEBATE OVER MULTICULTURALISM

Over the last three decades, discourse about Canadian national identity
has been framed within the debate concerning multiculturalism (see
Chapter 11) and its promise to recognize, respect and value cultural and
racial differences.[4] There are a multiplicity of responses to multiculturalism, both as ideology and as public policy (a policy on multiculturalism was introduced in the House of Commons by Prime Minister
Trudeau in 1971, and the Canadian Multiculturalism Act was passed in

1988). For many Canadians, contemporary multiculturalism poses a threat to the way that they have imagined and constructed Canadian identity. They hold on to an image of Canada as distinguished from other countries, and particularly the United States, by its French–English duality. Canadians want to resolve the French–English tensions without having to address the multicultural aspect of identity. Those who oppose multiculturalism hold that it is a fundamentally flawed approach to Canada's cultural and racial diversity. They perceive that support for the expression of ethnic and racial differences represents a serious threat to Euro-Canadian values and individual rights and freedoms, and ultimately leads to a society torn by division and cultural separation (Bissoondath, 1994; Gwyn, 1995).

On the other hand, others such as Kymlicka (1998) argue that multiculturalism is consistent with liberal democratic values and that it has been a positive force in the integration of ethno-racial communities. Moreover, Kymlicka asserts that because of its policy of multiculturalism, both at the federal level and as it has filtered down into public institutions such as the schools, Canada protects both individual and group rights more effectively than does any country that has not adopted multiculturalism.

Yet, another view of multiculturalism is that the policy and practice of multiculturalism continues to position certain ethno-racial groups at the margins, rather than in the mainstream of public culture and national identity. While "tolerating," "accommodating," "appreciating," and "celebrating" differences, it allows for the preservation of the cultural hegemony of the dominant cultural group. Many writers and theorists (Walcott, 1993; Goldberg, 1994; Mackey, 1996) have identified as a major weakness of multiculturalism its failure to deal with the problems of systemic racism in Canada. This race-based analysis documents the ways that multiculturalism as ideology has provided a veneer for liberal-pluralist discourse, in which democratic values such as individualism, tolerance, and equality are espoused and supported, without altering the core of the common culture or ensuring the rights of people of colour. This critique of multiculturalism points to its inability to dismantle systems of inequality and diminish White power and privilege.

The race-based analysis of multiculturalism has led to a new form of discourse labelled **"radical"** or **"critical" multiculturalism** (Shohat and Stam, 1994; Goldberg, 1994) or "insurgent multiculturalism" (quoted in St. Lewis, 1996:28). Critical multiculturalism moves away from a paradigm of pluralism premised on a hierarchical order of cultures that under certain conditions "allows" non-dominant cultures to participate in the dominant culture. This more pro-active, radical model of multiculturalism focusses on *empowerment* and *resistance* to forms of subjugation; the *politicization* and *mobilization* of marginalized groups; the *transformation* of social, cultural, and economic institutions; and the *dismantling* of dominant cultural hierarchies, structures and systems of representation.

RACISM AS A FIELD OF INQUIRY

Several trends in the study of racism can be identified. One of the most common responses has been neglect. The academic establishment, particularly in the social sciences, has been singularly remiss in undertaking research on racism, although some work on discrimination against Aboriginal peoples has been undertaken. Social anthropologists, in particular, have been in the forefront of research concerning Aboriginal rights to resources and land.

There are many reasons for the lack of attention to racism, but one important factor is that studies concentrating solely on racism did not appear until the late 1970s.[5] Growth in the field was slow, and the literature on race and racism in Canada remains limited. Another important factor is that race as a variable of differentiation is still considered a subset of ethnicity and ethnic relations. Thus, courses, books, and studies on "race and ethnic relations" remain popular. Race and ethnicity are not distinguished for the purposes of applied policy-oriented research.

One of the first research undertakings in the study of race and social racism in Canada was the demonstration of the existence of racism in Canadian society. Examples include Henry and Ginzberg's (1984) study of employment discrimination; studies of racism in education, such as those of Ramcharan (1974) and Adair and Rosenstock (1976); and studies of racial discrimination, such as Jain's and the beginning work of Li.[6] Much of the work published in the 1970s was undertaken by academics using traditional scholarly perspectives and methods to influence public policy.

Another trend was to consider race in studies of ethnic groups, particularly those of colour. Important work on the Chinese in British Columbia, Haitians in Montreal, and South Asians in Canada was done in the 1970s and continues to the present. These works reveal that it is not only culture and ethnicity that influence integration into a new host society, but also the forces of racism.[7]

More recently, scholarly research on racism has increased. For example, Reitz and Breton (1996) undertook a comparative analysis of racism and racial discrimination in Canada and the United States. Another reason is that more racial-minority scholars have been hired by universities and government agencies that have a research function.[8] An example of important work resulting from this is the Pendakur and Pendakur (1995) study of income differentials.

Three discernible trends can be identified in the current literature. The first is the use of a neo-Marxian political economy model in which the role of labour migration and labour exploitation is highlighted. Strongly influenced by the theoretical work of Miles (1989), this approach is best exemplified in Satzewich (1993), which brings together the results of a conference held on the subject of immigration, racism, and multiculturalism that was sponsored by the Social Research Unit of the University of Saskatchewan.

The second trend, also neo-Marxian, is research that uses a race, gender, or class paradigm to highlight the many factors involved in unequal power relations in societies such as Canada. Feminist scholars, especially feminist scholars of colour, are in the forefront of this approach.[9] In Canada as elsewhere, they have disputed the dynamics of the relationships of ethnicity and class, ethnicity and race, and all three as they relate to gender (Ng, 1993). Lastly, studies that use a cultural-studies approach and focus on questions of cultural, racial, and national identity are enjoying a modest success (Yon, 1991, 1995; Amit-Talai and Knowles, 1996).

One of the major reasons for the preponderance of attention to ethnicity and multiculturalism is Canada's immigration policies and demographic patterns. The aftermath of World War II resulted in substantial numbers of Europeans migrating to Canada. Not until the liberalization of immigration legislation in 1967 did substantial numbers of people of colour arrive in Canada. Thus, late-twentieth-century Canadian society was first diversified by the arrival of Europeans who were neither British nor French. A focus on ethnicity and the beginnings of multiculturalism became evident. Even today, "ethnic revitalization" is occurring in Canada (Herberg, 1989; Driedger, 1989; Breton et al., 1990). In addition to creating a substantial literature on ethnicity, Canadian scholarship has paid considerable attention to multiculturalism (e.g., Fleras and Elliott, 1992, 1996).

The policy of the present federal government is to consider the dynamics of racism in the context of multiculturalism. Multiculturalism, however, must be distinguished from racism and strategies to promote anti-racism. The essential question is, if federal legislation and policies recognize and legitimize cultural diversity, should

> multicultural initiatives focus on the perpetuation of culture or the enhancement of ethnoracial equality? If the latter, multiculturalism must accentuate the needs and aspirations of *racial* minorities.... However, does this mean that folkloric multiculturalism is obsolete and in danger of being replaced by an "instrumental" multiculturalism, with its commitment to race relations, social equality, and institutional accommodation? (Fleras and Elliott, 1992:6)

An emphasis on the needs of racial minorities in Canada is viewed with caution because of the government's fear that it would be perceived negatively by White mainstream and ethnic communities. It is unlikely, therefore, that the present government will ignore the celebration of cultural diversity in Canada.[10]

A considerable amount of good work has been done under the rubric of multiculturalism, and a legitimate case can be made for its benefits (Fleras and Elliott, 1992). However, racial inequalities and the social construction of racism should have pride of place at the level of the state, in public- and private-sector institutions, in teaching curricula and educational institutions, and in scholarly research.

RACE, GENDER, AND CLASS PARADIGMS IN CANADA

In Canada, as in other complex societies with heterogeneous populations, social relations are influenced by such factors as class, gender, and race. While the totality of social life can be explained only in terms of the interactions of these and other distinguishing characteristics, one characteristic is usually given prominence. The choice of factor is largely determined by the theoretical orientation of the analyst (Stasiulis, 1990).

Although race is an important segmenter of Canadian (and other) societies, class and gender also create significant inequities. Many modern paradigms of society include the "interlocking nature of relevant systems of domination and the varieties of consciousness that flow from them, with a view to understanding how they affect collective action" (Morris, 1992:361).

The interrelationships of class, race, ethnicity, and gender have especially been re-examined from the perspective of feminist neo-Marxism (Smith, 1987). Feminist neo-Marxists have criticized the ethnicity and class perspectives of sociology, in which the issues of gender and race are usually ignored. While Ng (1993) maintains that race and ethnicity can be taken together because of their constructed character, she concludes that "gender, race/ethnicity, and class are not fixed entities. They are socially constructed in and through the productive and reproductive relations in which we all participate. Thus, what constitutes sexism, racism, as well as class oppression, changes over time as productive relations change" (195).

Making a similar point, Khayatt (1994) argues that "unless the boundaries of race, gender, class and sexuality intersect to make visible the various nuances of each category, the usefulness of each becomes lost in a hierarchicalization of oppressions." In other words, these various categories of identity must be considered together, determining the way they intersect, the way they differ and, at the same time, taking into account the distinctiveness of individual experience.

Another Canadian approach to this area is represented by Calliste (1989, 1992), whose studies of Caribbean immigrant women show that historically they have been used as cheap domestic labour. The exclusion of black women from nursing in Canada before the late 1940s (Calliste, 1996) was rationalized by an ideological construction of racially specific femininity and sexuality, representing the opposite models of White, middle-class womanhood. A further example of the interrelationship between race and gender is manifested in the racism that continues to be experienced by Black nurses in Canadian hospitals (Calliste, 1996) in the 1990s.

Razack (1998) and Shakir (1995) point to the impact of gendered racism in the treatment of Aboriginal women and immigrant women of colour in the justice system. Both these theorists emphasize that gender can be culturalized and can replace race as the key interactive relationship (for example, consider the erroneous assumption that the passivity of South

Asian women and their position of submission to the patriarchy of their cultures accounts for spousal abuse).

Razack (1998), in analyzing the interlocking systems of race, gender, and class, identifies the complex ways in which systems of oppression support one another. She cites the example of domestic workers and the largely White professional women they work for as a symbiotic but hierarchical relationship.

Similarly, Bakan and Stasiulis (1995) demonstrate how the increasing demand for home child care in developed capitalist states and the controlled supply of Third World immigrant women work together to structure differences in citizenship rights across national boundaries.

THE FORMS OF RACISM

Because it is an exceedingly complex manifestation of human behaviour, racism takes many forms. The context within which it occurs largely determines the form it takes. In its simplest form, racism has three components: individual, systemic, and cultural or ideological. In individual racism, a further distinction must be made between an individual's attitudes and her or his behaviour. An individual might hold a set of attitudes about Black people — for example, they are lazy, unmotivated, or slow. These attitudes may remain at the level of thought, or they may result in a certain form of behaviour, such as "everyday racism," which includes small acts like not shaking a Black person's hand or not sitting next to a person of colour on a bus.

Another form of racism occurs in collectivities or organizations that have developed policies and practices that are, intentionally or unintentionally, discriminatory. Within police organizations, for example, the former policy requiring officers to be of a certain height and weight was discriminatory toward certain groups of people.

The overarching form of racism resides in cultural symbols and is expressed through language, religion, and art. "Cultural racism" refers to collective and mass beliefs about race that are woven into the fabric of the dominant culture. The use of the word "black" to denote something negative or evil (as in "blackmail") is an example of cultural racism.

At each of these three levels, the racism may be overtly expressed or take on a covert, subtle, or hidden form.

INDIVIDUAL RACISM

Individual racism involves both the attitudes held by an individual and the overt behaviour prompted by those attitudes. The attitudes are often obvious: extremely intolerant, bigoted individuals tend to be proud of their attitudes and articulate them overtly and publicly. In a society such as Canada's, however, most people are uncomfortable about expressing their attitudes openly because these attitudes run counter to the prevailing norms. They may show their attitudes by practising racial discrimination.

Table 2.1

THE FORMS OF RACISM

Type	Manifestations
Individual	Attitudes; everyday behaviour
Institutional/systemic	Policies and practices of an organization; rules woven into a social system
Cultural/ideological	Values embedded in dominant culture

Individual racism has been defined as the attitude, belief, or opinion that one's own racial group has superior values, customs, and norms and, conversely, that other racial groups possess inferior traits and attributes. Individual racist beliefs provide a lens through which one sees, interprets, and interacts with the world. Because it is rooted in the individual's belief system, racism is a form of prejudice, "an emotionally rigid attitude ... toward a group of people. It involves not only prejudgment but ... misjudgment as well. It is categorical thinking that systematically misinterprets the facts" (Wellman, 1977:24).

Prejudiced attitudes are largely unconscious and, as such, are unnoticed by most people. They are strongly connected to the ways in which social relations are structured:

> Racist attitudes are largely derivative in nature.... They do not spring up or survive in a vacuum ... but grow out of and are continually sustained by the structure of social relations of which they are largely a psychological reflection. (Parekh, 1987:viii)

Implicit in this notion is a rejection of earlier social psychology theories that suggest that racist thinking, **intolerance**, or prejudiced beliefs are rooted in certain deviant personality types (for example, the authoritarian personality) or related to low socioeconomic status. Wellman (1977) and others argue that middle-class Whites are trained to subscribe to "liberal" ideas of equality and therefore tend to verbalize tolerance, while holding ambivalent and sometimes conflicting attitudes.

In this view, prejudice needs to be placed in a broader sociological context because attitudinal manifestations of racial inequality are related to social, political, and economic stratifications that form social structures and arrangements. This approach shifts the focus on misconceptions that White people might have about "others" to an emphasis on measuring interpersonal, interracial animosity. It views the basis of racism as being the dominant position of White people in Western society and the benefits that result from this position. This analysis concludes that "personal prejudice is really a disguised way to defend privilege" (Wellman, 1977:39).

A central question about individual racism is: Do racist beliefs necessarily result in discriminatory behaviour and, if so, under what conditions? While there is some debate in the literature regarding the causal relationship between prejudice and discrimination, a body of research demonstrates a clear link (Howitt and McCabe, 1978). Researchers found that in circumstances in which behaviour has no observable victim, there was a clear correspondence between attitudes and behaviour. However, Howitt and Owusu-Bempah (1990) draw an important distinction: racism is not only something done by racists; it is a sociocultural system that achieves specific objectives. It is therefore important to move the conception of racism beyond a focus on interpersonal animosity.

Using a similar analysis, it can be argued that the racist ideology of individuals, like sexist attitudes, is only a symptom of the more serious malaise in the relationships between racial groups. Social and psychological considerations should be examined within the sociocultural context that produces and reproduces inequality and injustice (Howitt and Owusu-Bempah, 1990).

> Personal attitudes far from exhaust the catalogue of discriminatory behaviour.... Discrimination remains so pervasive and entrenched because it is not solely personal.... It permeates both power and private relationships....
> The racist, sexist or homophobe is not an aberrational figure in our culture.... It is the collective culture as much as individual citizens. (Hutchinson and Carpenter, 1992)

Racist beliefs and attitudes can also be considered as a continuum of weak to strong. A weak attitude merely uses and identifies racial classifications without necessarily prescribing any action. Reeves (1983) identifies weak racism to include beliefs:

- that races of human beings exist;
- that these races differ from one another;
- that the differences are deeply rooted and enduring;
- that the differences are significant, possibly because they appear in themselves to be explanatory, or because explanations of other social features may be inferred from them; and
- that the differences have social consequences, for example, for social policy.

There is no moral evaluation of differences, nor does any form of prescriptive action flow from them.

A medium racist attitude accords more favourable treatment to the alleged superior race while denying goods and services to the alleged inferior races. Medium racist belief systems may include:

- precise details of how and in what way the races differ;
- an explanation for the continuing existence of races and racial differences;

- reasons for the assumptions being thought significant in terms of social consequences that result or have resulted from racial differences; and
- the belief that differences between races make certain races superior or inferior and that races can be placed in some sort of rank order.

Finally, strong racist beliefs include a prescription for action that follows from all of the above beliefs: that the superior race is entitled to more favourable treatment than the inferior race.

EVERYDAY RACISM

Everyday racism involves the many and sometimes small ways in which racism is experienced by people of colour in their interactions with the dominant White group. It expresses itself in glances, gestures, forms of speech, and physical movements. Sometimes it is not even consciously experienced by its perpetrators, but it is immediately and painfully felt by its victims — the empty seat next to a person of colour, which is the last to be occupied in a crowded bus; the slight movement away from a person of colour in an elevator; the over-attention to the Black customer in the shop; the inability to make direct eye contact with a person of colour; the racist joke told at a meeting; and the ubiquitous question "Where did you come from?"

From a research perspective, these incidents are difficult to quantify because they are only revealed in the thoughts, feelings, and articulations of victims:

> It is very difficult to determine "objectively" the nature of everyday interaction between Whites and Blacks.... a variety of studies have shown that those who are discriminated against appear to have more insight into discrimination mechanisms than those who discriminate.... Blacks have a certain amount of expertise about racism through extensive experience with Whites. The latter, conversely, are often hardly aware of the racism in their own attitudes and behaviour. (Essed, 1990)

And, although people of colour are often sensitive to everyday racism, it may be so subtle that they are unaware of it. Research on racism has therefore tended to focus on what is more immediately visible and measurable. Thus racial discrimination in employment, in the media, and other more visible manifestations of racism have been studied.

In analyzing everyday racism, a further important distinction can be made between active and passive racism. Active racism includes

> all acts that — consciously or unconsciously — emerge directly from the motivation to exclude or to inferiorize Blacks because they are Black. Passive racism is complicity with someone else's racism. Laughing at a humiliating joke ... and "not hearing" others' racist comments are passively racist acts. (Essed, 1990)

INSTITUTIONAL AND SYSTEMIC RACISM

Institutional racism is manifested in the policies, practices, and procedures of various institutions, which may, directly or indirectly, consciously or unwittingly, promote, sustain, or entrench differential advantage or privilege for people of certain races. An example of institutional racism is the common practice of "word-of-mouth recruitment," which generally excludes racial minorities from the process.

Institutional racism generally encompasses overt individual acts of racism to which there is no serious organizational response, such as discriminatory hiring decisions based on the employer's **bias**. It also includes organizational policies and practices that, regardless of intent, are directly or indirectly disadvantageous to racial minorities, such as the lack of recognition of foreign credentials or the imposition of inflated educational requirements for a position. According to J.J. Jones,

> Institutional racism can be defined as those established laws, customs and practices which systematically reflect and produce racial inequalities in American society. If racist consequences accrue to institutional laws, customs or practices the institution is racist whether or not the individuals maintaining those practices have racist intentions. (Williams, 1985:131)

Systemic racism, although similar to institutional racism, refers more broadly to the laws, rules, and norms woven into the social system that result in an unequal distribution of economic, political, and social resources and rewards among various racial groups. It is the denial of access, participation, and equity to racial minorities for services such as education, employment, and housing. Systemic racism is manifested in the media by, for example, the negative representation of people of colour, the erasure of their voices and experiences, and the repetition of racist images and discourse.

CULTURAL AND IDEOLOGICAL RACISM

Cultural racism is sometimes difficult to isolate because it is deeply embedded in the society's value system. It consists of the tacit network of beliefs and values that encourage and justify discriminatory practices. Writers such as Lawrence (1982) are very specific in their connotation of cultural racism and cite the misunderstanding of the cultural patterns of some groups as a basis for it. Lawrence writes specifically about the perception of the Black, particularly Caribbean, family, which differs from the type of family considered "normal" by the dominant culture. If the family does not include a male breadwinner, a financially dependent wife, and their offspring, it is thought to be pathological or deviant. British politicians, for example, routinely display cultural racism when they claim that the "race problem" is caused by pathological cultural patterns (Lawrence, 1982). Some writers prefer the use of the term "ideological racism" (Reeves, 1983), but both terms refer to racism formulated as a set of values and ideas.

Essed (1990) argues that cultural racism precedes other forms of racism in society. It is reflected in everyday language — "whiteness" is associated with overwhelmingly positive connotations, while "blackness," in *Roget's Thesaurus*, has no fewer than sixty distinctively negative synonyms, twenty of which are related to race. It is reflected in the images generated by the mass media (racial minorities are often portrayed as problems) and by the arts (literature, poetry, and visual art). It is also manifested in religious doctrines, ideologies, and practices.

Cultural racism creates a "we and they" mentality in which one's own racial group is considered to be better than other groups. This ubiquitous tendency to view all peoples and cultures in terms of one's own cultural standards and values is known as **ethnocentrism** and plays a central role in racism.

Cultural racism is maintained through the socialization of the new generation. Children learn the cultural beliefs and values of their society at an early age. Ideas and beliefs about races and racism are included in this early learning (Ijaz and Ijaz, 1981; Milner, 1983).

Finally, an important component of ideological racism identified as the "new or modern racism" (Gilroy, 1987) provides the conceptual framework of this book. "Democratic racism" provides an important insight into why, in a democratic society, many forms of racism exist. As the title of this book indicates, the paradox is that both a liberal democratic value system *and* racist beliefs and behaviours — belief systems that should be in conflict with each other — nevertheless coexist.

Although the various forms of racism can be isolated for discussion purposes, in reality they form a complex dynamic of interrelated attitudes, feelings, and behaviours that are linked to the collective belief system and are expressed in institutional policies and practices. While institutional racism is for many theorists the focus of attention — because the very real discrimination that people of colour face often emanates from institutions — these institutions consist of individuals who make the policies and implement the actions. Institutional and systemic racism is therefore the result of a series of interactions between the individuals who function within the system and the forces of the system itself.

This approach is strongly influenced by Hall (1991) and others in viewing racism as a social construction of difference. It is based on the idea that minor physical and genetic differences between people can be used as a basis of social differentiation. Thus, social, cultural, and intellectual values are ascribed to these minute differences. These ascriptions lead to racial discrimination and inequality. Racism functions in society to maintain the power and privilege of certain groups at the expense of others. People of colour living as minorities in White-dominated societies are often treated as less than full citizens so that the balance of power relations will not be upset.

Racism takes many forms. At the individual level, prejudiced attitudes may be expressed in the many slights characteristic of everyday racism. It

Figure 2.1

THE DIMENSIONS OF RACISM

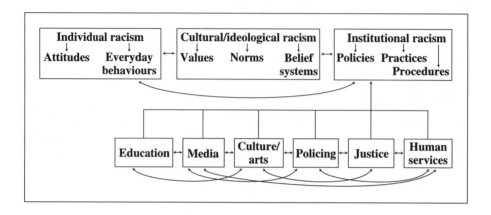

is demonstrated at the cultural and ideological level by the myths and stereotypes that circulate about the inferiority of certain kinds of people. And it is embedded in the policies and practices that regulate social, economic, political, and cultural institutions.

THE MEASUREMENT OF RACISM

One of the most problematic aspects of racism is measuring its many manifestations. What is acceptable as evidence that racism has occurred, and how can this evidence be quantified?

Little research has been conducted in Canada on the issue of measurement. Much evidence of racism must be culled from other indicators. As Weinfeld (1990) notes, data of adequate reliability and validity, transformed into recognized indicators and disseminated appropriately, are not available. Thus, most attempts to answer questions such as, "To what extent is Canada a racist society?" are based on partial snapshots, hunches, or the predispositions of the analyst.

Since racism and its many manifestations are now issues of central concern to contemporary social policy and practice, the question of measurement is a critical issue. Moreover, the media spend a great deal of time reporting, analyzing, and editorializing about racism. This attention leads people at all levels to pontificate on it, often with little knowledge of the subject, and increases or decreases in racism are frequently alleged. These public comments may be motivated by the political agendas of the speakers and writers who have a stake in this field.

Public spokespersons use different criteria to measure racism. Some cite poll results that show changes in attitudes; others cite economic criteria such as differences in income or employment, examples of discrimination in employment, or the number of cases brought to human rights commissions. Using different criteria to document racism leads to confusion about the meaning of the term and the ways in which it can be measured.

Clearly, a multidimensional approach to the measurement of racism is required, but even researchers in the field have relied on various approaches (Weinfeld, 1990). Neither the various spokespersons nor the academic researchers necessarily project an accurate picture. But what is an "accurate" picture?

How do we know, first, what racism is? Second, how can it be quantified not only for research purposes but for the development and implementation of anti-racist policies and practices? A review of the Ontario Human Rights Commission's disposition of complaints involving racism has shown that racial inequality is difficult to prove because of its hidden nature (Frideres and Reeves, 1989). If it is hard to demonstrate, how can it be measured?

In the first instance, it is again necessary to distinguish between overt individual forms of racism, such as the articulation of prejudicial attitudes, and the commonplace events and incidents that racial minorities confront daily. Attitudes can be studied and measured in a variety of ways. For example, a number of attitude studies undertaken in Canada show that from 12 to 16 percent of the population hold bigoted and intolerant attitudes (Henry, 1978). But how accurate are attitude surveys and polls as a measurement of racism?

In Canada, as elsewhere, studies of racism first focussed on prejudicial attitudes on the assumption that racism was caused solely by individuals acting on their negative feelings. More recently, a number of polls and surveys have considered the issues of racism and ethnicity. Polls have also been taken on matters relating to immigration. However, Gallup and similar polls are crude indicators, and their interpretation is often open to question. Questions asking for a perception of the increase in racism can be interpreted in many ways: a positive response can mean that the respondents have seen a greater number of racist incidents; it can also mean that a larger number of incidents are considered racist today, whereas formerly the respondents considered the incidents related to factors other than racism.

The first interpretation may mean that racism is on the rise, but the second may mean that a concern about racism and its negative effects is on the rise. Similarly, questions about the numbers of people who should be admitted to Canada give rise to various interpretations. People who respond negatively may simply be reflecting the view that Canada has more people than its economy can handle, which is not the same as the view that racial-minority immigration should be controlled.

Conversely, many Canadians pride themselves on their tolerance and respect for diversity and profess belief in the traditional democratic values of fairness and equality. Thus, their answers to pollsters' questions are unconsciously skewed to correspond to what they think a "liberal" response should be. Their ambivalent views are filtered out of the answers. The result is that a more positive response is projected. This is an example of ambivalent or aversive racism, in which people hold two opposing and contradictory attitudes — one friendly, the other hostile (Gaertner and Dovidio, 1986).

A further problem in measuring racism exists in relation to the results of polls and surveys. Since racial attitudes are frequently unconscious, unarticulated, and non-deliberate (Wellman, 1977; Barrett, 1987; Essed, 1990), "self-reports" of racial attitudes do not necessarily conform to behaviour (Phillips, 1971). A gap exists between attitude and behaviour, belief and action, prejudice and discrimination. But the extent of this divergence is not very clear (Barrett, 1987).

Several critical dimensions of the measurement conundrum, particularly with respect to polls and surveys, were revealed in an analysis of **anti-Semitism** in the United States (J.J. Goldberg, 1993). When representatives of major Jewish organizations met to draft a statement about anti-Semitism, a number of facts and figures were presented that seemed to indicate that anti-Semitism was greatly on the increase. One in five Americans, according to one poll, held strong anti-Semitic views; the number of bias crimes against Jews, ranging from graffiti to murder, seemed to have increased; and a number of constitutional challenges against hate-crime laws had been introduced in several states. The American Jewish Committee released a poll showing that 47 percent of New Yorkers, including 63 percent of Blacks, believed that "Jews have too much influence." A national poll revealed that 20 percent of Americans and 37 percent of Black Americans were anti-Semitic.

Although these poll results showed alarming numbers, other indicators of anti-Semitism presented a different picture. For example, overt discrimination against Jews in housing, jobs, and education had all but disappeared in the United States. Moreover, poll questions about Jews having too much influence are not necessarily indicators of anti-Semitism. Is perceived influence a measure of anti-Semitism or anti-Black prejudice? Increasingly, poll questions that allegedly test for negative stereotypes, such as the notion that "Jews stick together," are considered positive rather than negative traits.

In addition to challenging poll questions, this analysis also revealed that little attention is paid to longitudinal comparisons with earlier polling results. For example, the figure of 20 percent of Americans being anti-Semitic represents a drop of nearly one third from a 1964 result of 29 percent. The only indicator of anti-Semitism that does show an increase is the number of actual incidents — a total of 1879 in 1991, which consisted primarily of epithets and swastika daubings. This still amounts to five incidents per day in a total population of 250 million.

Although most poll and survey results do not appear to indicate any massive increase in prejudice, the vast majority of U.S. Jews (85 percent, compared with 45 percent in 1983) believe that "anti-Semitism is a serious problem in America today." This disparity is blamed by some on Jewish agencies who use anxiety about anti-Semitism as a means of fundraising. ("People don't give if you tell them everything's okay.") J.J. Goldberg (1993) concludes by noting that "the masses are driving the leadership.... Maybe it's time for the leadership to start leading, and tell their public the truth."

Although polls and attitude surveys present considerable obstacles to understanding the manifestations of racism, it is even more difficult to study everyday racism. Everyday racism must be studied from the perspective of the victims who experience it in looks, gestures, and forms of speech. Part of the problem may be that most researchers are White and have not themselves experienced these daily slights. However, the problem of measuring the hidden, innermost feelings and experiences of victims also plays a significant role in limiting research (Silvera, 1989).[11]

An additional, important factor is that evidence based on the everyday experiences of victims — "victim testimony" — is not the kind of evidence that authorities and decision-makers trust. Victims are believed to have "chips on their shoulders" and therefore not to be objective. Victim testimony has been collected by some task forces and commissions investigating aspects of racism in Canadian society. Although their reports have used public consultation to elicit data, they are not considered reliable studies of overt racism.

Some racial-minority leaders maintain that the denial of victim testimony is in itself a form of subtle racism. On the other hand, some minority leaders in responsible positions argue against research of any kind and for a reliance on victim testimony as the only acceptable documentation of racism. Clearly, there is a danger here of "throwing out the baby with the bath water," and a balanced perspective that includes both testimonials and research on measurement must be established.

MEASURING INSTITUTIONAL AND SYSTEMIC RACISM

It is difficult to study and measure covert racism in its institutional or systemic form. What is usually considered evidence is the consequences of alleged discrimination, rather than the intent to discriminate. One of the main problems with the concept of institutional racism is that it does not differentiate the structural features of institutions in society from the actions of groups of individuals. To what extent is racism embodied in institutions, and how can its institutional manifestation be measured?

Weinfeld (1990) has listed a large number of indicators of racism in all its forms. With respect to institutional racism, his list includes socioeconomic measures such as:

- *education:* level of attainment and areas of specialization;
- *occupation:* income; mobility; measures of unemployment, underemployment, labour-force participation, and poverty; workplace measures such as racial harassment;
- *representation rates:* in upper and middle levels of firms and organizations; degree of racial segregation in work settings and sectors, job **ghettoization**;
- *housing data:* residential segregation and quality of housing; incidents of discrimination by landlords and realtors.

It is almost impossible to answer the question: "Is racism on the increase?" because the answer largely depends on which of its many facets is being considered and by what method it is being measured. When public figures discuss the alarming increase in racism, they usually rely on snapshots of attitudes — polls or surveys. Such studies are often enough only crude indicators at best, and "remarkably uninformative; for the most part, they tell us about the relative readiness of sections of the population to subscribe to one set of verbal formula rather than another" (Zubaida, 1972).

Institutional, cultural, and individual racism feature in many of the incidents that occur in institutional contexts. The confluence of individual attitudes and cultural ideologies in institutional contexts results in innumerable examples of both intended and unintended racism. Although the three major forms of racism outlined in this chapter can be isolated for historical analyses, it is often difficult to identify the forms of racism that occur in everyday life. The ways in which racism is manifested are "so much a part of each other that they are often inseparable.... To see how white people do racism ... we cannot compartmentalize their thoughts and actions; to see the full picture, the three distinct concepts need to be combined" (Wellman, 1977:39).

SUMMARY

This chapter has reviewed the main theoretical formulations devised by social scientists in the United States, the United Kingdom, and Canada to explain the phenomenon of racism in modern society. There are essentially four main themes in the theoretical literature:

- *assimilation models*, developed earlier in this century, in which race is assumed to be part of ethnicity, and members of racial groups are therefore expected to assimilate into mainstream society with the same ease as did members of White ethnic groups;
- *race relations models*, in which race and racism are considered variables that segment or fractionalize groups in society;
- *anti-racist approaches*, in which society in general and institutions in particular are expected to challenge racism;
- *cultural studies perspectives*, in which race and racism are placed within the context of globalization and the increasing ethno-racial heterogeneity of complex societies.

Assimilation approaches generally assume consensus and homogeneity in society, whereas the later theories, especially those that are Marxian-derived, generally consider racism as a manifestation of class-derived conflict. The most recent theoretical themes in the literature stress the manner in which racism is embedded in the language, text, and cultural symbols of increasingly complex modern societies.

This chapter also defined three major forms of racism: *individual racism,* which can be considered in its attitudinal and behavioural dimensions; *institutional or systemic racism*; and *cultural or ideological racism.* The chapter concluded with a discussion of the difficulties and complexities of measuring racism.

NOTES

1. "Functionalist" in this context refers to the idea that society is composed of institutions, beliefs, and values, all of which function together to form a whole. Theories that emphasize the assimilation of ethnic and racial groups assume that these groups will ultimately fit into and become part of the larger society.
2. "Thatcherism" refers to the neoconservative approach of Prime Minister Margaret Thatcher's government in the United Kingdom in the 1980s.
3. Canadian scholars have written relatively little on racism, compared with their counterparts in the United States and United Kingdom. The dominant concern in Canadian scholarship, until very recently, has been ethnicity and multicultural studies. Notable exceptions were the publication of Bolaria and Li (1988) and Ramcharan (1982). Canadian scholars have now started to research and write more in this area.
4. Multiculturalism as both policy and ideology is contested in many countries in the ever-increasing globalization of the world. See, for example, Isajiw (1997).
5. Henry (1978) was one of the first attitude surveys published on this subject. Other factors responsible for the neglect in this field include the fact that racial-minority communities in the first instance expressed their concerns about racism to government; the absence of racial-minority researchers and faculty members; and the inability to obtain research funds for studies on racism in Canada because racism was considered an American problem.
6. Others include Henry and Ginzberg (1984), Ramcharan (1983), Adair and Rosenstock (1976), Anderson and Grant (1975), Jain (1981), and Hughes and Kallen (1974).
7. Labelle, LaRose, and Piche (1983), LaFerrière (1983), Ujimoto and Hirabayashi (1980), Warburton (1992), Anderson (1991), Buchignani and Indra (1986), James (1990), and Adachi (1976).
8. An even more recent trend in Canadian scholarship is the acceptance of a social construct model of racism, such as that taken in this book. This perspective is demonstrated in the recent work of Peter Li, whose study of housing and the racialization of the Chinese community in Vancouver is an important example of this approach. Another significant example is Audrey Kobayashi's (1990) work on the racialization of the law.
9. Ng (1993); Ng and Ramirez (1981); and Calliste (1989, 1992).
10. Irshad Manji, writing in the *Toronto Star*, July 5, 1992, noted that in the previous year, "the federal Department of Multiculturalism spent nearly as much on promoting heritage cultures as it did on fighting racism. Yet pursuing both goals at the same time, and with almost equal amounts of money is stupid: racism makes the benefits of promoting heritage cultures null and void. Racism reduces culture to bright outfits, cute accents and tongue-burning foods. It also limits the audiences of ethnic celebrations to those who'd come out and see Ukrainians dancing anyway. *Racism makes multiculturalism premature.*"
11. In the Canadian literature, Silvera (1989), which describes the experiences of Black domestics, comes closest to this kind of study.

REFERENCES

Adachi, K. (1976). *The Enemy That Never Was: A History of the Japanese Canadians.* Toronto: McClelland & Stewart.

Adair, J., and D. Rosenstock. (1976). *Multiracialism in the Classroom: A Survey of Inter-racial Attitudes in the Schools.* Ottawa: Secretary of State.

Allport, G. (1954). *The Nature of Prejudice.* New York: Doubleday.

Amit-Talai, V., and C. Knowles. (1996). *Resituating Identities: The Politics of Race, Ethnicity and Culture.* Peterborough, ON: Broadview Press.

Anderson, A., and J. Frideres. (1981). *Ethnicity in Canada: Theoretical Perspectives.* Toronto: Butterworths.

Anderson, K. (1991). *Vancouver's Chinatown: Racial Discourse in Canada, 1875–1980.* Montreal and Kingston: McGill-Queen's University Press.

Anderson, W., and R. Grant. (1975). *The Newcomers: Problems of Adjustment of West Indian Immigrant Children in Metro Toronto Schools.* North York, ON: York University.

Bakan, A., and D. Stasiulis. (1995). "Making the Match: Domestic Placement Agencies and the Racialization of Women's Household Work." *Signs: Journal of Women in Culture and Society* 20(2):303–35.

Banton, M. (1977). *The Idea of Race.* London: Tavistock.

———. (1983). *Racial and Ethnic Competition.* Cambridge and New York: Cambridge University Press.

Barrett, S. (1987). *Is God a Racist? The Right Wing in Canada.* Toronto: University of Toronto Press.

Ben-Tovin, G., and G. Gabriel. (1986). *The Local Politics of Race.* London: Macmillan.

Bennett, T. (1992). "Putting Policy into Cultural Studies." In L. Grossberg, C. Nelson, and P. Treichler (eds.), *Cultural Studies.* New York and London: Routledge. 23–34.

Bibby, R.W. (1990). *Mosaic Madness.* Toronto: Stoddart.

Bissoondath, N. (1994). *Selling Illusions: The Cult of Multiculturalism.* Toronto: Penguin.

Bolaria, B.S., and P. Li (eds.). (1988). *Racial Oppression in Canada.* 2nd ed. Toronto: Garamond.

Bourne, J., and A. Sivanandan. (1974). "Cheerleaders and Ombudsmen: The Sociology of Race Relations in Britain." *Race and Class* 21(4):331–52.

Brandt, G. (1986). *The Realization of Anti-Racist Teaching.* London: Falmer Press.

Breton, R. (1989). "Canadian Ethnicity in the Year 2000." In J. Frideres (ed.), *Multiculturalism and Intergroup Relations.* New York: Greenwood Press. 149–52.

Breton, R., W. Isajiw, W. Kalbach, and J. Reitz. (1990). *Ethnic Identity and Equality:Varieties of Experience in a Canadian City.* Toronto: University of Toronto Press.

Buchignani, N., and D. Indra. (1986). *Continuous Journey: A Social History of South Asians in Canada.* Toronto: McClelland & Stewart.

Calliste, A. (1989). "Canada's Immigration Policy and Domestics from the Caribbean: The Second Domestic Scheme." *Race, Class, Gender: Bonds and Barriers: Socialist Studies,* 5:133–65.

———. (1992). "Women of Exceptional Merit: Immigration of Caribbean Nurses to Canada." *Canadian Journal of Women and the Law* 6:85–102.

———. (1996). "Anti-racism Organizing and Resistance in Nursing." *CRSA/RCSA* 33(3):361–90.

Carmichael, S., and C. Hamilton. (1967). *Black Power: The Politics of Liberation in America.* New York: Random House.

CCCS (Centre for Contemporary Cultural Studies). (1982). *The Empire Strikes Back: Race and Racism in 70's Britain.* London: Hutchinson.

Cox, O. (1976). *Race Relations: Elements and Social Dynamics.* Detroit: Wayne State University Press.

Crenshaw, K. (1997). "Colour-blind Dreams and Racial Nitemares: Reconfiguring Racism in the Post–Civil Rights Era." In T. Morrison and C. Brodsky Lacour (eds.), *Birth of a Nation'hood: Gaze, Script, and Spectacle in the O.J. Simpson Case*. New York: Pantheon Books. 97–168.

Dei, G. (1996). "Critical Perspectives in Antiracism: An Introduction." *CRSA/RCSA* 33(3):247–67.

Dines, G. (1994). "What's Left of Multiculturalism? Race, Class, Gender in the Classroom?" *Race, Sex and Class* 1(2):23–24.

Drake, S.C. (1991). *Black Folk Here and There*. 2 vols. Los Angeles: Centre for Afro-American Studies and University of California Press.

Driedger, L. (ed.). 1989. *The Ethnic Factor: Identity in Diversity*. Toronto: McGraw-Hill Ryerson.

During, S. (ed.). (1994). *The Cultural Studies Reader*. London: Routledge.

Essed, P. (1990). *Everyday Racism: Reports from Women of Two Cultures*. Claremont, CA: Hunter House.

Fairclough, N. (1992). *Discourse and Social Change*. Cambridge: Polity Press.

Fanon, F. (1967). *Black Skin, White Masks*. New York: Grove Press.

Fine, M., L. Weiss, L. Powell, and L. Mun Wong. (1997). *Off White: Readings on Race, Power and Society*. London: Routledge.

Fiske, J. (1994). *Media Matters: Everyday Culture and Political Change*. London: Routledge.

Fleras, A. and J. Elliott. (1992). *Multiculturalism*. Scarborough, ON: Nelson.

———. (1996). *Unequal Relations: An Introduction to Race, Ethnic and Aboriginal Dynamics in Canada*. 2nd ed. Scarborough, ON: Prentice Hall.

Foucault, M. (1980). In *Power/Knowledge: Selected Interviews and Other Writings, 1972–1979*, ed. C. Gordon. New York: Pantheon.

Franklin, R.S. (1991). *Shadows of Race and Class*. Minneapolis: University of Minnesota Press.

Frideres, J. (ed.). (1989). *Multiculturalism and Intergroup Relations*. New York: Greenwood Press.

———, and W.J. Reeves. (1989). "The Ability to Implement Human Rights Legislation in Canada: A Research Note." *Canadian Review of Sociology and Anthropology* 26(May):311–32.

Gaertner, S.L., and J.F. Dovidio. (1986). "The Aversive Forms of Racism." In S.L. Gaertner and J.F. Dovidio (eds.), *Prejudice, Discrimination and Racism*. New York: Academic Press.

Gilroy, P. (1987). *There Ain't No Black in the Union Jack*. Chicago: University of Chicago Press.

Glazer, N., and D. Moynihan. (1975). *Ethnicity: Theory and Experience*. Cambridge, MA: Harvard University Press.

Globe and Mail. (1993). "How Did We Wind Up Aboard This Train?" (July 19):A12.

Goldberg, D. (1993). *Racist Culture: Philosophy and the Politics of Meaning*. Oxford: Blackwell.

——— (ed.). (1994). *Multiculturalism: A Critical Reader*. Oxford: Blackwell.

Goldberg, J.J. (1993). "Overanxious about Anti-Semitism." *Globe and Mail* (May 24).

Gwyn, R. (1995). *Nationalism without Walls*. Toronto: McClelland & Stewart.

Hall, S. (1991). "Old and New Identities: Old and New Ethnicities." In A. King (ed.), *Culture, Globalization and the World System*. Binghampton: Department of Art History, State University of New York.

———, et al. (1978). *Policing the Crisis*. London: Macmillan.

Henry, F. (1978). *The Dynamics of Racism in Toronto*. North York, ON: York University.

———, and E. Ginzberg. (1984). *Who Gets the Work? A Test of Racial Discrimination in Employment*. Toronto: Urban Alliance on Race Relations.

Herberg, E. (1989). *Ethnic Groups in Canada: Adaptations and Transitions.* Scarborough, ON: Nelson.

Howitt, D., and J. McCabe. (1978). "Attitudes to Predict Behaviour in Males." *British Journal of Social and Clinical Psychology* 17:285–86.

———, and J. Owusu-Bempah. (1990). "The Pragmatics of Institutional Racism: Beyond Words." *Human Relations* 43(9):885–99.

Hughes, D., and E. Kallen. (1974). *The Anatomy of Racism: Canadian Dimensions.* Montreal: Harvest House.

Hutcheon, L. (1988). *A Poetics of Postmodernism: History Theory, Fiction.* New York: Routledge.

———. (1991). *Splitting Images: Contemporary Canadian Ironies.* Toronto: Oxford University Press.

Hutchinson, A., and P. Carpenter. (1992). "Can Women Be Misogynous or Gays Homophobic?" *Toronto Star* (March 5):A23.

Ijaz, A., and H. Ijaz. (1981). "Ethnic Prejudice in Children." *Guidance and Counselling* 2(1)(September):28–39.

Isajiw, W.W. (ed.). (1997). *Multiculturalism in North America and Europe: Comparative Perspectives on Interethnic Relations and Social Incorporation.* Toronto: Canadian Scholars' Press.

Jain, H. (1981). *Race and Sex Discrimination in the Workplace in Canada: An Analysis of Theory and Research and Public Policy in Canada.* Ottawa: Employment and Immigration.

———. (1985). *Anti-Discrimination Staffing Policies: Implications of Human Rights Legislation for Employers and Trade Unions.* Ottawa: Secretary of State.

James, C. (1990). *Making It: Black Youth, Racism and Career Aspirations in a Big City.* Mosaic Press.

Jones, J.J. (1972). *Prejudice and Racism.* Reading, MA: Addison-Wesley.

Kellner, D. (1995). "Cultural Studies, Multiculturalism and Media Culture." In G. Dines and J. Humez (eds.), *Cultural Studies, Multiculturalism and Media Culture.* Thousand Oaks, CA: Sage.

Khayatt, D. (1994) "The Boundaries of Identity at the Intersection of Race, Class and Gender." *Canadian Women Studies* 14(2):6–12.

Kobayashi, A. (1990). "Racism and the Law." *Urban Geography* 11(5):447–73.

Kymlicka, W. (1998). *Finding Our Way: Rethinking Ethnocultural Relations in Canada.* Toronto: Oxford University Press.

Labelle, M., S. LaRose, and V. Piche. (1983). "Emigration et Immigration: Les Haitians au Québec." *Sociologie et Société* 15:73–88.

LaFerrière, M. (1983). "Blacks in Quebec: Minorities among Minorities." In C. Marrett and C. Leggon (eds.), *Research in Race and Ethnic Relations.* JAI Press.

Lawrence, E. (1982). "Just Plain Common Sense: The Roots of Racism." In CCCS, *The Empire Strikes Back: Race and Racism in 70's Britain.* London: Hutchinson.

Li, P. (1988). *The Chinese in Canada.* Toronto: Oxford University Press.

———, (ed.). (1990). *Race and Ethnic Relations in Canada.* Toronto: Oxford University Press.

Mackey, E. (1996). "Managing and Imagining Diversity: Multiculturalism and the Construction of National Identity in Canada." Ph.D. thesis, Department of Social Anthropology, University of Sussex.

Mayr, E. (1963). *Animal Species and Evolution.* Cambridge, MA: Harvard University Press.

McIntosh, P. (1990). "White Privilege: Unpacking the Invisible Knapsack." *Independent School* 49(2):31–36.

Miles, R. (1989). *Racism.* London: Routledge

———, and A. Phizacklea. (1984). *White Man's Country: Racism in British Politics.* London: Pluto Press.

Milner, D. (1983). *Children and Race: Ten Years Later*. London: Alan Sutton.

Montagu, A. (1964). *Man's Most Dangerous Myth: The Fallacy of Race*. Cleveland: World Publishing.

Morris, A. (1992). "Political Consciousness and Collective Action." In A. Morris and C. Mueller (eds.), *Frontiers in Social Movement Theory*. New Haven, CT: Yale University Press.

Myrdal, G. (1944). *An American Dilemma*. New York: McGraw-Hill.

Ng, R. (1993). "Sexism, Racism, Canadian Nationalism." In H. Bannerji (ed.), *Returning the Gaze: Essays on Racism, Feminism and Politics*. Toronto: Sister Vision Press.

———, and J. Ramirez. (1981). *Immigrant Housewives in Canada*. Toronto: Immigrant Women's Centre.

Omi, M., and H. Winant. (1993). "On the Theoretical Concept of Race." In C. McCarthy and W. Crichlow (eds.), *Race, Identity and Representation in Education*. New York: Routledge.

Parekh, B. (1987). "Preface." In J. Shaw et al. (eds.), *Strategies for Improving Race Relations: The Anglo-American Experience*. Manchester: Manchester University Press.

Park, R.E. (1950). *Race and Culture*. New York: Free Press.

Pendakur, K., and R. Pendakur. (1995). *The Colour of Money: Earnings Differentials among Ethnic Groups in Canada*. Strategic Research and Analysis. Ottawa: Department of Canadian Heritage.

Phillips, D. (1971). *Knowledge from What*. Chicago: Rand McNally.

Ramcharan, S. (1974). "Adaptation of West Indians in Canada." Ph.D. thesis. Department of Sociology, York University.

———. (1982). *Racism: NonWhites in Canada*. Toronto: Butterworths.

———. (1983). *Racism in Canada*. Toronto: Butterworths.

Razack, S. (1998). *Looking White People in the Eye: Gender, Race and Culture in Courtrooms and Classrooms*. Toronto: University of Toronto Press.

Reeves, F. (1983). *British Racial Discourse*. Cambridge: Cambridge University Press.

Reitz, J. (1980). *The Survival of Ethnic Groups*. Toronto: McGraw-Hill Ryerson.

———, and R. Breton (1996). *The Illusion of Difference: Realities of Ethnicity in Canada and the United States*. Ottawa: C.D. Howe Institute.

Rex, J. (1983). *Race Relations in Sociological Theory*. London: Routledge and Kegan Paul.

———, and R. Moore. (1967). *Race, Community and Conflict*. London: Oxford University Press.

———, and S. Tomlinson. (1979). *Colonial Immigrants in a British City: A Class Analysis*. London: Routledge and Kegan Paul.

St. Lewis, J. (1996). "Identity and Black Consciousness in North America." In J. Littleton (ed.), *Clash of Identities: Essays on Media, Manipulation, and Politics of the Self*. Toronto: Prentice Hall. 21–30.

Satzewich, V. (1989). "Racism and Canadian Immigration Policy: The Government's View of Caribbean Migration, 1962–66." *Canadian Ethnic Studies* 30(1):77–97.

———. (1993). *Deconstructing a Nation: Immigration, Multiculturalism and Racism in 90's Canada*. Halifax: Fernwood.

Shakir, U. (1995). *Presencing at the Boundary: Wife Assault in the South Asian Community*. Toronto: Multicultural Coalition for Access to Family Services.

Shohat, E., and R. Stam. (1994). *Unthinking Eurocentrism: Multiculturalism and the Media*. London: Routledge.

Silvera, M. (1989). *Silenced*. Toronto: Sister Vision Press.

Smith, D. (1987). *The Everyday World as Problematic: A Feminist Sociology*. Toronto: University of Toronto Press.

Smitherman-Donaldson, G., and T. van Dijk. (1988). *Discourse and Discrimination*. Detroit: Wayne State University.

Solomos, J. (1987). *The Roots of Urban Unrest*. Oxford: Pergamon Press.

————. (1993). *Race and Racism in Britain*. London: Macmillan.

Stasiulus, D. (1990). "Theorizing Connections: Gender, Race, Ethnicity and Class." In P. Li (ed.), *Race and Ethnic Relations in Canada*. Toronto: Oxford University Press.

Tator, C., F. Henry, and W. Mattis. (1998). *Challenging Racism in the Arts: Case Studies of Controversy and Conflict*. Toronto: University of Toronto Press.

Ujimoto, V., and G. Hirabayashi. (1980). *Visible Minorities and Multiculturalism: Asians in Canada*. Toronto: Butterworths.

UNESCO. (1972). *Statement on Race* (Ashley Montague). New York: Oxford University Press.

Walcott, R. (1993). "Critiquing Canadian Multiculturalism: Towards an Anti-Racist Agenda." Master's thesis, Department of Education, York University.

Warburton, R. (1992). "Neglected Aspects of Political Economy of Asian Racialization in British Columbia." In V. Satzewich (ed.), *Deconstructing a Nation: Immigration, Multiculturalism and Racism in 90's Canada*. Halifax: Fernwood.

Weinfeld, M. (1990). "Racism in Canada: A Multi-Dimensional Approach to Measurement." Paper prepared for Conference on Race Relations in the United Kingdom and Canada. North York, ON: York University (June).

Wellman, D. (1977). *Portraits of White Racism*. Cambridge: Cambridge University Press.

West, C. (1990). "The New Cultural Politics of Difference." In R. Ferguson (ed.), *Out There: Marginalization and Contemporary Culture*. New York: New Museum of Contemporary Art.

Wetherell, M., and J. Potter (1992). *Mapping the Language of Racism*. New York: Columbia University Press.

Williams. J. (1985). "Redefining Institutional Racism." *Ethnic and Racial Studies* 8(3)(July):323–47.

Yon, D. (1991). "Schooling and the Politics of Identity: A Study of Caribbean Students in a Toronto High School." In H. Diaz (ed.), *Forging Identities and Patterns of Development*. Toronto: Canadian Scholars' Press.

————. (1995). "Unstable Terrain: Explorations in Identity, Race and Culture in a Toronto High School." Ph.D. thesis, Department of Anthropology, York University.

Zubaida, S. (1972). "Sociologists and Race Relations." In *Proceedings of a Seminar: Problems and Prospects of Socio-legal Research*. Oxford: Nuffield College.

Chapter 3

▼▼▼▼▼▼▼▼▼▼▼

Racism in Canadian History

It always amazes me when people express surprise that there might be a "race problem" in Canada, or when they attribute the "problem" to a minority of prejudiced individuals. Racism is, and always has been, one of the bedrock institutions of Canadian society, embedded in the very fabric of our thinking, our personality. (Shadd, 1989)

The historical overview in this chapter focuses on the relationship between the dominant White majority group and people of colour. It examines four racial-minority groups — African Canadians (Blacks), Chinese Canadians, Japanese Canadians, and South Asian Canadians — that are the primary targets of racial bias and discrimination in Canada. (Aboriginal peoples are considered in the following chapter.) This chapter goes on to identify racism in Canada's immigration policies and practices during the past one hundred years. It then explores the evidence of racism in contemporary society, drawing on some of the studies and surveys conducted over the past fifteen years, identifying evidence of overt racism, which is manifested in racist attitudes, assumptions, and practices. The more extreme expressions of beliefs and actions of right-wing "hate groups" are also discussed. Finally, the chapter focusses on discrimination in employment and housing, strong indices of racial discrimination in Canadian society.

INTRODUCTION

Racism in Canada is generally considered a contemporary phenomenon linked to the recent arrival of people of colour. However, the legacy of racial prejudice, discrimination, and disadvantage has its origins in the earliest period of Canadian history. Since more detailed historical accounts of racism exist in other sources, this chapter examines only some of the most telling examples and evidence.

MANIFESTATIONS OF RACISM

AFRICAN (BLACK) CANADIANS

The enslavement of Africans and the racial segregation of and discrimination against "free" Black people is also part of the history of Canada (Alexander and Glaze, 1996). Black slavery was introduced into Canada by the French as early as 1608, and the first slave brought directly into New France from Africa came from Madagascar in 1629. In the St. Lawrence and Niagara regions of Upper Canada, slaves were brought by United Empire Loyalists during and after the American Revolution, and at least six of the sixteen legislators in the first Parliament of Upper Canada owned slaves (Hill, 1981; Lampert and Curtis, 1989). Although slavery did not reach major proportions in Upper Canada, primarily because the land did not lend itself to monocrop agriculture, it was nevertheless actively practised (Walker, 1980).

Contrary to popular belief, until the early nineteenth century — throughout the founding of the present Quebec, New Brunswick, Nova Scotia, and Ontario — there was never a time when Blacks were not held as slaves in Canada (Walker, 1980).

For even the three thousand Black Loyalists who had been emancipated in the American colonies in exchange for supporting the British and who entered Canada in 1783 as "free" persons, there was blatant discrimination. Although they had been promised treatment equal to the White Loyalists in the granting of land contracts, they were bitterly disappointed. While the British promised all Black and White Loyalists settling in Canada 100-acre lots, Blacks either received no land at all or were given barren 1-acre lots on the fringes of White Loyalist townships.

Deprived of the rights of British subjects, Black Loyalists found themselves desperate and destitute. Many were compelled to work as hired or indentured servants to White settlers. Because they were paid about one quarter the wages of White workers, they were deeply resented by unemployed Whites (Winks, 1971). The hostility led to Canada's first race riot in Shelbourne and Birchtown, Nova Scotia, in 1784. A mob destroyed Black property and drove Blacks out of the townships (Shepard, 1991).

The precariousness and vulnerability of their lives in Canada convinced about 1200 disillusioned Nova Scotian Blacks to accept an offer by the Sierra Leone Company to sail for West Africa in 1792. The loss to the Black community was significant; many of those who chose to leave were teachers, preachers, and community leaders (Walker, 1980).

After the passage of the U.S. Abolition Act in 1793, which classified any runaway slaves as free, many fugitives from the United States entered Upper Canada. Several thousand Black slaves escaping slavery found their way into Canada via the "Underground Railroad." Many of these early fugitives settled close to the border in the southwestern part of Ontario. Some chose to go to New Brunswick, and smaller numbers went to Montreal.

The passage of the second Fugitive Slave Act in the United States in 1850 brought a significant increase in the Black population of Canada.

There may have been sixty thousand Blacks in Canada by 1860 (Bolaria and Li, 1988). Their life in Canada was marked by overt prejudice and discrimination. In the 1850s, they were restricted in their ownership of property and were unable to secure education for their children because many White people were opposed to Black children in their schools. Blacks were exposed to ridicule and derision in the local newspapers. Throughout British North America, Blacks were thought, by some, to be responsible for "all the outrageous crimes, and two thirds of the minor ones" (Winks, 1971:248).

With the outbreak of the U.S. Civil War and the Emancipation Proclamation of 1863, many Canadian Blacks chose to return to the United States, recognizing that the value attributed to the colour of one's skin would continue to marginalize them in Canada. The discrimination and exploitation they experienced in almost every aspect of their lives led them to feel that Canada was an inhospitable environment for people of colour (Henry, 1974).

In the early 1900s, the Canadian government sought ways of denying access to Black Americans without directly antagonizing American officials. Although the government had undertaken an extensive advertising campaign to attract farmers from the United States, the Immigration Branch of the federal Department of the Interior informed its American agents that "the Canadian Government is not particularly desirous of encouraging the immigration of negroes" (Shepard, 1991:17). So, instead of placing an explicit ban on immigration, officials engaged in a campaign to discourage Black American applicants from settling on the Canadian prairies, and rejected them on medical or other grounds rather than race. A 1910 editorial in the *Edmonton Capitol* summarizes the attitude of the White community toward Black immigration:

> The Board of Trade has done well to call attention to the amount of negro immigration which is taking place into this district. It has already attained such proportions as to discourage White settlers from going into certain sections. The immigration department has no excuse for encouraging it at all.... We prefer to have the southern race problem left behind. The task of assimilating all the White people who enter our borders is quite a heavy enough one without the colour proposition being added. (Shepard, 1991:19)

J.S. Woodsworth, superintendent of the People's Mission in Winnipeg and later one of the founders of the Co-operative Commonwealth Federation (CCF), had the same general attitude toward people of colour in 1903: the "very qualities of intelligence and manliness which are the essentials for citizens in a democracy were systematically expunged from the Negro race." He argued that the American Black was still "cursed with the burden of his African ancestry.... All travellers speak of their impulsiveness, strong sexual passion and lack of willpower.... Hardly a desirable settler" (Troper, 1972:121).

Blacks who remained in Canada lived in largely segregated communities in Nova Scotia, New Brunswick, and Ontario (Winks, 1971). Racial disparity continued to be evident in the schools, government, the workplace, residential housing, and elsewhere. The Ontario legislature established segregated schools; legal challenges to this segregation failed, and separate schools continued. The legislation remained on the statute books until 1964, after Professor Harry Arthurs drew attention to it in a note in the *Canadian Bar Review* (Arthurs, 1963). Segregated schools were also a part of Black education in Nova Scotia, and to a lesser extent (because of a smaller population of Blacks) in New Brunswick. Segregated schools continued in Nova Scotia until the 1960s (Winks, 1978).

Residential segregation was widespread and legally enforced through the use of racially restrictive covenants attached to deeds and leases. Separation and refusal of service was commonplace in restaurants, theatres, and recreational facilities. Several court challenges were launched against these practices by Black Canadians; in one challenge, in 1919, a Quebec court ruled that racial discrimination was not contrary to public order or morality in Canada. The most celebrated case began with a refusal to serve a Black customer in a Montreal tavern in 1931. It ended in the Supreme Court of Canada in 1939, when the nation's highest tribunal concluded that racial discrimination was legally enforceable (Walker, 1985).

The racist attitudes of Whites in Canada were probably reinforced by the pseudo-scientific concept of race popular in Western Europe, Britain, and the United States in the late nineteenth century. The concept of White cultural, intellectual, and moral superiority over the Black race was widely held then and continued to flourish well into the twentieth century.

As the study of race was "scientifically" organized, as stereotypes of the "Negro" became more widely known in Canada, and as the forces gathered under the rubrics of nationalism and racism began to have their effect, "Negroes" in Canada found themselves sliding down an inclined plane from mere neglect to active dislike (Winks, 1971:292).

CHINESE CANADIANS

The first wave of Chinese to settle in Canada arrived in British Columbia in the 1850s in search of gold. By 1860, however, most of the mines were depleted, and the Chinese who did not return to China turned to other forms of labour. Chinese Canadians were hired for various projects in British Columbia, including the building of railways, bridges, and roads, and work in coal mines and mills (Baureiss, 1985).

In the 1880s, over 1500 labourers were recruited to help lay the track for the Canadian Pacific Railway (CPR) in British Columbia. The emigration was in the form of "Coolie-trade," in which companies advanced the passage ticket and a small sum of money to the Chinese, who, before leaving their country, would give bonds, contracting to work for a period of five to ten years. The companies would hold all the Chinese workers' earnings and were obligated only to provide the workers with the bare essentials (Creese, 1991).

The work assigned to the Chinese contract workers was brutally hard and dangerous. Accidents were frequent, with far more Chinese than Whites as victims. Many workers died from exhaustion and rock explosions and were buried in collapsed tunnels. Their living conditions were appalling. Food and shelter were in insufficient supply, and malnutrition was widespread. There was almost no medical attention, contributing to a high fatality rate from diseases such as scurvy and smallpox. It is estimated that there were six hundred deaths in British Columbia of Chinese labourers working on the construction of the railway (Lampkin, 1985).

After the CPR was completed, new industries, such as mining, fishing, and sawmills, required additional labourers. As the supply of manual labour from Europe and the United States began to dwindle, the Canadian government reluctantly permitted Chinese Canadian labourers to fill the demand for largely contract labour required by these industries. From 1881 to 1883, 13 245 Chinese male labourers were recruited to compensate for the shortage of White workers (Bolaria and Li, 1988). These immigrants were not permitted to bring their wives and children with them or to have sexual relations with White women, for fear of spreading the "yellow menace" (Chan, 1983).

Chinese workers were paid one quarter to one half less than their White counterparts. The living conditions were appalling, and from 1881 to 1885 hundreds of Chinese died from disease, malnutrition, and exhaustion (Lampkin, 1985). Bolaria and Li (1988) argue that the Chinese immigration during this period was encouraged solely for the purpose of labour exploitation. Immigrants were "welcomed" only so long as there was a shortage of White workers. As soon as there was a labour surplus, the Chinese immigrants were considered a threat to Canadian society and were subjected to intense racial bias and discrimination.

By the mid-1880s, governments were feeling pressure from the White population to limit further Chinese immigration. The federal government passed the first anti-Chinese bill in 1885. In addition, British Columbia passed several anti-Chinese bills to curtail the political and civil rights of the Chinese in the province. The Coal Mines Act of 1890, for example, prevented Chinese from working underground and from performing skilled jobs in coal mines.

Other provincial legislation, introduced as early as 1875, disenfranchised the Chinese so that they were prohibited from voting in provincial and municipal elections (S.B.C. 1875, c. 2). Disenfranchisement was applied to *citizens* as well (Tarnopolsky, 1991). The Chinese were further subjected to a number of discriminatory acts that made it difficult for them to acquire Crown lands, work in skilled jobs in the mines, and obtain liquor licences. They could not serve in public office; they could not serve on juries or work in the public service; they were barred from the professions of law and pharmacy and excluded from White labour unions (Li, 1988).

Differential wage rates were entrenched in union agreements that allowed lower minimum wages for "orientals" than for "occidental" workers. Differential Asian and White rates were legitimized by assumptions that different wages reflected the inherently different "value" of the labour. In a perverse form of contract compliance, private contractors working with the British Columbia government on federal projects were required by the government not to hire "orientals" (Creese, 1991).

As anti-Chinese sentiment and discrimination grew, Chinese Canadians found that almost the only areas of the labour market open to them were certain sectors of the service industry. Thus, throughout the early twentieth century, Chinese Canadians were forced to give up their position in the core labour market and to move into domestic service, laundries, and restaurants, where there was less likely to be competition from White workers and employers (Bolaria and Li, 1988). Even so, their presence sufficiently threatened the White community that, in 1907, the latent hostility erupted into brutal violence when large numbers of Whites in Vancouver invaded Chinatown and the Japanese quarter, smashing and destroying property.

One of the most bizarre discriminatory labour policies in Canada was a series of provincial laws preventing "oriental" males from hiring White females. The intent of the Saskatchewan Female Employment Act of 1912, for example, was to "protect" White women from the alleged danger of working for "orientals" (Tarnopolsky, 1991).

The refusal to accept the Chinese Canadians, as well as other racial groups, as full citizens manifested itself in yet another way. For the first two years of World War I, racial minorities and Aboriginal people were rejected for military service. Although the militia headquarters did not actually establish a colour-bar, local commanders were encouraged to turn away volunteers on the grounds of the inferiority of their race. Only as the war progressed and shortages began to impede Canada's war effort were racial-minority recruits admitted. Again, in World War II, Black volunteers, along with Canadians of Chinese, Japanese, and East Indian ancestry, were at first not accepted. These barriers were also removed in face of military requirements for more soldiers (Creese, 1991).

A further manifestation of racist ideology translated into racist practice was the concerted effort of British Columbia school boards to keep "Asians" (Chinese Canadian and Japanese Canadian children) out of the public schools. As Li notes:

> Institutional racism disrupted the life of the Chinese in Canada in many ways.... Over time, the social stigma attached to the Chinese as undesirable citizens and unwelcome workers became their defining characteristic. In this way, belonging to the Chinese race in itself became sufficient grounds for discrimination and mistreatment. (Li, 1988:47)

JAPANESE CANADIANS

Japanese Canadians experienced similar discriminatory treatment from the time they first settled in British Columbia in the 1870s. They were subjected to economic exploitation, paid lower wages than White labourers, barred from both the federal and provincial franchise, subjected to discriminatory housing covenants, and segregated in schools and public places (Lampkin, 1985).

In 1907, largely as a result of a significant increase in the number of Japanese entering Canada, and as a reaction to existing populations of Chinese and East Indians in Vancouver, an organization known as the Asiatic Exclusion League was formed. Its goal was to restrict Asian admission into Canada. The league was a forerunner to the right-wing extremist organizations that would become widespread in Canada in the 1920s and 1930s. Following the arrival of a ship carrying over a thousand Japanese and a few hundred Sikhs, the Asiatic Exclusion League carried out a major demonstration, which culminated in the worst race riot in British Columbia history (Adachi, 1976; Bolaria and Li, 1988).

After the riot, the Canadian government entered into negotiations with the Japanese government, ending with the "Gentlemen's Agreement" of 1908. Under this agreement, the Japanese government agreed to permit entry to only certain categories of persons. These included returning immigrants, their wives and children, immigrants engaged for personal or domestic service, and labourers under specific Canadian government contracts or contracts with Japanese Canadian farmers. A quota was fixed for all but the first group (Adachi, 1976).

Another example of racial discrimination targeting Japanese Canadians was the efforts of the British Columbia legislature to press the federal government to restrict fishing licences to Japanese Canadians in the 1920s. The ultimate intention of this pressure was to drive these people out of the fisheries (Adachi, 1976).

In the late 1930s, anti-Asian sentiment, which had been dormant for about a decade, was inflamed by Japan's invasion of China. Anti-Japanese feelings swept across North America and became virulent once again in British Columbia. The bombing of Pearl Harbor by Japan in 1941 brought it into war against the Allies, and the Canadian government took an unprecedented action (Adachi, 1976). Rejecting the counsel of Canada's senior police and military officers, the cabinet amended the Defence of Canada Regulations (Order in Council, P.C. 1486, February 24, 1942) to give the minister of justice the authority to remove "any and all persons" from any "protected" area in Canada and to detain such persons without trial (Sunahara, 1981).

Canadians of Japanese origin, including Canadian-born and naturalized citizens — men, women, and children — were expelled from the West Coast of British Columbia and their civil rights were suspended. Twenty-three thousand people of Japanese ancestry, 13 300 of them Canadian-born, were sent to relocation and detention camps in isolated areas in the interior of British Columbia, southern Alberta, and Manitoba.

They were relieved of their property, and 1200 fishing boats owned by Japanese Canadians and naturalized citizens were impounded. Japanese-language schools were closed. Houses, automobiles, and businesses were sold, and savings were impounded. For example, a disabled Japanese Canadian veteran of World War I was given $39.32 for nineteen acres of fertile land in the Fraser Valley, a two-storey house, four chicken houses, an electric incubator, and 2500 hens and roosters. He later received an additional $2209.70, after an appeal to the 1947 royal commission established to deal with Japanese Canadian claims for compensation. The settlement clearly did not approach the value of the confiscated property (Lampkin, 1985).

Men were incarcerated in jails and internment camps and were sent to work on road construction projects or sugar-beet farms in British Columbia, Alberta, Manitoba, and Ontario. Abandoned mining towns were re-opened to house the evacuees, who were forced to live in abysmal living conditions (Adachi, 1976).

For several years, conditions of virtual apartheid existed for Japanese Canadians (Adachi, 1976; Sunahara, 1981; Kobayashi, 1987). The reason given for this mass denial of rights was wartime security, but no Japanese Canadian was ever charged with sabotage or any other kind of disloyalty before, during, or after the war. The Canadian government did not release the Japanese Canadians until 1947, and it took another two years before they were able to resettle on the West Coast. It is now agreed that the prime factor in their internment was the latent racist feelings harboured by Canadian officials against Japanese Canadians (Ujimoto, 1988).

Sunahara (1981) summarizes the major factors leading to this unprecedented act of racism, including the powerful anti-Asian lobby in British Columbia and a federal cabinet and civil service predisposed to basing its policy on the views of that lobby. However, underlying these considerations were the racist attitudes prevalent among politicians, bureaucrats, and the public: the manifest superiority of the Caucasian race and its "natural" obligation to rule "inferior," less endowed, non-White peoples (Sunahara, 1981). Not until 1988 was "justice" finally achieved for those Japanese Canadians who were still living, when twelve thousand Japanese Canadians were paid $20 000 each as compensation for their internment. As well, they were given a formal apology by Parliament (Ujimoto, 1988).

SOUTH ASIAN CANADIANS

South Asians are people who were born or whose ancestors were born in the Indian subcontinent, and include people from India, Pakistan, Sri Lanka, Bhutan, and Bangladesh. It also includes people with roots in South Asia who have immigrated from Kenya, Tanzania, Uganda, the Caribbean nations, and other countries.

The first South Asians to enter Canada were Sikhs, who came to British Columbia in the late nineteenth century. By the early twentieth century, the small numbers of South Asians (approximately five thousand in 1908) were viewed with the same racial bias, hostility, and resentment as was directed at other minority racial groups (Buchignani and Indra, 1985).

As was the case with Chinese and Japanese immigrants, Whites reacted antagonistically to any sign that the non-White population was increasing. The South Asian presence in British Columbia was viewed as a "Hindu invasion." Articles and editorials appearing in British Columbia newspapers emphasized the importance of maintaining Anglo-Saxon superiority (Raj, 1980). The Victoria *Daily Colonist* issued the call:

> To prepare ourselves for the irrepressible conflict, Canada must remain a White Man's country. On this western frontier of the Empire will be the forefront of the coming struggle.... Therefore we ought to maintain this country for the Anglo-Saxon and those races which are able to assimilate themselves to them. If this is done, we believe that history will repeat itself and the supremacy of our race will continue. (Ward, 1978:259–60)

To ensure Anglo-Saxon supremacy, legislation was enacted to control the economic and social mobility of South Asians and to prevent more from coming. Even though citizens of India were British subjects, British Columbia in 1907 disenfranchised them. The government feared that the South Asians might participate in the provincial elections that year. Again, the message communicated by the press was designed to engender fear and emphasize that the White population needed to be protected against "Hindus." The effect of this paranoia was an amendment to the B.C. Election Act that added "Hindus" to other "Asian undesirables" (Raj, 1980).

The denial of the franchise had serious economic consequences for the South Asian community in British Columbia. Since the voters' list was the basis for both provincial and municipal contracts, South Asians were prevented from bidding on them. As also was the case with Chinese and Japanese, the denial of political rights meant that South Asians were unable to enter professions such as education, law, and pharmacy, and they could not engage in the sale of Crown timber.

They also experienced overt prejudice in the form of racial stereotyping and physical abuse. They were called "ragheads." They could not go to a movie in their native dress. People refused to sit next to them on trains. They could not own property in some sections of Vancouver. Discrimination in housing resulted in many South Asians living in very poor conditions (Bolaria and Li, 1988).

While it was estimated that only a small community of South Asians remained in British Columbia, they continued to press for a repeal of the discriminatory clause in the Elections Act. In 1947, they finally won the right to vote in federal and provincial elections. In 1948, the right was extended to municipal elections (Lampkin, 1985).

In each of these brief summaries of prejudice and discrimination — against Canadian Blacks, Chinese Canadians, Japanese Canadians, and South Asian Canadians — there is a common thread. Racism in Canada is, in large measure, related to the dominant group's need for cheap labour. It can be attributed to the division of labour under capitalism (Ng, 1993; Bolaria and Li, 1988); it is a function of social organization and power differences (Creese, 1993). Racism is deeply rooted in the legacy and ideology of "White settler" **colonialism**, which reinforces patterns of power and privilege based on racial distinctions (Creese, 1993).

IMMIGRATION POLICIES AND PRACTICES

FROM THE 1880S TO THE 1960S

Immigration first became a major issue in Canada in the late 1880s. By the late nineteenth century the labour needs of the country required large numbers of workers from abroad, so the federal government actively encouraged *White* immigrants to settle and farm the vast areas of the country recently brought under Canadian control. As a result, most immigrants came from Britain and the United States, but thousands of Italians, Finns, Ukrainians, and other Europeans also arrived. More workers, however, were still required, and many thousands of Chinese workers were recruited in the 1880s.

The White population was openly antagonistic toward the newcomers. As soon as the completion of the CPR was in sight, the federal government passed a highly discriminatory piece of legislation, entrenching racism for the first time in the laws of the land. The first anti-Chinese law, the Chinese Immigration Act, was passed in 1885.

A head tax was established on all Chinese males arriving in Canada (women and children were excluded from admission), partly in response to the demands of White workers, who wanted to eliminate job competition. The tax was set at $50 in 1888, and by 1903 it was $500. Under increasing pressure to "stem the flood" of Chinese immigration, the Canadian government passed the Chinese Exclusion Act (S.C. 1923, c. 38), which banned Chinese immigration from 1923 to 1947 (Bolaria and Li, 1988).

Additional restrictive immigration policies were imposed on other racial minorities. In 1907, British Columbia disenfranchised South Asians and the federal government passed an order-in-council requiring South Asians to have $200 in their possession upon arrival in Canada. Canada pressed the British and Indian governments to pass regulations and legislation to stop Indian immigration to Canada. These efforts failed, and as a result Canada passed an order-in-council restricting Indian immigration.

In 1908 the federal government passed the Continuous Passage Act, which stipulated that all immigrants must arrive by an uninterrupted journey, on through tickets, from their country of origin. As citizens of the British Empire, Indians should have had access to Canada, but immigration was made almost impossible by the act (Buchignani and Indra, 1985). Mackenzie King, in presenting a defence of the policy to British authorities, argued that "Canada should desire to restrict immigration from the orient is natural; that Canada should remain a White man's country is believed to be not only desirable for economic and social reasons, but highly necessary on political and national grounds" (King, 1908).

The government was careful not to explicitly bar a particular group from landing, for this might have jeopardized Canada's relations with the rest of the British Empire. Instead, the Continuous Passage Act amended the Immigration Act to allow the government to control East Indian immigration without having the appearance of doing so (Cohen, 1987). In addition, the policy also effectively barred Japanese and other "undesirables" from entry into Canada (Sampat-Mehta, 1984). The Chinese Exclusion Act, the Continuous Passage Act, and various regulations to restrict immigration were effective mechanisms for ensuring that almost no Asians or East Indians emigrated to Canada until after World War II.

The 1910 Immigration Act enshrined the government's discriminatory policies in law by creating an excluded class of immigrants deemed undesirable because of Canada's climate or its social, educational, labour, or other requirements — or because their customs or habits were deemed to result in a probable inability to become readily assimilated (Malarek, 1987). The legislation did not specify the countries that had sufficiently different customs or habits to be excluded. Thus it gave immigration officials wide discretion to exclude almost any prospective immigrant on the basis of race, national or ethnic origin, and creed.

Differential treatment based on race and ethnicity was firmly established as government policy. A list of preferred and non-preferred countries was established, and selection was carried out on the basis of whether applicants were from those countries on the "preferred" list: those with affinities to the United Kingdom and United States. Next in preference came immigrants from northern and western Europe, followed by those from central and eastern Europe, and then those from southern Europe. A special permit class included immigrants from Greece, Syria, and Turkey, and European Jews (Bolaria and Li, 1988).

When, in 1914, a shipload of four hundred would-be immigrants from India sailed directly from Calcutta and arrived in the Vancouver harbour aboard the Japanese freighter the *Komagata Maru*, they were denied entry. The passengers were held aboard the ship for nearly three months before the *Komagata Maru* was forced to return to India (Buchignani and Indra, 1985).

Throughout the history of Canadian immigration, overt and covert policies have excluded racial-minority women immigrants in the hope that excluding women would keep the total number of minority-group immigrants down. A 1927 report on "Oriental immigration activities" in British Columbia showed that between 1906 and 1925, 45 women and 41 children had entered Canada, compared with 4909 men (Lampkin, 1985).

The Great Depression, beginning in 1929, prompted the government to invoke a series of restrictive measures to further limit new immigrants to those from the preferred groups. Canadian immigration policy continued to be racist in the 1930s. The dominant and pervasive mindset underlying the policy and the administrative and political framework was "Whites only." White immigrants from Britain were given preferential treatment; next in preference were White immigrants from the United States and France. Only if these traditional sources of immigration proved insufficient would the government consider admitting White Europeans from countries other than France and Britain.

In 1942, when Adolf Hitler activated his "final solution" to eliminate the Jewish people, Canada closed its doors to refugees fleeing Europe. The ship *St. Louis,* carrying Jewish refugees from Europe, attempted to land in Halifax as well as many other ports in North and South America and was denied entrance to all ports. Of all Western countries, Canada admitted the fewest Jewish refugees (Abella and Troper, 1982).

The federal government did not, however, pass any legislation specifically restricting Jews. As was the case in restricting Black, East Indian, and Chinese immigrants, the government chose a more insidious approach by developing informal administrative measures to accomplish its goals. The informality of the practices that had such a devastating impact on Jewish immigration is exemplified in a memo to Prime Minister Mackenzie King prepared by the Department of External Affairs and Immigration in 1938:

> We do not want too many Jews, but in the present circumstances we do not want to say so. We do not want to legitimize the Aryan mythology by introducing any formal distinction for immigration purposes between Jews and non-Jews. The practical distinction, however, has to be made and should be drawn with discretion and sympathy by the competent authorities, without the need to lay down a formal policy. (Dirks, 1977:58)

Jews who were fortunate to have come in earlier waves of immigration did, however, experience widespread discrimination in employment, business, and education; for example, universities maintained restrictive entrance quotas. Other signs of anti-Semitism included restrictions on where Jews could live and buy property. Signs posted along the Toronto beaches warned "No Dogs or Jews Allowed." Many hotels and resorts had policies prohibiting Jews as guests (Abella and Troper, 1982).

As soon as the war ended, pressure was put on the government for a liberalization of immigration policy. In 1947, in a House of Commons debate, Mackenzie King affirmed Canada's need for a larger population and a "proactive" immigration policy. However, he cautioned his colleagues about the importance of selecting "desirable" immigrants, stating that the people of Canada

> do not wish, as a result of mass immigration, to make any fundamental alteration in the character of our population. Large-scale immigration from the Orient would change the fundamental composition of the Canadian population. Any considerable Oriental immigration would, moreover, be certain to give rise to social and economic problems of a character that might lead to serious difficulties in the field of international relations. (Malarek, 1987:15)

In 1952, s. 61 of the new Immigration Act gave the government the power to limit or prohibit the entry of immigrants for reasons of "nationality, citizenship, ethnic group, class or geographic area of origin, peculiar customs, habits, modes of life ... or probable inability to become readily assimilated." The act gave clear preferential status to all White immigrants.

In summarizing Canada's immigration policy until 1967, it can be said that the policy divided the world's population into two parts: preferred immigrants, who were of British and European ancestry and White; and the rest of the world, largely composed of people of colour. The Canadian government's discriminatory policy of immigration was based on the premise that Asians and other people of colour were "unassimilable," that is, they had genetic, cultural, and social traits that made them both inferior and unadaptable (Bolaria and Li, 1988).

The year 1967 marked the beginning of a series of radical reforms in immigration policy, largely as a result of changing demographics and economic pressure to replenish the labour supply. The traditional sources of labour were no longer producing sufficient numbers of immigrants as postwar Europe began to prosper. New labour needs were emerging in Canada; rapid industrialization and expanding new technologies required workers with high levels of skills and education. In response, Canada dropped its racially discriminatory immigration policies. Yet, despite reforms, in a 1975 brief to Parliament the Canadian Civil Liberties Association stated that during a 26-month period, approximately two thousand persons were allowed to enter Canada subject to the posting of cash bonds. All of them were non-Europeans, mostly Asians, South Americans, and West Indians. In no instance were such requirements made of Europeans (Mattis, 1990).

During the 1960s, a new Immigration Act introduced a point system whereby immigrants, regardless of origin or colour, were given points based on job training, experience, skills, level of education, knowledge of English or French, degree of demand for the applicant's occupation, and job offers. The new act opened the doors to immigration from previously excluded countries. While the act allowed for a more open immigration process, some argue that it maintained some of the racist administrative practices of earlier immigration policies (Cohen, 1987; Bolaria and Li, 1988).

FROM THE 1970S TO THE 1990S

New immigration policies opened the door to immigrants from areas that for the past two hundred years had been largely excluded — Asia, the Caribbean, Latin America, and Africa. The "point system" uses nine criteria to assess an applicant's chances of successful integration: age, occupational demand, vocational preparation, arranged employment, location, education, relatives in Canada, official-language competence, and personal suitability. Prospective immigrants are placed in three broad categories: economic, social, and humanitarian. From these categories, they are classified as independent immigrants, family-class immigrants, or convention refugees.

The changes incorporated into the 1978 Immigration Act are a result of a number of factors. First was internal pressure, in the form of a multicultural policy that recognized racial and cultural diversity as a fact of life in Canada. The policy affirmed the contributions of racial and ethnic minorities to the economic, social, and cultural development of Canada. Second, the increasing politicization and mobilization of minority groups led to new demands for a more accessible, non-discriminatory immigration policy. Third, pressure was exerted by human-rights activists and lawyers representing organizations such as the Canadian Civil Liberties Association.

A fourth factor was pressure from the international community to eradicate overt racism. Canada's international reputation was badly tarnished by its treatment of Japanese Canadians and Jewish refugees during World War II. Both the formal and informal methods of exclusion that had shaped Canada's immigration policy for over a hundred years were viewed as a contravention of international conventions.

Finally, and probably the most significant force for change, was the economic factor. Immigration from traditional source countries had declined in the 1960s. The postwar recovery of Europe and the establishment of the European Economic Community (EEC) gave Europeans freer access to economic opportunities in Europe and a sense of greater optimism: there was no longer a need to emigrate in order to find work. Also, the labour needs of Canada in the 1960s changed from a dependence on unskilled, manual labour toward the need for a more highly educated and skilled workforce. This fundamental alteration benefited people from developing countries because Europe was unable to supply these workers in sufficient numbers. The result of all the above factors was a dramatic change in the characteristics of immigrants to Canada in the past two decades.

Superficially, the change in immigration policy to a point system suggests that Canada's policy is motivated by equal access and tolerance. However, there may still be inequity, especially in the ways in which the policy is implemented. Richmond, for example, succinctly makes the point that

> Immigration policies need not completely exclude certain nationalities in order to warrant description as "racist." If the intended or unintended consequence of particular regulations is to put certain ethnic groups at a disadvantage while making it easier for others to gain admission, then such policies may be designated "quasi-racist" or systemic forms of discrimination, even though the admissions criteria make no reference to "race" as such. Thus, visa requirements, literacy tests, health regulations and medical examinations, quotas, preference for close relatives, patrial clauses, the location of immigration officers abroad, and even exclusions based on environmental considerations can have a differential impact on particular ethnic groups. (Richmond, 1994:155)

In a similar vein, Cohen (1987) points out that discrimination did not disappear from Canada's immigration policy. Despite the more universal system and the commitment to non-discrimination in the act's policy objectives, discrimination was still possible in the immigration process. Under the guise of a universal selection process, a myriad of seemingly neutral administrative procedures had an **adverse impact** on racial-minority immigrants and constituted differential treatment and racial discrimination.

In the first instance, visa offices were unevenly distributed in developing countries, and few resources were committed to them. Until 1990, there was only one visa office in India and one in China. Moreover, there were differences in processing time for assisted relatives (those sponsored by family members who are Canadian citizens) from developing regions, such as Pakistan, as compared with the United Kingdom. Although visitors from the United States were exempt from visa requirements, countries such as India and Jamaica, originally exempt, now required visas.

Immigration officers were given wide latitude and discretion, which allowed for individual prejudices and even overt racism in their decisions. For example, the point system's "personal suitability" category requires immigration officials to assess an immigrant's "adaptability, motivation, initiative, resourcefulness and other similar qualities" and entitles the officer to evaluate the applicant's cultural background and personal style. The officials, however, lacked an objective method to assess the qualifications that potential immigrants had acquired in other jurisdictions, especially developing countries (Malarek, 1987). A recently published book critically analyzes Canada's immigration laws and policies (Jakubowski, 1997). It provides a detailed chapter on the relationship of race to immigration policy and concludes that while Canadian immigration law is alleged to be nondiscriminatory, unfairness and inequity still characterize aspects of it.

Early in 1998, the minister of employment and immigration released a report entitled *Not Just Numbers*, which outlines policy changes in the areas of immigration and refugee determination. Although it proposed expanding family-class immigrants to include any known relatives that a Canadian citizen would be willing to sponsor, it also called for a new class of immigrants called "self-supporting," which would include skilled workers, entrepreneurs, and investor categories. Demonstrated proficiency in one of the official languages of the country as well as education, age, and experience requirements would have to be met. Potential immigrants without language proficiency would be required to pay for such training. The paper also called for a different method of refugee determination. The Immigration and Refugee Board, established in 1989, would be abolished, and refugee determinations would return to civil servants who had evaluated refugee claims prior to the establishment of the board.

A very brief consultative process was undertaken. The report engendered widespread criticism from spokespeople from immigrant communities who feared that their numbers would be severely reduced by the language requirement. Advocates of an open policy of immigration and a retention of the present method of refugee determination also objected to the proposed changes. At the time of writing, the government was considering the results of the consultation.

From the perspective of the public, immigration policy is a highly charged issue and one that lends itself to considerable controversy. As the results of the many polls demonstrate (see below, "Polls and Surveys"), large segments of the population do not support an open policy. In fact, a racist discourse of fear of immigration is part of the public agenda. In this discourse, racism is caused by both the numbers and the racial identities of immigrant populations. The argument here is that if immigration is curbed (particularly from the "Third World"), racism will decrease. However, racism existed well before the large-scale immigration of people of colour into Canada, as evidenced by the exploitative relationship between White colonizers and **Aboriginal peoples** throughout the history of this country.

Since the 1980s the majority of immigrants to Canada have come from Asia, Africa, Latin America, and the Caribbean. Anti-immigration attitudes are reflected not in obvious racial terms, but in a collection of myths such as:

- Immigrants take jobs away from Canadians.
- Immigrants are a drain on the economy.
- Immigrants are unskilled, uneducated, and live in poverty.
- Immigrants exploit the welfare system.
- Immigrants commit more crimes.

These statements are clearly fallacious. Numerous studies (e.g., Economic Council of Canada, 1991; Samuel, 1989, 1998) have concluded that immigrants make more jobs than they take. These studies have found that immigrants are more likely to be self-employed and that they bring a significant degree of skill, education, self-reliance, and innovative flair to the Canadian economy. Immigrants do not displace Canadian residents from jobs; they tend to take jobs that residents do not want. Since 1971, immigrants have paid more in taxes than they have used in services. Finally, immigrant rates of criminality are lower than those of the native-born population (Samuel, 1989).

Anti-immigration sentiment also views racism as the inevitable result of different cultures being brought into close proximity, prompting cultural jealousies and conflicts. Racism, however, is not made inevitable by cultural differences. There is no inescapable tension between people who are different. Racial conflict exists only when one group has power over another. The White majority in Canada has political, economic, and social control over most Canadian institutions. When **racial discrimination** is entrenched in a society's institutions and value systems, the social and economic exclusion of people of colour is to be expected.

Domestic Workers

Canada's domestic workers' program was established in 1955 to deal with the chronic shortage of workers prepared to accept low wages and undesirable working conditions. Initially the program targeted Black women from the Caribbean region, and later it focussed on women from the Philippines. Many of these women who entered Canada as "domestics" were in fact qualified teachers, nurses, and secretaries who were unable to immigrate to Canada because of racist immigration practices. Although they were able to seek other employment after a year's service, they generally faced significant discrimination in the labour market (Ng, 1992; Henry, 1968).

In 1973 their status changed, and the majority of workers came in on "work authorizations" as temporary workers. Their stay in Canada was entirely dependent on maintaining their jobs as domestics. By 1981, 87.9 percent of domestic workers had temporary work permits, and many of them could expect at some point to be asked to return to their country of origin. Securing permanent resident status from within Canada was discretionary (Task Force on Immigration Practices and Procedures, 1981). The government's immigrant domestic program was structured to allow domestic workers who had worked in Canada continuously for at least two years to apply for landed-immigrant status. But, in order to qualify, workers must demonstrate "self-sufficiency" or the potential to achieve "self-sufficiency." These decisions appear to be based on subjective criteria (Cohen, 1987).

The conditions in which many of the domestic workers are compelled to work underline their **marginal** status in the Canadian work force. Although unemployment-insurance premiums and Canada Pension Plan deductions are made from their paycheques, they are unlikely to secure benefits from their contributions (Silvera, 1993:204). They are denied the right to organize into a trade union and therefore lack the power to bargain collectively for better wages or working conditions. In Ontario, they are not covered by the province's health and safety legislation. In 1987 the Ontario government amended the Employment Standards Act to provide greater protection for domestic workers. Among other things, the amendments required domestic workers to be paid minimum wage and stipulated the work week. The provincial government's regulatory changes coexisted with Canada Employment and Immigration Guidelines. As late as 1992 Employment and Immigration established certain minimum requirements. The worker should receive $710 per month in Ontario with a deduction of $210 per month for room and board. However, as Silvera (1989) demonstrates in her book on Caribbean domestic workers, these entitlements are seen as bureaucratic jargon. The reality remains the same: the domestics remain intimidated; complaints are rarely laid. Their tenuous legal status in Canada leads many women to fear reporting employers who fail to comply with the regulations.

The federal government in February 1992 implemented a requirement for prospective domestic workers (nannies) that they have a Grade 12 education and at least six months' professional child-care experience. Critics suggest that this requirement places workers from Third World countries at a disadvantage. While most European workers would be able to meet the new criteria, countries such as the Philippines, India, and Jamaica (where most domestic workers currently come from) have no such training programs; and those with Grade 12 equivalency would be unlikely to want to work for minimum wage (Hernandez, 1992; Ng, 1992).

CONTEMPORARY RACISM

THE CHANGING NATURE OF CANADIAN SOCIETY

Despite the continuing residue of racial discrimination in Canada's immigration policies, a significant shift has occurred in the composition of Canadian society. This changing demographic pattern is largely the result of the ending of the most overt forms of racism in immigration policies and the opening up of immigration to Third World countries.[1]

Canada's population has become increasingly racially diverse. From what was a country largely inhabited by Whites and Aboriginal peoples, the population has changed to include people from more than seventy countries. In addition, the source countries from which immigrants come have dramatically altered. In 1961, 90 percent of Canada's immigrants came from European countries; between 1981 and 1991, this figure declined to 25 percent. Almost half of all immigrants who came to Canada between 1981 and 1991 were Asian-born.

By 1986, 38 percent of Canadians had at least one ancestor who was neither French nor English. In the same year, racial minorities accounted for 6.3 percent, or 1.6 million, of Canada's population. In 1991, the figure had increased to 9.6 percent, or 2.6 million. Projections indicated that the racial minority population will rise to 17.7 percent — 5.7 million people — in the year 2001.

More than two thirds of racial-minority immigrants to Canada come from Asia. Chinese comprise the most numerous group, with 1.3 million people, followed by South Asians (East Indians, Pakistanis, Sri Lankans,

Figure 3.1

RACIAL MINORITIES BY PROVINCE, 1986—2001 (PROJECTED)

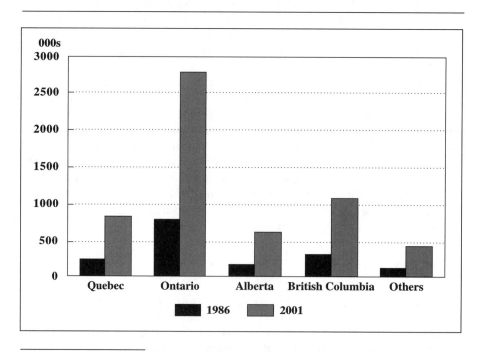

Source: T.J. Samuel, *Visible Minorities in Canada: A Projection.* Toronto: Race Relations Advisory Council on Advertising, Canadian Advertising Foundation, 1992.

Figure 3.2

ETHNICITY OF RACIAL MINORITIES, 1986

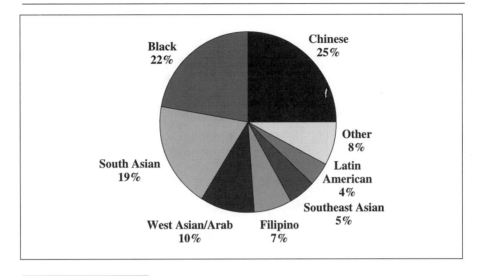

Source: T.J. Samuel, *Visible Minorities in Canada: A Projection*. Toronto: Race Relations Advisory Council on Advertising, Canadian Advertising Foundation, 1992.

Figure 3.3

ETHNICITY OF RACIAL MINORITIES, 1991

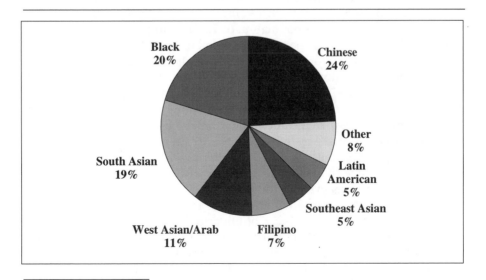

Source: T.J. Samuel, *Visible Minorities in Canada: A Projection*. Toronto: Race Relations Advisory Council on Advertising, Canadian Advertising Foundation, 1992. Percentages do not total 100 due to rounding.

Figure 3.4
ETHNICITY OF RACIAL MINORITIES, 2001 (PROJECTED)

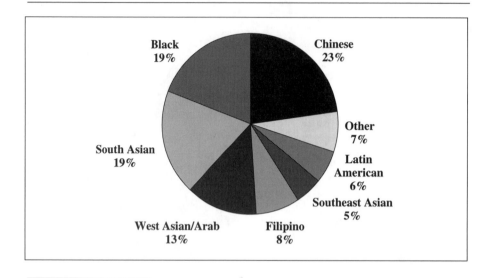

Source: T.J. Samuel, *Visible Minorities in Canada: A Projection*. Toronto: Race Relations Advisory Council on Advertising, Canadian Advertising Foundation, 1992.

and Bangladeshis) and Blacks, with 1.1 million each. The next most numerous groups are West Asians and Arabs, Filipinos, Southeast Asians (Indochinese), and Latin Americans. The number of Latin American immigrants was expected to grow fourfold by the turn of the century.

By 2001, about half the population of Toronto and two fifths of the population of Vancouver are expected to be racial minorities. About one quarter of the populations of Montreal, Edmonton, Calgary, and Winnipeg are expected to be racial minorities. In Ottawa–Hull and Windsor, one sixth of the populations will consist of racial minorities. Halifax, Kitchener, Hamilton, Victoria, and Regina will have racial-minority populations of 10–14 percent.

The figures above are taken from the Samuel projection of the numbers of racial minorities expected to live in Canada by the year 2001. Actual figures according to the most recent census of 1996 provide the following numbers.

These data show that about 10.7 percent of Canada's total population in 1996 was classified as "visible minority" by the census.[2] As in the earlier figures noted above, Asians, including those from Southeast Asia and South Asia, predominate. The provinces of Ontario, British Columbia, and Quebec have the most racial-minority inhabitants. There are also nearly 800 000 Aboriginal people in Canada. The largest cities in Canada also contain the most racial-minority people. In 1996, Toronto led the list with 1 338 095, followed by Vancouver with 564 600 and Montreal with 401 425 respectively.

Figure 3.5

RACIAL MINORITIES IN SELECTED CMAS, 1991 AND 2001 (PROJECTED)

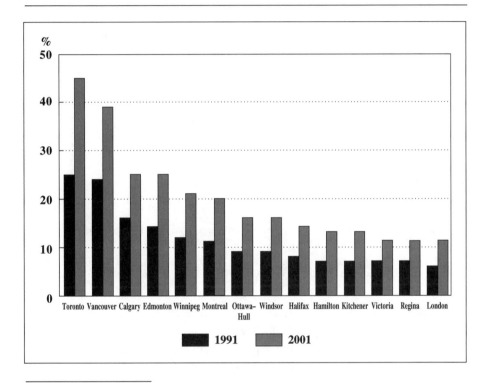

Source: T.J. Samuel, *Visible Minorities in Canada: A Projection.* Toronto: Race Relations Advisory Council on Advertising, Canadian Advertising Foundation, 1992.

There are many kinds of data one can turn to in assessing the impact of these changes on the composition and complexion of immigrants to Canada. One of the most important and reliable sources of data on racism is the direct experiences of the victims. This evidence is found in the numerous reports of task forces, commissions, and surveys that are often conducted by academics, public authorities, and ad hoc advisory committees. It is also found in the oral histories of people of colour. A growing body of literature documents the experiences of racial minorities. Although these kinds of data are sometimes dismissed as being too subjective, they are critical to the understanding of racism.

Another source of data is the polls and surveys that seek to measure racist attitudes among individuals or groups. In the past two decades, many such surveys have been initiated by government agencies, politicians, the media, and academics.

A third source is the research findings of academics and commissioned studies by universities and other public-sector agencies.

Table 3.1

VISIBLE MINORITIES IN CANADA
BY ETHNIC GROUP, 1996

	Number	Percentage
Total visible-minority population	3 197 480	99.9
Chinese	860 150	26.9
South Asian	670 585	21.0
Black	573 860	17.9
Arab/West Asian	244 665	7.7
Filipino	234 200	7.3
Latin American	176 975	5.5
Southeast Asian	172 765	5.4
Japanese	68 135	2.1
Korean	64 835	2.0
Visible minority, n.i.e.[a]	69 745	2.2
Multiple visible minority[b]	61 570	1.9

[a] Includes Pacific Islanders and other visible-minority groups. n.i.e. = not included elsewhere.

[b] Includes respondents who reported more than one visible-minority group.

Source: Data from Statistics Canada, *The Daily*, Cat. no. 11-001, February 17, 1998. Downloaded June 4, 1998, from <http://www.statcan.ca/Daily/English/980217/d980217.htm>. Percentages do not total 100 due to rounding.

Table 3.2

VISIBLE-MINORITY POPULATION OF CANADA,
BY PROVINCE, 1996

	Total population	Total visible-minority population	Visible minorities as % of total population	Geographic distribution of visible minorities
Canada	28 528 125	3 197 480	11.2	100.0
Newfoundland	547 155	3 815	0.7	0.1
Prince Edward Island	132 855	1 520	1.1	0.0
Nova Scotia	899 970	31 320	3.5	1.0
New Brunswick	729 625	7 995	1.1	0.3
Quebec	7 045 085	433 985	6.2	13.6
Ontario	10 542 790	1 682 045	15.8	52.6
Manitoba	1 100 295	77 355	7.0	2.4
Saskatchewan	976 615	26 945	2.8	0.8
Alberta	2 669 195	269 280	10.1	8.4
British Columbia	3 589 760	660 545	17.9	20.7
Yukon Territory	30 650	1 000	3.3	0.0
Northwest Territories	64 125	1 670	2.6	0.1

Source: Data from Statistics Canada, *The Daily*, Cat. no. 11-001, February 17, 1998. Downloaded June 4, 1998, from <http://www.statcan.ca/Daily/English/980217/d980217.htm>.

Table 3.3

VISIBLE-MINORITY POPULATION[a] OF CANADA, BY CENSUS METROPOLITAN AREAS, 1996

	Toronto	Vancouver	Montreal
Total population	4 232 905	1 813 935	3 287 645
Total visible-minority population[b]	1 338 095	564 600	401 425
Black	274 935	16 400	122 320
South Asian	329 840	120 140	46 165
Chinese	335 185	279 040	46 115
Korean	28 555	17 085	3 505
Japanese	17 055	21 880	2 310
Southeast Asian	46 510	20 370	37 600
Filipino	99 115	40 715	14 385
Arab/West Asian	72 160	18 155	73 950
Latin American	61 655	13 830	46 705
Visible minority, n.i.e.[c]	45 655	6 775	3 485
Multiple visible minority[d]	27 435	10 215	1 885

[a] The Employment Equity Act defines the visible-minority population as persons, other than Aboriginal peoples, who are non-Caucasian in race or non-white in colour.

[b] The visible-minority groups are based on categories used to define the visible-minority population under the Regulations to the Employment Equity Act.

[c] Not included elsewhere. Includes Pacific Islander groups or another write-in response likely to be a visible minority (e.g., West Indian, South American).

[d] Includes respondents who reported more than one visible-minority group.

Source: Data from Statistics Canada, *1996 Census of Canada*. Downloaded June 4, 1998, from <http://www.statcan.ca:80/english/Pgdb/People/Population/demo40e.htm>.

The following sections of this chapter examine the evidence of employment and housing discrimination. Employment discrimination has been singled out for special attention because it is perhaps the single most important arena in which racism flourishes. Barriers to access and equity in the workplace ultimately affect all other areas of social functioning. With respect to discrimination in housing, only limited research has been done.

VICTIMS' MANIFESTATIONS

Evidence of racism in Canada, particularly over the past two decades, can be found in a number of government-sponsored inquiries, task forces, and commissions, which have usually been established after a series of highly publicized events or incidents involving members of racial-minority communities. For example, in 1975, the Nova Scotia Human Rights Commission received more than eight hundred complaints of racial discrimination in the educational system. Most were from Black residents in several largely segregated Black communities.

In 1977, Walter Pitman, then president of Ryerson Polytechnical Institute, was appointed by the Municipality of Metropolitan Toronto to lead an inquiry into the reasons for an increase in the number of racial-minority persons being assaulted in Metropolitan Toronto. The Pitman Task Force found sufficient evidence of racism in the city to warrant action. Although subway attacks were the most obvious examples of racial violence, the task force found numerous instances of racial violence in parks and recreation areas, in public-housing complexes, in school playgrounds, on the streets, and in shopping plazas.

Its report described the vicious and continuous harassment of South Asian businesspeople, the verbal and physical harassment of children, and repeated attacks on the homes of racial-minority members and houses of worship belonging to the South Asian community. The task force found that a substantial number of Toronto's citizens lived in fear, were unwilling to use the subway, and felt uncomfortable and threatened in their own neighbourhoods. It also pointed to the failure of a number of institutions — municipal governments, the police, schools, the media, and social agencies — to respond to the problem.

In the same year, the annual report of the Ontario Human Rights Commission raised concerns about the dramatic increase in reported incidents of assaults and verbal abuse against racial minorities. Another report that year (Ubale, 1977), documenting a series of case histories of **racial incidents** as related by South Asian victims, indicated that the individuals responsible belonged to all groups and socioeconomic categories and even included police and immigration officers. Like Pitman, Ubale identified racism as the root cause and suggested that it was linked to the racial bias and discrimination of Canadian institutions.

Head (1981) conducted a study on the adaptation of racial-minority immigrants in Canadian society by analyzing their perceptions of discriminatory treatment in the areas of housing, employment, and access to community services. He identified a number of barriers that prevented racial minorities from gaining suitable employment, such as the requirement for "Canadian experience." More than half of the respondents indicated that their present employment was not the type of work they were seeking or trained for.

In terms of community services, both respondents and community agency staff reported that the services were inadequate. The problem areas included the lack of training for staff; the need to hire staff from Black, South Asian, and other immigrant groups; and the need for more ethno-specific agencies. Several staff workers noted that although their Black clients were usually reluctant to talk about problems resulting from racism, this was a major concern for many clients.

When respondents were asked about their perceptions of the extent of racial discrimination in Metropolitan Toronto, almost 90 percent of Blacks and 72.2 percent of South Asians felt "some" or a "great deal" of discrimination. In contrast, only 35.3 percent of European respondents felt "some" or "a great deal" of discrimination. Most Blacks (63.7 percent) and South

Asians (67.7 percent) reported having been subjected to racial discrimination in Toronto, while only 27.6 percent of the European-born respondents reported that they had experienced some form of ethnic discrimination.

Both Blacks and South Asians thought that racism was increasing. They felt only minimal acceptance by White Canadians and sensed that government agencies were reluctant to deal with racism. These perceptions were consistent with an earlier study carried out by Head (1975), which focussed on the impact of racism on the Black community in Canada.

In 1981, following the killing of a South Asian man in Vancouver, 1800 people demonstrated. The rally was a response to the growing incidence of violent attacks and the widespread racist activities of the Ku Klux Klan. During the rally, several people required hospitalization (Barrett, 1984).

In 1982, the federal government investigation into racial tensions in eleven urban communities across the country found that the racial climate was "tense." The study catalogued expressions of racism that ranged from the subtle acts of "polite racists" to the "sometimes violent" acts of racist zealots in each of these communities (Secretary of State, 1982).

In the same year, the Quebec Human Rights Commission investigated violence between Haitian-born cabbies and Whites in the taxi industry that resulted from the firing of twenty Black taxi drivers from one company. The inquiry found that customers regularly asked for and were given White drivers only. Moreover, many taxi companies were refusing to hire Blacks. The widespread discrimination against Black taxi drivers was found to be only the latest in a series of racial incidents.

Continuing racial tension in Vancouver resulted in the publication of an important survey documenting racist incidents involving South Asian Canadians in that city (Robson and Breems, 1985). It found that about half of Indo-Canadians (South Asians) had experienced at least one hostile incident in the two-year time frame of the study. The most frequently cited incidents involved name calling, verbal threats, and physical gestures, which occurred in cars, on the streets, in shopping malls, and in other public places. Graffiti was also frequently mentioned, and property damage was cited by 14 percent of the respondents; damage to cars and other stolen and damaged possessions were most often cited. Seven percent reported having suffered physical harm, and some of these respondents were in the company of young children when attacked.

Of particular interest in this study is the fact that over 70 percent of the South Asian respondents who reported incidents did nothing in response. The authors suggest that one reason for this is that there is no recourse or reporting mechanism in place for many of the more frequently experienced incidents, such as verbal harassment and graffiti. Another important finding of the study was that close contact between South Asians and members of the dominant culture had little impact. Members of the dominant culture who had the most racist attitudes were those living in areas with high concentrations of South Asian Canadians.

In the mid-1980s, the federal government established a parliamentary task force to examine the nature and extent of racism in Canadian society.

The catalyst for the task force was the cumulative effect of "racist incidents," which could no longer be ignored by the government. The report, *Equality Now,* was published in 1984. Authors of the briefs and witnesses who appeared before the task force described the devastating experiences and debilitating effects of racial prejudice and discrimination on the then approximately two million people of colour living in Canada in 1984. The racial barriers identified included both the intentional discriminatory behaviour of racist individuals and the systematic and systemic barriers created by the major institutions in Canadian society, including schools, employers, media, justice, and law enforcement.

The invisibility of racial minorities was one of the recurring themes of the briefs, which repeatedly argued that people of colour were excluded from participation in political, social, and economic institutions. They are invisible in the official history of Canada. Racial bias was demonstrated by the recurring questions regarding who is really a Canadian. Participants argued that racism in Canada is unyielding; it does not disappear in one or two or even three generations. Dozens of witnesses argued that racist ideology is woven into Canada's public policies, entrenched in programs, and built into the systems and cultural networks of the whole society. The briefs not only focussed on individual racism, but also identified the important role of education, policing, justice, the media, and the human-service delivery system in contributing to racism (*Equality Now*, 1984).

In the late 1980s, evidence of the growing intolerance and acts of discrimination were also documented in the annual reports of the Canadian Human Rights Commission. The 1989 report, for example, raised concerns about the nature of the controversy over whether Sikhs should be allowed to wear turbans in the Royal Canadian Mounted Police (RCMP). The issue resulted in petitions tabled in the Commons carrying the names of as many as 250 000 Canadians who supported the proposition "that a handful of Sikhs wearing turbans would 'crack up the RCMP'" (Camp, 1990). Racist pins and calendars depicting turban-clad Mounties appeared across Canada.

The commissioner of the RCMP warned Canadians that "racial violence will cut to the heart of the Canadian soul unless something is done quickly to stop intolerance.... Violence in some form seems inevitable without a concerted effort to combat racism" (Watson, 1990). He also said that he wasn't as worried about the "few dedicated racists" as about the "significant population of well-meaning, intelligent and educated people who are among the opponents of the changes that a multi-racial society inevitably brings" (Watson, 1990).

In 1991, two major incidents in Nova Scotia drew attention to the racism directed at its Black community. In Cole Harbour, a community east of Dartmouth, a fight between a Black and a White youth attending a high school led to a larger confrontation involving about fifty Black and White students and non-students. The RCMP were called in to investigate, and charges were laid against eighteen people, ten of whom were Black. The parents unanimously protested the arrest of the students from these communities and decided to unite to ease racial tensions. Eventually the charges were dropped, except those against five Black defendants.

Reactions to the incidents led to the mobilization of the Black community, and a series of studies and reports were commissioned to examine educational opportunities and labour participation rates among the residents of the three surrounding communities where Blacks lived. The findings of the studies led to the conclusion that the Black residents of the three areas were "significantly disadvantaged" compared with their White neighbours. The *Report of the Nova Scotia Advisory Group on Race Relations* (1991) found that racism was rampant in the province and in all levels of the school system. The report also focussed on the racial implications of unemployment among Blacks.

In the same year, another incident in Nova Scotia escalated into a series of racial disturbances. After Black youths were refused entrance to a downtown Halifax bar, a brawl ensued in which a Black youth was stabbed. More than a thousand people participated in a march and rally following the incident, to demand action to combat racism in Nova Scotia. In July 1991, the federal, provincial, and municipal governments and representatives from the Black community agreed to form an advisory group on race relations to deal with racism and racial discrimination in education, employment, media, policing, justice, and services.

The *Report of the Nova Scotia Advisory Group on Race Relations* (1991) provided the context for these incidents. It suggested that Blacks in the province had been excluded from all areas of mainstream life in the communities in which they, their parents, grandparents, and great grandparents were born. Racist attitudes converged with racist policies and practices to deprive Blacks and other minorities from access to housing, education, employment, and other services that most White Canadians take for granted, such as access to bars and restaurants. Bridgal Pachai, executive director of the Nova Scotia Human Rights Commission, suggested that "the story of Nova Scotia is a story of denial of opportunity and broken promises to minorities ... who just happen to be Blacks, Aboriginal people and Acadians" (Murray, 1991).

The responses of the White and Black communities to incidents of racial unrest underscored how the two groups (one with power and privilege, the other deprived of fundamental rights) understand racism. Many Blacks readily speak of the explosion of racial tension as inevitable in a racist society, whereas White individuals express shock and anger at the threat of increased racial violence.

In the summer of 1992, the premier of Ontario, Bob Rae, appointed a former Canadian ambassador to the United Nations, Stephen Lewis, to lead a special inquiry on race relations following a disturbance in Toronto a few weeks before. A night of violence and looting followed a peaceful protest by a mixed-race crowd of more than two thousand people decrying the acquittal of Los Angeles police officers whose beating of a Black man was caught on videotape. While the rioters were of all races, the provincial government saw it as a symptom of racial unrest and called for an investigation.

Lewis consulted widely with individuals and groups from racial minorities, particularly the Black community, across the province. He concluded in his report that the root of the problem was anti-Black racism:

> While it is obviously true that every visible minority community experiences the indignities and wounds of systemic discrimination throughout Ontario, it is the Black community which is the focus. It is Blacks who are being shot, it is Black youth that is unemployed in excessive numbers, it is Black students who are being inappropriately streamed in schools, it is Black kids who are disproportionately dropping out.... It is Black employees, professional and non-professional, on whom the doors of upward equity slam shut. (Lewis, 1992:2)

Concerns about racism and the justice system including the police shootings of Black men and the over-representation of Blacks in the prisons led the Ontario government to appoint a commission to inquire into racism in the justice system. (Its findings are discussed in Chapter 5 of this book.)

POLLS AND SURVEYS

One of the first surveys of racist attitudes in Canada included fifty-seven attitudinal items pertaining to racial prejudice (Henry, 1978). The findings revealed that 16 percent of the White mainstream population was extremely intolerant and 35 percent somewhat racist. At least 18 percent had very liberal views about race, and a further 30 percent were somewhat liberal.[3]

The attitudinal survey literature has been remarkably consistent over the more than twenty years since that first survey was done. Most of the surveys show that between 10 and 20 percent of Canadians are extremely intolerant of racial minorities. Another 20–35 percent are somewhat racist. Combining these two findings suggests that a majority of the population could be characterized as racist.

A decade after the Henry study, another survey found that between 7 and 20 percent of Canadians could be described as strongly racist in their views (Environics, 1988). Evidence of "hard core" racism included the following findings: 19 percent of Canadians agreed with "research findings" that Orientals were superior to Whites who were, in turn, superior to Blacks. Moreover, 13 percent of Canadians would exclude non-White groups from immigrating to Canada, 7 percent would not vote for a Black political candidate, and 9 percent would not vote for a Chinese candidate.

A 1989 survey conducted by researchers at the University of Toronto and York University was designed to determine whether there was a significant difference between the racial attitudes of decision-makers — legislators, lawyers, administrators, and police officers — and those of the general population. The survey found that 23 percent of the "elite" Canadians thought minority groups needed to get rid of "harmful and irritating faults," compared with 39 percent of the general population who held the same view. Half of the decision-makers and 70 percent of the general population felt that immigrants often bring discrimination upon themselves; 16 percent of the "elites" and almost one third of the general citizenry believed that "races are naturally unequal" (Gould, 1990).

A 1989 poll in British Columbia, which receives most of the racial-minority immigrants settling in the West, indicated that many residents believed that immigration does not bring economic advantages to the province. These perceptions were held despite the fact that shortly before, a highly publicized report by Employment and Immigration Canada found exactly the opposite to be the case. The report demonstrated that after ten years in Canada, Third World immigrants paid more taxes per capita than did western European immigrants. These perceptions were also not shaken by the well-reported findings of the province's central statistics bureau, which showed that Asian entrepreneurial immigrants contributed $122.9 million into the B.C. economy and $5.4 million into the Alberta economy in 1988. Although entrepreneurial immigrants from Asia created fifteen thousand jobs in Canada in 1988, nearly half of B.C.'s population thought there were too many immigrants of colour moving into the province.

In a Toronto survey in 1992, when asked how well their racial or cultural group was accepted, 80 percent of those surveyed in the Black Canadian community, 63 percent in the Chinese Canadian community, and 62 percent of the East Indian–Pakistani Canadian community felt there was some prejudice toward them in Toronto. Also, 73 percent of Blacks, 48 percent of Chinese, and 47 percent of East Indians–Pakistanis felt discriminated against in obtaining work, compared with 31 percent of Jews, 16 percent of Portuguese, and 15 percent of Italians. In terms of discrimination in the legal or court system, the survey found that 49 percent of Blacks felt they were discriminated against. Twenty-one percent of East Indians–Pakistanis felt this way, as did 9 percent of Chinese (*Toronto Star*, 1992).

A report by the Economic Council of Canada (1991) attempted to measure the changing attitudes toward prejudice over time by analyzing the results of sixty-two surveys taken from 1975 to 1990 by Gallup, Decima, Environics, and other polling organizations. The report found that respondents from communities with greater proportions of visible-minority immigrants were "likely to be more tolerant of racial and ethnic differences." The report also concluded that over time there were "diminishing levels of prejudice." However, the results should be approached with some caution, considering the unreliability and validity of the many data sources as well as the kind of statistical analysis performed, which tends to obscure important variables, such as the unit of analysis, the nature of the questions, the age distribution of the sample, the socioeconomic status of the respondents, their educational background, and their gender.

A survey by the federal immigration department of 1800 adults and fourteen focus groups showed a "growing acceptance" of attitudes and practices that show a dislike for "foreigners." One third of the respondents agreed it was important to "keep out people who are different from most Canadians," while more than half were "really worried that they may become a minority if immigration is unchecked." Almost half admitted there were too many immigrants, even though most underestimated how many people were admitted (*Globe and Mail,* 1992).

Given the extent of ethnocentrism in Canadian society, it is not surprising that these concerns are expressed. However, the number of people who hold these negative attitudes but are not expressing them far exceed those who do, for "fear of being stamped racists" (Samuel, 1988; Wellman, 1978).

In a national survey undertaken by Decima Research in October 1993 for the Canadian Council of Christian and Jews, many of the myths identified in Chapter 1 of this book were reflected in the responses of 1200 respondents. Nearly three quarters of respondents rejected the concept of Canada as a multicultural mosaic, and 72 percent believed that different racial and ethnic groups should try to adapt to Canadian society rather than preserve their original cultures. The survey found that 41 percent of respondents thought that Canada's immigration policy "allows too many people of different cultures and races to come to Canada," and 53 percent agreed with the statement that "some racial and ethnic groups don't make enough of an effort to fit into Canada." Half agreed with the statement: "I am sick and tired of some groups complaining about racism being directed at them," and 41 percent agreed they are "tired of ethnic minorities being given special treatment."

Ekos Research Associates conducted a number of surveys on immigration and used their results to advise the federal government on immigration policy. Their results in 1992 showed that 43 percent of Canadians believed that too many immigrants took advantage of social programs. By 1994, their polls revealed a steady increase (from 30 percent in 1988 to 53 percent in 1994) in Canadians who believed that there were "too many immigrants." More than one quarter of the sample also thought that too many "visible minorities" were being accepted. A 1996 poll indicated that 44 percent of respondents found immigration levels too high, and the same number said the levels were about right (*Globe and Mail,* 1996). The population appears to be evenly split on this issue, which has resulted in government policy to maintain the status quo.

A more sophisticated series of surveys have been undertaken by Berry and Kalin, who conducted two national surveys on attitudes toward multiculturalism. Although many more respondents were tolerant than intolerant, the latter group gave less positive ratings to visible-minority groups. This provides evidence of "differential evaluations of ethnic groups along racial lines, but predominantly among those who are the most generally prejudiced" (Berry and Kalin, 1997:9). Aboriginal people and those of Chinese origin were rated nearly as positively as those of European origin. Berry and Kalin's explanation is that while racism may be a factor in explaining why European groups are rated more positively than non-European groups, "it is clear that Canadians are not generally racist in the sense that they rate all non-European origin Canadians in the same way" (1997:10). Their general conclusions are in keeping with the less sophisticated polls reported above: that 5–20 percent of Canadians "respond negatively to attitude statements about inclusion and acceptance of racial others" (Berry and Kalin, 1997:11).

The findings of many of the polls and surveys undertaken on this subject demonstrate some of the paradoxes of racism in Canadian society.

HATE GROUPS

An ideology of White supremacy was long considered within the bounds of respectable, defensible opinion in Canada. In the colonial era, Aboriginal peoples were portrayed by church and state as "heathens" and "savages" and somehow less than human. These images provided justification for the extermination, segregation, and subjugation of Aboriginal peoples. The dehumanizing impact of such blatant propaganda is clearly evident today in the conditions of many Aboriginal communities (Frideres, 1983).

The 1920s and the 1930s saw the development of racist organizations such as the Ku Klux Klan (KKK), which openly promoted hatred against Catholics, Jews, Blacks, and other minorities. The original Klan was founded in Tennessee in 1866. It established bases in Alberta, Manitoba, Saskatchewan, British Columbia, and Ontario, feeding on Canadian anti-Semitism and the fear of Blacks and southern Europeans. While the KKK in Canada today appears to have only a handful of members, a network of other groups peddle hate propaganda, including the Heritage Front, the Liberty Lobby, the Church of the Creator, the Church of Jesus Christ–Aryan Nation, the Aryan Resistance Movement, and the Western Guard. All these groups share an ideology that supports the view that the Aryan, or White, race is superior to all others morally, intellectually, and culturally and that it is Whites' manifest destiny to dominate society.

Barrett (1987) made a significant contribution to understanding the recent activities of the extreme right in Canada. He found 130 organizations but under 600 members, many of whom belonged to more than one organization. Hate groups are usually coteries centred on a leader with a mailing list. Aside from holding meetings, they promote their ideology through distributing their literature widely. They hold rallies and parades, distribute buttons, paint slogans, establish dial-a-message telephone lines, demonstrate, and hold counter-demonstrations at the rallies of others. They may engage in paramilitary training, hold church services, or engage in political canvassing.

Another strategy used by these groups is to defend their activities by presenting themselves as defenders of free expression. Since they consider themselves to be promoting the principles of civil libertarianism, any attempts to curb their activities are portrayed as **censorship** and therefore anti-democratic.

Barrett (1987) suggests that the main elements of White supremacist ideology are anti-communism, anti-liberalism, racism, and anti-Semitism. White Supremacists perceive themselves as the "saviours of the White race and Western Christian civilization" (Barrett, 1987:90). They believe that the survival of White society in Canada is in jeopardy because of the practice of allowing "non-Aryans" into the country. The Ku Klux Klan suggests that one alternative to the problem of too many racial minorities in Canada is for the government to give "$35 000 to each coloured family as inducement to return to Pakistan, Africa, and elsewhere in the Third World" (Barrett, 1987). It suggests that Jews, too, should be included in this form of "ethnic cleansing," and that the expansion of the White race should be encouraged by providing financial incentives for White parents to have more children.

Barrett concludes that the ideology of the radical right does, to some extent, reflect "what the majority of people think and feel privately, albeit often unconsciously." While hate groups and hate propaganda may be regarded as marginal phenomena, the impact of such extremists is, according to Barrett, disproportionate to their numbers. They gain notoriety and apparent influence by combining strong stances on sensitive policies (such as immigration), which are controversial and have a substantial popular base, with continuous racist appeals couched in emotional, inflammatory rhetoric and threats of violence.

Since the publication of Barrett's pioneering work, the numbers of right-wing groups have proliferated in Canada. KKK branches are active in all of Canada's major cities. Offshoot groups such as the Heritage Front, the Church of the Creator, the Knights for White Rights, and the Aryan Nation are flourishing. Their presence is felt in the many telephone "hot lines" established throughout the country that spew forth hate messages, many of which are directed at Aboriginal peoples and racial minorities. Multiculturalism and immigration policies are also frequently criticized. The messages hammer home the theme, "Keep Canada White."

In the past decade, the League for Human Rights of B'nai B'rith (1992) has monitored the number and types of anti-Semitic incidents that have occurred in all regions of Canada. The data file includes a large variety of incidents, ranging from non-violent ones such as anti-Semitic graffiti to more violent incidents that involve damage to persons or property and the desecration of synagogues. A recent analysis of this file showed a "significant increase ... in the numbers of incidents of all kinds." The report noted that this may merely reflect a "growing tendency of intolerance." But, since longitudinal studies of intolerance are non-existent in Canada, it is not possible to determine whether either intolerance or racist behaviour has increased (Economic Council of Canada, 1991).

These racist incidents target not only the Jewish community. Hate-group activity and hate propaganda is directed at members of the Black, Chinese, and South Asian communities. Reports from various multicultural and anti-racist organizations and networks, as well as the cases in the human-rights commissions and courts, support the findings of the League for Human Rights of B'nai B'rith (British Columbia Organization to Fight Racism, 1992; Mock, 1992).

In the early 1990s, the Canadian Human Rights Commission began launching actions to prohibit telephone hate lines. In Vancouver, its action resulted in a tribunal ordering a telephone hate line off the air. Similarly, in

Toronto, the Heritage Front was issued with an injunction to stop producing hate messages. In Winnipeg, a human-rights tribunal ordered the Manitoba Knights of the KKK to cease airing its messages. The tribunal found "overwhelming uncontradicted evidence that the messages were likely to expose the persons involved to hatred and contempt by reason of their race, religion, national or ethnic origin, colour or sexual orientation." This decision included not only the Manitoba chapter of the KKK, but also "any other individuals who are member of or act in the name of the Knights of the Ku Klux Klan." In recent years, the Internet has been used as a primary vehicle for the dissemination of hate propaganda (Anti-Defamation League, 1997). One prominent Web site was controlled by Canadian Ernst Zundel, using a base in California. The Canadian Human Rights Commission had, at the time of this writing, launched a tribunal hearing challenging the legitimacy of this method of distributing hate materials.

By 1992, racist violence was increasing in many Canadian urban centres. For example, over a period of a few weeks in 1993, three Tamil refugees were beaten in Toronto. One died as the result of the injuries inflicted by his White assailants, and one was paralyzed. These incidents must be considered in the context of a long history of racist attitudes toward immigrants and refugees (or those perceived to be "foreigners" by virtue of the colour of their skin). In 1987, Canadians vehemently reacted to the arrival of a few boatloads of Tamil and Sikh refugees who entered Canada without following the normal procedures, while at the same time expressing little concern about the equally unorthodox arrival of significant numbers of Polish refugees.

Recent Research

The research on hate crimes and hate or bias incidents has increased in the last few years. Data from the United States, as well as the more limited data available in Canada, indicate that the majority of perpetrators of hate crimes or hate or bias incidents constitute a relatively homogeneous group. They are young, male, and tend to be involved in gangs (Gilmour, 1994). There is also some evidence that skinheads have been involved in anti-Semitic hate crimes against the Jewish community. Further evidence was found in a study which documented that most right wing violence was committed by skinheads, "and members of other neo-fascist groups such as the Western Guard and anti-communist nationalists". The majority of attacks were motivated by racism, anti-communism, and anti-Semitism (Ross, 1992).

Research also indicates that actual acts of violence or hate crimes committed against racial and other minorities have increased. A study commissioned to determine the nature and extent of hate activity in Metro Toronto (Mock, 1996) offered the following definitions of hate activity:

- hate/bias crime: "criminal offense against a person or property that is based solely on the victim's race, religion, nationality, ethnic origin or sexual orientation"; and

- hate/bias incidents: "incidents of harassment and other biased activity that is not criminal, including name calling, taunting, slurs, graffiti, derogatory or offensive material, vandalism and threatening or offensive behaviour based on the victim's race, creed, ethnicity or sexual orientation" (Mock, 1996:14).

The study examined a wide variety of statistical indicators. These included the data from the only three agencies that keep such records, including the Metro Toronto Police Hate Crimes Unit. Qualitative measures such as interviews, focus-group discussions, and reviews of other available literature were also used. The findings reveal that

> as the population of Metropolitan Toronto continues to become more diverse, and as a difficult economic times continue to fuel the backlash against immigrants and minority groups, the reported incidents of hate motivated activity have steadily increased. While these findings could be the result of increased awareness of reporting mechanisms ... it is unlikely, since the anecdotal evidence of the perceptions of community workers and caseworkers corroborates the statistical findings. (Mock, 1996:57)

Moreover, the groups most singled out were Jews, Blacks, and homosexuals.

> Reported anti-Semitic incidents are at an all time high, in 14 years of documentation by the League for Human Rights of B'nai B'rith Canada; and according to statistics gathered by the Metro Police, racially motivated incidents against Blacks and other people of colour, and hate motivated attacks on Gays and Lesbians have increased steadily over the last few years. (Mock, 1996:49)

In a comprehensive statistical analysis of hate crimes in Canada, Roberts (1995) estimated that the total number of hate crimes committed in 1994 in nine major urban centres in Canada was approximately sixty thousand, including crimes motivated by race hatred as well as ethnicity and religion.

In sum, although the research evidence does not generally support an increase in negative attitudes, there has apparently been an increase in actual behaviour as measured by the escalation of hate-related criminal activity.

It also appears that media reports may have an effect on generating more hate crimes and incidents. This is known as "the copy-cat effect." For example, an increase in anti-Semitic vandalism was reported after the airing of a program on racism, "Hearts of Hate," on CTV. Members of the Jewish community and Jewish organizations also report an increase in hate activity whenever a "hate monger such as Zundel, Droege, or Burdi was featured prominently in the media without any counterbalance." Other minority groups report similar events (Mock, 1996).

CASE STUDY 3.1

EMPLOYMENT DISCRIMINATION

One of the clearest demonstrations of racism in a society is the lack of access and equity experienced by people of colour in the workplace. A number of studies over the past two decades have documented the nature and extent of racial bias and discrimination in employment. One study, *Who Gets the Work?* (Henry and Ginzberg, 1984), examined access to employment. In this field research, evenly matched Black and White jobseekers were sent to apply for entry positions advertised in a major newspaper. An analysis of the results of several hundred applications and interviews revealed that White applicants received job offers three times more often than did Black applicants. In addition, telephone callers with accents, particularly those from South Asia and the Caribbean, were more often screened out when they phoned to inquire about a job vacancy.

A follow-up study to *Who Gets the Work?* focussed on the attitude, hiring, and management practices of large businesses and corporations in Toronto. This report, *No Discrimination Here*, documented the perceptions of employers and personnel managers in these organizations. In personnel interviews, recruitment, hiring, promotion, training, and termination practices, a high level of both racial prejudice and discrimination was demonstrated; 28 percent of the respondents felt that racial minorities did not have the ability to meet performance criteria as well as Whites did (Billingsley and Musynski, 1985).

Thus, racist behaviour stretches along a wide continuum. At one end are the overt and covert daily acts of discrimination involving a significant proportion of the mainstream community. At the other end of the continuum, one finds far more explicit and extreme racist activity in the form of hate propaganda and racial violence perpetrated by a small minority of the population.

DISCRIMINATION IN THE WORKPLACE

Concern over employment discrimination against people of colour, women, persons with disabilities, and Aboriginal peoples led the federal government to establish a royal commission on equality in employment (Abella, 1984). Its task was to inquire into the employment practices of eleven designated Crown and government-owned corporations and to explore the most effective means of promoting equality in employment for four groups: women, Native peoples, disabled persons, and racial minorities. Its findings echoed the conclusions of the report *Equality Now* (1984) that racial bias and discrimination were a pervasive reality in the employment system. The commissioner, Judge Rosalie Abella, observed that "strong measures were needed to remedy the impact of discriminatory attitudes and behaviour." The remedy she recommended was employment equity legislation (Abella, 1984).

Federal employment equity legislation for the four target groups identified by the Abella Commission was first introduced in 1986 and strengthened in 1995. In that year, the annual report of the president of the Treasury Board revealed that small progress had been made with respect to the hiring of members of employment equity targeted groups. For example, the percentage of women in the public service increased from 42.9 percent in 1988 to 47.4 percent in 1995. The percentage of Aboriginal representation increased from 1.7 to 2.2 percent, while visible-minority representation increased from 2.9 to 4.1 percent. In all of these categories, the available labour pool is much higher.

Although the federal government has attempted to increase its representation of minorities, downsizing as well as residual racist attitudes have not led to significant gains. In addition, minority-group employees complained in a survey that employment practices were unfair and racially biased. A number of complaints to the Canadian Human Rights Commission, including a class action representing more than one hundred employees of Health Canada, were made in the 1990s. Most involved professional employees who believe that they had not had equal access to promotional opportunities in the Public Service, particularly with respect to managerial positions. A tribunal of the commission found in favour of the complainants in the class action against Health Canada. In sum, there has been little real progress for minorities in the federal public service, largely due to the inability and unwillingness of this institution to respond to social and demographic imperatives.

At the level of the federally regulated private sector, more hiring has taken place. For example, in the banking sector, which has the best record of minority hiring, visible-minority representation has increased from 12.1 percent in 1989 to 13.7 percent in 1994. Communications rose from 5.3 to 7.2 percent; transportation from 3.8 to 4.3 percent, and all others from 3.7 to 6.2 percent (Samuel and Karam, 1996). Despite improvements in the overall position of racial minorities in the employment regulated by the federal act, these groups are still concentrated in the lower sectors of the industries. For example, in banking, visible minorities are over-represented in lower-level positions, such as tellers, and under-represented in the managerial ranks.

In the late 1990s, responding to an aging and short-staffed bureaucracy, the Public Service Commission announced that it was hiring more than two thousand new employees. Since a report showed that the availability rate of visible minorities in the labour force was 12 percent but only 4.1 percent were represented in the public service, it might be thought that such minorities were likely to be especially recruited (Samuel, 1998).

Members of racial-minority groups have higher levels of education than do other Canadians. For example, 23 percent had university degrees, compared with 14 percent of other Canadians. Moreover, racial minorities had consistently higher levels of education than did other workers in the lower-paying occupations. In the category of "semi-professionals and technicians," for instance, 32.3 percent of racial-minority employees had university degrees, compared with 18.3 percent of others.

Despite higher levels of education, members of racial-minority groups were paid lower salaries than were other Canadians. Reitz et al. (1981) demonstrated that considerable income disparities existed among various ethno–racial groups. People of colour, such as West Indians, and more recently arrived groups such as Portuguese, ranked lowest in incomes.

A decade later, the average salary for all levels of education for a member of a racial minority in both the upper and middle levels and other management occupations was approximately 18 percent lower than that of the total population (Employment and Immigration Canada, 1992:57). Even in the "other manual workers" category, including all levels of education, members of racial minorities earned nearly 10 percent less than all other manual workers. Another study, issued in 1995 and provocatively entitled "The Colour of Money," found that Aboriginal and visible-minority men earned significantly less income than did native-born and White immigrant men in Canada. The earnings differentials were not explained by socioeconomic variables such as education, place of schooling, occupation, and others, which were controlled for in this study. Even visible-minority men born in Canada suffered about a 10 percent earnings penalty. These differences were, however, not found among visible-minority women as compared with Canadian-born or immigrant White women. The researchers also noted that while there were clear-cut earning differentials between Whites and visible minorities, there was also a considerable degree of heterogeneity within each of these categories (Pendakur and Pendakur, 1995).

One of the key barriers preventing immigrants of colour from access and equity in the labour market is credentialism. Studies in Ontario (Ontario Ministry of Citizenship, 1989) and British Columbia (Fernando and Prasad, 1986) showed little recognition in Canada of the professional qualifications, credentials, and experience of immigrants. Thousands of immigrants find their university degrees and trade diplomas of little value in Canada. These barriers affect doctors, teachers, social workers, nurses, engineers, and others.

Public-sector agencies also show a lack of representation of racial minorities. An audit done for the Ontario public service in 1986 showed that 77 percent of civil servants were White and only 11.9 percent were racial minorities, most of whom were clustered in lower-level positions. In 1989, racial minorities formed only 4 percent of the Metropolitan Toronto Police Force. Almost all of them were cadets, constables, or in training; only three had the rank of inspector (Small, 1992). In 1998, the representation of racial minorities had shown insignificant gains: there were three staff inspectors, three senior police officers, and only 7.4 percent of the total uniformed employees were racial minorities (Metro Toronto Police Services, 1998). In the late 1980s, at the Toronto Board of Education, only 5 percent of the teaching staff were from racial minorities, but this figure increased to 8.5 percent with the inclusion of non-teaching staff. Only 6 percent were classified as managers. The Ontario Human Rights Commission had only one racial-minority director. The former Metropolitan Toronto Housing Authority, which dealt with large numbers of minority clients, had a minority contingent of only 16.7 percent, of whom 11 percent were at a middle- or senior-management level.

A survey of 672 corporate recruiters (*Currents*, 1989), hiring managers, and agency recruiters across Canada conducted by the Canadian Recruiters Guild concluded that there were gross deficiencies in Canada's recruitment and selection practices. It revealed that the moral, legal, and economic impact of recruitment was either not understood or simply ignored by recruiters.

A study undertaken by the Maritime School of Social Work at Dalhousie University in Halifax (Bambrough et al., 1992) tracked its racial-minority and Aboriginal graduates and found that minorities experienced considerable difficulty in obtaining employment after graduation. Acadian and Black graduates took several more weeks to find their first job, and Blacks had to apply to many more employers and undertake many more interviews to get a job offer. (In this respect, the study mirrors the results of *Who Gets the Work?*, which also found that Blacks and others had to make many more telephone calls than did Whites to obtain an interview.)

The study also found that upon graduation, Blacks found less desirable jobs than others, including limited or term positions and more part-time jobs. Of particular interest was the fact that Blacks were more often in jobs in which the chances for advancement were relatively low, as were salaries. The report concluded that "Black graduates have been less successful than the majority group in accessing the more prestigious social work jobs, such as those to be found in family counselling, hospital social work and in administrative/supervisory positions."

Harish Jain, who has done extensive research (Jain, 1988; Jain and Hackett, 1989) on employment discrimination in Canada, suggested that racial minorities, as well as women, Aboriginal peoples, and people with disabilities, encounter both entry-level and postemployment discrimination in the workplace. Jain (1985) argued that human-rights statutes across Canada were ineffective in ensuring **equality of opportunity** in the workplace. Jain identified numerous job barriers in the employment system, including narrow recruitment channels and procedures (such as word-of-mouth recruitment, inflated educational qualifications, biased testing, prejudice and stereotyping in the job interview process, poor performance evaluation, and lack of promotions, transfers, and/or salary increases). Unions are another potential source of both racism and sexism (Leah, 1989).

Non–English-speaking and racial-minority immigrant women are part of a segregated and marginalized workforce and are employed mainly in three areas: private domestic service, service industries, and light manufacturing. Many immigrant racial-minority women working in the public sector are employed as cleaners, cafeteria workers, nurses' aides, and lower-level clerical workers (Vorst et al., 1989). Brand (1987) observed that most Black women work at low-status jobs in homes and institutions and do "Black women's work."

Research on the Caribbean communities in Toronto (Henry, 1994) has yielded some interesting information on the continuing impact of racial discrimination on employment. More than one hundred in-depth interviews and many hundreds of hours of participant observation among persons of Caribbean origin in Toronto indicated that the community shows a fairly high level of institutional completeness, considering the recentness of Caribbean migration to Canada. Although there are no Caribbean-owned financial institutions within the community, most service and retail sectors have developed to the extent that goods and services of many kinds can be obtained from Caribbean-owned and -managed businesses.

One of the main reasons for private entrepreneurship among the community was the racial discrimination experienced by job seekers and workers employed in mainstream-owned and -managed firms. Difficulty in obtaining employment was often cited as a major reason for dissatisfaction with living in Canada. In addition, racial harassment on the job and the inability to advance in the company was cited as a contributory factor in private entrepreneurship. Restaurateurs, clothiers, and variety-shop owners said they were "fed up" with racial harassment.

A research project focussing on diversity, mobility and change among Black communities in Canada used primarily census data and made similar findings. It found that although Black people in Canada had levels of education similar to those of the total population, they had substantially lower incomes, were less likely to be self-employed, and were less likely to occupy senior management positions. Many more Blacks than Whites lived in poverty, and Black women had greater poverty rates than men (Torczyner, 1997).

A report on socioeconomic indicators of equality conducted among ethno-racial communities in Toronto in the early 1990s found that while the overall rate of unemployment in Metro Toronto was 9.6 percent, the unemployment rate of non-Europeans far exceeded this (Ornstein, 1997). For example, Africans had a 25.8 percent unemployment rate, followed by Mexicans and Central Americans at 24 percent and Tamils at 23.9 percent. Other groups with a higher than average unemployment rate included Arabs and West Asians, Sri Lankans, Vietnamese, and Aboriginal people. Jamaicans, especially youth between the ages of 15 and 24, had high rates of unemployment as compared with other youth in the same age category. The study also found a weak link between employment and education and concluded that groups with the most unemployment were not those with the least education; many non-European groups found it difficult to convert their educational qualifications into jobs.

Income is closely related to employment, and in the early 1990s Tamils, Sri Lankans, and Africans in Toronto had the lowest earnings (about $19 000), followed closely by East and Southeast Asians, Jamaicans, and South Americans. This figure is in sharp contrast to the average annual employment income of $31 300 and a mean annual income of $50 000. With respect to general indicators of poverty, 19 percent of all families in Toronto were living at or below the poverty line. The highest levels of poverty (33–37 percent) existed among Arabs, West Asians, Latin Americans, Blacks, and Africans. Three in five Toronto children from African nations lived in poverty, as did more than half the children of Jamaican, Iranian, other Arab and West Asian, and Central American parents. More than two fifths of Aboriginal children, as well as those of Tamil and Vietnamese origin, lived in poverty.

Ornstein (1997) concluded that many people in Toronto were affected by poverty and inequality. The report acknowledged that the groups most affected were those who found access to employment, housing, education, and other resources constrained due to a variety of economic and social factors.

Employment Agencies

Allegations of racial discrimination in the operations of employment agencies in accepting and referring certain clients have been a concern for more than two decades. In 1975, the Canadian Civil Liberties Association (CCLA) conducted a survey of randomly selected employment agencies. The CCLA told agency representatives that it represented an out-of-town firm planning to locate in their community and asked whether, among the services provided, the agencies would agree to refer only White people for the jobs that had to be filled. Of the fifteen employment agencies in Metro Toronto that received this request, eleven said they would screen out persons of colour.

The study was repeated in 1976, surveying employment agencies in Hamilton, Ottawa, and London. Again, eleven of the fifteen agencies indicated their willingness to fulfil discriminatory requests. In 1980, the CCLA surveyed ten agencies in Toronto, seven of whom expressed a willingness to abide by a "Whites only" restriction. In 1991, the CCLA repeated the survey for the fourth time, and of the fifteen agencies surveyed in four cities in Ontario, only three declared their unwillingness to accept discriminatory job orders.

Following are some examples of the agencies' responses.

> It is discrimination, but it can be done discreetly without anyone knowing. No problem with that.

> That's no problem, it's between you and me. I don't tell anyone; you don't tell anyone.

> You are paying to see the people you want to see.

> Absolutely — definitely ... that request is pretty standard here.

> That's not a problem. Appearance means a lot, whether it's colour or overweight people. (Rees, 1991)

Although the role of employment agencies in colluding with discriminatory employers had long been known to those who monitor race relations in Canada, the publicity surrounding a complaint laid with the Ontario Human Rights Commission against two employment agencies in Toronto brought this issue into the public arena. Although the commission found discriminatory information about job applicants in some files, it maintained that the agencies did not have a deliberate policy of discriminating against job applicants. Accordingly, a settlement was reached in which the agencies agreed to develop written policies against accepting discriminatory job requests from employers and to provide training for their employees in race relations and employment equity.

Both agencies also said they would establish three-year employment equity plans, with goals and timetables that provided for the elimination of barriers in recruiting, referral, and placement services. The chief commissioner of the human rights commission was quoted as saying that this settlement "will provide a blueprint for all employment agencies in the province." A number of critics, however, noted that the settlement was fairly limited and did not adequately encompass all the aspects of this complex issue.

SUMMARY

This chapter has provided an overview of the historical and contemporary evidence of racism in Canada. The examples cited demonstrate both

---

CASE STUDY 3.2

DISCRIMINATION IN HOUSING

Housing provides another example of how racial discrimination restricts people's choices with respect to accommodation. Although the evidence in Canada is scanty, racial discrimination in rental housing occurs in cities, especially in Toronto and Montreal, where the issue has been studied. Discrimination in Canadian rental accommodation would not be surprising, since the evidence from both the United Kingdom and the United States is overwhelming (Rex and Moore, 1967; Flett, 1979; Ward, 1978; Bristow, 1979).

LANDLORD EXCLUSIONARY PRACTICES

A study by the Canadian Council on Social Development has shown that two types of individual prejudice on the part of landlords lead to housing discrimination. In the first case, landlords hold negative stereotypes about certain groups and believe that such people will make bad tenants. In the second, landlords restrict occupancy on the grounds that their existing tenants would threaten to move out if members of a particular minority group were allowed in (Quann, 1979).

(continued)

CASE STUDY 3.2 *(continued)*

These and other types of prejudice restrict the chances of minority groups to live where they choose. Various methods are then used by rental agents and landlords to prevent members of minority groups from renting or purchasing property. Quann (1979) noted that discrimination may arise as an immediate response to the applicant's manner of speaking over the telephone. Others, who do not have a discernible accent, encounter discrimination when they arrive to see the apartment.

Discrimination appears to be more common in certain kinds of rental accommodation than in others. Owners of rooming houses seem to discriminate most frequently. In private homes, where the owner lives in the building, there is also a high level of discrimination. Most cases referred to human rights commissions concern these types of accommodation (Quann, 1979).

In the real estate industry, it was alleged that some companies and agents steered racial-minority clients away from certain areas and toward those already inhabited by minority groups. Although some minority-group members want to live in areas already inhabited by members of their group, if potential buyers are steered toward some areas and away from others, over-concentration may result.

Two significant research studies of racial discrimination in housing have been undertaken in Quebec. In 1981, Black and other racial-minority immigrants living in two sections of Montreal were sampled by census tracts and questioned about their experience with racial discrimination in housing (Teitlebaum and Bérubé, 1983). Twenty-two percent of respondents had personal experiences of discrimination, and many more had heard of the experiences of others. More than three quarters of those sampled had experienced the typical situation of being told that an apartment was "just rented." The study concluded that racial discrimination in housing in Montreal was severe and that it was not a temporary problem likely to disappear once the groups got to know each other. Housing segregation was on the increase in Montreal, it was concluded, largely as a result of the inability of racial-minority people to exercise free choice in their living arrangements.

A 1988 study undertaken by the Quebec Human Rights Commission used the methodology of field testing developed by Henry and Ginzberg (1984) in their study, *Who Gets the Work?* Matched pairs of White and Black actors, pretending that they were in search of accommodation, applied for apartments in the newspaper. The study controlled for sex, age, and social status and found that Black working-class applicants were the individuals most often rejected as tenants.

This methodology was also used in a pilot study in the mid-1980s to test racial discrimination against single professional women seeking accommodation in Toronto (Henry, 1989). The two women researchers (one Black, one White) represented themselves as having the same income, being the same age, and being in the same occupational group. Of the 73 cases tested, 31 showed blatant or overt discrimination. Discrimination was defined as occurring when the Black woman was told there was no vacancy while immediately afterward the White woman was told there was a vacancy. Discrimination was also revealed when different rental fees were quoted for the same accommodation.

(continued)

CASE STUDY 3.2 *(continued)*

Another method of discrimination is offering different availability dates. In some instances in the study the Black woman was told nothing would be available for five or six months, whereas the White woman was told that something would become available "next month." Clearly, it was hoped that the Black woman would be discouraged and not return.

In 10 of the 73 cases, it was difficult to determine with any degree of accuracy whether some evidence of discrimination or differential treatment had taken place. In only 32 of the 73 cases was there no difference in the treatment of or information offered to the researchers.

The results of this small study as well as those of the Quebec studies clearly indicate that significant housing discrimination exists. The methodology also reveals that most applicants do not know when they have been victims of discrimination. When landlords or rental agents act pleasantly but say that they have no vacancies, most applicants will readily accept that explanation. This is especially true in a city such as Toronto, which has gone through periods of extremely low vacancy rates.

Only when a White applicant applies to the same contact person and is shown an apartment, or told that a vacancy will come up in a month's time, or given an application form, or quoted a lower rental rate for the same apartment, does a racial-minority person realize that unequal treatment has occurred. Housing discrimination is even more subtle than employment discrimination, since in the latter case it can always be alleged that a job applicant's credentials are not adequate. When seeking accommodation, however, all one usually needs is the first and sometimes last month's rent.

Finally, another manifestation of racism in housing occurred in the 1990s in Vancouver. The arrival of large numbers of Hong Kong Chinese, many of whom were relatively wealthy, created a situation in which they were blamed for the increase in house prices. In fact, the increase in housing prices was a reflection of a number of social and demographic trends (Li, 1994). Moreover, their building of alleged "monster" homes reinforced the perception of Chinese immigrants as alien and unlike Canadians in their tastes and values.

A study of this issue demonstrated that a group can become "racialized" because of supposed social characteristics. "The controversy over 'unneighbourly' and the battle to preserve what some Caucasian Canadians consider to be a 'Canadian heritage' promotes a negative racial connotation for Chinese immigrants" (Li, 1994). Li argued that attempts by local residents to create zoning regulations prohibiting the building of such houses is an example of racism against the Chinese.

---

the highly complex nature of racism and the diverse forms it takes. There is a brief examination of how racial bias and discrimination have affected specific minority communities, including Black Canadians, Chinese Canadians, Japanese Canadians, East Indian Canadians, and Canadian Jews.

One sees repeated examples of individual racism when individuals, acting on racial prejudice and stereotypes, translate their negative attitudes into racist and discriminatory behaviour.

Racist ideology strongly influences the development of public policies and legislative enactments. The historical evidence demonstrates how racial bias and discriminatory practices have limited access to education, housing, and employment and have resulted in the denial of the fundamental civil rights to racial minorities in Canada. The development of restrictive and racist immigration policies lasting over one hundred years is compelling evidence of racism in Canada.

The last section of this chapter has documented some of the extensive data on employment and housing discrimination, further illustrating the extent to which racial bias and discrimination function and flourish in Canadian society. The history of racism in Canada can be characterized by the development and maintenance of policies and practices based on the marginalization, exclusion, segregation, and domination of racial minorities.

NOTES

1. This section is drawn from the projections of T.J. Samuel, *Visible Minorities in Canada: A Projection* (Toronto: Race Relations Advisory Council on Advertising, Canadian Advertising Foundation, 1992).
2. The term "visible minority" is used in the Census of Canada as well as in publications that use census or other government-generated data. It is used in this book when discussing such research.
3. Polling and survey data from other countries are similar to those of Canada. For example, a survey conducted in the European Union countries revealed that racism is rampant. The data showed that one third of respondents are racist; some admitted that they were "very" racist, and others reported being "quite racist" (*North Africa Journal*, 1998). Surveys on racism and attitudes toward immigrants in Australia revealed similar figures to those of Canada (see Adelman, et al., 1994).

REFERENCES

Abella, I., and H. Troper. (1982). *None Is Too Many*. Toronto: Lester and Orpen Dennys.

Abella, R. (1984). *Report of the Commission on Equality in Employment*. Ottawa: Supply and Services Canada.

Adachi, K. (1976). *The Enemy That Never Was: A History of the Japanese Canadians*. Toronto: McClelland & Stewart.

Adelman, H., A. Borowski, M. Burnstein, and L. Foster (eds.). (1994). *Immigration and Refugee Policy: Australia and Canada Compared*. Melbourne: Melbourne University Press.

Alexander, K., and A. Glaze. (1996). *Towards Freedom: The African Canadian Experience*. Toronto: Umbrella Press.

Anti-Defamation League (1997). *High Tech Hate: Extremist Use of the Internet*. New York: ADL.

Arthurs, H. (1963). "Civil Liberties and Public Schools: Segregation of Negro Students." *Canadian Bar Review* 4:453–57.

Bambrough, J., W. Bowden, and F. Wien. (1992). *Preliminary Results from the Survey of Graduates from the Maritime School of Social Work*. Halifax: Maritime School of Social Work, Dalhousie University.

Barrett, S. (1984). "White Supremists and Neo Fascists: Laboratories for the Analysis of Racism in Wider Society." In O. McKague (ed.), *Racism in Canada*. Saskatoon: Fifth House. 85–99.

———. (1987). *Is God a Racist? The Right Wing in Canada*. Toronto: University of Toronto Press.

Baureiss, G. (1985). "Discrimination and Response: The Chinese in Canada." In R. Bienvenue and J. Goldstein (eds.), *Ethnicity and Ethnic Relations in Canada*. 2nd ed. Toronto: Butterworths.

Berry, J.W., and R. Kalin. (1997). "Racism in Canada: Evidence from National Surveys." In L. Driedger and S. Halli (eds.), *Visible Minorities: Race and Racism in Canada*. Ottawa: Carleton University Press.

Billingsley, B., and L. Musynski. (1985). *No Discrimination Here*. Toronto: Social Planning Council of Metro Toronto and the Urban Alliance on Race Relations.

Bolaria, B.S., and P. Li. (1988). *Racial Oppression in Canada*. 2nd ed. Toronto: Garamond Press.

Brand, D. (1987). "Black Women and Work: The Impact of Racially Constructed Gender Roles on the Sexual Division of Labour." *Fireweed* 25:35.

Bristow, M. (1979). "Ugandan Asians, Racial Disadvantage and Housing Markets in Manchester and Birmingham." *New Community* 7(2):203–16.

British Columbia Organization to Fight Racism. (1992). *Canada 125*. Surrey, BC: BCOFR.

Buchignani, N., and D. Indra. (1985). *Continuous Journey: A Social History of South Asians in Canada*. Toronto: McClelland & Stewart.

Camp, D. (1990). "Diefenbaker Would Have Backed Turbans in the RCMP." *Toronto Star* (March 21):A25.

Canadian Civil Liberties Association. (1991). *Survey of Employment Agencies*. Toronto: CCLA.

Canadian Council of Christian and Jews. (1993). *Survey of Canadian Attitudes towards Ethnic and Race Relations in Canada*. Toronto: Decima Research.

Chan, A. (1983). *The Gold Mountain: The Chinese in the New World*. Vancouver: New Star.

Cohen, T. (1987). *Race Relations and the Law*. Toronto: Canadian Jewish Congress.

Creese, G. (1991). "Organizing against Racism in the Workplace: Chinese Workers in Vancouver before the Second World War." In O. McKague (ed.), *Racism in Canada*. Saskatoon: Fifth House.

———. (1993). "The Sociology of British Columbia." *BC Studies* 100(Winter 1993–94).

Currents: Readings in Race Relations. (1989). "Canada's Employment Discriminators." 5(2):18–21. Toronto: Urban Alliance on Race Relations.

Dirks, G. (1977). "Memorandum to Mackenzie King." In *Canada's Refugee Policy: Indifference or Opportunities?* Montreal and Kingston: McGill-Queen's University Press.

Economic Council of Canada. (1991). *Report*. Ottawa.

Employment and Immigration Canada. (1992). *Annual Report, Employment Equity*. Ottawa: Minister of Supply and Services.

Environics. (1988). *Focus Canada Survey*.

Equality Now: Report of the Parliamentary Task Force on the Participation of Visible Mi-norities in Canada. (1984). Ottawa: Queen's Printer.

Fernanado, T., and K. Prasad. (1986). *Multiculturalism and Employment Equity: Problems Facing Foreign-Trained Professionals and Tradespeople in British Columbia*. Vancouver: Affiliation of Multicultural Societies and Service Agencies of British Columbia.

Flett, H. (1979). "Dispersal Policies in Council Housing: Arguments and Evidence." *New Community* 7(2):184–94.

Frideres, J. (1983). *Native Peoples in Conflict*. Scarborough, ON: Prentice Hall.

Gilmour, G.A. (1994). *Hate-Motivated Violence: A Working Document*. Ottawa: Department of Justice. (May).

Globe and Mail. (1992). (October 14).

Globe and Mail. (1996). "Immigrant Levels Reflect Backlash." (October 30):A1.

Gould, T. (1990). "Who Do You Hate." *Toronto Life* (October).

Head, W. (1975). "The Black Presence in the Canadian Mosaic: A Study of Perception and the Practice of Discrimination against Blacks in Metropolitan Toronto." Toronto.

———. (1981). *Adaptation of Immigrants: Perceptions of Ethnic and Racial Discrimination*. North York, ON: York University.

Henry, F. (1968). "The West Indian Domestic Scheme in Canada." In *Social and Economic Studies*. Mona, Jamaica: University of the West Indies.

———. (1974). *The Forgotten Canadians: The Blacks of Nova Scotia*. Don Mills, ON: Longmans.

———. (1978). *Dynamics of Racism*. Ottawa: Secretary of State.

———. (1989). *Housing and Racial Discrimination in Canada: A Preliminary Assessment*. Ottawa: Ministry of Multiculturalism and Citizenship.

———. (1994). *The Caribbean Diaspora in Toronto: Learning to Live with Racism*. Toronto: University of Toronto Press.

———, and E. Ginzberg. (1984). *Who Gets the Work? A Test of Racial Discrimination in Employment*. Toronto: Urban Alliance on Race Relations and the Social Planning Council of Toronto.

Hernandez, C. (1992). "Nanny Rule Will Have Racist Outcome." *Toronto Star* (February 15).

Hill, D. (1981). *The Freedom Seekers: Blacks in Early Canada*. Agincourt, ON: Book Society of Canada.

Jain, H. (1985). *Anti-Discrimination Staffing Policies: Implications of Human Rights Legislation for Employers and Trade Unions*. Ottawa: Secretary of State.

———. (1988). "Affirmative Action/Employment Equity Programmes and Visible Minorities in Canada." *Currents: Readings in Race Relations* 5(1)(4):3–7.

———, and R. Hackett (1989). "Measuring Effectiveness of Employment Equity Programmes in Canada: Public Policy and a Survey." *Canadian Public Policy* 15(2):189–204.

Jakubowski, L.M. (1997). *Immigration and the Legalization of Racism*. Halifax: Fernwood.

King, W.L.M. (1908). *Report of the Commissioner Appointed to Enquire into the Methods by Which Oriental Labourers Have Been Induced to Come to Canada*. Ottawa: King's Printer.

Kobayashi, A. (1987). "From Tyranny to Justice: The Uprooting of the Japanese Canadians in 1941." *Tribune Juive* 5:28–35.

Lampert, R., and J. Curtis. (1989). "The Racial Attitudes of Canadians." In L. Tepperman and J. Curtis (eds.), *Readings in Sociology*. Toronto: McGraw-Hill Ryerson.

Lampkin, L. (1985). "Visible Minorities in Canada." Research paper for the Abella Royal Commission, *Equality in Employment*. Ottawa: Minister of Supply and Services Canada.

League for Human Rights of B'nai B'rith. (1992). *Annual Audit of Anti-Semitic Incidents*. Toronto.

Leah, R. (1989). "Linking the Struggles: Racism, Sexism and the Union Movement." In J. Vorst et al. (eds.), *Race, Class, Gender: Bonds and Barriers*. Toronto: Between the Lines.

Lewis, S. (1992). *Report on Race Relations to Premier Bob Rae*. Toronto: Queen's Printer. Excerpt on page 96 reproduced with permission from the Queen's Printer for Ontario.

Li, P. (1988). *The Chinese in Canada*. Rev. ed. Toronto: Oxford University Press.

———. (1994). "Unneighbourly Houses or Unwelcome Chinese: The Social Construction of Race in the Battle over 'Monster Homes' in Vancouver." *International Journal of Race and Ethnic Studies* 1–2:47–66.

Malarek, V. (1987). *Heaven's Gate: Canada's Immigration Fiasco*. Toronto: Macmillan.

Mattis, W. (1990). "Canadian Immigration Policy 1867–1990: More of the Same." Unpublished manuscript. Toronto.

Metro Toronto Police Services. (1998). *Reporting Data*. Toronto.

Mock, K. (1992). *Combatting Hate: Canadian Realities and Remedies*. Toronto: League for Human Rights, B'nai B'rith Canada.

———. (1996). *The Extent of Hate Activity and Racism in Metropolitan Toronto*. Toronto: Access and Equity Centre of the Municipality of Metropolitan Toronto. Excerpts on pages 101–102 reproduced with permission from Access and Equity Centre of the Municipality of Metropolitan Toronto and Dr. Karen Mock, League for Human Rights, B'nai B'rith, Canada.

Murray, M. (1991). *Toronto Star* (June 23).

Ng, R. (1992). "Managing Female Immigration: A Case of Institutionalized Sexism and Racism." *Canadian Women Studies* 12(3):20–23.

North Africa Journal. (1998). 18 (February 21).

Ontario Human Rights Commission. (1977). *Annual Report*. Toronto.

Ontario Ministry of Citizenship. (1989). *Access: Task Force on Access to Professions and Trades in Ontario*. Toronto.

Ornstein, M. (1997). *Report on Ethno-Racial Inequality in Metropolitan Toronto: Analysis of the 1991 Census*. Access and Equity Centre of the (former) Municipality of Metropolitan Toronto.

Pendakur, K., and R. Pendakur. (1995) *The Colour of Money: Earnings Differentials among Ethnic Groups in Canada*. Strategic Research and Analysis. Ottawa: Department of Canadian Heritage.

Pitman, W. (1977). *Now Is Not Too Late: Report on Race Relations in Metro Toronto*. Toronto: Council of Metropolitan Toronto.

Quann, D. (1979). *Racial Discrimination in Housing*. Ottawa: Canadian Council on Social Development.

Raj, S. (1980). "Some Aspects of East Indian Struggle in Canada, 1905–1947." In K. Ujimoto and G. Hirabayashi (eds.), *Visible Minorities and Multiculturalism: Asians in Canada*. Toronto: Butterworths.

Rees, T. (1991). "Racial Discrimination and Employment Agencies." *Currents: Readings in Race Relations* 7(2):16–19.

Reitz, J., L. Calzavara, and D. Dasko. (1981). *Ethnic Inequality and Segregation in Jobs*. Toronto: Centre for Urban and Community Studies, University of Toronto.

Report of the Nova Scotia Advisory Group on Race Relations. (1991). Halifax.

Rex, J., and J. Moore. (1967). *Race, Community and Conflict*. London: Oxford University Press.

Richmond, A.H. (1994). *Global Apartheid: Refugees, Racism and the New World Order*. Toronto: Oxford University Press.

Roberts, J. (1995). "Disproportionate Harm: Hate Crime in Canada: An Analysis of Recent Statistics." Ottawa: Department of Justice, Research, Statistics and Evaluation Directorate.

Robson, R., and B. Breems. (1985). *Ethnic Conflict in Vancouver*. Vancouver: B.C. Civil Liberties Association.

Ross, J.L. (1992). "Research Note: Contemporary Radical Right Wing Violence in Canada: A Quantitative Analysis." *Terrorism and Political Violence* 72(3)(Autumn).

Sampat-Mehta, R. (1984). "The First Fifty Years of South Asian Immigration: A Historical Perspective." In R. Ranungo (ed.), *South Asians in the Canadian Mosaic*. Montreal: Kala Bharati.

Samuel, T.J. (1988). *Immigration and Visible Minorities in the Year 2001: A Projection*. Ottawa: Centre for Immigration and Ethnocultural Studies.

———. (1989). "Canada's Visible Minorities and the Labour Market: Vision 2000." In O.P. Dwivedi et al., *Canada 2000: Race Relations and Public Policy*. Guelph: University of Guelph.

———. (1998). "Debunking Myths of Immigrants." *Toronto Star*, June 17.

———, and A. Karam. (1996). "Employment Equity and Visible Minorities in the Federal Workforce". Paper presented to Symposium on Immigration and Integration. Winnipeg (October 25–27).

Secretary of State. (1982). *Study of Racial Tensions in 11 Major Cities in Canada*. Ottawa: Secretary of State.

Shadd, A.S. (1989). "Institutionalized Racism and Canadian History: Note of a Black Canadian." Appendix in C. James (ed.), *Seeing Ourselves: Exploring Race, Ethnicity and Culture*. Toronto: Sheridan College.

Shepard, B. (1991). "Plain Racism: The Reaction against Oklahoma Black Immigration to the Canadian Plains." In O. McKague (ed.), *Racism in Canada*. Saskatoon: Fifth House.

Silvera, M. (1989). *Silenced*. 2nd ed. Toronto: Sister Vision Press.

———. (1993). "Speaking of Women's Lives and Imperialist Economics: Two Introductions from *Silenced*." In H. Bannerji (ed.), *The Gaze: Essays on Racism, Feminism and Politics*. Toronto: Sister Vision Press.

Small, P. (1992). "Promote Minorities, Report Tells Police." *Toronto Star* (September 11):A6.

Sunahara, A. (1981). *The Politics of Racism: The Uprooting of Japanese Canadians during the Second World War*. Toronto: James Lorimer.

Tarnopolsky, W. (1991). "Discrimination and the Law in Canada." In *Seminar on Race, Ethnic and Cultural Equity*. Vancouver: Western Judicial Centre.

Task Force on Immigration Practices and Procedures. (1981). *Domestic Workers on Employment Authorizations: A Report*. Ottawa.

Teitlebaum, B., and L. Bérubé. (1983). "La Discrimination raciale dans le logement à Montréal." *Collectiv Paroles* (Montreal) 22.

Torczyner, J.L. (1997). *Diversity, Mobility and Change: The Dynamics of Black Communities in Canada*. Montreal: McGill School of Social Work.

Toronto Star. (1992). "Minority Community Survey."

Troper, A. (1972). *Only Farmers Need Apply*. Toronto: Griffin House.

Ubale, B. (1977). *Equal Opportunity and Public Policy: A Report on Concerns of the South Asian Community regarding their Place in the Canadian Mosaic*. Toronto: Ontario Ministry of the Attorney General.

Ujimoto, K. (1988). "Racial Discrimination and Internment: Japanese in Canada." In B.S. Bolaria and P. Li (eds.), *Racial Oppression in Canada*. 2nd ed. Toronto: Garamond Press.

Vorst, J., et al. (1989). *Race, Class, Gender: Bonds and Barriers*. Toronto: Between the Lines.

Walker, J. (1980). *The History of Blacks in Canada: A Study Guide for Teachers and Students*. Ottawa: Minister of State for Multiculturalism.

———. (1985). *Race and the Historian: Some Lessons from Canadian Public Policy*. Waterloo: University of Waterloo.

Ward, P. (1978). *White Canadian Forever*. Montreal and Kingston: McGill–Queen's University Press.

Watson, P. (1990). "RCMP Chief Fears Violence if Racism Continues to Grow." *Toronto Star* (March 4):A1.

Wellman, D. (1978). *Portraits of White Racism*. Cambridge: Cambridge University Press.

Winks, R. (1971). *The Blacks in Canada: A History*. New Haven, CT: Yale University Press.

———. (1978). *The Blacks in Canada: A History*. New Haven, CT: Yale University Press.

Chapter 4

▼▼▼▼▼▼▼▼▼▼▼▼

Racism and Aboriginal Peoples

Let us have Christianity and civilization among the Indian tribes.... Let us have a wise and paternal government ... doing its utmost to help and elevate the Indian population who have been cast upon our case.... And Canada will be enabled to feel, in a truly patriotic spirit, our country has done its duty to the red man. (Alexander Morris, nineteenth-century treaty negotiator, as quoted in Cayo, 1997)

[T]he relationship that has developed over the last 400 years between Aboriginal and non-Aboriginal people in Canada ... has been ... built on a foundation of false promises — that Canada was for all intents and purposes an occupied land when the newcomers arrived from Europe; that the inhabitants were a wild, untutored and ignorant people given to strange customs and ungodly practices; that they would in time, through precept and example, come to appreciate the superior wisdom of the strangers and adopt their ways; or, alternatively, that they would be left behind in the march of progress and survive only as an anthropological footnote. (*Report of the Royal Commission on Aboriginal Peoples,* 1996)

This chapter examines the nature of Aboriginal–White relations in Canada from a historical perspective.[1] It examines the relationship from the perspective of differential values, assumptions, and beliefs and shows how the racist ideology of the dominant society continues to have a negative impact on Aboriginal peoples. Policies and practices that evolved between Aboriginal peoples and White society over the past four hundred years have been based on the assumption that Aboriginal people were inherently inferior and incapable of governing themselves. Therefore, actions deemed to be for their benefit could be carried out without their consent or involvement in design or implementation. Treaties and other agreements were, by and large, not covenants of trust and obligation but devices of state — formally acknowledged but frequently ignored.

Before the 1960s, Aboriginal people were treated as objects of policy paternalism and wardship. An assumption that has evolved since then is that they constitute an interest group, one among many in a pluralistic society. They have not been considered to have legitimate political authority as nations entitled to treatment as such.

This history of Aboriginal–White relations can perhaps be understood as occurring in four discrete periods (Miller, 1991). Apart from sporadic and intermittent Norse, Basque, and other European contacts beginning in A.D. 1000, a sustained non-Aboriginal presence has existed in Canada since the end of the fifteenth century, when European involvement focussed on developing the fisheries and the fur trade. Although there were exceptions, this early period was marked by many instances of mutual tolerance and respect.

The second period, which occurred during the eighteenth century, was dominated by trading and military alliances as France and England battled for imperial dominance over North America. This period was also marked by incidents of conflict, by increasing numbers of European immigrants, and by a steep decline in Aboriginal populations following the ravages of diseases to which they had little resistance.

The third period of displacement and assimilation began at various times throughout northern North America — in the Maritimes it had begun by the 1780s, in the interior of Quebec and Ontario after the end of the War of 1812, and on the West Coast by 1870. This period was marked by a continuing saga of expropriation, exclusion, discrimination, coercion, subjugation, oppression, deceit, theft, appropriation, and extreme regulation.

The fourth period, still in progress, has been described by the 1996 Royal Commission on Aboriginal Peoples as a period of negotiation and renewal that began after World War II and accelerated after publication of the federal government's White Paper in 1969.

INTRODUCTION

Before contact with Europeans, Aboriginal nations were fully independent and "organized in societies and occupying the land as their forefathers had done for centuries." These societies had varying degrees of sophistication. Many practised agricultural techniques and had established intricate systems of political and commercial alliances among themselves.

Most of these people had been in their locations for thousands of years; they spoke about fifty languages that have been classified into twelve families, of which six are exclusive to present-day British Columbia. The greater language diversity of the Pacific coast suggests much earlier settlement there than in the rest of the country (Dickason, 1992).

The ethnic diversity of the Aboriginal population was much greater than that of Europe. However, whether encountering the cultures of the Beothuk of Newfoundland, the Mi'kmaq of Nova Scotia, the Maliseet of New Brunswick, the Innu of northern Quebec, the Algonquin and Huron of Ontario, the Cree of Manitoba, the Chipewyan of Saskatchewan, the Sarsi or Blackfoot of Alberta, or the Haida, Nisga'a, or Tlingit of British Columbia, incoming Europeans found it difficult to recognize this diversity of economic and social organization, language, religion, and values, and labelled all Aboriginal peoples as "Indians" (Frideres, 1993). This inability to rec-ognize the huge diversity among Aboriginal peoples had reverberations throughout the long history of Aboriginal–White relations.

"DISCOVERY"

When the Europeans arrived in "the New World," they attempted to justi-fy their assumption of political sovereignty and title to Aboriginal lands on the basis of a reinterpretation of the doctrine of discovery. This doctrine was based on the notion of *terra nullius* — a Latin term referring to empty, es-sentially barren, and uninhabited land. Under norms of international law at the time of contact, the European "discovery" of such land gave the dis-covering nation immediate sovereignty and all rights and title to the land. Over the course of time, however, the concept of *terra nullius* was extend-ed to include lands that were not in possession of "civilized" peoples or that were not being put to proper, "civilized" use. Europeans were therefore legally justified in assuming full, sovereign ownership of the "discovered" lands, since Aboriginal peoples could not possibly have the civilized and Christian attributes that would enable them to assert sovereign ownership. Over time, these ethnocentric notions gained currency and were given fur-ther legitimacy by various court decisions, such as *St. Catharines Milling and Lumber Co. v. The Queen* (1887): "To maintain their position the appel-lants must assume that the Indians have a regular form of government, whereas nothing is more clear than that they have no government and no organization, and cannot be regarded as a nation capable of holding lands."

While European notions of property and government were used to jus-tify appropriating Aboriginal lands, a further self-serving justification was presented that argued that Europeans would use the land more productive-ly, produce a greater quantity of conveniences, and produce far greater op-portunities to work by expanding the division of labour (Tully, 1995).

These kinds of arguments, which distorted the reality of the situation, converted cultural *differences* into *inferiorities* and continue to have impact on government policy and court proceedings up to the present day.

Aboriginal belief systems, cultures, and forms of social organization dif-fer substantially from European patterns. These differences continue to be at the heart of the present struggle of Aboriginal peoples to reclaim posses-sion not only of their traditional lands, but also of their traditional cultures and forms of political organization.

CONTACT AND CO-OPERATION

The Aboriginal peoples' initial contacts with Europeans were through par-ticipation and partnerships in the fisheries and the fur trade. Until the eight-eenth century, the links between Aboriginal and non-Aboriginal societies were primarily commercial. They did not interfere in a major way with long-standing Aboriginal patterns of pursuing their livelihood and, in some ways, actually reinforced Aboriginal strengths in hunting, fishing, trapping, trading, and transporting. This commerce also appears to have strengthened Aboriginal social organization, enhancing the power of hereditary chiefs and generally enriching Aboriginal culture.

The social, cultural, and political differences between the two societies were respected, by and large. Each was regarded as distinct and autonomous, left to govern its own internal affairs but co-operating in areas of mutual interest. The relationship was characterized by considerable interdependence, a complementarity of roles, and some mutual benefit. However, trade also had destructive consequences. The first and most serious were epidemics of European origin, which began to decimate the Aboriginal population.

MILITARY ALLIANCES AND COMMERCIAL CO-OPERATION IN THE EIGHTEENTH CENTURY

The second phase of Aboriginal–White relations, which occurred in the 1700s, was dominated by a combination of commercial partnerships and military alliances as the French and English struggled for imperial dominance over North America.

This period marked a process of change that reflected imperial ambitions tempered by cautious realism. Although the Europeans preferred some form of sovereign control over the Aboriginal peoples, they often had to settle for a mixture of trading agreements, alliances, or simple neutrality. Similarly, while Aboriginal nations might have wished to assert their total independence, in practice they often found themselves reliant on European trade and military protection. In 1763, the Treaty of Paris ended the Seven Years' War and New France was ceded to Britain. The policy of the new colonial government was based on the Royal Proclamation of 1763, in which King George III instructed his colonial governments to ensure that Aboriginal peoples should not be disturbed in their lands, "but that, if at any time, any of the said Indians should be inclined to dispose of said land, the same shall be purchased for Us, in our Name, at some public Meeting or Assembly of the said Indians, to be held for that purpose" (*Report of the Royal Commission on Aboriginal Peoples*, 1996: Vol. 1, App. D).

Aboriginal–English relations had stabilized to the point where they could be seen to be grounded in two fundamental principles (Glavin, 1998). Under the first principle, while Aboriginal peoples were regarded as British subjects, they also were generally recognized as autonomous political units capable of having treaty relations with the Crown. The second principle acknowledged that Aboriginal nations were entitled to the territories in their possession, unless or until they ceded them to others.

The Crown therefore guaranteed that any Aboriginal lands not previously ceded or purchased by the British Crown were reserved for Aboriginal peoples, and that these lands could not be purchased or settled without the special leave and license of the Crown.

Paradoxically, however, the Royal Proclamation referred to Aboriginal lands as Crown lands, despite their prior occupation by Aboriginal nations. Thus, while setting out new rules for Aboriginal land cessions, the proclamation retained the colonial assumptions of the discovery doctrine.

DISPLACEMENT AND ASSIMILATION

The third phase of Aboriginal–White relations began at various times throughout North America during the eighteenth century. The past relationship of mutually beneficial co-operation and practical accommodation changed to a pervasive and sustained attack on the respectful, egalitarian nation-to-nation principles. Confronted with a powerful and growing colonial society, the strength of the Aboriginal nations declined. Colonial governments appeared to have neither the will nor the means to counter the illegal occupation of the remaining lands of the indigenous population. Encroachment became more common as the colonial economic base changed to an emphasis on agriculture and a decline in the importance of the fur trade and the traditional harvesting economy. In addition, Britain's normalization of relations with the United States after the War of 1812 no longer required its cultivation of Aboriginal peoples as military allies.

SOCIAL DARWINISM

Europeans' initial impressions of Aboriginal peoples as "savage" were reinforced by the scientific racism and Social Darwinism of the late nineteenth and early twentieth centuries. These views were reflected in many legal provisions concerning Aboriginal peoples, up to and including the 1951 federal Indian Act.

To justify their actions against Aboriginal peoples, the European settlers relied on a belief system that judged the original inhabitants to be inferior. Originally based on religious and philosophical grounds, this sense of moral and cultural superiority was further buttressed by pseudo-scientific theories of Social Darwinism that rested ultimately on ethnocentric and racist premises.

The isolationist–assimilationist strategy toward Aboriginal peoples was justified by beliefs in "progress" and in the evolutionary development of human cultures from lesser to greater states of civilization. The long-standing Western belief in Europe's racial and cultural superiority were given a scientific veneer to justify existing assumptions. This was accompanied by a belief in the destiny of European cultures to expand across North America and take over the whole land base.

Western society was seen to be at the forefront of evolutionary development, and Aboriginal peoples lagged far behind. As a result, Aboriginal peoples needed to be guided — even directed — to catch up, in a process of accelerated evolution. Consequently, a whole philosophy and belief system justified the establishment of unilateral decision-making and a centralized administrative system to merge the Aboriginal peoples into Western society.

The belief in the superiority of European culture and the desire to "civilize" and Christianize other cultures went hand in hand with the political and economic expansion of European imperialism. The characterization of Aboriginal peoples as "savage" and biologically inferior enabled Europeans to remain blind to the complexity of Aboriginal cultures, customs, beliefs, and traditions. At the same time, it permitted the imposition of European values and the control of Aboriginal peoples by outsiders.

CHRISTIANIZATION

The important role of the Christian church in supporting the systematic annihilation of Aboriginal values, norms, religions, and language has been well documented. The Jesuits and other missionaries, who believed that Aboriginal peoples should not be left in their "inferior" natural state, considered it their duty to replace Aboriginal cultures with Christian beliefs, values, rituals, and practices (Bolaria and Li, 1988).

There was general agreement that the propagation of Christianity entitled Europeans to intervene in the lives of the Aboriginal peoples and to exercise force, if necessary, to achieve this end. Combined with the legal doctrine of territorial rights of discovery, the notion of a Christian's duty to evangelize and civilize "Indians" provided a virtually open mandate for European colonization (Dyck, 1991).

The role of the churches was to "civilize and educate Native people," and the churches were given Aboriginal land to undertake this task (Powless, 1985). To the Jesuits, their mission was a war against satanic forces. A strong and enduring component of European conceptions of the inferiority of Aboriginal peoples was the conviction that they were heathen. As a result of this conviction, Europeans determined that it was their religious duty to convert Aboriginal peoples to Christianity.

Since most Whites viewed all aspects of tribal life and organization as culturally and morally inferior, missionaries made efforts to eliminate the matrilineal customs of Aboriginal societies and to promote the norms of the dominant European patrilineal society (Ng, 1993; Bienvenue and Goldstein, 1985). The perceived differences between men and women were used by nineteenth-century missionaries to organize the Aboriginal peoples into Euopean male and female roles. For example, a man's place was in the economic, food-production world, while a woman's was in the domestic, food-preparation world. This altered the prime economic unit from the tribe to the European version of the family — the nuclear family (Clubine, 1991:16) — which led to a deconstruction of traditional male–female relations among Aboriginal people and a reconstruction into male–female roles appropriate to and approved by colonial society (Ng, 1993:54).

CASE STUDY 4.1

RESIDENTIAL SCHOOLS

One of the most powerful examples of racist ideology and practice in Canada was the treatment of Aboriginal children in residential schools in many provinces.

Education was considered the most effective means to achieve the transformation of Aboriginal children into European–Canadians. Residential schools represent one of the starker examples of Canada's paternalism toward Aboriginal people, its civilizing strategy, and its stern assimilative determination. As a solution to the Indian "problem," education would, as Minister of Indian Affairs Frank Oliver predicted in 1908, "elevate the Indian from his condition of savagery" and "make him a self-supporting member of the state, and eventually a citizen in good standing."

The residential school system was an attempt by successive governments to appropriate and shape the future of Canadia's Aboriginal peoples by removing thousands of children from their homes and community and placing them in the care of strangers.

The common wisdom of the day maintained that Aboriginal children had to be rescued from their "evil surroundings" and "prejudicial influences." They should, therefore, be isolated from parents, family, and community, and kept constantly within "the circle of civilized conditions." Residential schools were conceived as an all-encompassing environment of resocialization. The schools were seen as a bridge from the Aboriginal world into non-Aboriginal communities. That passage was marked out in clear stages: separation, socialization, and finally assimilation through enfranchisement.

Residential schools were operated by missionary societies under the aegis of the federal government. Through a process of coercive assimilation, supported by the government agencies and churches that ran the schools, Aboriginal children were forbidden to speak their language, to practise their traditions and customs, and to learn about their history.

The residential schools suffered from appalling mismanagement and inferior educational services. Christian missionaries were more concerned with saving souls than with literacy education. Few had the qualification to teach. The inadequate education ensured that Aboriginal children could not in fact assimilate or compete on any basis of equity with their non-Aboriginal counterparts. The focus was merely on the acquisition of practical skills in order to function at the very bottom levels of the economic mainstream.

Underfunding (which resulted in an inadequate diet), overwork in non-academic activities to sustain the "self-supporting activities" of the institution, and overcrowding contributed to rampant ill health and tuberculosis among the children. This situation caused such a high death rate that *Saturday Night* magazine concluded, "Even war seldom shows as large a percentage of fatalities as does the education system we have imposed upon our Indian wards" (November 23, 1907). At one point it was estimated that "fifty percent of the children who passed through these schools did not live to benefit from the education which they had received therein" (Scott, 1914).

(continued)

CASE STUDY 4.1 *(continued)*

The persistent and unrelieved neglect of the children — hungry, malnourished, ill-clothed, dying of tuberculosis, and overworked — was compounded by harsh discipline, cruelty, and physical and sexual abuse. The system of transformation from "savage" to "civilized" was suffused with not just strict discipline and punishment but with a violent savagery. Children were frequently beaten severely with whips, rods, and fists; they were chained and shackled, bound hand and foot, and locked in closets, basements, and bathrooms, and they had their heads shaved or hair closely cropped.

In the 1960s, many residential schools were shut down; the last one closed in 1988. However, the abuses perpetrated in these schools continue to haunt the present.

> The survivors of the Indian residential school system have, in many cases, continued to have their lives shaped by the experiences in these schools. Persons who attended these schools continue to struggle with their identity after years of being taught to hate themselves and the culture. The residential school led to disruption in the transference of parenting skills from one generation to the next. Without these skills, many survivors had had difficulty raising their own children. In residential schools, they learned that adults often exert power and control through abuse. The lessons learned in childhood are often repeated in adulthood, with the result that many survivors of the residential school system often inflict abuse on their own children. (Ing, 1991)

Haig-Brown (1988), who documented the experiences of several Aboriginal people who were forced to attend residential schools over a period of sixty years, suggested that the cultural oppression and ethnocentric indoctrination of the educational process were a microcosm of the domination of Euro-Canadian culture over all aspects of Aboriginal life. Cummins (1992:3) stated that it is not unreasonable to conclude that one of the central goals of these schools was to "prepare children of subordinated groups for their status in life by rekindling shame from one generation to the next."

Psychologist Roland Chrisjohn defined the residential school "as an institution formed to make war on First Nations languages, religions and societies." In extensive interviews conducted with Aboriginal students, he found that those who attended these schools felt that the experience had deeply affected their sexual relations, their ability as parents, and their feelings about their religion and culture and had contributed to alcohol abuse, high levels of suicide, and wife abuse (Wilson, 1991).

According to Stanley McKay, a Cree–Ojibwa from Manitoba who is the first Aboriginal moderator of the United Church of Canada, residential schools collaborated in the cultural genocide of Aboriginal peoples. He considers his experiences in residential school as a form of incarceration: "My spirit was not broken but my anger is there. It is something that should not have happened. Some people were desperately scarred and wounded" (Roberts, 1993:A1).

(continued)

CASE STUDY 4.1 *(continued)*

The Assembly of First Nations, in its study of the impact of residential schools (1994), described Aboriginal children's experiences in terms of their emotional, mental, physical, and spiritual impact. The process of cultural **genocide** toward Aboriginal children was carried out by having their feelings ridiculed, their creativity and independent thinking stifled, their bodily needs ignored or violated, and their ways of life denied (Barman, 1996).

The residential schools did incredible damage. They resulted in loss of life, the denigration of culture, the destruction of self-respect and self-esteem, and the torture of families. The impact of these traumas on succeeding generations is overwhelming, as is the enormity of the cultural triumphalism that lay behind the enterprise.

Not only were residential schools an abject failure in assimilation, but they further marginalized generations of men and women not only from the Canadian mainstream but also from their own home environments.

Aboriginal peoples, deemed to be inferior, were schooled for inferiority, and as a result they indeed largely did end up at the bottom ranks of Canadian society. Outwardly espousing assimilation through education, the federal government provided neither the leadership nor the resources to achieve any other goal than the self-affirming prophecy inherent in racist rhetoric (Barman, 1996).

The doctrine of Euro-Canadian "superiority" and Aboriginal "inferiority" over several centuries has become "a created body of theory and practice" in which, for many generations, there has been a sustained social and material investment (Dyck, 1991).

LEGISLATION

As British imperial power became firmly established in northern North America following the War of 1812, the drive to assimilation took on a new intensity. This was the beginning of the great land-cession treaties, by which the British sought to extinguish the limited land rights they had previously recognized.

The displacement and assimilation of Aboriginal peoples throughout the nineteenth and early twentieth centuries was motivated largely by economics and was the most significant factor in developing and maintaining the reserve system (Bolaria and Li, 1988). The commercial economy, based on the fur trade and other natural resources, was pushed from centre stage and replaced by the drive for expansionary settlement and for agricultural and, later, industrial production. Aboriginal peoples clearly stood in the settlers' way, for they inhabited and claimed title to vast stretches of land.

The fundamental differences in world views can be seen in the very different ways in which the treaty process was approached. Aboriginal conceptions of how relations in human societies and with the natural world should be conducted assumed a relationship of equality among nations, in which each nation retained its autonomy and distinctiveness, each nation had a separate as well as a shared land base, and the natural world was respected (Dockstator, 1993).

The Aboriginal world view was of a universal sacred order made up of compacts and kinship relations among human beings, other living beings, and the creator. This concept of sharing with other forms of life is alien to Judeo-Christian thought. So is the Aboriginal position that they were not granted the right to give up their land. Aboriginal systems reflected an ideology of land use, not of individual land ownership. The Crown, to claim absolute title, would have to obtain surrender from past generations as well as those of the future. As far as Aboriginal peoples were concerned, when they signed treaties, they were not giving up their lands but sharing them (Dickason, 1992).

Aboriginal societies therefore operated on the assumption that they were maintaining a nation-to-nation relationship when they signed treaties. They expected that treaties would grow more valuable with time, as the parties came to know each other better, to trust one another, and to make the most of their treaty relationships.

Governments and courts in Canada, however, often considered treaties as instruments of surrender rather than as compacts of co-existence and mutual benefit. Property law, as created in liberal democracies such as Canada, severely restricts Aboriginal peoples' ability to institutionalize and render into legal form their unique relations with the land. The Canadian legal system has not been able to embrace Aboriginal ideas of tradition, of what has often been referred to as natural law. Canadian laws, based on the principle of adversarial relations, have not recognized Aboriginal customary laws, which are based on the principles of relations and consensus (Monture-Angus, 1995). These fundamentally different understandings have characterized all of the treaties.

The economic ambitions of the settlers became increasingly incompatible with the rights and ways of life of the Aboriginal peoples, on whose land this new development was to take place. Throughout the nineteenth century and into the twentieth, the British Crown and then the new Dominion of Canada entered into treaties in Ontario, the prairie provinces, and parts of the North, under which Indians agreed to the creation of reserves in exchange for sharing their lands and resources with the newcomers.

While the segregationist policy of creating reserves was being enacted, it was at the same time being supplemented by assimilationist policies, such as the 1857 Act to Encourage the Gradual Civilization of the Indian Tribes in this Province. It provided for the voluntary enfranchisement — the release from Indian status — of individuals of good character, as determined by a board of examiners. Upon enfranchisement, volunteers would no longer be considered "Indians" and would acquire instead the rights common to ordinary non-Aboriginal settlers. In addition, they would take a portion of tribal land with them.

This enfranchisement policy was a direct attack on the integrity and land base of Aboriginal communities. At the same time it was an assimilative strategy to move educated Indians away from the "backward" culture of the reserves. Aboriginal communities strongly opposed the Gradual Civilization Act and largely succeeded because only one man is known to have volunteered for enfranchisement in the two decades following passage of the act.

The federal Enfranchisement Act of 1869 interfered with tribal self-government by establishing the supremacy of bureaucratic authority over traditional leaders and restricted the jurisdiction of band councils to that of municipal governments. The act defined an "Indian" as possessing at least one-quarter Indian blood and expanded the differentiation between officially registered "status" Indians and non-registered "non-status" Indians. Indian status could also be lost through obtaining a university degree. In addition, Indian women married to non-Indian men lost their Indian status, thus maintaining European assumptions about women taking on the identity of their husbands. This discriminatory section of the Indian Act remained in place until 1985, surviving several court challenges (McMillan, 1995).

The 1876 Indian Act further strengthened the 1869 act's provisions instituting elected rather than traditional band councils. This act also positioned Aboriginal people as "wards" of the federal Department of Indian Affairs. Although the Indian Act was amended many times and underwent a major revision in 1951, its fundamental purpose was assimilation.

Meanwhile, as the assimilative and relocation policies were in force, Aboriginal peoples were starving, the Métis were struggling for recognition, and land claims were being ignored. The notion of accommodation with "savages" was unthinkable, at least in the realm of practical politics (Dickason, 1992). The Canadian government could disregard the concerns of Aboriginal people because they were considered inferior — they were "others," strangers.

From the moment that the federal government assumed jurisdiction over Aboriginal peoples, Canada's relationship with them has been based on cultural, social, economic, and political oppression. It has been characterized by an endless struggle against cultural annihilation and poverty (Duclos, 1990). Aboriginal peoples were displaced from the land that formed the basis of their culture, their way of life, and their livelihood. They were placed on reserves to provide land for newly arrived European immigrants and settlers from the United States.

Although the reserves were located in areas that the various tribes had long occupied, they were much smaller than the groups' previous territories. Land on the reserves could not be disposed of without the permission of the federal government. Aboriginal people were expected to survive on the reserves and not to rely on the resources or services available in settler communities. Traditional Aboriginal governments were supplemented by band councils that had little power or influence (Bienvenue and Goldstein, 1985).

CASE STUDY 4.2

THE INDIAN ACT

The Indian Act, first passed in 1876, is the legislation that has intruded on the lives and cultures of status Indians more than any other law. Though amended repeatedly, the act's fundamental provisions have scarcely changed. They give the state powers that range from defining how one is born or naturalized into "Indian" status to administering the estate of an Aboriginal person after death.

The 1876 Indian Act rested on the principle "that the aborigines are to be kept in a condition of tutelage and treated as wards or children of the State" (Department of the Interior, 1877: xiv). The act gave Parliament control over Indian political structures, landholding patterns, and resource and economic development. It covered almost every important aspect of the daily lives of Aboriginal peoples on reserves. The overall effect was to subject Aboriginal people to the almost unfettered rule of federal bureaucrats. The act imposed non-Aboriginal forms on traditional governance, landholding practices, and cultural practices.

The Indian Act provided a means of removing political sovereignty from indigenous people by introducing a system of indirect rule and segregation (Fleras and Elliott, 1992). The sweeping regulations under the act included prohibitions against owning land. Early clauses, which have only in recent years been eliminated, controlled every aspect of the lives and lifestyles of Aboriginal peoples, from denying them the right to vote to prohibiting them from purchasing and consuming alcohol (Bienvenue and Goldstein, 1985).

For example, the Indian Act of 1876 and various amendments up to the 1930s decreed that:

- The majority of Aboriginal people living on reserves could not vote in federal elections. (This was not changed until 1960.) Those who wished to have the franchise were forced to give up their status and lose all the benefits conferred by the Indian Act, including rights to land, homes, and community (Sharzer, 1985).
- Aboriginal people could not manage their own reserve lands or money and were under the supervision of federally appointed Indian Agents.
- All chiefs and band councillors were to be elected for three-year terms. Exclusionary and sexist, the act also decreed that only men were to be allowed to vote in band elections. (Aboriginal women were not given the right to vote in band elections until the 1951 Indian Act.)
- Protected reserve lands were to be converted to provincial lands upon the enfranchisement of an Indian.
- Aboriginal peoples did not have power to decide whether non-Indians could reside on or use reserve lands.
- Public authorities were given the power (in 1911) to expropriate reserve land without a surrender, as long as the expropriation was for the purpose of public works.
- No Aboriginal peoples could develop land without the agents' consent.
- For an Indian to be intoxicated on or off the reserve was an offence punishable by one month in jail.

(continued)

CASE STUDY 4.2 *(continued)*

- The sale of agricultural products was prohibited without official permission.

In 1885, a pass system was instituted by the federal government, prohibiting Aboriginal people from leaving their reserve without the written authorization of their agent. This move was designed to restrict parental visits to residential schools. The Indian Act was also amended to authorize the arrest of Indians found on reserves other than their home reserve. This amendment, supported by missionaries, had the effect of prohibiting communal sun dances, thirst dances, and ghost dances. This ban was extended to all forms of Aboriginal dances in 1906.

Another example of the concerted attack on Aboriginal cultural practices was the 1884 amendments to the Indian Act that banned the West Coast potlatch and other ceremonies. Potlatch "giveaways" were deemed incompatible with Euro-Canadian economic practices and the concept of private property. Using ritual, ceremony, and celebration, the potlatch provided a central organizing framework in which new leaders were installed, wealth was distributed, names were given and recorded, political councils were held and decisions made, history instruction was provided, and spiritual guidance was given. The Aboriginal peoples were not only denied an opportunity to participate in an important ceremonial festival but lost control over their political life (Ponting and Gibbons, 1980).

The Indian Act of 1927, in recognizing the failures and inadequacies of the coercive assimilationist strategy, tried to bolster it by providing even stronger measures to intervene in and control the affairs of Aboriginal societies. This included further efforts to develop an agricultural economy, in the expectation that social and cultural change would follow in its wake. In responding to Aboriginal political organizations pursuing land issues, especially in British Columbia, the act also made "raising a fund or providing money for the prosecution of any claim" a crime unless permission was obtained.

By the beginning of the twentieth century, the administration of "Indian affairs" had assumed a format that continued with few changes until after World War II. The Indian Act provided the Department of Indian Affairs with exclusive jurisdiction over Aboriginal people and gave its officers the authority to supervise most facets of their lives.

In summary, the Canadian government, through the Indian Act, imposed a form of institutionalized racism in the relationship between Canada and its Aboriginal peoples (Frideres, 1993; Bolaria and Li, 1988). The act was designed to promote coercive assimilation, in which Aboriginal peoples were expected to adopt the cultural attitudes and norms of the dominant culture and give up their own cultural traditions, histories, values, customs, and language (Richardson, 1993; Bolaria and Li, 1988). Aboriginal social and political institutions were systematically dismantled.

The Indian Act also set out to define "who was an Indian." Yet, as Daniel Raunet pointed out, "to ask the question in legal terms is in itself discriminatory.... People do not need legislation to know their origin or place on this earth" (in Ducharme, 1986). For the White lawgiver, the Indian was a person registered in an "Indian Register." Indian women who married non-status Indian men simply

(continued)

> **CASE STUDY 4.2** (*continued*)
>
> lost their status. These legal definitions relating to identity totally ignored the fact that Aboriginal peoples were not a monolithic group but represented extraordinarily diverse and distinct populations with different customs, traditions, histories, cultures, and languages (Ducharme, 1986).
>
>   The Indian Act persists as an essentially repressive instrument of containment (Fleras and Elliott, 1996). Founded on the ethnocentric certainties of the nineteenth century, it continues to interfere profoundly in the lives, cultures, and communities of First Nations peoples today.

In summary, throughout this period of displacement and assimilation, Aboriginal peoples were denied access to their traditional territories and often forced to move to new locations selected by colonial authorities. They were also displaced socially and culturally by being subjected to intense missionary activity and the establishment of schools that undermined Aboriginal parents' ability to pass on traditional values to their children. They had imposed upon them male-oriented Victorian values, while traditional activities such as significant dances and other ceremonies were attacked and made unlawful. They were also displaced politically, forced by colonial laws to abandon or at least disguise traditional governing structures and processes in favour of municipal-style institutions.

NEGOTIATION AND RENEWAL

After World War II, there was growing public and international concern about the racist treatment of Canada's Aboriginal peoples. Although the 1951 revisions to the Indian Act removed some of the more coercive instruments, the act retained its assimilative intent: the end of Aboriginal culture. Civilization was to be encouraged but not so blatantly forced on Aboriginal peoples (Miller, 1991).

     The 1969 White Paper on Indian Policy, introduced by Minister of Indian Affairs Jean Chrétien, argued that Canada's Indians were disadvantaged simply because they enjoyed a unique legal status. It therefore recommended the abolition of Indian status. Indians as Indians would therefore disappear and become just another element in a multicultural Canada (Miller, 1991). The controversy and opposition that the White Paper provoked also stimulated political mobilization and the reinforcement of a shared common history of "Indianness" — a history of being subjected to a form of tutelage that was intended to take Aboriginal people out of their existing social groups and to force them into mainstream Canadian society (Dyck, 1991).

     Although the federal government backed down from the White Paper, the paper's underlying philosophy continued to animate federal

CASE STUDY 4.3

THE PHYSICAL DISPLACEMENT AND RELOCATION OF ABORIGINAL PEOPLES

The displacement of Aboriginal peoples often took the form of deliberate initiatives by governments to move particular Aboriginal communities. Governments saw relocation as an apparent solution to a number of problems. Aboriginal lands with valuable resources were often expropriated when provincial and federal government agencies required them for the building of railways, roads, and dams (Bienvenue and Goldstein, 1985). The Métis in Saskatchewan, the Cree along James Bay, and many other Aboriginal groups were uprooted and relocated at the convenience and for the economic gain of various Canadian governments (Ducharme, 1986). In Manitoba and Saskatchewan, band councils claim to have lost over a million acres as a result of the government expropriation and sale of reserve lands (Kellough, 1980).

If Aboriginal communities appeared to be undernourished, then they could be moved to where game was more plentiful. If they were suffering severe health problems, they could be placed in new communities where health-care services and other amenities were available. Addressing Aboriginal medical and welfare problems in this way also provided an opportunity for governments to achieve their social objective of assimilation. If Aboriginal people were thought to be indolent, the new communities would provide education and training facilities. If they were in the way of expanding agricultural frontiers or happened to occupy land needed for urban settlements, they could be moved "for their own protection." And, if their traditional lands held natural resources — minerals to be exploited, forests to be cut, rivers to be drained — they could be relocated "in the national interest" (*Report of the Royal Commission on Aboriginal Peoples, 1996*).

Justified by this attitude of paternalism and employing the discourse of democratic racism, the practice of relocation by the Canadian government was widespread. Decisions were made with little or no consultation, and Aboriginal communities were relocated on short notice. Relocation has been described as the "last major pre-liberal policy thrust through which a distinctly paternalistic inclination can be seen." Many relocations were carried out to ease the administration and costs of government services. Examples include the centralization of the Mi'kmaq of Nova Scotia in the 1940s, and the movement of the Gwa'Sala and 'Nakwaxda'xw of British Columbia in 1964, the Mushuau Innu of Labrador to Davis Inlet in 1967, the Inuit of Hebron in Labrador, the Sayisi Dene in northern Labrador, and the Yukon First Nations.

Addressing the perceived needs of Aboriginal peoples often involved moving them "back to the land" from a more or less settled existence. Administrators attempted to encourage Aboriginal peoples to resume or relearn what was considered the traditional way of life. This approach was directed particularly at the Inuit. For the government, this paternalism was linked to another political motivation: the need to assert Canadian sovereignty in the High Arctic, which would be enhanced by effective occupation. The "first official Eskimo relocation project" involved the dispersal of Baffin Island Inuit to Devon Island between 1934 and 1947.

(continued)

CASE STUDY 4.3 *(continued)*

In a research study for the Royal Commission on Aboriginal Peoples, it was noted, "The analogy of human pawns being moved on an Arctic chessboard is perhaps never more strikingly illustrated than in the instance of Devon Island, of relocation of a small group of Inuit to form new sites in succession, as it suited the experimental interests of the Hudson's Bay Company, and set against the background of the geopolitical interests of the State" (*Report of the Royal Commission on Aboriginal Peoples, 1996*). Other Inuit relocations motivated by the same rationale included Nueltin Lake (1949), Henik Lake (1957–58), Rankin Inlet and Whale Cove, Banks Island (1951–52) and Baffin Island throughout the 1950s and 1960s.

Development relocation was carried out in the "public interest" for the purposes of agricultural expansion, urban development, mineral exploitation and hydroelectric power generation. Examples include:

- The Saugeen Ojibwa on Ontario's Bruce Peninsula throughout the latter half of the nineteenth century; they were moved to the Cape Croker Reserve to make way for the agricultural needs of European settlers.
- The Songhees, a Coast Salish people who were relocated to land near Esquimault to make way for the growth of Victoria, British Columbia, in 1910.
- The Métis community of Ste. Madeleine, Manitoba, which was relocated in the late 1930s to make room for cattle.
- The Ouje-Bougnoumou Cree of Quebec, who have been moved seven times since 1927, all to meet the needs of mining companies.
- The Churchill Falls project in Labrador, Alcan's Kemano hydroelectric project on the Fraser River, the Grand Rapids hydroelectric project on the Saskatchewan River, the Talston River Hydroelectric System in the Northwest Territories, and the northern Manitoba hydroelectric system resulted in the flooding of Aboriginal lands and forced relocation.

The impact of these relocations was disastrous. Not only did they impose dramatic changes on the Aboriginal way of life, family, and community structure, but they also resulted in the loss of economic livelihood and the swift establishment of welfare dependency, increased family violence, and a variety of social and health problems.

policy for years to come. The 1984 Nielson Task Force also provoked similar opposition when it recommended the dissolution of the Department of Indian Affairs and the devolution of the department's responsibilities to the provinces and band councils. The legacy of distrust was maintained as avenues of redress continued to be tightly controlled and regulated. Throughout the 1970s and 1980s, the federal government was generally not prepared to move beyond the limited strategies of administrative decentralization of programs and services and the granting of municipal-style governing powers to community-based Aboriginal governments.

There continue to the present day to be differing perspectives and objectives regarding self-government. On the one hand, Aboriginal leaders continue to push strongly for self-government as an inherent right, arguing that its roots lie in Aboriginal existence before contact. On the other hand, the notion of "existing Aboriginal and treaty rights" as recognized in Canada's constitution has, from a non-Aboriginal perspective, tended to be limited to those rights already recognized and defined by institutions such as the courts. The only requirement of government, therefore, is to enumerate and define them more precisely. From an Aboriginal perspective, however, the term includes many rights that have not yet been defined or recognized by non-Aboriginal society (Assembly of First Nations, 1994).

One of the more obvious criticisms of the present land-claims process is the federal government's conflict of interest in attempting to deal with these matters. On the one hand, the federal government has a fiduciary or trust-like responsibility toward Aboriginal people to act in their best interests, while on the other hand it seeks to act in its own best interest — to minimize its legal and financial obligations. It is in the position of being both judge and jury in dealing with claims against itself. It sets the criteria, decides what claims are acceptable, and controls the entire negotiating process, including funding support (Assembly of First Nations, 1994).

As a result of the criteria, processes, and costs, very few settlements have been reached. Aboriginal peoples are consequently questioning the viability of the claims mechanism as a means of obtaining their constitutionally protected Aboriginal and treaty rights. They see their political relationship with Canada as not much more than an extension of the racist and paternalistic attitude toward Aboriginal peoples that characterized Canada's colonial traditions.

With so few land claims being settled, the 1990s witnessed a number of acts of civil disobedience and conflict as a consequence of Aboriginal peoples' growing frustration with the process. Violent confrontations occurred in Akwesasne on the Quebec–Ontario border, Oka in Quebec, Gustafsen Lake in British Columbia, and Ipperwash in Ontario.

At the same time, however, there has been some movement toward a greater understanding and recognition of Aboriginal aspirations. It no longer seems so important that Aboriginal societies follow the evolutionary path toward assimilation within non-Aboriginal society.

Of particular significance is the establishment of the Tungavila Federation of Nunavut in 1999, after twenty-five years of negotiation. Covering over 350 000 square kilometres in the Eastern Arctic — a fifth of Canada's land mass — it comprises about 20 000 people, of whom 85 percent are Inuit. The territory will be self-governing, though not with the full powers of a province. The agreement provides financial compensation of $1.14 billion to be paid out over fourteen years, $13 million for a training trust fund, and royalties from mineral development (Frideres, 1993).

A second significant example is the 1998 treaty with the Nisga'a people in northwestern British Columbia. The first treaty in British Columbia between an Aboriginal people and government in almost 140 years, the treaty allows a form of government elected only by the Nisga'a people, with authority to make laws on culture, language, employment, public works, land use, traffic, and marriage. It will provide for health, child welfare, and education services, a police force that meets provincial standards, and a court system with jurisdiction over Nisga'a laws on Nisga'a lands. Non-Nisga'a people will be subject to the Nisga'a law on the Nisga'a lands, but they will also have the option of using the provincial court system.

The treaty gives the Nisga'a government power to tax Nisga'a citizens on Nisga'a land and to impose property taxes on non-Nisga'a residents. Income and sales tax exemptions that now exist under the Indian Act will be eliminated. The Canadian Charter of Rights and Freedoms and the Criminal Code remain paramount, and all Nisga'a regulations dealing with wildlife, the environment and all other areas must meet federal and provincial regulations. The treaty includes provisions that the deal is final and that future generations cannot demand more. The Nisga'a have agreed to give up historic rights granted them under the Indian Act (*Globe and Mail*, 1998). Unlike any other agreement, the treaty combines the Nisga'a land claims and recognition of a central Nisga'a Nation government, with powers to tax, regulate land use, and administer a justice system.

POPULATION

At the time of initial sustained contact with Europeans, the Aboriginal population of North America was estimated to be at least 500 000 (Dickason, 1992). The diseases brought to North America by Europeans from the late 1400s onward, such as smallpox, tuberculosis, influenza, scarlet fever, and measles, reduced the population drastically. Armed hostilities and starvation also claimed many lives, to the point that in 1871, the Aboriginal population was estimated to be about 100 000.

Since the 1940s, however, there has been a rapid growth in the Aboriginal population. Between 1981 and 1991, the on-reserve Indian population of Canada increased by one third, the off-reserve Indian population more than doubled, and the Inuit population increased by one third (Frideres, 1993). Aboriginal birth rates were much higher than those of the larger Canadian population, but even more important was the rapid decline of the infant mortality rate.

Defining and measuring Aboriginal ethnicity and the size and composition of Canada's Aboriginal population is not an easy task. Demographically, the Aboriginal population is quite different from the rest of the Canadian population: it is much younger and faster-growing, with fertility rates almost twice those of non-Aboriginal people and life expectancy rates averaging ten years less than those of the average Canadian (Norris, 1996).

Considerable discussion exists regarding the limitations and undercoverage of Canada's Aboriginal peoples in census data. Table 4.1 presents the most recently published data source of the current Aboriginal population by ethnicity and by province. Today, Canada's Aboriginal population has

Table 4.1

TOTAL ABORIGINAL POPULATION BY GROUP, 1996 CENSUS OF CANADA

Jurisdiction	Total Population	Aboriginal Population			
		Total Aboriginal[a]	North American Indian[b,c]	Métis[b]	Inuit[b]
Canada	28 528 125	799 010	544 290	210 190	41 080
Newfoundland	547 160	14 205	5 430	4 685	4 265
Prince Edward Island	132 855	950	825	120	15
Nova Scotia	899 970	12 380	11 340	860	210
New Brunswick	729 635	10 250	9 180	975	120
Quebec	7 045 080	71 415	47 600	16 075	8 300
Ontario	10 642 790	141 525	118 830	22 790	1 300
Manitoba	1 100 295	128 685	82 990	46 195	360
Saskatchewan	976 615	111 245	75 205	36 535	190
Alberta	2 669 195	122 840	72 645	50 745	795
British Columbia	3 689 755	139 655	113 315	26 750	815
Yukon	30 655	6 175	5 530	565	110
Northwest Territories	64 120	39 690	11 400	3 895	24 600

[a] The total of North American Indian, Métis, and Inuit do not equal the total Aboriginal because 6 415 persons reported identifying with more than one group.

[b] Single and mutiple responses have been changed.

[c] The counts for "North American Indian" may be affected by incomplete enumeration of 77 Indian reserves and settlements in the 1996 census, depending on the geographic area under study.

Source: Data from Statistics Canada, "Ethnic Origin, 1996," *1996 Census of Canada*, Cat. no. 93-315.

been considered to consist of four major groups: status Indians, who are registered under the Indian Act; non-status Indians, who have lost or never had status under the act; Métis, who are of mixed Aboriginal and non-Aboriginal ancestry; and Inuit. The Royal Commission on Aboriginal Peoples projected that by the year 2016, Canada's Aboriginal population would total up to 1.2 million.

THE ABUSE OF THE RIGHTS OF ABORIGINAL WOMEN AND CHILDREN

An example of racism against Aboriginal women and children is the relationship between child welfare agencies and Aboriginal families. Since the late 1970s, when provincial welfare programs were first extended to Aboriginal people living on reserves, the system has removed many Aboriginal children from their natural parents, their extended families, and their communities. These children were routinely placed in non-Aboriginal foster homes or given for adoption to non-Aboriginal families, with devastating emotional and psychological effects on the children, the parents, and the

Aboriginal community (Kline, 1992). Social workers, using middle-class norms to assess Aboriginal families, took significant numbers of children into "care" and placed them for adoption, ignoring the child adoption practices of the Aboriginal extended family (Johnson, 1983).

A study conducted by the Canadian Bar Association (1988) revealed that Aboriginal children in British Columbia and Ontario were eight times more likely to be apprehended by the child welfare system than were non-Aboriginal children. Aboriginal children represented 30 percent of the children in care in Alberta, and over 60 percent in Manitoba; similar figures existed in other parts of Canada.

Aboriginal women have been, and continue to be, the most victimized group in Canadian society. From birth, the Aboriginal woman must confront all forms of discrimination — gender, race, and class. Her very identity has been determined by a law established by White men. She is frequently the victim of systematic emotional, sexual, and physical abuse, perpetrated since childhood by fathers, foster and adoptive parents, husbands, teachers, priests, social workers, and police (Elizabeth Fry Society of Saskatchewan, 1992).

Submissions to the Royal Commission on Aboriginal Peoples documented the endemic violence against Aboriginal women. Briefs documented the high levels of sexual, physical, and psychological abuse they endured and the lack of transition homes or services in most of the communities in which they lived (*Report of the Royal Commission on Aboriginal* Peoples, 1996). Economically, they are more vulnerable than both non-Aboriginal women and Aboriginal men in relation to levels of income and employment opportunities (Fleras and Elliott, 1992).

CONCLUSION

The struggles, injustices, prejudice, and discrimination that have plagued Aboriginal peoples for more than three centuries are still grim realities today. The failure of Canada's racist policies toward Aboriginal peoples is reflected in high levels of unemployment: the jobless rate averages nearly 70 percent, and 62 percent of Aboriginal people living on reserves receive social assistance. Aboriginal peoples' income averages little more than half that of non-Aboriginals.

Aboriginal infant-mortality rates are more than double the Canadian rate. The functional illiteracy of the Aboriginal peoples is 45 percent, compared with the Canadian rate of 17 percent, and only 20 percent of Aboriginal children complete their high school education, compared with a national rate of 75 percent. The Aboriginal suicide rate is three times the national rate; for young people aged 17–24, the rate is seven times as high (Canadian Labour Congress, 1992).

Numerous government task forces and reports have documented systemic racism against Aboriginal peoples in the justice system, including the reports of the Donald Marshall Inquiry in Nova Scotia (1989), the Task Force on the Criminal Justice System and its Impact on the Indian and

Métis People of Alberta (1991), the Aboriginal Justice Inquiry of Manitoba (1991), the Saskatchewan Métis Justice Review Committee (1991), and the Law Reform Commission of Canada on Aboriginal Peoples and Criminal Justice (1988).

The Aboriginal population of all provincial prisons in 1989 was 57 percent of all inmates (*Report of the Aboriginal Justice Inquiry of Manitoba*, 1991). In 1988, Aboriginal people represented 4 percent of the national population, yet they constituted 10 percent of the federal penitentiary population. They make up almost all of the inmates in certain women's prisons in Yukon and Labrador, and over 70 percent in the Northwest Territories, Manitoba, and Saskatchewan. Aboriginal people account for 52 percent of all prison admissions in Manitoba; in Saskatchewan, 61 percent; in Alberta, 25 percent; and in British Columbia, 17 percent (Canadian Bar Association, 1988).

Economic disadvantage, underemployment, substance abuse, and other factors that are used to explain Aboriginal over-involvement in crime are not the source of the problem but symptoms of the problems of a society that is structured on discriminatory values, beliefs, and practices (Monture-Angus, 1995). As the *Report of the Aboriginal Justice Inquiry of Manitoba* (1991) concluded, the causes of Aboriginal criminal behaviour are rooted in the long history of discrimination and social inequality that has impoverished Aboriginal people and consigned them to the margins of society.

What can be concluded from this brief overview is that the legacy of centuries of dispossession, oppression, and exploitation directed at the Aboriginal peoples of Canada is reflected today in Aboriginal peoples' high rates of physical and mental illness, suicide, homicide, incarceration, unemployment, and poverty — the direct result of pervasive and intractable racism.

This brief overview of the relations that have evolved between Aboriginal peoples and White society over the last four hundred years also highlights some of the discursive forms of democratic racism that have been, and continue to be, expressed to justify the experiences and continued ill-treatment of Aboriginal peoples. They include:

- *The discourse of nationality:* The quotation of Alexander Morris, a nineteenth-century treaty negotiator, that begins this chapter, eloquently and crudely captures the application of nationalism and the notion of patriotic duty as the underlying rationale for a policy of assimilation. The notion of the "other" could not be tolerated by a society in the pursuit of a unifying national identity grounded on Western values.

- *The discourse of paternalism:* Alexander Morris's remark also captures the sense of dominance, superiority, and munificent benevolence of a colonial government intent on "Christianizing" and "civilizing" the Aboriginal peoples to retrieve them from their assumed inferior, unchristian, uncivilized state. Reinforced by the scientific racism of Social Darwinism and by the Christian duty to evangelize and civilize, non-Aboriginals were provided with a discourse to justify plundering

Aboriginal lands and destroying their cultures, languages, and traditions. Such a discourse also provided the framework for the Indian Act and the treatment of Aboriginal peoples as wards of the state.

- *The discourse of "blame the victim":* Notwithstanding four hundred years of policies and practices of displacement and oppression, with the result that Aboriginal peoples exist at the bottom ranks of Canadian society, the resolution of this state of affairs continues to focus on Aboriginal people themselves. In the words of Patricia Monture-Angus (1995): "When are those of you who inflict racism, who appropriate pain, who speak with no knowledge or respect when you ought to know to listen and accept, going to take hard looks at yourself instead of me? How can you continue to look to me to carry what is your responsibility?"

- *The discourse of multiculturalism:* In the context of Aboriginal peoples, this discourse began to be reflected in government policies of the 1970s and 1980s. These policies indicated a desire on the part of the federal government to decentralize and dismantle its obligations to Aboriginal peoples, and to deal with them as just another element in a multicultural Canada.

- *The discourse of a monolithic "other":* A constant theme in the history of Aboriginal–White relations is non-Aboriginals' inability to recognize the enormous complexity and sophistication of Aboriginal societies and the enormous ethnic, linguistic, cultural, and economic diversity of the Aboriginal population. Such a discourse imposed a common history of "Indianness" as determined and defined by mainstream Canadian society.

NOTE

1. There is a considerable literature on Aboriginal peoples in Canada. In addition to the references cited in this chapter, the reader is encouraged to consult J. Rick Ponting (ed.), *First Nations in Canada: Perspectives on Opportunity, Empowerment, and Self-Determination* (Toronto: McGraw-Hill Ryerson, 1997); V. Satzewich and T. Wotherspoon, *First Nations: Race, Class and Gender Relations* (Scarborough, ON: Nelson, 1993); and Darrell Buffalo, *Socio-Economic Indicators in Indian Reserves and Comparable Communities, 1971–1991* (Ottawa: Department of Indian Affairs and Northern Development, 1997).

REFERENCES

Assembly of First Nations. (1994). *Breaking the Silence*. Ottawa: Assembly of First Nations.

Barman, J. (1996). "Aboriginal Education at the Crossroads: The Legacy of Residential Schools and the Way Ahead." In D. Long and O. Dickason (eds.), *Visions of the Heart: Canadian Aboriginal Issues*. Toronto: Harcourt Brace.

Bienvenue, R., and J. Goldstein (eds.). (1985). *Ethnicity and Ethnic Relations in Canada*. Toronto: Butterworths.

Bolaria, B.S., and P. Li. (1988). *Racial Oppression in Canada*. 2nd ed. Toronto: Garamond Press.

Canadian Bar Association. (1988). *Aboriginal Rights in Canada: An Agenda for Action*. Ottawa: Special Committee Report.

Canadian Labour Congress. (1992). *19th Constitutional Convention: Aboriginal Rights Policy Statement*. Ottawa: CLC.

Cayo, D. (1997). "The Seventh Direction." *The New Brunswick Reader*. (July 12).

Clubine, C. (1991). *Racism, Assimilation and Indian Education in Upper Canada*. Unpublished manuscript. Ontario Institute of Education, Department of Sociology, University of Toronto.

Cummins, J. (1992). "Lies We Live By: National Identity and Social Justice." *International Journal of the Sociology of Language*.

Department of the Interior. (1877). *Annual Report for the Year Ended 30th June 1876*. Parliament, Sessional Papers, No. 11.

Dickason, O. (1992). *Canada's First Nations: A History of the Founding Peoples from Earliest Times*. Toronto: McClelland & Stewart.

Dockstator, M. (1993). *Towards an Understanding of Aboriginal Self-Government*. Osgoode Hall Law School, York University.

Ducharme, M. (1986). "The Segregation of Native People in Canada: Voluntary or Compulsory?" *Current Readings in Race Relations* 3(4):3–4.

Duclos, N. (1990). "Lessons of Difference: Feminist Theory on Cultural Diversity." *Buffalo Law Review* 38:325.

Dyck, N. (1991). *What Is the Indian "Problem": Tutelage and Resistance in Canadian Indian Administration*. St. John's: Institute of Social and Economic Research, Memorial University.

Elizabeth Fry Society of Saskatchewan. (1992). "Aboriginal Women in the Criminal Justice System." In *Western Judicial Education Centre on Racial, Ethnic, and Cultural Equity*. Saskatoon: WJEC.

Fleras, A., and J. Elliott. (1992). *The Nations Within: Aboriginal–State Relations in Canada, United States and New Zealand*. Toronto: Oxford University Press.

———. (1996). *Unequal Relations: An Introduction to Race, Ethnic and Aboriginal Dynamics in Canada*. 2nd ed. Scarborough, ON: Prentice Hall.

Frideres, J. (1993). *Native People in Canada: Contemporary Conflicts*. 4th ed. Scarborough, ON: Prentice Hall.

Glavin, T. (1998). "Death of an Ideology." *Globe and Mail*. August 8.

Globe and Mail. (1998). "Landmark Treaty Raises Inequality Concerns." July 17: A1.

Haig-Brown, C. (1988). *Resistance and Renewal: Surviving the Indian Residential School*. Vancouver: Tillicum Library.

Ing, N.R. (1991). "The Effects of Residential Schools on Native Child-rearing Practices." *Canadian Journal of Native Education* 18 (supplement).

Johnson, P. (1983). *Native Children and the Child Welfare System*. Toronto: James Lorimer.

Kellough, G. (1980). "From Colonialism to Economic Imperialism: The Experience of the Canadian Indian." In J. Harp and J. Hoffley (eds.), *Structural Inequality in Canada*. Scarborough, ON: Prentice Hall.

Kline, M. (1992). "Best-interests Ideology in First Nations Child Welfare Cases." *Osgoode Hall Law Journal* 30:375–425.

McMillan, A. (1995). *Native Peoples and Cultures of Canada: An Anthropological Overview*. Toronto: Douglas & McIntyre.

Miller, J. (1991). *Sweet Promises: A History of Indian–White Relations in Canada*. Toronto: University of Toronto Press.

Monture-Angus, P. (1995). *Thunder in My Soul: A Mohawk Woman Speaks*. Halifax: Fernwood.

Ng, R. (1993). "Racism, Sexism and Nation Building." In C. McCarthy and W. Crichlow (eds.), *Race, Identity and Representation in Education*. New York and London: Routledge.

Norris, M. (1996). "Contemporary Demography of Aboriginal Peoples in Canada." In D. Long and O. Dickason (eds.), *Visions of the Heart: Canadian Aboriginal Issues*. Toronto: Harcourt Brace.

Ponting, R., and R. Gibbons. (1980). *Out of Irrelevance*. Toronto: Butterworths.

Powless, C. (1985). "Native People and Employment: A National Tragedy." In *Research Studies of the Commission on Equality in Empowerment*. Ottawa: Department of Supply and Services Canada.

Report of the Aboriginal Justice Inquiry of Manitoba. (1991). Winnipeg.

Report of the Donald Marshall Inquiry in Nova Scotia. (1989). Halifax.

Report of the Royal Commission on Aboriginal Peoples. (1996). Ottawa.

Report of the Saskatchewan Métis Justice Review Committee. (1991). Regina.

Report of the Task Force on the Criminal Justice System and Its Impact on the Indian and Métis People of Alberta. (1991). Edmonton.

Richardson, B. (1993). *People of Terra Nullius: Betrayal and Rebirth in Aboriginal Canada*. Vancouver and Toronto: Douglas & McIntyre.

Roberts, D. (1993). "A Stranger in God's House." *Globe and Mail*. December 1:A1.

St. Catharines Milling and Lumber Co. v. The Queen. (1887). *Supreme Court Reports* 12: 577 at 596–597.

Scott, D. (1914). "Indian Affairs, 1867–1912." In A. Shortt and A.G. Doughty (eds.), *Canada and Its Provinces: A History of the Canadian People and Their Institutions*. Toronto: Glasgow, Brook.

Sharzer, S. (1985). "Native People: Some Issues." In *Research Studies of the Commission on Equality in Employment*. Ottawa: Department of Supply and Services Canada.

Tully, J. (1995). "Aboriginal Property and Western Theory: Recovering a Middle Ground." In E.F. Paul, F.D. Miller, and G. Paul (eds.), *Property Rights*. Cambridge: Cambridge University Press.

Wilson, D. (1991). "Native Bands Demand Action on School's Abuse of Children." *Globe and Mail*. June 19: A4.

PART
TWO

▼▼

Racism in Canadian Public-Sector Organizations

▼▼▼▼▼▼▼▼▼▼▼▼▼▼▼▼▼▼▼▼▼▼▼▼▼▼▼▼▼▼▼▼▼▼

This part examines a number of key institutions in Canadian society, particularly those that provide services to the public. The analysis of racism in the justice system, in policing, and in human services shows how the policies, programs, procedures, and delivery systems of these major institutions discriminate against people of colour. The discussions in these chapters illuminate the nature of racism in Canada as articulated in its organizational life.

▼▼

Chapter 5

▼▼▼▼▼▼▼▼▼▼▼

Racism and the Justice System

A Black youth faces a White-dominated system with White police, White lawyers and White Judge, and a White Crown attorney. (A Black youth at the Jamaican Canadian Association Conference, 1990)

This chapter examines the justice system[1] from the perspective of differential treatment and racism. The evidence from studies and the various official inquiries into the justice system will be discussed. Specific issues of concern include differential treatment in the courts, such as in the granting of bail and sentencing disparities, and the attitudes of justice system officials. The lack of minority representation in the justice system will also be highlighted. The chapter includes case studies of two views of racism in the justice system.

INTRODUCTION

In addressing the topic of racism in the justice system, particularly in the courts, Pomerant outlined a persistent problem with respect to the identification and validation of racism:

> Minority persons and groups often allege that discrimination is regularly encountered by them in their contacts with the Canadian criminal process. Unfortunately, its incidence is difficult to objectively verify.... A court can readily justify matters such as credibility findings, detention orders and harsh sentences by articulation of "legitimate factors" (1992:6).

Racial discrimination in Canada's justice system has not been extensively or systematically studied. Objective research evidence of differential treatment in the courts is confined to a very small number of studies. Part of the problem stems from the fact that the study of racial discrimination in the justice system in Canada is beset by a wide range of methodological constraints.[2] The most problematic is the absence of systematic and comprehensive forms of data collection and analysis. Only recently has there been any attempt to identify and document the effects of bias and discrimination in the institutional structures of Canadian society and in the justice system in particular.[3]

Moreover, it is only in fairly recent times that theorizing about the meaning of discrimination as defined by the legal system has taken a different perspective. Vizkelety notes that "as recently as 1985, the legal definition of discrimination in Canada was still beset by uncertainty" (1987:36). Human-rights tribunals were beginning to attach a more progressive meaning to the term, emphasizing its effects on victims rather than on the intent of the perpetrator, which, especially when it is seemingly motivated by attitudes or states of mind, is difficult to prove in a court. Some courts were, however, still clinging to the more traditional intent-based theory of discrimination. As recently as 1985, the Supreme Court of Canada reviewed two cases of employment discrimination and decided that discrimination need not be subjected to proof as to its intent but could be demonstrated by its effects (Vizkelety, 1987:50). (For historical cases, see Walker, 1997.)

RACIAL MINORITIES AND THE JUSTICE SYSTEM

Several commissions have outlined the problems of Aboriginal people with the justice system and show that racism appears to be widespread in the administration of justice in regard to Aboriginal people (see Chapter 4). Racism in the Canadian justice system also applies to racial minorities. The issue has been examined from the perspective of the minority perceptions of the justice system. If the perceptions even moderately reflect the extent of the problem, it can be concluded that racism is a major problem in the justice system.

In acknowledging the existence of racism in the justice system, the minister of state for multiculturalism and citizenship noted:

> Can we really be surprised that prosecutors and judges and Crown attorneys should discount eyewitness testimony and disbelieve evidence given under oath? Or that law enforcement officers should approach Native Canadians from the point of view of scepticism and conclude their investigation at the first convenient moment, whether or not all the ends are tied up neatly?... But injustice before the court does exist and, perhaps no less important, confidence in the justice system to eliminate that injustice does not. (Wiener, 1990)

With respect to racial minorities in Ontario, Lewis described the relationship between the justice system and minorities as "two solitudes in life"(1992:3). Lewis went on to recommend that a comprehensive review be conducted of Ontario's criminal justice process with a broad mandate that included the judiciary. In Nova Scotia, it was noted that

> by some unspoken societal consensus, a generalized negativity towards Blackness persistently links Black skin to criminality. All too frequently

Black skin colour becomes the initiating catalytic factor which jettisons Black people into the criminal justice system. It is also Black pigmentation that colours and preconditions and plots the quality of our trajectory through a system seemingly inimical to our interests. (Thornhill, 1988:68)

The problem of racism in the justice system was also acknowledged by the Law Reform Commission of Canada (1992), when it noted that "racism in the justice system is a consistently expressed and central concern to Canada's minorities." It is exemplified in the lack of jobs and positions of power and influence in the justice institutions. It is also evident in the lack of access to police protection and legal aid, police harassment, and differential treatment in sentencing. The commission went on to acknowledge that "the racism of which these groups speak mirrors attitudes and behaviour found in Canadian society as a whole" (Law Reform Commission of Canada, 1992:10).

Perhaps the most extensive research conducted on racism in the justice system was included in the *Report of the Commission on Systemic Racism in the Ontario Criminal Justice System* (1995). The commission found that many people both within and outside of the justice system believe that differential treatment takes place. One third of the White population, for example, believe that judges do not treat Blacks the same as Whites. Although the majority of judges and lawyers do not accept that differential treatment of Blacks takes place, at least one third of the judges did believe so, as did nearly 40 percent of defence counsel. With respect to prison admissions, both Black men and Black women were over-represented. White accused were more likely to be released by the police and less likely to be detained after a bail hearing. Blacks constituted not quite 3 percent of the population of Ontario, yet they accounted for 15 percent of the prison population. During the six-year period from 1986 to 1992, the Black imprisoned population increased by 204 percent! With regard to drug offences, the commission found that White accused were twice as likely as Black accused to be released by the police. Moreover, Black accused were three times more likely to be refused bail. It also found strong differences with regard to sentencing. Generally speaking, Whites found guilty were less likely to be sentenced to prison, and Whites were sentenced more lightly than Blacks even when they had a criminal record and a more serious record of past criminal activity. Far more Blacks were sent to prison for drug offences than were whites. The commission also found that racist behaviour, both systemic and individual, was directed primarily against Black prisoners and was rampant in the prisons.

The differential treatment of Aboriginal peoples and people of colour in Canada's criminal justice system has, therefore, been documented. It is evident in the perceptions of victims of discrimination in the justice system. The findings of the studies also indicate that minorities are treated differently at every stage of the process of dispensing justice. Differential treatment is meted out by the police, in the courts, and in the correctional system. Growing evidence confirms that differential assessments of Aboriginal peoples and racial minorities, leading to differential decisions, start at the point of entry into the system and continue to the point of exit (Razack, 1998; St. Lewis, 1996).

THE MANIFESTATIONS OF RACISM

It has been argued that the law that is the foundation of the practices and policies exercised by the courts is itself racist because the principles germane to its interpretation were developed during an era in which people of colour and other disadvantaged groups were barred from participating in society and the justice system. It is only in recent years that the central concept of discrimination has been redefined to include its effects as well as its intent (Vizkelety, 1987).

Many people understand law as being neutral. The fallacy of this approach becomes obvious when it is understood that laws maintained slavery and made it illegal for Blacks to learn to read and write and participate in public life. Laws also were used to restrict the entry of racial minorities into Canada, and the law was used to intern Japanese Canadians. Laws were also used to rob Aboriginal peoples of their land, history, and culture. Law cannot, therefore, be understood as a neutral construct. Both the common law and codified law are inherently political.

Law has ignored or omitted racism in its deliberations. But it is not as innocent of the charge of racism as it would claim. Kobayashi (1990:449) argues that the culpability of the law can be examined in many ways: "the law has been used through direct action, interpretation, silence and complicity. The law has been wielded as an instrument to create a common sense justification of racial differences, to reinforce common sense notions already deeply embedded within a cultural system of values."

Recent work in critical legal theory posits the need to establish a connection between law and culture, "situating legal theory within social, political, and economic conditions, and interpreting juridical procedures according to dominant ideologies" (Kobayashi, 1990:449).[4] Such contexts were not evident in traditional legal discourse because law, like other disci-

---

MANIFESTATIONS OF RACISM IN THE JUSTICE SYSTEM

Racially biased attitudes and practices of judges, jurors, lawyers, and other court officials
Biased jury-selection procedures
Sentencing disparities
Lack of representation
Perceived neutrality of law
Perceptions of guilt of minority accused
Discretion by Crown attorneys

plines, did not "address the meaning of law outside [its] own terms." The study of law in abstraction from the social relations and the social system that it purports to regulate will always be idealistic, artificial, and inherently biased. The legal system produces and reproduces the essential character of law as a means of rationalizing, normalizing, and legitimizing social control on behalf of those who hold power and the interests they represent (Razack, 1998; Williams, 1991).

The law that governs the Western world was largely developed in an era of enlightened liberalism, in which the individual was thought to be an autonomous, rational self, essentially unconnected to other selves, and dedicated to pursuing his or her own interests. Liberalism emphasized the capacity of every individual to claim rights, which were to be exercised without interference from the state, providing that the exercise of those rights did not impair the rights of another. Canada's justice system falls within the traditional belief that justice is blind and that all people are equal before the law. It does not recognize collective or group rights based on race, gender, or class because of its focus on individuals.

> Liberalism plays a foundation part in this process of normalizing and naturalizing racial dynamics and racist exclusions. As modernity's definitive doctrine of self and society, of morality and politics, liberalism serves to legitimate ideologically and to rationalize politico-economically prevailing sets of racialized conditions and racist exclusions. (Goldberg, 1993:1)

To argue, therefore, that an individual is disadvantaged because he or she is a member of a specific *group* goes against the liberal tradition. The concept of an "independent, decontextualized" individual, isolated from his or her various communities, leads to a view that dismisses the possibility that group membership alters and limits individual choices, opportunities, and rights (Razack, 1998:26). This becomes vitally important with respect to the law that governs the justice system, because of the stereotypical and racist beliefs held by many of its members. To present an individual as part of a community and to describe that community as disadvantaged, marginalized, and subject to racial discrimination is to pose a fundamental challenge to legal discourse.

The traditional liberal argument that the law is objective is held by many in the system. They fear that a more relativistic approach that identifies such characteristics as race and sex will shift the focus from justice to social activism. According to a former British Columbia assistant deputy attorney general, "It allows groups to bring to the floor their own sense of injustice whether it has anything to do with the crime or not.... The danger is that the law will become meaningless, and the subjective approach extended not just to minority groups but to any individual" (McDiarmid in Cunningham, 1997). Furthermore, it is difficult to prove empirically the claims of an individual that are based on his or her group membership, and courts almost always require this proof in making a determination. The personal experiences of individuals who are subjected to racism are often given little weight by court officials, who generally demand empirical proof of the allegation.

INITIAL CONTACT: THE POLICE

For most individuals, the police are the first point of contact with the justice system.[5] This first contact often influences a case's future developments and the decisions with respect to it.

Racial minorities often complain of overpolicing. Squad cars often cruise through communities that are densely populated by racial minorities. Despite this over-surveillance, racial-minority persons complain that they do not receive equal protection under the law. For example, a frequent complaint is that the response time of police is greater in racial-minority communities than it is for the general population (Jamaican Canadian Association, 1990).

At the Jamaican Canadian Association's 1990 Toronto conference, the concerns of Black youth were specifically examined. The youth stated unequivocally that they felt alienated from the systems that administer justice in Ontario. Conference participants stated that they bore the brunt of police arbitrary stops, searches, charges of resisting arrest, and use of force. Black youth talked extensively about the negative stereotyping of members of their community. For example, they said that when a group of them congregated in a public place, they were more likely to gain the attention of police officers than were a group of White youths. They explained that this occurs because of a prevailing stereotype that Black youths are believed to be criminals. When Black youths get together, police are thought to assume that they are plotting a crime.

As a result, the relationship between police and racial-minority communities is extremely tense, especially in urban areas. In Toronto and Montreal, several highly publicized shootings of Black youth have added to the tension.

REPRESENTATION

The lack of representation of racial minorities in the justice system contributes to the perpetuation of racial stereotypes in the system (Bickenbach, 1989). It leads racial minorities accused of committing a crime to perceive that justice will not be done when the system itself does not understand them. The fact that the police officer, courthouse personnel, and the judge are all White creates the perception that justice will not be done.

Hutchinson (1992) noted that although attempts were being made to address the gender imbalance in the judiciary, "the general commitment to diversify the legal profession and judiciary is woefully lacking. It is hardly surprising that almost all judges are White, when fewer than 3 percent of lawyers are members of a visible minority and fewer than 1 percent are Native Canadian."

In recent years, however, the number of racial minority and Aboriginal students in law schools has somewhat increased. As a result, there are now more minority lawyers in practice, especially in Ontario.

ATTITUDES AND PERCEPTIONS OF JUDGES AND LAWYERS

Many of the respondents interviewed in a study conducted as part of the Marshall inquiry (Head, 1991) voiced significant fears about racial discrimination in the courts. Several respondents felt that judges pose the problem, and there was criticism that Blacks are usually tried by White judges and White juries. A White legal aid lawyer expressed his concerns:

> There is an unmistakable change in the atmosphere when I enter the courtroom with a Black client. The hostility of court personnel, including judges and others, is unmistakable and is recognized by all including the alleged lawbreaker. It is impossible, under these conditions, for a Black client to receive equal justice. (Head, 1991)

The study, based on a sample of more than five hundred individuals, also found that Blacks showed a high level of distrust and hostility toward the criminal justice system. They expressed the view that Blacks were treated more harshly than Whites in "some instances."

In a project undertaken in Toronto, racial minorities' perceptions of the justice system were studied (Equal Opportunity Consultants, 1989). This study found that racial minorities criticized the criminal justice system for being unrepresentative of the increasingly diverse population of Ontario. It was repeatedly stressed that the overwhelming majority of judges, Crown attorneys, and other legal professionals were White, male, and mainstream Canadians.

Judges were especially criticized for stereotypical attitudes, behaviours, and views of racial minorities. In particular, members of the Black community consistently said that most judges believe that Black people are more prone to criminal behaviour, because they see so many of them in their courtrooms.

Minority lawyers interviewed as part of the same project said that some judges make racist comments from the bench. In one case, a lawyer requested a conditional discharge for a youth whose case had all the elements for a compassionate hearing. The presiding judge said: "I am not accepting that. People like him need to be sent to prison." In another case, a judge, while sentencing a tall, heavily built Black man convicted of trafficking a small amount of cocaine, stated: "I am afraid of you. I'm going to give you a year in prison."

In addition, minority respondents felt that some judges do not believe that racial-minority accused are "innocent until proven guilty." Some racial minorities believe that they must prove their innocence to the court, not the reverse. Moreover, in instances in which defence counsel recommend bail at a preliminary hearing, the judge often refuses to grant it for racial-minority offenders. A standard rationalization for the refusal to grant bail is that most racial minorities "can't raise the money." This raises some questions about what is "reasonable bail." For example, a minority lawyer argued that although the bail may be granted, it appears to be disproportionately high for members of racial-minority groups (Westmoreland Traore, 1982:23).

In Manitoba, a series of complaints against a particularly contentious member of the judiciary has taken place over a period of twenty years. The judge made disparaging remarks about women and Aboriginal peoples. In one instance, he said that it would be a "joyful result if residents of the Long Plains Indian Reserve killed each other off." Although the judge was suspended when the transcript of these remarks was made public, a formal judicial hearing into his conduct has not taken place because such a hearing would stir up "too much publicity; plus it would make the entire profession and system look bad." This excuse was offered by a former chief provincial judge of the province to the Manitoba Judicial Council (*Globe and Mail*, 1993).

Judicial misconduct has also been noted in a number of cases brought to the attention of the National Judicial Council. One such case is presented in a case study included in this chapter. In another incident, a federal judge was accused of making inappropriate comments about Aboriginal society by describing it as being in an "adolescent" state of development when compared with "non-Indian adult societies." The judicial council merely asked that the judge refrain from allowing his personal opinions to influence his judgements. No further sanctions were imposed (Hutchinson, 1998).

The embarrassment caused by these and other offensive comments by judges has led to the creation of a set of guidelines that provides standards for behaviour of federally appointed judges. The guidelines state that judges should keep their political opinions to themselves, stop making sexist and offensive remarks to women, and not make racist comments to visible minorities. The *Toronto Star* obtained a copy of this confidential document and noted that its adoption by the National Judicial Council was uncertain: "A vocal minority of judges are opposed to behavioural guidelines, arguing they would interfere with 'judicial independence' " (1997:A1).

Justices of the peace have also been criticized for their role in perpetuating racism in the justice system. Respondents in the Toronto study described the racist attitudes of many justices of the peace appointed by the system. The issues of bail and assessing the financial credibility of sponsors were specifically cited. Other examples included the laying of charges. In one case, a justice of the peace refused to lay charges that had been brought by racial-minority persons. In one such case a young, Black, male lawyer was assaulted by a police officer in a legal clinic. He went to a justice of the peace to lay a charge against the police officer without revealing that he was a lawyer. The justice of the peace refused to lay the charge and asked: "Were any of your bones broken?" Eventually, the lawyer was assured that the officer would be charged. He returned to the justice of the peace some days later and found, to his surprise, that the charge had not been laid. When the young man revealed that he was a lawyer by showing his law society membership card, the charge was laid instantly.

Racist attitudes are said to be found among other court personnel such as Crown and defence counsel as well as duty counsel. A frequent complaint is that both the Crown and the defence counsel often have not adequately prepared their cases involving racial minorities. Sometimes, inexperienced Crown counsel are assigned to prosecute high-profile cases involving minorities. Moreover, many Crown and defence counsel are thought to harbour racially biased attitudes. These attitudes are expressed in many ways, including counsel's submissions to the court. A frequent complaint is that counsel often advise racial minorities to plead guilty either because "no one will believe your story" or to expedite a case. Many racial minorities are not aware that a guilty plea guarantees a conviction. They therefore agree with their defence counsel's advice and find themselves with a criminal record for a crime they did not commit.

The consistent omission of information about the racial overtones of a case applies also to Crown attorneys, who have a considerable amount of discretion.[6] Although Crown attorneys do not initiate prosecutions, they play a crucial role in advising the police with respect to whether a *prima facie* case can be made from the accumulated evidence and whether prosecution is justified. They also have the power to withhold evidence until the trial and, as well, to proceed summarily or by indictment. Abusing their power by not recognizing or accepting the racial overtones of a case often leads to situations in which victims of racially motivated crimes find themselves the accused party in the criminal justice system (Westmoreland Traore, 1982:18).

Although much criticism is directed toward Crown attorneys and judges, one area in which defence counsel have been sharply criticized is their refusal to believe in the existence of racially motivated attacks. As in any criminal case, defence counsel face the challenge of advising their clients to the best of their ability. However, this task is made more difficult by the nature of the defence and the prevalent scepticism about the existence of racially motivated attacks. In these cases, victims are often dissuaded by their own defence counsel from raising questions of racism by being told that to do so would only make matters worse for them. For the same reason, counter-charges are very infrequent (Westmoreland Traore, 1982:27).

Victims of racially motivated incidents are therefore doubly jeopardized because of the systematic omission or suppression of vital information from the record of the court. Thus, the court is rarely forced to rule on the matter of racial motivation either as part of *mens rea*[7] or as a factor in sentencing. The victim therefore has little opportunity to obtain satisfaction from the court for racially motivated attacks.

SENTENCING DISPARITIES

One aspect of the justice system that has been extensively studied in the United States is differential sentencing. Members of racial-minority communities in Canada as well as in the United States have consistently alleged that

CASE STUDY 5.1

TWO VIEWS OF RACISM IN THE JUSTICE SYSTEM

Frances Henry has had a number of personal experiences in the courts, since she frequently appears as an expert witness on matters relating to challenging the jury on the cause of racial discrimination or with respect to Caribbean immigrants in Toronto. She has encountered several examples of bias among justice officials. Two cases are described here.

In the first case, elements of racial bias were noted in the attitudes of a federal judge. This example of bias is, however, somewhat mitigated by a very positive example in which a provincial judge was convinced of the need to challenge a jury on the cause of racial discrimination because the expert-witness testimony readily convinced him that action to combat racism in the system was required.

THE FEDERAL JUDGE

In a case involving a contempt charge against the leader of a right-wing extremist group, Henry and another expert witness, Professor Susan Erlich of the Department of Linguistics, Language and Literature, York University, were called to testify that the telephone hate-line messages produced by this group contained elements of racism toward racial-minority groups, gays, and other disadvantaged groups. During both the examination-in-chief and cross-examination, the judge frequently interjected with a variety of observations and questions:

- Henry's objectivity as a witness was called into question because the judge labelled her a "militant anti-racist" on the basis of her *curriculum vitae*, which includes not only many research-based books and papers on race relations but also membership in an anti-racist organization.
- In discussing the change from the designation "race relations" to "anti-racism," which Henry said occurred because it was recognized that the latter more accurately stated a position against a negative and destructive force in society, the judge countered by saying that it also suggested moving from a value-free designation to one invoking a value judgement. (Is one to assume therefore that Canadians should not take a stand against racism?)
- In saying that the messages provoked hatred and created the potential for social disruption, the judge went into a long and unnecessary diatribe about how he, as a French Canadian, did not take offence every time someone said something negative about his ethnic group. He pointed to a message about French Canadians that he said did not offend him. He continued by suggesting that perhaps groups maligned by the Heritage Front telephone messages should start their own telephone message lines.
- In questioning Erlich on the meaning of the term "minority group" in the context of the racial groups that the Heritage Front demeans, the judge posed a situation involving employment equity. He asked, if ten applicants were applying for a job and four were White males, would they not constitute a minority group?

(continued)

CASE STUDY 5.1 *(continued)*

THE PROVINCIAL JUDGE

In a very different case, a provincial judge was asked to rule on the applicability of challenging the jury for cause on racial discrimination. The case involved charges against a Black person. Again, Henry, as an expert witness, was asked to testify with respect to racism against Black people in Canadian society in general and in the justice system in particular. Throughout the lengthy testimony, the judge listened attentively, took copious notes, and asked many questions. After the examinations by the defence and the Crown attorney, the judge raised a number of important and substantial issues for the witness to comment upon.

In his decision finding in favour of the need to challenge for cause, the judge stated that he had been convinced by the expert witness testimony. His judgement began with the notion that the Canadian Charter of Rights and Freedoms guarantees a fair and public hearing. He further noted that this Charter guarantee is defeated by bigoted jurors who cannot provide that context: "If one or more jurors are so in the grip of bigoted thinking that the accused's colour outweighs for decisional purposes both the law and the evidence, the trial would be unfair" (Macdonald, 1993).

The judge summed up by noting that a significant dimension of racial bias is present in this society, such that a juror may not be indifferent and that a jury including one or more such persons is unlikely to be fair and impartial. Challenges for cause on racial prejudice were therefore "shown to be appropriate in order to ensure that this trial complies with Charter requirements."

ANALYSIS

The first case shows that an element of individual bias is apparently present in these officers of justice. While Crown attorneys are known to badger and harass witnesses and this seems to be part of the accepted norms of the courtroom, it becomes inappropriate when the badgering includes language and labels that signify bias. The second case is an example of a system working well. An open-minded judge was influenced by expert-witness testimony to use any and all legal means to inhibit contamination by potentially biased jurors. On the important issue of racism, the judge commented that

> quite apart from constitutional requirements which dictate the result in this case, it is appropriate and necessary for the court to respond to these significant concerns [of racism] so that everyone may have confidence that this court is truly everyone's court.

The exercise of discretion is the essence of the enforcement and application of laws. Due to the dominant character of executive and judicial action, which require the exercise of discretion, racism is more difficult to detect and challenge when it is related to executive or judicial action or inaction (Binavince, 1989). Yet, the consistent claims and experiences of minorities suggest that they are treated differently by the courts. This perception is held very strongly, particularly as it relates to sentencing.

CASE STUDY 5.2

THE SUPREME COURT JUDGE

Judge Corrine Sparks is the first Black woman to be appointed to the Bench in Nova Scotia. In December 1994, she presided over a case in which a Black youth, R.D.S., was charged with assaulting a White police officer during the arrest of his cousin. When R.D.S. arrived on the scene, he asked if he should call his cousin's mother. The arresting officer replied, "Shut up or you'll be under arrest too," at which point R.D.S. was placed in a choke hold and charged with striking the officer with his bike.

Judge Sparks found that a reasonable doubt existed and acquitted R.D.S. of all charges. After handing down the acquittal and while responding to the Crown's question as to why the police officer should lie, she made some comments about the relationship of Black youth and the police. She noted that strained relations exist between the police and the Black community and that police can sometimes over-react when dealing with Black youth. Claiming judicial bias, the Crown appealed her decision to the Nova Scotia Supreme Court, which held that these remarks could lead people to believe that the judge was biased. It reversed her acquittal decision. Its judgement noted that Judge Sparks's decision "flowed from a racially based bias against the police" (*Toronto Star*, September 27, 1997). The Nova Scotia Court of Appeal upheld the reversal. Thus, Judge Sparks was not only accused of judicial bias but had her decision reversed by two provincial courts. A defence team then appealed these decisions to the Supreme Court of Canada.

Up to this point, the case had created considerable reaction in the Black community as well as among segments of the legal establishment. It was also widely reported in the media. Judge Sparks's remarks, made after a decision was rendered, were not sufficient to claim judicial bias and were, in any case, true. Observers wondered, if a White judge had made these comments, would his or her decision have been appealed on grounds of bias? Accusing her of bias in a case involving a Black youth raised some doubt about the standard of judicial neutrality required of judges as well as their ability to refer to the common knowledge of racism. Moreover, there was a perception that this Black judge's behaviour was examined more than is usually necessary.

The case engendered further controversy when it reached the Supreme Court of Canada. Chief Justice Antonio Lamer made the following comments during the hearing on March 10, 1997 (these comments were taken from the video proceedings of the event).

> For many years when I was practising as a lawyer in Montreal, I had clients who were Chinese. Chinese were very much into gambling, they are tremendous gamblers.... If a Chinese is accused of illegal gambling, the casino in Terre des Hommes is constantly occupied by the Chinese community. Can I take that into account? Can I factor in that he is a Chinese and he says he wasn't gambling and the police who is non-Chinese — a non-Chinese police officer might have a bias against Chinese people? On the

(continued)

CASE STUDY 5.2 *(continued)*

other hand, Chinese people have a propensity for gambling. I'm just concerned how far down the slope we are going to go if we do this.

We will not classify people in a blanket way — all young Blacks are suspect of stealing cars. Why? Because they don't have money because they don't have jobs ... no jobs because they are Black and being discriminated against. Conclude, its more likely that a young non-White, Black or Afro-Canadian or Afro-American is going to steal the car if the police officer says he caught him stealing a car. It works both ways.

What if he was the owner of the car. Do we factor in the colour of the owner? The Black owner of a car, an Afro-Canadian owner of the car being stolen by another Afro-Canadian — you get into if there is a difference between that and a non–Afro-Canadian owner of a car and the African stealing the car. Must we factor in all of these things?

What if I take judicial notice of the fact that 95 percent — and I'm saying this and I have no facts — I wouldn't want to offend that community — that 95 percent of Gypsies are pickpockets. And I'm dealing with a pickpocketer and assessing the police officer's credibility. I'm just pretending — it's a hypothetical.

Every police officer ... is not the same colour as [the] person being arrested. There is racism. To some people, I'm a hunky. To others I am a frog. We are all subject to the intolerance of others but now talking of the credibility of a witness ... am I to say that if an English policeman arresting a French Canadian, we take into account that there are social tensions right now and factor them in every case because what applies here will be applicable in other areas. I'm wondering how far we're going.

The Supreme Court of Canada, in a 6–3 judgement, upheld the original acquittal granted by Judge Sparks. Dissenting judges, including the chief justice, said there should be a new trial for R.D.S. because the trial judge, Sparks, had stereotyped police as racists and liars.

The decision of the Supreme Court was hailed by many community and legal groups. Others, including a lead editorial in the *Ottawa Citizen*, were outraged, claiming that

the decision was disastrous. The defendant hadn't introduced any evidence of racism, or even alleged it, so Judge Sparks had effectively introduced evidence herself — to put it charitably, since the "evidence" was only her personal opinion — which the Crown wasn't given a chance to rebut. It flew in the face of our adversarial system of justice.... The justice system now allows judges to violate basic principles and introduce gross

(continued)

CASE STUDY 5.2 *(continued)*

---

stereotypes only if those stereotypes sit well with the political left. (Ottawa *Citizen*, 1998)

Several themes emerge from this important case. In the first instance, there is the assumption made by many members of the legal system that this particular judge should not have used her personal knowledge and experience of racism. There is also concern about the over-surveillance of a Black judge, particularly in a province in which people of colour are poorly represented in the legal establishment. These and many aspects of racism were then compounded by the inappropriate use of racial and ethnic stereotypes by the chief justice of the Supreme Court.

If the trial judge should not have used her personal experience of racism against Blacks in Nova Scotia, should the chief justice of the land have made such blatantly stereotypical comments about Chinese and Gypsies? Should he have trivialized the issues of racism by verbally playing with the relationship of colour to car theft? Should he have commented about his own experience in being called a "hunky" or a "frog" and compared that with racism against people of colour?

There are probably many people, especially in Quebec, who would agree that the ethnic factor should be taken into account in the example cited by the chief justice when an English Canadian police officer arrests a French Canadian.

After the publication of some of his remarks, the Chinese Canadian National Council lodged a complaint to the National Judicial Council against Chief Justice Lamer that said that he "racially stereotyped Chinese as 'tremendous gamblers'." In his defence, Lamer said that he was using these examples as "hypothetical examples of stereotypes, not factual assertions, and that I did not mean any offence by them" (*Toronto Star*, November 5, 1997). Furthermore, he noted that "I find it outrageous to be accused of stereotyping when I was actually giving examples of how wrong stereotyping would be." Chief Justice Lamer included an apology to the Chinese Canadian community in his letter to them and maintained that he had not intended to offend any group.

This case brings the powerful and important role of judges into sharp relief. It also questions their alleged impartiality, particularly in cases involving racism, sexism, homophobia, and other arenas of behaviour that have only recently been brought to public attention.

---

disparities between Whites and Blacks with respect to sentencing exist. Growing evidence suggests that racial minorities, particularly those of Afro-Caribbean origin in the United States and the United Kingdom, are treated differently and subjected to less favourable decisions than are White people at each stage of the process of dispensing justice. Differential assessments, leading to differential decisions, start at the point of entry and continue to the point of exit from the justice system (Petersilia, 1985; *Harvard Law Review*, 1988).

The differential sentencing of minorities was also identified as a problem in the Toronto study (Equal Opportunity Consultants, 1989). With respect to sentencing, lawyers cited several instances of differential sentencing:

- A young White woman was given 30 days for shoplifting, whereas a Black woman was given 90 days for the same offence; both were first offenders.
- In another case involving fraud, a group of Black youths each received six months, whereas in a very similar case, two months earlier, a White youth received 90 days.
- In another case, five youths — three Whites and two Blacks — were charged with possession of marijuana. The three Whites were fined $40 per joint, whereas the two Blacks were sent to jail for three days. (Equal Opportunity Consultants, 1989)

People working in the courts tend to regard these as isolated incidents. While sentence disparity plagues the entire justice system and has been the subject of much study, differential sentencing is particularly important to racial minorities. Ample anecdotal evidence shows that racial minorities tend to receive harsher sentences than do others charged with similar offences. The limited research evidence in Canada indicates that such allegations may be true, at least in those jurisdictions studied.

A study in Nova Scotia considered eight defendant variables, one of which was race. Legal information on the charge and on the defendant's prior convictions was obtained for over one thousand people who faced Criminal Code non-driving offences. The presence of counsel and the decisions made by the court were also examined. The study showed that the majority of defendants were young, single, male, and often unemployed. Race was determined by an observer in the courtroom. It was found that Black persons accounted for 15 percent of the defendants but less than 2 percent of the population of the province. Clients represented by legal aid lawyers rather than privately retained counsel were, for the most part, young, unemployed, and members of racial minorities. Of major significance was the finding on sentencing: "Sentencing patterns were significantly associated with the defendant's race, even when restricted to first offenders convicted of summary charges. White defendants received discharges in 23 percent of the cases, while a Black first offender never received a discharge" (Renner and Warner, 1981:72).

Ten or so years later, research conducted under the auspices of the Marshall inquiry showed virtually the same results. Among a sample of 177 cases of convictions for theft, including those of 51 Blacks and 126 non-Blacks, 11.1 percent of the Whites received an absolute discharge, whereas none of the Blacks did. Moreover, 15.7 percent of the Blacks received a conditional discharge, while among Whites the percentage was 27 percent. In addition, Blacks with a lengthy criminal record were more likely to be incarcerated than were non-Blacks with a similar record.

The study also showed that factors associated with discharges included having counsel, being employed, and having high levels of education. Since many young Nova Scotian Blacks do not meet these criteria, their low levels of discharges are explainable by the "role of adverse effects discrimination" (Royal Commission, 1989). Thus the traditional factors that influence sentencing cannot be applied to sectors of the population that either cannot or do not meet these criteria.

By far the most comprehensive empirical research on sentencing was conducted for the *Report of the Commission on Systemic Racism in the Ontario Criminal Justice System* (1995). The sample consisted of 488 convicted men classified by police as White and 383 classified as Black. Analysis revealed that more Black men than White men were sentenced within the whole sample and also within a subset of drug offences. Moreover, Whites who were found guilty were also given more lenient sentences than Blacks, even though they were more likely to have a criminal record or a record of more serious offences.

The report noted that the commission's "findings are highly suggestive, but taken alone do not establish direct racial discrimination in sentencing decisions" (*Report*, 1995:266). The study therefore controlled for such variables as the seriousness of the offence, the characteristics of the criminal incident, and the criminal history of the convicted men. It found that, taken together, the differential incarceration rates were not explained by these factors. With respect to imprisonment before trial and after conviction, the study found that 81 percent of "convicted men who had been denied bail, compared with 63 percent of those ordered released at a bail hearing and 16 percent of those released by the police, received a prison sentence" (1995:275). Nearly twice as many Whites as Black convicted men had already been released by the police.

One of the most important factors leading to differential rates of imprisonment relate to bail. Significantly more Black men were denied bail and subsequently spent more time in prison than did White men. The commission noted that "the conclusion is inescapable: some black accused who were imprisoned before trial would not have been jailed if they had been white, and some white accused who were freed before trial would have been detained had they been black" (*Report*, 1995:v).

Most evidence for this aspect of differential justice comes from fairly recent sources. However, Mosher (1998) revealed the historical evidence of racism in the criminal justice system, particularly with regard to sentencing disparities. Mosher studied the experience of Blacks and Asians in Ontario's criminal justice system during the period 1892–1961 and came to the conclusion that the period was characterized by systemic racism. He noted that the first drug laws were enacted to control the immigrant Chinese population and that these laws were strongly enforced between 1908 and 1930.

Public-order legislation also focussed "disproportionately on Asians and Blacks involved in gambling, prostitution and other immoral activities and Blacks were not only more likely to be convicted for the commission of such offences, but, when convicted, were sentenced to longer terms of imprisonment" (Mosher, 1998:197). Moreover, court officials attached little credibility to the testimony of racial-minority offenders, which would result in higher conviction rates. Racial-minority group members were also subject to more severe sentencing if their victims were White, but were sentenced more leniently if their victims were of their own minority group. Thus, despite the relatively small numbers of both groups in Canada during this period, their experiences with the justice system were extremely unfavourable and characterized by systemic bias.

JURY SELECTION PROCESSES

Jury bias has been identified as a major contributor to the perpetuation of racism in the justice system (Pomerant, 1992; Petersen, 1993). Jury selection is critical to the process of providing justice; in the Toronto study, many Black respondents singled out this issue as extremely important. Having a Black accused tried by a White jury did not, according to the perceptions of racial-minority people, fulfil the criterion of "trial by a jury of peers." The issue of the extent to which a jury is representative of the community raises questions about the appropriateness of the current practice of using voters' lists to select juries. Many minorities are not eligible to vote, so they are under-represented on voters' lists.

The use of voters' lists to compose a pool has also been called into question because the lists quickly become inaccurate. They fail to include persons who move into or exclude those who move out of the community after each election. They are also not updated until a new election is called. Jurors are required to be Canadian citizens, a qualification that effectively eliminates members of immigrant communities who have not been in the country long enough to qualify for citizenship. It also disqualifies people who came to this country as children and whose parents neglected to make them citizens as well as those who, for whatever reason, have failed to apply for citizenship.

Pomerant (1992) and others have argued that for equality in jury trials to have meaning, jury selection should provide reasonable and equal opportunities and means for the parties to challenge the selection pool. It is also necessary to challenge the selection of jury panels and exclude from service unqualified, incompetent, or morally biased prospective jurors. In addition, it is argued that minority jurors should have the same opportunities as anyone else to be chosen for service. Their minority status should not prevent them from being chosen.

The use of the peremptory challenge by either the Crown or the defence counsel can further limit the diversity of a jury. In one case, a jury was being selected for the trial of a police officer accused of shooting a Black person. A Black woman, after answering questions with respect to her impartiality, was declared impartial and accepted by the prosecutor. The defence counsel for the police officer promptly rejected her as a juror. The final jury included six men and six women, one of whom was Asian. The racial designation of the jurors became an issue in this case. A pre-trial motion put forward by the Crown argued that the Canadian Charter of Rights and Freedoms, which bans racial discrimination, should apply to jury selection so that lawyers could not reject potential jurors because of their race. The defence argued against the motion, and it was rejected by the judge, who noted that this would open up the selection procedure to too many factors. He noted that a jury should reflect the racial composition of a community but urged lawyers to "be guided by their own conscience" (*Toronto Star*, 1993b).

In this instance, a peremptory challenge was used in the selection process to keep a racial-minority person off the jury because the accused was a police officer. The challenge is most frequently used, however, to determine whether jurors hold prejudices or opinions that would bias their objectivity. Bias or racist attitudes were not usually questioned in the *voir dire*.[8] In the late 1980s, Frances Henry began testifying as an expert witness on racism to help lawyers argue for this process. In the first few cases, judges accepted the challenge in only two cases out of six. Slowly, a few judges accepted the challenge both with and without expert-witness testimony. In 1993, the Ontario Court of Appeal, hearing the appeal of *Regina v. Parks* (appealed because the challenge for cause on racism was not allowed), found that the challenge of racism for the Black accused was legitimate because of the prevalence of racism in the system.

The challenge for cause based upon the landmark *Parks* decision has now been used hundreds of times in criminal trials involving Black accused. Anywhere from 10 to 40 percent of jury panels have been excused as a result. Because the *Parks* decision applied only to Metropolitan Toronto, there was resistance from some judges in areas such as Durham and Peel counties, who claimed that while racism against Blacks might exist in Toronto, it was not present in these bordering communities. These judges clung to the idea that racism stops outside of Toronto's borders. They failed to recognize that residents in these areas read the same Toronto-based media, from which most people derive their information and which helps to formulate and reinforce misconceptions and racial stereotypes.

While testifying as an expert witness in a case involving a Black accused, Frances Henry and the lawyer who had retained her decided to mount a small-scale empirical study to prove to the judge who had stated that he would reject the challenge for cause on racism that racism was also prevalent in the Durham region. Using similar questions developed by an earlier Angus Reid poll on racial attitudes in Toronto, a sample of over two hundred people in Whitby, Ontario, were questioned. The study found, as did the Angus Reid poll, that nearly two thirds of respondents believed a link existed between an individual's race and a propensity toward criminal activity. Most frequently cited as having this propensity were Jamaicans (and other Blacks) as well as Vietnamese (Henry et al., 1996).

The finding that many people link racial status and crime has helped the court in deciding that the challenge for cause on racism is a necessary precaution to ensure a fair trial for Black accused. A number of important decisions have followed *Parks*. In *Regina v. Wilson*, the Ontario Court of Appeal decided that the challenge for cause on racism could be used outside the borders of Metropolitan Toronto.

The *Parks* decision also does not apply to non-Black racial minorities. While, increasingly, Crown prosecutors and judges have accepted its application to Vietnamese, Chinese, and other minority groups, some still demand an evidentiary foundation for its use for non-Black accused. A later decision on this issue established another landmark. The Supreme Court of Canada in *Regina v. Williams* in June 1998 decided that the challenge for cause on racism can be used in all cases, regardless of the ethnic or racial status of the accused, if there is evidence of widespread bias against the group to which the accused belongs. The court held that either evidence of the bias should be presented by the party seeking the challenge or a judge may simply take judicial notice of it.[9]

Tanovich et al. (1997) critically examines the use of the challenge for cause to potential jurors. Analyzing judicial decisions on jury selection emphasizing the use of the challenge for cause procedure, the book argues for the use of the challenge and provides statistics showing that between 11 and 59 percent of jurors were discharged after being challenged in cases involving sexual assault. Although no systematic study of the success rate of the challenge on racism has been published, Henry, who has often appeared as an expert witness in such cases, believes that the success rate is anywhere from 10 to 30 percent.

The issue of jury selection and bias is important because the jury verdict all but binds a trial jury, at least in terms of establishing guilt or innocence. The Rodney King case in the United States showed that an impartial jury is a critical factor in ensuring the community's confidence in the justice system. Ensuring that the jury itself does not detract from a fair trial is an important part of the preservation of democracy.

RESPONSES TO RACISM

LACK OF POLITICAL WILL

How has the justice system responded to allegations of inequity and racial bias? One of its agencies, the Law Reform Commission of Canada, noted in a 1992 publication that politicians had, for the past twenty years, refused to deal with racism in the criminal justice system due to a lack of political will. Former Supreme Court Judge Bertha Wilson, after calling attention to the issue of gender bias, went on to head an investigation on this aspect of inequity in the system. It is hoped that the recognition of gender bias signals an equal concern with racial bias. Judge Beverly MacLachlan later spoke out against racism and stereotyping in all the institutions of Canadian society. One form of response, therefore, has been the recognition of the issue by important agencies and high-profile members of the legal profession.

DENIAL

The above examples have been a few voices in the wilderness, however. There is still a persistent and considerable denial of racism in the courts. Judges and Crown counsel, on the rare occasions when they do address allegations of racism, invariably deny them. "Crown attorneys have no control over intake and arrest, we deal with everyone equally.... I have never noticed that one group is treated differently. I don't care whether someone is Black, White or green," said Stephen Leggett, head Crown counsel at a court in Toronto (*Toronto Star*, 1992). Others, such as defence counsel Peter Abrahams, believe that race makes a difference in the legal system.

> You find that Black youths are denied bail more often than their young White counterparts. The first question you're asked as a lawyer going into a hearing is whether your client is Black. Everybody knows that there is a racial element to a criminal trial. Police, Crown attorneys and judges are not immune to it. (*Toronto Star*, 1992)

The denial of racism in the justice system is not confined to the legal profession. There was considerable criticism of the then attorney general of Ontario, Howard Hampton, for creating a task force to investigate the issue in the early 1990s. A Progressive Conservative MPP angrily stated in the legislature that members of the justice system had been "slandered":

> You stated publicly that it was your opinion that the justice system was rife with systemic racism. Statements such as these slander the reputation of every judge, Crown attorney, justice of the peace and police officer who makes up the justice system. (*Toronto Star*, 1992)

Faced with continuing pressure from minority communities, especially Blacks, the government of Ontario announced some new initiatives for the justice system. A new system of developing jury pools to increase minority-group representation on juries was announced by the attorney general. The announcement was greeted with allegations of reverse racism and fears about the imposition of jury quotas (*Toronto Star*, 1993a). One of Canada's most prominent lawyers, Edward Greenspan, said that "there is something fundamentally wrong with the notion that 12 people of one colour can't fairly try an accused of a different colour." Hutchinson countered this argument tellingly:

> In a society that still divides power and opportunity along racial, class and other lines, it is a profound error to imagine that one's race and background does not give one a certain perspective on social values, how society works and what others think.... It is the privilege of the White establishment to pretend that race is not important and that it does not contribute heavily to the kinds of lives that people live. (Hutchinson, 1992)

While recognizing that the views of individuals are as diverse as their backgrounds, Hutchinson argued that there was at least a chance of an accused receiving a fairer and more balanced decision when it reflected "the views of the whole community, not only part of it" (*Toronto Star*, 1993a).

These and other concerns led the government of Ontario to appoint a commission to study racism in the criminal justice system. Some of its findings have already been noted above. This commission provided a unique opportunity for changes to be made in the justice system. Although appointed in 1992, the commission did not release its findings and report until December 1995. A new government in the province, less favourable to the implementation of changes in its justice system, has neglected the report and its many excellent recommendations. At the time of writing, the provincial government had not even responded to the report.

EMPLOYMENT EQUITY

In Ontario, pending employment-equity legislation forced a number of hiring and appointment measures to be taken. In the 1990s, a concerted effort was made to hire more minority lawyers in the public service and to appoint more to the judiciary. A Black Legal Aid Clinic was formed to provide services to the Black community; similar services were already available for the Chinese and Aboriginal communities. There was also a small increase in the number of racial-minority students being accepted into law schools, and the overall number of racial minority lawyers in practice increased marginally. In addition, a 'Black' legal firm was established in Toronto. The employment-equity legislation in Ontario was, however, the first piece of legislation to be revoked by the new government.

TRAINING

Only a limited amount of anti-racist training has been undertaken in the justice system. The Judicial Education Committee in Ontario, which had earlier sponsored gender training, agreed in principle to offer anti-racist training to judges but was constrained by lack of money. Some training was undertaken by Ministry of the Attorney General for staff such as Crown counsel and offices that fell under its jurisdiction, such as the Public Complaints Commission. For the most part, however, practising judges, defence and Crown counsel, and other members of the justice system have not had any comprehensive training in matters relating to the manifestations of racism in public systems.

SUMMARY

There is now sufficient evidence of racism in the justice system to suggest that it is of grave concern in Canada. It is also a serious problem in both the United States and the United Kingdom. Various public inquiries, task forces, and commissions have been conducted over the past decade, and the anecdotal evidence gathered in public consultations with individuals, organizations, and racial-minority communities reflects a growing sense of distrust and fear of the justice system in Canada. There is a fundamental absence of faith in the fairness of the system.

Racial unrest in the 1990s in Toronto, Montreal, Halifax, and other Canadian cities has been, in part, a response to the perception among Black people that they are the victims of racial bias and discrimination, which are widespread in law-enforcement agencies as well as in the courts. Allegations of police brutality and harassment are widespread. Several Black men have been killed by police in the past few years in Toronto, Montreal, and Ottawa. No police officers have been found guilty. Growing concerns have been expressed about the low numbers of racial minorities and Aboriginal peoples employed in the legal system as well as on juries.

The justice system in Canada is plagued by a systemic bias that results in the over-criminalization of particular groups in society.[10] Blacks (and other racial minorities) face discriminatory practices and procedures at every stage of the administration of justice. Over-criminalization is reinforced by the media, which consistently report the alleged criminal activities of racial-minority people. As most people learn about people different from themselves from the media, it is not surprising that many members of the public now make the link between race and the propensity toward criminal activity.

This chapter demonstrates how democratic racism is manifested within the justice system. It examines the value conflict between the ideals and principles of democratic liberalism that are central to the provision of justice and the racism that is reflected in the everyday discursive practices of judges, lawyers, jurors, witnesses, and others in the justice system.

The examples and case studies illustrate the fact that despite the philosophical foundation of democratic liberalism underpinning the justice system, the law is neither impartial nor value-neutral. It reflects the political, cultural, and social biases of those who create the law and administer it. Judges, juries, and lawyers are frequently not impartial, but subscribe to the same stereotypes and hold the same biases that exist in the broader Canadian society. Therefore, a critique of the legal system cannot be accomplished without recognizing that the law and its institutions are in a dialectical relationship with the broader society.

Democratic racism is manifested in courtroom discursive practices. Racism is denied by some of the personnel who administer the legal and justice systems. They find it difficult to acknowledge cultural, institutional, and systemic forms of racism, even where they are manifested so clearly in the formal and informal practices of the legal system. The discourse of colour blindness is very powerful in this system. However, justice is not colour blind, despite the fact that 64 percent of provincial division judges and 72 percent of general division judges believed that the courts treated White and racial-minority people in the same way (*Report of the Commission on Systemic Racism*, 1995:30). As one judge sincerely noted: "My experience is that the court is colour blind.... I can honestly say that the minority parties have been treated no differently than any other by judges, juries, courts staff, lawyers, etc." (1995:31).

In the same way, the liberal discourse that fairness is best achieved by treating everyone equally (or in the same way) is shown by the many examples in this chapter to be a myth. A more relativistic perspective argues that an accused's gender and race must be considered in any determination. There is some consensus among scholars that racial disparities in the criminal justice system have developed because policies, practices, and procedures have been adopted without systematic efforts being made to find out whether they have a differential effect on members of racial-minority communities. While a fundamental principle and discourse in justice is that the accused is presumed innocent, in the case of racial minorities and Aboriginal peoples there is often an assumption of guilt.

Racial discrimination is not limited to the justice system; it exists in virtually every other social institution. However, the justice system has a special responsibility to function with fairness and to show that discrimination in any form is a denial of the justice it claims to uphold.

NOTES

1. "Justice system" here refers to police institutions, the courts, and correctional facilities.
2. Racial or any other form of discrimination cannot be dealt with in civil law except in the province of Quebec. In all other provinces, discrimination is not considered to be a tort; that is, victims cannot claim costs for personal injury as a result of discriminatory actions. Discrimination falls under the exclusive jurisdiction of human-rights tribunals.
3. See *Report of the Commission on Systemic Racism in the Ontario Criminal Justice System* (1995).
4. In the same way, critical race theory can be applied to the legal system. Critical race theory is both an offshoot of, and a distinct entity from, the earlier movement called critical legal studies. It first emerged in the United States as a counter-legal discourse to the positivist liberal legal discourse of civil rights. Legal scholars of colour led the movement, which is based on a critique of liberalism and argues that critical legal theory fails to address racism deeply embedded in the fabric of American culture. Critical race theory provided another, less traditional theoretical framework and offered an ideology focussed on altering the bond between law and racial power, which later was applied to many other fields such as education, human services, and media (Billings, 1998).
5. Although this book contains a separate chapter on policing, it is necessary here to briefly review some material on police, who are the first point of contact before individuals reach the courts.
6. For a systematic presentation of the powers of Crown attorneys see Morris Manning, "Abuse of Power by Crown Attorneys," *Special Lectures of the Law Society of Upper Canada* (Toronto: LSUC, 1979).
7. *Mens rea* refers to the conscious intention of a person to commit a crime.
8. *Voir dire*: "to speak the truth."
9. The challenge for cause based on racial discrimination was upheld by the Ontario Court of Appeal in *Regina v. Parks*. Justice Doherty accepted the fact that bias among jury members is possible in a society in which "wide spread anti-Black racism is a grim reality" (*Toronto Star*, December 15, 1993:25).

Presumably the way has now been cleared for lawyers to use the challenge whenever appropriate. Although this judgement and that of the Provincial Court (Macdonald, 1993) have shown progress occurring in the justice system with respect to the issue of racism, it should also be noted that the Ontario attorney general appealed the Court of Appeal's decision to the Supreme Court of Canada and asked that court to condone trials in which people of colour are not allowed to question the jury on racism. The Supreme Court of Canada in April 1994 denied the province leave to appeal.

However, in June 1998, Frances Henry was involved in a challenge for cause on racism on behalf of a Vietnamese accused. Despite the Supreme Court decision in *Williams*, which stated that any minority had the right to challenge the jury on cause, the Crown attorney maintained that he required evidence to support the use of the challenge. Moreover, he hired another expert witness to counteract Henry's evidence. Furthermore, the judge did not intervene to reason with the Crown attorney in the light of the Supreme Court decision. This case reveals clearly that this system contains many members who are unwilling to accept that racism in its various guises not only exists in society but is played out within the justice system. The denial of racism is still evident despite major decisions, including those made by the Supreme Court of Canada.

10. A number of Marxist-oriented critiques of the justice system have been undertaken. Reiman (1984), for example, argues that the justice system should be viewed as a functional institution that maintains the status quo in the interests of the dominant class. He argues that the justice system is properly functioning for the dominant elite in society by maintaining their interests under the guise of legitimately controlling for law and order. Reiman asserts that the goal of the justice system is not to reduce crime or achieve justice, but to project to the public a visible image of the threat of crime, such as that of the activities of poor, Black youth. He suggests that society derives benefit from the existence of crime, and thus there is reason to believe that social institutions work to maintain rather than to eliminate crime.

Reiman's argument is that in order to maintain the image of a functioning justice system, laws are created that prohibit the acts of poor youth. These laws would increase the need for "criminals" to engage in secondary crime — for example, the drug addict's need to steal to pay for drugs. At the same time that certain behaviour is classified as criminal and delinquent, many acts of the wealthy are not treated as criminal. Reiman argues that there is an astounding incidence of disease, injury, and death due to hazards in the workplace and that this is the consequence of the refusal of management to pay for safety measures and of the government to enforce safety standards. He cites white-collar crime as an example of the selection process in defining criminal activity. His assertion is that the definition of crime benefits the economically advantaged while targeting the disadvantaged.

Moreover, Reiman argues that the broad discretion given to police, prosecutors, and judges who influence arrests, charges, and sentencing rates facilitates the creation of the public perception of "who is criminal." He asserts further that the demeaning prison experience is meant to create future crime by emasculating prisoners in a violent, unsafe environment. The stigmatization of prisoners ensures that ex-offenders will find it difficult to reintegrate into society. This, coupled with police harassment, ensures that ex-offenders will be targeted by police and "recriminalized." The justice system is designed to "maintain and encourage the existence of a stable and visible class of criminals."

Staples (1975) uses a colonial model to analyze race and the law. This type of historical analysis identifies the origins of racism that permeate modern racial and economic stratification. Staples argues that Blacks are not protected by the law because they have no power to enforce the law. The power to define what constitutes a crime is in the hands of the dominant members of society, and this power is a mechanism of racial subordination.

The colonial model assesses the Black community as an underdeveloped colony whose economics and politics are controlled by leaders of the racially dominant group. Staples contends that crime by Blacks and the treatment of Blacks by the legal system is a result of the neocolonialist structure of society.

The central theme of the arguments put forth by these theorists is the importance of ideological control for the maintenance of inequality in society.

REFERENCES

Bickenbach, J.E. (1989). "Lawyers, Law Professors, and Racism in Ontario." *Queen's Quarterly* 3(Autumn):585–98.

Billings, G.L. (1998). "Just What Is Critical Race Theory and What's It Doing in a Nice Field like Education?" *Qualitative Education* 11(1):7–24.

Binavince, E. (1989). "The Juridical Aspect of Race Relations: A Discussion Paper." In O.P. Dwivedi (ed.), *Canada 2000: Race Relations and Public Policy*. Guelph, ON: Department of Political Science, University of Guelph.

Cunningham, D. (1997) "We're Not Equal before the Law after All: British Columbia's Judges Are Told to Treat Minorities and Women Differently." *Western Report* 12(46)(December 15):35.

Equal Opportunity Consultants. (1989). *Perceptions of Racial Minorities Related to the Services of the Ministry of the Attorney General*. Toronto: Ontario Ministry of the Attorney General.

Globe and Mail. (1993). (June 28).

Goldberg, D. (1993). *Racist Culture and the Politics of Meaning*. Oxford: Blackwell.

Harvard Law Review. (1988). "Race and the Criminal Process." 101:1472–1641.

Head, W. (1991). "The Donald Marshall Prosecution: A Case Study of Racism and the Criminal Justice System." *Currents: Readings in Race Relations* 7(1)(April).

Henry, F., P. Hastings, and B. Freer. (1996). "Perceptions of Race and Crime in Ontario: Empirical Evidence from Toronto and the Durham Region." *Canadian Journal of Criminology* (October):469–76.

Hutchinson, A.C. (1992). *Globe and Mail* (December 3).

———. (1998). "Rules about Court Bias Should Apply to Judges, Too." *Toronto Star* (June 22).

Jamaican Canadian Association. (1990). Conference: "Meeting the Challenge — Police–Black Relations." Toronto.

Kobayashi, A. (1990). "Racism and the Law." *Urban Geography* 11(5):447–73.

Law Reform Commission of Canada. (1992). "Consultation Document." Ottawa: The Commission.

Lewis, S. (1992). *Report to the Premier of Ontario*. (June 9). Toronto.

Macdonald, J.A. (1993). *Decision on Challenge for Cause in Regina vs. Griffiths*. Toronto: Ontario Provincial Court. (August).

Mosher, C.L. (1998). *Discrimination and Denial: Systemic Racism in Ontario's Legal and Criminal Justice Systems, 1892–1961*. Toronto: University of Toronto Press.

Nova Scotia. (1989). *Royal Commission on the Donald Marshall, Jr., Prosecution*. "Digest of Findings and Recommendations." Halifax.

Ottawa Citizen. (1998). Editorial: "We Told You So." (February 28).

Petersen, C. (1993). "Institutionalized Racism: The Need for Reform of the Criminal Jury Selection Process." *McGill University Law Journal* 38:147–79.

Petersilia, J. (1985). "Racial Disparities in the Criminal Justice System: A Summary." *Crime and Delinquency* 31(1)(January):15–34.

Pomerant, D. (1992). *Jury Selection and Multicultural Issues.* Ottawa: Law Reform Commission of Canada.

Razack, S. (1998). *Looking White People in the Eye: Gender, Race and Culture in the Courtrooms and Classroom.* Toronto: University of Toronto Press.

Reiman, J.H. (1984). *The Rich Get Richer and the Poor Get Prison: Ideology, Class, and Criminal Justice.* New York: Wiley.

Renner, K.E., and A.H. Warner. (1981). "The Standard of Social Justice Applied to an Evaluation of Criminal Cases Appearing before the Halifax Courts." *Windsor Yearbook of Access to Justice.* Windsor, ON: University of Windsor.

Report of the Commission on Systemic Racism in the Ontario Criminal Justice System. (1995). Toronto: Queen's Printer.

Royal Commission on the Donald Marshall, Jr., Inquiry Report. (1989). Part 4. "The Sentencing Sub-Project." 128–31. Halifax: The Commission.

St. Lewis, J. (1996). "Racism and the Justice System." In C. James, *Perspectives on Racism and the Human Services Sector.* Toronto: University of Toronto Press. 104–19.

Staples, R. (1975). "White Racism, Black Crime, and American Justice: An Application of the Colonial Model to Explain Crime and Race." *Phylon* 36.

Tanovich, D.M., D.M. Paciocco, and S. Skurka. (1997). *Jury Selection in Criminal Cases: Skills, Science and the Law.* Concord, ON: Irwin Law.

Thornhill, E. (1988). "Presentation to the Donald Marshall Inquiry." In *Proceedings of Consultative Conference on Discrimination against Natives and Blacks in the Criminal Justice System and the Role of the Attorney General.* Halifax.

Toronto Star. (1992). (October 12):24.

———. (1993a). P. Moloney. "SIU Arrived Four Hours after Shootings Jury Told." A17.

———. (1993b). "Should Juries Reflect a Society's Racial Mix?" (May 22):D4.

———. (1997). "Judges Face Conduct Crackdown." (September 21):A1.

Vizkelety, B. (1987). *Proving Discrimination in Canada.* Toronto: Carswell.

Walker, J. St. G. (1997). *Race, Rights and the Law in the Supreme Court of Canada: Historical Case Studies.* Toronto: Osgoode Society for Canadian Legal History and Wilfrid Laurier University Press.

Westmoreland Traore, J. (1982). "Race Relations and the Criminal Justice System." Paper presented at a Conference on Justice and Minorities. Vancouver (April).

Wiener, J. (1990). "Speech to the Western Judicial Education Centre, Vancouver." (May 13).

Williams, P. (1991). *The Alchemy of Race and Rights: Diary of a Law Professor.* Cambridge, MA: Harvard University Press.

Chapter 6

▼▼▼▼▼▼▼▼▼▼▼

Racism and Policing

I must tell you, I don't think there's any Black that was born and raised in Toronto that doesn't know someone personally or hasn't personally experienced police harassment in some form or another. (Al Mercury, quoted in C. Lewis, 1992)

Racial Minorities experience the system differently. (Margaret Gittens, co-chair, Commission on Systemic Racism in the Ontario Criminal Justice System, 1996)

This chapter explores racism in policing institutions. It begins by examining attitudes and behaviours of policing and shows how police discretionary powers can lead to both the overpolicing and the underpolicing of minority communities. The chapter then discusses the racialization of crime and the criminalization of minorities. Police accountability, response to pressure from minority groups, professional competence, and its relationship to the representation of people of colour on police forces are also discussed. A brief overview of some of the issues relating to police culture and the public-complaints process is presented.

The second part of the chapter examines the responses of police services across the country. It concludes with a discussion of the initiatives taken by the police in such areas as policies, training, employment equity, community relations, community-based policing, and use-of-force guidelines.

INTRODUCTION

Policing in Canada today is carried out at three levels: municipal, provincial, and federal. There are at present about sixty thousand police officers in Canada. Policing institutions generally derive their authority from a Police Services Act or analogous legislation.

Police forces are mandated to enforce infractions against federal laws, including the Criminal Code, the Narcotic Control Act, and the Food and Drug Act. As well, police forces enforce provincial laws and municipal by-laws. Under police legislation, police officers are given broad discretionary powers in enforcing laws.

It is the duty of Royal Canadian Mounted Police, for example,

> to perform all duties that are assigned to peace officers in relation to the preservation of the peace, the prevention of crime, and of offences against the laws of Canada and the laws in force in any province in which they may be employed, and the apprehension of criminals and offenders and others who may be lawfully taken into custody. (Royal Canadian Mounted Police Act, S.C. 1986, c. r–9, s. 181(a))

In incorporating the need for community policing, the Ontario Police Services Act of 1990 required that policing in Ontario be provided in accordance with the following principles:

— the need to ensure the safety and security of all persons and property in Ontario;
— the importance of safeguarding the fundamental rights guaranteed by the Canadian Charter of Rights and Freedoms and the Ontario Human Rights Code;
— the need for co-operation between the providers of police services and the communities they serve;
— the importance of respect for victims of crime and understanding of their needs;
— the need for sensitivity to the pluralistic, multiracial, and multicultural character of Ontario; and
— the need to ensure that police forces are representative of the communities they serve.

These broad functions of policing were reframed in Ontario's Police Services Amendment Act, 1997, which identified the minimum core services as:

Crime prevention
Law enforcement
Assistance to victims of crime
Public order maintenance
Emergency response

What this list of functions reflects is an overall shift of responsibility for maintaining order from the community level to formal police agencies of social control. The assumption of a wide range of duties by police signals a concurrent decrease in community involvement (Griffiths and Verdun-Jones, 1994).

From such concepts as the preservation of peace and order, the prevention of crime, and the pursuit and apprehension of criminals to the concepts of representativeness, sensitivity to victims, awareness of the multiracial character of society, and the participation of the community in policing, it is understandable that a certain amount of uncertainty and ambiguity exists regarding the broad and sometimes conflicting roles that police play in modern society. This ambiguity is particularly salient in the context of racism and policing institutions.

No single area of Canadian life has perhaps caused more concern and more persistent tension and conflict than the relationships between the police and people of colour. For many years, people of colour have strongly indicated that policing in Canada was not carried out with an even hand, that they are the objects of a constant systemic pattern of harassment and unnecessary violence and insensitivity to their lifestyles and needs.

A survey carried out for the Royal Commission on the Donald Marshall Jr. Prosecution (Province of Nova Scotia, 1989), found that about 60 percent of respondents agreed that police discriminated against Blacks. In a similar survey conducted in Montreal, 53 percent of respondents agreed that the police mistreated citizens from ethnic minorities (Davis, 1990). A 1998 survey undertaken in Toronto found that 38 percent of respondents believed that Toronto police did not treat all racial and economic groups fairly (Grayson, 1998). One of the studies sponsored by the Commission on Systemic Racism in the Ontario Criminal Justice System found that a majority of Toronto residents were not confident that the police treated all members of society equally, and the vast majority of Blacks (79 percent) believed they were treated worse than Whites. These percentages represent a serious crisis of confidence and a widespread loss of faith in the fairness and impartiality of policing systems that purportedly exist to protect the rights of all individuals.

With respect to the treatment of Aboriginal peoples by police forces across Canada, a number of government reports, such as the *Report of the Royal Commission on the Donald Marshall Jr. Prosecution* in Nova Scotia (1989), the *Report of the Task Force on the Criminal Justice System and Its Impact on the Indian and Métis People of Alberta* (1991), the *Report on Aboriginal Peoples and Criminal Justice* by the Law Reform Commission of Canada (1991), and the *Report of the Aboriginal Justice Inquiry of Manitoba* (1991), have presented evidence of racism. The last study concluded that the "justice system has failed Manitoba's Aboriginal people on a massive scale."

A report to the Metropolitan Toronto Police Services Board on perceptions of policing in Metropolitan Toronto's Aboriginal community concluded:

> One thing that all Native people agree on is that there is a serious problem with policing in the Aboriginal community. There is a perception that the police are guilty of brutality, racism, false arrests, and numerous other offences against Native people. Compounding this is a great sense of helplessness — that there is no recourse for the Native community. There is no place to make a complaint and nobody will listen anyway. (Mukwe Ode First Nations Consulting, 1992)

Throughout the 1980s and 1990s, a number of government reports in Ontario were initiated in response to incidents involving racial minorities and police. Similarly, in Quebec, the task force report by J. Bellemare, *Investigation into Relations between the Police Forces, Visible and Other Ethnic*

Minorities (1988) was prepared in response to the serious injury and death of members of the Black community at the hands of the police.

The relationship between the police and people of colour will always, it seems, be a sensitive matter. In many ways, relations between the police and racial-minority communities can be seen as the flashpoint, the means to gauge the general temper of race relations in Canada. As Ungerleider (1992b) points out, considering not only the racial diversity of Canadian society but also inequalities in the distribution of wealth and power, the relations between the police and people of colour will always be extremely fragile because the police are the most visible embodiment of the dominant group's power.

Clearly, if one were to succeed in eliminating racism in the wider society, it would be much easier to attain a much more positive police–race-relations climate. The policing of Canada's racial-minority communities cannot be divorced from the way in which society at large views those communities. The attitudes of the police are a reflection not only of the current social views of people of colour, but also of the historical attitudes of the White majority. The consequence of this, as Ungerleider argues, is that the police are more likely to mistreat individuals who are stigmatized by the dominant society. These individuals are more likely to be subjected to small or gross indignities and mistreatment at the hands of the police. This police behaviour leads to accusations of both "overpolicing" and "underprotecting" of minorities.

THE DISCOURSE OF DEMOCRATIC RACISM AND POLICING

An underlying tenet of Canadian democracy is the obligation of its public institutions to explain and justify their activities in public. This accountability provides legitimacy to the democratic state. With regard to policing, it requires police forces to accept the notion of community control and participation in the decision-making processes of policing.

One of the major problems is that people of colour do not have access to, and are not able to participate in and influence, the decision-making processes of policing institutions. If the police are not directly accountable to the racially diverse communities they serve, they are less likely to reflect and respond to the needs and concerns of those communities.

Most Canadians know little about the operation of their police forces. Policing is still, in many ways and for many Canadians, a "closed" public institution, surrounded by mystery and secrecy. The isolation of the police from the racially diverse community they serve exists in part because relatively few members of the public have taken an active interest in the police. Many Canadians feel that public order is the responsibility of the police alone. This attitude also diminishes the sense of police community accountability — the police are encouraged to perceive themselves as the only organization of social control, as the sole protectors and guardians of society.

The police, however, have been criticized for not wishing to conform to this democratic obligation of accountability. It has been suggested that the notion of a democratically accountable police force is a contradiction in terms, when the police are empowered to infringe on the liberties of citizens and are legally entitled to use force and violence to uphold law and order. The police deal in and with conflict and are empowered by the state to do so (Cashmore and McLaughlin, 1991:110).

It has been suggested that rather than having a democratic notion of accountability — to a political process and to the community — the police tend to view their accountability in different terms. Within this policing ideology, an obligation to the political process — which is portrayed as partisan — is seen in negative terms. The police are seen as preferring to derive their legitimacy and authority from a general acceptance of the laws and regulations they enforce, the values they stand for, the morality they are supposed to support, and the order they maintain. It is toward this process of upholding legally defined standards that the police feel they are accountable. At the same time, it is within this broader framework that they feel they directly represent the "common good." This discourse of accountability to upholding the laws of the land rather than an accountability and responsiveness to the multiracial public they serve is a manifestation of democratic racism.

The police have also been criticized for capitalizing on societal tensions as a strategy for further mobilizing their legitimacy as society's crisis managers. The police, in wanting greater authority and resources as the sole protectors of order, have at the same time been promoting and feeding a fear of social uncertainty and disintegration.

In order to cope with public perceptions of increasing crime rates and public disorder, the police tend to demand even greater organizational and professional autonomy. The issue of democratic accountability is inevitably regarded by the police with some apprehension and resistance. It is resisted as an unnecessary and dangerous intrusion on their ability to do their increasingly difficult job. In opposition to notions of democratic accountability, the police are seen as promoting what has been called "the crisis conspiracy," in which urban centres are on the verge of collapsing into disorder and anarchy (Cashmore and McLaughlin, 1991).

The idea of chaos and crisis in every area of society, and the image of the police vainly trying to cope with the overwhelming demands of a society in turmoil, is a self-serving image that the police are likely to support in their requests for more resources and greater autonomy. They tend to substantiate these fears and continue to push the moral panic button by releasing crime statistics that focus on the explosion of violent crime. The imprecise manner in which people of colour have been linked to crime and disorder contributes to the image of certain racial minorities as being a major cause of this turmoil and therefore as subversive and unwanted elements in society.

The need for more democratic accountability and the reduction of police powers in this "urban battlefield" scenario are therefore seen as a wholly irrelevant, badly timed, and unnecessary intrusion. The police believe they need to be released from all the controls of government — all the political, legislative, bureaucratic, and financial fetters — so that they can better contain the explosion of violent crime.

The Metropolitan Toronto Police stated that they were "probably the most regulated group of working people in Ontario" (Metropolitan Toronto Police Association, 1992). They saw a number of government initiatives as "additional controls." These "arbitrary" actions "engendered a growing sense of frustration and anger among the police, especially front-line officers confronting increasing crime."

A protest against the Ontario government by the Metropolitan Toronto and provincial police associations in the fall of 1992 was in large part symptomatic of this police outrage at "political intervention." Attempts to introduce some mechanisms for greater democratic accountability were viewed as something that should be discouraged and nullified. Such intervention was either invalidated by the police as a socialist conspiracy or marginalized as resulting from the unreasonable demands of vociferous special-interest groups.

This job action in 1992 was launched in part to protest what the police association termed "the disproportionate representation of self-interest groups on government-appointed committees reviewing the police." The demands for greater democratic accountability tended to be seen as opposing the police and were therefore painted as subverting the democratic process. Notions of public accountability were consequently interpreted by the police as challenging the maintenance of law and order.

The demands for increasing police empowerment and greater professional autonomy are further promoted by the notion that policing is so specialized that nobody outside policing can be expected to comprehend its distinct and peculiar complexities. In this type of thinking, the police feel that any errancy or irregularities by police officers should be handled internally. That is why one of the demands made by the police associations in Ontario to the provincial government (in their protest of 1992) was for a review of the need for the Special Investigations Unit, a semi-autonomous unit under provincial jurisdiction that was established to investigate shootings by police.

In the crisis–conspiracy scenario, racial minorities are often depicted as principal protagonists. Suppressing drug dealers is easily translated to mean the suppression of racial minorities. Such a focus legitimizes the police role for the majority of Canadians. Race has therefore become a causal factor in the increase of violence and disorder. In maintaining law and order, the police have also been able at the same time to identify culpable villains.

In the summer of 1994, for example, the murderer of Vivi Leimonis, at a restaurant in a trendy part of Toronto, "became a representative of all the ills black men can inflict on white women. The colour of the perpetrators — three black men — seemed to be the most important aspect of the robbery and murder" (Foster, 1996). The focus was on the "other" — dangerous and sinister. As Michael Valpy, a columnist with *The Globe and Mail*, wrote, "the barbarians are outside the gates" (Valpy, 1994).

Margaret Cannon commented on the public reaction to the murder: "Nice people from good homes talked about sending people back to Africa. A majority of Canadians told a polling company that the immigration quotas were too high, that the refugee determination process was too easy, and that the immigration appeal process was obviously designed to permit dangerous felons to kill Canadians" (Cannon, 1995). In response to the call for shipping the suspects back to Jamaica, the then minister of immigration, Sergio Marchi, himself an immigrant, pointed out that they had been in Canada since childhood and therefore their Jamaican citizenship was, at best, technical. However, shortly afterward, the minister instructed the RCMP to ferret out the estimated six hundred individuals who were in hiding after having their deportation appeals denied.

This interconnectedness between race and crime appears to be reinforced by a survey of Canadian police officers about their greatest fears regarding the future. Police officials reported that they are fearful about two issues: "drug abuse and the likelihood of collective violence from disadvantaged visible minorities" (Bayley in Ungerleider, 1992b). When asked about the basis of their fears, police officials justified their fears with reference to "increased militancy in the pursuit of political goals, manifest in obstructive and deliberate law-breaking, as well as open disrespect for police in carrying out their duties," though they were unable to provide any concrete evidence in support of their claims.

If the policing ideology of accountability, as outlined above and as reflected in the statements of the Metropolitan Toronto Police Association, dictates police decision-making, it will clearly not require police to negotiate or justify their presence in neighbourhoods. Such notions of police accountability do not require the police to cultivate the consent of the community or to take into account the needs of the community. The police will need to be less responsive to changing expectations of policing and to the changing nature, needs, and concerns of the population.

THE MANIFESTATIONS OF RACISM

Police forces make many discretionary decisions about who they hire, what is to be done, the priorities assigned to activities, and the ways in which to carry out these activities. Some of the most important of these decisions are made in the course of enforcing the criminal law, such as decisions whether to arrest, search, and detain suspects and whether to investigate citizens' complaints. Each of these decisions may present opportunities for discrimination. It is generally accepted that such decisions should be related to societal conditions and needs. However, recent royal commissions and public inquiries have confirmed minority-group and Aboriginal concerns that these decisions have been biased in a manner that reflects selectivity based on race. Their reports have highlighted many of the inherently unfair and racist practices of police forces across the country.

MANIFESTATIONS OF RACISM IN POLICING	
Overpolicing	Police culture
Underpolicing	Poor police–community relations
Lack of representation	Racist attitudes and behaviour
Use of force	Lack of accountability
Racialization of crime	Lack of professional competence

The Commission on Systemic Racism in the Ontario Criminal Justice System (Province of Ontario, 1995), for example, reviewed police discretionary decisions that produced a disproportionate number of people of colour in the court and prison system. How the police exercise their discretion to stop and question people contributes to a lack of confidence in equal treatment. The commission's studies found that Black men were particularly vulnerable to being stopped by the police. About 43 percent of Black male residents, but only 25 percent of White and 19 percent of Chinese male residents, reported being stopped by the police in the previous two years.

Police discretionary actions may contribute significantly to racial inequality in imprisonment before trial. The police make the critical decision about whether to arrest an accused person, and in most circumstances they also decide to release or detain pending a bail hearing. In addition, the police prepare "show cause" reports that summarize information about the accused and the alleged offences. Crown attorneys generally use these reports when deciding if the state should seek the imprisonment of an accused and when making submissions to a justice at a bail hearing. This aspect of the police function, no less than the arrest and release powers, may be influenced by social constructions of Black people as more likely than White people to warrant detention before trial.

Exercise of the arrest power is highly discretionary and, except when the police obtain prior authorization in the form of a warrant, it is difficult to scrutinize. As the Law Reform Commission of Canada (1991) noted, this discretion and low visibility make the arrest power open to many types of abuse, including discriminatory treatment.

RACIST ATTITUDES AND BEHAVIOUR

Although extensive racism among the police is often alleged and anecdotal evidence of significant incidents has been offered, documented research evidence for this assertion is relatively slim. Most studies relate to police "personality" traits such as authoritarianism, dogmatism, and conservatism. The only study in Canada on this subject was undertaken by Ungerleider, who sampled 251 uniformed officers in two major municipalities in Canada. His study examined the judgements that police officers made about others. It found that 25 percent of the officers were either confused in their judgement of others or irrationally negative, and it concluded that "the existence of a large number of Canadian police officers who make irrational judgements about others is disquieting" (Ungerleider, 1992b).

Another perspective on this sensitive issue as to whether police officers are more likely to betray racist tendencies (above and beyond the occasional "bad apple" incident) has been put forward in a study of the Metropolitan Toronto Police Force that found no evidence of organized, intentional prejudice or bias against people of colour (Andrews, 1992). However, while acknowledging that the force had done a reasonable job of ensuring that those who are recruited did not display an overt bias, Andrews found

> that a change occurs after joining the Force. There was significant evidence that many police officers who are constantly in contact with the public develop strong feelings and beliefs as to attributes of individuals, based on factors such as appearance and racial background. These officers would no doubt be offended if their attitudes were described as potentially racist. Nevertheless, the same attitudes can and do produce a bias in behaviour which results in unequal treatment of individuals of different cultural or racial backgrounds.

What is evident here is not so much a symptom of personal belief as evidence of a developed culture and value system within the organization. As a result of work experience whereby police officers are exposed to an extremely selective cross-section of the population, an attitudinal bias toward people of colour may creep in.

The many commissions of inquiry on relations between the police and Aboriginal people all identified a state of hostility and distrust, which increased the likelihood of conflict and high arrest rates (Sukahara, 1992). In its investigation into the circumstances surrounding the shooting death of J.J. Harper by a Winnipeg police officer and the subsequent mishandling of the investigation, the Manitoba Aboriginal Justice Inquiry concluded that "racism played a part in the shooting of J.J. Harper and the events that followed" (Province of Manitoba, 1991).

OVERPOLICING

Policing priorities can be both formal and informal. Formal priorities are those that are specifically identified as priorities of a police force. Informal priorities are peculiar to an officer or a set of officers.

There is little disagreement that policing activities and resources ought to be focussed on areas of high risk, those having a high probability of criminal activity or requiring high levels of service. But what constitutes "high risk" or a "higher level of service"? For example, fraud and white-collar crimes are on the increase. These cases have overloaded the system to the point where the police have advised that many of these crimes will go un-investigated and that an affected private company should do the prelimi-nary investigation itself before going to the police. In other words, the ac-tions or functions of the police suggest that white-collar crimes can go unchecked, relative to other crimes. Most white-collar crimes are commit-ted by White people who occupy positions of power, rank, and confidence in an organization (Reiman, 1984). Thus, by choosing not to make white-collar crimes a priority, the police simultaneously remove a large segment of the community from potential criminal liability. The segment of the com-munity largely responsible for white-collar crime is underpoliced.

Who defines what is "high risk" or a "higher level of service"? This is not an objective exercise. As already noted, police race relations are influ-enced by the structural features of a society in which opportunities, re-wards, and constraints are unequally and unfairly distributed.

Canadian society is hierarchically stratified along a number of dimen-sions, including ascribed attributes such as skin colour, ethnicity, sex, and religion, as well as along such lines as economic and political power. As Ungerleider argues:

> The categorization of people in this way can provide a shared sense of identity as well as distinctive perceptual, normative and behavioural pat-terns. These differences are injected into society's policing process in-cluding affecting criminal justice — creating disputes about what behav-iours are to be considered criminal and how seriously particular criminal violations are to be regarded. (1992a)

The criminal justice system reflects and promotes the interests of the more powerful members of society. These members, in turn, exert influence to diminish the priority and resources given by the police to those criminal activities in which they themselves are more likely to engage (for example, white-collar crime) and to increase the priority given to "street" crimes, which are committed by less advantaged people.

"Overpolicing" refers to the extent to which police use discretion in the surveillance of a community and the apprehension of people within that community. Are police cruisers seen more frequently, for example, in com-munities that are densely populated by people of colour? Is the police pres-ence more clearly noticeable at any event involving people of colour? Are business establishments such as restaurants and clubs that are owned, man-aged, or patronized by Black people under more frequent police surveil-lance? Sometimes such police presence may be obvious and visible; at other times, unmarked cars and plain clothes hide their surveillance. One notable result of overpolicing is that charges tend to be more frequently laid against Blacks.

For example, the report of the Commission on Systemic Racism in the Ontario Criminal Justice System (Province of Ontario, 1995) noted the dis-cretionary changes in policing policies and strategies from the mid-1980s to more intensive policing of low-income areas with high proportions of

Blacks, as well as greater use of law enforcement as a primary strategy to control drug abuse. One of the consequences of these policing priorities has been a dramatic increase in prison admissions of Black people. Between 1986 and 1993 there was a 204 percent increase in the incarceration of Blacks, compared with a 23 percent increase for Whites. The 1992–93 statistics showed that Black people accounted for 15 percent of Ontario's prison population while forming only 3.1 percent of the province's general population.

Perhaps one of the most significant aspects of the commission's work was the study undertaken by the Canadian Centre for Justice Statistics to investigate the use of discretion in the remand process. Using Toronto for the study sample, the study examined imprisonment decisions for a sample of Black and White adult males charged with any of five offence types: drug charges, sexual assaults, bail violations, serious non-sexual assaults, and robbery. The sample, 821 adult males described by the police as Black and 832 adult males described as White, included equal numbers of Black and White accused for each of the five offences.

The study found that the over-representation of Black adults was much higher among those imprisoned before trial than among sentenced admissions. Although White men were imprisoned before trial at about the same rate as after sentence (approximately 329 per 100 000 persons in the population before trial, and 334 after sentence), the pre-trial admission rate of Black men was twice their sentenced admission rate (approximately 2136 per 100 000 before trial, and 1051 after sentence).

The data from the study revealed no evidence of differential treatment for some types of charges laid against White and Black accused, but substantial differences for other charges. Differential treatment was most pronounced for accused charged with drug offences. Within this subsample, White accused (60 percent) were twice as likely as Black accused (30 percent) to be released by the police. Black accused (31 percent) were three times more likely than White accused (10 percent) to be refused bail and ordered detained.

Further analysis of the drug-charge sample indicates separate patterns of discrimination at the police and court stages of pre-trial detention. Across the sample as a whole, the results of differential treatment evident at the police stage were subsequently transmitted into the court process. Police decisions to detain Black accused at a higher rate than White accused meant that the bail courts saw a significantly higher proportion of Black accused. Thus, even similar rates of denying bail at court resulted in larger proportions of Black accused being jailed before trial.

The commission's research appears to confirm the perception held by many members of racial-minority communities in Toronto that one of the reasons for the number of accused Blacks being totally out of proportion to their numbers in the total population is informal police priorities and actions. The "war on drugs," for example, and the consequent drug sweeps in poor and Black areas involve police techniques that entail significant numbers of people being arrested and charged when, in fact, only a few may be guilty. Drugs, both hard and soft, have been viewed by police as a reason for raids using overwhelming resources. As more and more Blacks crowd into the courtrooms, it is inevitable that the perception is encouraged that Blacks are more prone to criminal behaviour.

The overpolicing of racial minorities can be understood, therefore, within the larger sociopolitical context, in which the police contribute to the criminalization of marginalized individuals and groups by selecting what is "high risk" criminal behaviour. It can also be seen in the methods chosen to address that deviant behaviour.

This experience of overpolicing clearly contributes to the notion that certain racial groups, particularly Blacks, are more disposed to commit crimes than are Whites. The evidence presented by the Commission on Systemic Racism in the Ontario Criminal Justice System suggests that the discretionary actions of the police are not only racializing crime, but contributing to the public perception that Blacks are a high-crime group and the related notion that their criminality is an expression of their distinctive culture. This further reinforces the need for "overpolicing" and helps to further legitimize the differential treatment by the police toward members of the Black community.

Overpolicing can be seen, as well, in the discretionary decisions and behaviour of individual police officers. For example, the Race Relations and Policing Task Force (C. Lewis, 1992) heard numerous examples of the active harassment of racial minorities by police. The task force quoted one presenter: "Harassment is being released from prison, finding a job, to have a police officer come to your job and ask your employer, 'Why have you hired him, don't you know he's a criminal?' " This presenter went on to tell of racial-minority young people constantly being stopped by police on the street, especially after dark. She told the task force: "The questions are always being asked [by police]: 'Where are you going?' 'Where are you coming from?' "

The task force found that Black youth in particular tended to view police with distrust and fear, feelings said to be rooted in confrontations involving physical and verbal abuse by some police officers. The task force was told by several Black youths of police using racial slurs and exercising their right to use force in excessive or humiliating ways:

> We will talk about jay-walking. There are situations in Windsor where five people will walk across a street on a red light, which is jay-walking. If one or two of them are Black, they are the ones that will get the jay-walking ticket. If a Black is out going to work in the wee hours of the morning ... and most people working in the Big Three are out there at 5:30, 6:00 o'clock in the morning waiting for a bus ... he is apt to be harassed there. [The police] will go so far as to look in your lunch bag, and things of this nature. (C. Lewis, 1992)

This kind of anecdotal evidence, received by the Race Relations and Policing Task Force and other forums like it across Canada, make it abundantly clear that people of colour believe they are treated quite differently from the majority community by the police. Black people, it seems, are far more likely to be stopped and searched by the police and far less likely to be cautioned than are their White counterparts.

Other anecdotal evidence suggests that racial minorities are often charged and accused of crimes they did not commit. The police may arrest a racial-minority member who, they say, resembles someone they are searching for in connection with a crime. Blacks allege that identities are not carefully checked, and that to White police officers "all Blacks look alike." While these reports certainly acknowledge that the majority of police conduct themselves professionally, there continues to be ample evidence of improper and, sometimes, discriminatory behaviour by some police officers.

Racially prejudiced police behaviour has not been clearly defined in Canada, and as a result it is generally not seen as a disciplinary offence by police forces. In addition, since the impartiality of the complaints procedure is generally seen as being severely compromised (it entails the police investigating the police), few complaints of racial discrimination and harassment by police are actually made. Consequently, the nature and extent of overpolicing and the harassment of people of colour are difficult to quantify. Information about these issues largely depends on the kinds of anecdotal evidence presented to government-appointed task forces such as the ones cited above.

THE RACIALIZATION OF CRIME

Overpolicing clearly contributes to the notion that certain racial groups, particularly Blacks, are more disposed to commit crimes than are Whites and other races. Because of their interactions with the Black community, police and some members of the justice system commonly believe that Blacks are responsible for more crimes and that Blacks come from a crime-prone culture, notably Jamaica.

In the United Kingdom, the racialization of crime has been evident since the early 1970s, and it reached a high point in the early 1980s (Gilroy, 1987:72–109). The idea that Blacks are a high-crime group and the related notion that their criminality is an expression of their distinctive culture have become integral to British racism in the period since the "rivers of blood" speech by a member of Parliament, Enoch Powell, in objecting to Black emigration to Britain and suggesting the repatriation of existing citizens in 1968.

Crime — specifically acts of "mugging," robbery, drug charges, and street rioting — were understood to be the natural expressions of Black culture, which was defined as "a cycle in which the negative effects of black matriarchy and family pathology wrought destructive changes on the inner city by literally breeding deviancy out of deprivation and discrimination" (Gilroy, 1987:109–10).

In the United Kingdom the police began to suggest the ideas of Black criminality following the disturbances of the early 1980s:

> The police, aided by a hyperbolic mass media, were able to nail down their problem more precisely. Blacks, particularly young Blacks, were a new force in British society and one which, unless checked, could un-

dermine the nation's stability. A rush of lurid editorials, academic theses and television documentaries tended to confirm the police's premise: Blacks were a problem. (Cashmore and McLaughlin, 1991:3)

Similar patterns may be emerging in Canadian cities, particularly with respect to police interactions with the Black communities in Toronto and Montreal. As happened in an earlier period in the United Kingdom, Black crime appears to be becoming the central focus of police activity that leads directly to the reinforcement of a racist ideology. Such ideology directed at the Black community means that Black life, in a more general sense, is being examined and understood or misunderstood through the "lens which criminal signs and imagery provide" (Gilroy, 1987:76).

Another example of the racialization of crime by police in Canada relates to Hispanics. Prior to the provincial election in Ontario on June 2, 1999, the Toronto Police Association ran a subway poster that asked voters to "help fight crime by electing candidates who are prepared to take on the drug pushers, the pimps and the rapists ..." and showed a picture of a Hispanic gang. In a letter to the Hispanic community expressing his concerns regarding the inappropriateness of the poster, the mayor of Toronto, Mel Lastman, wrote: "To single out one race in an advertising campaign and draw parallels with gang warfare is unconscionable" (June 1, 1999).

Similarly, the overrepresentation of Aboriginal people in the criminal justice system is too often seen as a problem of a pathological community unable to cope and adjust to the rigours of contemporary society. The Aboriginal Justice Inquiry of Manitoba (Province of Manitoba, 1991) found that Aboriginal people were more likely to be charged with multiple offences by police. Twenty-two percent of Aboriginal people appearing in court faced four or more charges, compared with only 13 percent of non-Aboriginal people. Once arrested, Aboriginal people were found to be 1.34 times more likely than non-Aboriginal people to be held in jail before their court appearances, and once in pre-trial custody, Aboriginal people spent 1.5 times longer in custody before their trials.

Thus, the racialization of crime, in which Aboriginal people, Hispanics, and Blacks are increasingly identified with criminal behaviour, reinforces the need for "overpolicing" and helps to explain and legitimize the differential behaviour of police officers toward members of these communities.

UNDERPOLICING

Minority experiences and perceptions relate not only to situations of overpolicing. Members of racial minorities have consistently alleged that police often underpolice them — that is, police fail to protect them adequately or to respond to their requests for assistance. The Task Force on Race Relations and Policing in Ontario (C. Lewis, 1992) found, for example, that racial-minority battered women believed that they received less sensitivity from police than did White females who had been abused. They alleged that police were particularly slow in responding to their calls and that many police seemed to believe they somehow liked or deserved abuse from men.

Another example of the potential of underpolicing is the length of time that police take to respond to hate activity directed at people of colour. Again, anecdotal evidence has suggested long delays before the police have appeared. The result is that eyewitnesses may have forgotten details or, even worse, can no longer be contacted. In some instances, the attitude and manner of the police have left victims feeling that they were to blame for the harassment they had suffered.

Similar incidents are experienced by Aboriginal people, as noted in this quote from the Royal Commission on Aboriginal Peoples:

> If an Aboriginal woman calls the police because she is being assaulted, she is not always treated in the same manner as a non-Aboriginal woman making the same call. When we talk to women about calling the police for assistance, very often their response is, "Why bother, they will probably just ask me if I was drinking." Our women get this treatment from all aspects of the system. (*Report of the Royal Commission on Aboriginal Peoples,* 1996)

One of the more blatant and appalling examples of underpolicing is the Osborne case in Manitoba. In November 1971, several white youths gang-raped and murdered Helen Betty Osborne, a Cree teenager in The Pas. Not until a reinvestigation sixteen years later, in 1987, was one youth sentenced to life imprisonment, one companion acquitted, and a third granted immunity from prosecution for testifying. A subsequent inquiry revealed details of complicity between the RCMP and "respectable" white townspeople so that details of the original case were not investigated or made known (Province of Manitoba, 1991).

PROFESSIONAL COMPETENCE

When there is antipathy between the police and people of colour, mutual stereotypes, reinforced by ignorance, misunderstanding, and serious incidents of conflict, can develop that are unhelpful to both groups.

The knowledge that police officers have about the communities and peoples they are policing is too often acquired after they arrive in the community (Griffiths and Verdun-Jones, 1994). One of the findings of an inquiry into policing the Blood tribe in Alberta was that, although RCMP officers had not demonstrated any conscious bias in their interactions with band members, their behaviour was often perceived as insensitive and disrespectful.

In their submissions to the Ontario Task Force on Race Relations and Policing, "Ontario's police made it exceedingly clear that they consider themselves to be professionals. Members of the public, for their part, were no less adamant in demanding that police behave professionally" (C. Lewis, 1992). Although, as the task force noted, what each considered this to mean was an open question, the equitable treatment of the public they serve must be accepted as one of the basic yardsticks of professional conduct.

The police are constantly required to deal with an increasingly diverse public in situations in which the need for communication is matched only by manifold possibilities for confusion and insensitivity. In commenting on the gross deficiencies of police race-relations training in Ontario, Stephen Lewis, in his report to the premier of Ontario following the Yonge Street disturbances on May 4, 1992, stated:

> The situation, it seems to me, is grossly unfair to the police and to new recruits in particular. We have a society of immense diversity, with a complex proliferation of multiracial and multicultural sensibilities, and we don't prepare our police for dealing with it. These are areas where the exercise of judgement, and the development of skills for conflict resolution become every bit as important as the grasp of sophisticated technology. If we really believe in investing in our justice system, then the people who are on the front-lines deserve the best training possible. It is ultimately a test of management. The management of a police force in the 1990's requires qualitative shifts in training, and without those shifts, things go wrong.[1] (S. Lewis, 1992)

REPRESENTATION

Although there is widespread agreement that the composition of police forces should reflect the make-up of the general population, it clearly does not. In 1986, less than 2 percent of police officers in Canada were people of colour, even though these people formed 7 percent of the country's population (Jain, 1986). In 1998, while there were significant variations across the country, the greatest representation was in the Toronto Police Service, with just over 7.4 percent. However, in this city, people of colour represented almost 50 percent of the available labour pool. Police forces are clearly out of step with the general labour market. No police force in Canada has a complement of racial-minority employees close to parity with any reasonable community population or work-force criteria.

By the late 1970s, there was a general recognition that many police recruitment and hiring criteria and practices were inherently discriminatory. For example, height and weight restrictions that had no direct relationship to effective job performance unfairly discriminated against people of colour who were smaller in stature than other groups. Many tests and other entry criteria heavily favoured White, middle-class, Canadian-born and -educated applicants. Even the advertising of careers in police work was carried out in media that did not reach large segments of the racial-minority audience.

Accordingly, a number of police forces undertook special efforts to attract people of colour to police work, and the rate of recruitment improved. By the late 1970s, the Metropolitan Toronto Police, for example, began to advertise career opportunities in media aimed at minority groups. Many aspects of assessment tests and entry criteria for acceptance were adjusted. Minority police officers were given a higher profile. Notwithstanding these efforts, of the 299 new police recruits to the Toronto Police in 1996, only 27 were persons of colour.

Minority-group representation in police forces continues to be disproportionately low, especially in the upper ranks. And, while obvious attention must be spent on the recruitment and hiring of minority police officers, an important corollary is retaining them in the force once they have been hired.

An issue that has not received systematic study in Canada is whether minority officers leave police forces at the same rate as their White counterparts do. A report from the United States suggested that they do not (National Urban League, 1980). It also indicated that Whites might be drawn away from the police force by attractive alternatives, whereas Blacks would be pushed out by negative experiences.

POLICE CULTURE

Impediments continue to exist that make recruiting (and retaining) minority officers difficult. Some of these impediments are the attitudes of individual police officers that are revealed in overt manifestations of racism, such as verbal slurs or discriminatory acts by supervisors.

Other impediments to racial-minority recruitment include negative perceptions of policing among many racial-minority communities, which may make police work an unattractive career choice for them. Many racial-minority communities have a very different notion of the nature of policing from that generally understood by the police in Canada. For example, a study of police recruitment of minorities conducted in New York City (Hunt and Cohen, 1971) found fundamental differences in the perceptions of the police role between Whites and racial minorities. Minorities found the service aspects of police work more important than the pay, fringe benefits, or job security, compared with Whites. Whites, on the other hand, were attracted to police work by the concepts of law and order; minorities found this work repugnant. Minorities saw policing as an opportunity to help and serve others rather than simply to enforce the law.

Within this context, Andrews (1992) found that, over time, officers develop strong feelings and beliefs about the attributes of individuals, based on factors such as appearance and racial background that can and do produce a bias in behaviour and that, in turn, result in unequal treatment of individuals of different cultural or racial backgrounds.

From their initial consideration of policing as a career to their assignment as officers on patrol, police personnel are subjected to pressures that encourage their acceptance of a set of beliefs and values that may present an obstacle to better relations between them and the communities they serve. Ungerleider (1992b) identifies the following beliefs and values that influence the outlook of police officers toward the conduct of their work:

- a sincere commitment to a broadly based police role in society, centred on the enforcement of criminal law, the protection of the public, and the maintenance of order;
- a concern for the maintenance of police authority and control, and respect for that authority on the part of the public;
- a general belief that society and the court system are too lenient;

- a general belief that the press is unfair in its coverage of police matters;
- a strong action orientation; a belief that police must take action to resolve anxiety, uncertainty, and disorder;
- a tendency to respond to all public calls and to attempt to find solutions or at least to reassure the persons involved;
- a belief in the mutual support and backup, accompanied by non-interference and secrecy as far as the actions of other line officers are concerned;
- a general trust in the validity or appropriateness of police action, accompanied by a limited concern for the abuse of authority;
- among operational officers, a general distrust both of top management's understanding of the complexities and priorities of the operational role, and the likelihood that top management will protect an officer who is falsely accused by the public;
- a limited tolerance for deviance from broadly accepted social values and beliefs;
- a relatively rigid definition of what is "right" and "wrong" behaviour;
- a tendency to stereotype as hostile those people who question police authority; and
- a tendency to simplify events and to fit people and incidents into categories that can be dealt with through police action.

Chief among the factors identified by Ungerleider that help to sustain the beliefs and values of the police and to impede addressing the problems between the police and the citizens they serve is the part that "life on the street" plays in their experience. The "street" is exalted as a *raison d'être* of policing, and "street experience" is asserted to be the foundation of police knowledge.

However, police officers are inadequately prepared for the social realities they confront and the range of tasks they are called upon to perform "on the street," including mediating disputes between landlords and tenants or among family members, locating runaway children and missing persons, maintaining order during or following public events such as labour disputes or sporting contests, enforcing traffic regulations, and comforting the bereaved and victims of accidents and crime. Although the social realities that police officers face often require the knowledge and disposition of social workers, labour mediators, and counsellors, much of their preparation involves recipe-oriented information, largely devoted to understanding and applying the law. As Andrews (1992) noted in his audit of the Metropolitan Toronto Police Force,

> the culture of police forces in general tends to produce a "we and they" philosophy. Part of this is probably necessary, related to the need to maintain a detached view of the world being policed; part is brought about over time by virtue of the high level of contact with people who break the law; part is undoubtedly due to the image of policing as portrayed on television and in other media.

Police forces in Canada have generally followed a policing model in which crime fighting is seen as the principal activity. This notion of policing tends to increase the isolation of police officers from members of the public through its excessive emphasis on crime control and solution. This isolation can also lay the foundation for a more selective isolation from various minority groups.

COMPLAINTS PROCESS

There has been a persistent community demand for independent civilian-review boards to investigate complaints against the police. Not only should there be an impartial and fair complaints procedure in which citizens can feel free to voice their grievances, but the police force should not be placed in the untenable position of investigating itself.

The present system in Ontario, for example, entails an internal investigatory process that is monitored by external review. The public concern is that it is still inherently unfair because it is still dominated by the police themselves.

The lack of an effective, impartial, and independent complaints procedure is viewed as a major stumbling block in ensuring not only that police treat all members of the community in a non-discriminatory manner, but that there are also credible avenues of recourse available when individuals are unfairly treated. When this doesn't exist, minorities feel considerable distrust and suspicion of the integrity and openness of the process.

CASE STUDY 6.1

PUBLIC COMPLAINTS AGAINST THE POLICE

In 1997, a *Toronto Star* analysis (November 30 to December 2) found that 99 percent of the 5629 public complaints filed against Toronto police officers from 1992 to 1996 were dismissed. In 1996, 118 officers received more than one complaint and 8 had at least five complaints filed against them. Complaints are typically about allegations of excessive force, wrongful arrest, abusive language, and racial slurs.

Of the 5629 complaints, only 59 (just over 1 percent) resulted in the officer being disciplined. About one third of the 59 were demoted, one third were docked pay, and in the remaining third a letter of reprimand was placed on the officer's file. Of 114 completed criminal cases against Toronto police officers between 1992 to 1996, 34 led to convictions while the rest were a mixture of acquittals and charges withdrawn for lack of evidence. This 29 percent conviction rate contrasts with a much higher 85 percent conviction rate when civilians go to court on similar offences.

A not unusual example of the complaints process is the case of Dwight Drummond, a CityTV videographer, and a companion, who were subjected to

(continued)

CASE STUDY 6.1 *(continued)*

a "high-risk takedown" at gunpoint after reports of gunfire at a downtown street corner in Toronto in 1993. The police officers claimed an unidentified prostitute had fingered Drummond. No charges were laid. Drummond, who is Black and who had been stopped by the police before, believed his skin colour was a factor. He lodged a complaint. In 1995, a board of inquiry cleared the two officers. A move by the now-defunct Office of the Police Complaints Commission to appeal the decision was withdrawn after the office was closed at the end of 1997.

DISCUSSION

That 99 percent of public complaints against the police are dismissed raises the obvious concern about the apparent lack of objectivity when the police investigate and adjudicate themselves. It is inevitable that the public is left feeling suspicious that police interests are protected over those of the public or the complainant.

The impersonal, formalized, and highly legalistic manner in which police investigators respond to complaints inevitably diminishes the likelihood that complaints will be substantiated or even dealt with in a fair and unbiased fashion. In a study of complainants against the police (Landau, 1994), numerous instances were also reported of police actively discouraging complainants from going ahead with their complaints, discrediting witnesses, encouraging and coercing withdrawals, narrowly focussing on documentary and physical evidence, and giving too much weight to the subject officer's version of events.

Although there have been considerable efforts over the last two decades in Ontario to create an independent civilian complaints system that would be fair, readily accessible, objective, and unbiased, the Ontario Police Services Amendments Act of 1997, rather than strengthening the principles of public accountability and civic participation, appears to be a purposeful dismantling of the already inadequate complaints system. It reverts to the old system by placing most of the responsibility to adjudicate complaints on the accused officer's immediate supervisor and the chief of police.

This piece of legislation also restricts who can make a complaint and where the complaint can be made by directing that "a complaint may be made by a member of the public only if the complainant was directly affected by the police service or conduct that is the subject of the complaint." This means that witnesses to incidents of police misconduct or family members of victims or a community or legal representative cannot file a complaint on behalf of the victim. The act also requires that the complaint must be made to the "station or detachment of the police force to which the complaint relates."

In conforming with this legislation, the Toronto Police Service will disband the "independent" public complaints bureau and decentralize its investigating officers to the same police divisions as the officers they will be probing.

As the *Toronto Star* reported, many defence lawyers have for years been advising clients not even to bother filing a complaint. The number of complaints

(continued)

CASE STUDY 6.1 *(continued)*

steadily declined after 1992, from a high of 1286 in that year to 763 in 1997. With this new system, it will likely continue to decline as public awareness increases.

International experience indicates a "daunting record of police failure of self-regulation in the complaints area" (Goldsmith, 1991), and a review of the Toronto experience led Clare Lewis to question whether "the complaints process is merely another means of legitimizing inappropriate police conduct" (C. Lewis, 1992).

USE OF FORCE

Any discussion of policing must include the recognition of the extraordinary powers of police. Police officers are empowered by law to interfere with individual liberty in the most severe ways. They have the power to question, stop, search, use force, and kill people. This extreme power is sanctioned by the state, and therefore the police are the very real front-line enforcers of state power (Community Coalition Concerned about Civilian Oversight of Police, 1997).

Police shootings of Blacks in major urban centres such as Montreal and Toronto in recent years have brought the entire policing system under increasing suspicion by the Black community. Given the spate of police shootings of Blacks, the police use of firearms is of grave concern. The Lewis Task Force in Ontario recommended that police officers be limited to the use of deadly weapons in a "fleeing offender" situation and that the use of deadly force be limited to situations in which the fleeing person poses an immediate threat of death to police officers or others.

CASE STUDY 6.2

POLICE ACCOUNTABILITY AND THE USE OF FORCE: POLICE SHOOTINGS AND CIVILIAN REVIEW OF POLICE CONDUCT[2]

Between 1988 and 1992, eight Blacks and ten Whites were shot by the police in Toronto. Of the ten people shot by police in Montreal between 1988 and 1993, five were Black and three were Hispanic (Fleras and Elliott, 1996). There were ten fatal shootings by Toronto police between 1992 and 1997. All the dead were male, all were non-White, and many suffered from mental illness. They are Xie Pei Yang (shot April 13, 1997), Hugh Dawson (March 30, 1997), Edmond Yu (February 20, 1997), Wayne Williams (June 11, 1996), Andrew Bramwell (March 14,

(continued)

CASE STUDY 6.2 (continued)

1996), Tommy Barnett (January 10, 1996), Albert Moses (September 29, 1994), Ian Coley (April 20, 1993), Luis Vega (December 26, 1992), and Raymond Lawrence (May 2, 1992). In only one case did anyone other than police fire a shot. In one case an officer suffered an injury. In no case has an officer been charged.

As the Commission on Systemic Discrimination in the Ontario Criminal Justice System said, the shooting of Blacks had come to symbolize the ultimate manifestation of the systemic pattern of harassment that many Black people experience in Toronto, especially in their interactions with police. Such disproportionate numbers could not be dismissed as isolated incidents.

BACKGROUND

Civilian review of police conduct in response to the public outcry for greater public control of police conduct has a long and controversial history. The Report of the Ontario Royal Commission into Metropolitan Toronto Police Practices of 1976 identified some of the serious deficiencies with the then current system of handling civilian complaints about police conduct.

When two Black men were fatally shot by police in 1988, the Ontario government created the Task Force on Race Relations and Policing. The task force, chaired by Clare Lewis, reported that racial minorities did not believe they were policed fairly and that this problem could not be ignored. The Police Services Act of 1990 created the Special Investigations Unit (SIU) for the investigation of deaths and serious injury arising in the course of policing. However, in June 1992, Stephen Lewis, in a report to the Ontario government, noted the SIU's credibility problem and made further recommendations regarding its arm's-length status and resource requirements.

The reconstituted Task Force on Race Relations and Policing in 1993 expressed concerns again that the SIU differed markedly from the concept that was originally recommended.

In 1995, the Commission on Systemic Racism in the Ontario Criminal Justice System devoted considerable attention to the systemic responses to police shootings. The commission found that the response of the criminal justice system to shootings, for communities of colour, lacked accountability. It concluded that the establishment of the SIU had not improved police accountability in the use of force. Three basic problems were found to have frustrated the SIU in carrying out its mandate. They were, again, inadequate funding, a lack of co-operation from police services, and the refusal of individual officers to be interviewed. The commission made a number of recommendations, none of which had been implemented as of the time of writing.

In October 1996, the government asked Roderick McLeod, Q.C., to advise it on how the existing system of civilian oversight of police could be improved. Mr. Mcleod also made a number of recommendations respecting the SIU, none of which have so far been acted upon.

(continued)

CASE STUDY 6.2 *(continued)*

On September 23, 1997, the attorney general of Ontario appointed former superior court judge George W. Adams, Q.C. — an expert in mediation — to address once again concerns about both the difficulties encountered by the SIU during its investigations and the lack of clear procedures regarding the need for police to co-operate with the agency.

This initiative was required because, in many of the above-noted police shootings, it was perceived that investigations by the SIU were frustrated by controversies dealing with:

- delays and even refusals by police officers who were witnesses to the incident to complete notebooks and to attend SIU-requested interviews;
- delays by the police in notifying the SIU about the incident in question;
- access of unauthorized persons behind police lines prior to the arrival of the SIU, and failure to segregate involved officers from each other pending SIU interviews;
- police statements to the media about incidents, made without SIU approval; and
- interviews with and release of civilian witnesses by police officers without the consent of the SIU.

Following an extensive process of consultation, the recommendations made by Judge Adams in his report, released May 14, 1998, represented the common ground between all the parties who participated. Of the twenty-five recommendations, the major ones included:

- Both witness and "subject" officers (the focus of a criminal probe) should be segregated from each other to the extent practicable, so that they would not talk to each other until being interviewed by the SIU.
- Legislation should clearly spell out that witness officers give a statement "forthwith," unless there was a medical reason for the delay. Such delays should be a matter of hours, not days. Failure to comply would be treated as a "serious act of misconduct."
- In cases where there were no charges, the SIU should provide a written report that would be available to the public.
- More resources should be provided to the SIU so it could properly fulfil its mandate.

Other recommendations related to such issues as protecting the Charter rights of police officers, the completion of police notebooks, the training of police officers concerning SIU procedures, the provision of cross-cultural education opportunities for SIU investigators, and regular communication between the SIU, the police, and community groups. None of these recommendations had been implemented at the time of writing this book.

An example of the consequences of this lack of action is an $8.6 million lawsuit filed by the family of Manish Odhavji, who was fatally shot in the back by Toronto police while trying to avoid arrest on September 26, 1997. The lawsuit

(continued)

CASE STUDY 6.2 *(continued)*

---

accuses the Ministry of the Solicitor-General of "negligent supervision." This was justified, according to the statement of claim, because Ontario's solicitors-general had known for at least nine years that Toronto police officers had routinely refused to co-operate with the SIU, yet they had done nothing about it. Also named as defendants were the chief of police and the officers involved in the shooting (*Globe and Mail*, August 8, 1998). When the reputation for and public confidence in the appropriate and impartial conduct of police deteriorate, as they clearly had done as a result of these police shootings, other consequences result:

- increased public hostility toward the police;
- diminished moral authority and perceived legitimacy of the legal order;
- decreased public co-operation with the police; and
- increased crime rates.

As the *Report of the Commission on Systemic Racism in the Ontario Criminal Justice System* (Province of Ontario, 1995) stated: "Perhaps no incidents involving the criminal justice system generate as much public outcry, especially in the black community, as police shootings of civilians." In the past two decades, the number and circumstances of police shootings convinced many people of colour that they were disproportionately vulnerable to police violence. They concluded that the police are quicker to use their guns against men of colour and that the shootings were unduly harsh responses to the incidents under investigation.

The resulting deaths and injuries were perceived as a manifestation of the daily discrimination and harassment that many people of colour experience, especially in interactions with the police. In short, the shootings were perceived not as isolated incidents, but as part of a systemic pattern affecting the entire community.

If racism is an element that does pervade interactions between police and people of colour, then there is no reason to believe that those interactions resulting in the use of force and fatalities would be exempt from such racism. As the Urban Alliance on Race Relations argued, "It would be artificial and intellectually dishonest to assume that fatal interactions between police and racial minority communities do not, on occasion, manifest an element of racism on the part of the police" (Urban Alliance on Race Relations, 1995). However, the existing process of getting at the truth with respect to these police shootings has been broadly criticized for not permitting a full and complete inspection of the facts.

Effective investigations into police shootings must have the full co-operation of police officers. However, the SIU, which is responsible for investigating all civilian injuries and deaths involving police in the province, has been hampered in its ability to fulfil its role by a lack of co-operation from police services and the refusal of individual officers to be interviewed. When the process is so flawed as to be unable to provide the necessary reassurances to the public, suspicions and fears of racist policing can only be exacerbated.

Such obstruction and delay raise public suspicions that police "screen" or review the form and content of the information and evidence that is being transmitted. In regard to being interviewed by SIU investigators, officers have justified their refusal by reference to their constitutional right to remain silent. A police officer in these circumstances might well be a suspect, and a suspect has no obligation to answer questions from investigating officers.

However, as the Commission on Systemic Racism in the Ontario Criminal Justice System noted,

> A police officer who has used a weapon is not in the same position as other suspects. All police officers must accept that the authority to carry and use a firearm in the course of their employment entails a duty to explain completely any circumstances in which it is discharged. A refusal to provide such an explanation prevents the SIU from conducting the thorough investigation required by law, and thwarts the accountability that police officers must have to their superiors in carrying out their duties. Such accountability is crucial to public confidence. (Province of Ontario, 1995)

CASE STUDY 6.3

THE POLICE SHOOTING OF HUGH DAWSON

On Easter Sunday, March 30, 1997, a team of seven plainclothes Toronto police officers from the East Field Command Drug Squad used marked money to buy cocaine from Hugh George Dawson, a 31-year-old Jamaican-born father of two. Later, the team of officers in several unmarked vehicles moved in on Dawson's car, effectively trapping the Honda against the sidewalk.

The officers rushed the car with their firearms at the ready. They carried the standard police issue Glock .40-calibre pistol. One officer carried a shotgun. One of the officers smashed in the car's back window with a nightstick, while others went to the front windows of the car. One officer smashed one of the tinted windows with his service weapon. The gun discharged into the car, according to the *Toronto Star* (April 4, 1997).

The bullet smashed a window on the other side of the car, where the officer who was holding the shotgun was hit with the glass or bullet fragments. That officer reeled back, thinking he had been shot. Then a third officer opened fire at Dawson, who was sitting at the wheel alone in his car. He was hit at least six times. Dawson died at the scene with multiple gunshot wounds.

(continued)

CASE STUDY 6.3 *(continued)*

IMMEDIATE RESPONSE

After the shooting, amid some confusion, according to media reports, Dawson's body was moved well before the Special Investigations Unit — the civilian agency called into action whenever police in Ontario kill or seriously injure someone — had arrived on the scene.

The "subject" officers — those who fired the shots — and the "witness" officers were gone. Nevertheless, Police Chief David Boothby addressed reporters on the scene within hours of the shooting by reading a statement prepared by his legal staff. "A violent struggle ensued when the suspect attempted to seize an officer's firearms. This led to two officers discharging their firearms." The chief of police claimed his statement, given shortly after the shooting, had been approved by the SIU. Andre Marin, director of the SIU, was forced to hold a press conference contradicting the chief, saying, "Neither the lead investigator nor the communications advisor of the SIU, nor myself, saw that release, or approved it at the time." "Subject" officers have the right to remain silent, as guaranteed by the Canadian Charter of Rights and Freedoms.

The provincial legislation requires that police officers must "co-operate fully" with the SIU. However, not until ten days later did all the "witness" officers make themselves available to be interviewed by the SIU. These delays, in addition to the inability to compel even witness officers to give evidence, clearly demonstrate basic weaknesses in the SIU's ability to gather evidence in the face of police suspicion or hostility.

DISCUSSION

As Rosie DiManno noted in a column in the *Toronto Star* (April 11, 1997), "A cynic might suggest that [Police Chief] Boothby offered a *de facto* exculpation of the officers involved in the Dawson shooting, before the SIU investigators had even started examining the evidence, and long before any of the witness officers submitted to interviews." DiManno went on to suggest that given the need for a scenario that had already been planted by Boothby:

> a scenario prepared, in part, by the commanding officer of the drug cops involved, and perhaps even by a Metro Police Association lawyer who would later be retained to represent the subject officers — all the officers at the scene would have a convenient blueprint for their subsequent statements. Especially since those officers were free to take their sweet time — eight days — meeting, perhaps consulting, comparing notes, before they deigned to meet with the SIU. The point is not that these cops would necessarily undertake such a calculated, contrived plan. But it sure as hell could look that way. And removing the perception of a biased or contaminated investigation is precisely why the SIU exists, and why it is given its independent sole-investigator status.

(continued)

CASE STUDY 6.3 *(continued)*

Commenting on the Dawson shooting and the police shooting of a psychiatric patient, Edmund Yu, a week later, the Toronto Chinese-community newspaper *Sing Tao Daily* stated:

> Canada has repealed the death penalty a long time ago. There is no death punishment for a crime, no matter how serious. The police has the right to use the gun in critical circumstances for self protection, but this right should not be abused so that the public become shooting targets. Police officers who abuse the use of the gun, and after getting into trouble hide themselves behind the Charter of Rights to avoid criminal responsibility, are to be despised. Police officers who do not have adequate training and who cannot stay calm to handle the situation should be dismissed. Or else they will damage the image of the police and ruin police and community relations. (April 12, 1997)

RESPONSES

The disproportionately high number of Blacks who have been the victims of police shootings in major urban centres such as Toronto and Montreal over the past decade have provided the major impetus for changes in the policing system. It is a truism that many of these shootings could have been avoided if the police had been better prepared to deal with the realities of serving a multiracial population. Racial-minority distrust toward the police continues not only because of the shootings themselves, but even more because of the apparent lack of any clear strategy or response by the police and the criminal justice system as a whole to deal appropriately with them.

In too many instances the criminal justice system has reacted slowly and inappropriately, and in some cases it has initiated actions that further exacerbated police–community tensions. As the *Report of the Commission on Systemic Racism in the Ontario Criminal Justice System* noted, "The response of the criminal justice system to these tragic events has been seen as reflecting a lack of accountability" (Province of Ontario, 1995).

RACE RELATIONS POLICIES

Notwithstanding their sometimes inappropriate responses to crisis situations, police forces across Canada have implemented many of the recommendations contained in the numerous studies and reports produced over the past two decades that have addressed the issue of police–race relations. The major areas in which efforts have been made include policy, the training of police officers, the improvement of ethno-racial representation in police forces, community relations, the complaints process, and the use of force.

Policy statements are important in providing a foundation for policy and program development and as a reference point for service delivery. They also provide a clear public message of a corporate commitment to improving racial equity.

The Metropolitan Toronto Police Services Board's Race Relations Policy emerged from Standing Order No. 24, "Declaration of Concern and Intent," which was first developed in 1979 and whose key statement is that "every member of the Force must avoid any expression or display of prejudice, bigotry, discrimination, and sexual or racial harassment," and that any violation of this order will result in disciplinary action.

In 1990, the Standing Order was reaffirmed, together with a broader race relations policy that addressed community relations, employment equity, staff development and training, media relations, and public complaints. Published in booklet form, it has been widely distributed.

In Ontario, a race relations policy for police services was adopted in 1993. This was in direct response to the recommendation of the Lewis Task Force on Race Relations and Policing for a policy to assist police services in Ontario with race relations initiatives and to enhance community policing. Lewis also recommended that the policy be credible to all partner groups, clearly oppose racism and discrimination in the practice of policing, and promote a service orientation to policing (C. Lewis, 1992).

The Ontario Race Relations Policy for Police Services contains an introduction, a statement of principles, a statement of policy, specific objectives, and a glossary. The first statement of the policy defines the essence of the document: "The right of all Ontarians to equal rights and opportunities is enshrined in federal and provincial law." It goes on to articulate key principles of racial equality and fairness, community service and community policing, and accountability. More particularly, the policy makes the following commitments:

- Personnel at all levels, uniformed and civilian, must clearly understand that racially discriminatory behaviour, such as racial harassment, racial name-calling, racist graffiti, racial jokes, or racially biased hiring, is not tolerated and is considered grounds for disciplinary measures consistent with the Police Services Act.
- Police procedures and practices in every area of operations and administration — such as response to calls, investigation and arrest, crowd control, recruiting, hiring and promotion — must be free of discriminatory elements.
- The work force at all levels, whether uniformed or civilian, should reflect the racial diversity of the community.
- Personnel at all levels, both uniformed and civilian, must
  — understand racism in all its forms — overt, covert, and systemic — and have the skills to ensure that it is not manifested in their behaviour or any systems they manage;
  — understand, be sensitive to, and work positively with racial and cultural differences among people in the community and within the police service itself; and

— understand the principles of community policing and have the skills to implement them in their areas of responsibility.

- Mechanisms must be in place to promote and facilitate active, meaningful participation by the community, including racial minorities and Aboriginal peoples, in the planning of police services and the implementation and monitoring of this policy.
- Mechanisms for addressing racial complaints within the workplace or by members of the public against police personnel should be in place, known and accessible to citizens and police service personnel.
- All segments of the community and all police service personnel must be informed about this policy and its implementation.

In commenting on the police officers' familiarity with the race relations policy of the Metropolitan Toronto Police Force, Andrews (1992) found "a surprising variation in the level of familiarity.... Many police constables at the Divisional level were not familiar with the contents or intent of the total Policy.... There are no operating standards specified for the Policy so that compliance depended more on common sense situational application than it did upon statements of procedures."

Andrews also noted with surprise that among community groups there was not as much familiarity with the policy as one might expect. He suggested that while it may be important to have statements of policy or intent, it is the impact of these statements on police behaviour that is more important to the community.

This cautionary attitude toward the value of policy statements was perhaps reinforced by the conclusion of the 1992 report of the Ontario Task Force on Race Relations and Policing, which noted that "race relations and policing matters may still not be seen by some senior civil servants, some police services board members, and some senior police officers as real, significant, or worth the commitment of long-term planning and resources." Clearly, a structure and culture that is unable to accept racial diversity will not create policies to deal with it (Hunt and Cohen, 1971).

TRAINING

Training has been viewed as the primary remedy for improved police–race relations in Canada. Notwithstanding the massive human and financial resources being expended on such training programs, they still have not received the kind of rigorous scrutiny that is demanded. As Nadine Peppard has said, "the field of race relations training remains largely unexplored and ... little thought has been given to what the objectives of such training should be" (Peppard, 1983). These comments are perhaps even truer today than when they were first made in 1983. While there is increasing pressure for much more police–race relations training, there is still no clear answer to the question as to what, if any, effect race relations training has on police officers.

Is it realistic to hope for any meaningful improvements in police–race relations as a result of training? Too many programs have been poorly coordinated, superficial in content, and apparently ineffective. There are many reasons for this. First, there is no clear agreement as to what the goals are, except at the most general levels. Second, training has been provided in an organizational environment that has not always been particularly supportive. With few exceptions, there have not been the kinds of tangible organizational support systems and resources to put anti-racism and equity policies into meaningful policing practices that can reinforce training. Third, there is confusion as to whether attitudes, knowledge, or skills should be taught. Most of the training efforts seem to be dictated by some abstract notion of the general desirability of providing enlightenment on racial matters, not by the actual work-related requirements of policing.

There appear to be few examples in Canada of incorporating and translating the utility of race relations training into police work-related skills. If police race relations training was more clearly contextualized into the operational requirements of policing, the relationship between training and performance could be more firmly established and measurable objectives for the training could be set.

REPRESENTATION OF MINORITIES

What has been done to ensure that the recruitment and promotional processes of Canadian police forces will make them more representative of the multiracial population they serve?

Notwithstanding the resources that the Toronto Police Service devoted to minority recruitment over a number of years, Andrews (1992) found that the representation of people of colour on the force was about one third the level of their representation in the population as a whole. In addition, minority representation was heavily concentrated in the entry levels of the force.

Both Andrews and S. Lewis (1992) concluded that even the most advanced employment equity efforts would not significantly improve the racial diversity of police forces. Long debated and resisted in police circles is the consideration of such additional options as lateral entry, direct entry, and the application of innovative career-path plans such as the permanent specialization of uniformed officers, particularly at higher levels. As Andrews (1992) noted, other highly structured institutions, such as the military, have dealt with the need for and use of different skill sets in a very different way than police forces have. That fact alone makes it very difficult to accept the rationale that there are no alternatives to the present structure.

USE OF FIREARMS

In response to the concern that police officers do not always use only as much force as is necessary to bring a situation under control, recent efforts have been made to provide much clearer guidelines about the use of force, alternatives to lethal force, the filing of a report whenever guns are drawn or used, and the need to amend the "fleeing felon" provision of the Criminal Code.

In 1992, for example, Ontario introduced a new regulation stating that "a member of a police force shall not draw a handgun and discharge a firearm, unless he or she believes, on reasonable grounds, that to do so is necessary to protect against the loss of life or serious bodily harm."

However, part of the present confusion is that police officers are also governed by the Criminal Code, which allows a police officer to draw and discharge a firearm to apprehend a suspect who attempts to escape, unless escape can be prevented by less violent means. Many have urged changes to this section of the Code, which allows the use of lethal force against a fleeing felon who does not present a risk to life. Although the government of Canada indicated its commitment to change these provisions of the Criminal Code in the spring of 1994, it has yet to do so.

COMMUNITY RELATIONS

While the primary thrust of present police initiatives is the elimination of racism within existing police services to ensure an impartial police service, mechanisms are also being put in place that attempt to ensure that policing services are more responsive and sensitive to all sectors of the population.

A number of forces across Canada have implemented a variety of models of community policing and programs to "improve police–community race relations." Most of the programs have been designed primarily to improve the image of the police in the community. Many of them have depended on external sources of funding, and very few have been adequately evaluated as to their actual impact on police–minority relations.

Police–community relations have largely been characterized by public criticism of the police, on the one hand, and police efforts to counter that criticism, on the other. As community frustration intensifies, the police have generally responded by making minor adjustments to meet the immediate crisis and have avoided comprehensive plans for change in response to community needs and demands.

In addition, police–community relations programs have traditionally been developed by the police as a response to resolving police–community conflict. Programs emanating from this process have generally been designed to change community attitudes, opinions, and perceptions of the police through the provision of information, through "opportunities for positive police–community contact," and through the projection of the appearance of substantive change by the revision of superficial aspects of police operations, deployment modes, or supplemental services, without any change in basic police practices and enforcement policy.

When image improvement is the basic thrust of most police–community relations programs, it is not surprising that the programs have not generally led to direct and meaningful involvement of citizens in police policy-making. The potential weakness of expecting sustained citizen involvement in police policy-making or monitoring is the lack of resources within community groups to play an effective role. Minority groups, by their very nature, may also tend to find it difficult to use the formal political process to express concerns about discriminatory police conduct (Davis, 1990). Other factors that contribute to this lack of effective public participation are the lack of support from police leadership and the rank-and-file for this kind of involvement, and the lack of understanding among police personnel about the benefits of such programs.

SUMMARY

This chapter has highlighted some of the discursive barriers used by policing institutions in Canada in not dealing with racism. These discourses have included:

- *The discourse of accountability:* The police have generally articulated their accountability to the laws and regulations they enforce. It is to the formalized community standards, as expressed in the laws of the land, that the police feel they are accountable, rather than to the public they serve. Demands for greater public accountability have therefore been seen as challenging the maintenance of law and order and therefore constituting a threat to the state.
- *The discourse of moral panic:* The idea of chaos and dramatic change in society, and the image of the police vainly trying to cope as the sole defenders of law and order, are positions that help to strengthen the authority and autonomy of the police.
- *The discourse of denial:* The notion of racism in the provision of policing services has generally been dismissed by admissions that unfortunately there may be the occasional "bad apple."
- *The discourse of "blame the victim":* The provision of policing services to all sectors of society is presumed to be provided and applied equally and neutrally. Therefore, if charges tend to be proportionately more frequently laid against Blacks or Aboriginal people, it is because they are more criminally inclined. Such a conclusion ignores the discretionary changes in policing priorities and strategies, overpolicing, differential treatment, and many other factors. But the fact that these groups are now overrepresented in the criminal justice system reinforces the need for further "overpolicing" of these communities.

This chapter also explored racism and policing by looking at the attitudes and behaviours of the police as individuals, as well as looking at the ideologies, structures, and practices of law-enforcement organizations. The conflictual relationship between police and racial minorities — particularly Aboriginal peoples and Blacks — is also demonstrated by the evidence of several task forces established to examine racism among the police.

This chapter has analyzed the many manifestations of racial bias and discrimination and showed how deeply entrenched racism is within all areas of law enforcement. Some of the critical areas discussed include the overpolicing of minority communities, the racialization of crime and the criminalization of racial minorities, the lack of police accountability, the emphasis on law and order rather than provision of service, the use of excessive force, and the professional competence of the police. The last section of the chapter summarized some of the institutional responses by the police, including training, employment equity, and models of community policing.

NOTES

1. When granting permission for us to reprint this excerpt, the office of the Queen's Printer for Ontario requested that we include the following note: "As a result of both the 1992 Stephen Lewis and the 1992 Clare Lewis reports on policing and race relations, Ontario took strong action to improve the training of police officers. A permanently staffed Race Relations and Adult Education unit was formed at the Ontario Police College with the responsibility of ensuring the complete integration of anti-racism and anti-discrimination training into all courses. Training for recruits was extended from 47 to 60 days in order to meet the requirements of the recommendations from both reports. In addition, training in the use of force, conflict resolution and de-escalation (including dealing with the mentally ill), use of judgement, and other related areas was strengthened. These actions exceeded the recommendations contained in both reports."
2. A detailed study of police shooting of Black people was conducted by Professor H. Glasbeek of Osgoode Hall Law School for the Commission on Systemic Racism in the Ontario Criminal Justice System. The study, "A Report on Attorney General's Files, Prosecutions and Coroners' Inquests Arising out of Police Shootings in Ontario," can be found in the research documents published by the commission. A version of this study is also published in Abel and Sheehy (1996:324–29).

REFERENCES

Abel, J., and E. Sheehy. (1996). *Criminal Law and Procedure: Cases, Context, Critique.* Toronto: Captus Press.

Andrews, A. (1992). *Review of Race Relations Practices of the Metropolitan Toronto Police Force.* Toronto: Municipality of Metropolitan Toronto.

Bellamare, J. (1988). *Investigation into Relations between the Police Forces, Visible and Other Ethnic Minorities.* Montreal: Commission des Droits de la Personne du Québec.

Cannon, M. (1995). *Invisible Empire: Racism in Canada.* Toronto: Random House.

Cashmore, E., and E. McLaughlin (eds.). (1991). *Out of Order: Policing Black People.* London: Routledge.

Community Coalition Concerned about Civilian Oversight of Police. (1997). *In Search of Police Accountability.* Toronto.

Davis, K. (1990). "Controlling Racial Discrimination in Policing." *University of Toronto Faculty of Law Review* 51(2).

Fleras, A., and J. Elliott. (1996). *Unequal Relations: An Introduction to Race, Ethnic and Aboriginal Dynamics in Canada.* 2nd ed. Toronto: Prentice Hall.

Foster, C. (1996). *A Good Place to Come From: The Meaning of Being Black in Canada.* Toronto: HarperCollins.

Gilroy, P. (l987). *There Ain't No Black in the Union Jack.* Chicago: University of Chicago Press.

Gittens, M. (1996). *Press Release: Report of the Commission on Systemic Racism in the Ontario Criminal Justice System.* Toronto.

Goldsmith, A. (1991). *Complaints against the Police: The Trend to External Review.* Oxford: Clarendon Press.

Grayson, P. (1998). *Social Report Card.* Toronto: Institute for Social Research, York University.

Griffiths, C., and S. Verdun-Jones. (1994). *Canadian Criminal Justice.* Toronto: Harcourt Brace.

Hunt, I.C., and B. Cohen (1971). *Minority Recruiting in the New York City Police Department.* New York: Rand.

Jain, H. (1986). *Recruitment and Selection of Visible Minorities in Canadian Police Forces: A Survey of Selected Police Agencies.* Research and Working Paper Series. Hamilton, ON: Faculty of Business, McMaster University.

Landau, T. (1994). *Police Complaints against the Police: A View from Complainants.* Toronto: Centre for Criminology, University of Toronto.

Law Reform Commission of Canada. (1991). *Report on Aboriginal Peoples and Criminal Justice.* Ottawa.

Lewis, C. (1992). *Report of the Task Force on Race Relations and Policing.* Toronto: Government of Ontario.

Lewis, S. (1992). *Report to the Premier on Race Relations.* Toronto. Excerpt on page 186 reproduced with permission from the Queen's Printer for Ontario.

Metropolitan Toronto Police Association. (1992). "Brief to the Solicitor General of Ontario." November 11.

Mukwe Ode First Nations Consulting. (1992). *As We Were Told.* Toronto: Metropolitan Toronto Police Services Board.

National Urban League. (1980). *Staying Power: Keeping Minority Police Officers in the Force.* New York.

Peppard, N. (1983). "Race Relations Training." *Currents: Readings in Race Relations* (Toronto) 1(3):6–11.

Province of Alberta. (1991). *Report of the Task Force on the Criminal Justice System and Its Impact on the Indian and Métis People of Alberta.* Main report, vol. 1. Edmonton.

Province of Manitoba. (1991). *Report of the Aboriginal Justice Inquiry of Manitoba.* Winnipeg.

Province of Nova Scotia. (1989). *Report of the Royal Commission on the Donald Marshall Jr. Prosecution: Findings and Recommendations.* Vol. 1. Halifax.

Province of Ontario (1995). *Report of the Commission on Systemic Racism in the Ontario Criminal Justice System.* Toronto.

Reiman, J. (1984). *The Rich Get Richer and the Poor Get Prison.* New York: Macmillan.

Report of the Royal Commission on Aboriginal Peoples. (1996). Ottawa: Minister of Supply and Services.

Sukahara, D. (1992). "Public Inquiries into Policing." *Canadian Police College Journal.* 16:135–36.

Ungerleider, C. (1992a). "Intercultural Awareness and Sensitivity of Canadian Police Officers." *Canadian Public Administration* 32(4)(Winter):612–22.

———. (1992b). "Issues in Police Intercultural and Race Relations Training in Canada." Ottawa: Solicitor General of Canada. Excerpt on pages 187–88 reproduced with the permission of the Minister of Public Works and Government Services Canada, 1999.

Urban Alliance on Race Relations. (1995). "Police Shootings and Racism: Getting at the Truth." Submission to the Commission on Systemic Racism in the Ontario Criminal Justice System. Toronto.

Valpy, M. (1994). "A Nasty Serving of Cultural Apartheid." *Globe and Mail* (April 8).

Chapter 7

▼▼▼▼▼▼▼▼▼▼▼

Racism and Human-Service Delivery

No amount of tinkering can fix the problem. What is required is a massive shift in attitudes, a revolution which would see a multifaceted approach, including full funding for ethnocultural and racial-community agencies and a decision-making process that is controlled by people truly representative of the population. (Minna, 1991)

his chapter examines the dynamics of individual, institutional, and cultural racism as they are reflected in the policies and practices of traditional, mainstream, human-service organizations. Included in the analysis are a wide range of human services provided by social and health-care agencies such as family- and child-service agencies, mental-health clinics, child-care facilities, and child-welfare agencies. Although it does not specifically consider other human services such as hospital and community health clinics and community or recreational centres, the issues are very much the same in these settings.

This chapter also looks briefly at the critical challenges confronting ethno-cultural and racial-community-based organizations that are attempting to meet the needs of specific constituencies such as immigrants, refugees, African Canadians, Chinese, South Asians, and other communities. Some barriers that affect the delivery of service are analyzed, including lack of representation of people of colour in mainstream human-service organizations; the marginalization and differential treatment experienced by racial-minority practitioners in these agencies; and the racist ideology underpinning the provision of services and modes of treatment. A case study of a women's hostel, Nellie's, provides the reader with a clear illustration of how racism, in its many dimensions, operates in the context of a human-service agency.

INTRODUCTION

As is the case with other Canadian institutions and systems (e.g., education, law enforcement, government agencies, media), a growing body of evidence indicates that racist ideologies and practices affect the administration and operation of human-service organizations, the delivery of services to individual clients and communities, the allocation of resources, training, and education programs, and the access and participation of people of colour as clients or patients, managers, staff, and volunteers.

THE MANIFESTATIONS OF RACISM

Racial and cultural barriers influence the provision of services and the quality and appropriateness of those services. Racial bias and discrimination can be reflected in the allocation of resources by funders, who may ignore the dramatic rise in immigrants and refugees in recent decades and the particular needs of racial-minority groups and the agencies that serve them. An aspect of racism may be reflected in the view of funders that racially specific services are an unnecessary duplication of the programs and services offered by mainstream agencies.

Racist assumptions and practices may also influence the employment opportunities for minority social workers and health-care practitioners. Professional credentials acquired in other countries, for example, may not be recognized in Canada. Professional competency is therefore measured by standards and norms that undervalue the training received by many members of racial minorities.

Racial bias may also be reflected in the modes of treatment and approaches to problem resolution, which may ignore the effects of systemic racism on the client or fail to take into account cultural values, community norms, and indigenous resources. Racism may also influence the common assumption that views racial minorities from a "problem" perspective — either they have problems, or they are the cause of problems. A further example of racism commonly found in human-service organizations is the failure to provide services that are racially sensitive, culturally appropriate, and linguistically accessible.

The disempowering effects of racism in human-service organizations may be further compounded when a person of colour is also an immigrant

---

MANIFESTATIONS OF RACISM IN HUMAN SERVICES

Lack of access to appropriate programs and services
Ethnocentric values and counselling practices
Devaluing of the skills and credentials of minority practitioners
Inadequate funding for ethno-racial community-based agencies
Lack of minority representation in social agencies
Monocultural or ad hoc multicultural model of service delivery

or refugee. The effect of this double group identification is even greater marginalization and disadvantage. Women of colour who are immigrants are particularly vulnerable, as are the elderly.

A number of studies have drawn attention to these and other pervasive racial barriers, which exist in almost all the major traditional, mainstream, human-service delivery organizations across Canada (Calliste, 1996; Christensen, 1996; Shakir, 1995; Bambrough et al., 1992; Doyle and Visano, 1987).

EDUCATION AND TRAINING

Few undergraduate and postgraduate educational programs provide the skills and knowledge necessary for social workers, doctors, nurses, and other human-service practitioners from the dominant culture to confront racism in their professional values, norms, and practices. For example, faculties of social work, medicine, and nursing have resisted incorporating into their curriculum the study of racism. Moreover, the theories, methodologies, and traditional skills taught in these programs bear little relation to the needs of clients from diverse racial and cultural backgrounds (Christensen, 1996; Shakir, 1995; Canadian Asociation of Schools of Social Work, 1991; Agard, 1987).

An exploratory survey of a Task Force on Multicultural and Multiracial Issues in Social Work Education found that most accredited schools of social work in Canadian universities do not offer courses dealing with multicultural and multiracial issues (Canadian Association of Schools of Social Work, 1991). As a result of interviews with students, faculty, field instructors, administrators, and community representatives, the task force recommended changes to accreditation standards related to organizational structures, policies, curriculum content, student body, faculty, fieldwork, and community accountability.

A report of the Multicultural and Race Relations Division CAO, Municipality of Metropolitan Toronto, in 1994 identified a number of critical issues related to the curriculum of social work faculties, which rely heavily on Eurocentric practice models and fail to recognize that this paradigm is not the norm, but one of several norms. Most faculties of social work have resisted including in their core curriculum mandatory courses on antiracism, Aboriginal issues, and cross-cultural issues (Christensen, 1996). Some faculties have added optional courses that focus on "cultural awareness" or "ethnic-sensitivity" models of social work. These models have failed to examine the assimilationist assumptions of social-work practice upon which these models are based (McMahon and Allen-Meares, 1992).

One measure of determining how deeply racism penetrates any professional group is an analysis of the body of knowledge that underpins the training of its practitioners, in terms of both pre-service education and on-going professional development. A major survey of social-work literature, including most of the major journals in the field (McMahon and Allen-Meares, 1992), revealed that racism is deeply embedded in the theoretical and ideological frameworks underlying the practice of social work. The authors of the content analysis of over one hundred articles suggest that social-work literature conveys the impression of a non-critical and inward-looking professional literature. Central to the literature is the belief that immigrants and minorities should assimilate into the mainstream dominant culture.

Rather than focussing on anti-racism, the pervading models of "good practice" seem to focus on individual interventions with minority clients to assist them in adapting to their oppressive situation, or alternatively to "sensitize" social workers to the "different" cultural values and beliefs of minorities. Most of the literature ignores the macro-issues of racism as a systemic phenomenon and shows a general resistance to undertaking proactive transformative actions within a macro-context. On the basis of this review, the authors concluded that the literature portrays the profession as superficial in its anti-racist practice.

ACCESS TO SERVICES

Evidence of the failure of traditional, mainstream social and health-care agencies is provided by the findings of numerous task forces and consultations undertaken to assess the quality and accessibility of care and services provided to racial and ethno-cultural client groups by traditional human-service agencies (Shakir, 1995; British Columbia Task Force on Family Violence, 1992; James and Muhammad, 1992; Medeiros, 1991; *Canadian Task Force*, 1988).

In 1987, the Social Planning Council of Metropolitan Toronto publicly reported on a comprehensive study it had commissioned (Doyle and Visano, 1987). The findings suggested that while access to basic social and health services is a form of universal entitlement, mainstream agencies in the human-service delivery system failed to provide accessible and equitable services. The researchers identified many linguistic, cultural, and racial barriers and discriminatory practices, as well as an absence of strategies to address these obstacles. They found institutional discrimination reflected in indifferent attitudes and a lack of commitment to seek remedies for patterns of exclusion and inaccessibility.

Some of the barriers to health and social services identified by minority-group clients were lack of information about the services provided, the unavailability of service, the service providers' lack of knowledge of the linguistic and cultural needs of different groups, and the inappropriateness of treatment modes and counselling. There was a widespread perception that the difference in racial and cultural backgrounds between clients and White, Anglo human-service professionals frequently resulted in misconceptions and negative judgements being made by service providers. All these problems were made more acute by the general problems that all consumers experience, such as child-care and transportation costs, lengthy delays, and physical distance from agencies (Doyle and Visano, 1987).

Another significant finding of the study was the existence of "two solitudes," in which mainstream agencies and ethno-racial services exist side by side, with little interaction and co-ordination in planning and delivering services. ("Mainstream" agencies offer services to anyone in the community who meets general eligibility criteria; "ethno-racial" agencies provide services to people on the basis of membership in a particular racial or cultural group.)

Ethno-racial organizations act as brokers and advocates for minority populations by providing settlement and integration services, language interpretation for mainstream agencies, family counselling, and so on. Support services are offered in which practitioners from agencies accompany clients to other organizations, assist in helping interpret their needs, and represent them and their interests. These services exist largely because of the failure of traditional organizations to adequately respond to the changing needs of a multiracial and pluralistic society.

Services provided by many ethno-racial agencies that are often absent in the mainstream agencies include more flexible hours, with evening and weekend service; drop-in services; locations in accessible, informal settings, such as community centres; home visits; community outreach; advertising of services in the multicultural media; and group counselling (Bridgman, 1993).

REPRESENTATION

One of the most profound barriers to access and equity in human-service agencies is the absence of people of colour at every level, especially boards of directors. In a study (Murray et al., 1992), the boards of some 1200 non-profit organizations in Canada were surveyed. It was found that these boards were predominantly composed of people with British origins; 28 percent were at least three-quarters British. An additional 30 percent were at least half British. The next most common group was those of "other Northern European origins" (German, Dutch, Scandinavian), with 47 percent of boards having at least some representation from this group. French Canadians were well represented, on 47 percent of boards. People of colour, however, were almost entirely absent.

Racial-Minority Professionals in Mainstream Human-Service Organizations

People of colour who are professionals working in human-service organizations often confront biases, barriers, and conflicts totally unknown to mainstream practitioners. A study in Nova Scotia (Bambrough et al., 1992), revealed that Black social-work graduates from the Maritime School of Social Work found less desirable jobs than others, including limited or term positions and more part-time jobs. Moreover, once they obtained work, they found that their opportunities for advancement were relatively limited and their salary levels low. The report concluded that Black graduate social workers had been less successful than the majority group in accessing the more prestigious social-work jobs, including family counselling, hospital social work, and administrative or supervisory positions.

Another formidable manifestation of bias frequently encountered by minority workers is the fact that the knowledge, skills, and experience they have acquired in their home countries may not be recognized or may be significantly undervalued. Degrees earned abroad are often not accredited, and foreign-trained graduates have no access to retraining (Ontario Ministry of Citizenship, 1989). Almost a decade after the Task Force on Access to Professions and Trades in Ontario was concluded — with numerous recommendations and strategies for effectively assessing the skills and experience of immigrants — there was still no formal implementation of its recommendations.

A related concern is the fragile position of community workers, who play a pivotal role in providing services to racial and ethno-cultural communities but do not have formal degrees or certificates. Patricia O'Connor, of Toronto's George Brown College, pointed out that the implications of the regulation limiting certification to university graduates was that funding for publicly funded agencies might be contingent on hiring only those with the right credentials (Webster, 1992).

Social workers and other human-service practitioners from diverse racial and cultural communities may experience serious conflicts between their cultural values and those of the dominant culture, which influences the practices and priorities of their organization. Minority workers commonly function from a dual perspective: they understand both the needs and concerns of their own communities and the limitations of the programs of mainstream human-service organizations. On the other hand, mainstream social-work and health-care practitioners are trained to view their services as having universal applicability and accessibility. There is considerable pressure on racial-minority practitioners to conform with traditional agency practices (Calliste, 1996; Desai, 1996; Mental Health Coordinating Group of Scarborough, 1992).

Within human-service agencies, increasing the number of ethno-racial staff often signals a commitment to improving services to minority clients and a commitment to multiculturalism and anti-racism. But as Turney (1997) points out, an increase in staff from a particular group does not necessarily improve service delivery. Change often remains at an administrative level without fundamentally altering the delivery of services. Minority workers are frequently isolated and marginalized in mainstream agencies. They are concentrated at the entry levels or in front-line positions. Their primary role is to serve clients who share the same racial or cultural background, but they tend to have limited power and status in the organization. This practice can result in a kind of ghettoization, especially of staff who are people of colour, where all "problems with Blacks" are referred to the Black worker (Thomas, 1987). Racist attitudes and behaviours are considered a significant barrier to good working relationships between White and minority practitioners.

Racial Minorities in the Health-Care Delivery System

Head (1986) was the first to examine the extent of racial discrimination in some Toronto hospitals. His research findings confirmed the general perception of racial-minority women working in these institutions: racial-minority nurses were under-represented at the decision-making and supervisory levels. Despite having similar educational qualifications, most minority health-care workers were represented in the lower levels of the hierarchy. White nurses in the sample were twice as successful in gaining promotions as Blacks were. A considerable degree of apathy, hopelessness, and fear existed among Black respondents. Many were hesitant about participating in the study, for fear of being reprimanded or fired. More than half the Black respondents indicated they had been harassed by patients.

Calliste (1996) analyzed racism in nursing by focussing on the experiences of African Canadian nurses between 1990 and 1995. Calliste contends that the economic restructuring and rapid downsizing in the health-care system in the 1990s combined with both old and new forms of racism to have a disproportionate impact on female health-care workers of colour, particularly Black women who attempted to speak out about racism. They were more likely to be laid off, demoted, and dismissed. In recent years, Black nurses, with the support of organizations such as the Congress of Black Women, have been demanding institutional and systemic change to racism and other forms of social oppression operating in the health-care system.

In the 1990s, several human-rights complaints were filed with the Ontario Human Rights Commission against hospitals in Toronto. There were similar cases in Montreal. The recruitment, selection, and promotion practices in hospitals revealed a pattern of systemic racism in the workplace, leading to differential treatment of nurses of colour. An Ontario Human Rights Commission tribunal corroborated this finding (Hardill, 1993), citing the fact that in one hospital, during hiring, one reference check was the general norm for White applicant nurses, while three references were commonly checked before selecting Black nurses.

Calliste's study documents the manifestations of systemic racism experienced on the job by nurses of colour, including excessive monitoring and differential documentation. For example, personnel files for Black nurses frequently contained irrelevant personal information about their families, place of origin, and English proficiency. The study found that Black nurses were disciplined for minor or non-existent problems for which White nurses were not disciplined. The Ontario Nursing Association (Caissey, 1994:3) also concluded that nurses of colour were often over-supervised and subjected to differential treatment and had their employment terminated more often than did White nurses. Calliste labelled this "the racialialization of surveillance practices in nursing" (1996:371). In a number of interviews carried out in 1994 and 1996, Marshall and Minors (cited in Calliste, 1996) found that Black nurses were stereotyped as childlike, lazy, aggressive, uncommunicative, and trouble-makers. Calliste observed, "the black woman nurse becomes an 'undesirable' identity" (1996:369). In this context, harassment and other forms of discrimination aimed at nurses of colour by hospital management as well as patients are widespread phenomena.

FAMILY SERVICES

A study prepared by the Multicultural Coalition for Access to Family Services (MCAFS) in Metropolitan Toronto underlined some of the critical issues facing racial- and cultural-minority communities (Medeiros, 1991). It found an "appalling lack of services" in ten ethno-cultural and racial communities. The report concluded that methods of family-service delivery were based on "certain notions of family structure, values and what is taken as normal behaviour and functioning within society, as defined by White, middle-class Judeo-Christian standards" (Medeiros, 1991:12).

Fewer than 8 percent of staff at established mainstream agencies spoke a language other than English, and only 14 percent of front-line staff were identified as being from the ten communities studied. Whereas $14.6 million was allocated annually to Metro for family services, only $900 000 went to ethno-cultural agencies. "The issue is not just lack of money, but rather a complacent disregard for the needs and the rights of ethno-cultural and racial communities" — who represent 60 percent of the population of Metro (Medeiros, 1991:7). The study indicated that 62 percent of the established family-service agencies had no policies or practices to address the needs of ethno-cultural and racial communities.

A more recent study conducted by Shakir (1995) for the MCAFS, focussing on wife assault in the South Asian community, found that mainstream social services were shaped by the notion of "essentialized" difference. The notion of **essentialism** suggests that there is a particular "essence" associated with being a Black or Asian client; that is, there is a single interpretation, unchanging through "time, space, and different historical, social, political and personal contexts" (Grillo, 1995:19). Shakir contends that what is "appropriate" for South Asian women in terms of services is not just a matter of culturally specific values and norms; what needs to be understood is the context of the power imbalance in the relations between the South Asian community and the values, institutions, and practices of the dominant culture. As Shakir explains: "The family may be the locus of abuse for some women of South Asian origin but it is the Canadian context that defines the nature of that violence/abuse" (1995:19). Razack makes a similar observation, commenting that while cross-cultural service delivery is a goal for service providers from dominant groups, usually very little is known about the impact of racism on the lives of the women of colour with whom they work (Razack, 1998:84).

A further ideological barrier for women of colour and other non-European immigrant women is the assumption that their problems are rooted in the cultural values and norms of these cultures — that is, they are hierarchical, traditional, patriarchal, and display a high tolerance for violence toward women. However, two studies (Shakir, 1995; British Columbia Task

Force on Family Violence, 1992) demonstrate that contrary to stereotypes of the acceptance of violence against women in non-Western cultures, there is no tolerance for it anywhere.

The ideology and power structure of mainstream service delivery is reflected in the fact that the experiences of South Asians and other ethno-racial groups can only be accommodated as "special-interest" issues. Ethno-specific services are seen as either a duplication of mainstream services or defined by cultural imperatives, while mainstream services are defined as being a universal approach, that is, treating everyone as having common needs (Desai, 1996; Shakir, 1995).

One of the leading authorities in the field of social work, race, and ethnicity in the United Kingdom suggested that no amount of asserting the irrelevance of race, colour, and ethnicity alters the fact that racial discrimination and disadvantage chronically influence the circumstances of ethnic and racial minorities (Cheetham, 1982). The fact that multicultural or anti-racist policies have been established in many family-service agencies appears to have made little difference because mainstream agencies continue to function without making fundamental changes to their service-delivery systems and to the dominant cultural values underpinning their organizational practices (Bridgman, 1993).

In social work today, seemingly innocuous concepts of "self," "relationship," or "therapy" are "a site of struggle" (Cooper, 1997:127). Clinical models of treatment and intervention offered by mainstream human services commonly ignore or dismiss the strength and significance of group identity and loyalty. At the same time, they fail to recognize the supportive role that racial and ethno-specific groups play in helping ethno-cultural and racial minorities to confront social, economic, and political disadvantage and discrimination.

Much of the influential literature on family therapy has drawn a boundary around the nuclear family. Solutions to problems have been sought within this internal system, without taking into account the extended family maintained by many clients and the pressures placed on them by their environment. Yet, one cannot consider family dysfunction without considering the context of family life.

As a result of these barriers, many clients underutilize or terminate their involvement with an agency, finding the service delivery "too institutionalized, fragmented and culturally insensitive" (Agard, 1987). Their reasons for doing so are related to the biased nature of the services: "The services offered are frequently antagonistic or inappropriate to the life experiences of the culturally different client; they lack sensitivity and understanding; they are oppressive and discriminating toward minority clients" (Sue and Sue, 1990:7).

MENTAL-HEALTH SERVICES

The findings of a national task force to conduct hearings on access to mental-health services by immigrants indicated that health and social services for immigrants were highly fragmented and uncoordinated (*Canadian Task Force*, 1988) and that they had been developed without an overall plan for co-ordination with the mainstream service-delivery system. The task force identified numerous racial, cultural, and linguistic barriers that prevented the effective use of mental-health services. Ethno-cultural and racial groups and service providers agreed that the lack of a common language was the barrier that most interfered with assessment and treatment.

A survey conducted by a hospital in Toronto found that the need for more mental-health services among immigrant, refugee, and racial-minority women was greatest for those who had been sexually assaulted (Pilowsky, 1991). The report also found that the common barriers immigrant women faced when seeking mental-health services were language, a lack of personnel trained to be sensitive to people of different cultures and races, and a lack of free services and information.

The lack of professional, trained interpreters affects all areas of human-service delivery. In Ontario, limited efforts were made by the provincial government (Ontario Ministry of Citizenship, 1989) to support the training of cultural and linguistic interpreters. In some major hospitals, resources were allocated to hire trained interpreters. However, most social and health-care agencies rely on volunteers, family, or their own unqualified employees to interpret. Consequently, many patients or clients choose not to disclose personal and pertinent information, in order to avoid embarrassment. The translation may provide misleading data because of a lack of professional expertise (*Canadian Task Force*, 1988).

Another significant barrier between minority clients or patients and mainstream human-service delivery is the fact that many minority groups consider social and health concerns to be a collective problem, affecting others as well as the person seeking help. Members of both the immediate and extended family, especially elders, expect to be involved in the assessment of the problem and to play an active role in treatment. Although the centrality of the individual is an indispensable foundation of social work in Western societies, it is for some minorities an incomprehensible concept (Cheetham, 1982). In many immigrant cultures, independence from the family is not a primary goal. Enormous value is placed on interdependence, co-operation, and loyalty to the family. Each family member is expected to put the family's needs ahead of individual desires (British Columbia Task Force, 1992).

The formal and bureaucratic atmosphere of mental-health facilities and other social and health-care agencies creates an alienating environment. Sterile reception areas (often staffed by culturally insensitive staff), complex and confusing administrative forms, service-delivery information printed only in English, and inflexible office hours are common features of these clinics (Doyle and Visano, 1987).

Minority professionals have pointed out the profound difference in worldview that typically separates White interviewers from clients of colour (Sisskind, 1978). Racial stereotyping often skews the initial assessment of therapists, who may view traits such as aggressive behaviour as indicative of a personality disorder, when in fact they may be a normal response to living in a racist society. Professional norms as well as class-bound values are used to judge normality or deviance (Dominelli, 1989).

In one study, when therapists interviewed patients, they tended to assign diagnoses of depression to Whites and of schizophrenia to Blacks. When they used a standardized interview form, differences between Blacks and Whites disappeared. Another submission to the task force (Harambee Centres of Canada) identified racial stereotyping as a potential factor in biasing assessments (*Canadian Task Force*, 1988).

Traditional interviewing techniques in social work and the health sciences commonly emphasize professional distance between the client and the therapist, a non-directive style, and emphasis on verbal, emotional, and behaviourial expressiveness and self-disclosure. They also stress self-responsibility and examining past experiences. These techniques are rooted in a North American value system that may directly conflict with the client's cultural norms. Racial-minority clients whose lives have been marked by racism may well be disinclined to engage in self-disclosure with a White professional. For many minorities, sharing intimate aspects of one's experiences only occurs after a long and intense relationship has been established.

CHILDREN'S SERVICES

Racism in societal institutions has a significant impact on services to children and child-welfare policies and programs. It also has a profound affect on the self-image of racial-minority children.

In a study of African Canadian children (children of African heritage in Canada, regardless of place of birth) under the care of child-welfare agencies in Canada, Louis (1992) identified a number of ways in which the cumulative effects of the racism of bigoted peers, teachers, other adults, the media, and fellow African Canadians affects these children.

One of the most important effects of this negative socialization are that the African Canadian child's self-image becomes distorted, and a positive sense of racial identity is undermined before it has a chance to develop (Louis, 1992). Children begin to develop racial awareness at three to five years of age; they are aware of differences between racial groups and can recognize and label these differences. Children at this early age can also identify themselves in racial terms (Milner, 1975).

Louis (1992) observed that when African Canadian children were removed from their natural families, they entered into an almost exclusively White world (White social workers, lawyers, counsellors, doctors, judges, and court officials; foster families and adoptive parents are also often White). African Canadian children tended to be placed with White families. This uprooting of children from their own family and community and their placement in all-White environments can have a debilitating effect on the self-image and group identity of these children. They often feel insecure and unable to discuss their experiences with racism. Thus, however well intended the caregivers and the agencies, there is a general failure to recognize the unique problems facing these children in care and an absence of programs to address their needs. Numerous studies in the United Kingdom reached similar conclusions (Ahmed, 1981).

Children from oppressed racial and cultural groups tend to have pre-occupations different from those of their White peers. In order of concern, they have questions about their own identity; about racism and Whites; and about other groups. For White children, the order seems to be questions about people of colour; comments that reflect stereotypical or negative attitudes; and questions about their own identity (Derman-Sparks et al., 1980). These findings have significant implications for policies and practices involving racial-minority children from day care to child welfare.

BARRIERS AFFECTING WOMEN

Racism and sexism meet in the lives of women of colour and affect their daily experiences as well as their access to services. In cases of sexual assault or family violence, these women may be under even more pressure than Anglo-Canadian women not to report the incident, in order not to breach the solidarity of the community (British Columbia Task Force, 1992). On the other hand, they may be isolated and not have the traditional family-support networks. Immigrant and refugee women often are unaware of their legal rights; they fear that if they report their husbands for abuse, they might lose their landed-immigrant status and be sent back to their home country.

The lack of fluency in English creates another barrier that affects immigrants' access to protection and safety. Their first difficulty is finding out which services are available; the information is mostly available only in English. Linguistic, cultural, and racial barriers make it difficult for these women to seek help from social workers, police, counsellors, doctors, and religious leaders. In an Ontario study, 62.2 percent of the battered immigrant women interviewed cited a fear that they would lose "everything — house, children, reputation — everything I worked for" once they involved the police as an important reason for not calling the police. Also, 42.2 percent of the women cited fear that a husband or partner would be brutalized or victimized by the police as a reason for not calling the police (ARA Consultants, 1985).

Within the service-delivery system, from interactions with the police to experiences in the courts and access to shelters, these women are likely to encounter racial bias and discrimination. Social workers or judges may have mistaken and stereotypical attitudes, leading them to disbelieve the woman of colour, particularly if she is describing the conduct of a White person. For victims of abuse, racism adds another painful dimension to the experience and to the problem of finding help.

These barriers lead some researchers to conclude that victims of family and sexual violence from minority cultures confront not only the trivialization and denial that are the by-products of sexism, but also the denial that stems from the invisibility of racism in Canadian society (British Columbia Task Force, 1992).

CASE STUDY 7.1

NELLIE'S

This case study illustrates some of the major themes and issues identified in this chapter. It shows how human-service professionals and organizations, with established and significant track records in providing diverse and critically important services, are often unable to adapt their policies, programs, professional attitudes, and behaviours to control racism in its diverse forms.

Nellie's is a women's hostel in Toronto for battered and homeless women. It was co-founded in 1974 by June Callwood and Vicki Trerise. From 1991 to 1993 it was rocked by controversy, conflict, and internal strife. The focus of the dissension was racism in the organization. At the centre of the controversy was a woman of enormous prestige who, especially in the mainstream community, is viewed with great respect and affection.

Callwood, a journalist, broadcaster, and social activist, is widely revered for her involvement in and commitment to many social justice issues. She was a founding member of the Canadian Civil Liberties Association and several peace and feminist organizations, and the driving force behind Jessie's (a home for unwed mothers) and Casey House (an AIDS hospice). She was awarded the Order of Canada for her outstanding contributions to Canadian society.

BACKGROUND

Nellie's has provided an important community service in Toronto throughout its history, serving battered women, homeless women, women in emotional distress, prostitutes, destitute refugees, and incest survivors. As is the case with most human-service organizations in recent years, the ethno-cultural and racial composition of the clients has changed; more than half the clients are immigrants, refugees, and women of colour. In response to its changing client population, Nellie's recruited some women of colour as staff and board members. However, the nominal increase in representation did not address the fundamental conflict over race and power that emerged in the organization.

EVENTS

In the early 1990s, Nellie's became the focus of public attention as a result of actions that occurred in the organization. Allegations of racism surfaced and then escalated in the course of several months, and they were extensively reported by the media. The allegation of racism appeared to stem from two issues: a clash of ideologies over service and program-delivery issues, and a power struggle between staff and board members who were White and staff and board members who were women of colour.

(continued)

CASE STUDY 7.1 *(continued)*

It appears that the catalyst for the conflict was a difference of opinion about whether to provide programs and counselling for incest victims. Some staff wanted to provide services for women wanting help for suffering related to past abuses, and others believed that Nellie's current resources were insufficient to handle these clients. Those opposed to introducing this service were mainly women of colour who were relatively new to Nellie's. Those arguing for counselling were White workers who had been at the shelter for a longer period and felt that the agency should provide this service.

In staff meetings and board meetings, racial tension increased. Questions of who had the power to make critical decisions in the organization were raised. Staff members who were women of colour felt the need to coalesce for support and formed a caucus group. In a series of letters, the group expressed its perception that systemic racism was operating at Nellie's and expressed concern about the absence of a grievance mechanism to deal with their views on racial issues.

The Women of Colour Caucus argued that despite the fact that Nellie's was supposedly structured on a feminist collective model, in which all members had equal access to decision making, it operated on the basis of a subtle hierarchy of power and authority. Women of colour felt marginalized, isolated, and excluded. From their perspective, issues such as client access to culturally and racially appropriate services and equitable participation and representation in the workplace were ignored or deflected. Despite the efforts of the caucus to place the issue of racism on the organizational agenda, many of the White board and staff continued to deny the validity of these perceptions and dismissed the signs of a growing crisis in the organization.

Although June Callwood was not the central issue, she stood at the centre of the struggle. In the highly charged atmosphere of a board meeting at Nellie's, one of the staff read a document prepared by the caucus identifying a wide range of concerns, including racial inequities in the workplace, their colleagues' racist behaviour, and discriminatory barriers in the development and delivery of services. The demands called for improved equity hiring practices, a grievance policy, a strong anti-racism mission statement, and new evaluation and training procedures.

Following the reading of the document, Callwood responded with an angry criticism of the Black woman who had read it and disclosed that the woman had once been a Nellie's client. Callwood implied that the woman should have been grateful for the support and assistance the organization had given her, rather than complaining about racism. The board asked Callwood to apologize for the breach of confidentiality and the inappropriateness of her remarks. Michele Landsberg quotes Callwood as saying, "I blew it." She began by saying, "I was coerced into this apology.... Only a small part of it is sincere" (Landsberg, 1992b). At a subsequent board meeting, there was a call for Callwood's resignation.

In the spring of 1993, Callwood resigned from the board of Nellie's. In a special article in the *Toronto Star*, she suggested that she was the victim of tactics of "intimidation and naked aggression." She observed that "the tactics of intimidation which have been effective at Nellie's are not strategies that anyone can

(continued)

condone.... Such naked aggression only hardens differences and does the cause of racism serious damage" (Landsberg, 1992b).

The charges of racial bias and discrimination at Nellie's and Callwood's resignation created a furor in the mainstream community. Several editorials appeared in the press, and numerous articles were written by Callwood's media colleagues and friends, all denouncing the actions of the women of colour at Nellie's and defending Callwood's integrity (Thorsell, 1992; Dewar, 1993; Marchand, 1993). Pierre Berton (1992) wrote: "If June Callwood is a racist then so are we all."

In an eleven-page *Toronto Life* article about Nellie's, Elaine Dewar insinuated that the charges of racism against Callwood and Nellie's were totally fallacious, contrived by the caucus, and supported by other radicals outside the organization to gain power and control in the agency. She commented, "Anyone planning a run at Nellie's could surmise that if Callwood was pushed on the subject of racism, she might leave" (Dewar, 1993:35).

In far fewer numbers, articles appeared in the media analyzing the conflict from the perspective of the women of colour involved in the issue (Landsberg, 1992a; Barker and Wright, 1992; Benjamin et al., 1993).

ANALYSIS

Confronting and challenging racism in a human-service organization is fraught with risk and pain for the organization's clients, staff, and board of directors. The backlash effect and resistance often extend well beyond the organization; both the mainstream and the minority communities are implicated in the struggle. In this instance, the media played a critical role in reinforcing the position of the White group in Nellie's and helped mobilize public sentiment against the Women of Colour Caucus. By depicting those who were calling for change as radicals, reverse racists, and aggressive power-seeking individuals, the media further polarized the situation and reinforced the marginalization of people of colour in Canadian society.

The perspective of the White staff of Nellie's and June Callwood was that Nellie's provided important, effective programs and services and used a progressive, egalitarian model of service delivery that included everyone. Most of the White women in the organization were feminists and saw themselves as unbiased, fairminded individuals, committed to equality and dedicated to service.

As is the case with most White human-service professionals, they were confident of their professional skills and knowledge and believed that Nellie's current structure, norms, and mode of operation met the needs of the groups it was serving. While they recognized that the changing client group required some organizational adjustments (such as increasing the representation of women of colour in the agency), they saw no need for radical changes in the work environment, service-delivery model, or decision-making and administrative processes.

Thus, they were shocked when they were accused of racism in their attitudes and behaviour in relation to their organizational policies, practices, and structures.

(continued)

CASE STUDY 7.1 *(continued)*

They were unable to identify the subtle and overt ways in which they continued to exercise power and control and thus felt unjustly accused.

For the women of colour, there were significant costs in exposing the racism at Nellie's. Their demands for substantive change were met with a powerful back-lash, not only in their own organization, but in the mainstream community. The media were instrumental in devaluing and delegitimizing the concerns of the women of colour and reinforced the White-dominated status quo. In analyzing this issue, three prominent anti-racism practitioners observed:

> Anti-racism, like other struggles for social change, brings about division and emotional turmoil. Effective anti-racism work identifies resistance to change and lays bare on the one hand, holders of historic power and privi-lege that is based on skin colour, however relative that power may be, and on the other hand, powerlessness and internalized oppression of Black women and other women of colour. (Benjamin et al., 1993)

CONCLUSION

This case study demonstrates how racism, in all its diverse dimensions, affected a highly respected human-service agency such as Nellie's. It also provides a graph-ic illustration of the strategies commonly used to minimize the issue of racism in White-dominated organizations.

RESPONSES TO RACISM

Despite the fact that a growing number of mainstream human-service agen-cies have developed multicultural and anti-racism policies, have carried out cross-cultural and anti-racism training programs for staff and management, and have hired a few members of ethno-racial minorities, the ideology of social work reflects the deep tension and contradictions characteristic of democratic racism. On one hand, social work and health care are commit-ted to the promotion of the well-being and welfare of all members of soci-ety. On the other hand, mainstream human services continue to be shaped by "essentialized" concepts of difference, deficit cultures, hegemonic power imbalances, and Western therapy models that are alien to many non-dom-inant populations.

A racialized discourse underlies the practice of human services and re-flects the strong resistance of human-service theorists, practitioners, and educators to transformative models of social change. A number of discur-sive strategies are used in social work to resist dealing with racism (Dominelli, 1989). All of them operate in Case Study 7.1 and in the other examples cited in this chapter.

- *Denial strategies* are based on the idea that cultural, institutional, and systemic forms of racism do not exist in the human-service delivery system. They assume that while there may be isolated cases of racist attitudes, these are extremely rare in an otherwise civil society.
- *Universalism* in the context of human services assumes that people are essentially the same — that members of any ethno-racial group have similar problems, needs, and goals. This discourse ignores the the fact that the construct of **universality** does not carry an inherent meaning beyond a specific set of cultural, historical, political, and material conditions (Shakir, 1995).
- *Cultural awareness and ethno-specific sensitivity* focuses on changing the attitudes and behaviours of White human-service workers. However, racial inequality requires more than professional sensitivity to address the systemic forms of racism that affect the lives of minorities.
- *Patronizing approaches* appear to accept the principle of equality between Whites and people of colour. But when the power and privilege of White people are challenged, demands for substantive change are met with fierce resistance and the status quo is affirmed.
- *"Dumping" strategies* rely on placing the responsibility for eliminating racism on the shoulders of the victims. In this strategy, professionals see themselves as neutral players.
- *Decontextualization strategies* acknowledge the presence of racism "out there" in the external environment, but not "in here," in *this* organization. Decontextualization also operates in the form of treatment modes that focus on individual intervention, that is, on helping individuals assimilate or adapt to their oppression.

These responses are characteristic of organizations that operate on an assimilationist model of human-service delivery. This model recognizes that racial and cultural diversity exist in the broader community but views this reality as irrelevant in determining the role and mandate of the agency, the nature of the service delivered, the constituencies served, the professional staff hired, and the volunteers recruited.

In monocultural organizations, linguistic, cultural, and racial barriers to service delivery are neither identified nor addressed. Thus, the services provided by them remain inaccessible to multicultural and multiracial communities. The underlying assumption is that, despite the obvious differences in the cultural backgrounds and racial identities of clients, all people share common needs and desires and therefore require similar modes of service and intervention.

Many voluntary social agencies and some health-care organizations have attempted to respond to racial-minority demands for more accessible and equitable services by introducing a multicultural organizational model. The change, however, appears often to be cosmetic. New initiatives include the translation of communication materials, the recruitment of board members and volunteers from minority communities, and the hiring of one or two "ethnic" workers. Multicultural and anti-racism issues, while important, are considered separately from the day-to-day life of the organization. The needs and interests of minorities are dealt with on an ad hoc basis rather than being integrated into the structure, policies, programs, and practices of the organization.

The responsibility for change is often delegated to the front-line worker, who may function in a totally unsupportive environment. Concrete action to promote change is sometimes deferred, as the organization attempts to juggle competing demands and priorities. Racism is perceived to be an issue mainly in terms of minority client–mainstream professional interactions and relationships. Therefore, the primary responsibility of the agency is to provide opportunities for human relations–race relations sensitization-training programs for front-line staff.

Mainstream agencies continue to be ineffective in delivering services to ethno-cultural and racial communities. Despite some modifications in the policies of funding agencies such as the United Way and provincial governments, a significant shift is required in the policies and practices of funding bodies.

The controversy over the production of *Show Boat* (discussed in Chapter 9) provides an interesting insight into the limitations of some organizational responses to racism as it relates to human services. The United Way of Greater Toronto had attempted to develop a multicultural anti-racist policy and program to assist its member agencies in becoming "more accessible, responsive and reflective of the total community through a process they have called multicultural/anti-racist organizational development" (United Way of Greater Toronto, 1991).

The thrust of the policy was to encourage member agencies to develop more inclusive services and to identify racial and cultural barriers in their organizational structures and programs. The United Way prided itself on its "pro-active" approach in providing anti-racist training to its staff, reaching out to racial-minority communities, establishing advisory committees that included representatives from racial communities, recruiting racially and culturally diverse board members, and establishing what it considered to be a more equitable allocations process.

However, the United Way's decision to sponsor a performance of *Show Boat* as a fundraiser, in conjunction with one of its member agencies, the Canadian Institute for the Blind, created a wave of controversy, particularly among people of colour. The refusal of the organization to withdraw from sponsorship led many in the community and some members of the agency to question its commitment to anti-racism. Some argued that the United Way bowed to the interests of the marketplace and the power elite, who threatened to withdraw their financial support if the United Way cancelled its fundraising event. To protest the organization's position on *Show Boat*, the United Way's recently created Caribbean/Black Advisory Committee and several volunteers resigned from the agency.

ANALYSIS

White, Anglo-Canadian human-service practitioners have generally been unwilling to acknowledge that services developed to help those who are most vulnerable can work against the interests of racial and cultural minorities (Cheetham, 1982). White practitioners in the human services are often oblivious to racism as a powerful social force. They generally lack an understanding of racial minorities' daily struggle with prejudice and discrimination. A preference for homogeneity and assimilation runs deep in the institutions of Canadian society and clearly weaves its way into the human-service delivery system.

Ethno-cultural and racially specific community-based agencies have filled the huge service-delivery gap created by the failure of mainstream institutions to serve the needs of a multiracial, multicultural, immigrant population. Yet, these agencies are generally isolated from the mainstream delivery system and are often seen by funders as a duplication of services. They have undertaken the responsibility of providing more effective, responsive, and equitable services to minority communities, with little recognition or remuneration.

Although minority communities have great trust in this alternative form of human-service delivery, there has been an overwhelming lack of support from government and other funding bodies for community-based agencies. Generally the funding has been in the form of time-bound projects rather than operational funding.

SUMMARY

White human-service practitioners use a variety of rationales to deny, ignore, and minimize racism in their organizations, their professional values and practices, and their personal belief systems and relationships. The case study of Nellie's and the discussion of racism in hospitals demonstrate how mainstream agencies continue to operate within a universalist, assimilationist, monocultural model of service delivery that views the **pluralism** of Canadian society as being irrelevant to their mandates, policies, structures, and operations. Despite the growing number of anti-racism policies developed by agencies such as the United Way and municipal and provincial agencies, there is little evidence of a willingness to alter the ideology that shapes traditional human-service delivery.

REFERENCES

Agard, R. (1987). "Access to the Social Assistance Delivery System by Various Ethnocultural Groups." In *Social Assistance Review Committee Report*. Ontario Ministry of Community and Social Services.

Ahmed, S. (1981). "Children in Care: The Racial Dimension in Social Work Assessment." In J. Cheetham et al. (eds.), *Social and Community Work in a Multiracial Society*. London: Harper and Row.

ARA Consultants. (1985). *Wife Battering among Rural, Native and Immigrant Women*. Toronto: ARA Consultants.

Bambrough, J., W. Bowden, and F. Wien. (1992). *Preliminary Results from the Survey of Graduates from the Maritime School of Social Work*. Halifax: Maritime School of Social Work, Dalhousie University.

Barker, D., and C. Wright. (1992). "The Women of Colour on the Nellie's Saga." *Toronto Star* (September 3).

Benjamin, A., J. Rebick, and A. Go. (1993). "Racist Backlash Takes Subtle Form among Feminists." *Toronto Star* (April 30):A23.

Berton, P. (1992). "If Callwood Is a Racist Then So Are We All." *Toronto Star* (May 23):H3.

Bridgman, G. (1993). "The Place of Mainstream and Ethno-Racial Agencies in the Delivery of Family Services to Ethno-Racial Canadians." Master of Social Work thesis, Faculty of Graduate Studies, Graduate Program in Social Work, York University.

British Columbia Task Force on Family Violence. (1992). *Is Anyone Listening*.

Caissey, I. (1994). "Presentation to the City of North York's Community Race and Ethnic Relations Committee." Toronto, October 13.

Calliste, A. (1996). "Antiracism Organizing and Resistance in Nursing: African Canadian Women." *Canadian Review of Social Anthropology* 33(3):361–90.

Canadian Association of Schools of Social Work. (1991). *Social Work Education at the Crossroads: The Challenge of Diversity*. Report of the Task Force on Multicultural and Multiracial Issues in Social Work Education.

Canadian Task Force on Mental Health Issues Affecting Immigrants and Refugees in Canada. (1988). Ottawa: Ministries of Multiculturalism and Citizenship and Health and Welfare.

Cheetham, J. (1982). "Introduction to the Issues." In J. Cheetham (ed.), *Social Work and Ethnicity*. London: George Allen and Unwin.

Christensen, C.P. (1996). "The Impact of Racism on the Education of Social Service Workers." In C. James (ed.), *Perspectives on Racism and the Human Service Sector: A Case for Change*. Toronto: University of Toronto Press.

Cooper, A. (1997). "Thinking the Unthinkable: 'White Liberal' Defenses against Understanding in Anti-Racist Thinking." *Journal of Social Work Practice* 11(2):127–37.

Derman-Sparks, L., C.T. Higa, and W. Sparks. (1980). "Children, Race and Racism: How Race Awareness Develops." *Interracial Books for Children Bulletin* 11(3 & 4):3–9.

Desai, S. (1996). "Afterword." In C. James (ed.), *Perspectives on Racism and the Human Service Sector: A Case for Change*. Toronto: University of Toronto Press. 246–51.

Dewar, E. (1993). "Wrongful Dismissal." *Toronto Life* (March):32–46.

Dominelli, L. (1989). "An Uncaring Profession? An Examination of Racism in Social Work." *New Community* 15(3):391–403.

Doyle, R., and L. Visano. (1987). *Access to Health and Social Services for Members of Diverse Cultural and Racial Groups*. Reports 1 and 2. Toronto: Social Planning Council of Metropolitan Toronto.

Grillo, T. (1995). "Anti-Essentialism and Intersectionality: Tools to Dismantle the Master's House." *Berkeley Women's Law Journal* 10(1):19.

Hardill, K. (1993). "Discovering Fire Where the Smoke Is: Racism in the Health Care System." *Toward Justice in Health* 2(1):17–21.

Head, W. (1986). *Black Women's Work: Racism in the Health System*. Toronto: Ontario Human Rights Commission.

James, C., and H. Muhammad. (1992). *Children in Childcare Programs: Perception of Race and Race Related Issues*. Toronto: Multicultural and Race Relations Division and Children's Services of the Municipality of Metropolitan Toronto.

Landsberg, M. (1992a). "Callwood Furor Masks Real Racism Struggle at Nellie's." *Toronto Star* (July 18).

———. (1992b). "The Nellie's Furor: June Callwood Tells Her Side." *Toronto Star* (July 23):F1.

Louis, C. (1992). "Issues Affecting African-Canadian Children in Alternative Care." *Multiculturalism* (Toronto) 14(2 & 3):58–60.

McMahon, A., and P. Allen-Meares. (1992). "Is Social Work Racist? A Content Analysis of Recent Literature." *Social Work* 37(6) (November 6):533–39.

Marchand, P. (1993). "Callwood Denounces 'Bullying' by Self-Defined Weak." *Toronto Star* (June 21).

Medeiros, J. (1991). *Family Services for All*. Toronto: Multicultural Coalition for Access to Family Services.

Mental Health Coordinating Group of Scarborough. (1992). *Together for Change*. Scarborough.

Milner, D. (1975). *Children and Race*. London: Penguin.

Minna, M. (1991). "Social Service System Cheats Metro's Ethnics." *Toronto Star* (June 5):A23.

Municipality of Metropolitan Toronto, Multicultural and Race Relations Division. (1994). *Anti-Racist Social Work: The Time Is Now*. Report on the March 24 Forum. Toronto.

Murray, V., P. Bradshaw, and J. Wolpin. (1992). "Power in and around Non-Profit Boards: A Neglected Dimension of Governance." *Non-Profit Management and Leadership* 3(2):165–82.

Ontario Ministry of Citizenship. (1989). *Access*. Toronto: Task Force on Access to Professions and Trades in Ontario.

Pilowsky, J. (1991). *Community Consultation Report*. Toronto: Doctors Hospital, Multicultural Women's Programme.

Razack, S. (1998). *Looking White People in the Eye: Gender, Race, and Culture in the Courtrooms and Classrooms*. Toronto: University of Toronto Press.

Shakir, U. (1995). *Presencing at the Boundary: Wife Assault in the South Asian Community*. Toronto: Multicultural Coalition for Access to Family Services.

Sisskind, J. (1978). "Cross-cultural Issues in Mental Health." In *ERIC Reports*. Washington: U.S. Dept. of Education.

Sue, D., and D.W. Sue. (1990). "Issues and Concepts of Cross-Cultural Counselling." In *Counselling the Culturally Different: Theory and Practice*. New York: John Wiley and Son.

Thomas, B. (1987). *Multiculturalism at Work*. Toronto: YWCA.

Thorsell, W. (1992). "A Question of the Pot Calling the Kettle White." *Globe and Mail* (May 23):D6.

Turney, D. (1997). "Hearing Voices, Talking Difference: A Dialogic Approach to Anti-Oppressive Practice." *Journal of Social Work Practice* 11(2):115–25.

United Way of Greater Toronto (1991). *Action, Access and Diversity: A Guide to Multicultural/Anti-Racist Change for Social Service Agencies*. Toronto: United Way.

Webster, P. (1992). "Toronto Social Workers' Skills Buried by New Urban Realities." *Now Magazine* (Toronto)(October 1).

PART
THREE

▼▼

Racism in Educational and Cultural Organizations

▼▼▼▼▼▼▼▼▼▼▼▼▼▼▼▼▼▼▼▼▼▼▼▼▼▼▼▼▼▼▼▼▼▼▼▼▼▼▼

Part Three continues examining various institutional structures by analyzing racism in schools and universities, the media, and cultural and arts organizations — the major vehicles by which society's values, beliefs, and norms are developed, strengthened, and protected.
These institutions are the primary sites for the production and reproduction of racist values and ideology. The chapters in this part show how the myths and assumptions of democratic racism are employed to avoid acknowledging racism in Canada.

▼▼

Chapter 8

▼▼▼▼▼▼▼▼▼▼▼

Racism in Canadian Education

> Visible-minority students are exposed to discriminatory educational practices which, like a multitude of timeless voices, tells them loudly or softly that they are intellectually, emotionally, physically and morally inferior. (Thornhill, 1984:3)

> Including African and non-White scholars in one's intellectual cosmos does not necessarily mean a lowering of standards. When this university finally opens its gates and minds to non-White intellectuals, ideas and personnel, then visiting professors like me will cease to be one-year stands, interesting exotica or simple white elephants. (Lgundipe-Leslie, 1991)

This chapter analyzes the role of education in producing and reproducing racial bias and inequality. It focusses on the ways in which racism is reflected in the learning environment and continues to form an intrinsic part of the learning process within the school and the university. The negative effects of racist ideology and differential treatment on students of colour are examined.

An analysis of curriculum, including the hidden curriculum, provides some insight into the ways in which schools marginalize minority students and either exclude or minimize their experiences, history, and contributions to Canada as a nation. This marginalization, as the literature demonstrates, has a significant impact on the identities and self-esteem of racial-minority students at every level of the educational process.

The effects of educators' attitudes and expectations in influencing and limiting the learning of many racial-minority students are examined, as are the consequences for the students' academic and social performance.

Another manifestation of racism examined in this chapter is the dysfunctional relationship between educational institutions, racial-minority parents, and communities. This analysis is followed by a discussion of the overt expression of racism in the form of racial harassment (racial graffiti and physical and verbal abuse) and the more covert forms (e.g., the lack of an institutional response to educators' and students' continuing racist attitudes and behaviours, and the streaming of Black students into non-academic programs). Some trends and patterns in educational institutions' responses to racism are examined.

The chapter concludes with a analysis of the school and university as discursive space and of how racialized discourses used by educators reflect both institutional and individual resistance to addressing racism in the schools and universities.

INTRODUCTION

It is a strongly held conviction in Canada and other Western democracies that educational institutions play a central role in providing an environment that fosters the attainment of life opportunities for all students. The educational system is assumed to be the main instrument for acquiring the knowledge and skills that will ensure the students' full participation and integration into Canadian society. This belief holds true through primary, secondary, and postsecondary education. A significant body of evidence, however, demonstrates that educational institutions have preserved and perpetuated a system of structured inequality based on race. Although racial-minority and White students have similar career and professional aspirations when entering the school system, the outcomes are markedly different.

RACIST ATTITUDES IN CHILDREN

One of the key assumptions of many educators is that children enter school as "blank slates" with few preconceived assumptions, beliefs, and values. In relation to racial attitudes and social identity, this view has been challenged by a number of studies that find that White children prefer Whites and typically show negative attitudes toward Blacks, Asians, and Aboriginal peoples. By the time children enter school at the age of five, they have already been exposed to racially constructed images of social relations (Rizvi, 1993; Ijaz and Ijaz, 1986; Milner, 1983). The racist popular culture, which includes racist images and negative stereotypes of people of colour in films, television, books, and toys, has a strong influence on children's attitudes and perceptions. The portrayal of Blacks as criminals, Arabs and Asians as untrustworthy, and South Asians as terrorists, and the absence of people of colour in the stories children read, the pictures they see, and the music they hear, influence children's ideas about racial differences. The social environment and the daily experiences of children communicate both implicit and explicit messages (Aboud and Skerry, 1984; Ijaz and Ijaz, 1986).

Children become aware of differences in physical characteristics such as skin and hair colour between the ages of three and seven. At about the same time, they also begin to develop labels for racial groups, often based on oversimplification and misinformation. Lawrence Hirschfeld's study (1996) of racial attitudes suggests that children instinctively possess a way of forming beliefs about the world that leads them to believe that races exist and have certain qualities. Between the ages of four and seven, children form racial preferences, and by the ages of eight to twelve they deepen their understanding of the status associated with particular groups. At this stage, overtly prejudicial behaviours may emerge. This form of racism has a significant, enduring impact both on how White children see themselves and on how they perceive "others" (Essed, 1990). As well, it has a negative effect on the development of minority children's self-image and self-esteem (Milner, 1983).

THE MANIFESTATIONS OF RACISM

CURRICULUM

Curriculum has two dimensions: the formal curriculum and the hidden curriculum. The formal curriculum consists of content and the processes of instruction, which are shaped by the selection of educational materials such as books and teaching aids. It also embraces teaching practices and evaluation procedures, including assessment and placement practices. The hidden curriculum includes educators' personal values, their unquestioned assumptions and expectations, and the physical and social environment of the school and university.

In the context of both the school and the university, some key questions about racism in the curriculum are: What counts as knowledge? From what perspective does the teaching take place? What images are drawn upon? What learning materials are used? How is knowledge transmitted? What kinds of knowledge are absent, ignored, and denied?

Formal Curriculum

The issue of bias in the classics, for example, is a matter of concern not only in Canada, but also for anti-racist educators and advocates in the United States and Great Britain (Brandt, 1986; Lee, 1985; Council on Interracial Books for Children, 1980). There is increasing evidence that reading "literary classics" such as *Huckleberry Finn* and *The Merchant of Venice* without being prepared to deal with their racism does untold damage to minority children, who are further marginalized by the racist language, images, and concepts in these texts (Lee, 1985).

Educators at the primary, secondary, and university levels often fail to deal with the fact that literary texts do not transcend the contexts in which they are written and in which they are read (Pinar, 1993). The social, cultural, and political contexts of all authors, including William Shakespeare and Mark Twain, should form part of any teaching of literature. Equally important and often ignored are the perceptions, assumptions, understandings, and experiences that the student brings to the reading of the text.

Bias in the classics and the Eurocentrism that permeates other texts and teaching materials have an impact on the perceptions, attitudes, and behaviour of both minority and mainstream students (Council on Interracial Books for Children, 1980; Lee, 1985; Dei, 1996). For example, in a Kitchener–Waterloo, Ontario, high school classroom in which *The Merchant of Venice* was being studied, a Jewish student came to class one day to find swastikas painted on her desk. The teacher admonished the unknown perpetrators and called the custodian in to remove the offending graffiti. The student commented that the custodian cleaned the swastikas off her desk, "but no one cleaned them off me" (Ferri, 1986).

A Four-Level Government/African Canadian Working Group report (1992) argued that the assault on racial-minority students' identity is the direct consequence of bias and exclusion in curriculum content. This report and other authorities (Moodley, 1984; Cummins, 1992; Pratt, 1984; Lee, 1985; Solomon, 1992; Dei, 1996) share the view that the reproduction of knowledge in the classroom through curriculum and teaching practices perpetuates racist thinking among both White students and their teachers.

Racism in the curriculum manifests itself in subjects such as history, literature, social studies, geography, and science. The perspectives of novelists and poets who reflect the history and experiences of non-Western cultures are generally ignored in the Eurocentric curriculum. The history curriculum often exhibits a dominant-culture bias that expresses itself in the way history texts are written. There is an unwillingness to look beyond the study of British, American, or European history, and multicultural history is often considered as separate and distinct from Canadian history.

History in its textbook form is frequently nothing more than a representation of tradition (McGee, 1993); and tradition, as Raymond Williams (1977:115) suggests, is "always selected and thus presents us with a system of values disguised as a natural and transcendent process of cultural development." In other words, history is a reflection of the perceptions of those who tell the story, describe the events, and interpret them.

In the history curriculum, the history of people of colour typically begins when Whites "discover" them. Human civilization is portrayed as an evolutionary process, in which Euro-American culture — the Western legal

---

MANIFESTATIONS OF RACISM IN THE EDUCATIONAL SYSTEM

Racially biased attitudes and practices of teachers and administrators
Eurocentric curriculum
Racial harassment and racial incidents
Streaming of minority students (especially Blacks) into non-academic programs
Assimilationist culture of the school
Lack of representation
Devaluing of the role and participation of parents and the community

system, democratic forms of government, and a capitalist economy — is considered the "best" culture in the world. This perspective is also manifested in learning resources, which often fail to reflect alternative views. Until very recently, the history of slavery in Canada, the treatment of Chinese Canadians and other Asian immigrants, and the story of the abuse of Aboriginal children in residential schools (to a cite only a few examples) were not part of the history taught in schools.

At the level of the school and the university, science classes also provide opportunities for fostering racism in the classroom. Bias is reflected in the omission of people of colour from most scientific texts; their images and contributions to scientific development are absent. A more specific example of bias in the science curriculum is the study of theories of race that legitimize and provide justification of the superiority of the White "race." Teachers commonly resist critically discussing with their students the recent resurgence of theories of biological or scientific racism, which seek to link race with intelligence and other traits.

The importance of Eurocentric curriculum in reproducing racism in education is stressed in the following observation: "Until curriculum is studied less as a receptacle of texts than as activity, that is to say, as a vehicle of acquiring and exercising power, descriptions of curricular content in terms of their expression of universal values on the one hand, or pluralistic, secular identifier on the other, are insufficient signifiers of their historical realities" (Viswanathan, 1989:167).

However, within academia, curriculum is commonly considered sacrosanct by many professors. "Nobody can be told what and how to teach" is an oft-repeated sentiment. Yet, the Eurocentric nature of much of the current university's offering cannot be denied (Carty, 1991; Fleras, 1996; Razack, 1998).

Roxanna Ng, in analyzing racism in the university curricula, identified the need "to open up the spaces for previously silenced or marginalized voices to be heard" (1994: 44). Professors Joanne St. Lewis (1996), Linda Carty (1991), Carl James (1994), Shrene Razack (1998), and Himani Bannerji (1991), all professors of colour teaching in Canadian universities, observed that as people of colour working in academia, neither their presence nor their histories are recognized. The curriculum is devoid of their narratives.

Carty commented that "there is little difference between what we experience on the streets as Black women and the experiences we have inside the university ... the university's commonsense appeal to reason and science may take the rough edges off or sediment the particular behaviour, but the impact is no less severe" (1991: 15). Carl James suggested that one's sense of self (as a racial minority) will always be located within a set of meanings that are socially situated and defined by systems of cultural representation: "That I am a professor does not make me immune to the stereotypes and concomitant issues and problems that go along with being a racial minority, and a Black person in particular in this society" (1994:51).

Himani Bannerji, referring to her teaching experience in a Canadian university said: "The perception of the students is not neutral — it calls for responses from them and even decisions. I am an exception in the universities.... I am meant for another kind of work — but nonetheless I am in the classroom.... I am authority" (1991:72). Finally, Joanne St. Lewis commented, "The colour of my skin drives the engine of my public life. It defines relationships and sets out possibilities. Attitudes and beliefs make it real" (1996:28).

The Queen's University report on race relations (1991) identified a number of critical curriculum issues:

- the existence of course names that do not reflect their content (e.g., "The History of Political Thought" should be renamed "The History of *Western* Political Thought");
- the prevalence of core courses (required of majors students) that include only Eurocentric issues;
- the lack of anti-racist courses in the curriculum and the need to make these mandatory in some curricula;
- the need to hire faculty who can teach courses that do not have a Eurocentric focus;
- the need to introduce more interdisciplinary studies, such as Black studies and Native studies;
- the need to review science curricula to make the important point that even science is not value-free;
- the need to develop supplementary programs for minority students that would help them meet academic standards.

Hidden Curriculum

One of the most difficult aspects of racism to isolate and identify is the hidden curriculum, which embraces the social and cultural environment of the school and is formed by the personal, professional, and organizational assumptions, values, and norms of those working in it. The hidden curriculum is the tacit teaching of social and economic norms and expectations to students (Kehoe, 1984). It is often through the school's hidden curriculum that the **hegemony** of racism is experienced and through which Black pupils become marginalized (Brandt, 1986).

It is manifested, for example, in school calendars (in their choice of which holidays are celebrated and which are ignored), concerts and festivals, bulletin-board and hallway displays, the collections in school libraries, school clubs, and the kinds of behaviours tolerated (e.g., racial harassment). Solomon (1992) and Yon (1995) draw attention to the forging of racial-minority student subcultures as expressions of defiance and opposition to the closed, dominant, and hierarchical culture of the school. Cummins observes: "Just as particular forms of identity were being negotiated when Aboriginal children were beaten or starved for speaking their mother tongue, so today the curriculum and patterns of educator–student interaction in school either constrict or expand students' possibilities for identity formation" (1992:3).

The issue of self-esteem is also a critical issue for students who speak English as a second language (ESL). In Alberta, a study by Watt and Roessingh (1994) of ESL students revealed a school drop-out rate of 74 percent. At the beginning level, however, 95.5 percent of ESL students dropped out before attaining a high school diploma. Reasons cited for leaving school included lack of confidence in one's spoken English, ridicule by English-speaking classmates, lack of support from teachers, and teachers underestimating the student's potential.

PEDAGOGY

The most powerful examples of the hidden curriculum are the attitudes and practices of educators in the classroom. Several researchers have suggested that the learning difficulties of minority students are often pedagogically induced; that is, their learning is influenced by how the teaching is done (Cummins, 1988). Kehoe summed up the problem succinctly: "It is a fact rarely accepted that there is less wrong with the learner than with the process and institutions by which the learner is taught" (1984:64).

A complex relationship exists between educators' expectations and their conformity to these expectations in terms of their students' academic performance. A teacher or professor who holds stereotypical opinions about a particular racial group is likely to translate these biases into differential teaching techniques and classroom treatment (Mullard, 1984; Brandt, 1986; Shapson, 1990; Dei, 1996). In his interviews with Black Canadian students, Dei found that the dynamics of social difference and racism shape the processes and experiences of public schooling. Students indicated a high level of concern about the school's ability, through classroom pedagogy, texts, and everyday discourse, to misrepresent and negate the experiences of students of colour.

Many researchers (Alladin, 1996; Dei, 1996; Kehoe, 1984) argue that teachers may make subjective evaluations of the capabilities of their students for the purpose of grouping and that those assessments may be unrelated to academic potential. Kehoe (1984) cited a study showing that children who spoke in a dialect were about three times as likely not to respond to questions given in standard English as were children in the higher group who spoke standard English. Moreover, membership in these groupings remained unchanged from grade to grade.

Several studies have suggested that learning difficulties are often pedagogically induced, in that children designated "at risk" frequently receive instruction that confines them to a passive role and induces "learned helplessness" (Cummins, 1984). Cummins added that instruction that empowers students will encourage them "to become active generators of their own knowledge" (1988:143).

Following a similar perspective, Brandt (1986) suggested that certain pedagogic styles, such as reliance on didactic teaching, are inappropriate and must be examined to consider the extent to which it promotes collaborative learning, which involves not only teachers and students but the wider community's perspectives and "knowledge," especially that of marginalized groups. The benefits of co-operative, collaborative, group-centred learning as an effective teaching strategy at the level of the school and university is supported by a number of educators (Brandt, 1986; Dei, 1996).

The dynamic of race creates enormous resistance in classrooms that are controlled by teachers who continue to be deeply committed to what Solomon (1992) described as the dominant teaching paradigm of cultural assimilation.

The silence that generally pervades the classroom on the subject of racism echoes loudly in the attitudes of students, who daily struggle to affirm their identities in an institutionalized culture that denies their feelings, stories, and experiences. McGee (1993) argued that educators must begin to take responsibility for the effects of their pedagogical and curricular decisions. In discussing the need for transforming changes in pedagogical practices, Razack proposed that the critical educator "takes as central the inner histories and experiences of the students themselves" (1998:42), endeavouring to promote critical reflection of everyday experiences. She contends that students (and others) who develop critical-thinking skills are better positioned to challenge oppressive practices.

ASSESSMENT, PLACEMENT, AND STREAMING

One of the largest barriers to educational equity is the system of assessment and placement. A significant body of data indicates that psychological assessment and placement procedures are riddled with racial, cultural, and linguistic biases (Cummins, 1988; Samuda and Kong, 1986).

Samuda et al. (1980) surveyed the assessment methods used for minority and immigrant children in many Ontario schools and found that the traditional classification was based on the presumption of internal pathology or deficits. It is now generally accepted that "objective" tests are not as "culture free" or "culture fair" as test manufacturers would have one believe. Test materials are developed to assess children of the mainstream culture and do not accurately reflect the learning potential and achievement of students from minority cultures.

In a study of four hundred assessments of students enrolled in English as a second language programs in a western Canadian city, Cummins (1992) found that the psychologists lacked the knowledge to assess the children's academic potential and that the tests were frequently culturally biased. The psychologists were oriented to locate the cause of an academic problem in the minority child, which prevented a critical scrutiny of a variety of other possible contributors to the child's difficulty. The psychologists' training resulted in a "tunnel vision" that did not consider the experiential realities of the children.

Cummins (1988) believes that racially biased assessments emanate from psychologists who frequently lack the knowledge base required to assess the student's academic potential. The assessments' Eurocentric orientation and lack of sensitivity to the children's cultural backgrounds and linguistic skills provided results that were significantly different from those of the children upon whom the test was normed. Cummins argued that institutionalized racism is apparent both in the lack of awareness of the educational psychologists and in the failure of the institutions that trained these psychologists to make them aware of the knowledge gaps and their consequences.

Even educators who are genuinely committed to anti-racist and intercultural education may lack important information, which leads them to make poor decisions regarding minority students. For example, a teacher may hold the view that using two languages in the home confuses bilingual children and consequently may advise parents to speak only English.

Cummins's research (1988, 1992) suggests that power and status relations between minority and majority groups exert a major influence on school performance. Minority students are disempowered educationally in very much the same way as their communities are disempowered by interactions with societal institutions. Minority students are "empowered" or "disabled" as a direct result of their interactions with educators in schools.

The streaming of Black students into low-level academic programs and the placement of large numbers of Black students in vocational programs have been issues of debate for more than a decade. In Ontario, in consultations with the Stephen Lewis Task Force (Lewis, 1992) and the Four-Level Study (1992), many Black community leaders argued that despite tense relations with the police, many more young Blacks are injured in the classroom than on the streets. Toronto high school teacher Lennox Farrell suggested that "this is the only community where our youth has a lower level of education than their parents" (O'Malley, 1992:A19).

The Toronto Board of Education (1987) undertook two major studies of the progress of Black students compared with that of Whites and Asians in high school. It found a dramatically higher percentage of Blacks in basic school programs, which emphasize vocational rather than academic training. One out of every thirty-three Asian students was enrolled in a basic program, whereas the number for Whites was one in ten. For Blacks, it was one in five (O'Malley, 1992:A19).

At a conference on facilitating the academic success of Black children in Canada in the spring of 1992, educators considered supportive alternative models for incorporating Black education into schools. Their concern was expressed in the repeated observation of Black educators that "Black students are not failing school; the school system is failing" (Walker, 1991).

At the level of the university, problems associated with streaming reduce the number of minority students who are in a position to qualify for postsecondary education. What seems clear is that the attitudes, policies, and practices in the school greatly affect minorities' opportunities for higher education. They also have some impact on the choice of specialization or faculty for those minorities who are successful. For example, the large numbers of Southeast Asians in computer science reflects, in part, a secondary school system that commonly labels this group of students as "good" at math and sciences.

SCHOOL–COMMUNITY RELATIONS

The unequal relationship between educational institutions, parents, and the community is another manifestation of systemic racism. The notion that parents' involvement and responsibilities cease once the child has entered the school gate is a form of disempowerment that continues to be a common feature of school life in Canada. Many racial-minority parents perceive schools as requiring no input and tolerating no interference from outside. Cummins argued that minority students are empowered in the school context to the extent that parents and communities are themselves empowered through their interactions with the school: "When educators involve minority parents as partners in their children's education, parents appear to develop a sense of efficacy that communicates itself to children with positive academic consequences" (1988:141).

A number of other factors hinder the relationship between the school and the Black community. For example, many Black parents express dissatisfaction with the school's unilateral handling of discipline and curriculum matters. They describe communication with the school as one-way, non-transactional, and initiated only when the school reports disciplinary problems. In the area of program placement, parents appear to be unaware of and uninvolved in critical decisions affecting their children's educational welfare (Solomon, 1992).

Rather than practising a collaborative approach, school authorities tend to favour a more exclusionary approach to parent and community participation in the school. Many educators (and other professionals) seem to believe that a collaborative relationship with parents will reduce their independence and that their professional competence is being challenged.

Similarly, it has been suggested that racial minorities do not have the opportunity to contribute in a meaningful way to policy planning and implementation. Often their involvement is limited to superficial encounters with the system, in which their suggestions are solicited but then disregarded: "We carry on, business as usual, speculating, diagnosing, examining, studying, implementing and remedying, without once ever consulting the victims" (Thornhill, in Samuda and Kong, 1986:289).

What is required are more visible partnerships that involve a greater sharing of power. White teachers must recognize that they cannot make crucial educational decisions or carry out initiatives alone; they have a responsibility to enlist the guidance of parents and community members who are knowledgeable and competent to provide this help (Buchignani, 1984).

RACIAL INCIDENTS AND HARASSMENT IN THE SCHOOL ENVIRONMENT

Racial harassment is one of the most painful manifestations of racism. In Canada, there is no accurate assessment of the frequency, nature, or distribution of racial harassment, nor is there any documented analysis of either perpetrators or victims. However, a body of impressionistic evidence is provided by students, parents, minority communities, and in some cases, boards of education reports. Some educators believe that the number of racial incidents in Canada's schools has steadily increased in recent years. Teachers and principals are filing reports about racially motivated occurrences with greater frequency than ever before (Kohane, 1992).

Racial harassment in educational institutions includes racial slurs, ethnic and racial jokes, and racist graffiti. It is expressed in racial conflict and tension between groups and by threats and physical assaults on minority students and teachers. It has become so serious that in Edmonton the police chief stated that his department was contacting various minority groups to defuse potentially violent situations in the city's public schools. In one instance, forty people arrived at a high school armed with crowbars and baseball bats to avenge an alleged attack on an East Indian student (Oake, 1991).

One of the barriers to dealing with these kinds of incidents is institutional resistance, a general unwillingness to acknowledge and report racial conflict, harassment, or violence. McCaskell (1993) reported that teachers were reluctant to report racist incidents because they didn't want to be seen as lacking control over their classes; department heads did not report them because it "looked bad"; principals were reluctant to report them because they reflected negatively on their school; and superintendents did not report them because superintendents were supposed to provide leadership. McCaskell concluded that racial incidents and hate activity, although known at an informal level, do not become institutional knowledge, despite a requirement by boards to report such incidents.

The result of this individual and institutional denial is that a range of inappropriate responses have been adopted by boards of education. First, the most common response has been to ignore or redefine the "racial" dimension of these incidents — "There's no problem here." Second, informal policies have emerged as ad hoc responses to individual incidents of harassment. There appear to be significant problems in implementing these policies. Finally, a "multicultural approach" uses the curriculum to emphasize tolerance and respect for other cultures and racial groups.

Hatcher and Troyna (1993) lack confidence in most of these approaches, arguing that there is no empirical evidence of their effectiveness. In their discussion of racial harassment and conflict in schools, they provided a multidimensional framework for analyzing a racial incident. They concluded that a constellation of factors and influences contribute to the understanding of any racial confrontation, including structural racism and differential power relations between groups; ideological beliefs and attitudes;

cultural values and understandings; institutional values, procedures, and practices; children's subcultures; the specific experiences of the individuals; the context and history of the incident; and the details and nature of the incident (1993:197).

CASE STUDY 8.1

RACISM IN NOVA SCOTIA'S EDUCATIONAL SYSTEM: COLE HARBOUR

BACKGROUND

Education has been one of the critical sites of contestation against racism for Black activists in Nova Scotia. As early as the 1800s, the Black community was petitioning the provincial government for equal education (Winks, 1978). The formal segregation of Black and White students continued in Nova Scotia's educational system until the 1960s. However, even after legislated desegregation, there were still seven formal Black school districts and three exclusively Black schools in the province.

In 1975, the Preston communities filed a class action suit with the Nova Scotia Human Rights Commission against the Halifax County School Board because they felt that Black youth were receiving inadequate facilities and education. In 1979, the Cole Harbour District High School was established, and students from four communities began to be bused to the school. (Three of them were largely White middle-class; the other, North Preston, was a completely Black community.) In 1999, North Preston, now part of Halifax, remained a segregated community.

EVENTS

In 1989, a snowball fight sparked a brawl in which Black and White students fought against each other with chains. Eighteen students were charged, ten of whom were Black, although many of the charges were dropped amid claims that the Black students were being singled out by the RCMP. By late 1990, a year and half after the fighting, the government still had not investigated racism in the province's educational system, supporting the Halifax County–Bedford District School Board's claim that the fight was not a racial incident and its denial that racism existed in the school system (Kakembo and Upshaw, 1998). The incident received national media attention. Several steps were taken: a group of black parents demanded a royal commission of inquiry into systemic racism in the educational system, and members of the community organized a week-long fast to force the province to undertake this inquiry (Walkom, 1997).

(continued)

CASE STUDY 8.1 *(continued)*

In 1991, directly as a result of the mobilization of the Black community demanding action on racism in the educational system, a series of studies were conducted. The findings of the inquiry led to the conclusion that racism was rampant in all levels of the school system (BLAC, 1994).[1] BLAC (the Black Learners Advisory Committee) identified the same inequities in the education system that had existed for Black learners since the 1970s. Some of the critical issues and needs that were catalogued include: Black teachers unable to get jobs and promotions; the need for Black role models and anti-racism training; the need to eliminate racism in the curriculum, which required staff and research resources; the need to consolidate and disseminate information on the successes of African Canadian education innovations; the need to identify the barriers to Black students in rural Nova Scotia; streaming; lack of teacher sensitivity to Black students; and the need for a more culturally diverse and inclusive curriculum (Kakembo and Upshaw, 1998).

In October and December of 1996, there were further altercations between Blacks and Whites at the Cole Harbour District High School, and the police and RCMP were called in. Some witnesses of the second incident said that the brawl was not racially motivated and accused police of targeting Black students (*Maclean's*, 1996:25). In 1997, the racially troubled high school was the scene of another violent fight, which resulted in three students and a teacher having to go to hospital. The altercation involved about forty Black and White students. The school suspended twelve students. The following day, some of the suspended students returned with their parents, demanding explanations, which led to some heated arguments and further conflict.

Three months before the altercations (August 1997), the Halifax regional board had received a report by Professor Blye Frank of Mount Saint Vincent University. The report warned of a volatile climate in the school, with Black students feeling rejected by teachers and White students feeling that Black students received special treatment. After examining the situation at Cole Harbour, Frank came up with more than seventy recommendations, including the hiring of more racial-minority staff, the addition of anti-racism courses, peer leadership programs, and the development of a literacy campaign, among others. Ironically, the school board had shelved the report two weeks before the riots, baulking at the cost of implementing the recommendations (Bergman, 1997). Education officials decided to shut the school down immediately and consult parents and teachers about the next course of action.

Both the principal of the school and the superintendent appeared willing to attribute the primary blame for the altercation to the Black parents and students who returned to the school the day after the students were expelled. Superintendent Don Trider said, "We have reached our limit. We have tried to broaden our approach in an educational, social way ... and now there is a tremendous amount of anger involved" (Cox, 1997).

Both teachers and parents refused to support the option put forth by the superintendent to close the school for the rest of the year and disperse students to other

(continued)

CASE STUDY 8.1 *(continued)*

schools. The principal argued that the school's problems were not about racism but resulted from the "tribalism" of the four distinct and separate communities that "don't understand one another." He rejected the notion that some of his teachers had racist attitudes that were reflected in discriminatory behaviours toward Black students (Walkom, 1997). After a week of being shut down, the school was re-opened with eight security guards policing the halls, a shorter school day, and no lunch hours or free periods.

ANALYSIS

Cole Harbour represents a classic example of organizational and institutional denial and resistance by people at all levels of the system. In the external review conducted by Professor Frank a teacher said, "It is like a big festering sore and all it takes is one small brush against that wound to make it pain.... And when it hurts, horrible things begin to happen in this school" (Cox, 1997). The reality of racism in the Nova Scotia educational system goes well beyond the ten years of problems experienced in one school, but reflects the struggles of Black students over two hundred years. The educational system failed to investigate the underlying causes of the tensions and conflicts in the schools; it failed to challenge systemic racism; it refused to institutionalize changes in the hiring practices, curriculum, and pedagogical practices.

Esmeralda Thornhill, chair of Black Canadian Studies at Dalhousie University, suggested that the incidents of racial conflict at Cole Harbour and other schools are not isolated phenomena but exist on a continuum and are part of an unbroken set of interlocking conditions. She observed: "We're talking about the reality of racism here and the reality is that it kills the spirit, it distorts, stuns aspirations and if your sense of identity is not strong, it would make you want to self destruct" (quoted in Bains, 1997).

POSTSCRIPT

In an effort to tackle some of the problems themselves, students at Cole Harbour District High School created a newspaper, *Cava-Chronicle*, that is not only an in-house vehicle for communication, but is distributed to five diverse communities that feed into the school. It tackles racism head-on. and through the control of their own newspaper Black and White students have come together to tell their own stories to each other and their respective communities. The project is assisted by parents, a school guidance counsellor, and the director of King's College School of Journalism (Thorne, 1998).

BLAC continues to work toward achieving educational equity for Black students, in partnership with parents, students, school boards, Black community organizations, and government agencies. The BLAC Report on Education compelled the Nova Scotia government to acknowledge the existence of systemic racism in the educational system and served as a guide for establishing new educational policies and programs and developing further recommendations (Kakembo and Upshaw, 1998).

UNIVERSITIES: A CHILLY CLIMATE FOR MINORITIES[2]

On university campuses across the country, minority students have complained that the campus is often a hostile learning environment. Aboriginal students on Winnipeg's campuses say that they face acts of racism as brutal as any that occur in the poverty-stricken city. They are constantly bombarded with racist acts, from death threats spray-painted on the elevator walls to insensitivity from professors; in class, people often won't sit beside Aboriginal students. A third-year student from the Peguis First Nation said that in one incident, a sociology professor presented a theory in class about why Aboriginal people are more prone to alcoholism, a remark that hurt students in his class (*Edmonton Journal,* January 9, 1994, as cited in Alladin, 1996:15).

Many universities have received student complaints of racial harassment from fellow students, technical and administrative staff, and faculty. At York University a few years ago, a group of Black students, claiming that they had been harassed by security guards, staged a protest at the president's door. (The university responded quickly by agreeing to hire another staff member at its Centre for Race and Ethnic Relations and to provide training for the guards.)

Students at a number of campuses have complained of harassment in the residences, cafeterias, and other public places on campus. Graffiti smeared on washroom walls and other surfaces are often racist. Racial-minority students sometimes react to this hostility by forming racially and ethnically based student associations, claiming particular space in public places (such as the "Black table" in the cafeteria), and generally socializing only with each other.

Razack (1998) suggested that in many universities there is a chilly climate in terms of attempting to alter racialized forms of power. Many academic institutions have remained committed to the notion that race and class must not count. Those universities that have recognized the existence of a "racial problem" on campus and the corresponding need for a response were largely motivated by a continuing racial crisis.

During the mid-1980s, for example, York University established a committee on race and ethnic relations only because a graduate student in a residence was consistently subjected to racial harassment. The student was first told by the manager of the residence that she was "too sensitive." When she complained to her department, little was done, other than to give her a hearing. Concluding that the university was not prepared to deal with the issue, she mobilized her fellow students of colour. Student pressure finally led to the creation of a committee to look into the complaint. The committee was divided in its view of the issue, and its report, awkwardly split into a majority and a minority section, was rejected. Another committee had to be established. Its detailed report (York University, 1989) included many important structural recommendations, but few were implemented in more than tokenistic terms.

CASE STUDY 8.2

THE CONTROVERSY AT THE UNIVERSITY OF BRITISH COLUMBIA

BACKGROUND

In 1992, a major controversy erupted on the campus of the University of British Columbia that is, in many ways, a good example of a "chilly" climate with respect to gender and race relations. The controversy began when a group of graduate students notified the then dean of graduate studies that the department of political science marginalized and demeaned women and students of colour. Although the allegation was denied by the head of the department, who complained that the language used by the graduate students was inflammatory and perhaps even slanderous, a committee was established to examine curriculum changes and a meeting took place with the dean and some of the grieved students.

A year or so later, a female graduate student of colour in the same department mentioned to a faculty member that the students in her tutorial were now beginning to take her seriously because she had given them their first set of marks. He replied, "Yeah, now they probably think you are just one big, bad, black bitch" (Martin, 1996). The student filed a complaint with the sexual harassment office of the university and doubted the sincerity of the faculty member's apology. The issue escalated as other students lodged complaints of racism and the woman student made demands of the university, including the payment of a sum of money and an upgrade of some of her grades. As the issue went public, the university, fearing more bad publicity, set up a committee to identify and hire an outside consultant to investigate the charges.

A Vancouver lawyer, Joan McEwen, was hired in 1994 to conduct the investigation and was given wide latitude to investigate whether there was any basis for the allegations of racism and sexism in the department of political science. Her investigation and report took ten months to complete, at a cost of $246 364. Ms. McEwen's report indicated that five complainants experienced sexism and/or racism. Among her recommendations was one that the department close its graduate admissions until all students were given educational equity. The then president of the university accepted the recommendations, at the advice of the graduate dean.

The dean of arts who initially hired the lawyer, however, disagreed not only with the report's conclusions but also with its methodology and tendered her resignation. The media made the most of these events, and the issue received widespread national press coverage. The campus was in an uproar; meetings, telephone calls, and discussions abounded as the dispute further polarized those allied with both right- and left-wing positions.

Finally, in October 1995, the ban on graduate admissions was lifted and the department began to restructure its organization and curriculum. The dean of arts, who was herself heavily involved in these proceedings, wrote and published a

(continued)

CASE STUDY 8.2 (*continued*)

book, *Racism, Sexism and the University* (Marchak, 1996). The book was highly controversial; some critics argued that it lacked objectivity and reflected an ideology linked to the traditional values and discourses of the university.

ANALYSIS

This incident reveals some of the difficulties a large organization has when it is accused of racism. In the first instance, there was the denial of racism, and because the members of the organization did not take the charges seriously, their reaction was bureaucratic and slow. Quick dialogue was a band-aid approach, whereas a mediated solution might have averted some of the fallout. Moreover, when an investigation was launched, some members of the organization did not accept its findings. Nor was the organization able to defuse some of the negative publicity it received from the media. This incident provides an excellent example of a "chilly" university climate while demonstrating the inability of a large organization to deal with complaints of sexism and racism.

HATE ACTIVITY ON CAMPUSES

One of the exacerbating factors in creating a hostile climate for minorities is the increasing presence of hate groups on campuses. Racist extremists and **Holocaust** deniers have been able to make significant inroads in both schools and universities. During the past few years, Holocaust deniers have intensified their efforts to influence students by placing ads denying the Holocaust in campus newspapers. They have also begun to make active use of computer bulletin boards. At the University of Toronto, the radio station gave the Heritage Front a half hour of free interview time to promote their message, thus unwittingly facilitating student recruitment to their cause.

The University of British Columbia has been inundated with hate propaganda in the form of copies of the *Ball Report*, published by Samisdat Publishers, who also produce Holocaust denial propaganda authored by Ernst Zundel and other neo-Nazis. Among other examples is the case of Robert O'Driscoll, an English professor at St. Michael's College, University of Toronto, who published two books claiming that there is a vast conspiracy of Jewish financiers, communists, Freemasons, and Mormons to enslave the world.

In another case, Professor Joseph Fletcher of the Department of Political Science at the University of Toronto invited a member of the Heritage Front to his class in order to give his students direct experience of hate groups and their leaders. The action was severely criticized by members of the student body as well as a number of community groups who argued that the appearance of hatemongers in a classroom lent credibility to the work of such right-wing groups.

The work of Professor Philippe Rushton, professor of psychology at the University of Western Ontario, involves hierarchical racial classifications. Rushton has published several articles in reputable psychology journals that conclude that there are inherited racial differences, including greater intelligence for Orientals and less for Blacks. His research has received significant criticism. The Rushton case has generated significant controversy, highlighting the tension between two competing ideals: protection of the rights and freedom of tenured faculty, regardless of the nature of the research or its impact, and the right of racial-minority students to learn in an environment free of racial bias.[3]

The Society for Academic Freedom and Scholarship, with more than three hundred members from across Canada, supports the right of faculty to teach students or carry out research as they choose, and to speak freely both on campus and elsewhere (Fleras, 1996; Granatstein, 1994). Richard Devlin (1993), in examining this tension, observes that in the university, the democratic vision of substantive equality is opposed to a more pluralistic and inclusive education that leads to new norms of professional responsibility.

RESPONSES TO RACISM IN THE SCHOOLS

For most of Canada's history, including the first seven decades of this century, the issue of racism was totally absent from the agendas of educational institutions and completely invisible to most White educators. Assimilation — the complete absorption of different ethnic and racial groups into the majority culture — was considered the appropriate model both for educational institutions and for the broader society.

Although the educational system had no formal policy on monoculturalism, this pervasive and coercive ideology influenced the training of educators, the practice of teaching, the content and context of learning, the hiring and promotion practices of boards, and the cultural values and norms underpinning all areas of school life. Students from diverse backgrounds were expected to leave their cultural, religious, and racial identities at the front door of the school.

The assimilationist approach to education ignored the fact that large numbers of children experienced racial bias and discrimination both outside and inside the school. The monocultural approach to education, which operated unchallenged until the mid-1970s, continues to influence education today in many Canadian educational institutions (Tator and Henry, 1991; Thomas, 1984; Shapson, 1990; Cummins, 1986; Fleras and Elliott, 1992).

In 1971, largely in response to demographic, social, and political pressures, the federal policy of multiculturalism was declared. The government's commitment to preserve and promote Canada's cultural diversity and to overcome barriers to full participation was a catalyst for school systems to begin examining their policies and practices.

MULTICULTURAL EDUCATION

Multiculturalism, as government policy and later as legislation, provided the moral and empirical foundation on which to move away from the monocultural, assimilationist orientation. Many school boards gradually developed policies, programs, and practices intended to create a learning environment that respected the cultures of all students. Initiatives were introduced that focussed on the histories, traditions, and lifestyles of diverse cultures. Cultural pluralism, or multicultural education in its most effective expression, acknowledged the reality of diversity in Canadian society and aimed to produce students who were more tolerant, respectful, and understanding of cultural differences. The major thrust of the multicultural approach was attitudinal change.

An empirical study of multicultural ideologies and programs in six countries in the 1970s concluded that three key assumptions underpinned multicultural education:

- learning about one's culture and ethnic roots will improve one's educational achievement;
- learning about one's culture and its traditions will promote equality of opportunity; and
- learning about other cultures will reduce children's (and adults') prejudice and discrimination toward those from different cultural and ethnic backgrounds (Bullivant, 1981:236).

However, after almost two decades of multicultural education in Canada, the limitations of this approach have become increasingly apparent. Multiculturalism's policies and programs relied on untested assumptions about culture and its transmission (Kehoe, 1979).

Multicultural education in many educational jurisdictions tended to focus on a "museum" and "monolithic" approach to the study of complex and constantly evolving cultures. Educators taught students about the material and exotic dimensions of culture, such as food, festivals, and folktales, rather than the values and belief systems that underlie cultural diversity. Important factors shaping cultural identity, such as racial, linguistic, religious, regional, socioeconomic, and gender differences, were often ignored (Moodley, 1984). Moreover, the teachers often had very little knowledge or understanding of other cultures, which inadvertently led both teachers and students to trivialize and stereotype different ethnic and racial groups.

Perhaps the most serious weakness of multicultural education was its failure to acknowledge that racism was endemic in Canadian society. While schools attempted to "respond to special needs" by affirming ethnic-minority children's background, culture, and language, celebrating festivals, and teaching "mother" (heritage) languages, "multicultural" history, and non-Western music, the real problem of racial inequality was ignored. In a growing number of boards of education in the 1980s, many parents and representatives of diverse racial and ethnic groups urged trustees to make radical changes to an educational system that they believed was disadvantaging their children. They maintained that the fundamental issues were not so much cultural as racial; not lifestyles but life chances; not heritage but competence; not diversity but disparity; not prejudice but discrimination. As one parent expressed it in the foreword to the Toronto Board of Education's *Policy on Race Relations* (1979): "The issues facing the colour of my skin are more pressing than those facing my culture."

The huge body of literature documenting the limitations of multicultural education in Great Britain and the United States (Mullard, 1984; Brandt, 1986; Troyna, 1987) supported the concerns of parents and advocacy groups in Canada. A consensus developed that educational policies centred on promoting cultural diversity did little to address racial inequities and were an inadequate vehicle for challenging the racism inherent in the school system.

The basis of multicultural education was a problem paradigm, which in itself was racist. The underlying assumption was that racial- and cultural-minority children in the educational system suffer because they are "socially disadvantaged." According to this perspective, many minority children seem to suffer from a negative self-concept and low esteem, resulting in defective perceptual, cognitive, and linguistic skills that were often exacerbated by the negative, non-supportive values of their social and family background (Kowalczewski, 1982). The duty of the schools (especially those with high concentrations of minority students) therefore was to provide a curriculum relevant to the needs of such disadvantaged groups, in order to enhance their self-image and to promote racial harmony and mutual tolerance.

Both monocultural and multicultural education ignored the role of educational institutions in the generation and reproduction of racism (Cummins, 1992; Moodley, 1984; Thomas, 1984; Wright and Tsuji, 1984). These approaches ignored the reality of racism as a powerful and pervasive force that shaped all of Canada's institutions. Thus, the racial conflicts in the wider society were mirrored in the educational system (Solomon, 1992).

ANTI-RACISM EDUCATION

Anti-racism education as both a theoretical and a practical approach to institutional and systemic racism was formulated in both the United States and Great Britain. It first appeared in the Canadian educational context in the late 1980s and is still evolving. The shift to this model was largely the result of the persistence of minority communities, especially Black parents, in drawing attention to the way racism limited the academic progress and circumscribed the life chances of their children.

The central thrust of anti-racism education is to change institutional and organizational policies and practices that have a discriminatory impact and to change individual attitudes and behaviours that reinforce racial bias and inequality. Anti-racism education is based on the principle that race, despite the concept's lack of scientific foundation, is anchored in the experiences of racial minorities in society and in the school, and that anti-racism is a tool for social change (Dei, 1996). It has motivated some boards of education to develop new policies and has acted as a catalyst for the gradual introduction of various initiatives, including the training of educators in anti-racism; reviews of personnel practices; an analysis of assessment and placement procedures; the introduction of employment equity strategies; a review of curriculum materials to identify for racial bias, and the development of anti-racism curriculum resources and strategies.

Largely in response to the Stephen Lewis report (Lewis, 1992) and the demands of racial-minority communities for greater racial equity, Ontario introduced two new measures. First, a legislative act required all boards of education in Ontario to develop and implement anti-racism policies in their schools. However, no additional funds would be allocated to the school boards to develop and implement these policies (Lewington, 1993). One positive feature of the new measures were proposed changes in the teacher-selection process at university faculties of education. The faculties were required to develop new admission criteria that would increase the representation of minority groups. These criteria included a recognition of the experience acquired by teachers trained outside of Canada.

The second initiative involved a destreaming process, in which grade 9 students would no longer be separated into academic and vocational streams. The streaming would be delayed until grade 10.

These pro-active responses to racism were largely revoked by the Conservative Ontario government of Premier Mike Harris in the late 1990s. As well, as the various task forces and studies cited in this chapter demonstrate, anti-racism has not transformed the educational system, nor has it resulted in the dismantling of racist practices.

BLACK-FOCUSSED SCHOOLS

The failure of the mainstream school system to provide equitable education to Black students has led to the development of another alternative model of education: "Black-focussed" schools. The concept of such a Black–African-centred school has been a matter of intense public debate in Ontario. Advocates of Black-focussed schools argue that the current educational structure inhibits the maximum social and intellectual development of many Black students; therefore, a need exists for a more radical approach to racism.

In Metropolitan Toronto, government officials and members of the Black community recommended that a Black junior high school be established in each of the area's six municipalities. The proposed separate Black schools would be administered and have a curriculum designed and implemented by skilled Black educators.

The concept of a Black-focussed school is based on the view that mainstream schools are not neutral terrain. They pass on the values and norms of the dominant culture; they inculcate Western worldviews and devalue non-Western forms of knowledge. Dei (1996) contends that the model of an African-centred school suggests that there are relevant African-based cultural values and epistemic constructs — such as the concepts of community, traditions of mutuality, and communal bonding — that provide a solid educational foundation on which to promote both academic and social success.

TEACHER TRAINING

Teacher training is provided by the university, and the knowledge, values, and norms acquired by educators will be passed on to students. Rosenberg suggested that in teacher education, discussions about the power and privilege of Whiteness go "underground" (1997:87). Difference is seen as being variation, or as Mohanty argued, cultural and racial differences bypass both power and history to suggest "a harmonious, empty pluralism" (1993:42). Within the school and the university, educators and students bring conflicting experiential frameworks that influence the construction of school knowledge. The contradictory and conflicting issues of race, ethnicity, gender, and sexuality, among other social markers, influence how identities are lived within the school and university (Yon, 1995).

Dei argued that faculties of education need to begin providing new knowledge and skills that will equip them and their future students with the ability to challenge the status quo and question why things are the way they are. Teachers need to develop an understanding of the multiple roles that students occupy in the school system and society; how social hierarchies are established; and the ways in which male-centric, Eurocentric power structures function in schools (Dei, 1996).

Recent research on the responses of prospective teachers to attempts to introduce anti-racism into their educational programs has revealed tensions and resistance. This resistance is reflected in teachers' negative responses to the integration of anti-racism, pedagogy, and curriculum in their practices and their resistance to racial-minority peers and educators (Solomon, 1992; Solomon and Levine-Rasky, 1996; Hankivsky, 1996).

RESPONSES BY THE UNIVERSITY

Until fairly recently, racism was not on the public agenda in institutions of higher learning, largely because its existence was denied; and there were few if any champions of the cause. Meininger (1990) suggested a number of reasons for this lack of interest:

- Minority students are generally very concerned about their vulnerability and have usually kept experiences of racism to themselves. In addition, until recently universities did not have complaint or grievance mechanisms that dealt with racial harassment and other forms of racism.
- Few members of the faculty had any expertise in race and ethnic relations. Those who did tended to examine the issue elsewhere in society, rather than in their own back yard.
- Staff associations and unions were busy with bread-and-butter issues, rather than ideological and systemic issues.
- Academic administrators and managers respond primarily as a result of political pressure or evidence of conflict. Since pressure to create equity and equality for racial-minority students did not exist, it was not on the academic administrative agenda.
- The women's movement, which urged equity and curriculum change, had not yet made its mark.
- The general slowness of institutional change, and the *particular slowness of institutional change at universities*, also contributed to the lack of response to racial and other equity-related issues.[4]

Finally, universities have been subject to financial constraints, as have the other institutions that depend largely on public financing. It has therefore been necessary to increase the number of part-time faculty who are hired to teach specific courses for one to three years. They are not eligible for tenure protection and are not protected by collective agreements. As a result of their feeling of powerlessness they do not challenge the status quo: "If people feel vulnerable, you can be sure they won't articulate beliefs that challenge the status quo" (Sweet, 1993).

RACE AND REPRESENTATION

Canadian universities, especially those in Ontario, grew rapidly during the 1960s and 1970s and expanded their faculties enormously. Financial constraints increasingly affected their ability to hire new faculty and resulted in fewer opportunities to hire women, racial minorities, and other disadvantaged groups. Today, relatively little hiring occurs, except in a few "growth" fields, such as computer studies and management. Thus the demand for representational faculty and staff hiring has come at a time when major growth (except, paradoxically, in student enrolments) has become severely limited. The universities are, therefore, in a conundrum because racial-minority student enrolments are increasing while financial constraints prevent substantive hiring.

Nevertheless universities, like other institutions, are required to review their hiring policies and practices. Many have done employee work-force audits, and their results with respect to minorities, women, and other disadvantaged groups are less than impressive. For example, at the University of Toronto, Canada's largest university, the numbers reveal a pattern of inequity.

In the early 1990s, visible-minority student enrolment at the University of Toronto was almost 40 percent, yet less than 10 percent of its faculty were members of racial-minority groups. Even more revealing was the fact that this 10 percent were heavily concentrated in a few fields, such as engineering and computer sciences (*University of Toronto Employment Equity Annual Report*, 1992–1993). Disciplines such as the social sciences had very few minority faculty, and the sociology department did not have a single Black faculty member.

Razack (1998) pointed to the fact that in the Ontario Institute for Studies in Education/University of Toronto Faculty of Education there is a lack of access and equity for racial minorities. Out of a faculty body of 120, there were four members of colour, and this number had not changed in a decade. She observed that this inequity makes the learning environment less comfortable for both faculty and students of colour. Razack also noted that there was an increase in the number of incidents in which Black students and faculty were threatened and assaulted.

At York University, the figures differed only slightly. Even fewer faculty members were members of racial minorities — 6.4 percent were from racial-minority groups — and at all academic levels, including graduate assistants, there were more racial-minority men than women. At other employee levels, one third of parking and security personnel were racial minorities, as were 20 percent of unionized staff, 16 percent of teaching assistants, 9 percent of part-time faculty, and 8.8 percent of professional and managerial staff. Moreover, East Asians constituted by far the largest pool of minority employees in all sectors, with the exception of the "other manual" category, where Blacks were nearly three quarters of the racial-minority employees.

RESISTANCE TO CHANGE: DISCURSIVE BARRIERS TO ANTI-RACISM IN THE SCHOOL AND UNIVERSITY

Yon suggested that schooling should be understood as discursive space, a terrain in which there are a variety of discourses that "overlap, compete and sometimes collide with one another" (1995:312). Discourses on race and racism converse with concerns with national identity, multiculturalism, ethnicity, and culture, as well as gender and sexual orientation. They are mixed with the discourses of colour blindness, equal opportunity, and balkanization.

The conflict between the ideology of democratic liberalism and the racist ideology of the dominant culture — democratic racism — is manifested in the racist discourse that operates in educational institutions. The school and university are discursive spaces. They reflect a terrain of tension and conflict: tension between the everyday experiences of minority students and educators of colour, and the attitudes and practices of those who have the power to redefine that reality (White administrators and educators).

While lip service is paid to the need to ensure equality of opportunity for all students in the classroom, in reality, individuals, organizations, and institutions are far more committed (at a subconscious level) to maintaining the status quo, that is, the cultural hegemony of the dominant culture with which most educators identify. In other words, many educators resist anti-racism and equity initiatives because they are unwilling to question their own belief and value systems, teaching practices, and positions of power and privilege within the school and the society. Thus, they are unable to examine the relational aspects of cultural and racial differences and the power dynamics constructed around ideas about differences. Acknowledging that ethno-racial differences make a difference in the lives of their students is to concede that Euro-Canadian hegemony continues to function and organize the structures within which the delivery of education operates (Dei, 1996).

Some of the discursive forms and coded language in which resistance is expressed include the following.

The Discourse of Denial

This discourse reflects a refusal to accept the existence of racism in its cultural and institutional forms. "I am not a racist, and racism is not a problem in this school." The evidence of racism in the lives and on the life chances of children of colour is indicated by the effort made by the educator and the school to suppress the processes of "othering" — the marginalizing effects of ignoring the experiences, histories, and cultures of minority students in the classroom, texts, and classroom pedagogy.

The Discourse of Decontextualization

In this discourse, there is an acknowledgement of the existence of racism but it is interpreted as an isolated and aberrant phenomenon limited to the beliefs and behaviours of deviant individuals. It is believed that "students enter the school with 'blank slates'." The position of power and privilege that White educators enjoy in the classroom is neither acknowledged nor understood. Their own racial and cultural identities are generally invisible. Thus racism is decontextualized in terms of what counts as knowledge and how it is taught.

The Discourse of Colour Blindness

Educators' attitudes toward racial minorities are expressed in assertive statements about colour blindness, neutrality, and objectivity. "I never see a child's colour. I treat all children the same." The refusal of educators to recognize that racism is part of the "baggage" that racial-minority children carry with them, and the refusal to recognize racism as part of the daily policies, programs, and practices of the educational system, are part of the psychological and cultural power of racial constructions on the lives of students of colour as well as educators (James, 1994).

The Discourse of "Blame the Victim"

This discourse is framed around the notion that equal opportunity is assumed to exist in all areas of the educational system. Thus, the lack of success of Black students, for example, is often attributed to dysfunctional families or culturally deficient or disadvantaged communities (Sleeter, 1993). This view is reflected in statements such as: "Education is not really valued in the Black community as it is in 'Canadian' culture." At the level of the university, this discourse is articulated in relation to questions of representation and meritocracy. Pro-active measures to ensure that barriers to minorities are dismantled has led to the common refrain: "We must not lower our standards. All hiring and promotions should be based on merit."

The Discourse of Binary Polarization

This is the discourse of fragmentation into "we"–"they" groups. "We" represent the White dominant culture of the school; "they" are the students, families, and communities who are the "other," possessing "different" values, beliefs, and norms. "The problem with 'our' Black/Asian students is that they do not really try to fit in."

The Discourse of Balkanization

The view here is that paying too much attention to "differences" leads to division, disharmony, and disorder in society and in the classroom. "First they want us to do away with Christmas concerts. Soon we'll be wearing turbans. Before long, we won't know what a Canadian is" (see Yon, 1995; McCarthy, 1993; Solomon, 1992; Brandt, 1986; Lee, 1985).

The Discourse of Tolerance

The emphasis on tolerance suggests that while one should accept the idiosyncrasies of the "others" (students or faculty who are culturally or racially "different"), the dominant way is superior. "We try to accommodate their different norms, but it is not always possible or desirable."

The Discourse of Tradition and Universalism

This form of resistance is formulated on the premise that the traditional core curriculum should remained unchanged. "Western civilization represents the best of human knowledge and forms the basis of cultural literacy and educational competence."

The Discourse of Political Correctness

Demands for inclusion, representation, and equity are deflected, resisted, and dismissed as authoritarian, repressive, and a threat to academic freedom. "The standards, values, and intellectual integrity of the university are in danger."

SUMMARY

This chapter has identified some complex and far-reaching consequences of racism in the educational system. The findings of task forces, surveys, and studies, and the testimonies of racial-minority students, parents, teachers, and academics from all parts of Canada, document the impact of racial bias and racist practices on both educators of colour and racial-minority students. This chapter has illustrated how racism is woven into the formal curriculum and influences the ways in which knowledge is structured, valued, and transmitted. Examples of bias in curriculum content have been provided to show how teaching materials and subject matter can minimize the contributions of racial minorities.

Also notable is the importance of the hidden curriculum in creating a negative and hostile physical and social environment for students of colour. Racism in the schools and universities is reflected in the ethnocentric attitudes, assumptions, practices, and everyday discourses of White teachers, professors, and others in educational institutions who fail to acknowledge their own racial biases and the systemic racism that is so pervasive. The evidence of racism in educational institutions is demonstrated by the failure of boards and schools to develop an inclusive and equitable relationship with racial-minority parents and communities. It is reflected in the failure of teacher training programs to provide students with the necessary knowledge, understanding, and skill to effectively manage a multiracial classroom. This analysis of racism demonstrates how, for both minority students and educators, the school and the university can be non-supportive and even threatening environments.

Biased assessment and placement procedures are some of the most powerful forms of differential treatment in the educational system and affect the educational achievement of racial-minority groups, especially Black students.

There are various institutional responses to racism. This chapter has considered assimilationism, examined the multicultural model and its ineffectiveness in addressing racism, and investigated the anti-racist orientation to education. The concept of separate schools for Black students has been put forth as an alternative model. The concluding section of the chapter summarizes some of the common forms of liberal discourse that circulate within the school and university and cover up the need to address the racism woven into the educational system.

NOTES

1. The Black Learners Advisory Committee (BLAC) was established in 1990 to address historical problems for Black students in Nova Scotia dating back two centuries. In 1994, it produced the *BLAC Report on Education: Redressing Inequity — Empowering Black Learners.*
2. The term "chilly climate" was introduced by Bernice Sandler (1986).
3. For a more detailed analysis of the controversy over Rushton, see Ziegler et al. (1991).
4. An example of this slowness of institutional change is the Ontario Council of Universities' recommendation that the "zero tolerance" policy against sexual and racial harassment developed by the previous NDP provincial government be rejected because it contravenes academic freedom and freedom of expression (*Toronto Star*, February 7, 1994).

REFERENCES

Aboud, F., and S. Skerry. (1984). "The Development of Ethnic Attitudes." *Journal of Cross-Cultural Psychology* 15:3–34.

Alladin, I. (ed.). (1996). *Racism in Canadian Schools.* Toronto: Harcourt Brace.

Bains, A. (1997). "Fight at Auburn High." *This Magazine.* (July/August):22–27.

Bannerji, H. (1991). "But Who Speaks for Us? Experience and Agency in Conventional Feminist Paradigms." In H. Bannerji, L. Carty, K. Dehli, S. Heald, and K. Himmanji, *Unsettling Relations: The University as a Site of Struggle.* Women's Press. 67–108.

Bergman, B. (1997). "Zero Tolerance: A Nova Scotia High School Copes with Racism." *Maclean's Magazine* (October 20):18.

BLAC (Black Learners Advisory Committee). (1994). *BLAC Report on Education: Redressing Inequality — Empowering Black Learners.* Halifax: Black Learners Advisory Committee.

Brandt, G. (1986). *The Realization of Anti-Racist Education.* London, Falmer Press.

Buchignani, N. (1984). "Educational Strategies to Increase Racial Tolerance." *Currents: Readings in Race Relations* (Toronto) 2(3):13–20.

Bullivant, T. (1981). *The Pluralist Dilemma in Education: Six Case Studies.* Sydney, Australia: George Allen and Unwin.

Carty, L. (1991). "Black Women in Academia: A Statement from the Periphery." In H. Bannerji, L. Carty, K. Dehli, S. Heald, and K. Himmanji, *Unsettling Relations: The University as a Site of Struggle.* Women's Press. 6–13.

Council on Interracial Books for Children. (1980). *Guidelines for Selecting Bias-free Textbooks for Children.* New York: The Council.

Cox, K. (1997). "School Turns to Law to Curb Violence." *Toronto Star* (October 4):A10.

Cummins, J. (1984). *Bilingualism and Special Education: Issues in Assessment and Pedagogy.* Clevedon, UK: Multilingual Matters; San Diego: College Hill Press.

———. (1986). "Empowering Minority Students: A Framework for Intervention." *Harvard Educational Review* 56(1).

———. (1988). "From Multicultural to Anti-Racist Education." In T. Suutnabb-Kangas and J. Cummins (eds.), *Minority Education: From Shame to Struggle.* Clevedon, UK: Multilingual Matters.

———. (1992). "Lies We Live By: National Identity and Social Justice." *International Journal of the Sociology of Language.*

Dei, G. (1996). *Anti-Racism Education: Theory and Practice*. Halifax: Fernwood.

Devlin, R. (1993). "A Counter-Attack in Defence of Political Correctness." *Toronto Star* (March 8):A5.

Essed, P. (1990). *Everyday Racism: Reports from Women of Two Cultures*. Claremont, CA: Hunter House.

Ferri, J. (1986). "Are Teachers to Blame if Play Arouses Racism?" *Toronto Star* (July 16).

Fleras, A. (1996). "Behind the Ivory Walls: Racism/Anti-Racism in Academe." In I. Alladin (ed.), *Racism in Canadian Schools*. Toronto: Harcourt Brace. 62–89.

Fleras, A., and J. Elliott. (1992). *Multiculturalism in Canada*. Scarborough: Nelson.

Four-Level Government/African Canadian Community Working Group. (1992). *Towards a New Beginning: Report of the Four-Level Government/African Canadian Community Working Group*. Toronto.

Granatstein, J.L. (1994). "Universities Strangled by 'PC' Politicians." *Canadian Speeches: Issues of the Day*. (July 2–8).

Hankivsky, O. (1996). *Resistance to Change: Exploring the Dynamics of Backlash*. London: Centre for Research on Violence against Women and Children.

Hatcher, R., and B. Troyna. (1993). "Racialization and Children." In C. McCarthy and W. Crichlow (eds.), *Race, Identity, Representation in Education*. New York and London: Routledge.

Hirschfeld, L. (1996). *Race in the Making: Cognition, Culture, and the Child's Construction of Human Kinds*. Cambridge, MA: MIT Press.

Ijaz, A., and H. Ijaz. (1986). "The Development of Ethnic Prejudice in Children." *Guidance and Counselling* 2(1) (September):28–39.

James, C. (1994). "The Paradox of Power and Privilege: Race, Gender and Occupational Position." *Canadian Woman Studies: Race and Gender* 14(2):37–51.

Kakembo, P., and R. Upshaw. (1998). "The Emergence of the Black Learners Advisory Committee in Nova Scotia." In V. D'Oyley and C. James, *Re/Visioning: Canadian Perspectives on the Education of Africans in the Late 20th Century*. Toronto: Captus Press.

Kehoe, J. (1979). "Effective Tools for Combating Racism in the Schools." Keynote Address to the Third Annual Human Rights and Liberties Institute. Vancouver.

———. (1984). *A Handbook for Enhancing the Multicultural Climate of the School*. Vancouver: WEDG.

Kohane, J. (1992). "Educator Calls for Racism Education to Begin as Early as Possible." *Canadian Jewish News* (December 10):42.

Kowalczewski, P.S. (1982). "Race and Education: Racism, Diversity and Inequality, Implications for Multicultural Education." *Oxford Review of Education* 8(2):145–61.

Lee, E. (1985). *Letters to Marcia: A Teacher's Guide to Anti-Racist Education*. Toronto: Cross-Cultural Communication Centre.

Lewington, J. (1993). "Ontario Attacks Racism in the Classroom." *Globe and Mail* (July 16):A6.

Lewis, S. (1992). *Report on Racism Presented to the Premier of Ontario*. Toronto: Queen's Printer for Ontario.

Lgundipe-Leslie, M. (1991). "Forum," *University of Toronto Bulletin* 16(September 9).

Maclean's Magazine. (1996). "Black Students from Cole Harbour District High School Charged for Role in Fight." (December 23):25.

McCarthy, C. (1993). "After the Canon: Knowledge and Ideological Representation in the Multicultural Discourse on Curriculum Reform." In C. McCarthy and W. Crichlow (eds.), *Race, Identity and Representation in Education*. New York and London: Routledge.

McCaskell, T. (1993). Presentation to the Community Forum Sponsored by the Metropolitan Toronto Council Committee to Combat Hate Group Activity.

McGee, P. (1993). "Decolonization and the Curriculum of English." In C. McCarthy and W. Crichlow (eds.), *Race, Identity and Representation in Education*. New York and London: Routledge.

Marchak, P. (1996). *Racism, Sexism and the University: The Political Science Affair at the University of British Columbia*. Montreal and Kingston: McGill-Queen's University Press.

Martin, S. (1996). "Sex, Race and Recrimination at UBC." *Globe and Mail* (September 28): D5.

Meininger, T. (1990). "Visible Minorities and the Universities: Some Obstacles and Challenges on the Road to Social Justice." Unpublished paper. York University.

Milner, D. (1983). *Children and Race: Ten Years Later*. London: Alan Sutton.

Mohanty, C.T. (1993). *Beyond a Dream: Deferred Multicultural Education and the Politics of Excellence*. Minneapolis: University of Minnesota Press.

Moodley, K. (1984). "The Ambiguities of Multicultural Education." *Currents: Readings in Race Relations* (Toronto) 2(3):5–7.

Mullard, C. (1984). *Anti-Racist Education: The Three O's*. Cardiff: National Association for Multiracial Education.

Ng, R. (1994). "Sexism and Racism in the University: Analyzing a Personal Experience in the University." *Racism and Gender* 14(2)(Spring):41–46.

Oake, G. (1991). "Racism Hits Edmonton Schools." *Toronto Star* (December 12).

O'Malley, S. (1992). "Demand Quality Education, Black Parents Told." *Globe and Mail* (August 20):A1, A19.

Pinar, W. (1993). "Notes on Understanding the Curriculum as Critical Text." In C. McCarthy and W. Crichlow (eds.), *Race, Identity and Representation in Education*. New York and London: Routledge.

Pratt, D. (1984). "Bias in Text Books: Progress and Problems." In R.J. Samuda et al. (eds.), *Multiculturalism in Canada: Social and Educational Perspectives*. Toronto: Allyn and Bacon.

Queen's University. (1991). *Towards Diversity and Equity at Queen's: A Strategy for Change*. Final Report of the Principal's Advisory Committee on Race Relations. *Queen's Gazette* supplement (April 8).

Razack, S. (1998). *Looking White People in the Eye: Gender, Race and Culture in Courtrooms and Classrooms*. Toronto: University of Toronto Press.

Rizvi, F. (1993). "Children and the Grammar of Popular Racism." In C. McCarthy and W. Crichlow (eds.), *Race, Identity and Representation in Education*. New York and London: Routledge.

Rosenberg, P. (1997). "Underground Discourses: Exploring Whiteness in Teacher Education." In M. Fine, L. Weis, L. Powell, and L. Mun Wong (eds.), *Off White*. London: Routledge. 79–89.

St. Lewis, J. (1996). "Identity and Black Consciousness in North America." In J. Littleton (ed.), *Clash of Identities: Essays on Media, Manipulation and Politics of Self*. Englewood Cliffs, NJ: Prentice Hall. 21–30.

Samuda, R.J., D. Crawford, C. Philip, and W. Tinglen. (1980). *Testing, Assessment, and Counselling of Minority Students: Current Methods in Ontario*. Toronto: Ontario Ministry of Education.

———, and S.L. Kong. (1986). *Multicultural Education: Programmes and Methods*. Kingston, ON: Intercultural Social Sciences Publications.

Sandler, B. (1986). *The Campus Climate Revisited: Chilly for Women Faculty, Administrators, and Graduate Students*. Washington, DC: Project on the Status and Education of Women, Association of American Colleges.

Shapson, S. (1990). *Multicultural Education: A Research Paper to Inform Policy Development*. Burnaby, BC: Faculty of Education, Simon Fraser University.

Sleeter, C. (1993). "How White Teachers Construct Race." In C. McCarthy and W. Crichlow (eds.), *Race, Identity and Representation in Education*. New York and London: Routledge.

Solomon, P. (1992). *Black Resistance in High School: Forging a Separatist Culture*. Albany: State University of New York Press.

———, and C. Levine-Rasky. (1996). "Transforming Teacher Education." *CRSA/RCSA* 33(3):337–59.

Sweet, L. (1993). "Academic Angst: The Professional Privilege of Tenure — A Job for Life." *Toronto Star* (July 18):B1.

Tator, C., and F. Henry. (1991). *Multicultural Education: Translating Policy into Practice*. Ottawa: Ministry of Multiculturalism and Citizenship.

Thomas, B. (1984). "Principles of Anti-Racist Education." *Currents: Readings in Race Relations* (Toronto) 2(3):20–23.

Thorne, S. (1998). "Student Newspaper Aims to Bridge Racial Gap." *Canadian Press* (January 15).

Thornhill, E. (1984). "Fight Racism Starting with the School." *Currents: Readings in Race Relations* (Toronto) 2(3):3–7.

Toronto Board of Education. (1979). *Policy on Race Relations*.

———. (1987). *Consultative Committee on the Education of Black Students in Toronto Schools*. Toronto: Board of Education for the City of Toronto.

Troyna, B. (1987). "Race and Education: Two Perspectives for Change." In B. Troyna (ed.), *Racial Inequality in Education*. London: Routledge.

University of Toronto Employment Equity Annual Report. (1992–1993). Toronto: University of Toronto.

Viswanathan, G. (1989). *Masks of Conquest: Literary Study and British Rule in India*. New York: Columbia University Press.

Walker, S. (1991). "Schools Don't Do Enough for Blacks, Educators Say." *Toronto Star* (April 15).

Walkom, T. (1997). "Hateful Times at Cole Harbour High." *Toronto Star*. October 12:A1

Watt, D., and H. Roessingh. (1994). *ESL Dropout: The Myth of Educational Equity*. Calgary: Faculty of Education, University of Calgary.

Williams, R. (1977). *Marxism and Literature*. Oxford: Oxford University Press.

Winks, R. (1978). *Blacks in Canada*. New Haven, CT: Yale University Press.

Wright, E., and G. Tsuji. (1984). *The Grade 9 Survey*. Research Paper 174. Toronto: Information Services Division of the Toronto Board of Education.

Yon, D. (1995). "Unstable Terrain: Explorations in Identity, Race, Culture." Ph.D. dissertation, graduate program in Social Anthropology, York University.

York University. (1989). *Report of the President's Committee on Race and Ethnic Relations*. North York, ON: York University.

Ziegler, M., et al. (1991). "Philippe Rushton and the Growing Acceptance of 'Race-Science'." In O. McKague (ed.), *Racism in Canada*. Saskatoon: Fifth House.

Chapter 9

▼▼▼▼▼▼▼▼▼▼▼▼

Racism in Arts and Culture

The core of racism in the arts remains constant: the refusal to treat as valid cultural experience, knowledge or expertise of an artist of colour — wedded to the belief that Eurocentric values are better. (Nourbese Philip, 1992:225)

This chapter explores the nature of cultural racism as ideology and practice in cultural production.[1] Cultural production is one way in which society gives voice to racism, recycling ideas, images, and discourses about Canada's people of colour and Aboriginal peoples. The debates over cultural representation deal with fundamental and deeply felt issues about the nature of Canadian culture and national identity. This analysis of popular or mass culture and "high culture" explores why the images created and presented by mainstream writers, producers, directors, curators, and others involved in cultural production often are not the images that Africans, Asian Canadians, and Aboriginal peoples would present of themselves. The practice of cultural appropriation — the use of another culture's images or experiences by artists from the dominant culture — is analyzed as an example of racist ideology and practice.

This chapter's case study of the Royal Ontario Museum's exhibit "Into the Heart of Africa" highlights issues such as cultural appropriation, Eurocentrism, misrepresentation, and power relations. A second case study, of the musical *Show Boat,* focusses on representation, stereotyping, marginalization, freedom of expression, and censorship. These two case studies demonstrate the power of the dominant culture to create, reproduce, and transmit certain cultural forms while marginalizing and erasing the images, voices, and experiences of people of colour. The third case study involves a small conference for Aboriginal writers and writers of colour that created a major controversy that received national (mostly negative) attention from the media and much of the literary establishment.

This chapter identifies both ideological and structural barriers to the access, participation, and representation of people of colour in the arts and Canadian cultural institutions, and explores the struggles of minority artists and performers to find space for their work on the "representational stage" of Canadian culture (Mackey, 1995:403).

INTRODUCTION

Viewing an exhibit of paintings in an art gallery or of cultural artifacts in a museum, reading a literary work, watching a theatrical performance, or listening to a symphony is to experience an art form, cultural object, or event that has been brought into being through a complex process. Cultural production involves an interaction of values, ideas, and organizational practices shaped by concrete social and historical conditions. It incorporates an intricate nexus of groups and institutions including patrons, publishers and producers, curators and administrators, corporations and boards of trustees, advertising agencies and media organizations, funding agencies and government bodies, consumers and audiences. The machinery of cultural production includes cultural industries that produce cultural products for profit, not-for-profit organizations, and public-sector bureaucracies (Becker, 1994; J. Hall and Neitz, 1993).

Cultural production and creative processes define and structure "maps of meaning" (S. Hall, 1977), articulate and communicate authoritative messages, and transmit powerful symbols, icons, images, and ideas through which we "live" culture (Bhabha, 1990). These messages and meanings ultimately become a part of the collective belief and value system of a people.

Both high culture and popular or mass culture produce "codes of recognition," such as stereotypical images, out of which individual, communal, and national identities are forged. The arts, the music industry, theatre, literature, film, print, and broadcast industries provide a society with a sense of what it means to be a man or woman, poor or privileged, Aboriginal Canadian or African Canadian. Cultural production provides the lens through which people view themselves and the world, communicating powerful messages about the core values, norms, cultural hierarchies, and central narratives of mainstream society. Meaning is constructed across the bar of differences (racial, cultural, gender, sexual orientation, and so on).

Cultural products and practices mirror the larger social processes; cultural representations echo social realities (Pieterse, 1992). Thus, all forms of cultural production must be understood in the context of how they were produced, by whom, at what historical moment, and with what social, economic, and political impact. Cultural practices cannot be separated from the environment in which they find expression.

Cultural production provides a vehicle through which dominant cultural ideologies are promoted, sustained, and reinforced, although these beliefs appear invisible and natural to those who are immersed in it. Access to cultural production is created or limited by the dominant cultural institutions such as museums, galleries, publishing houses, academies, and theatres. Mainstream cultural institutions often function as gatekeepers, determining the acceptable conventions by which cultural productions are sponsored and distributed, as well as determining how their aesthetic and market value are assessed (Li, 1994).

Culture and cultural production are increasingly being defined by economic forces, and the penetration of the commodity culture is a key ingredient in shaping systems of representation and structures of cultural meaning. There is a new intersection between commerce, advertising, and consumption. The penetration of commodity culture into every aspect of daily life has become a major axis in the relationship between mass culture and high culture. The gap between these two worlds is rapidly diminishing (Becker, 1994).

However, cultural production is also an important source and site of struggle against a dominant culture significantly influenced by the legacy of its Eurocentric heritage. The arts and popular culture offer the possibility not only for the creative contributions of artists from diverse ethno-racial communities, but also provide a powerful vehicle for new constructions of Canadian identity and new forms of social relations.

In the past decade, as the case studies in this chapter demonstrate, there has been a crisis in representation in which the traditional modes of cultural production are no longer acceptable to many marginalized groups in Canadian society. As a consequence, there is greater scrutiny, criticism, and contestation of the roles, functions, and meanings of cultural institutions (Hutcheon, 1994).

MANIFESTATIONS OF RACISM IN THE PRODUCTION OF CULTURAL ART FORMS

Canada's mainstream cultural institutions include museums and art galleries, theatres, film-production houses, publishers, ballet and opera companies, symphonies, arts councils and artists, and writers' and performers' unions and professional associations. Each of these cultural systems contributes in different ways to the marginalization of people of colour.

These cultural institutions define "great works of art," "literary classics," and "world-class music." They determine who is selected to direct, produce, or perform in artistic productions and where these productions will be presented; which authors are deemed worthy of publication; which artists' works are given public exhibitions in the major galleries; whose music is played in concert halls; whose music gets recorded and played on

---

MANIFESTATIONS OF RACISM IN CULTURAL INSTITUTIONS

Lack of access to funding
Marginalization of minority cultures
Cultural appropriation of people of colour
Eurocentric aesthetic values
Negative images and stereotyping

Invisibility of images, narratives, and voices of people of colour
Lack of minority-group representation on boards, arts councils, unions, and professional organizations

mainstream radio; and whose voices and images become part of television programming. They reflect the funding policies and practices of government agencies and private foundations and the ethno-racial representativeness of those who work in cultural organizations in the public and private sectors. As well, the dominance of White culture is manifested in the power relationship between mainstream cultural organizations, ethno-racial communities, and artists of colour.

What are the images of people of colour projected on the screen and from the stage? The casting of actors is frequently based on assumptions made by casting agents, producers, and directors who believe that skin colour determines an actor's suitability for a part. It raises questions about "who has the power to define whom, and when, and how" (McCarthy and Crichlow, 1993:xvi).

Culture and cultural expression are the mirror in which racism is both reflected and reproduced. The racism in various aspects of the arts, such as literature, visual art, film, dance, and theatre, emanates from the racism embedded in the dominant culture's values and institutions. Cultural racism finds its expression primarily in the perceptions, attitudes, values, and norms of White males, who have controlled and shaped cultural life in Canada. A Eurocentric bias provides the lens through which White decision-makers in Canadian cultural organizations and institutions filter their view of the world, establish priorities, assess the quality of art forms, allocate resources, and determine who will be the audience or consumer of their cultural products (Mackey, 1995; Li, 1994).

Cultural racism is one of the most important frameworks of interpretation and meaning for racial thought in society (Essed, 1990:44). It is so deeply ingrained in the symbolic systems of society that it is almost always denied. In a sense, cultural racism is the most invisible form of racism, because it is seamlessly woven into the collective belief and value systems of the dominant group. White culture is an "invisible veil" that envelops Canadians (Katz, 1978:10).

Cultural racism is an ideology that divides society into "in" and "out" groups — "us" and "them." Images of undesirable "otherness," conveyed in a wide diversity of art forms, shape perceptions, discourse, and identity (Hall, 1992). The cultural images in the stories, narratives, and photographs created by the arts (and transmitted via the media and education) become the building blocks of social reality (Lubiano, 1992). Culture is the central mechanism through which the dominant group reaffirms itself through image and representation, and it is the vehicle through which marginalized groups are excluded. In this way, arts and cultural organizations and the authorities within these systems play a significant role in the production and reproduction of racism in a society (Nourbese Philip, 1993; Morrison, 1992; Ferguson, 1990).

CULTURAL APPROPRIATION

Cultural racism in the arts is the marginalization of the cultures of "others," so that the dominant group's cultural images, symbols, and norms remain intact. Conversely, culturally creative expressions developed by people of colour are appropriated and interpreted by White visual artists, producers, musicians, and writers. This phenomenon is called "cultural appropriation."

The controversy over cultural appropriation has spilled over into many arenas. Curators, authors, theatrical producers, and visual artists incorporate into their creations stories, histories, and images derived from cultures that are not theirs. When members of the dominant culture benefit materially from the production and dissemination of the history, traditions, and experiences of other cultural groups, it is as if a party were being held in a house that's been in a family's possession as far back as memory serves, and the family is not included in the celebration (Williams, 1992). Furthermore, "the issue of appropriation has to do with access; it is rooted in the problem of access. For 300 years ... women ... people of colour, have had no access to many institutions in this country" (Williams, 1992:6).

Governor General's Award–winning writer Dionne Brand made the point that cultural appropriation is not about personal accusation but rather views the issue in the context of a critical category. Brand argued that cultural appropriation "looks at the location of the text, and the author, in the world at given historical moments. These moments are moments of gendering, race(ing) and class making, (othering), moments rooted in colonial conquest, slavery and economic exploitation" (quoted in Rundle, 1997:13). Nourbese Philip (1992) asserted that if writers are drawn to write about another culture, they must do so from a point of humility and a willingness to learn, and not with a sense of entitlement or exploitation.

In each of this chapter's case studies ("Into the Heart of Africa," "*Show Boat*," and the "Writing Thru Race Conference"), the subject of cultural appropriation was central to the debate and controversy surrounding the three cultural events.

The protest against the exhibit "Into the Heart of Africa" at the Royal Ontario Museum highlighted a number of contentious issues that museums are confronting across North America, the United Kingdom, and elsewhere. Those who opposed the exhibit argued that it was an example of a cultural production that contributes to cultural racism by the ways in which the artifacts were acquired; by the value attributed to the artifacts; by the context and content of the exhibit that displayed the artifacts; and by the nature of the relationship between the artifacts, the institution, and the living cultures and communities for whom these artifacts have special meaning. These issues raise fundamental questions about "the very status of museums as historical, cultural theatres of memory. Whose memory? For what purposes?" (Clifford, 1990:141).

CULTURAL APPROPRIATION IN OTHER ART FORMS

In recent years, cultural appropriation has created controversy concerning White artists who interpret the experiences of the "others," including

CASE STUDY 9.1

INTO THE HEART OF AFRICA

"Into the Heart of Africa" was an exhibition, mounted by the Royal Ontario Museum (ROM), consisting of about 375 artifacts from central and west Africa that had been stored by the ROM for over one hundred years. It opened in November 1989 and closed in August 1990. Ostensibly, the theme of the exhibit was the impact of colonialism on Africa, particularly at the height of the colonial period.

The exhibit included such items as photographs of Canadian missionaries and military stations, reproductions of newspaper articles, scales that had been used to measure gold dust for the colonizers, spears that White soldiers brought home after their battles against Africans, traditional beaded jewellery, and masks. Many of these relics were acquired by Canadian soldiers who participated in Britain's colonial campaign in late-nineteenth-century Africa. Other artifacts had been acquired by Canadian missionaries while attempting to bring "Christianity, civilization, and commerce" to Africans. These artifacts, many of which had significant financial value and all of which had enormous cultural value to those societies from whom they were taken, were eventually donated to the ROM.

The curator, Dr. Jeanne Cannizzo, a specialist in African art, suggested that the show was intended to examine both Canadian and African sensibilities. The objects in the ROM collection were an expression "not only of the world view of those who chose to make and use them, but also of those who chose to collect and exhibit them" (Cannizzo, 1991:151). She stressed her desire to illustrate the social history that provided the context of the exhibit and to expose the racist assumptions of the Canadians involved in the colonization and Christianization of Africa. Her intent was also to show that White Canada had a somewhat less than perfect understanding of the complexity and richness of African societies.

Despite these positive intentions, the exhibit became the most controversial show in the history of the ROM. From the perspective of those who opposed the exhibit, "Into the Heart of Africa" was a demonstration of cultural racism and appropriation in which images, stories, and voices of Africans were silenced and the real story of colonization remained misinterpreted and misunderstood.

One of the many problems with the exhibit was the strong use of irony to deliver the message (Butler, 1993). For example, the exhibit relied on a liberal use of quotation marks around words and phrases such as "the unknown continent" and "barbarous" people and the dramatization of a White missionary bringing "light" to a continent "full of Muslims, and animists and fetishists." The quotation marks were meant to inform the viewer about the racist assumptions underlying these labels. However, what the curator and the ROM failed to recognize was that the irony of the exhibit's texts required a certain degree of shared knowledge between the curator and the observer (Butler, 1993). Many visitors did not understand these subtleties and interpreted the images and phrases such as "barbarous customs" literally. This is reflected in the comment of one visitor who thanked the ROM for the lovely show on "primitive Africa" (Crean, 1991:26).

On the other hand, many members of minority communities in Toronto, as well as visitors from Africa who clearly understood the irony, felt that the exhibit only

(continued)

CASE STUDY 9.1 *(continued)*

reinforced racist stereotypes and assumptions. Some of the most controversial objects included an engraving depicting Lord Beresford thrusting his sword into a Zulu man. The engraving was accompanied by its original caption: "Lord Beresford's encounter with a Zulu." Near the engraving was a display of Zulu spears and shields. Beside it was another picture of Zulu soldiers, who were described as "savages." Still another photograph showed a missionary giving African women "a lesson in how to wash clothes." A flyer distributed by members of the Coalition for the Truth about Africa to communicate their concerns about the exhibit's racist images posed the question: "Did Africans not know how to wash before the arrival of the Europeans?"

An audio-visual slide show in the exhibit, entitled "In Livingstone's Footsteps," provided viewers with a simulation of a lecture that missionaries might have delivered to a congregation of worshippers in the nineteenth and early twentieth centuries, during the missionization of Africa. The lecture contains highly derogatory, culturally racist, and paternalistic language. As Crean (1991) pointed out, although a caption at the entrance to the room and an oral disclaimer by the narrator at the beginning and end of the show explained that this was a fictional re-enactment, most viewers would likely have missed this important piece of information because relatively few of them would have sat through the entire presentation.

A visitor from Uganda noted that

the show gives an overwhelming colonial impression. If the ROM is trying to say that these are historical facts and we're ashamed of them, that message doesn't come through.

The exhibit's irony was clearly inappropriate for many Blacks. A young student said:

I look at those spears and shields and all I can think of is how did they get them? By killing Africans, that's how. What am I supposed to feel?

A prominent member of Toronto's Black community, Charles Roach, questioned the ROM's objectives:

I have to ask what is the ROM's objective in presenting Africa in 1990 from the perspective of the missionaries? Why show the colonials trampling through Africa imposing their lifestyle on the people? To me, it's a form of cultural genocide and I put it in the larger context of what's happening to Black people in Toronto — the police shootings and the discrimination we face. (Roach, 1990)

In glorifying acts like the slaying of the Zulus — the precursor to apartheid and the enslavement of Africans in South Africa — the exhibit had a chilling effect, Roach found.

Other members of the Coalition for the Truth about Africa commented on the likelihood of children misreading the irony of the messages. A teacher who visited

(continued)

CASE STUDY 9.1 (continued)

the exhibit twice with classes analyzed the negative impact of the exhibit. She found the tour guides unable to explain or interpret the exhibits without sharing their racist assumptions and understandings. One guide leading a group of students explained that "the missionaries civilized the pagans of Africa" and that the Zulu were "an extremely vicious tribe" (McMelland, 1990:10). Another guide, on a subsequent visit by this teacher with a grade 5 class, explained that missionaries taught the Africans to carve wood and that a mask had been used to practise "barbaric rituals, vicious, barbaric rituals." Another guide offered her view on how crazy African girls were to put pieces of ivory through their noses.

Susan Crean identifies a related problem with this exhibit:

By presenting the African collection through the history of its donors, by giving pride of place to the personal stories of the White Canadians who happened to bring them to Canada, Cannizzo creates a context in which that history is claimed rather than criticized and rejected, showcased even while she tut-tuts from between the lines. (1991:121)

Members of the Black community not only protested against the images in the exhibit but saw the same marginalization in the exclusionary process used by the ROM in developing the exhibit. They criticized the museum for not consulting the community more widely.

After developing promotional materials for the exhibit, the ROM hired a consultant from the Black community to review these materials. The consultant voiced concern about both the stereotypical language and inappropriate images in the brochure. These concerns were expressed by other people who saw the brochure. At this point, educators with the Toronto Board of Education initiated discussions with the ROM because it was intended that students in this board's jurisdiction would visit the exhibit. The board identified a number of concerns about the promotion, including stereotyping, the use of irony, and the ethnocentric perspective of many of the displays and captions (Lalla and Myers, 1990:6).

The ROM subsequently created focus groups, which also voiced concern about both the direction of the show and the inappropriate language of the brochure. The ROM agreed to redo the brochure (at a cost of $28 000). The groups were also concerned that there was no contemporary content in the exhibit. In response, an African historian was hired to develop, with the community, programs that included lectures, music and dance performances, workshops, and films, which were presented at the ROM after the exhibit was launched, in February 1990.

At a reception for selected members of the Black community to preview the completed exhibit, further concerns were expressed. Some guests felt that they had been invited to simply "rubber stamp" the exhibit, rather than being invited to comment. The previewers, primarily visual artists and writers, objected to words and phrases such as "dark continent" and "mysterious land" (Da Breo, 1989–90).

(continued)

CASE STUDY 9.1 *(continued)*

EVENTS

"Into the Heart of Africa" opened at the ROM in November 1989. Opinions and feelings among some members of the Black community ran high, and sixteen Black groups in Toronto formed The Coalition for the Truth about Africa. The coalition began to picket in front of the ROM early in March 1990. It concentrated its efforts on Saturdays, a particularly busy day for the museum. As many as fifty demonstrators, carrying placards and distributing pamphlets, appeared early in the mornings. Several of the demonstrators read speeches, using a bullhorn to attract the crowds. They called the ROM the "Racist Ontario Museum," and while they did not demand, in the first instance, the closure of the exhibit, they urged the museum to change or clarify the offending explanatory texts. Failing that, however, they demanded that the show be closed. The ROM responded by saying that it had no plans to change the show in any way, that it was historically accurate, and that people were simply reacting to it in different ways. Its director was also quoted as saying that the museum would stand by its curator and the exhibit. Jeanne Cannizzo, in the meantime, kept a low profile and declined to speak about the controversy (Butler, 1993).

On at least two occasions, the demonstrations became violent. In one instance, a few of the demonstrators raised their voices to visitors attempting to enter the museum. Officials called the police, who tried to break up the demonstration. As a result, thirty-five police officers and fifty demonstrators were involved in a violent confrontation. Two demonstrators were arrested, and two police officers and several demonstrators were hurt. The ROM responded to this incident by applying for and receiving an injunction from the Supreme Court of Ontario to prevent protesters from picketing within fifty feet of the museum's entrance. The following day, more than seventy-five people, chanting "ROM is Racist Ontario Museum," continued the demonstrations.

As a result of the confrontations, educators from the Toronto Board of Education concluded that "Into the Heart of Africa" had no direct educational value for elementary students, and if secondary students viewed the exhibit, they were to be given extensive preparation (Lalla and Myers, 1990:4).

ANALYSIS

A controversial museum exhibition became the focus for a major ideological and physical confrontation between the Black community of Toronto and one of its leading cultural and educational institutions.

Although the museum took steps to involve a few members of the Black community, in doing so it also apparently made several significant errors. First, the community involvement occurred after the exhibition had been fully mounted and after brochures and flyers describing the exhibition had already been printed. Second, although the ROM invited representatives of the Black artistic community to comment, it did not seek the views of a broadly based cross-section of Toronto's Black population. Third, it chose to ignore the concerns of those who were consulted.

(continued)

CASE STUDY 9.1 *(continued)*

Once the coalition had been formed and had begun its demonstrations, the ROM appeared to "dig in its heels" and consistently refused to meet the demonstrators' demands. Neither did the ROM show much sensitivity to the perspectives of the Black community and others who shared their concerns. Instead, its officials continued to affirm their support of the exhibit and appeared to take offence at the attempts made to interfere (as they saw it) with their museum and curatorial roles.

After several months, Cannizzo broke her silence and attempted to justify the exhibition. Seven months after the show was launched, she stated that "the exhibition does not promote colonialism or glorify imperialism.... It should help all Canadians to understand the historical roots of racism" (Cannizzo, 1990). Her article did not demonstrate particular sensitivity to the concerns of the Black community.

Exacerbating the tense situation was the media coverage of these events. A number of feature pieces were written, most of which were critical of the protesters, who were characterized as radicals, bullies, blackmailers, terrorists, and revisionists. An art critic wrote that the "price of popularity must sometimes be paid for at the cost of integrity." He went on to observe that this show "caused a minor uproar here" (Hume, 1989). He observed: "Some members of the Black community considered it racist. It wasn't, of course."

Journalists in most of the mainstream newspapers and magazines dismissed the protest as the work of "radicals." A headline in *The Globe and Mail* read, "ROM Adds Insult to Injury in Debacle over African Show," (Drainie, 1991); *The Toronto Star* accused the "self-righteous left" (Hume, 1990); and the *Toronto Sun* concluded: "Why are we so bloody eager to be held hostage by the ravers from the political left? They won big on this one, you know" (Blatchford, 1990).

For the Black community and its representatives, the incident merely confirmed that

> as long as institutions and individuals fail to understand how thoroughly racism permeates the very underpinnings of Western thought, then despite all the good will in the world, catastrophes like "Into the Heart of Africa" will continue to happen. Intentions, particularly the good ones, continue to pave the way to hell. And to Africa. (Nourbese Philip, 1992)

CONSEQUENCES

"Into the Heart of Africa" was scheduled to tour several museums in Canada and the United States. The controversy led to the cancellation of the exhibit by the other museums. In response, the director of the ROM, John MacNeill, commented: "the controversy which surrounded this exhibition and led to the cancellation of the tour impinges on the freedom of all museums to maintain intellectual honesty, scientific and historical integrity and academic freedom."

(continued)

CASE STUDY 9.1 *(continued)*

CONCLUSION

This case study crystallizes many of the issues related to cultural racism and cultural appropriation. Nourbese Philip (1993) suggested that at the heart of the ROM controversy were changing beliefs about the role and function of museums and other cultural institutions, especially the issue of who should have the power to represent and control images created by "others." The traditional values and practices of institutions such as museums are difficult to change.

One analyst posed an important question about the ROM controversy: Would the institution have supported a more critical approach to the subject? Would it have risked offending its important patrons, some of whom donated artifacts to the collection? (Butler, 1993:57).

The ROM controversy also illustrated how the past converges with the present. The protesters saw a relationship between the symbolic domination, reflected in the colonial images of the exhibit, and the sense of powerlessness experienced daily by Black people in Canada. The linkage between racism in various sectors of society was made by a critic who emphasized the importance of understanding how the struggles with the ROM and the Metropolitan Toronto Police were welded together: "Inside the ROM is institutional racism and outside is the brutal reality" (Roach, 1990).

This case study also emphasizes the intrinsic link between colonialism and cultural racism. The process employed by the ROM to conceptualize and develop "Into the Heart of Africa" was based on the colonial model of objectification. Mitchell suggested that the West habitually renders the world as object or, more specifically, "the world as exhibition" (1989:219–22), and argues that this process of organizing and ordering the world is identical to the logic and processes of colonialism. The outcome of this process is the domination of the body, spirit, and soul of the "others."

Objectification is also very much a part of the way in which Africans in the exhibit were depicted. The lens of the camera held by the missionary or colonizer captures the "object" (the women washing clothes), but the "objects" are rendered powerless and silent. They appear not to challenge their oppression. The exhibit was totally "devoid of images and voices of resistance" to colonial subjugation (Butler, 1993:63). There are numerous examples in the history of Africa in which Africans resisted domination both physically and in writing. This should have been included in the narrative.

Crean summarized the cultural racism of the exhibit by stating that "Into the Heart of Africa" was "a classic case of a cultural institution unable to see its own bias and unprepared to examine its own cultural assumptions" (1991:127).

In the final analysis, "Into the Heart of Africa" was a classic example of a situation in which the possibility for growth and change was lost to the moment, as the cultural power of the museum and other institutions was used to preserve a tradition of silencing and marginalization. The ROM, as a "historical-cultural theatre of memory" (Clifford, 1990), chose to respect and showcase

(continued)

CASE STUDY 9.1 (*continued*)

one set of life histories — that of the "defenders of the Empire." In so doing, it discarded the experiences of Africans and the histories of African Canadians. Thus the exhibition did not really go into the "heart of Africa" but gave pre-eminence to the story of those Canadian who went "out of Africa," taking home "souvenirs" of their journey.

Asians, Asian Canadians, Africans, Black Canadians, and Aboriginal peoples. Protests against this practice have been countered by cries of censorship from White artists and cultural producers.

For example, many mainstream writers object to the Canada Council's and Women's Press's guidelines on cultural appropriation. They suggest that these policies jeopardize their right to freedom of expression (Paris, 1992). The Writers Union of Canada's commitment to support the rights of racial-minority writers to greater freedom of expression and access has not been well received by many mainstream writers. June Callwood, a co-founder of the union, warned her colleagues of the dangerous emotional-

---

Figure 9.1

TWO PROCESSES OF CULTURAL APPROPRIATION

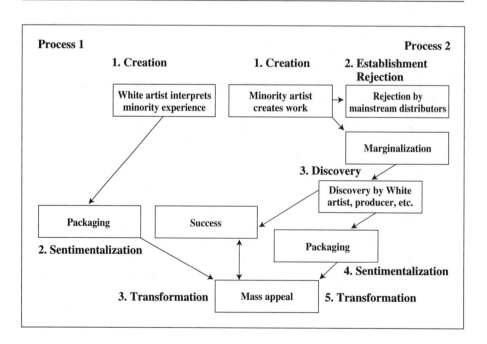

ism in the positions and strategies used by writers of colour to assert their own freedom of expression while undermining the freedom of mainstream writers. She referred to these efforts as the acts of the "self-defined weak" that include "bullying and intimidation" (Callwood, 1993).

The defences of freedom of expression and artistic licence are challenged by many artists of colour. In a world dominated by White values, images, and norms, where people of colour are either absent from most cultural production or misrepresented as racial or gender anomalies, it has been observed that

> it is critical for disenfranchised racial minorities to maintain possession and control over the telling of their stories and histories.... Any representation of ourselves and our cultural experiences done by an outsider would be from a comparatively superficial perspective, simply because he/she hasn't had the experience of surviving racial oppression — complete with all its complications, consequences, and contradictions. (Browning, 1992:33)

Thus, Browning (1992) concluded that White artists and writers who attempt to speak on behalf of the "others" or who believe that they can interpret their experiences are perpetuating their own positions of privilege and dominance.

Building on this analysis, Nourbese Philip (1992) drew attention to one of the central paradoxes in cultural appropriation. While there is a profound lack of respect for artists of colour and their **aesthetics**, there is generally a strong approval of the White artist who culturally appropriates those traditions and benefits from them (for example, see the case study of *Show Boat*).

Brant (1990) holds the view that the truth is not told by the many White writers who use their hundreds of years of colonial supremacy to speak for Aboriginal peoples.

> I do not say that only Indians can write about Indians. But you can't steal my stories and call them your own. You can't steal my spirit and call it your own. This is the history of North America — stolen property, stolen lives, stolen dreams and stolen spirituality.... If your history is one of cultural domination you must be aware ... you have to tell the truth about your role, your history, your internalized domination and supremacy.

The concern over cultural appropriation is part of a broader struggle, that of power — the power of White cultural authorities to publish a literary work, to produce a theatrical production, to select and organize an exhibition, to determine what music will be played and what performers will be chosen.

MARGINALIZATION OF PEOPLE OF COLOUR IN PUBLIC CULTURE

People of colour confront both subtle and overt barriers as they attempt to move from the margins of mainstream culture into the centre. The title of the book *Out There* (Ferguson, 1990), suggests that the power of the centre depends on the relatively unchallenged authority of the dominant culture.

In other words, cultural racism is maintained by silencing artists, writers, and musicians of colour who, having been relegated to a place outside the dominant culture, find it difficult to challenge dominant modes of cultural production and dissemination.

The racism of cultural institutions has been characterized as a form of organizational apartheid that in the past relegated Aboriginal art to museums and the category of "anthropology," while White artistic productions went to public galleries and were categorized as "art." This devaluing of the art of Aboriginal peoples and artists of colour is considered by some to be not only cultural domination but cultural genocide (Danzker, 1991).

A further example of cultural racism is the canon of "great works" by White, mainly male, writers and dramatists that is incorporated in the curricula of educational institutions and considered the only material appropriate for mainstream audiences. It is assumed that this body of writing represents the best of human culture and creativity. Cultural racism is reflected in "objective" and "neutral" reviews of literary, arts, and entertainment critics who defend their judgements by maintaining that universal criteria and standards can be applied to all creative arts, thereby ignoring their own cultural and ideological frameworks and biases. Racism is sometimes hidden in efforts to stifle debate about representation, access, and equity. Those who challenge racist attitudes, policies, or practices are often accused of "censorship," and their concerns are dismissed as examples of "political correctness."

Efforts to change or challenge these assumptions are generally met with fierce resistance. For example, when the Art Gallery of Ontario (AGO) established a task force to examine the issue of representation both from the perspective of governance — who sits on the board and who is hired for senior management positions — and in terms of the extent to which the AGO supported artists who reflected the diversity of Ontario, the media argued that the Ontario government had gone too far. It implied that the AGO must "show and publicize the work of current Ontario artists even if the AGO curators think that, at the moment, most of their work is mediocre" (Fulford, 1992). The implicit assumption appeared to be that all art that does not fit within the Euro-American tradition is *ipso facto* inferior.

These assumptions were in evidence in an exhibit at the Vancouver Art Gallery (VAG). In 1991, the Artists' Coalition for Local Colour held a protest outside the gallery. The coalition was formed primarily by South Asian artists and cultural workers in response to the VAG's decision to mount an exhibit of South Asian art imported from the United Kingdom. The coalition argued that this was a blatant example of the systemic racism of the organization and resulted in a lack of access, participation, and equity for local artists of colour. Moreover, the VAG decided that, in light of the controversy, it would celebrate the opening with a private viewing of the collection rather than a formal opening event. No members of the South Asian community were invited to the opening.

REPRESENTATION AND MISREPRESENTATION

The case study *"Show Boat"* looks closely at the issues of representation, misrepresentation, marginalization, stereotyping, cultural appropriation, freedom of expression, and the **commodification** of cultural production.

Here, "representation" concerns not only the inclusion or omission of images of people of colour in art. It indicates who controls the production and transmission of ideas, images, and discourse in art and society.

CASE STUDY 9.2

SHOW BOAT

In the winter of 1993, Live Entertainment Corporation, which had an exclusive contract to manage the new North York Municipal Arts Centre in Ontario, announced that a production of the musical *Show Boat* would launch the opening of this important new institution. The play is based on a 1926 novel by American writer Edna Ferber.

Show Boat chronicles the lives of a White southern family and the performers who work on a boat that travels on the Mississippi River over four decades, entertaining White audiences in the southern and midwestern regions of the United States. The play begins during the postemancipation period and continues through the first decades of the twentieth century. In the world depicted in the novel, Blacks exist as backdrop. Almost every reference to them in the novel employs demeaning and derogatory stereotypes:

> The cook was a woolly-headed Black with a rolling protuberant eye and the quick temper of his calling.

> A simple ignorant soul, the Black man, and ... somewhat savage ...

> One drop of nigger blood makes you a nigger in these parts ...

> I kind of smell a nigger in the woodpile here in more ways than one.

> Eight months of flies and niggers and dirty mud-tracking loafers is enough for me, Captain Hawks. I'm thankful to get back for a few weeks where I can live like a decent white woman.

> Long before white-aproned Jo, breakfast bell in hand, emerged head first from the little doorway beneath the stage back of the orchestra pit, like an amiable black python from its lair ... (Ferber, 1926)

The Jamaican Canadian Society, in stating its position on *Show Boat*, wrote that it is a musical based on a novel filled with degrading images of Blacks.

(continued)

CASE STUDY 9.2 *(continued)*

The words leap off the page and hit one in the face like a ton of bricks and plant deleterious images in the minds of readers such as "shiftless Joe" ... "teeth gleaming and eyes rolling." There are no redeeming descriptions of Blacks in the novel; throughout they are portrayed as dimwitted, childlike, animalistic, lazy, drunk and irresponsible. Nowhere in the novel or in any of the subsequent plays or films is the horrifying reality of Black peoples' suffering experiences throughout this period. (Coalition to Stop *Show Boat*, 1993)

The musical first appeared in 1927 and was revised and restaged numerous times, with productions in the United States, the United Kingdom, and Canada. Two film versions were also based on the novel. Each version retained the negative and demeaning stereotypes of Blacks happily singing and dancing. Only the character Joe, played by Paul Robeson, laments his plight in the famous song, "Ol' Man River." The opening line of the song, in its earliest rendition, begins: "Niggers all work on the Mississippi." This was later changed to "Darkies" and then "Colored" and finally "We all work." However, in most productions, while he moves White audiences with his music, Joe remains a lazy, good-natured "negro." He displays no rage or resistance. The other Black characters are equally passive figures who never challenge their oppression.

EVENTS

A large and diverse segment of Toronto's Black community launched a protest shortly after learning about the decision to produce *Show Boat*. A coalition was formed to "Stop *Show Boat*." Its concern centred on the ways in which the various productions of the play distorted the memory, history, and experiences of Black people who lived through slavery and the Reconstruction period. Opposition to the play was based, in part, on the fact that it romanticized and trivialized one of the most oppressive periods of Western civilization and misrepresented the deep emotions, conditions, and experiences of Blacks in those horrific times.

Show Boat is an example of both misrepresentation and cultural appropriation. In this instance, White writers, producers, directors, composers, and lyricists assume the right to create and transmit inaccurate and stereotypical images of "others." The music of *Show Boat* is drawn largely from the rich musical traditions of Afro-American culture. The appropriation of this music by the dominant culture for its own use and profit, while at the same time portraying Africans and Afro-Americans as a people bereft of culture, was a common practice in a racist society (Nourbese Philip, 1993).

The Black community, the Coalition to Stop *Show Boat*, and other groups argued that the decision to mount this controversial musical in a public municipal arts theatre in a municipality in which thousands of Blacks live indicated a staggering lack of sensitivity toward the community. The continued racism and oppression that were an everyday reality for Black Canadians were considered irrelevant by the

(continued)

CASE STUDY 9.2 *(continued)*

decision-makers of Live Entertainment Productions as well as the mayor of North York and other politicians who gave absolute freedom to the producers in all aspects of management of the North York Performing Arts Centre.

The Coalition to Stop *Show Boat* argued that Blacks in the various versions of *Show Boat* are viewed as backdrops, props, and stage dressing and provide a "colourful" context for the lives of the White people in the story. In every production of the musical, Black characters have functioned as singing caricatures, enhancing the picture of a people who are happy in their condition. Their portrayal is incidental to the story. When they do appear, they are depicted as passive, cheerful, ignorant, singing and dancing stereotypes.

Although recent revisions of the play removed some of the more offensive stereotypes and problematic language, the critics of *Show Boat* argued that the play was designed for White audiences and that all of its productions have perpetuated the same myths and misconceptions about Black people that existed in its first production. The protesters argued that the play reinforced the negative images of Blacks that are part of the mainstream culture and that influence the way in which White people see and interact with Black people daily (Lee, 1993; Auguste, 1993a). The chair of the African Heritage Educators' Network wrote:

> We Africans in the diaspora define ourselves. When we cry out in anguish over our suffering under the yoke of "artistic license," our pain cannot be trivialized by dominant groups' attempts to define us. (Farrell, 1993)

The chair of the Coalition to Stop *Show Boat* expressed a similar view of the musical:

> *Show Boat* has resonated in the Black community.... It is the symbol of systemic and cultural racism. It symbolizes what we suffer in our daily lives, no matter what we have achieved in this society, no matter who we are. (Henry, 1993:54)

However, the producers of *Show Boat* and a significant cross-section of the media, including many editorial writers, journalists, and theatre critics, were unsympathetic. One of Canada's most respected writers suggested that it was "dangerous nonsense" to describe *Show Boat* as racist; he urged the producers not to "scrub *Show Boat* too clean," that is, not to remove the overt racist language and stereotypes (Berton, 1993). He meant that the racism of the play belongs there because of the historical context in which the story was written.

THE CENSORSHIP DEBATE

The backlash to the protest against *Show Boat* was linked to the rhetoric of censorship and political correctness. The Black community's call for greater sensitivity and responsibility in the selection of cultural productions in publicly funded institutions was seen as a violation of freedom of expression. The protesters were considered to

(continued)

CASE STUDY 9.2 *(continued)*

be undermining one of the fundamental and sacrosanct values underpinning a democratic society. Editorials published in *The Toronto Star*, *The Globe and Mail*, and the *Toronto Sun* were highly critical of the Black community's position on *Show Boat*, suggesting that what was being called for was the rewriting of history as well as the stifling of creative expression.

Some questioned whether the media's strong stand in support of the production — particularly that of the three Toronto newspapers — was influenced by their vested interest in the production. Each of the newspapers received significant revenues from the show's advertisements, which appeared daily for several months. One of *The Toronto Star*'s own columnists noted, "Live Entertainment Corporation of Canada are among the *Star*'s half-dozen biggest advertisers" (Slinger, 1993). Nourbese Philip (1992) observed that the quantum leap from racism to censorship was "neither random nor unexpected." The issue of censorship is central to the dominant cultures of liberal democracies like Canada. In these cultures, "censorship becomes a significant and talismanic cultural icon around which all debates about the 'individual freedom of man' swirl."

The Coalition to Stop *Show Boat* argued that calling for a play to be boycotted was not a condonation of censorship. It was, rather, a calling into question of the social responsibility and morality of dedicating a publicly funded building, in one of the most racially diverse cities in the world, with a production that demeaned a large segment of that community. Farrell (1993) suggested that the real and initial concerns about *Show Boat* concerned a hierarchy of rights: the rights of a producer to artistic freedom versus the rights of a community not to be hurt, not to have its children hurt by stereotypes. *Show Boat* revealed the fundamental tension that exists in democratic liberal societies: the tension between the competing principles of an individual's right to freedom of expression and the right of communities to be protected from forms of speech that do harm.

The questions remain: what constitutes harm, and who will make this definition for the purpose of determining what legally may be said or done in the public domain? Many groups, including Jews, have argued powerfully, with respect to hate propaganda, for example, that the risk of ignoring hate groups is greater than the risk of regulating them. In the same way, women's groups and others have vigorously opposed the production and dissemination of pornography. They have argued that pornography has the potential to cause serious harm to women and children. In each of these examples, freedom is not viewed as an absolute right. It is tempered with the notion of justice and the protection of the rights and freedoms of those who are most vulnerable.

Landsberg (1993) posed the question, "Why is it censorship to protest a demeaning and irrelevant theatrical production?" She observed that these protests have provided a valuable form of public education and free speech. Similarly, the director of the Simon Wiesenthal Centre of Canada wrote: "The Black community has every right to protest what it sees as a racist vehicle" (Littman, 1993).

REPRESENTATION AND THE ROLE OF AUDIENCE

For the largely White audiences attending *Show Boat*, the glitz and glamour of the show — the high quality of acting, the lavish sets, the beautiful costumes, the

(continued)

CASE STUDY 9.2 *(continued)*

familiar "stirring" music, and the power of the spectacle — all served to render the racist images, characterizations, plot, and subplots invisible. The Anglo audiences remained fixed in their own sociocultural location. What viewers saw were the images, preconceptions, and attitudes that are part of the "White gaze" — the White experiential frame of reference.

The White audience felt comfortable with the "sanitized" representation of Blacks in this version of the play, that is, as largely one-dimensional, stereotypical figures who function as an entertaining backdrop to the central narrative. The only Black character who has any real role in this story is Julie, who is half-White, and she disappears in Act II before the act is half over and is not seen again. The rest of the Black actors essentially appear only to sing and dance.

For many in the Black community who have been marked as "outsiders" and rendered invisible in everyday discourses of positive recognition and affirmation, controlling the production of negative images and cultural misrepresentations became a stridently self-conscious strategy for challenging a cultural form of expression that they felt was harmful to their community. As teacher Clem Marshall suggested, there is an intrinsic link between art and life, and "*Show Boat* as art has spilled into our lives" (Marshall, 1993).

CONSEQUENCES

Three additional factors increased the stakes in this debate and demonstrated the ripple effect of cultural racism into other institutional arenas. First, a North York Board of Education trustee publicly expressed her concern about the play: "Most of the plays that portray Black or any other ethnic groups in a negative way are always done by a White man, and usually always [sic] a Jewish person is doing plays that denigrate us" (Valpy, 1993). Although she soon publicly apologized for her insensitivity to the Jewish community, the spectre of Black anti-Semitism heightened tensions and misunderstanding between the two communities. Members of the Jewish community took exception to editorials and other articles appearing in a Black community newspaper that they felt were indicative of Black anti-Semitism. Similarly, individuals in the Black community spoke about their pain, frustration, and anger at having racism ignored by the Jewish community and others (Auguste, 1993a, 1993b).

A second factor in the controversy was the intention of several voluntary organizations to sponsor the performance of *Show Boat* for fundraising purposes. One of them, the United Way of Metropolitan Toronto, had prided itself on its anti-racism position, policy, and practices. When the controversy arose, the board of the United Way, after considerable discussion, chose to proceed with their fundraiser. To protest the United Way action, 19 of the 22 members of its Black and Caribbean Fundraising Committee resigned, as did several other volunteers. The United Way position led to the questioning of the organization's commitment to anti-racism. Further questions were raised by some members of the Black community about whether there were fundamental inequities in the allocations process for funding the Black community's human-service agencies.

(continued)

CASE STUDY 9.2 *(continued)*

The third factor was the intention of Live Entertainment to bring in 200 000 students to see the production. The corporation indicated that it planned to produce "educational" packages to "enlighten" students about the history of slavery and the Reconstruction period after they had seen the show. The materials were to be developed by an Afro-American academic who had been retained to act as the primary consultant for the educational program. In response to the plan to develop these programs, critics protested both the choice of the play and the development of educational materials based on a racist text. In a letter to Ontario's minister of education, they stated that

> creating the opportunity for the school-going community to be entertained at the expense of some of its members is not the best strategy for helping eliminate racism. To argue that seeing *Show Boat* would itself be a lesson in racism is to argue that one learns best about radiation by being continually exposed to it. Likewise the central impetus for the show is entertainment and economic gain. It was never intended to be educational.... Any educational package accompanying the show would therefore be at best inadequate and inappropriate. (Ijaz, 1993)

In a similar way, Black educators argued that

> It is inappropriate for the producers of *Show Boat* to use the educational system of Ontario to make a dollar over the objection of the Black community and at the expense of the self-esteem of Black children and youth. To allow *Show Boat* materials into the schools is systemic racism that says "I have political and financial power over you, even if you object." (Black Educators' Working Group, 1993)

CONCLUSION

This case study demonstrates how cultural racism functions and how pervasive its impact is on both the dominant culture and marginalized groups. It demonstrates how invisible cultural racism can be to White people and how acutely present it is in the lives of people of colour. It also clarifies the links between racism in one sector, such as the arts, and other arenas, such as the media, education, and the marketplace.

The *Show Boat* controversy continues to reverberate with significant consequences for all the protagonists, including the Black community, the Jewish community, the United Way and other agencies that sponsored *Show Boat*, the media, boards of education, municipal and provincial government agencies, and other cultural agencies. *Show Boat* is a clear example of how the cultural power and racist ideology of individuals and institutions converge to further marginalize, exclude, and silence people of colour.

The relationship between White cultural professionals and people of colour in the arts reproduces the symbolic bias of colonial domination (Butler, 1993). In the

(continued)

CASE STUDY 9.2 *(continued)*

examples of "Into the Heart of Africa" and *Show Boat*, the conflict between the interests of producers and the Black and other communities who challenged the power of the dominant culture was constrained by further acts of marginalization and exclusion. This process has been described as

> the act of conceptualizing, inscribing, and interacting with "others" on terms not of their choosing; in making them into pliant objects and silenced subjects of our scripts and scenarios; in assuming the capacity to "represent" them. (Comaroff and Comaroff, 1991:15)

ALLOCATION OF GRANTS AND RESOURCES BY FUNDING AGENCIES

Historically, the policies and practices of arts councils — by virtue of their neglect and lack of support of minority artists, artistic organizations, and projects — have been a powerful vehicle for perpetuating racism in the arts. It has been extremely difficult for writers, artists, musicians, directors, producers, and performers of colour to receive grants from arts councils and government agencies because they are perceived to be unable to meet Eurocentric aesthetic standards. They often find themselves relegated to the margins of the arts and labelled as "not professional." Funding organizations have tended to view Black, Asian, and Aboriginal Canadian artists and cultural companies as "exotic" or "folkloric." As a result, it has been thought that they should be supported through multicultural funding agencies rather than expect to share in the limited resources of arts councils (Li, 1994).

In essence, two distinct policies operate to provide unequal support structures: to arts within the dominant culture, and to art produced by Aboriginal artists and artists of colour. "These two art worlds operate within separate infrastructures and rules and standards; and the source and magnitude of funding are different ... and the art works of these two art worlds carry unequal market value and social status" (Li, 1994).

As the 1980s drew to a close, escalating demands were made by Aboriginal, Black/African, and Asian artists and writers for funding agencies to address cultural and racial barriers in their structures. They were urged to identify representation in their staffing, the composition of their juries and panels, and their criteria of professionalism, quality, and excellence. Critics of these "relentlessly White" organizations argued that "in a country where a working artist is almost by definition a government funded artist, this situation amounted to cultural apartheid" (Bailey, 1992:22). Nourbese Philip shared the grave concern about funding agencies: "The divide between the lived reality of the Black artist and the funding policies of arts councils, between the Black artist and the art world in general, is so great as to be almost unbridgeable" (1992:227).

Arts funding is premised on two notions of culture that are mutually exclusive: one views culture as art, to be funded by arts councils; the other understands culture as an anthropological phenomenon that should be funded primarily by agencies such as multiculturalism and citizenship at the federal level and ministries of culture or citizenship at provincial levels (Wong, 1991). The assumption underpinning the second approach is that works of art produced by people of colour fail to meet professional standards of excellence. Only when artists of colour "prove" themselves in the context of the norms and models of White elites can they overcome the great divide (West, 1990).

A review of some of the activities of art councils illustrates the above points. Between 1990 and 1992, research carried out by three of Canada's major arts councils — the Canada Council, the Ontario Arts Council, and the Toronto Arts Council — resulted in reports dealing with racism in arts-funding organizations and containing various approaches and strategies for dealing with it.[2] In addition, Metropolitan Toronto's Department of Cultural Affairs held consultations on the funding of ethno-racial and Aboriginal arts organizations. In each case it was recognized that significant barriers confronted artists of colour. However, common to the approaches taken by each of these funding organizations was some attempt to distance the organization from the issues of race and racism and to focus on cultural barriers. The organizations seemed to have difficulty dealing with one of the most powerful components of cultural racism — the Eurocentrism of the arts in Canada. They also generally refrained from dealing with the specifics of systemic racism.

The Canada Council, for example, failed to support the committee's finding that "systemic racism is a result of the everyday functioning of all Canadian institutions" and rejected its call for an organizational review of the Canada Council. The Ontario Arts Council report and recommendations were based on a "diversity" paradigm; "racism" appeared only once in the document. The Toronto Arts Council used the terminology of cultural equity and referred to "specific" cultural communities to indicate differences based on culture, ethnicity, gender, language, race, and sexual orientation. However, specific systems and patterns of exclusion and discrimination are only hinted at (Bailey, 1992).

With respect to the issues of access and equity to funding, a noted Canadian recording artist and composer commented:

> It seems that only Caucasians are allowed to sit in judgement as experts on Chinese, African, African-Canadian, South Asian, Aboriginal, Indonesian, Korean, Japanese ... music, deciding who gets the grants and whose music is valuable to whose community. Until we have representation on these juries, we will only be tokens. (Nolan, 1992:28)

One of the issues raised by ethno-racial communities and artists of colour in the consultation by Metropolitan Toronto's Cultural Affairs Division was the question of professional standards. Many have suggested that the criteria and standards used by funders often screen out applicants belonging to racial communities by using Eurocentric aesthetics as a yardstick.

EUROCENTRIC FORMS OF CULTURAL CRITICISM

All cultural criticism is ideological — influenced by judgements and affected by a particular set of values and beliefs. When cultural critics offer a judgement on a text, art exhibit, or theatrical performance, they do so in some social, cultural, and/or institutional context. The relevant context might include one or more categories, such as gender, race, class, sexual orientation, and regional background.

A cultural critic who functions in the centre of the dominant culture feels safe in a cocoon of adherence to the notions of "objectivity" and "neutrality." Cultural criticisms are based on the assumption that a body of universal criteria and standards can be applied to *all* literary and art analysis. But the concepts of "universalism," "objectivity," and "neutrality" are contested categories.

From the perspective of many women and people of colour, the content and parameters of the universal are never all-inclusive. Non-western, non-European cultural forms are rarely seen as part of the corpus of great aesthetics (Tator et al., 1998; Jordan and Weedon, 1995; Nourbese Philip, 1992). They are often labelled and dismissed as "ethnic," "folkloric," "primitive," "community-based" art — as part of the world of the "Other" (Walcott, 1996; Li, 1994).

Arun Mukherjee, a professor of Canadian literature with a particular focus on writers of colour, points to the Eurocentric and racist nature of Canadian literary nationalism, which implies that the Canadian identity is defined in settler or colonial terms. There is a pressing need for cultural criticism that respects and understands the contexts from which First Nations writers and writers of colour speak — the historical, religious, literary, and cultural traditions that inform a piece of work (Mukherjee, 1994–95).

INSTITUTIONAL RESPONSES

The lack of access and the barriers to writers and artists of colour have recently begun to receive more attention from funding bodies, museums, writers' unions, publishing houses, and other cultural agencies. This chapter's case studies, "Into the Heart of Africa," "*Show Boat,*" and "The Writing Thru Race Conference," demonstrate that cultural production is indeed an important site of struggle. Racial-minority and Aboriginal communities are becoming more insistent that their cultural rights be respected and that the cultural appropriation of their experiences by White power brokers in cultural organizations be challenged.

CASE STUDY 9.3

THE "WRITING THRU RACE" CONFERENCE

BACKGROUND

In the summer of 1994 the Writers' Union of Canada (TWUC) sponsored the "Writing Thru Race" conference, which brought together 180 First Nations writers and writers of colour for a three-day meeting in Vancouver. Participation in the conference's daytime events was by invitation and was restricted to writers of colour and First Nations writers.

The conference came about because a number of racial-minority members of TWUC stated that the concerns of minority and Aboriginal writers — cultural appropriation, lack of access to grants and publishing facilities, and other issues — needed to be examined in some detail. The decision to hold a national conference created controversy within TWUC, since several members were against minority writers meeting by themselves.

In the weeks leading up to the conference, another controversial move made more headlines. Without warning, the federal heritage minister withdrew government funding for the conference. Pressured by the Reform Party's intense criticism in Parliament, the minister announced that his government could not support an "exclusive" conference. According to Roy Miki, chair of the Racial Minorities Writers Committee and chair of the conference, he learned of the retraction of funding by reading the newspaper. Neither he, nor any other member of the union was officially informed by Heritage Canada.

The Canada Council, the City of Vancouver, and the Ontario Arts Council maintained their financial support for the conference, despite mounting public pressure against the event. Union members began raising funds on their own; executive members and members of the Racial Minorities Writers Committee took an active fundraising role.

THE CONFERENCE

The opening evening was a public event. It attracted about 225 people, including some media personnel. The participants were an extraordinarily diverse group, with substantial numbers of First Nations writers, African Canadians, and artists of South Asian and Southeast Asian origins. A handful of Whites chose to attend the evening meetings. The atmosphere was extremely jubilant. People described their elation at being able to translate a vision into reality and to have overcome so many obstacles that were strewn in their path.

During the days, panels and workshops were held on a wide variety of themes, including "Emergence of First Nations Writers and Storytellers in a Multicultural Urban Environment; Reading and Writing Thru Race: Theory and Practice; The Teaching of Canadian Minority Writing; Writing for Children; The Effects of

(continued)

CASE STUDY 9.3 *(continued)*

Racism; Finding One's Own Identity; Access, Equity and Publishing; Writing in Mother Tongue" and other topics. The evening sessions which included readings were open to the public.

The conference afforded a safe space for Aboriginal writers and writers of colour to assert both their need and their right to have their identities and differences recognized, respected, and affirmed. The participants sought an acknowledgement of their distinct cultural, racial, linguistic, and other defining characteristics. They hoped to discover collective strategies to dismantle the ideological, attitudinal, organizational, and institutional barriers that keep writers of colour, First Nations writers, and writers from non-dominant cultural backgrounds from full and equal participation in the mainstream of Canadian culture.

ANALYSIS

The conference, with its attention directed at issues of identity, difference, and racism, appeared to pose a significant threat to the Eurocentric values, assumptions, and beliefs that have formed the central core of Canadian cultural identity and aesthetic representations. This sense of peril is reflected in a statement written by fourteen White authors who, a few months before the conference, in an attempt to silence the debate on racism in Canadian literature, wrote that fellow members of the Writers' Union of Canada should "shut the f—k up" on the issue (Clarke, 1994:48).

The resistance, conflict, and anger over the decision to hold such a conference expressed at TWUC meetings spilled out across the pages of the national media; and was then incorporated into the speeches and acts of politicians. This acute response to a conference of just over two hundred people reflected a deeper state of political and cultural tension, uncertainty, and anxiety. It drew attention to issues that became increasingly contentious and problematic in the last decades of the twentieth century. Among its other contributions, the conference brought these questions into sharp focus:

- What is Canadian culture?
- What does it mean to be Canadian?
- Who is included in the construction of the notions of "we" and "our," in relation to definitions of culture and the Canadian state?
- How should the state organize itself in relation to public policies and programs dealing with diversity and pluralism, access and equity, and anti-racism?
- Who really belongs in the mainstream of Canadian life?
- How shall we deal with our cultural, racial, linguistic, and religious differences and other social markers such as gender, sexual orientation, and class differences?
- Whose cultural knowledge, values, traditions, and histories should be recognized, and whose cultures should be given pre-eminence?

(continued)

CASE STUDY 9.3 (*continued*)

- How do the above issues affect cultural production and aesthetic representations?

For First Nations writers and writers of colour, the Writing Thru Race Conference provided the space and place for developing individual and collective strategies to deal with the racism that had long been embedded in the fabric of their personal and professional lives. The conference also represented a significant shift in the way in which racism in cultural production had been resisted and challenged. In incorporating an exclusionary policy, designed to reflect and respond to the needs and interests of First Nations writers and writers of colour, the conference organizers were pursuing a deliberate strategy of moving away from multicultural inclusionary paradigms that often function as a cover or distraction from the "unpleasant" matter of racism (McFarlane, 1995).

Contrary to the dominant public discourse that emanates from the cultural elite, a conference for a group of people who share a common body of interests and concerns is not a commitment to a lifetime of separation and exclusion from the mainstream culture. Nor does it represent the dismantling of Canadian culture or national identity. It is, rather, a manifestation of the need of every oppressed group to come together in a safe space where its members can share their disappointments, pain, and anger; celebrate what they have created and accomplished; mobilize, energize, and empower each other; and explore, as individuals and collectivities, new strategies and tools for dismantling barriers and crossing boundaries.

The resistance of the White writing and publishing industry to the conference reflects how threatened the literary elite is by the challenge to extend the definition of "we" to include those who differ in race, ethnicity, and other social markers. The outcry from various constituencies, including government, media, and literary critics against this conference and earlier initiatives suggests that the discourse of pluralism, inclusion, and equality have been a facade to mask the power, position, and privilege of the dominant cultural community. Both individuals and cultural agencies resist change, particularly change that threatens their own power base within a context of inclusiveness.

Ultimately, however, the conference was an act of affirmation and recognition as well as an act of defiance and protest. For First Nations writers and writers of colour, it was an affirmation and recognition of their identity as critical participants in what Lenore Keeshig-Tobias called a "cultural revolution" (Griffith, 1994), redefining what it means to be Canadian, what it means to be a Canadian writer, and the literary landscape of Canada. The conference was also an act of defiance against Eurocentric ideologies and exclusionary practices. It was an act of resistance to the notions of liberalism and pluralism that perpetuate White power and privilege within the arts.

In response to these concerns, arts organizations such as the Toronto Arts Council, the Ontario Arts Council, the Canada Council, and a limited number of galleries and museums, including the Royal Ontario Museum, the Vancouver Art Gallery, and the Art Gallery of Ontario, have established advisory committees consisting of people of colour. Some have also attempted to increase the representation of racial minorities in their administrative structures. Among book publishers, The Women's Press has developed anti-racist guidelines.

Since the controversy over the Writing Thru Race Conference, there has been an outpouring of outstanding literature by writers of colour and Aboriginal writers. These writers are winning major awards in Canada (for example, in 1997, Dionne Brand won a Governor General's Literary Award). As George Elliot Clarke writes: "'A fresh breeze is blowing' through the halls of Canadian literature. The doors and windows of the grand, old slightly musty, Victorian mansion are opening slowly to admit new accents and fresh scents" (1994:48).

With respect to exhibits, there have been some small changes at the ROM. According to key respondents in the museum community, consultation is now routinely done on all exhibits and programs that "deal with ethno-cultural subject matter." (One could raise the question: What in a museum does *not* fall in this category?) African and African Canadian scholars were called on to examine the museum's African collections. Similarly, a First Nations artist was consulted on the museum's reinterpretation of its Haida and Nisga'a crest poles. However, there is little evidence of structural change in the staffing, management, or governance of this institution.

There appear to be no major shifts in the views of many cultural authorities. For example, three years after the "Into the Heart of Africa" exhibition closed, T. Cuyler Young (1993), the former director of the ROM, wrote about what he had learned from the controversy over the exhibition. He said that the controversy was really about a small group of radicals motivated by an unstated personal and political agenda unrelated to the exhibition.

SUMMARY

This chapter has analyzed the powerful role of cultural organizations in contributing to democratic racism. The racism found in various forms of cultural production and transmission emanates from the dominant culture's value system. Although artistic expression and cultural production are framed in the context of liberal values such as universalism and freedom of expression, Eurocentric assumptions and standards strongly influence the decisions of cultural producers in terms of what artists, writers, musicians, and actors are supported and whose voices, words, and images are excluded or silenced. Each of the cultural events examined in this chapter's case studies reflect a struggle between those with privilege, power, and voice, and those seeking to gain control over the production of images and systems of representation that misrepresent or exclude them.

The analysis in this chapter also demonstrates how the discourses of liberalism, such as freedom of expression and universalism, are frequently used to silence dissent by minorities. The examples and case studies cited support the view of many people of colour and Aboriginal peoples that freedom of expression appears to be mainly limited to the rights of those who already exercise power. On the question of universalism, groups who find their culture excluded from mainstream theatre, museums, and publishing houses challenge the assumption that dominant cultural traditions and practices have universal appeal.

Democratic racism is also demonstrated by the response of cultural authorities to the demands by African Canadians, Asian Canadians, Aboriginal artists, and their communities for greater sensitivity, accountability, and accessibility, which were met with either indifference, or a barrage of criticism and racist discourse by cultural elite and the media. Cultural authorities within Livent, the ROM, and the literary establishment vigorously and continuously denied the possibility that racism was entrenched in their cultural institutions and individual practices. From their position of power and privilege, and from their social location of "Whiteness," racism was invisible to them.

In almost every example cited in this chapter, efforts on the part of minority groups to identify racism in art forms and cultural productions resulted in both overt and subtle attacks on those who voiced concerns and called for change. In the cases of "Into the Heart of Africa" and "Show Boat," people who opposed these productions were labelled "radicals," "activists," and "troublemakers." Those who supported the Writing Thru Race Conference were portrayed as a threat to Canada's most cherished democratic values, traditions, and sense of national identity.

This chapter also illustrates the interlocking nature of various forms of racism. For example, the intrinsic relationship between racist ideology and the practices of the mass media is linked to the cultural and racial assumptions driving various cultural organizations and disciplines. The presence of the police at the protests against the ROM and Show Boat communicate the message that dissent is undemocratic and dangerous. Educational institutions often become another vehicle for the production and dissemination of culture. In the examples of the ROM and Show Boat, the participation of students became an important issue in the debate.

Racism in the arts is also inextricably linked to the marketplace and propelled by the economic interests of the corporate elite. In the case of Show Boat, the profit motive was the central force driving the producers as well as the media. Racism in the arts is like racism in the other institutions of Canadian society; it is ultimately about the power of the dominant group to control cultural forms of expression.

Racism in cultural production dramatically illustrates the tension between the competing ideologies of racism and liberalism. On the one hand, North American society has a great attachment to the ideal of unrestricted artistic licence for those who work in the arts and in cultural organizations. On the other hand, the act of protesting, resisting, and challenging the power of those who control cultural expression is a tool in the fight against marginalization, exclusion, and erasure.

Racial-minority artists and communities believe that freedom of expression should not become the talisman under which White cultural institutions maintain and reproduce racist discourse and representation. They are using cultural production as a vehicle to call on a democratic society to live up to its promise of equality and justice for all.

NOTES

1. For an in-depth study of racism in the arts, an analysis of the cultural politics of difference, and an expanded analysis of the case studies in this chapter, see Tator, Henry, and Mattis (1998).
2. The three documents are Canada Council (1992), Ontario Arts Council (1990), and Toronto Arts Council (1992).

REFERENCES

Auguste, A. (1993a). "If They Come for Me in the Morning." *Share Magazine* (Toronto) (April 1):8.

———. (1993b). "Tired of Being Your Niggers." *Share Magazine* (Toronto) (April 29).

Bailey, C. (1992). "Fright the Power." *Fuse* 15(6):24.

Becker, C. (ed.). (1994). *The Subversive Imagination: Artists, Society and Social Responsibility.* New York: Routledge.

Berton, P. (1993). "Let's Not Scrub *Show Boat* Too Clean." *Toronto Star* (March 20):K3.

Bhabha, H. (ed.). (1990). *Nation and Narration.* London: Routledge.

Black Educators' Working Group. (1993). "Letter to Premier Bob Rae." (June 18).

Blatchford, C. (1990). "A Surrender to Vile Harangues." *Toronto Sun* (November 30):5.

Brant, B. (1990). "From the Outside Looking In: Racism and Writing." Panel Discussion, Gay Cultural Festival, Vancouver (August).

Browning, F. (1992). "Self-Determination and Cultural Appropriation." *Fuse* 15(4):31–35.

Butler, S. (1993). "Contested Representations: Revisiting 'Into the Heart of Africa.'" Master's thesis, Department of Anthropology, York University.

Callwood, J. (1993). "Journalism and the Blight of Censorship." *Globe and Mail* (June 28):A13.

Canada Council. (1992). *Recommendations of the Advisory Committee for Racial Equality in the Arts and the Response of the Canada Council.* Ottawa.

Cannizzo, J. (1990). "Into the Heart of a Controversy." *Toronto Star* (June 5):A17.

———. (1991). "Exhibiting Cultures: Into the Heart of Africa." *Visual Anthropology Review* 7(1):150–60.

Clarke, G. (1994). "After Word." *Possibilities Literary Art Magazine.* 1(2):48.

Clifford, J. (1990). "On Collecting Art and Culture." In R. Ferguson et al. (eds.), *Out There: Marginalization and Contemporary Culture.* New York: Museum of Contemporary Art.

Coalition to Stop *Show Boat.* (1993). "Reply of Coalition to Stop *Show Boat* to Garth Drabinsky's March 11, 1993 Press Release." (May 3).

Comaroff, J., and J. Comaroff. (1991). *Of Revelation and Revolution: Christianity, Colonialism, and Consciousness in South Africa.* Vol. 1. Chicago: University of Chicago Press.

Crean, S. (1991). "Taking the Missionary Position." In O. McKague (ed.), *Racism in Canada.* Saskatoon: Fifth House.

Da Breo, H. (1989–90). "Royal Spoils: The Museum Confronts Its Colonial Past." *Fuse* (Winter):28–36.

Danzker, J. (1991). "Cultural Apartheid." In O. McKague (ed.), *Racism in Canada*. Saskatoon: Fifth House.

Drainie, B. (1991). "ROM Adds Insult to Injury in Debacle over African Show." *Globe and Mail* (April 19).

Essed, P. (1990). *Everyday Racism*. Claremont, CA: Hunter House.

Farrell, V. (1993). "Staging *Show Boat* Is Power Play." *Share* (May 6):9.

Ferber, E. (1926). *Show Boat*. New York: Doubleday.

Ferguson, R., et al. (eds.). (1990). *Out There: Marginalization and Contemporary Culture*. New York: Museum of Contemporary Art.

Fulford, R. (1992). "Robert Fulford Ponders the Growing Strength of the Hruska Principle." *Globe and Mail* (September 30):C1.

Griffith, K. (1994). " 'Minority Writers' Conference Claims Revolutionary Success." *Vancouver Sun* (July 4):A2.

Hall, J., and M. Neitz. (1993). *Culture: Sociological Perspectives*. Englewood Cliffs, NJ: Prentice Hall.

Hall, S. (1977). "Culture, the Media and the Ideological Effect." In J. Curran, M. Gurevitch, and J. Woollacott (eds.), *Mass Communication and Society*. London: Edward Arnold. 315–48.

———. (1992). *Reproducing Ideologies: Essays on Culture and Politics*.

Henry, J. (1993). "Presentation by the Co-Chair of the Coalition to Stop *Show Boat*." Toronto: Seneca College (June 15).

Hume, C. (1989). "ROM Looks into the Heart of Darkness." *Toronto Star* (November 17):E3, E22.

———. (1990). "Rejection of ROM Show Not a Defeat for Racism." *Toronto Star* (September 29):F3.

Hutcheon, L. (1994). *Irony's Edge: The Theory and Politics of Irony*. London: Routledge.

Ijaz, A. (1993). "Educators against *Show Boat*." *Share* (May 27):1.

Jordan, G., and C. Weedon. (1995). *Cultural Politics: Class, Race and the Postmodern World*. Oxford, UK, and Cambridge, MA: Blackwell.

Katz, J.(1978). *White Awareness: Handbook for Anti-Racist Teaching*. Norman: University of Oklahoma Press.

Lalla, H., and J. Myers. (1990). *Report on the Royal Ontario Museum's Exhibit "Into the Heart of Africa."* Toronto: Toronto Board of Education.

Landsberg, M. (1993). "Blacks, Jews Must Join Forces to Sink *Show Boat*." *Toronto Star* (June 12):H1.

Lee, A. (1993). "Only White Sensibilities Matter." *Toronto Star* (May 28):A25.

Li, P. (1994). "A World Apart: The Multicultural World of Visible Minorities and the Art World of Canada." *Canadian Review of Sociology and Anthropology* 31(4)(November).

Littman, S. (1993). "Victims Can Be Racists Too: Blacks Have Right to Proclaim Their Fears over *Show Boat*." *Toronto Star* (June 22):A17.

Lubiano, W. (1992). "Black Ladies, Welfare Queens, and State Minstrels: Ideological War by Narrative Means." In T. Morrison (ed.), *Race-ing, Engendering Power*. New York: Pantheon Books.

Mackey, E. (1995). "Postmodernism and Cultural Politics in a Multicultural Nation: Contests over Truth in the Into the Heart of Africa Controversy." *Public Culture*. 7(2)(Winter):403–31.

Marshall, C. (1993). "Racism and Popular Culture." Lecture, November 10, York University.

McCarthy, C., and W. Crichlow (eds.). (1993). *Race, Identity and Representation in Education*. New York and London: Routledge.

McFarlane, S. (1995). "The Haunt of Race: Canada's Multiculturalism: The Politics of Incorporation and Writing Thru Race." *Fuse* 18(3)(Spring)18–31.

McMelland, J. (1990). "Uncovering a Hidden Curriculum." *Role Call* (April 10).

Mitchell, T. (1989). "The World as Exhibition." *Society for Comparative Study of Society and History* 31(2):217–36.

Morrison, T. (1992). *Playing in the Dark: Whiteness and the Literary Imagination*. Cambridge, MA: Harvard University Press.

Mukherjee, A. (1994–95). "Teaching Racial Minority Writing: Problems and Possibilities." *Paragraph: The Canadian Fiction Review* 16(3)(Winter and Spring).

Nolan, F. (1992). "Letter to Alan Gottlieb, Canada Council." *Fuse* 15(6):28.

Nourbese Philip, M. (1992). *Frontiers: Essays and Writings on Racism and Culture*. Stratford, ON: Mercury Press.

———. (1993). *Showing Grit, Showboating North of the 44th Parallel*. Toronto: Poui Publications.

Ontario Arts Council. (1990). *Consultations with Artists in a Culturally Diverse Society*. Toronto.

Paris, E. (1992). "A Letter to the Thought Police." *Globe and Mail* (March 31).

Pieterse, N. (1992). *White Images of Africans and Blacks in Western Culture*. London and New Haven: Yale University Press.

Roach, C. (1990). "Into the Heart of the Controversy." *Toronto Sun* (June 5):A17.

Rundle, L. (1997). "From Novel to Film: *The English Patient* Distorted." *Issue* 43:9–13.

Slinger, J. (1993). "*Show Boat* Sponsorship Casts Shadow over the *Star*." *Toronto Star* (April 20):A2.

Tator, C., F. Henry, and W. Mattis (1998). *Challenging Racism in the Arts: Case Studies in Controversy and Conflict*. Toronto: University of Toronto Press.

Toronto Arts Council. (1992). *Cultural Equity: Report from the Toronto Arts Council*. Toronto.

Valpy, M. (1993). "The Storm around *Show Boat*." *Globe and Mail* (March 12):2.

Walcott, R. (1996). "Lament for a Nation: The Racial Geography of 'The Oh! Canada Project'." *Fuse* 19(4)(Summer):15–23.

West, C. (1990). "The New Cultural Politics of Difference." In R. Ferguson et al. (eds.), *Out There: Marginalization and Contemporary Culture*. New York: Museum of Contemporary Art.

Williams, S. (1992). "The Appropriation of Noise." *Fuse* 15(6):15–17.

Wong, P. (1991). "Yellow Peril Reconsidered." *Fuse* 14(Fall):1–2, 48–49.

Young, C. (1993). "Into the Heart of Africa: The Director's Perspective." *Curator* 36(3):174–88.

Chapter 10

▼▼▼▼▼▼▼▼▼▼▼▼▼

Racism in the Media

> When visible minorities do appear in our newspapers and TV public affairs programming, they emerge as villains in a variety of ways — as caricatures from a colonial past; as extensions of foreign entities; or, in the Canadian context, as troubled immigrants in a dazzling array of trouble spots; hassling police, stumping immigration authorities, cheating on welfare, or battling among themselves or with their own families. (Siddiqui, 1993)

This chapter continues the examination of cultural racism by examining how the media reinforce racist ideology and practices through the production of racist discourse. It begins with a discussion of the role and function of the media and then moves to a summary analysis of some of the indicators of racism in the media. The chapter then presents an examination of the ways in which the image-makers of the Canadian media industries marginalize people of colour, reducing them to invisible status and devaluing their images in and contributions to Canadian society.

This chapter looks at the power of the media to produce and transmit the message that people of colour, especially Blacks, create social problems and jeopardize the harmony and unity of Canadian society. The example of the "racialization of crime" by the media shows how the media indulge in overt and subtle misrepresentation and stereotyping in order to influence popular opinion. The examples cited also demonstrate the close relationships and common interests of the media and elite groups such as the corporate sector and the police. Each of the major sectors of the media are reviewed by using data based on the practices of certain media organizations, and some of the initiatives developed as a response to racism in the media are considered.

The last section of the chapter examines discursive strategies used by the media that further reinforce the marginalization and racialization of people of colour. Throughout this analysis, the underlying theme is the tension between a social institution that is the cornerstone of a democratic society and the racism that is woven into its everyday practices.

INTRODUCTION

The electronic and print media have become major transmitters of society's cultural standards, myths, values, roles, and images. In theory, the media provide for the free flow and exchange of ideas, opinions, and information. As such, they represent the key instruments by which a democratic society's ideals are produced and perpetuated. In a liberal democracy, media institutions are expected to reflect alternative viewpoints, remain neutral and objective, and provide free and equitable access to all groups and classes.

In reality, however, while espousing democratic values of fairness, equality, and freedom of expression, the media reinforce and reproduce racism in a number of ways: negative stereotyping, the racialization of issues such as crime and immigration, Eurocentric and ethnocentric judgements, and the marginalization of people of colour in all aspects of media production.

ROLE AND FUNCTION OF THE MEDIA

The media, as a system and process of mass communication, incorporate a number of functions, including information processing and reproduction, education, socialization, entertainment, employment, and advertising. Media institutions are expected to reflect alternative viewpoints, to remain neutral and objective, and to provide free and equitable access to all groups and classes. The media in general, and television in particular, hold up a mirror in which society can see itself reflected. But who is reflected in the mirror?

The media reach out and touch people of every socioeconomic level, transcending differences in age, educational background, and occupational status. The media set norms, create stereotypes, build leaders, set priorities, and educate the public in matters of national interest and concern. Because of their wide-ranging exposure, the written and electronic media have an important role in guiding, shaping, and transforming the way we look at the world ("perceptions"), how we understand it ("conceptions"), and the manner in which we experience and relate to it ("reality") (Fleras and Elliott, 1992:234).

For many people, the mass media are a crucial source of beliefs and values from which they develop a picture of their social worlds. According to Hannerz the media are machineries of meaning (1992:26). Radio, television, the print media, and other cultural forms (e.g., art, literature, films, and theatre) provide the elements out of which we form our identities — our sense of what it means to be male/female, our sense of ethnicity, of class and race, of nationality, of "us" and "them" (Kellner, 1995). Because of the marginalization of racial-minority communities from mainstream society, many White people rely almost entirely on the media for their information about minorities and the issues that concern their communities. The relationship between the White community and these groups is therefore large-

---

MANIFESTATIONS OF RACISM IN THE MEDIA

Stereotypical portrayal and misrepresentation
Invisibility of people of colour in the news, advertising, and programming
Lack of representation at all levels of media operations
Racialization of people of colour as social problems
Reproduction of White values, norms, and images
Biased attitudes and practices of media professionals

---

ly filtered through the perceptions, assumptions, values, and beliefs of journalists and other media professionals.

THE MANIFESTATIONS OF RACISM

INVISIBILITY OF PEOPLE OF COLOUR

A brief submitted to a parliamentary subcommittee on equality rights stated that people of colour are invisible in the Canadian media: "The relative absence of minority men and women in the Canadian media is remarkable" (Canadian Ethnocultural Council, 1985:92). It observed that the unequal status of racial minorities in the media was reflected by their absence from on-air roles, such as anchors, reporters, experts, or actors, and their lack of representation at all levels of staffing operations, production, and decision-making positions in communications. Their limited participation is the result of both overt bias and systemic discrimination. Examples of systemic discrimination cited in the brief include the reliance on referrals in hiring from White producers, writers, and editors; the lack of comprehensive outreach programs for the employment and training of people of colour, and the lack of recognition for qualifications and experience gained outside of Canada.

A Black Canadian actor succinctly addressed the issue of invisibility by paraphrasing a famous quotation and question: "Mirror, mirror on the wall, tell me if I exist at all." The mirror is the media polished and held up by the image-makers — advertisers, radio-station owners, private and public television executives, producers, writers, artistic directors, publishers, editors, and journalists (Gomez, 1983:13).

This invisibility of people of colour is reflected in a study of programming conducted by Deverell (1986) that remains relevant today. Several types of programs were monitored on two Canadian networks, including local newscasts, network broadcasts, children's programs, drama, variety programs, and commercials. In addition, theatres were asked to list their plays for the 1984–85 season and the number of roles in the plays, and to note whether any of the roles were played by performers who were members of visible-minority groups. Radio location managers of all Canadian Broadcasting Corporation (CBC) radio locations were surveyed to indicate the type of program produced and the number of on-microphone people employed, and to tally which of those people were members of audible or visible-minority groups. The findings revealed that although approximately one third of all Canadians are non-British and non-French, less than 3 percent of such Canadians appeared on the stage, less than 3 percent were in commercials, and 5.5 percent were television principals.

The invisibility of people of colour in the print media is reflected in the hiring practices of media organizations. A study of recruitment procedures and promotion channels for women and minorities was conducted in forty-one English-language newspapers in Ontario in 1986. Across the entire sample, people of colour, persons with a disability, and Aboriginal peoples were negligible as newsroom employees. Of the 1731 full-time newsroom employees in the sample, thirty were from the above groups. Word-of-mouth recruitment excludes a wide range of suitable applicants. Promotion channels across all the newspapers tended to be from within. Yet, *The Toronto Star* was the only paper with a policy aimed at removing barriers to the employment and advancement of women and minorities (Mayers, 1986). Almost a decade later, Cecil Foster, reflecting on his experience as the only Black writer in the newsroom at *The Globe and Mail* for ten years and in the six years since he left from 1989 to 1995, is quoted as saying (in Manji, 1995): "When I left 100% of the Black staff went out."

In a study of the extent of the appearances of people of colour and Aboriginal peoples in national evening news programs, particularly their participation on CBC's "The National" and CTV's "National Evening News," almost all stories in which people of colour appeared were those in which the stories were about non-Whites. There were few stories of general interest, such as sports, taxes, or political issues, in which people of colour were included. During the four weeks in which these programs were monitored, only twenty of 725 interviews solicited the opinions of racial minorities for subjects not related specifically to stories or people from their communities (Perigoe and Lazar, 1992). A recent study conducted by the Canadian Islamic Congress (1998) found that Canadian Muslims rarely appear in the press, as indicated by the lack of coverage of their achievements and events. At the international level, Muslims are in the press too much.

In a similar study of Canadian newspapers (Miller and Prince, 1994), an audit of a random week's edition of six major dailies (*The Vancouver Sun, The Calgary Herald, The Winnipeg Free Press, The Toronto Sun,* and *The Montreal Gazette*) assessed the amount and types of coverage of people of colour. Their analysis revealed that stereotyping and negative coverage were common in terms of both language and images. Local stories were 49 percent negative. Over half dealt with either athletes or entertainers. The study concluded that if people of colour are in the news, "they are probably in trouble of some sort, and few make any contribution to business or have noteworthy lifestyles."

In representations made to the Canadian Radio-television and Telecommunications Commission by racial and ethnocultural minorities, one brief suggested: "We are here simply to point out that what we see on the television screens ... makes us feel as if we are in a foreign land, not one in which we are participating citizens" (CRTC, 1986:26).

The misrepresentation, invisibility, and marginalization of people of colour by the media communicates the message that they are not full participants in Canadian society. Salome Bey, a prominent Black entertainer, maintained that

> Canada today is a country where men, women and children of colour want to be seen and reflected as a vibrant and valuable component of the cultural reality of Canada, in the arts, and ... everywhere. But instead our people have run headlong into the harsh realities of institutionalized indifference, insensitivity and ignorance that degrades us and our children. (Bey, 1983:5)

A parliamentary task force looking at racism in Canadian society heard dozens of briefs from people of colour that racism in the media was reflected by their invisibility in terms of both their images and their representation in media organizations. Groups from across Canada spoke with a single voice about the need for people of colour to have access to, participation in, and equity in the print and electronic media, on media boards and commissions, and on self-regulating bodies such as press councils. Lynda Armstrong, a Black performer, commented, "The White-only mentality of the Canadian establishment is weird when you consider that this is one of the most racially diverse societies on earth.... What we get in Canadian media is a fantasy" (*Equality Now*, 1984:91). She reflected that one of the ironic aspects of the discrimination she faced as a professional performer who happened to be Black is that she was also a fifth-generation Canadian. Yet the colour barrier continued to deny her access to the entertainment and advertising industries.

One of the primary factors in this invisibility is cultural racism and the belief in the concept of the "rightness of Whiteness." Whiteness is considered the universal (hidden) norm and allows one to think and speak as if Whiteness described and defined the world. An example of this mindset is reflected in the comments of the president of a major brewer, who, when asked why there were no non-Whites in his company's commercials, responded: "White sells" (*Equality Now*, 1984:91). This attitude characterizes the collective belief system and influences the norms and practices of the media.

STEREOTYPICAL PORTRAYAL

Studies of the media (Fleras, 1995; Hall et al., 1978; Troyna, 1984; Fleras and Elliott, 1992; Granzberg, 1982; Ginzberg, 1985; Khaki and Prasad, 1988) demonstrate that the media, in general, produce a negative view of people of colour.[1] This is not a new phenomenon. Mosher (1998), commenting on racism in the criminal justice system of Ontario, revealed that the media have had an instrumental role in racializing crime for more than a hundred years. He found that the racialization of crime that is so prevalent today was also present in media coverage of an earlier period. Canadian newspapers routinely described the race of offenders, which "served to identify Asians and Blacks as alien ... and justified to a certain extent their differential treatment by the criminal justice system" (Mosher, 1998:126). He cites headlines such as:

> Chinese gambled; These 18 Chinks were Roped in ... (*Toronto Daily Star*, March 29, 1909)

> Warm Pipe Scorches Chink Opium User (*Toronto Daily Star*, April 3, 1916)

> No More Chicken Dinners or Watermelon Feeds ... (Hamilton *Spectator*, August 26, 1909)

> The Black Burglar (*Globe*, November 20, 1900)

> Negro Thieves Given Stiff Sentences (*Windsor Evening Record*, October 20, 1912)

In addition, Mosher noted that court reporters often focussed on the racial identity of accused persons and witnesses. For example, an article described "two hundred pounds of Julius Wagstaffe, a jet-black import from North Carolina...." In some instances, the Black accuseds' speech was rendered in dialect in the body of the article and their comments were ridiculed and trivialized. There is therefore "extensive evidence of the stereotyping of Asians and Blacks and the racialization of crime in the media, especially between 1892 and 1930" (Mosher, 1998:134).

Contrary to myth, journalists, editors, broadcasters, and directors of media organizations are not always neutral, impartial, objective, and unbiased. The media often select events that are atypical, present them in a stereotypical fashion, and contrast them with "White behaviour" (Hall et al., 1975). The broadcaster, reporter, camera person, and editor have a context that affects the way in which they interpret images, events, and situations. This context influences what they choose to film or air, what they select, and what eventually becomes part of the story. Media professionals are often guided by a need to focus on the sensational, extraordinary, and exotic, which sell well in the marketplace. They are influenced by their own connections to the groups and institutions that have power and influence.

A pervasive theme of both news and programming is the portrayal of people of colour as "the outsiders within," reinforcing the "we–they" mindset. Research establishes the close connection between the media's conception of and construction of stories on race-related issues and their impact on public opinion (van Dijk, 1991). The writer and critic bell hooks (1990) suggests that stereotypes of people of colour are developed to "serve as substitutions for reality." They are contrived images that are developed and projected onto the "others."

One of the most common and persistent examples of racism in the media is the frequency with which racial minorities are singled out as "having problems" that require a disproportionate amount of political attention or public resources to solve or as "creating problems." *They* make unacceptable demands that threaten the political, social, or moral order of society (Fleras and Elliott, 1996; van Dijk, 1991; Hall et al., 1975).

When visible minorities do appear in Canadian newspapers and TV public-affairs programming, they emerge as villains in a variety of ways — as caricatures from a colonial past; as extensions of foreign entities; or, in the Canadian context, as troubled immigrants in a dazzling array of trouble spots: hassling police, stumping immigration authorities, cheating on welfare, or battling among themselves or with their own families (Siddiqui, 1993:D1).

An example of how the media negatively stereotype people of colour is the coverage of the Sikh community by the mass media in Vancouver. Press coverage of issues of concern to this community are sensationalized, and Sikhs are commonly depicted as militants, terrorists, and disposed to violence. For example, in *The Province* newspaper in Vancouver, headlines of articles covering Sikh issues included "Guns Alarm Cops" (March 27, 1985); "Close Watch on City Sikhs" (October 20, 1985); and "Sikh Militancy Grows" (November 7, 1985). The articles conjured images of conflict, civil unrest, violent confrontation, terrorism, and destruction of property. In turn, the repetition of these images and stereotypes reinforces prejudice

Table 10.1

IMAGES OF VARIOUS MINORITY GROUPS

Aboriginal Peoples	Blacks	Asians
✓ Savages	✓ Drug addicts	✓ Untrustworthy
✓ Alcoholics	✓ Pimps	✓ Menacing
✓ Uncivilized	✓ Prostitutes	✓ Unscrupulous
✓ Uncultured	✓ Entertainers	✓ Subhuman
✓ Murderers	✓ Athletes	✓ Submissive
✓ Noble	✓ Drug dealers	✓ Maiming
✓ Needing a White saviour	✓ Murderers	✓ Quaint
✓ Victim	✓ Gangsters	✓ Gangsters
	✓ Butlers and maids	✓ Prostitutes
	✓ Simple-minded	✓ Cooks
	✓ Inconsequential	✓ Store vendors
	✓ Savages	
	✓ Primitive	
	✓ Needing a White saviour	

against not only Sikhs but all South Asians (Khaki and Prasad, 1988). The impact of media stereotyping is highlighted in the case study on the racialization of crime.

CASE STUDY 10.1

THE RACIALIZATION OF CRIME

By examining the media's coverage of crime, one can see how the media shape public understanding and opinion formation and document the way in which racial identity is linked to deviance and crime, particularly among Black males (Daniel and Allen, 1988; Hall et al., 1978; van Dijk, 1991).

Hall et al. (1975) identified two definitions of crime. First is the official definition, constructed by agencies responsible for crime control — the police, government agencies, and the courts. The second and equally powerful definition is the media's construction of crime. The portrayal of crime in the mass media plays a significant role in shaping public definitions of the "crime problem." The media explanations of crime are overlaid with racist ideologies that serve to "knit together ... the enigma of crime and its causation" (Hall et al., 1975:15).

Following the urban disturbances of the early 1980s in the United Kingdom, the idea of Black criminality received considerable attention by the media.

> The police, aided by a hyperbolic mass media, were able to nail down their problem more precisely. Blacks, particularly young blacks, were a new force in British society and one which, unless checked, could undermine the nation's stability. A rush of lurid editorials, academic theses and television documentaries tended to confirm the police's premise: blacks were a problem. (Cashmore and McLaughlin, 1991:3)

As Black crime becomes an increasing focus of police activity, the media become willing partners in fostering the racialization of crime. As a consequence, Black life in a general sense becomes increasingly interpreted or misinterpreted by the media through the "lens which criminal signs and imagery provide" (Gilroy, 1987:76).

Although the circumstances and social environment in Canada are not totally comparable to events unfolding in the United Kingdom, the United States, and the Netherlands, there is nevertheless a similar pattern of the racialization of crime, developed primarily by the police but communicated and perpetuated by the Canadian media.

EXAMPLES OF RACIALIZATION

A particularly striking example of the media's role in fostering the racialization of crime was a three-part series published by *The Globe and Mail* on Jamaican crime. The first article in this series (Appleby, 1992a), entitled "Island Crime Wave Spills Over: Criminal Subculture Exported to Canada," began with a description of life in a Kingston slum:

(continued)

CASE STUDY 10.1 *(continued)*

It's a sweltering Friday night — an ideal time for a plainclothes cop on the intelligence unit to look around. On one corner, Detective Corporal Mark Allen chats briefly with a man recovering from a bullet wound in the neck. It was a drive-by shooting, apparently motiveless. On another a woman complains that a gang of robber rapists is terrorizing the neighbourhood. He stops in a doorway to speak with a mother whose two teen-aged sons were recently slain ... Jamaica's crime rate is among the world's highest ... "I've never seen violence to this extent — to kill for no apparent reason," said a Western diplomat. (Appleby, 1992a)

The article went on to note that although it was now unpopular to discuss Black crime in Toronto, it was quite clear that "this criminal subculture has been exported" and is in evidence on the streets of Toronto and, to a lesser extent, in Montreal. Named and unnamed Toronto police sources were quoted as saying that Black crime was no myth; it was a reality "which manifests itself in arrest records" and proof that "a volatile group of young Jamaican males has altered Toronto's criminal landscape ... in an explosion of guns and crack cocaine."

Meanwhile, local Jamaican police sources maintained that this was strictly a Canadian problem and was caused by "riffraff" who migrate. Local Jamaican experts were quoted as saying that crack cocaine use was the result of the hopelessness of life among the poor and the breakdown of the family. It ended by offering another "expert" opinion: Jamaicans are aggressive and violence-prone.

The theory goes back to the movement of slaves from West Africa.... [The ones] who were offloaded in Jamaica ... were rebellious on the trip and it was the first opportunity to offload them.

The argument was pursued in the second article, in which a number of Jamaican authorities and institutions were blamed for this violent culture. It began by describing the "police heavy-handedness in one of the world's most violent cultures." Examples of "wholesale corruption and complicity in the drug trade" followed (Appleby, 1992b).

Finally, in the third article, a "divide and rule" reasoning was pursued, as disputes between Trinidadians and Jamaicans were revealed and a Trinidadian woman was quoted: "*Pressed*, she says: 'I don't know why Jamaicans are different. They just are.'" Although this article focussed on Jamaican youth in Toronto, even some born there, it nevertheless provided further explanations of the breakdowns in Jamaican society, including traditional political rivalries between its two major political parties and the "erosion of church authority" (Appleby, 1992c).

To further add to the confusion, the writer revealed that the relationship between traditional explanations and criminal youth in Toronto was unclear, especially as more experts were cited to show that the majority of criminals were now Toronto-born. Returning to the theme of Jamaican crime, the article cited American police officials as solemnly maintaining that "Toronto's a major centre, no doubt about it."

(continued)

CASE STUDY 10.1 *(continued)*

Building on the same theme, *The Globe and Mail*, some months later, reported on prostitution in Halifax. The subhead of the article read: "Prostitution: Halifax Police Have Set Their Sights on Black Pimps Who Are Sending Hundreds of Local Teenagers to Sell Their Bodies on the Streets across Canada." According to the reporter, most of the young *White* prostitutes worked for a "loosely organized community of Nova Scotia *Black* men" (italics added) (Jones, 1993). A letter to the editor a few weeks later succinctly identified the racism underlying the article and the header:

> The insinuation that a pimp's skin colour is in any way relevant is as preposterous as suggesting a prostitute's skin colour might predispose her to such a vocation. *The Globe and Mail* should be more sensitive. (Joffe, 1993)

In 1992, a tabloid in Montreal published a six-page section titled "Whites Are Fed Up with Blacks" (because of the many crimes they commit). Details of many police–Black-community encounters were provided. Black-community leaders in the city condemned the paper for "painting all Blacks as criminals" and asked that the government press charges of hate propaganda against the tabloid. A prominent member of the community, whose picture was printed with the caption "Asshole of the week," sued the paper. Hotline radio shows were, however, deluged with callers who agreed with the article. Callers said that "Blacks are parasites of society.... They should be sent back to their islands.... Blacks are genetically prone to violence" (*Toronto Star*, August 6, 1992).

In October 1992, the Metropolitan Toronto Police Association called for a job action to protest a new rule in which police were required to complete a report after unholstering a gun. The subtext of this job action was a protest over the issue of "race relations." While the media reported this event in great detail, a feature article in *The Toronto Star* written by Carsten Stroud added further fuel to the issue of the racialization of crime by arguing that "cops are right to resent and resist the kinds of restrictions that the NDP and the [Black] activists are trying to place on them." Stroud saw the police protest purely in terms of the escalating confrontation between police and Black youth:

> This is a war that's going to get a lot nastier before it gets better, because, make no mistake about it, the Metro police are the angriest police force I've seen outside of New York City. Why? For anyone who sees a Black kid being thrown into a cruiser and automatically thinks "racist cop," the obvious answer is because the forces of goodness and racial justice have finally jerked their leashes and the cops don't like it. (Stroud, 1992)

The implication throughout this article is that the bad behaviour of Black youth is being defended unrealistically by Black activists such as Dudley Laws and the Black Action Defence Committee, who do not represent the majority of the Black community. The police anger is further exacerbated by the NDP government, which is allegedly overinfluenced by these radical activists (or so the article claims) in its efforts to challenge the authority and restrict the powers of the police.

(continued)

CASE STUDY 10.1 *(continued)*

A columnist working at the Montreal *Gazette* provided a similar perspective on the racialization of crime. Writing about a disturbance that broke out in Montreal following a parade celebrating Caribbean culture, he observed:

> A profoundly disturbing fact has emerged: If you're Black, you're subject to immense scrutiny by the public and the media. It is disturbing because only one factor directs this spotlight — the colour of your skin. Specifically Black skin. It's a scrutiny that nurtures a level of myth and misconception that defies logic because it ignores or devalues an array of hard facts about the history and the diversity of Canada's Black population. (Chandwani, 1994)

A major study of video violence revealed Blacks, who make up 12 percent of the U.S. population, were portrayed as aggressors in 25 percent of violent videos. Forty-seven percent of the victims in these violent videos were white women (Krieger, 1998:C2).

ANALYSIS

As soon as people of colour, especially Black people, are associated with a criminal act, the event becomes newsworthy and is given significant coverage. Van Dijk (1991) suggested that the same crime committed by Whites would be ignored or given less attention. "Black crime," as it is frequently referred to, is perceived as posing a greater threat to the dominant White population. Explanations of criminal activity, although the crimes are the acts of individuals, are frequently interpreted as a form of "group crime" for which the entire Black community is held responsible. The perspectives and "expert" opinions of White authorities (especially the police) are usually considered more reliable and unbiased than those of a person of colour.

The marginalization and stigmatization of people of colour in the media follows the same demarcation of "them" and "us" discussed elsewhere in this book. The subtext of the discourse is that minorities and immigrants are aggressive, unlawful, disrespectful of democratic laws and values, and demanding of special treatment (van Dijk, 1991).

In many of the examples cited above, the media appear to work hand in hand with law-enforcement agencies in reporting criminal activities. In some police forces, the communication or public-affairs unit provides a continuous flow of information to local media organizations. For example, every morning CityTV in Toronto shows video clips of crimes committed overnight. The video is provided by the Metropolitan Toronto Police Force. Press releases are also distributed by the police to newspapers, radio, and television stations daily, providing statistics and data relating mainly to criminal activity.

The impact of this close relationship between the police and the media is that internalized racist perceptions, attitudes, and assumptions underlying police behaviour are reinforced by the biases of journalists, editors, newscasters, and their producers. Each institution's self-interests are served by this arrangement. Thus, for example, significantly more coverage was given to isolated incidents of violence during the Caribana festivities in Toronto in August 1992 than to the festival itself. For an in-depth analysis of the racialization of crime in the print media, see Henry (forthcoming).

MISREPRESENTATION IN THE PRINT MEDIA

The first study to identify and document racism in the print media in Canada was made in 1977 by Rosenfeld and Spina, who examined *The Toronto Sun*'s coverage of issues relating to immigration and racial and ethnic communities. In their review of the newspaper, they found considerable evidence of racial bias and discrimination. Their analysis revealed that *The Toronto Sun* presented the reader with a single, prejudiced view of the world.

In 1982, the Canadian Arab Federation commissioned a study on the image of Arabs in political cartoons (Mouammar, 1986). Cartoons were gathered from three major Toronto dailies from 1972 to 1982. The study found that Arabs were repeatedly portrayed as bloodthirsty terrorists who were blackmailing the West. They were depicted in the cartoons as ignorant, cruel, and backward. One cartoon after another over the ten-year period portrayed Arabs in a negative and stereotypical manner, using images suggesting that the Arab was tyrannical, untrustworthy, amoral, irrational, and the architect of international terrorism. The researcher pointed to the danger of this kind of racism by suggesting that the foundations of the Holocaust were laid by German caricaturists who commonly depicted Jews in a similar fashion (Mouammar, 1986:13).

Ginzberg's (1985) content analysis of *The Toronto Sun* was precipitated by the escalating concern and frustration felt by a number of racial-minority groups in the community who perceived that the *Sun* had consistently and repeatedly portrayed people of colour and Aboriginal peoples in a negative manner. In addition, there was a perception that the *Sun* had repeatedly distorted issues in which these communities were involved, including race relations, immigration, discrimination in employment and education, apartheid, and affirmative action. There had been a long history of minority groups expressing concerns about biased, inaccurate, and unbalanced portrayals of visible minorities to the management of this paper. In 1984, the Native Action Committee on the Media developed an information package concerning the racist coverage by *The Toronto Sun* of Aboriginal peoples. The committee's analysis of the *Sun*'s articles concluded that the coverage had caused hatred and misunderstanding toward Aboriginal peoples among the "majority society" by its racist commentaries. The *Sun* made no attempt to respond to these concerns.

Ginzberg (1985) studied over two hundred editorials and columns covering the period 1978–85. The framework for the analysis was based on the work of Gordon Allport (1954), which emphasized that prejudice is not a single thought or behaviour, but a pattern or system of behaviours that are not independent of each other. When one is present, others are also likely to be present. Allport suggested that the components of prejudice include, first, negative stereotyping, which is an exaggerated, overgeneralized belief, unsubstantiated opinion, or uncritical judgement about a group of persons. Its function is to justify conduct in relation to that group of persons. Stereotypes, through repetition, become embedded in people's attitudes, reflected in their behaviour, and woven into the culture of the majority group. They can also deprive persons from racial groups of their sense of self-worth.

Stereotypes were found repeatedly in the *Sun*. People of Indo-Pakistani origin were depicted as violent, weak, passive, submissive, and barbaric. Gandhi was called a "cunning and charismatic witch doctor." One writer made the astounding statement, "Democracy is beyond the aptitude of the majority of Asians." Arabs were violent, uncivilized, and primitive: "A tendency to violence in the settlement of disputes characterizes the typical Muslim male." Aboriginal peoples were portrayed as immoral, drunks, useless, and primitive. Blacks were depicted as immoral, savage, uncivilized, and superstitious.

A second component of prejudice that appeared regularly in the columns and editorials of *The Toronto Sun* was the writers' attempts to persistently rationalize or deny their prejudice. For example, "Gandhi did not seek peace but power"; "Apartheid represents a successful plan to save South African cities from the squalor that affects Bombay, Delhi and Calcutta through the huge, uncontrolled flux of the rural poor."

A third component of prejudice woven into the words and images used by *Sun* writers was a belief in biological racism. A view frequently shared in the newspaper was that the White race is genetically superior to non-White races:

> Those awful riots are caused by Black people who seem to be subhuman in their total lack of civility.... The Blacks of North America have diverged widely from their distant relatives in Africa. In their music and dancing and in their athletic prowess some specific genetic distinctions shine through the environmental influences. (Mackenzie Porter, July 15, 1978; cited in Ginzberg, 1985)

> Too many Afro-Asians abroad, even some of those with august rank of diplomat, possess only a veneer of civilization. (Porter, April 23, 1984; cited in Ginzberg, 1985)

Ginzberg found many examples of demagogy, a fourth component of prejudice. Repeatedly, statements appeared in the writings of editors and columnists that were likely to incite fear and hatred. The most blatant example of demagogy was found in "Our Nuremberg," in which the editorialist claimed that Toronto was gradually evolving its own set of Nuremberg race laws. Words like "gestapo," "fascist-like," "police state," "jackbooters," and "human-rights storm troopers" served to incite fear, on the part of the *Sun's* readers, of human-rights policies and race-relations initiatives.

The study concluded that *The Toronto Sun* had indeed violated the fundamental freedom and responsibility that society had entrusted to the press. The potential impact of a publication that has a daily circulation of over 300 000 readers — and on Sundays more than 460 000 — is enormous.

A smaller-scale study of *The Globe and Mail's* coverage of the immigration issue was conducted in 1985–86 (Ducharme, 1986). Of seventy articles written from 1980 to 1985, twelve were considered to be biased or slanted. About 86 percent of the articles focussed on the numbers of immigrants and refugees entering Canada. News stories on immigration levels and quotas appeared once a month, on average, in the five-year period, with varying figures and contradictory estimates. Misuse of language was also noted; there was a reliance on clichés and stereotypes, such as "floods of refugees"; the need to "stem the tide of illegal aliens"; the "luring" of entrepreneurs into Canada; immigrants and refugees who "wreck" and "gatecrash" the system; the "surge" in the number of immigrants; and "job stealers."

The researcher drew attention to the way in which both the headlines and the use of language frequently distorted, confused, or hid reality. The emphasis was placed on the sensational details of immigration policy, rather than on comprehensive understanding and analysis.

In promoting and sustaining the values of the dominant White society, the media often draw a line between the "First World" and the "Third World," between the "West" and the "non-West," the "North" and the "South." This line of demarcation is created by the constant production of images that distinguish the positive attributes, capacities, and strengths of the West from those of the countries of the East or the Third World. The First World is rational, progressive, efficient, moral, modern, scientifically and technologically ordered, and on the side of the good and right, whereas the Third World is linked with racialized premises; it is defined as traditional, underdeveloped, overpopulated, irrational, disordered, and uncivilized (Goldberg, 1993).

CASE STUDY 10.2

THE JOURNALISTIC RIGHT TO MALIGN MINORITIES

Doug Collins, a journalist in British Columbia, has been a regular columnist with various newspapers for two decades. He has had a long history of attacking racial minorities and Aboriginal peoples, among others, in his columns for the *Vancouver Sun* and Vancouver's *North Shore News*. Some examples of the overt prejudice in his articles follow.

On immigration:

The result is that Vancouver is becoming a suburb of Asia; Toronto, once the Queen City of English Canada, has become the tower of Babel, with every race except ours bawling for special rights and receiving them. Montreal is a target for the enlightened folk of Haiti. And the politicians wouldn't care if voodooism became the leading religion. (Collins, 1991)

On education:

The Third World is occupying the classrooms of much of the Lower Mainland. This is clear from the statistics and the pictures on TV. Hardly a White

(continued)

CASE STUDY 10.2 *(continued)*

face in sight. Which should tell you something about why we have to have free lunches. But no one wants to say it. (Collins, 1992a)

On Aboriginal peoples:

What saving the country boils down to is handing out more dough to the French and the ever-squawking Indians who know they are dealing with dummies and never had it so good until we turned up and showed them the wheel. (Collins, 1992b)

On the Holocaust:

The issue is whether the Holocaust took place. In other words, whether the Hitler regime deliberately set out to kill all the Jews it could get its hands on, and that 6 000 000 died as a result. More and more, I am coming to the conclusion that it [the Holocaust] didn't. (Daring thoughts that could land a guy in jail in this free country of ours!) (Collins, 1988)

ANALYSIS

Robin Ridington, an anthropologist, launched a complaint against the journalist with the British Columbia Press Council. His concern over Collins was based on an understanding that a journalist's language

conveys messages through the complex associations and implications of its metaphors and unstated assumptions. If a journalist's language violates the experiential reality of a minority or identifiable group within a society, it creates a conflict between public reality and the personal experience of those who come to be identified as deviant. (Ridington, 1986:6)

In his brief to the press council, he argued that

the language used by Doug Collins and supported by the *North Shore News* editorially tells the people of the *North Shore News* that it is normal to deprecate members of their community because of the ethnic group to which they belong. It implies that members of certain ethnic or other identifiable groups are inherently inferior to others as Canadians. (Ridington, 1986:7)

The press council dismissed the complaint, which led Ridington to conclude that print journalists appear to have the right to malign minority groups and be validated by their own self-regulatory institution. As a result of the complaint to the press council, the newspaper threatened the university at which Ridington was a professor with legal action, and Collins continued to attack him personally in his columns.

(continued)

CASE STUDY 10.2 *(continued)*

In 1993, the British Columbia Organization to Fight Racism (BCOFR) was appalled when it learned that the governor general of Canada had presented Doug Collins with an award that honours Canadians who have made a significant contribution to their fellow citizens, their community, or Canada. Collins was described by the member of Parliament for North Vancouver, who presented him with the medal, as a "controversial columnist for the *North Shore News* who forces people to think for themselves and re-evaluate commonly held opinions." The BCOFR circulated a petition to rescind the medal (BCOFR, 1993).

In addition to being criticized for publishing the articles cited above, Doug Collins has been accused of anti-Semitism in his published work. The Canadian Jewish Congress filed a complaint with the British Columbia Human Rights Commission in 1994 alleging that at least one of Collins's articles, "Hollywood Propaganda," was likely to expose Jewish people to hatred and contempt. The complaint eventually reached a Human Rights Tribunal, which determined that while Collins's writings were "nasty" and "obviously anti-Semitic," they did not expose Jews to hatred and contempt as specified in the Human Rights Code.

MARGINALIZATION IN PROGRAMMING

In a study by Granzberg (1982), 360 hours of prime-time television programming on two major Canadian networks and one American network were examined. The study concluded that the portrayal of racial minorities was characterized by misrepresentation and stereotyping. Minorities were depicted as being weak and unstable. They were shown as being less maritally stable, less important, less gainfully employed, and less heroic than White people.

Studies conducted in the United States and the United Kingdom on the portrayal of racial minorities in the daily press found a scarcity of news stories that challenged racial stereotypes. According to van Dijk (1991), in a comprehensive analysis of racism in the media, White newsmakers are more likely to report stories that confirm their preconceptions of Blacks as drug pushers, criminals, and troublemakers.

Daniel and Allen (1988) showed that this phenomenon also applies to leading news magazines. Comparing the coverage of Blacks in *Time* and *Newsweek* with issues of concern identified by Black organizations such as the National Urban League, they found that topics that are of critical concern to Blacks, such as maintaining civil-rights gains or alleviating poverty, were not at all the focus of these news magazines. Van Dijk (1991) argued that given the fact that White elites control the content and structure of the media, it may be expected that the White press shares in the overall system that sustains White group dominance.

A classic example of the kind of misrepresentation indulged in by the electronic media was a feature on a public-affairs program, aired on a national Canadian network, called "Campus Giveaway." The program was filmed at the University of Toronto. By using distorted statistics and erroneous information, it communicated the notion that Chinese students were depriving Canadians of their rightful places in the university. The assumption was that anyone who was not White had to be an immigrant or "foreigner." In reality, although almost all the faces filmed belonged to individuals of Chinese descent, every individual was either a Canadian citizen or a permanent resident. Despite this, the viewer was left with the distorted impression that deserving Anglo-Canadians could not find places in medical and engineering schools because these "outsiders" were taking their place.

In recent years, although racial minorities are seen more frequently in television programming, particularly on U.S. networks, some disturbing patterns of the marginalization of racial minorities are emerging. The television critic for *The Globe and Mail*, John Haslett Cuff, observed that where Black people were central to a television show they tended to be portrayed (even more one-dimensionally than is TV's norm) as "victim, villain, buffoon or cuddly, folksy types" (Cuff, 1990).

Historically, the predominant images of Black people portrayed on both American television networks and the Hollywood film industry have been those of criminals, rioters, thieves, drug addicts, pimps, and prostitutes (Cuff, 1992). Five years later, in 1997, the stereotypical images had not improved much; Cuff commented: "The two predominant images of the black male on prime-time television are that of the super-hero/athlete and the crotch-grabbing buffoon. In between there's the hipster and outlaw and the solid working-class type, but these are largely secondary characters, supporting roles" (Cuff, 1997). Making a similar point, Adilman (1998) questioned why there are no Black characters in Canadian TV series. He attributed the blame for the black-out to broadcasters, cable companies, and federal broadcast regulators, who meanwhile imported fictionalized stereotypes of American entertainment: "Canadian Blacks have their own rich stories — and experiences different from those of American Blacks — that are not being told on TV" (1998:M2).

Some of the most popular programs on television in the 1990s were virtually devoid of people of colour. The U.S. programs that portrayed an overwhelmingly White society included *Beverly Hills 90210*, *Friends*, *Melrose Place*, *Party of Five*, *Seinfeld*, *The X-Files*, *Grace under Fire*, *Roseanne*, and *Caroline in the City*. On the rare occasions when people of colour do appear on mainstream television, they are placed in stereotypical roles, filtered through a prism of the White gaze (Morrison and Brodsky Lacour, 1997).

Open-Line Shows

Open-line radio and television shows, which have become increasingly popular, often provide an opportunity for hosts, listeners, and viewers to publicly disseminate racist beliefs. An example of this occurred in April

1985, during Gary Bannerman's daily call-in radio program in Vancouver. The program that day provided the host and his listeners with an opportunity to express derogatory and demeaning views about Aboriginal peoples. The program was supposed to discuss self-government and land claims, but the host chose instead to start the show by delivering a diatribe against Native peoples:

> Every Native Indian alive today has got everything to do with the tragedy of the Native peoples, the fact that they have the highest rates of incest in Canada, the highest rates of crime, and misery and poverty and failure, you name it.... They have privileges that the average Canadian doesn't have, endless privileges, whether it comes to fisheries, handouts, meetings, grants. And what do they do with them? The brother has a child with his sister, is what they do with them. (Ridington, 1986:44)

In response to the mood and assumptions established by the host, callers supported and legitimized his racist comments. Under the guise of "fair comment," Bannerman abused the principle of free expression (Khaki and Prasad, 1988).

Ridington's (1986) study concluded that the very nature of call-in shows, which are growing in popularity in Canada, is a matter of concern with respect to race relations. It pointed out that the call-and-response format of radio and TV shows is a form of reality management, in which hosts (or columnists) "call" their audience in a language that establishes their assumptive world. The respondents (telephone callers or letter writers) are encouraged to speak in a manner and language consistent with the host's or columnist's perceptions. Responses that oppose this assumptive world appear to be deviant.

In the late 1990s, Howard Stern, a controversial American journalist of the "shock jock" school, broadcast on stations in both Toronto and Montreal. Stern used pejorative language by calling French Canadians "scumbags" and "peckerheads" and made degrading comments about women and ethno-racial minorities.

An appeal was made to the Canadian Broadcasting Standards Council, which ruled that Stern violated both its code of ethics as well as its sex-role portrayal code. It asked the two stations that carried his program to ensure that Stern did not make offensive comments again. Both stations failed to heed this request; their ratings had markedly improved because of Stern's shows. The Canadian Radio-television and Telecommunications Commission (CRTC), unlike the Standards Council, had the power to stop the show by revoking the licences of the broadcasters who aired Stern's program or by failing to renew them or citing the stations for contempt. At the time of writing the CRTC had, however, done nothing, seeming to fear that the issue of censorship would be invoked by the many thousands of people who listened to Stern's programs. At the same time, the agency was criticized:

> If we believe as a nation that broadcasting standards are worth having, then we must be willing to enforce them. The industry has shown that it isn't up

to the task. If the CRTC is unwilling to act, then it might as well abandon the pretence of having radio ethics.... So, no one has been willing to take responsibility for the pollution of our airwaves. (*Toronto Star*, 1997)

In 1998, CityTV in Toronto and CHOM radio in Montreal decided not to carry the Howard Stern show. He continues to broadcast on Q107 radio in Toronto (MediaWatch, 1998).

LACK OF ACCESS TO MASS MEDIA

Many institutions have ready access to the media. As a result, a significant proportion of news coverage deals with information that emanates from government agencies, politicians, police forces, school boards, commissions, chambers of commerce, and labour federations (Siddiqui, 1993). This contrasts sharply with the lack of access of people of colour in making their viewpoints and voices heard. Hall et al. (1975) argued that media professionals (editors, journalists, broadcasters, and producers) and their institutions control access between the elites of power and the mass audience. By controlling the qualitative aspects of the information that will become the audience's news; by determining the events that will dominate the "agenda" of news programs, newspapers, and public discussion; and by selecting which "expert" opinion will be solicited, the media assume the function of gatekeepers and agenda setters.

Black musicians and their promoters have identified significant racial barriers in their access to the Canadian broadcasting system. Despite the growing popularity of Black dance music that extends well beyond the African Canadian community, in Canada, there is little opportunity for it to be heard on commercial radio stations in Canada. African Canadian music professionals have complained since the 1960s about the failure of mainstream radio to play Black dance music, particularly the music of local musicians. Over a period of more than a decade (from 1984 to 1998), efforts were made to acquire a radio licence for an FM station that would focus on playing Black dance music and serve the listening needs of the African Canadian community in the greater Toronto area. This issue was highlighted in 1990, in a battle for what was then Toronto's last available FM radio licence. The award of the licence to a country-music station dashed the hopes of hundreds of thousands of Metro-area fans of Black music.

The decision by the CRTC was opposed by three of the commissioners, including chief commissioner Keith Spicer. He wrote in his dissenting opinion that he regretted the missed opportunity to serve the public interest "by opening other minds to a vital and growing dimension of Toronto." He further stated that an opportunity was missed to "embrace these [multicultural and racial] communities by echoing new themes, new accents, new values, new music" (*Globe and Mail*, 1990). A *Toronto Star* editorial concluded:

> By rejecting dance music such as rhythm and blues, reggae, rap, calypso, salsa, and other Afro and Caribbean styles, the Commission dis-

played a woeful ignorance of the varied multicultural community that constitutes Metropolitan Toronto. It doesn't appear to understand that the once predominantly White days of Hogtown are no more. (*Toronto Star*, 1990)

As even the chief commissioner noted in his dissenting opinion, the decision did not pay sufficient attention to the principles of the Multiculturalism Act (to promote policies, programs, and practices that enhance the ability of individuals and communities of all origins to contribute to the continuing evolution of Canada) or the Broadcasting Policy (CRTC, 1986), which states that the CRTC's policy is to increase access by ethnic groups to conventional radio and television and to cable services.

In a round of CRTC hearing applications for a vacant FM licence in the spring of 1997, two applicants, the Milestone group, which had deep roots in the Black community and was composed of African Canadians, and the Robert Wood group, which had helped pioneer the idea of a Black music station and was committed to employment equity in its organization, lost again to another mainstream applicant, this time the CBC. Milestone appealed the decision and lost. However, the appeal paved the way for the possibility that Milestone could obtain a licence for a former Peterborough, Ontario, AM frequency. However, as yet, there has been no successful assault on the colour bar of the broadcast industry (Foster, 1997). Royson James, in discussing this CRTC decision, observed:

> Every day, this type of thing happens to poor, vulnerable people who face the crushing weight of a power-driven society. Only here, it bears the imprimatur of the state and carries the blessings of the usual guardians of public policy. (James, 1998:A16)

RACISM IN THE ADVERTISING INDUSTRY

Benjamin Singer (1995) suggests that advertising is more than a cultural icon, it is a controversial social institution. Advertising plays a crucial economic role in the media as a primary source of income. In 1992, the estimated revenue from advertising by the major media groups, such as broadcasting, newspapers and magazines, directories, and outdoor advertising, was $9 billion. In a less tangible but equally significant way, advertising has enormous power, not only over mass media organizations, but also in establishing "desirable" societal standards and styles of living.

Advertising, in its multiplicity of forms, provides many of the images and experiences people take for granted. It paints a picture of our social world. Day after day, the White images circulated in newspapers and magazines, on radio and television and on the movie screen, mould impressions and shape perceptions. C. Wright Mills observed that the mass media have "not only filtered into our experience of external realities, they have entered into our very experience of ourselves" (1962:217), providing our society with new identities and new aspirations of what we should be like. Since advertising is geared to White consumers, audiences are reminded of who counts, who is reflected in the mirror, and who is cast outside the mainstream of society.

Non-Representation

The first Canadian study of the representation of people of colour in advertising was carried out by Elkin (1971) on behalf of the Ontario Human Rights Commission. The study examined the representation of visible minorities in TV commercials and revealed that only 3.7 percent of television ads contained a minority performer — usually in a group or crowd scene. A follow-up study in 1980 found only forty-eight visible-minority persons among the two thousand people in the commercials, and the majority of these were children or high-profile American sports and entertainment figures.

In 1982, a two-phase research project commissioned by the federal government was designed to determine the attitudes of Canadians toward the use of people of colour in TV advertising and provide a content analysis of commercials. This analysis revealed that only 10 percent of the over six hundred commercials viewed included racial-minority performers; again, most were either children or people in crowd scenes (PEAC Media Research, 1982).

In the second phase of the study, small groups of viewers in various regions across Canada (both White and non-White) were exposed to sixteen recent commercials. Half of the ads contained White characters only, and the remainder contained multiracial characters. The findings of the survey challenged many of the basic assumptions held by advertisers, many of whom assumed that using Black or Asian actors would have a negative effect on White viewers. The study found no significant differences in viewers' responses that could be attributed to the presence or absence of visible minorities. Regardless of the racial characteristics of the actors, participants in the research stressed the importance of the creative quality and realism of the commercials. There was also some concern expressed on the part of the non-White viewers about the stereotyped roles played by most non-White actors in these commercials.

Niemi and Salgado (1989) conducted an analysis of billboard advertising in Montreal subway stations. A total of 311 billboards were analyzed; of the 163 billboards depicting people, only 10 showed an individual from a visible-minority community. Of the 44 advertisers, only one included a person of colour, and that was the Ministry of Tourism in Ontario. The researchers argued that this "Whitewashing" of advertising reflected both ethnocentrism and discrimination. They suggested that the invisibility of racial minorities denied their existence, devalued their contribution to society, and trivialized their aspirations to participate as full members of society. The exclusion of racial minorities helped perpetuate the "White face" of Canada, "leaving others with feelings of rejection, of marginality and of non-belonging" (Niemi and Salgado, 1989:28).

A nationwide study conducted by the Canadian Advertising Foundation in 1992 found that 70 percent of Canadians thought that advertising was still "too geared toward White consumers" and failed to reflect the cosmopolitan reality of Canada in the 1990s. The poll found that 36 percent of respondents thought negatively about companies that excluded racial minorities from their advertising. The chairman of the firm that conducted the poll said that "Canada is a multicultural country. Our advertising should reflect that, but right now our advertisers are behind the times" (Goldfarb, 1992). The advertising industry, like other media industries, remains trapped in its self-defeating stereotypes.

In March 1998, an exhibition was mounted in Montreal tracing the evolution of Black images in advertising over the last one hundred years. The show, called "Négripub Paris et Négripub Quebec," was brought from Paris as part of Quebec's Black History Month, and demonstrated the connection between the blatantly racist images of early advertisements and the more subtle, negative imagery in current ones. The exhibit, for example, included a 1921 poster showing a Black woman feeding her baby rum to promote St. Christopher's rum. It also included a more recent poster, created by the Quebec education ministry to emphasize the benefits of education, showing television personality Gregory Charles emerging from a chest as a white hand helps him out. In another ad, the newspaper *La Presse* publicized the knowledge it dispenses by using a picture of two black football players and the slogan "One day the whole world will want to know" (Contenta, 1998:A6).

Stereotyping

Another common manifestation of racism is stereotyping. Aunt Jemima, for example, has appeared on boxes of pancake mix for over one hundred years. The smiling Black woman, whose head until recently was wrapped in a kerchief, is reminiscent of a mammy/servant ready to prepare pancakes for a White family. Rastus is still the Cream of Wheat chef, and Uncle Ben (the negative association is with Uncle Tom, a deeply offensive image to Black people) is still the smiling, grandfatherly Black man who has been pictured on boxes of rice for more than a half century. These images, created decades ago, are woven into popular culture. As Craig Neville, a Washington advertising analyst, stated, "These are symbols that are so ingrained in the society and culture that most people do not even notice them any more.... These symbols promote stereotypes" (Graham, 1993).

In the same article, sociologist Gaynelle Grant commented that "the very nature of advertising is to alter how we look at ourselves and things in our environment ... and advertising that perpetrates negativity — like Blacks as smiling, simple-minded servants — affects the way our culture regards Black people."

RESPONSES TO RACISM IN THE MEDIA

The many above examples provide a significant body of evidence that racism in the media exists and that it is reflected in almost every part of the mass communication system in Canada. The following section considers some of the responses to this reality.

COMMUNITY ADVOCACY

There are many examples in Canada of the significant role of the community as a change agent. In reaction to a racist program on a public-affairs show aired by a TV network, a national protest was spearheaded by Chinese Canadian communities across Canada. It had the support and participation of many other community groups and individuals from a wide diversity of racial and cultural backgrounds. After a seven-month campaign, the president of CTV issued a public apology.

The Nisga'a Tribal Council, which had a 100-year-history of lobbying on behalf of Aboriginal issues, together with the Musqueam Band, filed a complaint with the CRTC against the Gary Bannerman program discussed earlier. The CRTC strongly condemned the radio station and its hosts and urged the station to institute controls immediately. The council also filed a complaint with the Ministry of Justice. However, the inadequate response of the media and the legal and justice systems to this and several similar incidents of racism in the media resulted in the formation of the Ad Hoc Media Committee for Better Race Relations in Vancouver, a coalition of Jewish, Indo-Canadian, Chinese, and Black communities, in 1985.

In 1986–87, Khaki and Prasad (1988) conducted a survey of racism and the media to examine the portrayal of visible minorities and Aboriginal peoples in the media. The intent of the study was to create a greater awareness of the concerns of these groups regarding negative coverage in the media and to foster a more positive relationship between minorities and the media.

In Ontario over the last fifteen years, community advocacy committees have been formed both to respond to particular racial incidents and to deal with the general problems of bias and discrimination in advertising, programming, and news coverage. For example, as the result of a racist incident involving a Toronto broadcaster on a weekly jazz radio program, an intensive and extensive lobbying process was set in motion. This ultimately led to a community advisory committee being established to assist the senior management of this station and to create new policies and practices that gradually led to changes in programming, hiring practices, and news coverage.

In the field of advertising, an effective strategy was developed by the Urban Alliance on Race Relations in Toronto in 1984 to deal with the almost total exclusion of racial minorities in advertising and promotions by major retail stores in Metropolitan Toronto. Seven companies were targeted, all of which were frequented by large numbers of visible-minority shoppers. A mail-back campaign was instituted after many lobbying attempts by individuals and organizations failed to produce any changes in the glossy brochures and ads distributed daily. Letters were sent to each of the targeted companies, informing them of the campaign and of the reasons for it (Tator, 1984).

Details of the campaign were then distributed to race relations organizations and community groups across Metropolitan Toronto. Their co-operation and support were solicited. They were asked to mail back every catalogue, flyer, and promotion that did not reflect the multiracial composition of Metro, with a note to the president and advertising managers explaining why. Press releases were distributed, announcing the campaign. A content analysis of the ads six months later revealed positive results. Although there were no subsequent attempts to measure the representation of people of colour in advertising, evidence suggests that the numbers of racial minorities used in private-sector advertising have increased.

PUBLIC-SECTOR RESPONSES

Ontario developed guidelines concerning the portrayal of visible minorities in government advertising and communications in 1983. In 1984, the federal government introduced similar guidelines, largely as a result of lobbying efforts by community groups and organizations, who urged government agencies to ensure that their ads and promotions reflected Canada's racial and cultural diversity. However, several years after the establishment of these guidelines, no mechanisms were in place to monitor or evaluate the governments' performance and their implementation of these guidelines. For a brief period, the government of Ontario established an advisory committee composed of community representatives and civil servants who had full-time management positions in provincial ministries, but the committee was allowed to fade away.

In 1986, a task force on broadcasting policy affirmed that Canadian broadcasting should contribute toward "safeguarding, enriching and strengthening the cultural, political, social and economic fabric of Canada." The CRTC's policy recognizes the importance of multicultural programming. Briefs presented to the task force were united in the view that cultural and racial minorities did not want multicultural programming confined to special ethnic television and radio services. They expected public broadcasters, particularly the CBC, to take the lead. The task force recommended that the CRTC create a special class of licences for minority groups that would make them responsible for program context. It recommended that the right of access to the broadcasting system by Aboriginal Canadians and other Canadians, including diverse multicultural and multiracial groups, be established in the act.

Under federal legislation, Crown corporations such as the CBC are required to report to Parliament each year their progress toward employment equity goals for racial minorities. However, this legislation does not affect other electronic or print media.

ANALYSIS

This chapter's analysis of racism in the media reveals that the vast majority of media organizations fail to respond to the daily challenges that confront them in a multiracial, pluralistic society. Decision-makers generally have ignored or denied the existence of the racial bias and discriminatory practices in all sectors of the media. The coverage of issues affecting racial minorities is filtered through the stereotypes, misconceptions, and erroneous assumptions of largely White reporters, advertisers, journalists, editors, programmers, and producers. The media's images reinforce cultural racism, the collective belief system that divides society into "them" and "us" and sustains White group dominance.

Racism is manifested in the professional attitudes and behaviours of journalists, broadcasters, editors, publishers, program producers, directors, advertising managers, and marketing executives. It is reflected in the way in which issues are dealt with in the slant of a news story or in the use of imagery that promotes negative stereotyping (e.g., Asians are associated with gangs, Blacks and Jamaicans with crime, Tamils with immigration violations, Sikhs and Muslims with terrorism, refugees with welfare abuse). Racial bias is expressed in Eurocentric and ethnocentric values and norms that lead advertisers to conclude that using racial minorities in an advertising campaign will have a negative impact on White consumers. It is evidenced in newspaper headlines that sensationalize issues (e.g., "Immigration Policy Called Risk to Canadian Educators' Jobs" and "Quotas, Quotas and more Quotas"). It is reflected in the lack of access to media institutions as demonstrated in a series of decisions taken by the CRTC over a period of ten years related to the refusal to grant licences to applicants who are committed to opening up the airwaves to Blacks and other ethno-racial minorities.

Siddiqui (1993) identified some of the institutional barriers in media organizations that influence their coverage of racial and cultural issues:

- Although they are on the frontiers of news, journalists are rarely on the cusp of social change.
- Pretensions notwithstanding, the media are "the establishment."
- The media are not good at hearing the voices of the unorganized.
- The media's black-and-white, no greys-in-between, view of the world hurts minorities.
- Most media think of minorities only in the context of their ethnicity. Reporters and editors value their views on race relations but not on larger Canadian or world issues.
- Although race relations is clearly one of the most important issues of our time, most media do not cover it or cover it "on the run," looking for an easy hit.

Other indicators of racism in the media include the lack of recognition attributed to the qualifications and experience gained outside of Canada by media professionals; the absence of outreach and training opportunities for minorities; the way in which "facts" and "events" are selected and subsequently transformed into "news"; and the absence of programming that features the social, cultural, political, and economic contributions of people of colour.

Barriers to racial equity in the media may have the appearance of neutral practices, but in reality they reflect a preformulation of the ideas, opinions, and assumptions of the White power elite in society. Mass communication in Canada has been influenced and controlled by one dominant group and reflects its norms and values.

Racism is found in the daily operations of media organizations across the country and in every area of mass communications. As several of the studies cited in this chapter clearly demonstrate, it stems, at least in part, from the ethnocentrism that pervades the industry. The "we–they" way of thinking leads members of the dominant group to believe that the perceptions, feelings, and judgements of their group are appropriate and normative, while the beliefs and norms of "others" have less value and merit (Essed, 1991). As in other sectors, racism in the media has resulted in the denial of access, participation, and equity for racial minorities.

MEDIA REFLECT AND REPRODUCE WHITE IDEOLOGY

Cultural production, including the media, is increasingly influenced by commerce and the penetration of commodity culture into every facet of life (Giroux, 1994). Canadian newspapers, magazines, and television and radio stations (with the exception of public agencies such as the CBC) are generally owned by corporate interests and are structured to sustain the economic interests of business and government elites (van Dijk, 1991; Hall et al., 1975). The economic conditions in the marketplace, including market structure, competition, and linkages to other markets, have a profound influence on the production of media culture (Kellner, 1995). Most media function as corporations, serving the needs of their shareholders and other financial backers (Fleras, 1995; Wilson and Gutierrez, 1995).

Van Dijk (1991) stated that the reproduction of racism by the media, particularly the press, takes the specific form of "elite racism." His thesis was that since the dominant White media's values are inextricably linked to political, social, and corporate elite groups, it is also in their interest to play a role in producing and generating consensus. He argued that the mass media have nearly exclusive control over the resources required to produce popular opinion, especially in the area of race and ethnic relations. Van Dijk suggested that the media use distinct strategies to weaken the positions, issues, and ideas advocated by minority groups that threaten the status quo.

This analysis is consistent with that of Fleras and Elliott (1996), who observed that the media operate as powerful agents of domination, control, and propaganda. Media images of what is desirable or acceptable are absorbed, with little understanding and awareness of the indoctrination process. Thus, the media are able to establish the boundaries of social discourse, from which priorities are set and public agendas are established and perpetuated.

One example of the influence of the power elite to shape the media's discourse is the debate over employment equity, a federally legislated program (but repealed by the Ontario government in 1995) for overcoming employment barriers affecting people of colour, Aboriginal peoples, women, and people with disabilities. Most media organizations reflect the position of the corporate elite by misrepresenting employment equity as a risk to the operation of a free marketplace, a violation of the merit principle, and a threat to White males.

RACIST DISCOURSE IN THE MEDIA: SILENCING AND MARGINALIZING MINORITY DISSENT

FREEDOM OF SPEECH

There exists in the media a significant resistance to altering the power of the dominant culture. Attempts by racial minorities to protest and resist racist images and discourse in the media are frequently challenged by the media. These protests are seen by the corporate elite as attempts to suppress freedom of expression and are equated with censorship. What is frequently ignored is the connection between the championing of freedom of expression and the freedom of the marketplace to operate without constraint. Van Dijk (1991) argued that freedom of expression is closely linked to freedom of enterprise.

Many see the issue of freedom of speech in the context of the lack of access that people of colour and other groups have to the communication networks. The numerous examples cited in this chapter indicate that racial minorities are largely excluded from participation in public discourse. As Nourbese Philip suggests:

> Freedom of expression in this society is underwritten not by the free flow of information, but by the fact that there are those who are powerful enough in society to make *their* voices, *their* version of history, and *their* viewpoints heard. (1993:66)

In the same way, Hill argued that the way in which "freedom of speech" is applied is really just a reference to the rights and privileges that very few groups in this society possess, in terms of their access to the media (1992:17). The norms, values, and assumptions of White, male-dominated institutions continue to prevent the mass media from fairly and accurately reflecting and representing the multiracial reality of Canadian society. A former editor of the Ottawa *Citizen*, Irshad Manji (1995) made the point that media organizations can't claim to be on the front lines of freedom of expression when their White-dominated workplaces and cultures do not provide employment opportunities for people with different experiences and backgrounds. The composition of these media organizations restricts the free flow of different views.

The following section provides an example of how "freedom of expression" by the media leads to a racialized discourse by the media and limits the freedom of minorities to engage in social critique and dissent. In examining the media coverage of controversies over three cultural events, the Writing Thru Race Conference, "Into the Heart of Africa," and *Show Boat* (see the case studies in Chapter 9), it is clear that particular rhetorical devices were used to describe and analyze both the cultural events and the activities of the protesters. The press employed a discourse aimed at delegitimizing dissent and stifling debate.

In the case of the three events mentioned above, the three major Toronto newspapers created a "media event" around the protests. The term "media event" refers to the way in which the print and broadcast coverage of a particular issue that "is not a mere representation of what happened, but it has its own reality, which gathers up into itself the reality of the event that may or may not have preceded it" (Fiske, 1994:2). This phenomenon suggests that it is no longer credible to rely on a clear relationship between a "real" event and its mediated representation. Accordingly, it is not possible to argue that the "real" is more important, more accurate, or more true than the representation.

Drawing upon the analytical framework of Wetherell and Potter (1992) for identifying racist discourse, the following themes are some of the standard rhetorical devices used by journalists and editors in their critique of the protests.

Theme 1: Describing protesters as "extremists," "militants," "leftists," "zealots," who are engaging in protest activities to further their own agendas, interests, and political goals. They are few in number and are not representative of the "ordinary" members of the community. They are illogical and poorly informed.

There are numerous examples of this discursive strategy. Regarding the media's coverage of "Into the Heart of Africa," Christopher Hume, art critic of *The Toronto Star*, wrote that "either the protesters have not seen the show or they are deliberately distorting the truth to suit their own ends" (Hume, 1990). He went on to add: "If the coalition members were better informed they would have realized the organizers of Into the Heart of Africa were on their side." Christie Blatchford, a feature writer in *The Toronto Sun*, concluded her condemnation of the coalition with the comment: "Why are we so bloody eager to be held hostage by the ravers from the political left?" (Blatchford, 1990). Bronwyn Drainie, in *The Globe and Mail*, referred to "a small number of radical blacks" who viewed the exhibit as a "perpetuation of old racist attitudes.... More moderate blacks, while not deeming the show racist in intent ..." (Drainie, 1991).

Journalists described the protesters against *Show Boat* with similar negative connotations. Michael Coren (1995) in *The Globe and Mail* called them "unelected zealots." Pierre Berton (1993) in *The Toronto Star* characterized the protesters' message as "the silly argument ... made by a small group of activists." Allan Fotheringham (1993) in *The Toronto Sun* referred to the Coalition as "the goofies who are screaming racism" and told them they should "read some history." He described them as "instant experts who make a living out of protesting." In the same newspaper, Linda Barnard (1993) attacked one of the key players in the protest against *Show Boat*, North York Board of Education trustee Stephanie Payne, asking rhetorically if she was "a nasty, mean-spirited woman or is she simply dumb as a post?" An editorial, again in the same paper (April 8, 1993) commented: "We can't let them cook up some evil plot that this is something the Jews are doing to the blacks. Nonsense! It just goes to show how you have to check the hands for muck of those throwing the charge of racism. There really isn't much of a reason to pretend this is a major protest. What it is really is an excuse to agitate and get attention."

Theme 2: Constructing the minority group as oppressor and accusing its members of engaging in "reverse racism," violating the rights of others.

Responding to the Writing Thru Race Conference, Richard Gwyn of *The Toronto Star* described the conference as "an example of racism practised by those who suffer from it. All these noble intentions seem to be turning us into the hell of a 'systematically racist society'" (Gwyn, 1994). *The Toronto Star*'s editorial of April 5, 1994, took a similar position, stating that "reverse discrimination does not cure injustice, but rather feeds it." *The Toronto Sun* referred to the controversy as a "race war in the making" (May 25, 1994).

Regarding *Show Boat*, The *Globe and Mail*'s editor-in-chief, William Thorsell, wrote: "The apparent issue is race — the allegation by some Black people in Toronto that *Show Boat* demeans them. But the real issue is power. *Show Boat* is just a vehicle to advance the campaign of some blacks in Toronto for more power in the life in the city, in particular the City of North York" (Thorsell, 1993). He was implying here that the desire for the power to exercise some control over racist representation is somehow negative and improper. Three years later, in response to a similar controversy, Thorsell wrote, "In retrospect it was all the more clear that the struggle over *Show Boat* was not about race but power and protesters were using *Show Boat* as a vehicle in the contest for more power in the community at large" (Thorsell, 1996).

Theme 3: Alleging that protesters are challenging the principles, values, and norms of a liberal democratic society (such as truth, rationality, freedom of expression, individualism, academic freedom, the integrity of history).

In *The Globe and Mail*, Michael Valpy (1993a) suggested that the Coalition for the Truth about Africa, in trying to shut the ROM exhibit down, were proposing "the death of memory, the death of education. Censorship." Donna LaFramboise (1990), in *The Toronto Star*, meanwhile, chastised the Coalition for apparently believing that their interpretation was the one and only truth. "There is something truly appalling about believing that only you have the right story ..." Another *Toronto Star* journalist reported that the protesters "seem to have willingly misread the exhibit" and that "their attack on the exhibition challenges both academic freedom and the integrity of history" (Cayley, 1990). This writer seemed offended by the name of the Coalition. He argued that "by calling themselves the 'Truth about Africa' the protesters were contending that there was only one truth about Africa."

Robert Fulford, the culture critic of *The Globe and Mail*, said of the Writing Thru Race Conference: "Now the Writers' Union of Canada wants to tell us that closed is open, limited is free, exclusion is inclusion and private is public. The old liberal pluralism holds that each of us has rights as an individual: this is the idea that has animated social progress for generations. The new multiculturalism ... focuses on the rights of groups" (Fulford, 1994).

Theme 4:   Trivializing and dismissing the concerns of minorities about racism in cultural production and other systemic forms of inequality, and alleging that minorities are hyper-sensitive about race.

Philip Marchand, a feature writer in *The Toronto Star*, noted that "whatever the good effects the [Writing Thru Race] conference might have had for its participants, it is undeniably part of a recent trend toward intensifying racial and ethnic consciousness" (Marchand, 1994). Drawing upon the same theme, Richard Gwyn of the same paper commented: "We are at risk of institutionalizing racism in Canada ... this often happens as a by-product of attempts to combat racism or to advantage the disadvantaged. But the effect of their actions can be to create a hyper-consciousness about race" (Gwyn, 1994). Sid Adilman, *The Toronto Star*'s entertainment critic, dismissed the concerns of the African Canadian community about ROM's "Into the Heart of Africa" exhibition, noting that the museum's "wishy-washy board stood inert in the face of loud protests by black activists against its superb exhibition" (Adilman, 1990).

William Littler, the same newspaper's music critic, wrote that the Coalition to Stop *Show Boat*'s objective was an attempt to "rewrite history" (Littler, 1993). The ubiquitous Pierre Berton suggested that "a great fuss has been made about the use of the word 'nigger' " (Berton, 1993).

Theme 5:   Implying that the actions of the protesters themselves create division, tension, and conflict, which disturb the harmony, cohesiveness, and stability of society. These activities are also linked to the policies of multiculturalism, which support the "balkanization" of Canada.

An editorial in *The Globe and Mail*, critiquing the Writing Thru Race Conference, focussed on the premise that the policy of multiculturalism is a powerful force underpinning the conference: "As much as we share the revulsion to a publicly-funded racially exclusive conference ... it must be admitted this is entirely consistent with public policy." In the same paper, Michael Valpy (1994) described the conference as advancing the notion of "apartheid.... Why are 800-some members of the union marching along with this cultural dismemberment of Canada?"

All these examples suggest that the press constructs a discursive pattern in which the following elements are found: (1) protesters are depicted as outsiders, or "others"; (2) the pain experienced by a minority community is dismissed as irrelevant; (3) the existence of systemic racism is denied; (4) the motives of the protesters are belittled; (5) individual leaders are personally attacked; (6) the protesters' actions are equated with disruptive and dysfunctional behaviour; (7) the protesters are considered not to have acquired "Canadian" social values or adopted "Canadian" norms; (8) expressions of dissent and resistance are described as threatening the social order, harmony, and social equilibrium of Canadian society. This discourse is also used by cultural institutions and cultural producers, as demonstrated throughout this book.

As is clear from the preceding discussion, the majority of the mainstream media coverage was critical of the protest groups and dismissive of their actions. However, it is important to stress that media discourse, as well as that of institutional cultural authorities, was often markedly ambivalent and contradictory. It seems that critics, editors, and journalists are of two minds. Attitudinal shifts are observable in the writing of journalists we have quoted. For example, Valpy (1994) was totally dismissive of the concerns of First Nations writers and writers of colour in holding the Writing Thru Race Conference, but earlier he wrote concerning *Show Boat* that "history is going to remember the insensitivity of the Centre's opening, not the artistic merit of what took place there" (Valpy, 1993b). Other writers demonstrated similar kinds of contradictions in their approach and analyses of these cultural controversies.

What is clear, however, is that the issue of race and racism was largely invisible to the White-dominated press and other cultural institutions. Their own position of power and privilege, associated with *their* "Whiteness," was ignored. Their beliefs, assumptions, and values went unnoticed.

In this context, it is important to underscore the influence of the media's ideological positions, narrative strategies, and image construction on the formation of individual, group, and national identity. The implicit and explicit messages buried in media discourse point to the central conflict between a vision of Canadian culture and identity as heterogeneous, racially and culturally divided, and fragmented, versus the dominant ideology of Canadian culture as homogeneous, unified, and harmonious.

CONCLUSION

Ensuring greater access, participation, and equity in the mass communications industries continues to challenge Canadian society. The responsibility for change belongs both to the individuals working in the advertising, print, and electronic media and to the media organizations. Advertisers, editors, journalists, and broadcasters have personal biases; their attitudes, perceptions, and values are influenced by numerous social and cultural factors. However, professional standards should prevent these attitudes from being expressed in their work.

Policies to promote fairness and equity must address the under-representation of minorities in all areas of mass communication. Without greater access to employment opportunities, racial minorities will continue to have virtually no influence in determining how they are represented by others.

Research findings and the work of anti-racism advocates and practitioners suggest that there are a number of barriers to change:

- Freedom of the press is considered so sacred a trust that the media believe they have the right to communicate racist content in both print and broadcasts.
- The diverse and diffuse nature of the media makes them difficult to target, access, and penetrate.
- Self-regulating media agencies are either non-existent or extremely weak. Unions, press councils, and advertising boards exercise limited power and authority over media corporations.
- Significant resources are needed to effectively lobby such agencies as the CRTC. Regulations are complex and demand a high level of expertise.
- There is an absence of consistent monitoring processes and mechanisms in the media.
- Advocacy across Canada is erratic and generally limited to reactions to specific incidents.
- Few substantive, practical media anti-racism models and strategies exist. Where new approaches have been initiated, there is little dissemination of information.
- The law and the justice system provide only limited redress for libel and defamation.

SUMMARY

This chapter examined the ways in which the mass media in Canada have perpetuated and reproduced racism while maintaining the image of being neutral, objective, and unbiased purveyors of the truth. Racism in the media is reflected in racist discourse and the everyday practices of media organizations. Media professionals are often guided by their need to support special and powerful interests, such as government and business, to promote their positions and agendas.

Numerous examples were provided of how the media create and reinforce negative stereotypes of people of colour in order to influence public opinion. Racism is manifested in the under-representation of racial minorities in the advertising, print, and electronic media. People of colour are not in decision-making positions, they are largely invisible in newsrooms, and they have less access to television and radio programming.

Democratic racism is reflected in the media in a profound tension between the belief that the media represent the cornerstone of a democratic liberal society and the key instrument by which its ideals are produced and disseminated, and the actual role of the media as purveyors of racist discourse, supporters of the powerful White political, economic, and cultural elite, and vehicles for reinforcing White cultural hegemony.

NOTE

1. At the time of writing this book, two new studies are in progress: Henry (forthcoming) and Henry and Tator (forthcoming).

REFERENCES

Adilman, S. (1990). "Bad Guys Discrediting Integrity of the Board." *Toronto Star* (December 24):C5.

———. (1998). "Why No Black Characters in Canadian TV Series?" *Toronto Star* (March 21):M2.

Allport, G. (1954). *The Nature of Prejudice*. New York: Doubleday.

Appleby, T. (1992a). "Island Crime Wave Spills Over." *Globe and Mail* (July 10):A7.

———. (1992b). "The Twisted Arm of the Law." *Globe and Mail* (July 11):A1, A7.

———. (1992c). "Identifying the Problem." *Globe and Mail* (July 13):A1, A6.

Barnard, L. (1993). "Missing the Boat." *Toronto Sun* (May 21):73.

BCOFR (British Columbia Organization to Fight Racism). (1993). "Petition." Surrey, BC.

Berton, Pierre. (1993). "Let's Not Scrub Show Boat Too Clean." *Toronto Star* (March 20):K3.

Bey, S. (1983). "Visible Minorities in the Media." *Currents: Readings in Race Relations* (Toronto) 1(2):5–8.

Blatchford, C. (1990). "A Surrender to Vile Harangues." *Toronto Sun* (November 30):5.

Canadian Ethnocultural Council. (1985). "Brief to the Parliamentary Subcommittee on Equality Rights." Ottawa.

Canadian Islamic Congress. (1998). *Anti-Islam in the Media: A Case Study*. Waterloo, ON.

Cashmore, E., and E. McLaughlin (eds.). (1991). *Out of Order: Policing Black People*. London: Routledge.

Cayley, D. (1990). "Trouble out of Africa." *Toronto Star* (August 10).

Chandwani, A. (1994). "Do Blacks Attract Unfair Scrutiny?" *Toronto Star* (July 13):A14.

Collins, D. (1988). *North Shore News* (August 7).

———. (1991). *North Shore News* (September 11).

———. (1992a). *North Shore News* (January 22).

———. (1992b). *North Shore News* (August 26).

Contenta, C. (1998). "Exhibit Traces 100-Year Evolution of Images of Blacks in Advertising." *Toronto Star* (February 3):A6.

Coren, M. 1995. "Livent Court Case Really about Government Accountability." *Globe and Mail* (January 30).

CRTC. (1986). *Report of the Task Force on Broadcasting Policy*. Ottawa.

Cuff, J.H. (1990). *Globe and Mail* (August 21):C1.

———. (1992). "Putting a Lid on the Mean Streets." *Globe and Mail* (May 9).

———. (1997). "Black Sitcoms Play on Stereotypes." *Globe and Mail* (April 16):C2.

Daniel, J., and A. Allen. (1988). "Newsmagazines, Public Policy and the Black Agenda." In G. Smitherman-Donaldson and T.A. van Dijk (eds.), *Discourse and Discrimination*. Detroit: Wayne State University Press.

Deverell, R. (1986). *Equal Opportunities to Perform: The Alliance of Canadian Cinema, Television and Radio Artists*. Ottawa: Secretary of State.

Drainie, B. 1991. "ROM Adds Insult to Injury in Debacle over African Show." *Globe and Mail* (April 4).

Ducharme, M. (1986). "The Coverage of Canadian Immigration Policy in *The Globe and Mail*." *Currents: Readings in Race Relations* (Toronto) 3(3):6–11.

Elkin, F. (1971). *The Employment of Visible Minority Groups in Mass Media Advertising*. Toronto: Ontario Human Rights Commission.

Equality Now. (1984). Report of the Special Committee on Visible Minorities in Canadian Society. Ottawa.

Essed, E. (1991). *Understanding Everyday Racism*. Newbury Park, CA: Sage.

Fiske, J. (1994). *Media Matters: Everyday Culture and Political Change*. Minneapolis: University of Minnesota Press.

Fleras, A.(1995). "'Please Adjust Your Set': Media and Minorities in a Multicultural Society." In B. Singer (ed.), *Communications in Canadian Society*. 4th ed. Scarborough, ON: Nelson, 406–31.

———, and J. Elliott. (1992). *Multiculturalism in Canada*. Scarborough, ON: Nelson.

———, and J. Elliott. (1996). *Unequal Relations: An Introduction to Race, Ethnic and Aboriginal Relations in Canada*. 2nd ed. Scarborough, ON: Prentice Hall.

Foster, C. (1997). "Colour Barrier Remains." *Toronto Star*. (April 21):A18.

Fotheringham, A. (1993). "A Resounding Attack on Racism." *Toronto Sun* (October 19):12.

Fulford, R. (1994). "George Orwell Call Your Office." *Globe and Mail* (March 30):C1.

Gilroy, P. (1987). *There Ain't No Black in the Union Jack*. Chicago: University of Chicago Press.

Ginzberg, E. (1985). *Power without Responsibility: The Press We Don't Deserve*. Toronto: Urban Alliance on Race Relations.

Giroux, Henri. (1994). "World without Borders: Buying Social Change." In C. Becker (ed.), *The Subversive Imagination: Artists, Society and Social Responsibility*. New York: Routledge. 187–207.

Globe and Mail. (1990). "A License Denied to Dance Music." Editorial. (August 11).

Goldberg, D. (1993). *Racist Culture: Philosophy and the Politics of Meaning*. Oxford, UK: Blackwell.

Goldfarb, M. (1992). "Ads Still Too Geared to Whites, Poll Finds." *Toronto Star* (December 15):D1.

Gomez, H. (1983). "The Invisible Visible Minorities." *Currents: Readings in Race Relations* (Toronto) 1(2):12–13.

Graham, R. (1993). "We Are What We Eat and the Box It Comes In." *Toronto Star* (January 30):D5.

Granzberg, G. (1982). *The Portrayal of Visible Minorities by Canadian Television during the 1982 Prime-Time Season*. Ottawa: Secretary of State.

Gwyn, R. (1994). "Good Intentions Pave Canada's Road to Racist Hell." *Toronto Star*. July 8.

Hall, S., C. Critcher, T. Jefferson, J. Clarke, and B. Roberts. (1975). *Newsmaking and Crime*. Paper presented at NACRO Conference on Crime and the Media, Birmingham: Centre for Contemporary Cultural Studies, University of Birmingham.

————. (1978). *Policing the Crisis: Mugging, the State and Law and Order*. London: Methuen.

Hannerz, U. (1992). *Cultural Complexity: Studies in Social Meaning*. New York: Columbia University Press.

Henry, F. (forthcoming). *The Racialization of Crime by the Print Media*. Toronto: School of Journalism, Ryerson Polytechnic University.

————, and C. Tator. (forthcoming). *Racial Stereotyping in the National Press*. Ottawa: Canadian Race Relations Foundation.

Hill, R. (1992). "One Part Per Million: Native Voices and White Appropriation." *Fuse* 15(3):17.

hooks, b. (1990). *Yearning: Race, Gender, and Cultural Politics*. Boston: South End Press.

Hume, C. (1990). "ROM Critics Confusing Content with Context." *Toronto Star*. May 19: H6.

James, R. (1998). "CBC Celebrates, Others Mourn." *Toronto Star* (April 19):A16.

Joffe, H. (1993). "Offensive Premise." Letter to the Editor. *Globe and Mail* (May 1).

Jones, D. (1993). "Skirmishes in the Skin Trade." *Globe and Mail* (April 24):D3.

Kellner, D. (1995). "Cultural Studies, Multiculturalism and Media Culture." In G. Dines and J. Humez (eds.), *Cultural Studies, Multiculturalism and Media Culture*. Thousand Oaks, CA: Sage.

Khaki, A., and K. Prasad. (1988). *Depiction and Perception: Native Indians and Visible Minorities in the Media*. Vancouver: Ad Hoc Media Committee for Better Race Relations.

Krieger, L. (1998). "Stereotypes Pervade Music Videos Study Finds." *Globe and Mail* (April 8):C2.

LaFramboise, Donna. (1990). "ROM Protesters Miss Own Point." *Toronto Star*. October 22.

Littler, William. (1993). "*Show Boat* Set the Standard for Musicals." *Toronto Star* (October 16).

Manji, I. (1995). *Metro Report on Racial Minorities in the Media*. Municipality of Metropolitan Toronto.

Marchand, Philip. 1994. "Politics the Real CanLit Power Fuel." *Toronto Star* (July 5).

Mayers, A. (1986). "Minorities in Ontario Newsrooms." MBA thesis, McMaster University.

MediaWatch. (1998). *Bulletin* (Toronto) (August and October).

Miller, J., and K. Prince. (1994). *The Imperfect Mirror: Analysis of Minority Pictures and News in Six Canadian Newspapers*. Toronto: School of Journalism, Ryerson Polytechnic University.

Mills, C.W. (1962). "The Mass Society." In E. Josephson and M. Josephson (eds.), *Man Alone*. New York: Dell.

Morrison, T., and C. Brodsky Lacour (1997). *Birth of a Nation'hood: Gaze, Script, and Spectacle in the O.J. Simpson Case*. New York: Pantheon Books.

Mosher, C.L. (1998). *Discrimination and Denial: Systemic Racism in Ontario's Legal and Criminal Justice Systems, 1892–1961*. Toronto: University of Toronto Press.

Mouammar, M. (1986). "When Cartoons Are Not Funny." *Currents: Readings in Race Relations* (Toronto) 3(3):20–21.

Niemi, F., and M. Salgado. (1989). *Un visage français, oui, mais ... multicultural et multiracial, aussi!* Montreal: Centre for Research Action on Race Relations.

Nourbese Philip, M. (1993). *Showing Grit: Showboating North of the 44th Parallel*. Toronto: Poui Publications.

PEAC Media Research. (1982). *The Presence and Portrayal of Non-Whites in English-Language Television Advertising in Canada*. Ottawa: Secretary of State.

Perigoe, R., and B. Lazar. (1992). "Visible Minorities and Native Canadians in National Television News Programs." In M. Grenier (ed.), *Critical Studies of Canadian Mass Media*. Toronto: Butterworths.

Ridington, R. (1986). "Texts That Harm: Journalism in British Columbia." *Currents: Readings in Race Relations* (Toronto) 3(4)(Summer).

Rosenfeld, M., and M. Spina. (1977). *All the News That's Fit to Print: A Study of the Toronto Press's Coverage of Immigration, Ethnic Communities and Racism.* Toronto: Cross-Cultural Communication Centre.

Siddiqui, H. (1993). "Media and Race: Failing to Mix the Message." *Toronto Star* (April 24):D1, D5.

Singer, B. (1995). "Advertising: A Sociocultural Force." In B. Singer (ed.), *Communications in Canadian Society.* 4th ed. Scarborough, ON: Nelson. 122–38.

Stroud, C. (1992). "Handcuffing the Police." *Toronto Star* (October 17):C1.

Tator, C. (1984). "Mail Back Campaign." *Currents: Readings in Race Relations* (Toronto) 3(4)(Summer).

Thorsell, W. (1993). "In America's Bazaar of Competing Interests, Power Is the Only Currency." *Globe and Mail* (October 16):D1.

———. (1996). "Angels in America Has Powerful Parallels in Canada." *Globe and Mail* (September 28).

Toronto Star. (1990). "Music for Everyone." Editorial. (August 10).

———. (1997). "CRTC Should Intervene in Howard Stern Case." (December 23):A20.

Troyna, B. (1984). "Media and Race Relations." In E. Cashmore (ed.), *Dictionary of Race and Ethnic Relations.* London: Routledge.

Valpy, M. (1993a). "The Storm around Show Boat." *Globe and Mail* (March 12):A2.

———. (1993b). "There's Something Better Than *Show Boat.*" *Globe and Mail* (October 19).

———. (1994). "A Nasty Serving of Cultural Apartheid." *Globe and Mail* (April 8).

van Dijk, T. (1991). *Racism and the Press.* London: Routledge.

Wetherell, M., and J. Potter. (1992). *Mapping the Language of Racism.* New York: Columbia University Press.

Wilson, C., and F. Gutierrez. (1995). *Race, Multiculturalism and the Media.* London: Sage.

PART
FOUR

▼▼

The Impact of Democratic Racism on Canadian Institutions and Culture

▼▼▼▼▼▼▼▼▼▼▼▼▼▼▼▼

This part analyzes the impact of democratic racism on Canadian organizations and institutions. Chapter 11 describes and analyzes government responses to racism, and stresses the inadequacies of laws, public policies, and state agencies in dismantling structural inequality. Chapter 12 examines the powerful methods used to resist anti-racist change in organizational culture, policies, and practices. Chapter 13 discusses the ways in which democratic racism has maintained racial inequality. The concluding pages of this book identify some strategies for change.

▼▼

Chapter 11

▼▼▼▼▼▼▼▼▼▼▼▼▼

State Responses to
Racism in Canada

The law has been used through direct action, interpretation, silence and complicity. The law has been wielded as an instrument to create a common-sense justification of racial differences, to reinforce common-sense notions already deeply embedded within a cultural system of values ... and to form new social constructions. (Kobayashi, 1990: 40)

T his chapter explores the conflicting role of the Canadian state in both promoting and controlling racism. Public policies intended to ameliorate inequality each play a role in maintaining this conflict. On the one hand, the democratic state has a special responsibility to assert leadership and guard against the tyranny of the majority. Legislative action is the state's primary tool to promote and achieve equality and justice for all, regardless of race and colour.

On the other hand, legislation and the subordinate activities of the state can neither eliminate nor effectively control racism because the legacy of racism is so interwoven in the national culture, in its commonsense ideology and its public discourse. In this chapter, three major state responses are analyzed as case studies: multiculturalism legislation policy, the Canadian Charter of Rights and Freedoms, and human-rights codes and commissions.[1] The discussion considers the extent to which each of these political responses has delivered on its promise to diminish the legitimacy and impact of racial bias and discrimination in Canadian society.

The chapter proposes new ways of understanding the complex relationships between the state, the dominant culture, and ethno-racial minorities, particularly with respect to this book's central concern: the response to racism in a liberal democratic society. The principal thesis of this chapter is that despite the fact that state responses have been developed that specifically acknowledge Canada's culturally and racially diverse population and recognize the existence of bias and discrimination, these responses have largely failed to achieve the goal of eliminating or even controlling racial bias and discrimination. They have failed precisely because they have been framed within a liberal framework and tradition.

INTRODUCTION

The state has many functions and responsibilities. One of its main roles is to proscribe behaviour. It also influences public opinion through its public-policy and legislative functions and helps thereby to define national ideology. Among its many responsibilities is the responsibility to support the social, cultural, and economic development of communities that suffer racial discrimination, by helping them to achieve full participation, access, and equity.

THE STATE'S ROLE AS PUBLIC-POLICY-MAKER AND DECISION-MAKER

The influence of state policies and practices at various levels (federal, provincial, and municipal) is critical to the eradication of racism and the promotion of racial equity. As such, the state has a special responsibility to assert leadership.

The fundamental rights and freedoms to which Canada adheres include the right of all residents to full and equal participation in the cultural, social, economic, and political life of the country. This right is based on the principle of the fundamental equality of individuals. The rights of equality of access, equality of opportunity, and equality of outcomes for all communities are therefore implicit. They are entrenched in a number of state policies and statutes, as well as in the international covenants to which Canada is a signatory.

The ideal of racial equity is a relatively new and still fragile tradition in Canada because racism has only recently been acknowledged as a serious social concern. Both federal and provincial governments have, however, enacted legislation that reflects their abhorrence of racism as a form of behaviour antithetical to a democratic state. The legislation includes the Canadian Charter of Rights and Freedoms, the Canadian Multiculturalism Act, and provincial human-rights and labour codes.

Racism is a humiliating and debilitating experience for its victims. Its destructive forces affect individuals, groups, and communities, rendering them powerless and disadvantaged. Racism also is a threat to the viability and stability of the broader society. This has been recognized by many countries; Canada has, therefore, participated in international movements to stem racism and guarantee human rights.

INTERNATIONAL DECLARATIONS OF HUMAN RIGHTS

The Canadian government has participated in several international declarations concerning human rights. The Universal Declaration on Human Rights was the first international covenant protecting human rights to be ratified by Canada. Since then, the United Nations has adopted a number of international covenants on human rights, including the International Convention on the Elimination of All Forms of Racial Discrimination, which was ratified in 1970. The convention is based on the conviction that any doctrine of superiority based on racial differentiation is scientifically false, morally condemnable, socially unjust, and dangerous.

Signing these international conventions creates the impression that Canada is committed to the development of an equitable society based on fairness and non-discrimination. International human-rights covenants provide Canada with global standards to which all federal legislation is expected to conform, but they do not bind the provinces. Moreover, most international instruments respecting human rights do not constitute a legally binding set of rules, and many contain no enforcement mechanisms.

The following case studies examine three state interventions in issues of racial and cultural difference in the context of inequality. Although each of these responses has been framed within a "liberal" democratic framework, the analyses contained within the studies suggest that the state has largely failed to address the deeply rooted nature of racism and systemic discrimination.

CASE STUDY 11.1

MULTICULTURALISM POLICY AND LEGISLATION

BACKGROUND

Multiculturalism as state policy had its official beginnings in 1971, when Prime Minister Pierre Trudeau announced in Parliament that his government had accepted the recommendations of the Royal Commission on Bilingualism and Biculturalism (Fleras and Elliott, 1992). Recognizing that Canada was both culturally and ethnically a "plural" society, in that it contained Canadians of British and French origin, Aboriginal peoples, and "others," the commission recommended that Canada's diversity be recognized and maintained. "Multiculturalism within a bilingual framework commends itself to the government as the most suitable means of assuring the cultural freedom of Canadians."

Since then, the policy has become enshrined in the federal Multiculturalism Act, and a Ministry of Multiculturalism was established. The act committed the government to a policy of preserving and enhancing the multicultural identity and heritage of Canadians, while working to achieve the equality of all Canadians in economic, social, cultural, and political life.

Subsection 3(2)(a) of the act recognizes discrimination in Canadian society and articulates the federal government's commitment to ensure that no unfair barriers exist to employment and career advancement. The act commits federal institutions to enhance the ability of individuals and communities to contribute to Canadian society by ensuring that government policies and programs respond to the needs of all Canadians. Subsection 3(2)(c) provides assurances that government services will be delivered in an accessible manner to everyone (Multiculturalism and Citizenship, Canada 1989–90).

(continued)

CASE STUDY 11.1 *(continued)*

The act requires federal government agencies to develop and implement multicultural and racial-equality policies and programs as they apply to their respective mandates. Examples of initiatives cited in the 1991 annual report tabled in Parliament include:

- The solicitor-general established a police race-relations centre to serve as a resource both to federal and provincial police forces.
- The Canada Council audited its advisory committees and juries to ensure that they reflected Canadian diversity, and it increased support to minority artists.
- Employment and Immigration increased its funding of programs for immigrant integration.
- The Federal Business Development Bank established ethnocultural advisory committees to assist small businesses owned by minorities and immigrants.

As a result of changes in the leadership of the government of Canada in July 1993, multiculturalism was subsumed into the Heritage Canada ministry.

Federal multicultural initiatives have been described as providing symbolic support, setting the tone for what is acceptable ("behaviour clues"), establishing a legal basis for action, and sending out signals regarding the notion of justice and equality. By legitimizing the presence of racial minorities, multiculturalism has furthered Canada's experience with nation-building from a mosaic of cultures and races (Tepper, 1988).

DISCUSSION

Scholars such as Mackey (1996), Wallace (1994), and Bhabha (1990) contend that multiculturalism as state policy constructs a concept of a common dominant (English Canadian culture), in relation to which all other cultures are "multicultural." A norm is created by the dominant culture that suggests "these other cultures are fine, but we must be able to locate them within our own grid" (Bhabha, 1990:208). The political and public discourse affirms a faith in a pluralistic society but, at the same time, resists the demands that the articulation of cultural and racial differences makes upon a democratic liberal society — inclusion, equity, and empowerment. Itwaru and Ksonzek assert that multiculturalism, while fostering the illusion of tolerance and respect, "conceals the inner chambers of assimilation" (1994:14).

In this sense, multiculturalism as state policy is a strategy of containment rather than change. Walcott (1993) argued that symbolic multiculturalism is a way of maintaining existing hegemonic practices. Similarly, Wallace (1994) suggested that the intent of symbolic multiculturalism as public policy is to counter or neutralize the growing cultural, political, economic, and social demands of minorities for access and equity within all sectors of Canadian society. While "tolerating," "accommodating," "appreciating," and "celebrating" differences, multiculturalism allows for the preservation of the cultural hegemony of the dominant cultural group.

(continued)

CASE STUDY 11.1 *(continued)*

The concept of tolerance is central to the state ideology of multiculturalism. It implies positions of superiority and inferiority in implicitly assuming that some attributes and behaviours associated with minority groups need to be accepted, condoned, or sanctioned. In other words, "We tolerate only that of which we disapprove." Thus, acceptance by the dominant culture is dependent on the good will, forbearance, and benevolence of those who do the tolerating. Taylor (1994) and Walzer (1997) argued that modern philosophers writing on tolerance see it as a minimal form of recognition of an individual or group. Mirchandani and Tastsoglou (forthcoming) contend that the construct of tolerance entrenched in multicultural policy posed little challenge to the (racist) status quo because a ceiling of tolerance is established. "The call for individuals or groups to place a 'limit' on tolerance implies the self-definition of these individuals or groups as 'guardians' of the social order" (Mirchandani and Tastsoglou:11). James (1995) observed that the tolerant national self is seen as tolerating "others"; the characterizing of non-Anglos and immigrants as "others" reflects the way in which Canadians understand diversity. The "others" — including people of colour, Aboriginal peoples, immigrants, and gays and lesbians — lie outside the borders of Canadian identity.

The language of the Multiculturalism Act reflects this ambivalence toward the "others" — it is mainly passive, non-coercive, and non-threatening.[2] It relies on the concepts of tolerance, harmony, and unity within a paradigm of diversity. It is a discourse that presumes that justice and equity exist, although they are sometimes flawed by the biased attitudes and behaviours of aberrant individuals.

The Multiculturalism Act focusses on limiting diversity to symbolic rather than political or transformative kinds of change. As Angel (1988) observed, the other ethnic groups will always remain as individual groups, but will not "be incorporated into the political arena as groups. The government will not establish another power base that might upset the existing balance between French-speaking and English-speaking Canadians" (Angel, 1988:27). Mackey (1996) provided support for this position with information contained in the *Legislative Briefing Book* (obtained through an Access to Information request), which describes the act clause by clause and suggests answers to potential questions that might be raised by members of the Opposition during debate over the proposed Multiculturalism Act. In the responses prepared by the Corporate Policy Branch (1988:21), three important points are emphasized: (1) the policy is meant to be "highly symbolic"; (2) "the Bill's approach to equity is adversarial"; and (3) the act is a "non-coercive" approach that emphasizes "cooperation, encouragement, awareness and persuasion" (Mackey, 1996). The act, despite its incorporation of "race relations" and reference to discrimination and barriers, is still primarily a symbolic state intervention into the politics of diversity (Mackey, 1996).

In 1986 the federal government began using a new discourse: "Multiculturalism means business" (Fleras and Elliott, 1996; Calof, 1997). In this context, multiculturalism is a means of providing opportunities for new areas of consumerism and market penetration. Cultural diversity is considered a consumer resource in the global economy.

(continued)

CASE STUDY 11.1 *(continued)*

The failure of the Multiculturalism Act to live up to its promise of dealing with racial inequality has led to a race-based critique of multiculturalism. The act was supposed to signal a change in the official policy of multiculturalism from its primary focus (in the multicultural policy of 1971), on cultural preservation and retention, to a recognition and affirmation of the rights of people of colour to full participation in Canadian society.

Many writers and theorists (Mackey, 1996; Goldberg, 1994; Walcott, 1993) identified as a major weakness in multiculturalism its failure to deal with the problems of systemic racism in Canada. This race-based analysis argues that multiculturalism as state policy has provided a veneer for liberal-pluralist discourse, in which democratic values such as individualism, tolerance, and equality are espoused and supported, without altering the core of the common culture or ensuring the rights of people of colour. This critique of multiculturalism points to its inadequacies, including its inability to dismantle systems of inequality and diminish White power and privilege. Creese (1993–94) observed that despite multiculturalism, the legacy of "White settler" colonialism continues to provide some citizens with greater entitlements and the freedom to define who is a "real citizen" in Canada.

A race-based analysis asserts that multiculturalism fosters "a festive aura of imagined consensus" (Moodley, 1983). Multiculturalism focusses on "saris, samosas, and steel-bands" in order to diffuse the "three R's": "resistance, rebellion and rejection" (Mullard, 1982). A little local colour is "tolerated" and even encouraged because it provides vibrancy and vitality to what remains as the "core" culture.

Multicultural discourse as articulated in the act and other policies is founded on the premise of social order rather than conflict, and thus "it does not recognize, or provide any way of understanding existing structural disadvantages and the clashes which will occur as such inequalities are addressed" (Harding, 1995).

CASE STUDY 11.2

THE CANADIAN CHARTER OF RIGHTS AND FREEDOMS

BACKGROUND

The Canadian Bill of Rights was introduced by Prime Minister John G. Diefenbaker in 1960. Although it prohibited racial discrimination, it neither had constitutional status nor applied to provincial jurisdictions. Thus, prior to the enactment of the Constitution Act of 1982, the courts gave the Canadian Bill of Rights a very

(continued)

CASE STUDY 11.2 *(continued)*

narrow interpretation. Constitutional questions about racial equality were resolved according to the "implied bill of rights" flowing from the constitutional division of powers. It is instructive that the "Fathers of Confederation" did not find it necessary to address the issue of racial equality in the provisions of the British North America Act. At the time, racial inequality was considered to be normative, and therefore the notion of providing constitutional guarantees to achieve racial equality was contrary to the collective ideology of the times.

In 1982, after a lengthy and controversial consulting process, the Canadian Charter of Rights and Freedoms was enshrined in Canada's constitution. For the first time in Canada's constitutional history, racial discrimination became unconstitutional. Enshrining the Charter in the constitution was hailed as a triumph that was expected to put an end to many forms of overt racial discrimination in society.[3]

Section 15(1) of the Charter of Rights (the equity rights clause) came into effect in 1985 and is perhaps the most significant equality provision in the Charter.[4] It reads:

> Every individual is equal before and under the law and has the right to the equal protection and equal benefit of the law without discrimination and, in particular, without discrimination based on race, national or ethnic origin, colour, religion, sex, age or mental or physical ability.

In prohibiting discrimination, section 15(1) provides five separate equality rights, namely: a right to equality before the law; a right to equality under the law; a right to equal benefit of the law; a right to equal protection of the law; a right not to be discriminated against. It also protects affirmative action programs from constitutional litigation. Arguably, section 15(2) recognizes societal inequalities and permits affirmative action measures as a mechanism to assure equity for all Canadians.

DISCUSSION

While the Charter outlaws discrimination on the basis of race, it is seriously flawed in a number of important ways.[5] Section 1 establishes protection for all Canadians of certain basic rights and freedoms essential to a liberal democratic society. These include the protection of fundamental freedoms, democratic rights, legal rights, equality rights, Canada's multicultural heritage, Native rights, and the official languages of Canada. At the same time, however, the rights guaranteed in the Charter are subject to certain limitations: they should be reasonable, prescribed by law, demonstrably justified, and in keeping with the standards of a free and democratic society. Three of these four criteria included in Section 1 are subjective and open to differing interpretations. The views of ethno-racial minorities and other disadvantaged groups may be very different from those of the state on what is considered to be "reasonable" and "demonstrably justified" and on what meets the standards of a "free and democratic society."

(continued)

CASE STUDY 11.2 *(continued)*

The Charter does not define discrimination, racism, or race. Such definitions and interpretations have been left to the courts. Judges, justices, and lawyers have neither the expertise nor the training in social science to make determinations about the invisible network of racist discourses, beliefs, values, and norms that operate in a liberal democratic society. Many judges deny the existence of systemic racism. The courts are thus ill-prepared to define the meanings and conditions of racial discrimination.

When a charge of racial discrimination has been made against an institution, a "cause of action" must initially be defined for the case to be heard in the courts. Essentially, a litigant must frame a legal claim within the legal parameter of a "cause of action." When the cause of a legal action involves racism and discrimination, it is virtually impossible to present an argument without a legal definition of such terms. Constitutional litigation involves a process of language, interpretation, and meaning.

Matas (1990) made a strong argument that the Charter is an inadequate and imperfect instrument for effectively addressing the problem of racism. He suggested that, while the Charter prohibits racial discrimination in law (section 15 (1)), it does not require governments or legislatures to promote racial equality. The Charter is a passive instrument. It does not require governments or legislatures to do anything; it merely prevents them from doing certain things. Thus, a government that did absolutely nothing about racial equality would be in full compliance with the Charter. Positive efforts to combat racial discrimination are completely absent from the Charter. Thus, the Charter is a passive rather than a proactive tool in combating discrimination. The Charter prohibits racial discrimination in law, but it requires neither Parliament nor legislatures to design policies and programs to eliminate racial equality. There is no constitutional mandate to eradicate or even control racism.

For example, the Charter does not prevent one group of citizens from discriminating against another. As long as governments are not actively promoting inequality, they can legally wash their hands of what goes on in society at large (Matas, 1990). The real threat to equality does not come from legislative action but from the actions of private persons working within systems and organizations. Thus, the equality provisions in the Charter fail to address some of the real arenas of inequality in society.

Many of the same arguments can be made in discussing the weaknesses in the constitutional equality-rights process. For example, the constitutional equality-rights system, through its procedures, makes the same flawed assertion as does the human-rights system, that is, equality exists; only the lapses from it need to be addressed. However, Kallen (1982) contended that there is a covert status hierarchy among the enumerated minorities who are eligible to receive specified protection for their human rights in section 15. Ethnic and multicultural minorities, Aboriginal peoples, and women have specified human-rights protection under other Charter provisions (sections 25, 27, and 28, respectively), whereas other enumerated minorities (such as racial minorities) do not.

Lack of a support structure for victims of inequality and the absence of a public agency with a capacity to challenge inequalities on behalf of a disadvantaged

(continued)

CASE STUDY 11.2 *(continued)*

group is another major deficiency in the Charter. Perhaps one of the most important limitations of the Charter is the lack of guaranteed funding necessary to pursue a challenge. To raise an important Charter issue, a litigant must be willing and able to fight its case in the Supreme Court of Canada. To attempt a challenge of federal legislation on Charter grounds can cost $100 000 or more. Few citizens have the necessary funds. The absence of sufficient resources for minority groups exacerbates social inequalities.[6] This diminishes the section 15 provision and ensures that court actions are largely brought by wealthy litigants. It can be argued that a significant reason for the lack of Charter challenges by people of colour is that justice is economically inaccessible.

A further limitation of the Charter in relation to the protection of minority rights is the passivity of the courts. Gibson argued that the Charter "stands against a backdrop of the courts' passive tradition of self-restraint" (1985:39). Historically, the courts have deferred to democratically elected representatives. This weakness is clearly demonstrated in the repeal of the Employment Equity Act by the government of Ontario.

In sum, section 15 provides an inadequate guarantee against discrimination. Regardless of Supreme Court decisions and strong judicial statements condemning discrimination, the courts are an ineffective arena for enforcing or ensuring equality in Canada. Racial inequality cannot be eradicated by one act of legislation in one mainstream institution in society. The alleged importance of the Charter maintains the ideological fiction that the legal system can control the broader systemic biases found in Canadian society. Thus, the Charter can be said to be an instrument of the ideology of democratic racism in providing a liberal solution consistent with a liberal democratic society's view of the world. However, it provides only a template, without the authority required to implement racial equality.

CASE STUDY 11.3

HUMAN-RIGHTS CODES AND COMMISSIONS

BACKGROUND

Ontario's Racial Discrimination Act of 1944 was the first provincial legislation to prohibit racial discrimination. In 1962, the Ontario Human Rights Code was the first such provincial legislation to be enacted. The code prohibited discrimination on the grounds of race, creed, colour, nationality, ancestry, or place of origin. Today, all the provinces, two of the three territories (at the time of writing, Nunavut had just been established), and the federal government have a

(continued)

CASE STUDY 11.3 *(continued)*

human-rights code and most have a human-rights commission to administer their codes.

Provincial human-rights codes have quasi-constitutional status. The Canadian Human Rights Code is, of course, subject to the Canadian Charter of Rights and Freedoms, which in section 52 states that the Constitution is the supreme law of Canada.

Human-rights laws are codes of conduct to which society is expected to adhere. Although the prohibited grounds of discrimination vary from province to province, several jurisdictions prohibit discrimination in accommodation, facilities, services, contracts, and employment. All the codes prohibit discrimination on the basis of race, creed, colour, ethnicity, religion, gender, and, in Ontario, sexual orientation.

Canada's system of human rights is activated by the complaint mechanism. Under various human-rights codes, claims must be handled by a human-rights commission, which investigates claims and attempts to settle them by conciliation and mediation. If this is not possible, the commission either dismisses the claim or sends it to hearings conducted by a human-rights board of inquiry. The board of inquiry is a quasi-judicial tribunal and an independent body.

If a claim goes to a board of inquiry, lawyers acting for the commission present the case and argue for the "appropriate" remedy. Boards of inquiry make decisions to uphold or reject claims and can order redress, such as back pay and damages (Ontario Human Rights Code Review Task Force, 1992:17).

DISCUSSION

The present model of human rights has been criticized (Day, 1990; Duclos, 1990; *Equality Now*, 1984) for being a reactive model that comes into play only when a complaint is launched. Critics argue that commissions do not have a sufficiently broad mandate to combat discrimination effectively. A principal criticism is that a complaint-motivated system cannot effectively address a problem that is so widespread in society.

The Canadian human-rights commissioner reinforced the criticism of the complaint model: "I am convinced that one of the reasons our scheme of human-rights laws has become prey to bureaucratic delays and judicial haggling is that it is so predominantly a complaint-driven model," which requires several conditions to be met: a victim must come forward; that person must be able to relate particular actions to one or more of the forbidden types of discrimination; and the treatment must be demonstrably discriminatory, not just unfair or different. He proposed that the commissions complement the complaint system by creating a non-discriminatory environment that includes employment equity (Yalden, 1990:2).

In resolving human-rights complaints, the present model allows for persuasion and conciliation where necessary and, alternatively, for punitive measures when such persuasion fails. Human-rights commissions are therefore under tremendous pressure to settle complaints. In attempting to reach conciliation, staff are often unaware of the impact of their behaviour on victims. In the hearings of a task force

(continued)

CASE STUDY 11.3 *(continued)*

---

established to examine the procedures of the Ontario Human Rights Commission, delegations representing various community groups stated that the "process can be coercive and unfair. Claimants argued that sometimes they are specifically told that if they do not accept a settlement, which in their view is unjust, their case will be dismissed by the commission. Since they have no other choice, they feel forced to accept the settlement" (Ontario Human Rights Code Review Task Force, 1992:116). Often, settlements involve the payment of a certain sum of money. Several people believe that such settlements are offensive and unprincipled, as it appears that human rights are being bought and that the underlying questions of discrimination are not being addressed.

This complaint-driven approach is viewed as inadequate in addressing the complex, pervasive, and intractable forms of racism in Canadian society. A re-evaluation of the "effectiveness of a human rights system that is based on a model developed in the 1960's" (Mendes, 1997:2.v.) is clearly called for. Analyzing statistics for the various commissions, Mendes came to the conclusion that, due to a variety of factors, including the inability to deal with race complaints, there is a general tendency for "race complaints to be treated differently than other complaints ... they are dismissed more frequently than cases based on other grounds of discrimination." He concluded his analysis of human-rights commissions by noting that

> the human-rights system existing in most jurisdictions in Canada is not affording the victims of discrimination the recourse necessary to enforce their rights. In particular, cases of racial discrimination are proving to be too much for the present system to handle. (Mendes, 1997)

Two other reviews of the structure of human-rights commissions in Ontario and British Columbia have suggested a radical reorganization of the commissions and their operations (Ontario Human Rights Code Review Task Force, 1992; Black, 1994).

In each of the above government responses to racism, the state failed to provide adequate mechanisms for addressing the inequities experienced by racial-minority communities. The liberal discourses on multiculturalism, rights, and equality are largely framed on a passive model of state intervention that ignores collective or group rights based on race. Despite the espousal of equality as a guiding principle, these policies do not offer a means of ensuring social justice and equity for people of colour (St. Lewis, 1996; Goldberg, 1993).

In addition to its assumed role of providing leadership in combating racism and inequality in society and as a guarantor of human rights, the state also has a direct role in terms of its responsibility as an

- employer;
- purchaser of goods and services; and
- provider of services.

THE STATE AS EMPLOYER: EMPLOYMENT EQUITY

At the federal level, employment equity became law in 1986 and applies to Crown corporations and federally regulated employers with one hundred or more employees. The purpose of the Employment Equity Act was to "achieve equality in the workplace, and to correct the conditions of disadvantage in employment experienced by designated groups — women, aboriginal peoples, persons with disabilities, and members of visible minorities in Canada" (Employment and Immigration Canada, 1988). Employment equity legislation provided a framework to support a diverse work force. It was intended to change the workplace by identifying systemic barriers in policies and practices that may appear neutral and that, while not necessarily discriminatory in intent, are discriminatory in effect or result. The goal of employment equity was fair treatment and equitable representation throughout the workplace.[7]

Equality in employment means that no one is denied opportunities for reasons that have nothing to do with inherent ability (Abella, 1984). The act required all federally regulated employers to file an annual report with the Canadian Employment and Immigration Commission. The report was to provide information on the representation of all employees and members of **designated groups** (visible minorities, women, persons with disabilities, and Aboriginal peoples) by occupational group and salary range and on those hired, promoted, or terminated. In addition to filing an annual report, employers are required to prepare an annual employment equity plan, including goals and timetables, and to retain this plan for at least three years. The Employment Equity Act was revised and adopted by the Parliament in 1995, strengthening the legislation and bringing the public service, the RCMP, and the military under the purview of the act.

In passing the act, the government cited the need to avoid more bureaucratic regulation and argued that all that was required were procedures involving publicly accessible data collection on individual employers; critical public opinion was to be the driving force for change (Reitz, 1988).

Enforcement by public opinion was not effective. The lack of progress of the designated groups in employment was documented in the 1996 annual report of the Canadian Human Rights Commission, which documented, in stark numbers, the huge gap between the government's commitment to a public service that mirrors the diversity of the Canadian population and its dismal record in promoting minorities.[8] According to a study done by John Samuel for the Canadian Human Rights Commission, in 1995 the availability rate of visible minorities in the Canadian labour force was nearly 12 percent, while in the public service it was only 4.1 percent. In examining some of the reasons for this failure, Senator Noel Kinsella, formerly a senior bureaucrat with Heritage Canada, said, "Institutions act as collective memory carrying forward values, principles and traditions" (Samuel and Karam, 1996).

When the Ontario government repealed the provincial Employment Act (1995), it used the language of enlightenment and constructed a liberal discourse — rationality, progress, individual rights, and responsibilities — replete with code phrases designed to evoke anger against the strategy of employment equity.

The bill called "An Act to Repeal Job Quotas and to Restore Merit-Based Employment Practices" communicated clearly a broader political and ideological agenda that set out to eliminate equity and anti-racism policies and programs. The government's rhetoric represented a vocabulary disassociated from both a historical context and contemporary social conditions. Confronted with the demands of women, Aboriginal peoples, people of colour, and persons with disabilities for the "affirmative" correction of historical injustices, the government became the partisan of equality ("let everyone be treated in the same way"), ignoring the way in which inherited positions of privilege, entitlement, and power are maintained.

The rhetoric of the Ontario government implied that persons of colour (as well as women, persons with disabilities, and Aboriginal peoples) who had been selected or promoted were chosen on the basis of criteria other than merit. The name of the act itself suggested that the employment equity legislation required employers to hire unqualified candidates, and that merit was being judged solely on the basis of the colour of one's skin.

THE STATE AS PURCHASER OF GOODS AND SERVICES: CONTRACT COMPLIANCE

Contract compliance is a method of influencing private companies to implement an employment equity program. Under contract compliance, a vendor's contract is contingent on the existence of an equity program. The penalty for non-compliance is loss of the contract with the federal government.

The federal government has specific criteria governing contract compliance. A company must design and implement a program that will identify and take steps to remove barriers in the selection, hiring, promotion, and training of select minority groups. As in employment equity, compliance is largely voluntary; each company is expected to establish special programs in areas where imbalances exist (Jain, 1988).

This program can be criticized on many grounds. For example, the equity programs are not legislated and operate at the discretion of government, and government conducts only random audits of companies that have promised to implement employment equity programs. This allows companies to avoid developing a program until an audit occurs. What develops, therefore, is a cycle of delay in which federal bureaucrats and their corporate counterparts negotiate to delay the implementation of employment equity.

Some companies that supply highly specialized services are not audited. Corporate clients are permitted to set their own goals and timetables to match what is considered reasonable for their peculiar settings, but anti-racism is not a high priority for some companies. Since the government has not applied a criterion of success to this process, companies proceed at their own, often slow, pace.

THE STATE AS PROVIDER AND FUNDER OF SERVICES

Communities affected by racial discrimination continue to feel excluded from public services. They also perceive little support in their efforts to develop the community infrastructures and support systems required to meet the needs of their communities (*Equality Now*, 1984). Studies carried out in the past decade on access to government services (Mock and Maseman, 1987) suggest that racial minorities and Aboriginal peoples do not have equal access to or participate adequately in government programs and services.

Notwithstanding this concern, all levels of government for many years have provided some support to racial-minority, community-based service organizations. Generally, however, the funding is in the form of short-term project support. Despite varying levels of support and varying criteria, this support is a recognition by the state that racial-minority organizations play a critical role in ensuring that the community derives equal benefit from public service.

From one perspective, such support is an appropriate bridging strategy, until all communities are adequately served by public structures and programs. On the other hand, it encourages the development of parallel services that existing public institutions should be offering. The question of whether satisfactory service can be effected only by separate provision continues to be debated. Would separate service agencies along racial lines meet minority needs, or would they further fragment the state's delivery system? Would matching rather than mixing racial clients provide more emphatic help to people in need? Is "separate services" a euphemism for segregation?

Another concern is that in providing support to racial-minority organizations, the level of public support is grossly deficient. Separate services have become synonymous with inferior services. Expecting far too much for far too little, minority organizations have been exploited by the state as an expedient way to deliver public services to people of colour (Doyle and Visano, 1987).

Arrangements made within public organizations determine to whom services are provided, facilities are made available, and resources are allocated. The attitudes and actions of those who direct these institutions determine who gets what, where, and when. Since people of colour are generally absent from the key decision-making processes in these organizations and in the delivery of services, to what extent do public institutions treat people of colour less favourably?

Although considerable resources have been expended on the training of public servants in "multiculturalism," "race relations," or "managing diversity," to what extent have the special needs of minorities been identified? And to what extent have they been adequately considered and provided for? To what extent have the resources of the state been reallocated in favour of minorities as part of a commitment to equity? Within a framework of genuine, equal sharing of public resources, it appears that the scale on which this has been done by any state agency or institution in Canada is insignificant in addressing the imbalances caused by racially discriminatory policies, programs, and practices.

Initiatives taken to measure and address racial minorities' inequalities of access to public programs and services in Canada have been tentative and piecemeal.

CONCLUSION

In many ways, the role of the State in responding to issues of racism and inequality has had to fit within the context of an imagined national culture consisting of a unique blend of English and French cultures, and an identity built on English and French values. As a result, three categories of citizens were recognized: English Canadians, French Canadians, and "others" (Fleras and Elliott, 1992). Only the first two groups had constitutional rights. The construction of undesirable "otherness" has persisted as Canadians have continued to struggle for a national identity (Mackey, 1996). This notion of "otherness" can be seen from three interlocking perspectives:

- "Otherness" provides the dominant White culture with unmarked, invisible privilege and power;
- Issues are deflected in a way which suggests that these "others" threaten the democratic fabric of Canadian society;
- There is a reassertion of individual rights and identity over collective identity and group rights.

Those positioned within the privileged discourses and intent on maintaining their power assert their claim on the liberal values of individualism, equal opportunities, tolerance, and so on. In so doing, they construct a view of ethno-racial minorities who do not share these values and therefore are outside the boundaries of the common culture of the state. Anglo-European culture dominance asserts its entitlement and authority, defining all others as "ethnics," "minorities," "immigrants," and "visible minorities," who are then marginalized and rendered subordinate to its unmarked centre. The power elite determines which differences and which similarities are allowed in the public domain (Suvendrini and Pugliese, 1997; Mackey, 1996). That authority "to define crucial homogeneities and differences" is defended within the liberal discourse of equality and progress (Asad, 1979:627).

For many Canadians, the increasing pluralism of Canadian society poses a threat to the way they have imagined and constructed Canadian identity. They hold on to an image of Canada distinguished from other countries, particularly the United States, by its French–English duality.

Many Anglo-Canadians and others fear that multiculturalism will never provide a solution to the issue of national identity. Canadians want to resolve French–English tensions without having to address the multicultural issue of identity. One scholar argued that Canada is a nation in which "state-sanctioned proliferation of cultural difference itself is seen to be its defining characteristic" (Mackey, 1996:11).

Multiculturalism as state policy embraces, in theory, the notion of cultural and racial diversity. Ethno-racial minorities are declared to be part of the "imagined" community of Canada (Anderson, 1983).[9] However, in reality, the policy and practice of multiculturalism continues to position certain ethno-racial groups at the margins rather than in the mainstream of public culture and national identity.

The "symbolic multiculturalism" of state policy does not consider the necessity of restructuring or the need for a reconceptualization of the power relations between cultural and racial communities based on the premise that communities and societies do not exist autonomously but are deeply woven together in a web of interrelationships.

Liberal pluralist discourse is unable to move beyond "tolerance," "sensitivity," or "understanding" of the "others." The state's construction of symbolic multiculturalism as a mechanism for maintaining the status quo can be seen in many forms of public discourse around issues of race, culture, difference, politics, and identity. This discourse is not restricted to the public declarations of policy-makers, legislators, and bureaucrats. It is also reflected in the language and practices employed by the state through its institutions and systems, including justice and law enforcement, print and electronic media, cultural and educational institutions, and public-sector corporations (Tator et al., 1998).

Minorities are seldom invited into the mainstream discourse of Canadian public–core–common culture. The select few are considered to be models and are imagined as being different from others of their kind. In contrast, the airing of diverse perspectives by people of colour on issues related to multiculturalism and racism is commonly dismissed, deflected, or ignored. In a liberal democracy, justice and equality are already assumed to exist. Therefore, ethno-racial minorities' demands for access and inclusion are seen as "radical," "unreasonable," "undemocratic," and a threat to cherished democratic, liberal values. The small gains made by minorities and women are seen by the dominant groups as being "too expensive" economically and ideologically. Dissent by the oppressed is considered disruptive and dangerous.

The "symbolic multiculturalism" of state policies holds to a paradigm of pluralism premised on a hierarchical order of cultures that under certain conditions "allows" or "tolerates" non-dominant cultures to participate in the dominant culture. Such an approach imagines minority communities as "special-interest groups," not as active and full participants in the state and part of its shared history. This paradigm represents notions of tolerance and accommodation, but not of equity and justice. It holds to a unified and static concept of identities and communities as fixed sets of experiences, meanings, and practices rather than of identities as dynamic, fluid, multiple, and historically situated. In summary, state policies continue to be largely centred on the maintenance of the status quo.

SUMMARY

This chapter has analyzed the roles and functions of the state as law-giver, policy-maker, employer, purchaser, and provider of goods and services. It has argued that public policies, including the Canadian Multiculturalism Act, the Canadian Charter of Rights and Freedoms, and human-rights codes and commissions have been inadequate instruments to address racial inequality in Canadian society. The discourse of liberalism underlying these policies — the rhetoric of rights, reasonableness, freedoms, equality, standards, tolerance, understanding, and so forth, that is incorporated into all of these state responses to some extent — is in itself a limiting factor in the struggle to control racism.

Although these state responses are vastly different from the more overtly racist and assimilationist policies of earlier governments, the ideology and discourse of racism that are deeply embedded in the collective belief, value, and normative system of Canadian society affect the way in which laws are interpreted and implemented. The Multiculturalism Act, the Employment Equity Act, and the Charter of Rights and Freedoms and human-rights commissions may be significant steps on the path to racial equality, but they are not instruments of societal transformation. Despite the government's recognition of ethno-racial diversity through public policies on multiculturalism, minority rights, and equity, social inequality not only continues to operate but is actually reproduced and legitimated through the state.

The notions of tolerance, accommodation, diversity, and equality are woven into the rhetoric of federal, provincial, and municipal politicians and other public authorities. At the same time, their discourses, policies, and practices reflect a deep ambivalence to undertaking the tasks required to attain racial equity. This conflict has shaped the way in which state policies have been constituted and the way in which they have been implemented.

This analysis points to a central paradox of modern liberal societies, first identified by Goldberg (1993). As modernity increasingly commits itself to the ideals and principles of equality, tolerance, and freedom, new racial identities and new forms of racism and exclusion proliferate.

Racialized public discourses concerning multiculturalism, rights and freedoms, and employment equity tend to employ ill-defined ideas and implicit notions regarding culture, differences, race, and racism, which when operationalized function socially and politically to marginalize ethno-racial minorities. Democratic racism is manifested in both subtle and overt forms of the discourse that shapes the very policies and practices designed to ameliorate racial inequality.

NOTES

1. Most provinces in Canada have appointed an ombudsperson to handle the complaints of citizens who believe they have been treated unjustly by an agency of government. The office of the ombudsperson cannot deal with individual complaints of racism, but it has investigated complaints against provincial human-rights commissions, primarily regarding long delays in their management of cases.

2. The emphasis is on passive rather than active verbs:

> (1) a. *recognize and promote* the understanding that multiculturalism reflects the cultural and racial diversity of Canadian society and acknowledges the freedom of all members of Canadian society to preserve, enhance and share their cultural heritage;
> b. *recognize and promote* the understanding of multiculturalism is a fundamental characteristic of the Canadian heritage and identity and that it provides an invaluable resource in the shaping of Canada's future;
> c. *promote* the full and equitable participation of individuals and communities of all origins in the continuing evolution and shaping of all aspects of Canadian society and assist them in the elimination of any barrier to such participation;
> d. *recognize* the existence of communities whose members share a common origin and their historic contribution to Canadian society, and enhance their development;
> e. *ensure* that all individuals receive equal treatment and equal protection under the law, while respecting and valuing their diversity;
> f. *encourage and assist* the social, cultural, economic and political institutions of Canada to be both respectful and inclusive of Canada's multicultural character;
> g. *promote* the understanding and creativity that arise from the interaction between individuals and communities of different origins;
> h. *foster* the recognition and appreciation of the diverse cultures of Canadian society and promote the reflection and evolving expressions of those cultures;
> i. *preserve and enhance* the use of languages other than English and French, while strengthening the status and use of official languages of Canada; and
> j. *advance* multiculturalism throughout Canada in harmony with the national commitment to the official languages of Canada.

> (2) It is further declared to be the policy of the government of Canada that all federal institutions shall
> a. *ensure* that Canadians of all origins have an equal opportunity to obtain employment and advancement in those institutions;
> b. *promote* policies, programs and practices that enhance the ability of individuals and communities of all origins to contribute to the continuing evolution of Canada;
> c. *promote* policies, programs and practices that enhance the understanding of and respect for diversity of the members of Canadian society;
> d. *collect* statistical data in order to enable the development of policies, programs and practices that are sensitive and responsive to the multicultural reality of Canada;
> e. *make use*, as appropriate, of the language skills and cultural understanding of individuals of all origins; and
> f. generally, carry on their activities in a manner that is sensitive and responsive to the multicultural reality of Canada. (Canadian Heritage — Multiculturalism Program, 1990)

3. The Charter has not been extensively used in race cases. For a complete review, see Mendes (1997).
4. Because of the far-reaching significance of the equality rights guaranteed in section 15, the federal and provincial governments gave themselves three years to change their laws and policies to comply with the Charter. Thus, while the rest of the Charter came into effect in 1982, section 15 came into effect three years later.

5. It is indeed paradoxical that the Charter, with all its identifiable weaknesses, has nevertheless been perceived negatively by people who fear its power. Judge Rosalie Abella, for example, notes that "in less than a generation, this remedy for discrimination has been seen to be sufficiently powerful that people struggle urgently to find a remedy from equality. How ironic that 'equality-seeker' has become a pejorative term, denoting someone whose claim to fairness is a menace to the nation's economy and psyche" (*Toronto Star*, October 26:A20).

6. The Charter Challenges Program, supported by the federal government, provides some financial assistance to disadvantaged groups who wish to pursue Charter cases.

7. Equitable representation depends on the following factors: the number of designated group members in the working-age population in a certain geographical area, the number of trained or skilled members who are employable or can be readily available, and the equal opportunities for change that exist in each workplace.

8. In March 1987, visible minorities made up 2.7 percent of Canada's public service and 6.3 percent of the Canadian population. By March 1996, their share of government employment had risen to 4.5 percent, but their representation in the population was 13 percent. In management, minorities held only 2.3 percent of the executive positions in the public service (Samuel and Karam, 1996).

9. Anderson used the term "imagined community" to define the concept of "nation." A nation is "imagined" because the members of even a very small state do not know each other, yet in "the minds of each lives the image of their communion" (1983:15). Moreover, a nation is imagined as a community because "regardless of the actual inequality and exploitation that may prevail ... the nation is always conceived as a deep, horizontal comradeship" (1983:16).

REFERENCES

Abella, R. (1984). *Equality in Employment: The Report of the Commission on Equality in Employment*. Ottawa: Supply and Services Canada.

Anderson, B. (1983). *Imagined Communities*. London: Verso.

Angel, S. (1988). "The Multiculturalism Act of 1988." *Multiculturalism* 11(3):25–27.

Asad, T. (1979). "Anthropology and the Analysis of Ideology." *Man* 14:607–27.

Bhabha H.K. (1990). "The Third Space." In Jonathan Rutherford (ed.), *Identity: Community Culture and Difference*. London: Lawrence and Wishart. 207–21.

Black, B. (1994). *Report on Human Rights in British Columbia*. B.C. Human Rights Review, Communications Branch, Ministry Responsible for Multiculturalism and Human Rights. Government of British Columbia.

Calof, J. (1997). "The Role of Ethnic Minorities in Building a Strong Economy and a More Vital Country." In A. Cardoza and L. Musto (eds.), *The Battle over Multiculturalism: Does It Help or Hinder Canadian Identity?* Ottawa: Pearson-Shoyama Institute.

Canadian Heritage — Multiculturalism Program. (1990). *The Canadian Multiculturalism Act: A Guide for Canadians*. Ottawa: Multiculturalism and Citizenship Canada. Excerpt on page 350 reproduced with the permission of the Minister of Public Works and Government Services Canada and the Minister of Canadian Heritage, 1999.

Corporate Policy Branch of Multiculturalism and Citizenship Canada. (1988). "Canadian Multiculturalism Act Briefing Book: Clause by Clause Analysis." Unpublished document released under Access to Information Act.

Creese, G. (1993–94). "The Sociology of British Columbia." *BC Studies* Special Issue no. 100 (Winter).

Day, S. (1990). *Human Rights in Canada: Into the 1990s and Beyond*. Ottawa: Human Rights Research and Education Centre.

Doyle, R., and L. Visano. (1987). *Access to Health and Social Services for Members of Diverse Cultural and Racial Groups*. Toronto: Social Planning Council.

Duclos, N. (1990). "Lessons of Difference: Feminist Theory on Cultural Diversity." *Buffalo Law Review* 38:325.

Employment and Immigration Canada. (1988). *Annual Report, Employment Equity Act*. Ottawa: Minister of Supply and Services.

Equality Now. (1984). Report of the Special Committee on Visible Minorities in Canadian Society. Ottawa: Government of Canada.

Fleras, A., and J.L. Elliott. (1992). *Multiculturalism in Canada: The Challenge of Diversity*. Scarborough, ON: Nelson.

———. (1996). *Unequal Relations: An Introduction to Race, Ethnic and Aboriginal Dynamics in Canada*. 2nd ed. Scarborough, ON: Prentice Hall.

Gibson, D. (1985). "Protection of Minority Rights under the Canadian Charter of Rights and Freedoms." In N. Nelville and A. Kornberg (eds.), *Minorities and the Canadian State*. Oakville, ON: Mosaic Press.

Goldberg, D. (1993). *Racist Culture: Philosophy and the Politics of Meaning*. Oxford: Blackwell.

——— (ed). (1994). *Multiculturalism: A Critical Reader*. Cambridge, MA: Blackwell.

Harding, S. (1995). "Multiculturalism in Australia: Moving Race/Ethnic Relations from Extermination to Celebration?" *Race, Gender, and Class* 3(1)(Fall):7–26.

Itwaru, A., and N. Ksonzek. (1994). *Closed Entrances: Canadian Culture and Imperialism*. Toronto: TSAR.

Jain, H. (1988). "Affirmative Action Employment Equity Programmes and Visible Minorities in Canada." *Currents: Readings in Race Relations* 5(1)(4):3.

James, C. (1995). "Multiculturalism and Anti-Racism Education in Canada." *Race, Gender and Class: An Interdisciplinary and Multicultural Journal* 2(3)(Spring):31–48.

Kallen, E. (1982). "Ethnicity and Human Rights in Canada." In P. Li, (ed.), *Race and Ethnic Relations in Canada*. Toronto: Oxford University Press.

Kobayashi, A. (1990). "Racism and the Law." *Urban Geography* 11(5):447–73.

Mackey, E. (1996). "Managing and Imagining Diversity: Multiculturalism and the Construction of National Identity in Canada." D.Phil. Social Anthropology, University of Sussex.

Matas, D. (1990). "The Charter and Racism." *Constitutional Forum* 2:82.

Mendes, E. (ed.). (1997) *Racial Discrimination and the Law: Law and Practice*. Toronto: Carswell.

Mirchandani, K., and E. Tastsoglou. (forthcoming). "Toward a Diversity beyond Tolerance." *Journal of Status in Political Economy*.

Mock, K., and V. Maseman. (1987). *Access to Government Services*. Toronto: Ontario Ministry of Citizenship.

Moodley, K. (1983). "Canadian Multiculturalism as Ideology." *Ethnic and Racial Studies* 6(3):320–31.

Mullard, C. (1982). "Multiracial Education in Britain: From Assimilation to Cultural Pluralism." In J. Tierney (ed.), *Race, Migration and Schooling*. London: Holt, Rinehart and Winston.

Multiculturalism and Citizenship Canada. (1989–90). *Annual Report of the Operation of the Canadian Multiculturalism Act*. Ottawa.

Ontario Human Rights Code Review Task Force. (1992). *Achieving Equality: A Report on Human Rights Reform*. Toronto: Ministry of Citizenship.

Reitz, J. (1988). "Less Racial Discrimination in Canada, or Simply Less Racial Conflict? Implications of Comparisons with Britain." *Canadian Public Policy* 14(4):424–41.

Samuel, T.J., and A. Karam. (1996). "Employment Equity and Visible Minorities in the Federal Workforce." Paper presented at the Symposium on Immigration and Integration. Montreal: CERIS.

St. Lewis, J. (1996). "Race, Racism and the Justice System." In C. James (ed.), *Perspectives on Racism and the Human Services Sector*. Toronto: University of Toronto Press. 104–19.

Suvendrini, P., and J. Pugliese. (1997). "Racial Suicide: The Re-Licensing of Racism in Australia." *Race and Class* 39(2)(October–December):1–19.

Tator, C., F. Henry, and W. Mattis. (1998). *Racism in the Arts: Case Studies of Controversy and Conflict*. Toronto: University of Toronto.

Taylor, C. (1994). "Examining the Politics of Recognition." In A. Gutman (ed.), *Multiculturalism*. Princeton, NJ: Princeton University Press.

Tepper, E. (1988). "Changing Canada: The Institutional Response to Polyethnicity." In *Review of Demography and Its Implications for Economic and Social Policy*. Ottawa: Carleton University.

Walcott, R. (1993). "Critiquing Canadian Multiculturalism: Towards an Anti-racist Agenda." Master's thesis, Graduate Department of Education, York University.

Wallace, M. (1994). "The Search for the 'Good Enough' Mammy: Multiculturalism, Popular Culture and Psychoanalysis." In D. Goldberg (ed.), *Multiculturalism: A Critical Reader*. Cambridge, MA: Blackwell. 259–68.

Walzer, M. (1997). *On Toleration*. New Haven, CT: Yale University Press.

Yalden, M. (1990). "Canadian Human Rights and Multiculturalism." *Currents: Readings in Race Relations* (Toronto) 6(1):2.

Chapter 12

▼▼▼▼▼▼▼▼▼▼▼▼▼

Organizational Resistance to Anti-Racism

White people still invite people of colour to participate in social actions as subordinate to the organization as a whole. The bureaucratic machinery to ensure continuity is withheld from people of colour. We remain a peripheral validation of the lack of racism in White organizations. (Maracle, 1993:128)

This chapter examines change within institutions and institutions' effectiveness in dismantling racism within their organizations. Various forms of organizational resistance are analyzed as examples of institutionally specific forms of democratic racism. These are the commonly used mechanisms that have been employed in organizations to maintain racist behaviour and practices and to resist, evade, or sabotage anti-racism initiatives. The chapter concludes by noting that a race-conscious model of organizations is required and by describing three models of organizational change: assimilationist, multicultural, and anti-racist.

INTRODUCTION

An organization can be defined in various ways: in terms of its structure, its function, or a multitude of other characteristics. For our purposes, "organization" is defined as a sociopolitical system in which people act together under an imposed structure and ideology and use a specific set of technologies to achieve a specific objective. Henry Giroux has clarified the importance of ideology in organizational life, observing:

Ideology has to be conceived as both source and effect of social and institutional practices as they operate within a society that is characterized by relations of domination, a society in which men and women are basically unfree in both objective and subjective terms. (Giroux, 1988)

The dominant theme of this definition is that an organization is a social system in which people do specific jobs. An important aspect of the definition is the fact that an organization is a social construct; it does not have a physical existence. Furthermore, an organization is a series of subsystems that are inextricably linked. A change in any one of the subsystems affects the entire organization.

Organizations are social systems within which individuals act through a network of social relations. Behaviours in this social system are influenced by the organization's values, the values of the individuals within the organization, their functional responsibilities, and the society's prevailing ideology, which determines what is considered "right" and "proper." One of the important characteristics of organizations is that they resist change. This aspect of organizational behaviour is discussed in this chapter.

RESISTANCE TO CHANGE[1]

Resistance is human behaviour that either actively or passively attempts to undermine any aspect of the change initiative. The ideology of democratic racism, which sustains two conflicting values — one that espouses fairness, equity, tolerance, and justice; another that maintains and reproduces racism — has been instrumental in sabotaging efforts to eradicate racism. The opposition shows itself not through an overt display of intolerance but through subtle, sustained, and refined resistance to anti-racism.

The arguments of democratic racism may be applied at a number of points and take many forms. Figure 12.1 shows the points at which resistance may occur.

While resistance is generic to all large-scale change initiatives, a major factor of resistance to anti-racism change is rooted in the extent to which organizational leaders believe that "anti-racism" is a legitimate force to motivate change. Resistance to anti-racism initiatives in organizations takes many forms:

1. Reluctance to create an anti-racist vision
2. Lack of commitment
3. Inadequate policies
4. Inadequate training
5. Lack of representation
6. Limited access to goods, programs, and services
7. Absence of sanctions
8. Lack of individual accountability
9. Structural rigidity
10. Ineffective monitoring and evaluation mechanisms
11. Insufficient resources
12. Tokenism
13. Minority change agents
14. Lack of organizational accountability
15. Limited public accountability
16. Deceptive dominant discourses

Figure 12.1

THE CYCLE OF RESISTANCE

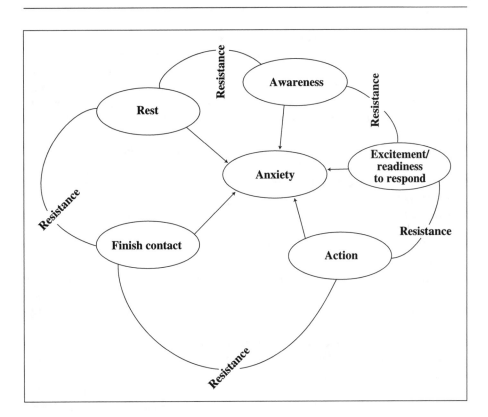

RELUCTANCE TO CREATE AN ANTI-RACIST VISION

The need for a clear and concise vision statement is critical to the success of an organization. A vision statement sets out the organization's goal and binds it and its members to work toward achieving that goal.

Very few of the organizations examined earlier in this book have explicitly incorporated anti-racism in their visions. Such an omission occurs partly because anti-racism is not considered important to the overall mandate of the organization. When an organization consciously omits anti-racism from its vision statement, it clearly wishes to retain a reactive stance to anti-racism. Even if the organization has progressive programs, the absence of a vision statement shaped by anti-racism principles and goals results in an inadequate framework for the changes required. When an organization responds purely on the basis of political or social pressures, it is often unwilling to link the change process to its mandate. On the other hand, anti-racism as a guiding organizational framework suggests a commitment to examine not only programs and practices, but also the ideology motivating those programs and practices.

LACK OF COMMITMENT

A commitment to anti-racism is a desire on the part of decision-makers and power-brokers to act consistently and systematically to challenge and redress racism. Lack of commitment is illustrated in many ways; for example, many organizations embark on anti-racism initiatives through coercion rather than by design. Thus, forces either within the organization or outside it demand a response in order for the organization to maintain its credibility.

A common form of coercion is a race-related complaint to a human-rights commission. Many of these complaints originate in organizations whose managers maintain that "there are no problems here" — an approach that results either from willful blindness or from ignorance of the manifestations of racism in organizations. The coercion resulting from the settlement of a human-rights case does not require an organization to change its ideology, but only to create programs or develop practices that give the appearance of change.

Lack of commitment is demonstrated when formal studies exposing racism in an organization result in management adopting a defensive position. This defensiveness takes various forms: discrediting the findings, suggesting that the researchers misinterpreted the mandate or overstepped the boundaries of the project, and "sanitizing" the results so that they do not appear so "negative." The latter strategy allows management to practise damage control by deflecting attention from the issue. A striking example of this strategy occurred when a government-ministry unit asked that the word "racism" be removed from a final report investigating employee complaints of racial discrimination.[2]

Often, vision statements are vague, "motherhood" statements of high-sounding principles that are difficult to put into practice. The intent of the organization (to maintain the status quo) is often masked in the vision statement because the organization has mastered the vocabulary of multiculturalism. The words become empty promises, nothing more than symbolic gestures. Thus, the commitment to anti-racism rarely goes further than a *verbal* commitment to equality, which in most cases means equality of opportunity rather than a commitment to action and equity.

None of the organizations examined in the previous chapters was committed to both the process and the content of anti-racism change. Although all sectors of society have responded to the pressures motivating change, organizational structures have remained untouched; the ideological underpinnings of their actions have remained intact.

Of those organizations that do recognize the need to respond to racism, most choose not to use the term anti-racism. They prefer instead labels such as "multiculturalism," "managing diversity," and "race relations."

Their strategy may be identified as one of resistance. Avoiding the term "anti-racism" circumvents the need to identify "racism."

Adopting euphemisms provides the organization with a rationale for limiting its responses to cosmetic changes. Multicultural approaches suggest that gaining an understanding of other cultures is sufficient to combat racism. Diversity labels cushion the organization by allowing it to hide behind the rationalization that managing diversity is all that is required. Such a view implies that racism results from diversity, and that it can be managed. Thus, racism is considered something to be "managed," not necessarily opposed. A more constructive approach would be one in which racism is acknowledged and anti-racist strategies are adopted.

Resistance to anti-racism is often very subtle. It may entail the setting of unrealistic goals. It may show itself in the context of last-minute, crisis-oriented planning, such as appending anti-racism plans to other plans, after all the other plans have been made. It may exist in the simplistic "fix it now" mentality; and it may show its preference for delay in making requests for how-to guides and more data.

INADEQUATE POLICIES

In all areas of organizational and institutional life, there is an intrinsic relationship between policy and practice. Every institution is governed by a policy, "whether stated or unstated" (Brandt, 1986:103). Although Brandt found no organization with an explicitly racist policy, strong evidence of its existence indicated covert racist policies that reflected deeply entrenched values, ideals, and assumptions. In each institution Brandt studied, racist ideologies influenced policies as well as individual behaviours and organizational practices.

In reviewing the formation of policies aimed at eliminating racism in the past two decades in Canada, it is possible to conclude that policies do not always lead to substantive and sustained change. Many of the policy documents are framed in the context of racial and cultural diversity and pluralism. Issues are conceptualized in terms of improving "relations" between racial and ethno-cultural groups, and there is often a reliance on rhetoric and euphemisms such as "race and ethnic relations" and "multicultural and race relations." Policy statements often lack specificity and clarity in relation to their goals, objectives, and implementation strategies.

For example, the focus of both the policy and policy implementation in many educational agencies is, on the one hand, the "needs" of racial- and cultural-minority students, and on the other hand, the "problems" of racial-minority students. Thus, it is not the educational system that is the "problem"; the problem is the difficulties that racial-minority students create for the system. The language of many of the policies suggests a preoccupation with creating, promoting, and encouraging greater tolerance, understanding, and harmony among racial-minority students and staff, rather than ensuring fairness and equity as the outcomes.

A survey of policy development and implementation sponsored by the Ontario Ministry of Education (Mock and Masemann, 1989) found that 39 boards had a policy and that 25 boards were currently developing policies. A study of these policies revealed that most school boards preferred positive language in the policy document and that there was a strong reluctance to refer to "anti-racist education."

Many educators have viewed the concept of anti-racism as too polemical and political and leading to unnecessary conflict and resistance (Tator and Henry, 1991). Instead, policy statements and documents choose to ignore, deny, and deflect the reality and persistence of racism in educational structures, processes, and ideologies.

A study of policy implementation in schools and boards noted that the desired outcome of many race relations policies in boards of education is the maintenance of the status quo — racial harmony — rather than systematic and systemic change (Anderson and Fullan, 1984). But policy-driven goals such as racial harmony, tolerance, and understanding, while appearing positive, avoid the need to deconstruct racist ideology, practices, and procedures.

Even an institution's use of the term "anti-racism" in policy documents does not necessarily ensure that it is supportive of or committed to actions and initiatives that will produce substantive change. In some cases, the issue of racism is framed in such a way that it fails to take into account how racism is specifically linked to the role and function of the organization (such as the school) or institution (for example, a board of education).

Another common weakness of policy documents is that they neglect to delineate the ways in which an anti-racism agenda will be pursued throughout all levels of the organization. The most common flaw, however, is the failure to link the anti-racism policy to the mission and mandate of the organization. For example, policing organizations have developed policies that fail to be explicit about the nature of the problem they are seeking to address. They have also not been specific about the kind of changes expected to occur at the various levels in the policing organization. As a result, many police officers appear to believe that their force's race relations policy is inconsistent with the work of policing and that it does not further the goal of law enforcement, "to serve and protect."

An audit of the Metropolitan Toronto Police Force (Andrews, 1992) found that most of the force's race relations policies, programs, and undertakings were framed in a way that encouraged the view that the force itself did not really require fundamental ideological or structural changes. The report suggested that efforts were mainly directed toward changes that affected only the fringe of the daily operations of policing. It identified attempts to engage in some form of accommodation of differences in the community. However, what was really required was a commitment to changing the values and culture of the institution.

Similarly, policies in human-service agencies do not appear to have transformed those agencies in Canada. For example, although the United Way of Greater Toronto had been involved in promoting multicultural and anti-racist organizational development in its social agencies for more than six years,[3] most of the area's ethno-cultural and racial communities continued to experience an "appalling lack of services" (Medeiros, 1991).

What is the potential for a policy to serve as an agent of individual or institutional change? Policies are perhaps a useful starting point, but policy statements in and of themselves are of limited value in actually combating racism. They cannot function as mechanisms to promote change.

INADEQUATE TRAINING

Training is the development of specific skills to meet policy and program objectives. Most programs for combating racism fail to meet these specifications. By and large, these programs have been ineffective because they treat anti-racism like any other subject — as something to be learned by employees in a three-hour, one-day, or, at most, three-day workshop. Learning about racism is placed in the same category as developing skills to manage a new computer program. Training is commonly delivered by trainers who are inexperienced and unskilled in anti-racism theory and practice. Often the training is unrelated to the daily roles and functions of the participants.

Training has drawn upon many different models, from developing cultural sensitivity and racial awareness to creating management skills for managing diversity and implementing employment equity. Some of these approaches are briefly described below.

Human-Awareness Training

Human-awareness training models perceive the goal of training to be the promotion of positive relations between the organization and groups from different cultural backgrounds. These programs focus on acquiring sensitivity to the values, customs, and practices of different groups. Most race relations training programs use some combination of human-awareness training with cultural-awareness training, and both are based on three false premises. The first assumption is that when people understand the customs of another group, they will be able to deal with them more effectively. Second is the assumption that an understanding of the complexities of culture can be learned in a few hours of training. Third is the assumption that only those who come into daily contact with racial minorities need to be trained.

Cultural-Awareness Training

The goal of cultural-awareness training is similar to that of human-awareness training. It has a strong emphasis on transmitting information about ethnic groups and their cultural patterns. This emphasis on transmitting "snapshots" of cultural information ignores the more important study of the complexities of culture. The crucial problems experienced by people of colour in organizations and institutions are not simply the result of a White lack of understanding of non-European cultures. Cultural-awareness or cross-cultural training commonly ignores the systemic and individual barriers created by racism. It ignores power relations between dominant and subordinate groups. Razack argued that cross-cultural training has tended to rely on a superficial understanding of cultural differences by viewing cultures as monolithic "unchanging essences, innate characteristics — the knowledge of which enables us to predict behaviour" (1998:8).

Race-Awareness Training

The premise of race-awareness training is that racism is a White problem. The purpose of the training is to help participants examine their attitudes and behaviours and understand the implications of their own racism. The participants' energy is directed toward self-examination rather than toward fundamental changes in the structure and ideology of the organization. Self-examination is only the initial phase of problem identification. Effective training should move on to show ways in which the entire organizational ideology can be challenged.

Legislative Compliance

The goal of legislative-compliance training is merely to understand human-rights and employment equity legislation so that the organization and its employees can comply with it. These programs rarely address the issue of racism or seek to change racist attitudes and behaviours.

Managing Diversity

Whereas legislative compliance stresses the avoidance of unlawful discrimination, managing diversity focusses on organizational management. These training programs see racism as simply a management problem, something that can be managed, controlled, and contained. Thus, the emphasis is on changing institutions by providing people-management skills, interviewing skills, and so on. These programs are not designed to bring about a greater understanding of race issues per se, but attempt to relate general understandings about diversity to the professional and practical world of the organization.

Many organizations in Canada have been fearful of even using the term "anti-racism" in their definition of training. For the most part, the objectives of their training are to enhance sensitivity and understanding, to provide ethno-racial information on diverse groups, or to provide knowledge and tools to manage employment equity programs. Basic to these approaches is the view that racism stems simply from a failure of Whites to understand Blacks and other groups. Many organizations feel that once they have offered such training, they have met the goals of an anti-racist organization.

A further flaw in many of the training programs is that the initiative is introduced into an organizational environment that is not particularly supportive. As a result, it is usually front-line staff who receive the training. Thus, training is generally provided to new police recruits, teachers, and human-service providers, but rarely to supervisors and senior managers.

Little research on training has occurred in Canada. The evidence from the United Kingdom and the United States, however, as well as the experience of anti-racist trainers in Canada, suggests that training as currently constituted has little chance of success in creating an anti-racist environment. In Canada, police–race relations training has been studied by Ungerleider and McGregor (1992), who examined studies of interventions designed to "change the attitudes and behaviours of police and military personnel towards minority groups." The study found that a small measure of attitudinal or behaviourial change was exhibited by little more than half of the training participants. In many instances, however, the impact of the training was minimal, compared with the effects of learning by experience, by absorbing the values of the occupational culture, and other factors.

Training is perhaps the most common institutional response to racism. It is often used by organizations because it is an easy way to show that some action is being taken to improve the organizational climate for racial-minority members. However, it does little to change the ideology that creates the framework within which the organization operates. That ideology is, for the most part, drawn from and influenced by the value system of the larger, mainstream society.

The value conflict that characterizes democratic racism is as evident in organizations as it is in the wider society of which they are a part. Training does not challenge that ideology; at best, it tinkers with it. Training is merely an organizational mechanism to adjust to the changing environment without changing or transforming any aspect of it. Thus, it is an essential element of an assimilationist organizational model, but it does little to move an organization toward anti-racism.

LACK OF REPRESENTATION

The evidence of widespread and systemic racial discrimination in employment in the public and private sectors is inimical to the fundamental tenets of a liberal democratic society. However, it is in this area of organizational change that resistance is most evident. Even *proposed* race-conscious measures generate enormous tension, hostility, and dissension within organizations.

In the limited number of institutions in which either anti-racism or employment equity programs are in place — such as some boards of education, universities, and police forces — there have been negative reactions, especially from White males. With the implementation of the

Employment Equity Act and the contract compliance program at the federal level of government, it is clear that huge obstacles will be faced. The inadequacy of the legislative and regulatory requirements, the lack of monitoring of implementation of employment equity programs, and weak enforcement mechanisms are some of the significant flaws in the current approach to equity. Even more problematic is the powerful backlash to these initiatives, across every sector, manifested in the attitudes and behaviours of many White male able-bodied employers, managers, and staff. Yet a further tension in the effective implementation of employment equity, as well as other public policies such as multiculturalism, is the demands of some White ethnic groups, religious minorities, gays and lesbians, among other marginalized groups, for public recognition of their distinctive identities, needs, and rights (Kymlicka, 1998).

In many institutions, such as universities, the media, police forces, and other public-sector agencies, initiatives designed to fundamentally alter discriminatory barriers are rigorously opposed. Resistance is framed within the ideological construct of a set of beliefs that rationalize and justify the maintenance of the status quo. Efforts to increase the representation of people of colour in the work force, as well as in appointments to boards, commissions, and other public bodies, are thus deflected.

An example of this type of resistance occurred in the Toronto Fire Department. Over 90 percent of the department's employees in the 1990s were White males. To redress this situation, the personnel committee of the Toronto City Council recommended that the department give preference in the hiring of thirteen *qualified* women and racial-minority candidates, ahead of the White men who had scored slightly higher in the qualification process. Despite the facts that the thirteen candidates were drawn from a pool of 140 fully qualified individuals selected from four thousand applicants and that all the candidates had passed the physical, health, and aptitude tests, the chief of the department protested vigorously. The motion was defeated by city council. Two years later, the Ontario Human Rights Commission filed a complaint accusing the union that represents Toronto firefighters of using its influence to block the employment of women and people of colour and creating a "poisoned work environment." Many of the arguments against employment equity used by the firefighters, the media, and more recently the Ontario government in its rescinding of the Employment Equity Act, were based on the following myths.

Employment Equity Is Reverse Discrimination.

According to this view, employment equity requires employers to discriminate against better-qualified Whites and gives an unfair advantage to people of colour. However, what is required is not reverse discrimination but the end of a long history of employment practices that result in preferential treatment for White males.

Employment Equity Ignores the Merit Principle.

This myth is perhaps the most widely believed and promoted. It is based on the assumption that employment equity and other anti-discrimination measures will result in the hiring and appointment of unqualified individuals and bring an end to the merit principle. In reality, however, equity programs do not require the abandonment of standards and qualifications. Rather, they eliminate irrelevant criteria such as the colour of one's skin, cultural background, disability, and gender.

Employment Equity Stigmatizes Minorities.

According to this misconception, minorities will never know if they have been selected on the basis of their qualifications or because of their group membership. One could argue that White males for two hundred years should have been asking themselves the same question. Implicit in the above assumption is the perception that there are no meritorious persons in this group. As one observer noted,

> Do all those corporate directors, bankers, etc., who got their job for extra-neous reasons — first because they were somebody's son, second, because they were male, third because they were Protestant, and fourth because they were White — feel demeaned thereby? It would be interesting to ask them — or to ask the same question of those doctors who managed to get into good medical schools because there were quotas keeping out Jews, the skilled tradesmen who were admitted to the union because two members of their families recommended them and so on. (Green, 1981:79)

Clearly implicit in the standard critique of these pro-active programs is the notion that being rewarded is the natural result of being part of the majority or the elite. Rewards are only demeaning when one is a member of a minority or a marginalized group (for example, women).

Equality Is Best Achieved through the Free Market.

Although abundant evidence demonstrates that the free market does not lead to equality (Abella, 1984), this view is still widely held. However, at the current pace of change it would take women and minorities hundreds of years to achieve equality with White able-bodied males. The reliance on slow measures such as education, information sharing, and dialogue with employers will not reverse the centuries of bias and disadvantage that are built into employment systems and are generally invisible to all but those who suffer from their adverse impacts.

Fairness Is Best Achieved by Treating Everyone in the Same Way.

Opponents of equity measures argue that in a democratic society, treating everyone equally is sufficient to ensure fairness in the workplace. However, as Abella pointed out, "We now know that to treat everyone in the same way may offend the notion of equality"(1984:3). She suggested that ignoring differences and refusing to accommodate them is a denial of equal access and opportunity; it is discrimination.

Employment Equity Means Hiring by Quotas.

Although mandatory quotas are not required in employment equity programs, a widespread perception exists that governments require specific numbers of racial minorities to be hired, promoted, or appointed in specific organizations. Instead, employment equity in Canada requires employers to set goals for their organization, taking into account the number of qualified individuals from target groups that are available in the potential workforce as well as the composition of the internal workforce. Flexible goals and timetables are used to establish benchmarks toward representative hiring and promotion.

Finally, concerning employment equity as a strategy to eliminate racism, there is some doubt about its efficacy in achieving this goal. The experience of the authors suggests that employment equity measures generate such a racist backlash that many people of colour suffer even greater discrimination after their introduction. Moreover, employment equity programs include other designated groups (women, Aboriginal peoples, people with disabilities), so the potential for competition among these groups for the limited number of available positions is very high. Thus, as a strategy for dealing with racism, employment equity must be combined with other approaches to be effective.

LIMITED ACCESS TO GOODS, PROGRAMS, AND SERVICES

The lack of access to goods and services has been illustrated in the chapters dealing with institutional racism. The lack of support for ethno-racial agencies in the human-service delivery system is an example of the failure of government and other funding bodies to address racism in the mainstream delivery system. Another manifestation of the lack of access to goods, programs, and services is the power of mainstream cultural and arts organizations to marginalize and exclude racial minorities in the production and transmission of literature, music, visual art, dance, theatre, and film. The Eurocentric funding criteria and priorities of arts councils relegate artists of colour to the margins of the dominant culture. The streaming of Black students in schools and bias in curricula and teaching methods further demonstrate the lack of access and equity for racial minorities in the educational system. The absence of people of colour in print and electronic media organizations, and the racialization of their communities in the images and stories transmitted by the mainstream media, reinforce racism in Canadian institutions.

ABSENCE OF SANCTIONS

Rewards and sanctions are important ways of changing behaviour in organizations. No organizations in Canada, however, are known to impose wage sanctions on staff or management for racist behaviour. Typically, the sanctions that do exist are those mandated by race relations or anti-racism policies, but few of them include staff accountability mechanisms. Even where anti-racism policies exist, adequate sanctions have been lacking; and, where sanctions are in place, they tend to be weak and ineffective.

In the early 1990s, the Ontario Human Rights Commission instituted a system authorizing organizations to conduct internal investigations of complaints based on prohibited grounds of discrimination. Organizations are free to develop strategies to respond to such complaints as they see fit. Unfortunately, most organizations do not have the expertise to conduct such investigations; moreover, complaints, unless they are serious, are likely to be dismissed. Sanctions are likely to be inadequate, and continuous monitoring may be non-existent. In some situations, the victim of discrimination may be punished and labelled a troublemaker.

LACK OF INDIVIDUAL ACCOUNTABILITY

Many organizations assume that their members are fair-minded — that they subscribe to the principles of equity and equality of treatment. This assumption leads to a lack of individual accountability. Few organizations require their employees to be held accountable for racist behaviour. Even organizations that have an anti-racism policy believe that their employees are tolerant and without prejudice. For example, there are few mechanisms to deal with teachers or administrators who are alleged to have demonstrated racist attitudes or behaviours. In many schools and boards, students, parents, and the community have little recourse.

A common problem with many organizational responses to racism is that individual members are not held accountable for their actions. Sanctions and accountability differ. Sanctions are penalties imposed for an infraction of organizational policies and norms. Accountability, on the other hand, refers to the assignment of responsibility for a specific set of actions for which non-compliance may result in specific sanctions. Thus, there can be accountability without sanctions.

It is difficult to find job descriptions that specifically prescribe anti-racist behaviour. Most often, the expectation is that those employed as equity practitioners[4] are the only ones accountable. The task of creating equity in the organization is frequently understood to be the job of the equity practitioner and no else. As Thomas noted in a review of the implementation of the Toronto Board of Education's policy and program, race relations is often perceived by the rest of the organization to be the work of the adviser on race relations: "It is where all the complaints, disputes, questions, and fears about racism go, even if they are connected to personnel or curriculum.... Whose business is race relations anyway?" (1984:18).

There are therefore two competing philosophies of equity in the organization. Since most members are considered tolerant, there is a need to prove that intolerance or racism was, in fact, intended. Since racism is defined very narrowly by senior decision-makers in most organizations, it becomes necessary to prove that employees, policies, and practices *intended* to discriminate or otherwise act in a racist manner. Often this results in a situation in which the innocence of the offender, already reinforced by the ideology of fairness, must be protected. Thus, an individual's reputation must not be tarnished by allegations of racism, nor must his or her fairness and objectivity be questioned. Anti-racism policies therefore provide an investigatory framework for which there is a strong presumption of innocence.

The presumption of innocence at the investigatory stage is peculiar to anti-racism allegations. A police investigation, on the other hand, is directed by a strong presumption of non-innocence. When a police officer arrests a suspect, it is usually assumed that the suspect is the correct person, and evidence is gathered to prove the police case. At the investigative stage in a charge of racism, however, the result of the presumption of innocence is a search for alternative explanations for the act of racism. Any other "reasonable" explanation negates a claim of racism, not simply for that case, but for all cases like it, regardless of the parties involved. The elusive nature of racism means that an alternative explanation can almost always be found. Thus, the notion of impact is eradicated and the result is a reduction of individual accountability for actions that have a racist impact.

In addition, in racially hostile work environments, those most affected by racism are unlikely to complain about it. Overt racism may be so entrenched in the organization's operation that victims are expected to comply. In correctional institutions, for example, both inmates and staff often engage in overt racist acts. Minority staff find it difficult to complain for fear of reprisal, despite the existence of a policy forbidding racist acts.

STRUCTURAL RIGIDITY

Anti-racism requires fundamental changes to the structure of organizations. Yet, a characteristic response is the maintenance and preservation of traditional structures. Sometimes organizations respond to the challenge by creating advisory bodies but not altering the basic structure of the organization. By definition, these bodies have limited power and exist at the discretion of those who appointed them.

Anti-racism is rarely considered important in the restructuring of ministries and government departments. The restructuring of the federal government in 1993 proceeded without much attention to anti-racism. Thus, anti-racism initiatives and policies operate at the periphery. They are not considered "really" important by senior decision-makers. When they are initiated, they are "add-ons." For example, pay equity legislation proceeded with little discussion of the relationship between race, gender, and pay.

INEFFECTIVE MONITORING AND EVALUATION MECHANISMS

The pursuit of racial equality demands that the mechanisms for measuring change be put in place. It means moving from discussing the principles of equality of opportunity to measuring achievement.

Equal-opportunity policies, mass "sensitization" training programs, and glossy public-relations campaigns are not especially effective unless they are combined with concrete programs that are regularly monitored and evaluated and publicly reported. The use of effective monitoring systems — which can be mere progress reports — can begin to provide information on whether the goals of a program are being reached.

The most important measure of any initiative is its results. Extensive efforts to implement training and develop procedures, data-collection systems, report forms, and finely written policy statements are meaningless unless measurable improvement takes place. Just as the success of a private business is evaluated in terms of increases in sales, the only realistic basis for evaluating a program to increase equity for racial minorities is its actual impact on these groups.

In Canada, the little evaluation that has been done on race relations training programs has focussed on evaluations by participants. The key indicator of effective training seems to be whether the participants found the trainers credible, balanced, and fair. The effectiveness of training for better interracial attitudes has, however, provided ambivalent results.

Efforts are needed to develop appropriate methods of "impact evaluation" — that is, measures of the extent to which an anti-racism initiative produces various results. The emphasis must be on an initiative's "return on investment" in relation to predetermined goals. From that basis, one can begin to establish legitimate and meaningful performance standards. The emphasis must be on determining whether the activity had the impact that it set out to have.

Measuring results with some degree of comfort and certainty requires the goals to be defined in specific, concrete, and realizable terms. Measuring results is impossible when the goals and objectives are nebulous generalizations.

INSUFFICIENT RESOURCES

The anti-racism initiatives discussed above suffer from inadequate resources, both material and human. To achieve a racially just and equitable society requires large-scale change and concerted commitment. In periods of economic restraint, many programs are cut due to lack of funds. Anti-racist initiatives are often the most vulnerable and often the first programs to be reduced or eliminated.

At the federal level, the Multiculturalism Act makes no provision for the multiculturalism department to dictate the scope of activities performed by individual ministries with respect to anti-racism. The multiculturalism department functions as an internal consulting body to government and as a minor funding body to organizations. It does not have the statutory power or substantial financial resources to intervene in government affairs, and the net effect is that government institutions are free to undertake whatever initiatives they deem sufficient.

TOKENISM

Tokenism often involves the practice of appointing or hiring one or two members of designated minority groups for relatively powerless positions in order to demonstrate the organization's tolerance of diversity. Tokenism circumvents substantive change. It is the most commonly used organizational mechanism to resist pressures for change and is "an essential element in the ideological hegemony of the institutional process of racism" (Phillips and Blumberg, 1983:34).

With respect to the employment of racial minorities, tokenism takes several forms. For example, minorities may be ghettoized in certain positions. The segregation of ethnic-minority employees is well documented (Reitz et al., 1981, 1982). Women of all ethnic and racial backgrounds are employed in factories as wage workers. Increasingly, Black men are hired as security guards and Black women are found in segregated occupations such as nursing aide, factory worker, and food-service provider. In addition to these well-known methods of segregation is the racialization of occupation.

Stereotypes about the skills of certain groups of people have structured the occupational categories in which minorities tend to be found. Many organizations today hire minorities for specific types of jobs. It is common to find a disproportionate number of persons from Southeast Asia employed in jobs that involve computation, such as computer programming and accounting. A disproportionate number of Black people employed in the public service are in jobs related to racism, anti-racism, equity, diversity, and so on.

This kind of job ghettoization of racial-minority professionals is partly related to a reluctance to value the universal skills that people of colour possess. It is also related to the desire of many firms to relegate minorities to occupational categories in which they are deemed to be efficient workers. Thus, Asians are thought to be especially good at math-related jobs, and Blacks, because of their size and alleged strength, are thought to do well at security. (When both physical strength *and* quick thinking are required — as in policing and firefighting — Blacks, oddly enough, are often not considered.)

MINORITY CHANGE AGENTS

The people in an organization who are responsible for initiating and developing strategies for change have been called "change agents." Their position is fraught with difficulties, since change agents rarely occupy a position of power in the hierarchical structure of the organization. Although they are responsible for advocating and implementing new policies and practices, their role is often marginal.

Their role may evoke resistance. For example, change agents of colour engaged in anti-racism work, purely because of their identity, elicit resistance from White members of the organization. To organizational leaders, change agents of colour represent a paradox. On the one hand, White people see them as "successful," unlike others of their community. Implicit in this assumption is that the individual does not possess the negative qualities of members of his group. On the other hand, change agents of colour represent the targets of racism. Consequently, resistance is engendered in ways that White people engaged in this same work do not experience.

Change agents of colour are particularly subject to scrutiny and to challenges of their position. They are seen as "looking for problems." They are subject to accusations such as "having a chip on their shoulder" or seen as "being too sensitive." Their knowledge, skills, resilience, and ability to mediate between various groups is constantly tested. Their "objectivity" is questioned, and their "favouritism" toward their own group, or toward racial minorities in general, is suspected. Their boundaries of responsibility are narrowed or expanded, depending on the situation.

Their methodologies or strategies are often held suspect. Their reports are often censored and altered until they are unrecognizable, as issues are restated so as not to sound so "negative," or their recommendations are set aside because they are viewed as being unrealistic, inaccurate, or unreasonable. All of these behaviours are manifestations of resistance to the anti-racism effort, exacerbated by the presence of minority change agents.

Even when persons of colour hold positions of power, their words and actions are closely scrutinized and their actions are frequently criticized. The intense criticism and the overwhelming scrutiny by the media, members of the police establishment, and others of Susan Eng, former chair of the Metropolitan Toronto Police Service Commission, is a powerful example of the vulnerability of people of colour who achieve positions of power. Another minority member of that board, in reacting to criticism of comments he made to a Bermuda newspaper about the well-documented problems between the police and Toronto's Black community, noted:

> This is what happens, in part, when people of colour make comments about a situation that exists. I expect it is still not nice for us to say these things, as if I should be grateful for having the opportunity to say anything at all. The vituperative, hostile reaction is so out of proportion. (Minors, 1993)

The lack of support and the powerlessness experienced by change agents result in a significant incidence of "burnout." Individuals suffer both physical and emotional exhaustion in their work as change agents; their "suffering or stress is a natural consequence of the dilemmas and paradoxes inherent in playing or resisting the token role" (Phillips and Blumberg, 1983:36).

LACK OF ORGANIZATIONAL ACCOUNTABILITY

Many of Canada's public institutions appear to have become increasingly bureaucratized, institutionalized, specialized, and isolated not only from the public, but from each other. They often operate as if they were separate and distinct from the larger society and far removed from the concerns and issues of importance to people of colour. Functioning in this framework results in a lack of accountability not only to the public but also to the political process (see, for example, the Cole Harbour case study in Chapter 8).

The criminal justice system is one institution that has been criticized for assuming that it can pursue the goal of upholding community standards only by being above the community. Its legitimacy is gained from a general acceptance of the laws and regulations it enforces, the values it embraces, the morality it is supposed to support, and the order it maintains. Many other professional groups, such as those in education, human services, and the media, feel a stronger sense of accountability to their self-defined codes of conduct than to those they serve.

Public-sector organizations are administered by bureaucrats whose roles, functions, and responsibilities appear to be largely unaffected by the issue of racism in their systems. Bureaucrats perform with relative autonomy, and most of their jobs involve making informed decisions in the interest of preserving democratic institutions. They are technocrats whose judgements are valued and trusted, and they are probably among the most mobile of public servants. Their judgements help determine the priorities of governments and other public-sector institutions. The judgements and ideology of senior bureaucrats dictate what is fair, reasonable, and achievable in the organization. As a group, therefore, they are perhaps the least accountable but most trusted of all public servants. They are the most capable of designing strategies to undermine any attempt to achieve a different conception of equity. In a government ministry, for example, some well-designed anti-racism training models developed with the help of international experts in the field were quietly "killed" by a handful of senior bureaucrats who thought them too radical.[5]

LIMITED PUBLIC ACCOUNTABILITY

An underlying tenet of Canadian democracy is the obligation of its public institutions to explain and justify their activities. This accountability might be said to provide legitimacy to the democratic state. It entails an acceptance of the notion of community participation in and control of the decision-making processes of public institutions.

But how does a public-sector organization develop these relationships? How does it include a diverse clientele, a diverse group of constituents, in the system? What are the mechanisms for bringing the community into the decision-making process? Do the institutions and organizations examined in this book demonstrate public accountability?

A number of public-sector agencies have responded to this issue by initiating a range of public-consultation mechanisms. These mechanisms have included:

- needs-assessment surveys
- consultation with key informants
- opinion polls
- community focus groups
- advisory councils and committees
- commissions and task forces
- public hearings
- conferences and workshops
- public information programs
- advertising
- neighbourhood meetings
- support to community groups
- telephone information hotlines
- community relations offices

Although many of these activities have been useful, others have not. Their objectives have frequently lacked clarity, their implementation has often been ineffective, and their impact has rarely been evaluated with any rigour.

There exists in racial-minority communities an increasing sense of mistrust, apathy, and anger toward these exercises, especially toward community consultations. Reactions such as "We have been consulted to death" and "What happened to our recommendations?" are the result of too many minor, cosmetic improvements. Community consultations require the expenditure of enormous time and resources by community groups and organizations that are already hard pressed. The growing scepticism and distrust of consultation initiatives are the result of the widespread view that public institutions are simply "going through the motions," that they continue to devote most of their resources to support "mainstream" organizations.

The spirit and commitment with which public consultations are carried out are therefore questioned. When goals are not clearly identified, when expectations are not articulated, and when no substantive action is initiated as a result of the exercise, these consultations are considered pseudo-democratic exercises to distract minorities from the real organizational goal of maintaining the status quo. When attempts to improve community relations involve the community in an unplanned, undisciplined, and unprofessional manner, community participation in the decision-making processes of public institutions is undermined.

DECEPTIVE DOMINANT DISCOURSES

Individual, institutional, and organizational resistance are clearly demonstrated by the kind of discourses that operate within organizational cul-

Figure 12.2
ADDRESSING RESISTANCE AND ENLISTING SUPPORT

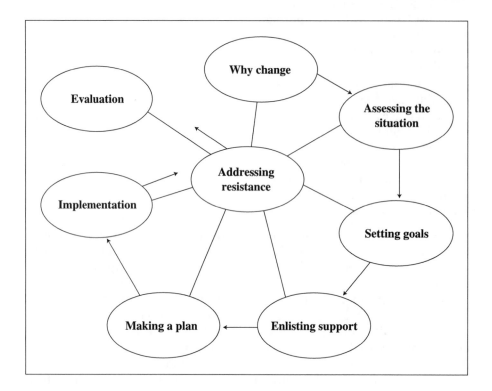

tures. Rhetorical strategies are used to establish, sustain, and reinforce inequalities and oppressive power relations. Discourses include explanations, accounts, rationalizations, justifications, and hidden codes of meaning. These discursive tactics serve to mask the reality of racism in various settings: social agencies' structures and programs, health-care practices, law-enforcement codes of conduct, the unexamined beliefs and assumptions of judges, the pedagogical practices of educators, the priorities of cultural workers, the norms of journalists and broadcasters, the development and implementation of public policies, and the allocation of bureaucrats and politicians.

Although explicitly derogatory statements, slurs, and epithets can be uttered in each of the sectors described in the preceding chapters, they are less commonly heard today. The more elusive nature of dominant discourse allows it to easily mask its racialized ideas (Wetherell and Potter, 1992). Major actors in each of these institutions present themselves as defenders of liberal ideals and principles, "Canadian" values, and national identity.

The appeal is not to prejudice, but to the preservation of a harmonious cultural pluralism. The discourses of "equal opportunities," "colour-blindness," "tolerance," "merit," "reverse discrimination," and "political correctness" create an organizational climate that prevents active engagement with racial and other forms of inequality. Discourse as social practice reinforces the status quo.

RACE-CONSCIOUS THEORY OF ORGANIZATIONS

Overcoming resistance to anti-racist change can best be accomplished in an organization that has become conscious of race as a social construction. In a race-conscious theory of organizations, the nature of social relations is influenced by race. Interests deemed legitimate have a racial component. Compliance, and the risks of non-compliance, are assessed in terms of the importance and legitimacy of the interests, power, and/or lack thereof, as well as social status both within the organization and outside of it. To what extent are Canadian organizations race conscious? Most organizations fall within a continuum that starts at monoculturalism, then gradually changes to assimilationism or multiculturalism, and finally assumes an anti-racist organizational stance. The majority of Canadian organizations appear to fall within the first two categories. Few, if any, have developed a genuine anti-racist model of organizational behaviour.

THREE ORGANIZATIONAL PARADIGMS OF CHANGE

In a heterogeneous society, race affects every aspect of organizational life. For this reason, some analysts view organizations along a race–cultural continuum in order to categorize organizational responses to racism. These approaches have a variety of labels but are identified here as assimilationist (exclusionary, monocultural, ethnocentric, homogeneous); multicultural (add-on); and anti-racist (racial equity) approaches. Each of these approaches has very different implications for the organization's development of strategies and initiatives to deal with racial bias and discrimination.

The various institutional responses to racism are based on different assumptions about the nature of racism and reflect broader perspectives underlying people's thoughts and behaviour. They also reflect the ideology of the organization, that is, the collective belief and value system woven through the institution, shaping and affecting all its aspects. More than one model may operate concurrently, particularly in large and complex organizations. For example, a board of education might have a very innovative approach in one unit, such as curriculum development, and an extremely resistant approach in the department responsible for placement and assessment issues.

Figure 12.3

A RACE-CONSCIOUS THEORY OF ORGANIZATIONS

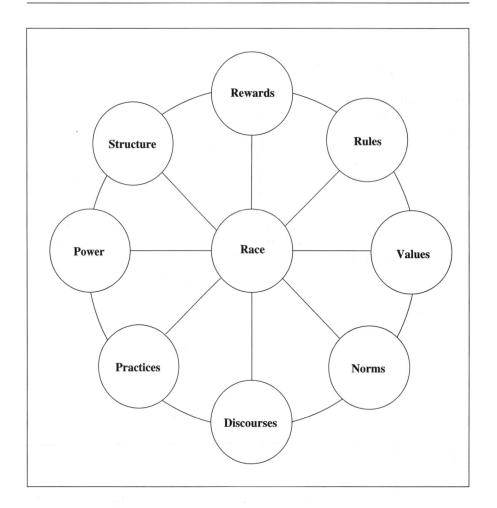

ASSIMILATIONISM

Organizations that do not recognize racial and cultural diversity generally operate on the assumption of homogeneity among people. They assume, for example, that even in a predominantly multiracial society such as Canada, individuals belonging to racial minorities have been assimilated into the mainstream of Canadian society.

Consequently, these organizations have a monocultural perspective (Jackson and Holvino, 1989). Their policies and practices are expressed in universal terms that emphasize the underlying values and norms of the dominant culture. Such organizations focus on preserving and maintaining the control of those in power, and their efforts are directed toward protecting the status quo (usually reflecting the interests of White males, but not always). The existing mission, policies, and practices of the assimilationist institution are perceived as the only "right" ones, and no consideration is given to other groups' perspectives or interests. Thus, the concerns of racial and cultural minorities are constantly ignored or deflected (Jones, 1986). There is no sense of accountability to external constituencies.

Mighty (1992) suggested that this form of cultural imperialism often unconsciously but sometimes consciously seeks to homogenize non-dominant cultures and transform them into a single one. It fails to consider both the sociocultural context in which the organizations operate and the diversity of perspectives that coexist within them. They undertake no efforts to respond to diversity issues in general. Moreover, there is a total absence of interest in addressing the issues or concerns of racial minorities or the other constituencies that the organization is supposed to serve. Assimilationist organizations do not see the need to participate in any fundamental alteration of their organizational culture (Jackson and Holvino, 1989).

This paradigm continues to be widespread (Adler, 1993; McDonald, 1991). Assimilationist institutions may recognize that racial diversity exists in society, but they perceive its impact as negative. They assume that their way of viewing the world is the best way and that all other perspectives are essentially inferior (Adler, 1993; Kanter, 1977).

Assimilationist organizations try to minimize diversity by selecting a workforce that is as homogeneous as possible. When external pressures such as anti-racism policies or employment equity are imposed, organizational decision-makers may find themselves coerced into allowing a few members of racial minorities to gain access to their organizations. They then seek to assimilate the newcomers into their world (Jackson and Holvino, 1989).

The biases in such organizations' perspectives are reflected in inequitable policies, inaccessible services, and discriminatory practices, all of which are considered immutable. "Outsiders" must conform without disturbing the existing organizational culture. As a result, newcomers are usually confined to the lower ranks of the organization, where they remain powerless to change the status quo. Occasionally, the recruitment of a "token" woman or racial minority into a higher-level position may occur after ensuring that the person is an exceptional member of the out-group, a team player who will conform to the organizational culture and not challenge the status quo (Mighty, 1992; Jackson and Holvino, 1989; Kanter, 1977).

MULTICULTURALISM

The principle underlying multicultural change strategies is a willingness to make limited modifications in the organization or institution but not to alter its fundamental structure, mission, and culture. A variety of initiatives may be undertaken from time to time, such as recruiting a "minority" for a staff position or as a member of the board, and translating print or audio materials into various languages.

Multicultural organizations and their members learn to master the equity rhetoric while engaging in cosmetic changes. Homeostasis characterizes these organizations, and it is very often reactive rather than proactive. Diversity is useful in such organizations. For example, they may draw on ethno-racial staff to assist in the translation of materials or to work with members of their own culture.

These organizations see diversity as a product and are therefore image-conscious. They often proclaim their programs and initiatives. They therefore make a point of hiring minorities, most of whom will have responsibility without power, limited control, and impressive titles without access to the centres of power. In many cases, these minorities will be physically and structurally isolated from the rest of the organization.

In this type of organization there is a recognition that certain changes must be made in order to comply with new policies, regulations, or legislation. However, issues related to racism are considered distinct from the day-to-day life of the organization. The needs, interests, and perspectives of racial minorities are dealt with on an ad hoc basis rather than being integrated into the programs and services of the organization.

Responsibility for change is often delegated to the front-line worker, who may then function in an unsupportive environment. The multicultural organization may seek to remove some discriminatory barriers by providing greater access to racial minorities, but its members are expected to conform to the dominant group's values and world view (Jackson and Holvino, 1989).

Despite recognizing diversity, multicultural organizations rarely make conscious efforts to create organizational climates that support diversity or establish systems that enable different types of employees to succeed (Copeland, 1988). For example, they may introduce training initiatives in relation to human rights, cross-cultural or intercultural activities, race relations, anti-racism, organizational management, or employment equity. But, while the training creates an awareness of diversity, it rarely creates new behavioural norms and organizational procedures that would promote access, participation, and equity; eliminate discrimination; and effectively manage diversity (Equal Opportunity Consultants, 1990).

ANTI-RACISM

An anti-racist organization is not one in which racism is absent. Rather, it takes a proactive stand against racism in all its forms. It is oppositional in nature and addresses racism at both the organizational and individual levels. Commitment in anti-racist organizations is based on an acknowledgement that racism exists, that it manifests itself in various forms at the individual, institutional, and systemic levels, and that it is embedded in the mass culture of the dominant group. An anti-racist perspective begins by accepting that the perceptions of people of colour are real and that there may be a multiplicity of realities in any one event.

The anti-racism approach to change is based on a commitment to eradicate all forms of social oppression and racial disadvantage in the organization. The anti-racist organization includes members of racial minorities as full and equal participants. It follows through on decisions that affect its broader social responsibilities and external relationships.

Anti-racism emphasizes a holistic approach to the development of anti-racist ideologies, goals, policies, and practices. As an organizational response it requires the formation of new organizational structures; the introduction of new cultural norms and value systems; changes in power dynamics; the implementation of new employment systems; substantive changes in services delivered; support for new roles and relationships at all levels of the organization; new patterns and more inclusive styles of leadership and decision-making; and the reallocation of resources. Strategic planning, organizational audits and reviews, and monitoring and accountability systems are all considered an integral part of the management of anti-racist change.

Of prime importance in the anti-racist institutional process is a commitment to the empowerment of racial minorities both within the organization and outside of it. Policy development and new mission statements are not considered an end in themselves; adequate attention, priority, and resources are given to implementation strategies and programs. Effective monitoring mechanisms are put in place to ensure accountability throughout the organization. Evaluation of the change effort is an ongoing process. Resistance to change is anticipated, and strategies to overcome it are planned.

Finally, anti-racism recognizes that no institution operates in isolation from other institutions and that racism in one arena of social life, such as education, will affect others, such as employment; that racism in police forces can be fostered by the media and in turn that the media can be influenced by market forces and government "propaganda." Thus, the anti-racist approach to change seeks to encourage and facilitate linkages and partnerships among institutions in order to identify and dismantle racial barriers and racial inequalities. (For more detail on diagnosing and removing institutional racism, see Table 12.1.)

SUMMARY

This chapter has presented reasons why organizations have been slow in enacting anti-racist initiatives. It is suggested that although organizations generally resist change, they are especially reluctant to initiate and implement anti-racist change. The reasons for this include a lack of vision or mandate, a lack of upper-level managerial commitment, inadequate policies, a lack of individual accountability, insufficient resources, and the maintenance of deceptive discourses that reflect dominant culture ideology.

Table 12.1

A MODEL FOR DIAGNOSING AND REMOVING INSTITUTIONAL RACISM AND OTHER BARRIERS TO ETHNO-RACIAL ACCESS

Indicators for Measuring Institutional Racism

Employment	Service Provision	Purchasing
1. Is there an over- or under-representation of ethno-racial minority employees in some job categories?	1. Do services present barriers to ethno-racial access? Are these barriers located in occupational practices and procedures or in staff attitudes or behaviour, or are they simply the outcome of decisions on different ethno-racial groups?	1. Is there evidence of denial of contracts to minority business?
2. Is there consistent over- or underemployment of ethno-racial minority employees in terms of matching job qualifications (e.g., education, experience) with job category?	2. Do the organization s communications materials and methods present barriers to ethno-racial communities (e.g., lack of translation, inappropriate portrayal, racial insensitivity, cultural inappropriateness)?	2. Is there evidence of past discrimination in the contracting customs, systems, etc.?
3. Do employee evaluations show consistent biases in favour of or against a particular race?	3. To what extent, and how, does the organization target information to and receive information from ethno-racial communities?	3. Do contracting requirements have a disproportionately negative impact on minority businesses?
4. Does race affect the degree of agreement between employees and their supervisors on the employee evaluations?	4. To what extent do the organization s communications strategies recognize the specific information needs of and barriers to information experienced by ethno-racial communities?	4. Is there a failure to distribute bidding information to potential minority businesses?
5. Does race affect the type of employment actions taken?	5. Do the information materials portray ethno-racial diversity?	5. What is the percentage of contractors that are minority-owned?
6. Is there differential access to in-service training?	6. Are ethno-racial communities involved in planning, designing, developing, and delivering information activities?	6. Is there a lack of notification of bid opportunities?
7. Is there differential enrolment in in-service training?	7. Are the service-delivery processes equitably reflective of the ethno-racial communities?	7. Is there a repeated use of a restricted number of vendors?
8. Are there adequate mechanisms to handle discrimination complaints?	8. In what way are services sensitive to the life experiences and reflective of the needs of various ethno-racial communities?	8. How large is the minority-business supplier base?
9. What are the findings of grievance settlements?	9. Do ethno-racial communities participate in the planning, design, and delivery of services?	
10. Are there policies and procedures to facilitate employee relations?	10. Do ethno-racial communities receive equal benefit from the services?	
11. Is there a failure to recruit ethno-racial minorities?		
12. What are the hiring criteria?		
13. Is there consistent hiring of non-minorities?		
14. Is there an employment equity plan?		
15. Is race an important functional variable within the organization from both the employees and employers perspective?		

(continued)

Table 12.1 *(continued)*

Categories of Information Required for this Paradigm		
Employment	**Service Provision**	**Purchasing**
1. Demographic statistics and ethno-racial work-force profile. 2. Policies and practices: job and performance factors. 3. Employer—employee relations. 4. Administrative procedures. 5. Perceptions of personnel and organization climate.	1. Demographic statistics. 2. Percentage of minority clients served by program, i.e., their under- or overutilization of the program. 3. Percentage of resources allocated to minority communities. 4. Communications efforts to reach minority communities. 5. Level of participation by minorities in the decision-making process.	1. Demographic statistics. 2. Percentage of minority firms in the private sector by industry sector. 3. Percentage of the organization s contractors (and prime subcontractors) that are minority-owned. 4. Percentage of total contracting purchasing dollars that goes to minority contractors.

Some organizations are not accountable to the public, nor do they listen to the requests made of them, especially by members of minority groups. Even agencies of government whose mandate is anti-racism lack the resources and especially the power to influence the decisions of other ministries. Anti-racist initiatives must have a strong organizational commitment in order to reach their goal.

The chapter concludes with a discussion of various models of organizational change and notes that most Canadian organizations can be described as either assimilationist or multicultural. Few have moved to a genuine race-conscious or anti-racist model of organizational behaviour.

NOTES

1. Many of this chapter's examples of organizational resistance are drawn from the authors' experiences in working with public- and private-sector institutions.
2. This incident occurred when the authors were working with an agency of government.
3. In 1986, the United Way of Greater Toronto first piloted its Multicultural/Anti-Racist Organizational Development Program, which was designed to assist health and social service agencies in identifying and dismantling barriers to the full participation of ethno-racial groups as volunteers, staff, and clients. Its goal was to enhance the capacity of agencies to respond effectively to the needs of a diverse community.
4. The term "equity practitioner" is used here to mean any individual involved in the pursuit of equity. Such a person could exist in an organization under a variety of labels, including adviser on race relations, employment equity, human rights, cross-cultural issues, diversity, or intercultural communications.
5. Personal communication from the expert contracted by a ministry of government.

REFERENCES

Abella, R. (1984). *Report of the Commission on Equality in Employment*. Ottawa: Supply and Services Canada.

Adler, N.J. (1993). *Human Resource Management in the Global* Economy. Kingston: Industrial Relations Centre, Queen's University.

Anderson, S., and M. Fullan. (1984). *Policy Implementation Issues for Multicultural Education at the School Board Level*. Toronto: Ontario Institute for Studies in Education.

Andrews, A. (1992). *Review of Race Relations Practices of the Metropolitan Toronto Police Force*. Toronto: Municipality of Metropolitan Toronto.

Brandt, G. (1986). *The Realization of Anti-Racist Teaching*. London: Falmer Press.

Copeland, L. (1988). "Learning to Manage a Multicultural Work Force." *Training* (May):31–35.

Equal Opportunity Consultants. (1990). *Race Relations Training Review*. Toronto: Ontario Ministry of the Solicitor General, Race Relations and Policing Unit. Unpublished.

Giroux, H. (1988). "Theory, Resistance and Education." In K. Weiler (ed.), *Women Teaching for Change: Gender, Class and Power*. South Hadley, MA: Bergin and Garvey.

Green, P. (1981). "The New Individualism." *Christianity and Crisis* 41(March 30):79.

Jackson, B.W., and E. Holvino. (1989). *Working with Multicultural Organizations: Matching Theory and Practice*. Proceedings of Workshop on Diversity: Implications for Education and Training. Toronto. 109–21.

Jones, E.W. (1986). "Black Managers: The Dream Deferred." *Harvard Business Review* (May–June):84–93.

Kanter, R.M. (1977). *Men and Women of the Corporations*. New York: Basic Books.

Kymlicka, W. (1998). *Finding Our Way: Rethinking Ethnocultural Relations in Canada*. Toronto, New York, and Oxford: Oxford University Press.

Maracle, L. (1993). "Racism, Sexism and Patriarchy." In H. Bannerji (ed.), *Returning the Gaze: Essays on Racism, Feminism and Politics*. Toronto: Sister Vision Press. 122–30.

McDonald, B. (1991). *Managing Diversity: A Guide to Effective Staff Management*. Winnipeg: Cross Cultural Communications International.

Medeiros, J. (1991). *Family Services for All*. Toronto: Multicultural Coalition for Access to Family Services.

Mighty, E.J. (1992). "Managing Workforce Diversity: Institutionalization and Strategic Choice in the Adoption of Employment Equity." Ph.D. dissertation, York University.

Minors, A. (1993). *Toronto Star* (September 6):A7.

Mock, K., and V. Masemann. (1989). *Survey of Race and Ethnocultural Equity Policy Development and Implementation in Ontario School Boards*. Toronto: Ontario Ministry of Education.

Phillips, W., Jr., and R. Blumberg. (1983). "Tokenism and Organizational Change." *Integrateducation* 20(1 & 2) (March):34–39.

Razack, S. (1998). *Looking White People in the Eye: Gender, Race and Culture in Courtrooms and Classrooms*. Toronto: University of Toronto Press.

Reitz, J., et al. (1981). *Inequality and Segregation in Jobs*. Toronto: Centre for Urban and Community Studies, University of Toronto.

———. (1982). *Ethnic Group Control of Jobs*. Toronto: Centre for Urban and Community Studies, University of Toronto.

Tator, C., and F. Henry. (1991). *Multicultural Education: Translating Policy into Practice*. Ottawa: Multiculturalism Canada.

Thomas, B. (1984). *Race Relations Program Review*. Toronto: Toronto Board of Education.

Ungerleider, C., and E. McGregor. (1992). *Issues in Police Intercultural and Intercultural Race Relations Training in Canada*. Ottawa: Canadian Centre for Police Race Relations.

Wetherell, M., and J. Potter. (1992). *Mapping the Language of Racism*. New York: Columbia University Press.

Chapter 13

▼▼▼▼▼▼▼▼▼▼▼▼▼

The Paradox of
Democratic Racism

> In general the talk around race ... has only moved as far as its own nega-
> tion; "I am not a racist" ... becomes a common and accepted disclaimer
> on the tip of everyone's tongue.... This allows for the avoidance of deep
> questioning and critical thinking. (Farman, 1992:7)

This concluding chapter of the book briefly summarizes the ways in
which democratic racism is expressed in individual ideologies, public discourses, organizational and institutional values and practices, and the collective beliefs, assumptions, and norms shared by the dominant culture of
Canadian society. The second part of this chapter discusses anti-racist
strategies. These approaches have been developed in the context of a pervasive denial of racism and a strong resistance to a fundamental alteration
in the positions of power and privilege that White Canadians occupy in relation to persons of colour.

INTRODUCTION

The various forms of resistance to anti-racism — lack of commitment; inadequate policies, programs, and practices; insufficient resources, monitoring, and evaluation; lack of individual, organizational, and public accountability; and deceptive discourses — are strongly influenced by democratic
racism and the values associated with it. These values fuel the action or inaction of the individuals working in institutions of Canadian society. These
values also, to a significant extent, explain the cognitive dissonances and
ambivalences manifested in the attitudes and behaviours of so many institutional players. The organizations and institutions described in this text
are filled with individuals who are deeply committed to their professional
work, who are regarded as highly skilled practitioners, who believe themselves to be liberal human beings — and yet they unknowingly, unwittingly contribute to racial inequality.

One of the main reasons why organizations, and the individuals who work for them, fail to move toward an anti-racist model of organizational change is the overarching ideology of democratic racism. Its values provide a justification for avoiding any action that might lead an organization to make progressive changes that not only challenge racism but deconstruct it.

The hegemonic ideology of democratic racism is articulated, transmitted, and reproduced in every sector of Canadian society. "It is in ... ideology that we live, move, and have our being" (McCarthy, 1993). And it is in language that ideology is disseminated and reinforced. Teun van Dijk (1991) maintains that language is never neutral. It is not simply a reflection of marginalization, discrimination, and racism, but it actually constructs oppression. Code words exist that, in themselves, do not have a racial meaning but do have a racial connotation that is understood by all — a meaning that has been socially constructed by the dominant culture.

In each of the central institutions of Canadian society analyzed in this book, racist discourse that includes myths and misconceptions continues to be generated, recycled, and replayed. These myths reinforce the racist attitudes and behaviours of individuals; fortify biased and discriminatory organizational policies, practices, and processes; and weave their way into societal belief and value systems. These processes result in collective denial, distancing, defensiveness, and a determination to maintain the status quo — the structural privilege of Whiteness.

The myths that form the basis of democratic racism include the following:

- *The Discourse of Denial:* "Canada is not a racist society; this is not a racist institution; he or she is not a racist; I am not a racist."
- *The Discourse of Colour Blindness:* "I never notice skin colour."
- *The Discourse of Equal Opportunity:* "All we need to do is treat everyone the same and fairness will be ensured."
- *The Discourse of Blaming the Victim:* "They lack the motivation to succeed"; "They don't really try to adapt their cultural values to 'our' society."
- *The Discourse of White Victimization:* "White European immigrants have also experienced prejudice and discrimination"; "All immigrant groups must expect to start at the bottom of the social and economic ladder."
- *The Discourse of Reverse Racism:* "Programs like employment equity and anti-racism policies incorporate authoritarian principles and methods that are antithetical to liberal democratic society."
- *The Discourse of Binary Polarization:* "We are 'Canadian-Canadians' — law-abiding, hardworking, contributing members of society"; they are the "others."
- *The Discourse of Immigrants, Balkanization, and Racism:* "Immigrants take jobs away from Canadians; immigrants commit more crime; immigrants are a drain on the economy; immigrants exploit the welfare system."
- *The Discourse of Moral Panic:* "We are in a state of crisis and disorder and are under siege; we have lost control; there is a serious threat to *our* 'civilized' society."

- *The Discourse of Multiculturalism:* Tolerance, accommodation, harmony, and diversity: "In a multicultural society *we* should try to be sensitive, to tolerate and accommodate different cultural values; but there are limits to *our* tolerance."
- *The Discourse of Liberal Values:* Individualism, truth, tradition, universalism, and freedom of expression: "The rights of the individual should override collective rights; there is a noble Euro-American tradition; there is a universal form of expression that includes and transcends all cultural and racial boundaries; there is an 'authentic' history that *we* are obliged to learn and share; we must establish what is the truth; freedom of expression is one of the most cherished of all of *our* values; it cannot be compromised because some minority group is unhappy with the position taken by a journalist, politician, curator, or educator."
- *The Discourse of National Identity:* "Real Canadians are willing to put their other cultural identities behind them; Canada should define itself on the basis of a single, unifying Canadian-Canadian culture."

In each of the institutional sectors examined earlier in this book, the various forms of racism have been shown to influence the manner in which organizations are structured. This book has attempted to make clear that the ideology of democratic racism reinforces and maintains racism in these institutions. It has demonstrated that the discourses of tolerance, equality of opportunity, reverse discrimination, and colour-blindness often conflict with the realities of injustice, inequity, and racial discrimination. These rhetorical strategies create a climate that prevents any kind of effective engagement with racial inequality. The next section of this chapter summarizes how democratic racism is manifested in Canada's major social institutions.

THE MANIFESTATIONS OF DEMOCRATIC RACISM

EDUCATION

In the area of education, racism is woven into the formal and informal curriculum, influencing the ways in which knowledge is structured, valued, and transmitted. Racial bias is reflected in the attitudes, assumptions, and behaviour of educators. Racism in education mirrors the racism of the dominant culture. It is reflected in the learning environment and forms an intrinsic part of the learning process. The evidence of racist ideology and differential treatment that negatively affects students of colour is documented by studies and reports and recorded in the testimonies of students and parents.

Educational practices that maintain Eurocentric biases and ignore the histories and contributions of racial-minority groups are maintained by a value system that allegedly emphasizes fairness and equality for all students. Canada's educational system is based on the premise that a well-constructed learning environment benefits students of all racial and cultural backgrounds. Despite this strongly held democratic liberal principle, substantial numbers of racial-minority students are disadvantaged and treated as though they were inferior. This is democratic racism.

Inequity and differential treatment continues at the university level. Lack of minority representation in faculties and administrations, the teaching of a Eurocentric curriculum, the absence of critical anti-racism pedagogy, the stereotyping of minority students and faculty, and incidents of harassment and overt racism continue to plague minority-group students. These practices are maintained in an institution that prides itself on its academic freedom and emphasis on freedom of expression. The latter freedom has enabled faculty to conduct research that allegedly demonstrates the inequality of races, allowed students to publicly insult members of racial minorities, and encouraged administrators to ignore issues that relate to inequity. The usual response of the university has been to deny and resist change in the name of academic freedom, freedom of expression, and the merit principle. These basic tenets of democracy allow racism to continue to flourish in the academic environment.

THE MEDIA

The media are regarded as a pillar of democratic society and the key instrument by which its ideals are produced and perpetuated. Democracy depends on a free flow and exchange of ideas, opinions, and information. In a liberal democracy, media institutions are expected to reflect alternative viewpoints and to provide equitable access to all groups.

In reality, the media are directed by the marketplace and are therefore subject to its constraints and demands. As a result, the Canadian media industries marginalize people of colour by making them invisible, devaluing their contributions, and perpetuating the White face of Canada. Media organizations play a key role in producing and disseminating the myth that people of colour, especially Blacks, threaten a well-ordered society, create social problems, and generally jeopardize the harmony of Canada.

Television cameras often show close-ups of Blacks in both the foreground and background of scenes in which the topic is crime. The media create and reinforce negative and stereotypical images to influence public opinion. Thus, issues such as crime, immigration, and housing become racialized and result in the further marginalization and exclusion of people of colour. Freedom of the press provides a licence for journalists, editors, and broadcasters to communicate racist views.

Yet, as the president of the Canadian Broadcasting Corporation stated in the introduction to the CBC's *Journalism Policy*:

> Freedom of the press ... is a cornerstone of our society, since freedom itself cannot flourish without the full flow and exchange of ideas, opinion and information. This is a tradition central to the democratic ideal and it has been accepted in that context as vital to the defence of individual liberty. (Canadian Broadcasting Corporation, 1982)

Freedom of the press has, however, continued to allow the media to include ideas, images, and words that demean and malign people of colour and that encourage fear and hatred against them.

THE ARTS

In the arts — literature, sculpture, painting, music, theatre, dance, and other creative achievements — work generated by people of colour is often judged inferior and relegated to the margins of mainstream public culture. Cultural appropriation — the use of another culture's images or experiences by artists from the dominant culture — is a particularly important example of the ways in which the culture, traditions, and history of minority-group artists are valued only after they have been appropriated. The prevailing ideology of cultural racism leads to the view that true art can only be produced by those with Eurocentric aesthetic values; all others produce folklore and exotica.

As is the case in the media, freedom of expression provides a rationale for silencing certain voices and ignoring particular images. Attempts to protest and resist the dominant culture's marginalization, stereotyping, and objectification of people of colour in theatre, film, television programming, and writing are met with allegations of censorship and political correctness.

POLICING

In the area of law enforcement, many racist attitudes and behaviours lead to a polarization between police and racial-minority communities. The culture of policing is based on a "we–they" mindset and emphasizes law and order, a concept that conflicts with the idea of a service-oriented police force. Citizens' demands for change are frequently seen by the police as challenging the maintenance of law and order and therefore a threat to the security of the state.

In addition, the police play an important role in the racialization of crime and the criminalization of minorities. The overpolicing of racial-minority communities leads to a substantial number of charges being laid against their members, which in turn leads to the view that members of these groups commit more crimes than others do. This unsubstantiated notion creates a negative, destructive, and unfair image that is disseminated among the public by the media. The racial minority (especially the Black) as criminal is a construct particularly well suited to the production and reproduction of racist ideology.

One of the major barriers to an improvement in police–race relations is the fact that people of colour do not have access to, and are not able to participate in, the decision-making processes of policing institutions. If the police are not directly accountable to the diverse communities they serve, they are less likely to reflect and respond to the concerns of these communities.

The fall 1992 protest against the Ontario government by the Metropolitan Toronto Police Association was symptomatic of police outrage at "political intervention." The government's attempts to introduce mechanisms for greater community accountability were actions that, in the association's view, should be discouraged. They were considered either a socialist conspiracy or the result of unreasonable demands by special-interest groups. The demands for greater accountability tended to be seen as opposing the police and therefore as subverting the democratic process.

THE JUSTICE SYSTEM

The justice system, which is intended to dispense "justice" fairly and without bias, has been severely criticized for its inability to do so. Specific issues of concern include alleged differential treatment in the courts — in the granting of bail, in sentencing disparities, in jury selection procedures, and in the attitudes of justice officials. Members of the legal profession, including the judiciary, have been cited for their prejudiced and biased attitudes toward various groups, despite their duty to be impartial. In minority communities, especially among Blacks, there is a fundamental absence of faith in the fairness of the system.

The justice system espouses an ideology based on long-established laws and historical and legal precedents. For example, mandatory anti-sexism training for judges was rejected by the justice minister "because of constitutional guarantees of judicial independence" (Canadian Press, 1993). Evidence continues to show that adherence to these honourable traditions and guarantees works to the disadvantage of, and dispenses injustice to, persons of colour.

HUMAN SERVICES

Social-service and health-care organizations are characterized by a lack of representation of people of colour. Those who are employed by these organizations experience marginalization and differential treatment. The prevailing ideology of human services is exclusionary and racist. It is based on the provision of appropriate service to all, regardless of colour or creed, yet its delivery is inconsistent with these principles. The assumption of a common set of needs among very different groups, which is usually accepted as a basic requirement for the equal and accessible provision of services, can have a negative impact on minority clients. People of colour often find the traditional mainstream human-service delivery system inaccessible and inequitable.

Current modes of service continue to reflect the values, norms, and practices of the dominant culture and therefore are of limited effectiveness for people coming from diverse racial and cultural backgrounds. By limiting the role and resources of ethno-racial agencies, funders and other institutional authorities have perpetuated inequality within the system. Mainstream organizations remain unable or unwilling to provide the special social and health-care services that many ethno-racial communities require.

Moreover, these helping professions are staffed by people who have been socialized to believe that since all human beings are equal and valuable, their needs can be met by the same methods and procedures. Therefore, minority-group workers employed in mainstream services frequently find themselves isolated and marginalized, their skills and credentials undervalued.

THE STATE

At the level of the state there is also evidence to demonstrate fundamental value conflicts. As Kobayashi (1990:447) pointedly argued, "The law itself has been an instrument used in the construction of racism as a hegemonic social relationship." Despite the development of human-rights legislation and codes, the glaring inadequacies of the Canadian Charter of Rights and Freedoms, the Multiculturalism Act, the Employment Equity Act, human-rights codes and commissions, government ministries, and public agencies at all levels demonstrate a lack of commitment to truly eliminate racism.

The conflict of values that characterizes the hegemonic ideology called "democratic racism" is at the root of racial inequality in Canadian society. The very values that define a democracy — freedom of expression, reliance on merit, the rights of individuals, the primacy of human dignity, and the rights of all citizens to equality — are used to combat, resist, and denigrate efforts to deconstruct racial barriers and inequalities. There is a constant and profound moral tension between the reality of the everyday experiences of people of colour and the responses of those who have the power to redefine that reality. White politicians, bureaucrats, educators, judges, journalists, social workers, cultural administrators, the corporate elite, and others pay lip service to the ideal of racial equality but are far more committed to maintaining the status quo.

The transformation of Canadian institutions and the organizations that serve them into anti-racist bodies is hindered by their reliance on the traditional values that such changes allegedly threaten. The paradox of "democratic racism" is that in the midst of a society that professes racial equality, there is racial inequality; instead of fairness, there is unfairness; instead of freedom of speech, there is the silencing of voices advocating change; instead of impartiality, bias; instead of multiculturalism, ethnocentrism. Diversity becomes assimilation, the rule of law results in injustice, service means lack of access, and protection increases the vulnerability of racial-minority communities.

STRATEGIES FOR CHANGE

Given the evidence of the collective denial of racism in Canadian society, what alternatives can be offered? What strategies can be implemented?

The complex, interactive nature of the Canadian social structure means that no single institutional response, policy, program, or other type of intervention can ensure that racism will be eliminated or even reduced. This book has identified numerous measures that have been undertaken, such as state policies on multiculturalism, human rights, immigration, and employment equity, as well as institutional initiatives in education, policing, human services, and the media. Some measures have had the appearance of success in the short term, but none has succeeded in controlling racism in a way that ensures full access, participation, and equity for people of colour.

Most of the approaches to combat racism in Canada have, in practice, been "too little, too late," too superficial, too simplistic. They have frequently been underfunded, short-term, ad hoc, and isolated interventions that lack co-ordination and do not address "root causes." Having been framed in an ideology of democratic racism, they have too often addressed symptoms without changing the conditions that produced the symptoms in the first place.

Although there are no sure formulas, the following strategic approaches to democratic racism hold hope for change:

- developing reflective skills and practices;
- responding to allegations of racism;
- empowering communities;
- monitoring anti-racism initiatives; and
- emphasizing the role of institutions.

The following pages offer some tentative suggestions in each of these areas to address inequalities and racist attitudes and behaviours.

DEVELOPING REFLECTIVE PRACTICES

For racism to have a less detrimental effect, it must be brought into the light and openly examined as a feature of the discourses, events, and experiences it influences, even in the most subtle ways (Dyson, 1994). What is lacking in the rhetoric of institutional and state "authorities" is a conceptualization of racism that uncovers its deeply rooted nature.

Moreover, what is required is to incorporate into this conceptual framework an understanding not only of how racism works on its victims, but of its effect on those who, perhaps unknowingly and unwittingly, are its perpetrators. For members of the White dominant culture, who are frequently unable to move beyond their own experiential framework, the collective values, assumptions, and beliefs operating beneath the coded language of liberalism and democracy remain invisible.

The position of White power and privilege allows many to evade the issue of race and racism and the powerlessness of the "others." The rhetoric of pluralism and inclusion does not address the tangible, everyday experiences of marginalization and exclusion. Most Whites are unable to "imagine" racism as a pervasive reality that affects the daily minutiae of living, working, thinking, and feeling (Srivastava, 1993). They are unable to see or deconstruct the racism that is woven into the discourses that are part of their professional and personal lives.

Caroline Knowles pointed out that the "lived dimensions" of racism transcend its administrative details. "An investigation of racism requires that it be grasped at the micro level, at the interface between the existential and administrative" forms of racism (1996:48).

The White professional — social worker, teacher, academic, administrator, employer, judge, law enforcement officer, lawyer, politician, bureaucrat, editor, journalist, broadcaster and cultural producer, curator, writer — is often reluctant to engage in critical self-reflection. There is an unwillingness to consider how these professionals' social locations or social identities influence the ways in which they function in their professional lives (Bonnett, 1993; Solomon and Levine-Rasky, 1996; Solomon and Brown, 1998). The conflicting ideologies and discourses operating in each of these sectors (media, the arts, justice, policing, government, human services, the private corporation) reflect unquestioned beliefs, assumptions, and interpretations about the racialization of differences.

Michelle Fine (1997) provided a powerful example of how the "professional socialization" of law students fundamentally alters their critical awareness of race and gender. She described how women law students, who began their first year with concerns about issues of social justice (e.g., generic use of "he," sexist jokes, differential participation by race and gender), by the third year patterned their political attitudes after those of White men. By graduation, "the vast difference in visions for the future by race and gender" (1997:61) had disappeared. Moreover, for the silenced White women, and women and men of colour, the critique of inequalities turned inward, against the self, and was reflected in lower grades, worsened mental health, and more conservative ideologies and politics. "Social critique by race/gender does not age very well within educational institutions" (1997:61).

Solomon and Levine-Rasky (1996) argued that in the training of teachers there is an urgent need to uncover the ideological entrenchment, contradictions, and resistance of prospective teachers as it relates to issues of race, racism, and anti-racism. Teachers must develop tools with which to critique the educational process, the society, and the self. "Issues of ethnicity and race must be integrated into the mainstream dialogues of teacher education" (1996:349). Carl James (1994) made a similar point, suggesting that teachers must constantly be critically self-reflective, "reflecting on our socialization, our biography, our worldview, and on how these impact on our practices" (1994:27).

In the same way, the training of journalists, police, human-service workers, MBAs, art administrators, and other professionals must provide opportunities for acquiring "critical literacy" (Wood, 1985) skills, that is, the ability to recognize and critique political, cultural, and economic structures that oppress marginalized peoples. They must be professionally socialized and given the knowledge and tools to deconstruct the meaning of the disabling discourses that surround them, such as the theories of "neutrality," "colour-blindness," and "professional competence and authority."

As has been demonstrated throughout this text, often the training of these professionals and practitioners has not prepared them for what Solomon and Levine-Rasky call "**reflective practice**." Thus, both pre-service training programs in postsecondary educational institutions and in-service professional development programs in organizations must play a pro-active role in developing self-reflective skills and ensuring that students and other participants gain the tools required to engage in social transformation.

RESPONDING TO ALLEGATIONS OF RACISM

Democratic racism allows individuals to hold and espouse liberal democratic values while believing and practising racist ideology. This form of racism is often subtle, elusive, and insidious. It is usually invisible to White people and readily apparent to people of colour. Thus, allegations of racism in organizations elicit anger, disbelief, and pain. Every allegation of racism has both individual and organizational consequences. In developing strategies to deal with racism, the individual is an essential part of the equation.

Allegations of racism are accompanied by a series of emotional responses from both the complainant and the subject of the complaint. These allegations often remain unresolved because people become involved in trying to prove that an incident was or was not discrimination. The individual accused of racism commonly believes that racism cannot occur without an intent to discriminate. Often the immediate organizational response is denial, expressed in a number of counter-productive behaviours. The person who alleges racism generally feels isolated, unsupported, and vulnerable. He or she may have expended enormous energy in trying to decide whether to launch a complaint or bring the issue to the attention of the organization.

Thus, in the first stage, the response to allegations of racism must begin by identifying and acknowledging the deeply felt emotions of both parties. Exposing these feelings and rigorously addressing them allows the incident to be used to create opportunities both to build individual relationships and to facilitate organizational growth.

The second stage is to uncover the underlying facts upon which these emotions are built. The social facts underpinning racism cannot be readily understood by White Canadians, who do not experience discrimination based on the colour of their skin. Thus it is very difficult for many White Canadians to understand the impact of constant, everyday racism on persons of colour and to identify the ways in which bias, exclusion, marginalization, and differential treatment function in their organizations. On the other hand, racism shapes the intellectual, professional, and personal lives of many people of colour. These distinctly different social realities must be taken into account in trying to determine the social facts underlying an allegation of racism.

The third stage requires a commitment to negotiate, implement, and institutionalize change. Finding common ground and identifying the mutual interests of the parties is an essential part of rebuilding relationships. Both the individuals and the organization must be able to identify the benefits of seeking a resolution to race-related conflicts. Often the experience and expertise of the community provide organizations with an important resource for developing effective strategies. Finally, it should be emphasized that this same process could have been applied in the many examples cited in the text, in which it is not an individual who is the aggrieved party, but the community as a whole that feels victimized by a set of racialized behaviours or actions.

EMPOWERING COMMUNITIES

Organized opposition by the offended group and/or community is a major catalyst to change. If societal institutions are to be free of racism, they need to be pushed to this level of change by organized, direct community action.

In a democratic society, when there is contestation and conflict over injustices, dissent should be valued as long as it occurs within socially approved limits. Public-sector support for anti-racism community advocacy and lobbying activities should be seen as necessary processes if democracy is to work. Competition in Canadian society is encouraged and institutionalized. Only when resources are scarce and inequitably distributed can such competition lead to disintegrative forms of conflict. Canadian democratic values encourage political dissent and opposition, again as long as they are expressed through proper channels and the conflict is "peaceful." Constructive conflict includes the recognition of different needs and interests (individual and collective) and provides for participation, negotiation, arbitration, and settlement. The establishment of such mechanisms may avoid violent confrontation.

A racial incident or series of incidents can act as triggers to direct reaction by the community, which often becomes the most salient agent of institutional and societal change. Thus, opposition and conflict may play a beneficial role in initiating the process of change toward racial equity.

A society in which integration is more advanced will have greater group interaction. As a result it may also experience more frequent incidents of behaviourial discrimination. However, the increasing number of such cases might indicate an improvement, rather than a worsening, in racial equality. Thus, ensuing conflicts should be recognized as signs of progress, not deterioration, because efforts to reduce racial inequalities may increase the short-term potential for conflict (Benyon and Solomos, 1987:156). In Canada, a society that promotes the democratic racist myths of progress through dialogue, mediation, and conciliation, the reduction of racial inequalities through increased racial conflict and tension will clearly be an uncomfortable but perhaps inevitable new direction.

The achievement of racial equity will not come about as a result of a rational, intellectual process of understanding. Nor will it occur through an "in-

visible hand" of organizational dynamics. Anti-racism efforts need to acknowledge the full complexity of the system they are attempting to change
and to locate those efforts in the context of the obstacles to racial equity. Anti-
racism strategies need to address the institutional constraints and the personal and occupational ideologies and values underlying democratic racism.

Although national and international conditions can precipitate social
change, a major impetus has been and will continue to be community pressure. It is therefore misleading to denude the pursuit of racial equity of any
political dimension. Social change is often precipitated by political imperatives. Does it matter whether the motivation is prevention, fear, moral
panic, or altruism? Does it matter whether the response is based on attempts to appease, to defuse discontent, to manage a crisis, to repair the
meritocratic credibility of institutions, or to avoid the development of separate institutions along lines of race?

What does matter is that the response will have an appreciable impact
on reducing racial injustice.

The case studies cited in this book show that the initial response of
Canadian institutions and organizations to demands for change is to make
cosmetic changes, and even then to make them only to defuse protest. Real
improvements come about only through sustained external pressure.

Parekh, in writing about anti-racism efforts in the United States, concluded that no reform had been secured without powerful and constant
Black pressure.

> It was the Black agitation, initially the non-violent civil rights campaigns
> and the later riots, that activated the moral impulse, energized and mo-
> bilized the liberals, provided a political counterweight to the highly in-
> fluential racial lobby, threatened disorder, changed the equations of
> White self-interest and resulted in reforms. (1987:x).

Parekh argued that no American reform was secure unless Black organizations and their leaders were able to consolidate, defend, and build on
it. His analysis of the American experience suggests that reforms secured in
the teeth of opposition by vested interests are fragile, vulnerable to subver-
sion, and generally lack the resources to implement them. Moreover, they
are unlikely to be fruitful and achieve the desired goal unless they are carefully formulated and part of a well-conceived strategy.

The frenzy of activity on March 21 each year — the day set aside to
commemorate the International Day for the Elimination of Racial Discrimination — is symbolic of the kinds of institutional initiatives that are often
little more than public-relations exercises. "Eliminate racism," "Remove
racial discrimination," "Create equality of opportunity," "Manage diversity,"
and "Implement anti-racist training" are empty slogans, incapable either of
guiding those who genuinely wish to help or of restraining those determined to resist them.

One of the most important conclusions that can be drawn from the
anti-racism activities described in this book is that immediate, consistent,

and well-developed community mobilization and action strategies can be highly successful in influencing political, institutional, and social action. Progress toward race equity is therefore unlikely to be attained unless concerned citizens and communities are able to co-operate to combat racism.

Community infrastructures and support systems need to be in place to combat racism, to monitor organizational and institutional initiatives, to ensure their implementation, and to overcome resistance, both systemic and individual.

Parekh (1987) also contended that any progress toward race equity is achieved only by sustained and direct community involvement. Sustained community advocacy and lobbying activities require:

- *organizational resources:* financial and human;
- *legitimacy:* support from the media and other communities;
- *expertise:* legal, media, and organizational; and
- *leadership:* training and development.

Political representation and the participation of people of colour in the decisions that affect them must also be regarded as necessary preconditions for the non-violent resolution of racism in Canadian society. For example, the issue of police behaviour raises questions that go to the heart of democratic accountability and government by consent. People of colour must be represented in the police force at all ranks and on the boards that manage them.

The use of police or the armed forces to deal with protest reflects a "legitimation crisis" in which inequalities of power and status undermine loyalty and create contradictions that threaten social integration. When such conflicts result in violent protest and a coercive response by authorities, they undermine the moral basis of society and the integrity of the state. Only through a comprehensive approach that addresses the underlying conditions that foster democratic racism and that facilitates constructive responses will a repetition of such crises in the future be avoided. The first precondition is that people of colour must participate in the decision-making process.

MONITORING ANTI-RACISM INITIATIVES

Public policies on multiculturalism and race relations, legislation on employment equity and human rights, and systems and agencies to promote racial equality have all had the impact on altering the appearance, if not the reality, of racial inequality in Canada. Canadians, including people of colour, are encouraged to believe in the myths of colour-blindness, meritocracy tolerance, and racial harmony. The maintenance of these democratic racist myths continues to hamper citizens' readiness to measure and dismantle racism. Although the extent of racial discrimination and inequality in Canada is similar to that of the United States and the United Kingdom, Canada has not yet experienced the level of violence and unrest that these other countries have.

A number of institutions and agencies in all sectors of Canadian life are articulating finely worded commitments and policies with regard to equity issues. Unfortunately, these commitments have seldom been translated into good practices. The pursuit of racial equality in Canada appears to be hampered by an inability to translate policy into time- and cost-efficient procedures that have a measurable impact on controlling racial disadvantage and discrimination. There is a danger that the impetus and commitment to equity will unravel in a collection of uncertain, cumbersome, and misdirected activities that do not achieve any real results in removing racial inequalities. These responses may indeed reinforce and even exacerbate the existing racial inequality.

The activity that has taken place in Canada in the last while in pursuit of racial equity has largely consisted of determining whether racism is occurring, how it is occurring and to what extent, and how it may be prevented. Although data on these issues are far from adequate and considerable research is still required, more emphasis should be placed on analyzing the issues from the perspective of outcomes.

The most important measure of any initiative is its *results*. Extensive efforts to implement training and develop procedures, data-collection systems, report forms, and finely written policy statements are worse than meaningless unless the end product is measurable improvement. Just as the success of a private business is evaluated in terms of increases in sales, the only realistic basis for evaluating a program to combat racism and increase racial equity is its actual impact on these issues. To accelerate the process of change, more careful consideration needs to be given to particular issues in sectors in which there is a real prospect of effecting change quickly.

In addition to focussing on strategic targeting, any strategy for improving policy and practices must incorporate mechanisms for monitoring and measuring their impact. In other words, initiatives must show definable results that reduce racial injustices in a measurable way. New techniques and mechanisms are required to assess whether anti-racist policies and practices are in fact achieving racial equity. There is a lack of rigorous monitoring in the field of anti-racism in Canada, and few criteria of evaluation have been developed. The consequence of this is that limited public dollars and community energies are wasted on irrelevant exercises that do little to control or eliminate racism.

Too many community activities are concerned with "promoting," "encouraging," "co-ordinating," "heightening," "improving," and other similarly imprecise and vaguely worded objectives. Sometimes, project evaluation consists merely of a loose "process evaluation" activity in which, for example, conference participants are asked to rate the speakers. The little evaluation that has been done on training programs indicates that efforts are needed to develop appropriate methods of "impact evaluation"—that is, evaluations of the extent to which anti-racism initiatives produce desirable outcomes. In terms of measuring results, the emphasis should be on an initiative's "return on investment" in relation to predetermined goals. Only then can legitimate and meaningful performance standards be established.

To be able to measure the results with some degree of comfort and certitude requires stated goals to be defined in specific, concrete, and realizable terms. Measuring outcomes is impossible if the goals and objectives consist of nebulous generalizations.

There is a need in Canada to collect and disseminate the information — about strategies, technology, and technical skills — that is required to achieve racial equity. Unfortunately, the degree of information sharing in Canada across institutional, racial, and geographical boundaries is relatively insignificant. This isolation, which results in an ignorance of other effective initiatives, methods, programs, and approaches, separates Canadians from the international community.

Canada cannot afford to persist in pursuing racial equity on an insecure foundation of inadequate knowledge. Nor can it, through its public and private sectors and its social agencies and institutions, afford to continue to devote resources to "improving opportunity" for people of colour if the impact on these persons continues to be negligible.

The failure to address the problem of racism in Canadian society might therefore be said to be largely due to a lack of information about the problem. A coherent response is more likely, and more likely to be effective, if Canadians have complete information on the extent and nature of racism. If effective preventive measures are to be formulated, then this kind of basic data is critical.

EMPHASIZING THE ROLE OF MAJOR INSTITUTIONS

The first task of an institution committed to racial equity is to make a clear statement that racism in any form will not be tolerated. Unfortunately, most major Canadian institutions operate as if the realities of a racially diverse population have nothing to do with the way they carry out their activities. They rely on "traditional management initiatives" or respond to incidents in an ad hoc manner.

In focussing on institutional strategies and in light of the previous observation regarding community involvement, an important factor is the degree to which an institution is open to *community pressure*. Some institutional sectors are more closed off from the public than are others. For example, the police are more accountable to the public because they are supported by tax dollars. Other public-sector agencies are accountable to elected representatives, who are concerned with staying in office. The education system is accountable as a public service and has additional obligations to parents.

Other public-sector institutions, however, such as the justice system, are less easily affected by public pressure. The tradition of judicial independence is difficult to overcome when combating racial inequalities in the justice system.

Similarly the tradition of freedom of speech is frequently used by the media to protect and defend themselves from community pressures. In addition, since the media are not highly organized, the mechanisms for seeking public redress are either ineffectual or non-existent.

Universities and colleges have decentralized authority structures, and old academic traditions guide their culture. Often, greater priority is given to the tradition than to the students or the broader population.

Museums and cultural institutions are also susceptible to isolation from the public they serve. The structure of and representation on the boards of these institutions suggest that they are not accountable to the larger community. The boards and staff of these institutions have not gained a clear understanding "of the invisible, but omniscient 'we' that such institutions embody to this day" (Tchen, 1993:4).

The case studies cited in this book indicate institutional ill-preparedness in dealing with racism, even when problems resulting from it have continued over years, for example, at Cole Harbour High School and other educational institutions, in the Toronto police force, in hospitals, in immigration policies, and in media organizations. Strategies must be developed that respond to racism that is the outcome both of individual beliefs and behaviours and of collective values and norms that form part of the organizational culture. Institutional-change strategies are fundamentally "local" in their orientation, in that they focus on one organization at a time. This is not to suggest, however, that there is not a generic organizational-response model.

Progress toward racial equity can be measured by the degree to which an organization:

- develops a discourse that is free of the ambiguities and ambivalences that have characterized racialized discursive practices in most organizational and institutional sectors;
- supports the development of self-reflective attitudes and reflective practices that lead to greater individual and organizational accountability in the process of social transformation;
- reflects the contributions and interests of all ethno-racial groups in Canada in its mission, operations, and service delivery;
- acts on a commitment to eradicate all forms of racial discrimination and disadvantage within itself;
- involves members of all its racial groups as full participants in all its levels; and
- fulfils its broader external responsibilities to promote racial equity.

In moving toward this ideal, appropriate organizational responses include:

- an immediate and strong condemnation of racism, and of those responsible for it, by the head of the organization;
- the development of a coherent implementation strategy to combat racism within the organization. This strategy should not merely deal with managing individual incidents, but strive to overcome the causes of racial incidents and eradicate systemic and structural discrimination in the organization;

- the establishment of an internal monitoring mechanism to record and monitor racism in all its forms; and
- taking action against those responsible for racism, serving notice on perpetrators, and informing the victims of all actions being taken.

Internal monitoring systems are generally located in organizations' human-resource policies and programs. They generally involve the filing of complaints, a multi-step procedure to attempt to resolve them, and a final decision by a senior official. In some organizations, an independent arbitrator is appointed to adjudicate complaints. In union settings, the collective agreement often includes a non-discrimination clause that subjects any discrimination complaint to grievance and arbitration procedures. In the Ontario Public Service Employees Union, for example, this procedure culminates in a hearing before the Crown Employees Grievance Settlement Board.

A "coherent strategy" for addressing systemic issues may include structural diagnosis (e.g., data collection and problem identification, customer or client audits, and employment equity audits), public and policy commitments, the appointment of an adviser and/or committee, the establishment of goals and timetables, training, monitoring, and evaluation.

Developing a coherent anti-racist strategy for an organization therefore entails:

- a total system effort that must be comprehensive, systematic, and long-term; and
- clearly enunciated goals, not so much concerned with maintaining order and harmony as with responding to grievances and correcting inequities.

Within the organization and its activities, the responsibility for race equity initiatives should reside not with one person or office, but with all the organization's members. The development of anti-racism values that could be integrated in the organization's culture and procedures should be considered. In summary, achieving race equity and a racism-free organization entails:

- an acknowledgement that racism exists in the organization and that certain groups have been, and continue to be, hurt by it;
- an acknowledgement of the need to move beyond racially inexplicit analyses that deflect the issue of racism by interpreting it in human-relations or cultural terms; and
- an acknowledgement of the need to move beyond policy statements and articulations of principles. Organizational and administrative measures will be required to provide appropriate conditions for progress toward race equity. Guidelines and procedures that include clearly identified responsibilities and accountability measures are required.

It may seem superfluous to state that the first step for all organizations, particularly those in the public sector, is to establish the need for a service for people of colour. It is clearly of major importance that the needs of the community be accurately assessed by systematic studies.

Second, in order to establish the relevance of services for people of colour, service provision must be monitored. A regular check must be made to ensure that a correspondence between need and service does in fact exist. The assessment must include the collection of data on the racial origins of clients, staff, and decision-makers.

The organizational arrangements of both public and private institutions determine the people or groups to whom services are provided, facilities are made available, and resources are allocated. The attitudes, actions, and practices of those who control these institutions determine who gets what, where, and when. Given the fact that people of colour are generally absent from these organizations' key decision-making processes and in the delivery of services, to what extent do the institutions treat them less favourably?

To what extent have the different and special needs of people of colour been identified and quantified? And to what extent have they been adequately considered and provided for? To what extent have existing resources been redirected in favour of people of colour as part of a commitment to equality?

The pursuit of racial equality also demands that institutional mechanisms for measuring change be in place. Formal employment equity policies, mass "sensitization" training programs, and glossy public-relations campaigns are generally ineffective unless they are combined with concrete programs that are regularly monitored, evaluated, and reported on publicly. Effective monitoring systems can begin to provide the information needed to answer the question of whether progress is occurring.

Increasing the amount of resources for anti-racism in and of itself is not a measurement of progress. Increasing the amount of "feel good" rhetoric contributes only to further obscuring the measurement of progress. Collecting evidence, although dry and tedious, is certainly cheaper and more honest than performing glamorous public-relations exercises. More resources should be devoted to research and evaluation and less to "communications strategies."

Ensuring that the multiracial dimension of Canadian society is incorporated into organizational decision-making in a comprehensive and systematic manner is not that difficult. But if it is not addressed directly, the notions of democratic racism and assumed equality will continue to be a major obstacle to race equity and will continue to contribute to the disadvantaged position of people of colour in Canada.

SUMMARY

Although all the strategies identified in this chapter are positive mechanisms for dismantling racism in organizations and institutions, they must be linked to a comprehensive transformation of the cultural values and norms that shape Canadian society.

Clearly, Canada's racial heterogeneity has been, is, and will continue to be a demographic and social reality. However, racial inequality and injustice continue to limit the participation of people of colour. Despite the existence of a variety of policies, programs, and other initiatives, the evidence in this book suggests that racist ideologies and racial barriers to equity in organizations and social structures have not been significantly reduced; that membership in the dominant White culture confers cultural, political, and economic power; and that racist ideology and discourse operate freely, without constraint.

The existence of democratic racism suggests that we can expect increasing resistance and backlash from those who now enjoy the power and privilege of membership in the dominant group to efforts by people of colour and other anti-racism advocates to alter the status quo. Simultaneously, those who are deprived of their rights as Canadians can be expected to become increasingly impatient with the slow rate of change.

Dealing with racism in an effective way requires us to deal with the dissonance in values that underlies our current understanding of democracy. At this point in the history of Canada, we have an opportunity to redefine and redistribute power and to eradicate the structured inequality propelled by the hegemonic ideology that we have called democratic racism.

REFERENCES

Benyon, J., and J. Solomos. (1987). *The Roots of Urban Unrest*. Oxford: Pergamon Press.

Bonnett, A. (1993). "Contours of Crisis: Anti-racism and Reflexivity." In P. Jackson and J. Penrose (eds.), *Construction of Race, Place and Nation*. London: University of London College Press. 163–80.

Canadian Broadcasting Corporation. (1982). *Journalism Policy*. Toronto: CBC.

Canadian Press. (1993). "Judges' Training Program Rejected." *Toronto Star* (September 8):A6.

Dyson, M. (1994). "Essentialism and the Complexities of Racial Identity." In D. Goldberg (ed.), *Multiculturalism: A Critical Reader*. Cambridge, MA: Blackwell. 218–29.

Farman, A. (1992). "An Archaeology of Interracial Relations." *Fuse* 15(3)(Winter):7–11.

Fine, M. (1997). "Witnessing Whiteness." In M. Fine, L. Weiss, L. Powell, and L. Mun Wong (eds.), *Off White: Readings on Race, Power, and Society*. London: Routledge. 57–65.

James, C. (1994). "I Don't Want to Talk about It." *Orbit*. 25(2):26–28.

Knowles, C. (1996). "Racism, Biography and Psychiatry." In V. Amit-Talai and C. Knowles (eds.), *Re-Situating Identities: The Politics of Race, Ethnicity, and Culture*. Peterborough, ON: Broadview Press.

Kobayashi, A. (1990). "Racism and the Law." *Urban Geography* 2(5):447–73.

McCarthy, C. (1993). "After the Canon." In C. McCarthy and W. Crichlow (eds.), *Race, Identity and Representation in Education*. New York and London: Routledge.

Parekh, B. (1987). In J. Shaw et al. (eds.), *Strategies for Improving Race Relations*. Manchester: Manchester University Press.

Solomon, P., and C. Levine-Rasky. (1996). "Transforming Teacher Education." *CRSA/RCSA* 33(3):337–59.

————, and D. Brown. (1998). "From Badness to Sickness: Pathological Conceptions of Black Student Culture and Behaviour." In V. D'Oyley and C. James (eds.), *Re/Visioning: Canadian Perspectives on the Education of Africans in the Late 20th Century.* Toronto: Captus Press. 104–19.

Srivastava, A. (1993). "Re-Imaging Racism: South Asian Women Writers." In H. Bannerji (ed.), *Returning the Gaze: Essays on Racism, Feminism, and Politics.* Sister Vision Press. 103–21.

Tchen, J.K.W. (1993). "What Are We Doing Now for the Year 2010?!? Museums and the Problems of Technospeak, Possessive Individualism, and Social Alienation." *Getting to 2010: Directors and Educators Visualize the Future.* Fort Worth, TX: Association of American Museums.

van Dijk, T. (1991). *Racism and the Press.* London: Routledge.

Wood, P. (1985). "Schooling in a Democracy: Transformation or Reproduction." In F. Rizvi (ed.), *Multiculturalism as an Educational Policy.* Geelong, Victoria, Australia: Deakin University.

Appendix A

▼▼▼▼▼▼▼▼▼▼▼▼▼▼

Racial Groups in Canada

Various racial groups make up the Canadian population. They are categorized by Statistics Canada as follows:

Aboriginal: Métis, Inuit, status and non-status Canadian Indian, North and South American Native peoples

Black: African Black, American Black, Canadian Black, West Indian and Caribbean Black, other Black

East Asian: Chinese, Fijian, Japanese, Korean, Polynesian

South Asian: Bangladeshi, Indian (India), Pakistani, Sri Lankan

Southeast Asian: Burmese, Cambodian, Filipino, Laotian, Malaysian, Thai, Vietnamese

West Asian: Arab, Armenian, Egyptian, Iranian, Israeli, Lebanese, North African Arab, Palestinian, Syrian, Turkish

White: British, European, South, Central, and North Americans of Caucasian background, Russian, Ukrainian, others of Caucasian background

Other: Mixed racial heritage; racial groups not referred to above

One of the challenges in discussing the issues of race and racism is achieving a common understanding of the terminology. The definitions, interpretations, and meanings of terms vary considerably. As our understanding of racism evolves, the pursuit of a language that is more specific, concrete, and clear will also evolve. For example, the term "visible minority" is a classification created by the Canadian state. "Visible minority" as a label refers to the categories of both native and foreign-born, non-white, non-Caucasoid, non-Aboriginal individuals. Many scholars (Synnott and Howes, 1996; Carty and Brand, 1993) argue that the term serves to homogenize and essentialize groups and ignores crucial differences in power, culture, history, and even visibility. Although colour remains the nucleus of the race classification system, it bears little relation to the actual skin tones of human beings. Many minorities who are not included in the concept are also very visible and experience disadvantage and discrimination. The term implies being "visible" from the norm, not part of normative mainstream society (which, of course, is presumed to be White). Being termed "visible" tends to reinforce the permanence of that status. Even the term "minority" is problematic, as it suggests being less than the majority. In parts of the country, and now in Toronto, this is no longer the reality in terms of population numbers. It is important to emphasize that both individual and collective forms of ethno-racial identity exist in a constant state of transformation. Moreover, some visible minorities may not view visibility as a significant criterion of self-identification. Some may consider language, religion, or history as a more important sign of identity rather than visibility.[1]

NOTE

1. Audrey Kobayashi (1992) explores the problem of formulations of ethnic definition and its importance to ethno-racial communities, researchers, politicians, policy-makers, and others.

REFERENCES

Carty, L., and D. Brand. (1993). "Visible Minority Women: A Creation of the Canadian State." In H. Bannerji (ed.), *Returning the Gaze: Essays on Racism, Feminism and Politics*. Toronto: Sister Vision Press. 167–81.

Kobayashi, A. (1992). "Challenges of Measuring an Ethnic World: Science, Politics and Reality." Proceedings of the Joint Canada–United States Conference on the Measurement of Ethnicity, April 1–3, Statistics Canada.

Synnott, A., and D. Howes. (1996). "Canada's Visible Minorities: Identity and Representation." In V. Amit-Talai and C. Knowles (eds.), *Re-Situating Identities: The Politics of Race, Ethnicity, Culture*. Peterborough, ON: Broadview Press. 137–60.

Glossary

▼▼▼▼▼▼▼▼▼▼

One of the difficulties in discussing racism is arriving at a common understanding of terminology. Unfortunately, the definitions and interpretations of terms vary considerably. Racism is an elusive and volatile issue, and our understanding of it continues to evolve. As such it is inevitable that our understanding of common, agreed-upon terms will also evolve.

Labelling groups of people is a difficult task because of the emotional significance of the names by which groups of people choose to identify themselves in Canadian society. And racism, by its very definition, addresses the evolving nature of that identity.

Another issue that needs to be considered in framing a discussion of racism is the scientific argument that there is only one "race" to which all members of human society belong, whatever their origin, colour, or other physical features. Anti-racism in this context is therefore concerned with eradicating the notions of race and racism and the myths of multiple "races" that have been used as the justification for one group to exert power over another.

The following glossary of terms is offered, not as the final word on the topic, but to explain the common words and phrases now being used in the constantly changing discussion on racism.

Aboriginal peoples In Canada, status Indians, non-status Indians, Inuit, and Métis.

adverse impact The extent to which policies, procedures, and practices disproportionately exclude certain groups.

aesthetics The "refined" appreciation of beauty in the arts. The object of study for aesthetics is the art object itself, in isolation from the historical-cultural context of its production. The study of aesthetics, or the analysis of what constitutes beauty, is a branch of philosophy.

affirmative action A set of explicit actions or programs designed to eliminate systemic forms of discrimination by increasing the opportunities of individuals and groups who have historically been excluded from full participation in and access to such areas as employment and education.

anti-racism A process of identifying and eradicating racism in all its various forms.

anti-racism education A perspective that addresses all aspects of the educational system and school practices, including all areas of the curriculum, and is aimed at understanding and eradicating racism in all its various forms.

anti-Semitism The body of unconscious or openly hostile attitudes and behaviour directed at individual Jews or the Jewish people, leading to social, economic, institutional, religious, cultural, or political discrimination. Anti-Semitism has also been expressed through acts of physical violence and through the organized destruction of entire communities.

appropriation The claiming of rights to language, subject matter, and authority that are outside one's personal experience. The term also refers to the process by which members of relatively privileged groups "raid" the culture of marginalized groups, abstracting cultural practices or artifacts from their historically specific contexts.

assimilation A process by which an individual or group completely adopts — or is absorbed by — the culture, values, and patterns of another social, religious, linguistic, or national group.

attitude A consistent pattern of thought, belief, or emotion toward a fact, concept, situation, or group of people.

bias An opinion, preference, prejudice, or inclination formed without reasonable justification that then influences an individual's or group's ability to evaluate a particular situation objectively or accurately; an unfounded preference for or against.

censorship The suppression of information and ideas — such as literature, the performing arts, criminal court cases, and ideologies — that are considered unacceptable or dangerous for political, moral, or religious reasons.

colonialism A process by which a foreign power dominates and exploits an indigenous group by appropriating its land and extracting the wealth from it while using the group as cheap labour. Also refers to a specific era of European expansion into overseas territories between the sixteenth and twentieth centuries, during which European states planted settlements in distant territories and achieved economic, military, political, and cultural hegemony in much of Asia, Africa, and the Americas.

commodification The process of turning a thing into a commodity, that is, into an object or service that can be bought or sold in the marketplace.

contract compliance Compliance as a result of a binding, written agreement between two or more parties. Within the context of anti-racism, it normally entails compliance with an anti-discrimination clause that may ask companies to take definite steps such as employment equity to redress imbalances in the workforce. Failure to comply or act in good faith could result in penalties or exclusion from future contracts.

cultural artifacts Human-created objects of any kind, including books, visual art, theatre, television, print media, tools, toys, clothing, furniture, and so on. Scholars also use the term as a way of broadening the study of culture by including aspects that are not usually included, such as verbal, visual, and auditory forms of discourse.

cultural studies The study of cultural practices, of systems of representation and communication, and of the relationship between culture and asymmetrical power relations. It is an interdisciplinary approach that draws from anthropology, sociology, history, semiotics, literature, art, theatre, film criticism, psychoanalysis, feminism, and Third World studies, to name only a few sources. This approach is used to critically examine the dominant culture and the role that mainstream cultural institutions and the media play in the legitimization, production, and entrenchment of systems of inequality. Cultural studies emphasize the roles of both "high" and popular culture in the transmission and reproduction of values. It also examines the processes of resistance by which women, people of colour, and other marginalized groups are challenging hegemonic (*see below*) cultural practices.

culture The totality of the ideas, beliefs, values, knowledge, and way of life of a group of people who share a certain historical, religious, racial, linguistic, ethnic, or social background. Manifestations of culture include art, laws, institutions, and customs. Culture is transmitted and reinforced, and it changes over time.

Culture may refer to a lifestyle of a group of people who tacitly acknowledge their differences from others in terms of beliefs, values, world views, and attitudes about what is right, good, and important.

Culture is a complex and dynamic organization of meaning, knowledge, artifacts, and symbols that guide human behaviour, account for shared patterns of thought and action, and contribute to human, social, and physical survival.

democratic racism An ideology that permits and sustains the ability to justify the maintaining of two apparently conflicting values. One set of values consists of a commitment to a democratic society motivated by egalitarian values of fairness, justice, and equality. Conflicting with these liberal values are attitudes and behaviours including negative feelings about people of colour, which have the potential for differential treatment or discrimination against them.

designated groups Social groups whose members have historically been denied equal access to such areas as employment, accommodation, health care, and education because of their membership in the group. Under employment equity legislation, the designated groups have been identified as women, visible minorities, Aboriginal peoples, and persons with disabilities.

disadvantage Unfavourable and unequal access to resources such as employment, education, and social services.

discourse The production of knowledge through language and social practices, especially ways of producing meaning in an interactive association between words and their denotative capacity and especially their connotative capacity.

discrimination The denial of equal treatment and opportunities to individuals or groups with respect to education, accommodation, health care, employment, services, goods, and facilities. Discrimination may occur on the basis of race, nationality, gender, age, religion, political affiliation, marital or family status, physical or psychiatric disability, or sexual orientation.

dominant/majority group The group of people in a given society that is largest in number or that successfully shapes or controls other groups through social, economic, cultural, political, or religious power. In Canada, the term has generally referred to White, Anglo-Saxon, Protestant males.

employment equity A set of practices designed to identify and eliminate discriminatory policies and practices that create unfair or unequal employment opportunities and to provide equitable opportunities in employment for designated groups. Employment equity means more than treating persons in the same way; it also requires special measures and the accommodation of differences. Thus, the quality of the results, not the equality of treatment, is important.

equality of opportunity The rights of individuals to be free from discrimination when competing for opportunities or services.

equity The rights of individuals to an equitable share of the goods and services in society. In order to ensure equality of outcome, equity programs treat groups differently when the situation in society precludes equal treatment. Equity programs are more inclined to accept the priority of collective rights over individual rights.

essentialism The practice of reducing the complex identity of a particular group to a series of simplified characteristics and denying individual qualities. Also, the simplistic reduction of an idea or process.

ethnic group A community maintained by a shared heritage, culture, language, or religion; a group bound together by ties of cultural homogeneity, with a prevailing loyalty and adherence to certain beliefs, attitudes, and customs.

ethnocentrism A tendency to view events from the perspective of one's own culture, with a corresponding tendency to misunderstand or diminish other groups and regard them as inferior.

Eurocentrism Refers to a complex system of beliefs that upholds the supremacy of Europe's cultural values, ideas, and peoples. European culture is seen as the vehicle for progress toward liberalism and democracy. Eurocentrism minimizes the role of Europeans in maintaining the oppressive systems of colonialism and racism.

exclusion A process of disempowering, degrading, or disenfranchising a group by discriminatory practices and behaviour.

genocide Deliberate actions of a nation or group of people to exterminate another nation or group.

ghettoization The conscious or unconscious act of isolating members of an ethnic or racial minority group from the larger community.

harassment A persistent and continuing communication (in any form) of negative attitudes, beliefs, or actions toward an individual or group, with the intention of disparaging that person or group. Forms of harassment include name-calling, jokes and slurs, graffiti, insults, threats, discourteous treatment, and written and physical abuse.

hegemony Social, cultural, religious, or moral traditions and ideas that reinforce the power of the dominant group at the expense of other groups.

Holocaust A widespread destruction and loss of life; particularly refers to the genocidal extermination of six million European Jews in concentration camps during World War II.

identity A subjective sense of coherence, consistency, and continuity of self, rooted in both personal and group history.

ideology A complex set of ideas that attempts to explain, justify, legitimate, and perpetuate the circumstances in which a collectivity finds itself. It provides a basis for guiding behaviour, making sense of the world, imparting meaning to life, instilling a common bond among group members, and explaining situations.

inclusion A situation that exists when disadvantaged communities and designated group members share power and decision-making at all levels in projects, programs, and institutions.

institutions Organizational arrangements and practices through which collective actions are taken (e.g., government, business, media, education, health and social services).

integration The process that allows groups and individuals to become full participants in the social, economic, cultural, and political life of a society while at the same time enabling them to retain their own cultural identity.

intolerance An unwillingness to consider and/or respect the beliefs and practices of others. Racial intolerance prevents members of other racial groups from sharing equally and benefiting fully from the opportunities available in a community, while religious intolerance refuses to respect the religious beliefs of others.

mainstream In the context of anti-racism, the dominant culture and the political, social, educational, cultural, and economic institutions through which its power is maintained.

marginal The status of groups who do not have full and equal access to the social, economic, cultural, and political institutions of society.

minority group A group of people that is either relatively small in number or has little or no access to social, political, or economic power.

multiculturalism An ideology that holds that racial, cultural, religious, and linguistic diversity is an integral, beneficial, and necessary part of Canadian society and identity. It is an official policy operating in various social institutions and levels of government, including the federal government.

oppression The domination of certain individuals or groups by others through the use of physical, psychological, social, cultural, or economic force.

people of colour *See racial minority.*

pluralism An approach in which some degree of cultural, linguistic, ethnic, religious, or other group distinction is maintained and valued by individuals.

prejudice A mental state or attitude of prejudging, generally unfavourably, by attributing to every member of a group characteristics falsely attributed to the group as a whole.

race A socially constructed category used to classify humankind according to common ancestry and reliant on differentiation by such physical characteristics as colour of skin, hair texture, stature, and facial characteristics.

race relations The quality and pattern of interactions between people who are racially different.

racial discrimination Any distinction, exclusion, restriction, or preference based on race that has the purpose of nullifying or impairing the recognition, enjoyment, or exercise, on an equal footing, of human rights and fundamental freedoms in the political, economic, social, cultural, or any other field of public life.

racial incident An incident in which there is an element of racial motivation, or one that includes an allegation of racial motivation made by any person. Racial incidents may involve verbal abuse (such as banter, jokes, name-calling, harassment, teasing, discourteous treatment), defacement of property, or physical abuse and assault.

racial minority A group of persons who because of their physical characteristics are subjected to differential treatment. Their minority status is the result of a lack of access to power, privilege, and prestige in relation to the majority group.

racism A system in which one group of people exercises power over another group on the basis of skin colour; an implicit or explicit set of beliefs, erroneous assumptions, and actions based on an ideology of the inherent superiority of one racial group over another, and evident in organizational or institutional structures and programs as well as in individual thought or behaviour patterns.

Individual racism is a form of racial discrimination that stems from conscious, personal prejudice.

Systemic racism consists of policies and practices, entrenched in established institutions, that result in the exclusion or advancement of specific groups of people. It manifests itself in two ways: (1) institutional racism: racial discrimination that derives from individuals carrying out the dictates of others who are prejudiced or of a prejudiced society; and (2) structural racism: inequalities rooted in the system-wide operation of a society that exclude substantial numbers of members of particular groups from significant participation in major social institutions.

Cultural racism is deeply embedded in the value system of a society. It represents the tacit network of beliefs and values that encourages and justifies discriminatory actions, behaviours, and practices.

racist An individual, institution, or organization whose beliefs, actions, or programs imply or state that certain races have distinctive negative or inferior characteristics.

racist discourse The ways in which society gives voice to racism, including explanations, narratives, codes of meaning, accounts, images, and social practices that have the effect of establishing, sustaining, and reinforcing oppressive power relations.

racist ideology The whole range of concepts, ideas, images, and institutions that provide the framework of interpretation and meaning for racial thought in society. It creates and preserves a system of dominance based on race and is communicated and reproduced through agencies of socialization and cultural transmission such as the mass media, schools, and universities, religious doctrines, symbols and images, art, music, and literature.

radical/critical multiculturalism A form of multiculturalism that calls for a radical restructuring of the power relations between ethno-racial communities and that challenges the hierarchical structure of society. Radical multiculturalism focuses on empowering communities and transforming systems of representation, institutional and structural centres of power, and discourses. Multiculturalism in this context suggests that diversity can be meaningful only within the construct of social justice and equity.

reflective practice Critical thinking and rethinking about issues that are often taken for granted. Also involves deconstructing feelings, events, situations, and experiences by peeling away the various levels of meaning attached to them through the passage of time.

representation The process of giving abstract ideological concepts concrete forms (examples: representations of women, workers, Blacks). Representations include all kinds of imagery and discourse, and involve constructions of reality taken from specific points of view. Representation is a social process of making sense within all available signifying systems: speech, writing, print, video, film, tape, and so on.

skin colour Skin colour carries with it more than the signification of colour: it also includes a set of meanings attached to the cultural traits of those who are a certain colour.

stereotype A false or generalized conception of a group of people that results in an unconscious or conscious categorization of each member of that group, without regard for individual differences.

text Any communication product or work of art. Includes not only books, plays, and poetry, but also media representations, films, and visual art forms. Textual analysis involves studying how particular written, oral, or visual cultural artifacts generate meaning, taking into account their social and political contexts.

universality A level of understanding that transcends all human boundaries of culture and nation. Universality is a critical quality of expression and comprehension traditionally valued in literature and art. Universality has, however, been defined in specific Eurocentric rather than truly universal terms. The Eurocentrically influenced notion of universality has been disseminated globally through the forces of colonialism.

Whiteness A social construction that has created a racial hierarchy that has shaped all the social, cultural, educational, political, and economic institutions of society. Whiteness is linked to domination and is a form of race privilege that is invisible to White people who are not conscious of its power. Whiteness, as defined within a cultural studies perspective, is description, symbol, experience, and ideology.

Index

▼▼▼▼▼▼

Reader Reply Card

We are interested in your reaction to *The Colour of Democracy: Racism in Canadian Society,* Second Edition, by Frances Henry, Carol Tator, Winston Mattis, and Tim Rees. You can help us to improve this book in future editions by completing this questionnaire.

1. What was your reason for using this book?

    ❏ university course   ❏ college course   ❏ continuing education course
    ❏ professional   ❏ personal   ❏ other _____
    ❏ development   interest   _____

2. If you are a student, please identify your school and the course in which you used this book.

3. Which chapters or parts of this book did you use? Which did you omit?

4. What did you like best about this book?

5. What did you like least about this book?

6. Please identify any topics you think should be added to future editions.

7. Please add any comments or suggestions.

8. May we contact you for further information?

    Name:_____

    Address: _____

    _____

    Phone: _____

    E-mail: _____

(fold here and tape shut)

MAIL ⇒ POSTE

Canada Post Corporation / Société canadienne des postes

Postage paid
If mailed in Canada

Port payé
si posté au Canada

**Business
Reply**

**Réponse
d'affaires**

0116870399   01

0116870399-M8Z4X6-BR01

Larry Gillevet
Director of Product Development
HARCOURT CANADA LTD.
55 HORNER AVENUE
TORONTO, ONTARIO
M8Z 9Z9